MW01280149

The Eisenach Epistle Selections V1: The First Sunday In Advent To Trinity Sunday

Richard Charles Henry Lenski

THE EISENACH
EPISTLE SELECTIONS

Made Ready for Pulpit Work

BY

R. C. H. LENSKI

VOLUME I

The First Sunday in Advent to Trinity
Sunday

1914
LUTHERAN BOOK CONCERN
Columbus, Ohio

INDEX.

		PAGE				PAGE
Acts	3, 1-16.......	II, 39	Phil.	1, 12-21.......	I, 338
"	4, 1-12.......	II, 53	"	1, 27-2, 4......	I, 322
"	4, 32-35.......	II, 12	Col.	3, 1- 4.......	I, 607
"	5, 34-42.......	II, 64	1 Thess.	5, 14-24.......	II, 323
"	8, 26-38.......	II, 74	2 Thess.	3, 6-13.......	II, 204
"	16, 9-15.......	II, 163	1 Tim.	1, 12-17.......	II, 192
"	16, 16-32.......	II, 99	"	2, 1- 6.......	I, 594
"	17, 16-34.......	II, 114	"	4, 4-11.......	II, 311
"	20, 17-38.......	II, 132	"	6, 6-12.......	II, 87
Rom.	1, 13-20.......	I, 249	2 Tim.	2, 8-13.......	I, 576
"	7, 7-16.......	I, 269	"	4, 5- 8.......	I, 56
"	8, 1- 9.......	I, 287	Heb.	1, 1- 6.......	I, 110
"	8, 24-32.......	I, 147	"	4, 9-13.......	II, 231
"	8, 33-39.......	II, 150	"	4, 15-16.......	I, 377
"	10, 1-15.......	II, 22	"	10, 19-25.......	I, 11
"	14, 1- 9.......	II, 269	"	10, 32-39.......	II, 337
1 Cor.	1, 21-31.......	I, 357	"	12, 1- 6.......	I, 451
"	2, 6-16.......	I, 227	"	12, 18-24.......	II, 216
"	3, 11-23.......	II, 381	"	13, 1- 9.......	II, 208
"	10, 16-17.......	I, 467	James	2, 10-17.......	II, 243
"	15, 12-20.......	I, 506	"	4, 13-17.......	I, 173
"	15, 54-58.......	I, 519	"	5, 13-20.......	II, 254
2 Cor.	3, 12-18.......	I, 302	1 Pet.	1, 3- 9.......	I, 531
"	4, 3- 6.......	I, 190	"	1, 13-16.......	I, 406
"	5, 1- 9.......	I, 128	"	1, 17-25.......	I, 432
"	5, 14-21.......	I, 482	"	2, 1-10.......	II, 174
"	6, 14-7, 1......	I, 208	2 Pet.	1, 3-11.......	I, 31
"	7, 4-10.......	I, 417	1 John	1, 1- 4.......	I, 72
"	9, 6-11.......	II, 397	"	2, 12-17.......	I, 388
Eph.	1, 3-14.......	I, 645	"	3, 1- 5.......	I, 91
"	1, 15-23.......	I, 616	"	4, 9-14.......	I, 562
"	2, 4-10.......	I, 546	Rev.	2, 8-11.......	II, 351
"	2, 19-22.......	I, 632	"	7, 9-17.......	II, 366
"	6, 1- 9.......	II, 283			

iii

FOREWORD.

THE cordial reception accorded the author's *Eisenach Gospel Selections* induced him to prepare in a similar manner the *Eisenach Epistle Selections*. The excellence of these texts, as far as their choice is concerned, is beyond question. They are extensively used in the churches of Germany, and are finding equal favor in our midst. The epistles especially present both the finest doctrinal and practical texts for regular Sunday morning preaching.

The author has followed the same general lines in this work as in the one on the gospels. He has kept the needs and requirements of the pulpit worker before him throughout, endeavoring to furnish as much useful material as possible for the actual production of sermons. Each text, when possible, is divided into its main parts, and these are given appropriate captions. In the "Homiletical Hints," instead of a collection of brief thoughts, the author has preferred to furnish a variety of thoughts more fully elaborated. In many cases the source is indicated, in others the thought has been recast and no special credit is accorded. The number of outlines for sermons has been limited to six for each text, except the last two. The Greek text used in the exegesis is that of Wescott & Hort; the English, the Revised Version as published together with the Greek text by Harper & Brothers, New York, in the edition of 1882. Throughout this work *Die neuen epistolishen Perikopen der Eisenacher*

1

Konferenz by O. Reylaender have been critically compared. Reylaender parcelled out the texts, using nine assistants to help him. He makes no effort whatever to link the texts together, and the work of some of his assistants is inferior both exegetically and doctrinally. The Book of Concord (Jacob's translation) has again been used with all diligence. It is not necessary to name all the exegetical authors whose works were consulted, as in most cases their names are inserted in connection with their views. The majority of them as well as all the homiletical writers are Germans; if therefore the purists discover a Germanism here and there they may remember that it would be phenomenal if, working to such an extent from German sources, no Germanisms should have crept in. Three series of sermons on the Eisnach epistles have been published: *Schriftgedanken fuer unsere Zeit,* two small volumes by M. Riemer; *"Herr, was willst Du, dass ich tun soll?"* two larger volumes by Johann Rump; and *Die Epistolischen Lektionen* by A. Matthes. These three together with the work of Langsdorff, the unpublished sermons by Rev. C. C. Hein of Columbus, O., and others like Koegel, two volumes of sermons on Romans, and Dryander, on St. John, have been utilized for the "Homiletical Hints." No man could hope to present a flawless exegesis on so many texts, some of them presenting special difficulties, and even less could he expect to accord with every idea of his critical readers. A comparison of the great exegetes with each other is sufficient to cure all lesser men of any prideful thoughts in this regard. The author has carefully examined every position taken and has striven to keep safely within the bounds of the Confessions and the analogy of faith. On grammatical questions he has consulted the *Grammar of New Testament Greek* by Friedrich Blass, translated by Henry St. John Thackery (Macmillan and Co., London); *Grammatik des neutestamentlichen Sprachidioms,* by Winer, the sixth edition; the new and handy little volume, *Kurzgefasste Grammatik des neutestamentlichen Griechisch* by A. T. Robertson, translated into German by Hermann Stocks; *Einleitung in die Sprache des Neuen Tes-*

taments, by J. H. Moulton; *Neutestamentliche Grammatik. Das Griechish des Neuen Testaments im Zusammenhang mit der Volkssprache,* by Ludwig Rademacher; and the author's colleague, F. W. Stellhorn, D. D., professor of exegesis in the Evangelical Lutheran Seminary at Columbus, O.

The preacher's throne is his pulpit; the highest function which any man can perform is to act as God's embassador in proclaiming his Gospel. To aid somewhat in this greatest work in the world is the author's aim and purpose, and for this he prays God's blessing upon his humble efforts.

THE AUTHOR.

COLUMBUS, OHIO, September 1, 1913.

THE CHRISTMAS CYCLE.

THE CHRISTMAS CYCLE.

INTRODUCTORY.

First Sunday in Advent to Sunday After New Year.

Five great cycles comprise the first half of the Christian church year as the Lutheran Liturgies with their Introits, Versicles, Collects, Graduals, and Scripture Lessons (epistles and gospels) set this before us. They center about the five great Christian festivals, Christmas, Epiphany, Good Friday, Easter, and Pentecost. Sometimes only three cycles are counted, Christmas and Epiphany being combined into one, Lent and Easter likewise; but for our purpose the division into five for the first half of the church year will be found preferable. The second half of the church year constitutes one grand cycle, with several well-defined divisions indicating a natural and appropriate line of progress.

The regular Scripture Lessons for each festival and Sunday comprise the old epistle and gospel selections which have come down to us from ancient times. These constitute two lines of pericopes which are used for a double purpose, to be read at the altar or lectern in the liturgical part of the service, and to be preached on as texts from the pulpit. Of the two texts thus given for each festival and Sunday the chief one is the gospel text, since this especially lends character to the day for which it is set; the epistle selection is always secondary. The Eisenach gospel and epistle selections follow the same general course as the old texts, and thus harmonize well with all the old liturgical parts of each festival and Sunday. The intention in these new texts is not to duplicate as closely as possible the old texts, nor is it to follow entirely different lines. As regards the latter point we must remember that each of the great festivals is so distinctive that any text at all appropriately chosen for it must bring out that distinctive

7

feature. Besides this, some of the Sundays have come to bear a stamp of their own, for instance Palm Sunday, Rogate, the Tenth Sunday after Trinity, *etc.*, so that distinctive texts are required also for these Sundays. The Eisenach gospel and epistle selections meet these requirements fully, and at the same time are especially chosen as texts for preaching. In this respect they present the advantage that each text not only fits in a general way its proper place in the church year, but each is at the same time so linked to the one following that all the texts in a cycle constitute one well-rounded whole, dominated by one central thought, and in the case of the festival cycles circling about the message of the festival text.

The gospel texts in the Eisenach selections for the first half of the church year present **the great deeds of God for our salvation.** This is the subject also for the epistle selections, which, of course, are secondary and subordinate to the gospel texts. The epistles carry out the thought after the manner of the apostolic Epistles generally. This is clearly seen in the three texts which form the heart of the Christmas cycle in the epistle series. Three texts are chosen from the apostolic letters which especially mention the great fact of the manifestation of the Son of God as our Savior. The entire Christmas series of nine texts divides naturally into three sections. The first presents the Advent idea in epistolary selections, leading us up to the Christmas festival; the second section we have already described; the third combines the Christmas blessings with the thought of time involved in the closing and opening of a year.

Thus the nine texts are grouped as follows: The First Sunday in Advent, opening up the entire church year, shows us once more, in a comprehensive manner as befits the day and its significance: *the fundamentals of the Christian life,* into which the Advent season means to lead us anew. Or, following the specific injunction contained in the text: *Advent bids us draw near again with fulness of faith.*

The Second Sunday in Advent keeps in view the special significance of the day as reminding us of the second coming of Christ. We who are to make ready for that coming see here once more: *the course of the Christian life,* which is to lead us to our great goal on the last day. Here too we may take out one prominent thought of the text as its dominating note for this day: *the abundant entrance into the eternal kingdom of our Lord and Savior Jesus Christ.*

The Third Sunday in Advent usually shows us, in the gospel selections both old and new, the figure of John the Baptist. In his place our epistle text puts the apostle St. Paul and his disciple Timothy. Paul speaks of his end, and this makes the burden of the text: *the close of the faithful Christian life,* which this new Advent season would aid us in reaching. Or, following the grand statement contained in the text itself: *the crown of righteousness which is laid up for all who have loved the Savior's appearing.* A glance at this grouping shows that the three texts go together in the order given and form a whole.

The same thing is true of the next three texts, in which the Christmas cycle reaches its climax. The Fourth Sunday in Advent is drawn to the Christmas Festival and filled with Christmas glory. It proclaims, on the very eve of the festival: *the Word of life was manifested for our joy.* Now follows the Christmas Festival itself with this announcement reiterated in the following form: *Christ, the sinless Son of God, was manifested in human flesh for the salvation of us sinners;* or, if a briefer statement is desired: *Christ manifested for our salvation.* The Day after Christmas adds yet one more necessary thought, with great fulness and emphasis, when it shows us: *the incomparable glory of him who was born in Bethlehem.* Again we see the three texts go together, the one amplifying and intensifying the glorious Christmas message of the other.

Three more texts remain and they too are closely related. Christ has appeared in the fulness of time, and time is swiftly running its course. A year is ending, another begins, and presently we shall be in it. But we carry the Christmas grace with us. The Sunday after Christmas shows us: *the future is bright for us,* since we have a house not made with hands, eternal, in the heavens. New Year's Day goes a great step farther: *the future is certain for us,* for we rest on the eternal grace of God which cannot fail. One more thought completes this little circle, and the Sunday after New Year adds it: *the future is all in God's hands for us,* and we rejoice to submit everything wholly to his will.

In this advance survey of the texts of the Christmas cycle, just as in our study of the subsequent cycles, our aim is to define in a general way, and yet as closely as possible, the significance of each text in its particular place. Many texts are exceedingly rich, and some of them so extensive that the preacher will hardly be able to utilize all the contents in detail. But this makes it the more necessary to fix the central thought which each text in its respective place conveys, and thus to view it from the particular angle in the series in which it occurs. The preacher is, of course, free to follow some other line of thought contained in any individual text, as he may deem most profitable for his people and the special circumstances in which he and they may find themselves. But aside from such liberties, for which there may be more or less justification, the regular mode of procedure with a well-chosen series of texts for a particular section of the church year will be the one here attempted, and for ordinary homiletical purposes, with the church year as the preacher's guide, the author has never found anything more satisfactory and fruitful in the actual performance of his pulpit work. The testimony of many others who have used the author's *Eisenach Gospel Selections* in the past few years is altogether to the same effect.

THE FIRST SUNDAY IN ADVENT.

Heb. 10, 19-25.

The second word in this text (οὖν) marks its general character. It is a conclusion based on the extensive elaboration in the previous chapters. Because of the length of this elaboration and the importance of what it presents, a brief but pithy recapitulation ushers in the conclusion now founded upon.it. This is in two members: ἔχοντες παρρησίαν . . . καὶ (ἔχοντες) ἱερέα μέγαν. With a double sweep the holy writer takes in the great objective facts of our salvation, in order at once to apply them to our hearts and lives. This he does with the three exhortative subjunctives προσερχώμεθα, κατέχωμεν, καὶ κατανοῶμεν. They take in *"faith,"* "the confession of our *hope,"* "*love* and good works" (note the trio: faith, hope, and charity), in other words the whole range of the life under the grace of God. This shows the character and scope of the text: it is like a mighty open-in chord in the grand symphony that is to follow in the texts of the coming Sundays and festivals. All the chief tones are blended together in one great harmony at the very start. And the echo in our hearts must be full and strong, for ἔχοντες means that *we* have the treasures of God's grace, and the προσερχώμεθα following shows what *we*, having them, can and shall now do.

The text is comprehensive, and in this respect fits well the Sunday at the head of the whole church year, which properly takes in a wide range. There is uplift and joy both in the words that tell us what we have, and in those that outline the life we in consequence should live; and this too is appropriate for the First Sunday in Advent. In the closing words: "Ye see the day drawing nigh," we have a brief reference to the second advent of Christ. It

11

is like the reference in the old epistle for the day (Rom. 13, 11-14): "Knowing the time, that now it is high time to awake out of sleep . . . The night is far spent, the day is at hand." This reminder adds its note of solemnity, and is thus very acceptable, although we would not advise that it control the entire sermon. Summing up the message which this text offers for the First Sunday in Advent, we have here before us: *The fundamentals of the Christian life,* into which Advent leads us anew. Or, if we wish to single out one word of the text, as marking the contents of the whole, the admonition: *Let us draw near with fulness of faith.*

Our first great possession.

The first words of the first text for the church year have a peculiar fitness: **Having therefore, brethren, etc.,** ἔχοντες οὖν ἀδελφοί; they resemble the opening word in the Sermon on the Mount and that in the First Psalm: "Blessed!" Thank God, we *have* some things; they are there, positive treasures, and cannot be removed or annulled; they are there even if we should fail to realize their objective presence and their true value. The ἔχων, however, indicates that a personal possession of these treasures and a full enjoyment of their blessedness is intended. Christ and his salvation exist indeed, and that for all men, but for those who are the ἀδελφοί the fullest appropriation has taken place. Every ἀδελφός is a partner in this infinite wealth. Whatever real or imaginary advantages are found in other brotherhoods and possessions, none can compare with what this brotherhood carries with it.

The closing part of the second section of the Epistle to the Hebrews is ushered in with the words: "Having then a great high priest," and the appended admonition reads: "Let us therefore draw near with boldness unto the throne of grace." See chapter 4, 14 and 16. In our text these words are repeated, and that with redoubled force because of the full elaboration which has intervened.

The holy writer has shown us with great fulness the divine basis of our salvation, namely the heavenly High Priest himself and his eternal work. These two, the great person and his mighty work as thus set before us *in extenso*, are now put side by side in a brief recapitulation: "Having therefore, brethren, **boldness to enter into the holy place by the blood of Jesus,** by the way which he dedicated for us, a new and living way, through the veil, that is to say, his flesh; and having **a great priest** over the house of God; let us draw near, *etc.*" Τὰ ἅγια, the holy places, are like the Holy and the Holy of Holies in the old Jewish temple at Jerusalem. None but priests dared to enter there, and into the second none but the high priest, and he not without blood. Heb. 9, 7. The statement that we, the ἀδελφοί, now have boldness to enter τὰ ἅγια implies that we are considered priests. And indeed, we are nothing less: "But ye are an elect race, a royal priesthood, a holy nation, a people for God's own possession, *etc*," 1 Pet. 2, 9; "ye also . . . are built up a spiritual house, to be a holy priesthood, to offer up spiritual sacrifices, acceptable to God through Jesus Christ," verse 5. As such "priests" we have not only the right, but also **boldness to enter** into the holy place, παρρησίαν εἰς τὴν εἴσοδον τῶν ἁγίων, really: for the entering into of the holy places. The same thing is mentioned Eph. 3, 12: "In whom (namely Christ Jesus) we have boldness and access in confidence." Παρρησία denotes the liberty to tell everything (πᾶς ῥῆσις), openness and boldness in speech; we have full and free access to the communion with God who is ever ready to hear us. And this boldness we have **by the blood of Jesus.** The words are emphatic, standing at the end of the clause, and a striking explanation follows them, as we shall see in a moment. This Advent text bids us enter the portals of salvation anew, with the fullest confidence and assurance based on the blood of Jesus. As the Jewish high priest bore the atoning blood of the sacrifice when he entered the Holy of Holies, so we must come with blood, and this the blood of Jesus which is the true propitiation for our sins. Without this blood we could have only fear, terror, despair, and no boldness. Any man who makes bold to face God without "the blood of Jesus" will find his boldness a frightful presumption; the wrath of God will overwhelm him. His boldness will turn into dismay, for "no one cometh unto the Father, but by me," John 14, 6, *i. e.*, by my blood. In the new dispensation each one of us is to perform constantly the priestly act of drawing nigh unto God, but only with the blood upon us which God himself designed for our cleansing, the blood of the Lamb of God; this makes us acceptable to God, for "the blood of Jesus his Son cleanseth us from all sin," 1 John 1, 7. This interpretation is preferred because the entire text involves the priestly function of believers; also as already ἀδελφοί or believes theirs is a renewed and constant approach with boldness to the holy place. Another exegesis makes ἐν τῷ αἵματι Ἰησοῦ only the objective basis of the παρρησία, which indeed it is, but even this when taken in its full meaning includes our appropriation of Christ's atoning work. The latter, we hold, must here be included, and the best construction is to take ἐν τῷ αἵματι Ἰησοῦ as a modifier of the entire phrase ἔχοντες παρρησίαν εἰς τὴν εἴσοδον τῶν ἁγίων; we indeed have boldness for the entrance into the holy places only in the power or virtue of the blood of Jesus.

The εἴσοδον τῶν ἁγίων is described by a relative clause, which shows us how the blood of Jesus prepared the entrance for us, and thus brings out the supreme importance of this blood: **by the way which he dedicated for us, a new and living way, through the veil, that is to say, his flesh.** Jesus "dedicated" the entrance for us. Εἴσοδος, together with its apposition ὁδός, is objectively "the entrance" itself, although it may include also the act, "the entering in," and this subjective element, strongly brought out by the term "boldness," must here be included, for the thought here is not only that the way is ready for us, but ready, "dedicated," opened for us actually to use, in fact we are urged to use it. The verb ἐγκαινίζω = make new or dedicate; τὰ ἐγκαίνια = Feast of Dedication, celebrated annually by the Jews in commemoration of the cleansing of the temple after its desecration by Antiochus Epiphanes. Ἡμῖν shows that the entrance was dedicated for our benefit, opened up for our immediate use from the first moment of its completion. That was indeed a glorious dedicatory act when Jesus opened the portals of the "entrance" and revealed it as **a new and living way.** Πρόσφατος = etymologically "freshly killed," but in later Greek it has lost this meaning and stands simply for what is new, recent, fresh. The "entrance" we are to use boldly as our possession is one altogether "new," original, without counterpart, absolutely unique, the wonderful result of God's highest wisdom and love. — Its second remarkable attribute is **living,** for Jesus himself is "the way . . . and the life," John 14, 6. The very first step on this way is the new birth or regeneration, John 3, 5. Not only does it lead to eternal life by terminating in that life as its goal, but it is life itself, deliverance from sin and death, and by its life-power it fills us with life and bears us onward as a living force to the glorious presence of God. All other "ways" are lifeless, dead, and they end in death. Bengel points to the *opera mortua* as the opposite of this "living way." — **Through the veil, that is to say, his flesh,** at once recalls the old Jewish temple with its veil before the Holy of Holies, through which only the high priest entered once a year bearing the blood. That veil itself the Jewish high priest could not remove; he could not open up the way for all to approach God directly; he could only act for them as an intermediary entering in behind the veil in their behalf. The death of Jesus at once rent in two this veil, showing that its purpose had come to an end. Matth. 27, 50. The veil was only a type, a symbol, and now we see what it stood for: "the veil, that is to say, his flesh." The way to "the holy place," the presence of God and the blessed union and communion with Him (as the old temple symbolized it in its Holy of Holies and the veil) leads through "the flesh" of Jesus, God's Son. Διὰ τοῦ καταπετάσματος may be construed with ὁδόν, which is the apposition to εἴσοδον; οὖσαν or ἄγουσαν would then be supplied: the way being, or leading, through the veil. The idea would be that for every believer the way to the holy place still leads through "the veil," or "the flesh" of Christ. Since, however, the rending and removing of the veil was one act, performed once for all, a simpler and more satisfactory thought as well as construction results by construing διὰ τοῦ καταπετάσματος κτλ. with the verb ἐνεκαίνισεν = he dedicated through the veil, *etc.* The dedicatory act of Christ consisted of his opening up the way through his flesh, in the wondrous sacrifice on Calvary, when he gave his flesh and shed his blood in death for the sins of the world. If one wants to take care here of the thought that the veil in the temple was rent in twain, which veil signifies Christ's flesh, he may say that Christ's flesh was rent in death. If the entire removal of the veil is taken into account, one may add, that the flesh of Christ in its humiliation had served its purpose when Christ died, and so was removed, being transferred to the state of exaltation. But these are thoughts which the text itself does not express, at most only suggests. The essential thing is that for us ἀδελφοί, fellow believers of the holy writer, we are shown what we have: a wonderful way to come to God, opened and dedicated by Jesus, which we may use with bold assurance; it is the way ἐν τῷ αἵματι, or διὰ τῆς σαρκὸς αὐτοῦ, the way of his bloody sacrifice on the cross. Having this way, we can indeed draw near with the fullest confidence and assurance, even as we are here urged to do.

Our second great possession.

And having a great priest over the house of God, ἱερέα μέγαν, which the Septuagint occasionally uses instead of ἀρχιερεύς. This "priest" is "great" indeed, "for such a high priest became us, holy, guileless, undefiled, separated from sinners, and made higher than the heavens . . . a Son, perfected for evermore." Heb. 7, 26 and 28. Indeed, he is God's own Son; he accomplished in fact what all preceding priests only wrought in symbols and types;

his priesthood is everlasting, and his sacrifice both of infinite value and eternal effect, producing an "eternal redemption," Heb. 9, 12. **The house of God** is defined in Heb. 3, 6: "whose house are we." In the entire passage Heb. 3, 1-6 we are shown the relation of Christ the Apostle and High Priest to this "house," he being the Son who himself built it and produced it, namely the church of true believers, as compared with Moses, the servant (not Son) in that "house" of old. Eph. 2, 19-22 carries the same thought: "So then ye are no more strangers and sojourners, but ye are fellow-citizens with the saints, and of the household of God, being built upon the foundation of the apostles and prophets, Christ Jesus himself being the chief corner stone; in whom each several building, fitly framed together, groweth into a holy temple in the Lord; in whom ye also are builded together for a habitation of God in the Spirit." What the functions of this great Priest in his own house are we can gather from the entire previous description of Jesus the High Priest, especially Heb. 3, 1-6; 7, 25; *etc.* As the Son he has complete power to bestow every gift upon us and to secure for us all the fulness of the divine grace, John 1, 16.

The first exhortation.

Let us draw near, προσερχώμεθα (subj. in exhortation, as also κατέχωμεν and κατανοῶμεν), a liturgical term harmonizing with ρεραντισμένοι and λελουσμένοι. We have the free access — let us use it; we have the boldness (the right to come boldly) — let us exercise it! Enter into the full and free communion with God which invites you, into all the blessings and enjoyments which belong to you. The call is to the ἀδελφοί who have already followed it in the past; for them it signifies a continuation in their approach to God and his grace in Christ, and thus an augmentation of their spiritual possessions. There is an ever continuing stream of blessings flowing from the holy place; having taken we may ever take more and more; we will never

2

reach the end. But this call to present believers is not meant to exclude the others who are not yet brethren in the faith. The blood of Christ and the entrance through the veil has been prepared for all men; none are excluded. Hence this call must be preached so as to appeal also to those still without, that seeing the grace of God and the blessedness of the ἀδελφοί they may be attracted and brought to join them. — The call to ʽdraw near is one thing, the manner in which this is to be done is the next: **with a true heart in fulness of faith** (marginal reading R. V.: *full assurance*). Ἡ καρδία, here the seat of consciousness, will, *etc.*, hence the inner self. God always looks at the heart; his eyes penetrate it through and through. Hence the admonition: Come with a true *heart*, one which really is what it professes to be. Ἀληθής = "true" in the sense of actual; used of persons it means reliable, trustworthy; φίλος ἀληθής, a reliable friend who does what he says; while ἀληθινός = true in the sense of genuine; used of persons it means to be what one claims; φίλος ἀληθινός, a genuine friend, one rightly so named. The ἀληθινὴ καρδία then is opposed to the heart that is false, hypocritical, not in earnest, merely pretending, making a profession not warranted by the real intentions. Let every man examine his own heart that it be found "true" indeed. — The "true heart" goes well together with "fulness of faith," for which the margin offers "full assurance of faith." Faith is a fixed term, denoting trust in Jesus Christ and his merits. Πληροφορία adds the idea of certainty, and of such certainty in full measure. It is the counterpart to the "boldness" in the previous verse. "The blood of Jesus," the way "through the veil of his flesh," and the "great priest" all demand faith on our part, but more than this; for so all-sufficient are these for our salvation, so mighty and glorious, that nothing less than "fulness of faith" will comport with them, a faith fully certain of its ground, not ignorant or doubting, not moved by the world or any human argument or objection, but, laughing these to scorn, confidently, joyfully entering into the holy place with the blood of Jesus. But many a

heart lacks this full assurance of faith, and needs the very
stimulation this text offers anew. James 1, 6, *etc.*

A second statement is added as to how we should
draw near: **having our hearts sprinkled from an evil
conscience, and our body washed with pure water.** It
is possible to draw the second of these two participal clauses
to the following verb κατέχωμεν: "and having our body
washed with pure water, let us hold fast." The marginal
reading offers this arrangement, but it destroys the fine
balance between the modifiers here introduced, and the
sense of the clauses is likewise against a separation of the
participles. How are we to draw near? The answer is
given by μετά and ἐν, a pair of prepositions with their objects (each of these with one modifier), and by ῥεραντισμένοι
and λελουσμένοι, a pair of participles (each with an accusative of specification and one additional modifier); besides
this fine balance, which must not be destroyed, the two
participles refer to lustrations and are thus related closely
in meaning as well as form (both perfect passive). —
Heart and "body" correspond; not "heart" and "flesh," the
counterpart of the latter being "spirit." The "heart"
is properly mentioned where the conscience is concerned;
the inner man is meant, but, of course, so that the cleansing
affects the entire man. The **body** is properly mentioned
where the sacramental washing of Baptism is concerned,
since the water touches the body; and again, this washing
affects the entire man. "Heart" and "body" are here considered as going together. The cleansing of the heart may
indeed take place without the immediate washing of the
body, but this will surely follow ere long; the washing of
the body, however, with sacramental water always includes
the cleansing of the heart; in infants the two are simultaneous. Both verbs, ῥαντίζω and λούω, recall vividly the O.
T. cleansing of the high priest before performing his great
duties: he was sprinkled with blood, Ex. 29, 21; Lev. 8, 30;
and he was washed with water, Ex. 40, 12 *etc.;* 30, 19 *etc.;*
Lev. 8, 6; 16, 4 and 24. The implication then is that in
drawing near to God we are exercising priestly preroga-

tives of the loftiest kind, and hence must be clean through
and through, inwardly and outwardly; nothing less will
suffice.   The cleansing fluid for the heart is mentioned
1 Pet. 1, 2: "sprinkling of the blood of Jesus Christ;" Heb.
12, 24: "the blood of sprinkling that speaketh better than
that of Abel;" 1 John 1, 7.   Christ indeed shed his blood for
all men, but now for every individual there must follow a
sprinkling of the heart with this blood, an application of it
to each one, an appropriation of its atoning merit by faith.
This inward sprinkling is justification through the redemption that is in Christ Jesus, Rom. 3, 24. — To **sprinkle
from an evil conscience** is a pregnant expression = to
sprinkle and thus free from an evil conscience.   Evil conscience is here taken in its true sense: as long as sin and
guilt rest upon us we have an evil conscience.   Even if it
sleeps awhile and becomes seared, in the end it will fill us
with accusation and condemnation.   This is changed the
moment Christ's blood washes away our guilt.   Being justified by faith we have peace with God — the evil conscience
is gone.   When the risen Savior greeted his disciples with
"Peace be unto you," he showed them his wounds by which
he had shed his blood; then were they filled with joy.
Luke 24, 40-41.   And we may well ask, How could any
one draw near to the holy place as long as his evil conscience
remains?   That would drive him into outer darkness. —
There is only one washing of the body known in the new
dispensation, it is the sacramental washing of Baptism.
Jesus said to his disciples: "Already ye are clean because
of the word which I have spoken unto you."   The water
of Baptism is joined with this same Word of Christ.   This
Word itself has cleansing power, but it comes to us not only
by means of the ear (preaching and teaching), but also in
connection with the divinely ordained elements of water
in Baptism and of bread and wine in the Holy Supper.
Baptism is here mentioned, not so much because in general
and for infants it is the first means for their cleansing, but
because for all believers it is the means of grace which sets
their spiritual cleansing restore them after the manner of

the O. T. priestly lustrations. "Christ also loved the church, and gave himself up for it; that he might sanctify it, having cleansed it by the washing of water with the word, that he might present the church to himself a glorious church, not having spot or wrinkle or any such thing; but that it should be holy and without blemish." Eph. 5, 25-27. Here Paul shows how Baptism acts upon us in making us fit to appear before Christ. We may also recall "the house of God" in verse 22, in which we all live as "brethren" and children of God. Here again Baptism has its important function: "Ye are all sons of God, through faith, in Christ Jesus. For as many of you as were baptized into Christ did put on Christ." Gal. 3, 26-27.

Thus then let us draw near to God and confidently enter into communion with him anew in this church year: with a sincere heart, in confident faith, justified and pardoned of all guilt, baptized in the Savior's name. We are the royal priesthood of God, let us use fully our heavenly prerogatives.

The second exhortation.

Let us hold fast the confession of our hope that it waver not, is a repetition of the admonition in 4, 15: κρατῶμεν τῆς ὁμολογίας, substituting the verb κατέχω for κρατέω, and adding the significant genitive τῆς ἐλπίδος to ὁμολογία. The latter signifies our inward and outward consent to the Gospel; it signifies a positive declaration of the truth we hold and of the faith we hold it with. The idea is that every justified and baptized believer is naturally and as a matter of course a confessor. And the confession is here described as "the confession of hope;" in 3, 6 we have "the glorying of hope," a confession also, but full of exultation. Hope points to the future, to the fulfilment of all the great promises of Christ, which the believer confidently expects. —But in both κατέχωμεν, "let us hold fast," and in ἀκλινῆ, "that it waver not," we have the thought of assault upon our confession. Verses 32-38 furnish a vivid picture of what these hostile forces are able to do in forcing upon the confessors "a great conflict of sufferings," making them "a gazingstock both by reproaches and affliction," "spoiling them of their possessions," *etc.* In another form, but with the same fundamental sense, the admonition to hold fast our confession is repeated: "Cast not away therefore your boldness, which hath great recompense of reward;" followed by the firm declaration: "But we are not of them which shrink back unto perdition; but of them that have faith unto the saving of the soul." We are to keep on believing and confessing, no matter what men may do to us. Whatever we may be called upon to forfeit, our hope is to be undisturbed, "knowing that ye yourselves have a better possession and an abiding one." If ever we grow weak and hesitate the grace of God is to be our fountain of strength. Ἀκλινῆ is predicative and emphatic, standing at the end: we are to hold our confession as an unwavering one, unbending, unyielding, or, as the R. V. has it, since the subjunctive of the verbs points to the future: "that it waver not;" Luther, very finely: *"und nicht wanken."* John the Baptist may serve as our example; he laid his head upon the block in the prime of his early manhood, and Jesus praised him as not being a reed shaken by the wind, not wavering. Chapter 11 of this Epistle furnishes the classic galaxy of unwavering believers and confessors. Let us hold fast as did they.

A special reason is added: **for he is faithful that promised,** πιστός, trustworthy. 1 Cor. 1, 9: "God is faithful, through whom ye were called into the fellowship of his Son Jesus Christ our Lord." 1 Thess. 5, 24: "Faithful is he that calleth you, who will also do it." 1 Cor. 10, 13 refers especially to the temptation which might induce us to deny: "But God is faithful, who will not suffer you to be tempted above that ye are able; but will with the temptation make also the way to escape, that ye may be able to endure it." Ἐπαγγειλάμενος (aor. part.) refers to the hope just mentioned, which for the faithful confessor embraces all that he may yet expect, not only future glory, but also grace, blessing, help, support, *etc.,* now as he may have need of it;

"der sie", die Hoffnung, "verheissen hat." On the one hand κατέχωμεν, let us hold fast, implying the danger of letting go, the dire results of which are pictured in verses 26-31; on the other hand πιστός, absolute trustworthiness, God never lets go what he has promised. If any confessor ever becomes a denier, the fault is wholly his own. This consideration is indeed a mighty motive, an impulse, a strengthening power to the believer when assailed. The gracious and faithful God, who has given us all that verses 19-21 declare, certainly will not now prove unfaithful, will not forget a single promise, or omit a single thing we may need in our trial.

The third exhortation.

This exhortation presupposes the relation of brotherhood, verse 19, hence it rounds out the circle of our duties: the first exhortation looks to God and bids us draw nigh to him in the proper manner; the second looks to the world and bids us hold fast our confession unwaveringly; and now this third looks to our brethren and bids us stimulate them. There is here an implication which must not be overlooked: if I am to consider my brethren in a certain manner, I must first consider myself. Should I be slack in good works, how could I then stir up others to such works; my conduct would rather confirm them in their unfruitful course. Our remissness causes double damage, to ourselves and to others; our faithfulness and zeal produces double fruit, our own good works, and a stimulation of others to like good works. **And let us consider one another to provoke unto love and good works** — παροξυσμός usually in an evil sense, an excitation to anger, bitterness, an inflammation; here however in a good sense, making the exhortation the more striking for its unusualness. Ἀλλήλους makes the action reciprocal; each is to observe the other to see where and how he can excite the other to love and good works; and as this must largely be done by each brother himself exercising love and good works, there will be a constantly increasing stream from a double source. It will be seen at once that this is the opposite of that malicious regarding of others which results in all manner of evil thoughts, words, and works. On this point St. Paul writes Gal. 6, 4: "But let each man prove his own work, and then shall he have his glorying in regard of himself alone, and not of his neighbor. For each man shall bear his own burden." The expression **love and good works** is especially fine, showing the true source of all good works, namely love the fruit of faith, and the true fruit of love, namely works good in the sight of God. Both are introduced here after faith and justification have been mentioned, for love and good works flow from faith. "Oh," writes Luther, "it is a living, efficacious, active thing that we have in faith, so that it is impossible for it not to do good works without intermission. It also does not ask whether good works are to be done; but before the question is asked it has wrought them, and is always busy. But he who does not produce such works is a faithless man, and gropes and looks about after faith and good works, and knows neither what faith nor what good works are, yet meanwhile babbles and prates, in many words, concerning faith and good works." *Formula of Concord,* Jacobs, 585, 10 *etc.* Love and good works always belong together, as fire and the light and heat it emits. Often the two are compressed into the one word love: "By this shall all men know that ye my disciples, if ye have love one to another," John 13, 35. Nor need we trouble here because love to men generally is not mentioned. He who loves his brethren aright will desire to love all men in the same way, and this is the very best motive for love and kindliness to them all. Alas, that the love which provokes is so weak; and when we meet it we often fail to respond to it, and thus discourage it instead of strengthening it.

The positive injunction is followed by the negative: **not forsaking the assembling of ourselves together.** It has been well said that love and good works must have their root in God, in the constant influx of power from the Holy Spirit and the means of grace, and that therefore the assembling of ourselves for worship is here introduced.

Yet this is only suggested. The idea put forth here is not of the means of grace or of divine worship, but of brotherhood and the exercise of fellowship in the Christian assembly. Ἐπισυναγωγή is used, instead of συναγωγή, most likely to distinguish the Christian assembly from that of the Jews usually designated by the latter term. Ἑαυτῶν, which is stronger than ἡμῶν, "the assembling of our own selves," suggests as the opposite the assembling of others hostile to the Christians, of Jews or idolaters for their worship, just as now there are many gatherings, secret as well as open, opposed to the spirit and truth of the church. The participle ἐγκαταλείποντες is strong, = desert, leave alone or abandon, as in a contest; compare Matth. 27, 41: "My God, my God, why hast thou forsaken me?" 2 Tim. 4, 10 and 16; 2 Cor. 4, 9. Repeated action is meant (present participle), hence not the one act of apostasy, as some have interpreted. Hence also the reference to actual conditions among the first readers of this Epistle: **as the custom of some is.** What produced this "custom" we are left to surmise; and the fear of men, the lack of brotherly love, indifference, *etc.*, have been suggested, much as they to-day explain the same custom as it still prevails with all the dangers it involves. For if we keep apart we certainly will not be able to provoke each other to love and good works. Scattered coals always lose their heat, and only heaped-up coals fire each other. Especially is this the case as regards divine service, where with the voice of worship we exhort each other and our very presence helps to stimulate. On the other hand to abandon our brethren means to weaken their hands and to strengthen the forces of unbelief, error, worldliness, *etc.* To do this is to be a kind of traitor to the cause once espoused. — **But exhorting** *one another,* παρακαλοῦντες, repeated action; the verb signifies to call to one's side, to encourage, cheer *(zureden; gute Worte geben),* not then to rebuke, chastise or anything like that. Thus to exhort is part of the παροξυσμός required in this case, the proper conduct, in this instance, of a brother deserving that name and cognizant of his high prerogatives and blessed duties.

A special motive is introduced for the brethren to exhort one another not only the wayward and indifferent, but all, lest also the faithful ones grow slack: **and so much the more, as ye see the day drawing nigh.** There is no question but what ἡ ἡμέρα (often termed "that day") is the same as ἡμέρα κρίσεως, Matth. 10, 15; 11, 24; 12, 36; ἐσχάτη ἡμέρα, John 6, 40 (*dies illa, dies irae*). It is a mistake to make "the day," or its equivalent terms, mean *any* day of judgment, as the *Luth. Com.* does. Some do this in order to escape the objection, that if the Hebrews "saw the day drawing nigh," and this "day" is taken as the end of the world, then the holy writer must have erred, as the end of the world still lay far in the distant future. That Paul, and in fact the entire early church, erred in looking for the second advent of Christ as near at hand, is boldly claimed by not a few. Riehm quotes Heb. 3, 9 for his conjecture that the first Christians supposed the time from the resurrection of Christ till his return to judgment would be exactly as long as the time Israel spent in the wilderness journeying to Canaan; and Daechsel reprints this wild conjecture in his *Bibelwerk*. But all such notions are without foundation in fact. Paul, the writer of Hebrews, and the early church did not fix the time of "the day," but were as ignorant of its exact date as we are; they knew only that it was at hand, that it might come at any time, even in their own lives, and they spoke and acted accordingly, just as we must to-day; only we know, what they did not and could not know, that 19 centuries have elapsed and the Lord has not yet come. For them there were vivid signs of the coming of "the day," just as there have been all through the ages, and still are at the present time. How many of these signs there shall be altogether, no man knew nor knows now; nor with what rapidity they shall follow each other, especially also at the last. The writer of Hebrews could point to what his readers were seeing (βλέπετε): the tribulations gathering for the Jews as the destruction of Jerusalem approached, the rebellions and turbulence which broke out ever afresh, and the defections in the ranks of the Christians. These were indeed signs of the Lord's coming, and were intended for just what this Epistle used them for; and so with the added signs which have occurred since, the accounts of which have come down to us, and the signs which still flare in men's eyes. The longer the Lord delays the more we should know that "the day" is nearer than ever. What a mistake then to disregard the blessings he has vouchsafed to us, to abandon our brethren, our priveleges, and our duties, and to let the world ensnare us. Let not that day find us unprepared!

HOMILETICAL HINTS.

A new year always appears like a new portal into which we enter. Yet mere changes of time, even when these are from one year to another, do not of themselves bring us to anything new. Your life may be just as dark, dreary, hopeless, and broken in the new year as it was in the old. The Christian new year is a different thing; it opens a portal that does lead to something new: the great portal of God's grace in Christ Jesus. This gate leads into nothing less than a new life for those who have dwelt, alas, too long in the old desert of sin and fear under an evil conscience. It conducts them into God's kingdom, where the blood of Christ cleanseth us from all sin, and where we are made kings and priests unto God. And for those who have seen this portal before and have entered it long ere this, it still leads on to that which is new: new knowledge, new power, new comfort, new joy, new visions of hope and glory. And this wondrous portal stands open for us once more in our text for to-day. Let us draw near with a true heart in fulness of faith and enter by the grace of God.

Our text mentions many things that are necessary for us as we enter the new church year. We may think that each of these is to be embodied in a new resolution on our part, but new resolutions will not carry us very far. They reach only as far as our own strength reaches. It is a mistake for us to turn every admonition of God at once into a new resolution. God's admonitions are intended first of all to show us what we lack, in order that we may seek the heavenly power which will give us that very thing which we lack.

Our text is found for the First Sunday in Advent also in the fine series of Epistle texts selected by Nitzsch. Langsdorff in analyzing the thought has the following to say: The first Sunday in Advent is the gate-keeper for the whole church year, and must have a text according. Our text presents first the salvation which Christ obtained for us (19-20), and then our appropriation of that salvation (21 *etc.*). This makes the text very fitting for the first Sunday in the church year. Besides that it is full of advent thoughts. It announces anew that the kingdom of God has come unto us, for here we are shown that Christ has prepared a new way for us into the holy place, by giving himself for the sins of the world, and the way is ready for us to enter upon. The text also bids us prepare the way of the Lord, by using the means of grace in true faith, and by continuing in faith, love, and hope to the end. The great riches of the text reveal in advance with what abundance the table will be set for us in the coming year.

The old Advent hymn of Paul Gerhardt rings through many of the sermons preached on this text:

"Say with what salutation
Shall I Thine Advent greet?"

The old blood-theology is decried by many modern pulpits, but the gateway of our New Year is marked again by Christ's sacrificial blood. — Only with blood in his hands did the high priest of the Jews enter into the Holy of Holies; and only with the blood of Christ may we now venture into the holy presence of God.

Wherever faith is absent, our evil conscience is present; things then are not right between God and us. Most men live in a sort of flight from God, shrinking from contact with him, and fearing to get near to him, instead of seeking him in faith and truth. Faith in Christ's atoning blood makes us glad to be near God.

Let us hold fast the confession of our hope in the new church year, and let our motto be: I shall abide in the house of the Lord forever! Let all things shake and fall, do thou stand firm; for hope maketh not ashamed, the hope that rests on our faithful God and his promises. Many are the delusive visions with which the world lures on the wanderers in the desert; but they are all empty shadows, dissolving in smoke and vapor. Woe to him, who is deceived thereby! And thou, lone wanderer following the cross, art greeted on every side with jeers and mockeries: Where now is thy God? Answer them by the Psalmist's cry to his own soul: "Why art thou cast down, O my soul? and why art thou disquieted in me? hope thou in God: for I shall yet praise him for the help of his countenance." Ps. 42, 5.

It seems at first glance to be a mere outward thing, and therefore quite secondary and inferior, this attendance upon the services in God's house. And yet how vital for us to keep ever in closest touch with the preaching of God's Word, with the blood of the Holy Sacrament, with the people of God who are united in confessing the Gospel. In drawing near to Christ inwardly, we must draw near outwardly too, for Christ is found where his Word resounds and where men truly gather in his name. And so it is not accidental that the matter of attending worship should be appended to the grand thoughts of our text. As the year opens anew, let this admonition be deeply impressed.

Every new Advent season brings the whole world and us one mighty step nearer to that day of days when all our hopes shall be eternally fulfilled.

The First Sunday in Advent sets before us anew:

The Open Portals of Salvation.

with the call:

I. *To behold them;*

II. *To enter them.*

The New Message of the New Church Year:

I. *Follow the new way!*
1. Which Christ dedicated by his blood.
2. Which Christ bids us enter upon in true faith.

II. *Follow with new courage.*
1. Your heart divinely cleansed.
2. Your heart faithful in confession.
3. Your heart joyful in hope.

Adapted from Riemer.

Christian Boldness in Drawing Nigh Unto God.

I. *From what does it grow?*
1. The blood shed for us.
2. The invitation extended to us.

II. *In what does it consist?*
1. The assurance of faith.
2. A good conscience.

III. *How does it show itself?*
1. By an unwavering confession.
2. By faithful attachment to the brethren.
3. By joyful expectation of the Lord.

God's Gifts of Grace Are Spread Out Before Us Once More.

I. *Draw near and behold them.*
II. *Believe and receive them.*
III. *Enjoy and preserve them.*

Suggested by Deichert.

Draw Near With a True Heart|

I. *The way is open.*
II. *Our High Priest calls us.*
III. *Faith suffices.*
IV. *No evil conscience to deter us.*
V. *The world unable to hold us.*
VI. *Many brethren to encourage us.*
VII. *The Lord himself coming to meet us.*

Faith's Advent Vision.

I. *An open heaven above us.*
II. *A host of believers about us.*
III. *A glorious consummation before us.*

THE SECOND SUNDAY IN ADVENT.

2 Pet. 1, 3-11.

Two words occupying prominent positions in the preceding text, meet us again in this one: ἀδελφοί, verse 10, and εἴσοδος, verse 11, the latter, however, restricted to the the eternal kingdom. These links are, of course, welcome, and we willingly make use of them. But the connection of this text with the foregoing is to be sought in its general contents. In the former, reconciliation and justification occupy the foremost place; in this one the Christian life stands in the forefront. Manifestly it would be improper to reverse the two texts. — For the second Sunday in Advent we ought to keep in mind that this text is from Peter's Second Epistle, in which the παρουσία is prominently put before the readers; the close of the Epistle, chapter 3, 7-14 should be allowed to cast its light upon the beginning, for the whole was written with these closing thoughts in mind, to which verse 11 also refers: "For thus shall be richly supplied unto you the entrance into the eternal kingdom of our Lord and Savior Jesus Christ." — Another observation of value is that the word "knowledge," ἐπίγνωσις and γνῶσις, runs through our Epistle. Read the entire letter and note how much rests and hinges on this one word. "Knowledge" here is the heart-knowledge of faith; and in the text its opposite is brought out: "blind, seeing only what is near, having forgotten," verse 9. It is this light of faith that is here emphasized, and it should shine brightly upon the entire Christian life, lifting it up into the full richness which belongs to it. — In correlating the first three texts for Advent, we may do one of two things: refer either to the body of what each text contains, or to the special point which each text in a few striking words

31

presents for the Sunday for which it is selected. If the former is done, this text will describe: *the course of the Christian life which Advent bids us once more to follow,* especially in view of the glorious end. If we prefer the latter, we may place the emphasis on the last verse: *the abundant entrance into the eternal kingdom of our Lord and Savior Jesus Christ.*

Like the former text this one sets before us first of all the great grace which has been granted to us; then comes the admonition as to what should follow on our part; finally we are shown the blessed consequences of heeding the admonition.

The divine grace which has been granted to us.

It is well to glance at Peter's First Epistle and its opening paragraph, verses 3-12. There too the grace of God in Christ Jesus is shown the reader, but in a way to fit and illumine all that follows in that Epistle. So it is here in the shorter Second Epistle with verses 3 and 4. This introduction looks to what follows, namely the perversions of the Gospel introduced by the false prophets who taught a doctrine of libertinism, making the Gospel a cloak for all manner of loose living. Over against this St. Peter sets the grace of God in Christ Jesus as productive of nothing but a life full of Christian grace and virtues.

Seeing that his divine power hath granted unto us all things that pertain unto life and godliness, etc. The first question to decide is whether the genitive absolute τῆς θείας δυνάμεως δεδωρημένης (middle, not passive) introduced by ὡς belongs to the foregoing or to what follows, ἐπιχορηγήσατε. The punctuation in both the R. and A. Versions shows that the two bodies of translators chose the former alternative. But commentators generally consider this a mistake on the ground that it interferes with the run of the thought in the entire first eleven verses, and also on the ground that the salutations in all the letters are not thus amplified or connected with the body of what follows. Whatever weight the latter consideration may

have — an exception might be possible — the former
argument is entirely convincing. This means that we begin a new sentence with the third verse and make it include
all that follows up to the end of the seventh verse, placing
a semicolon after the fourth verse where the A. and the
R. V. show a period. — The granting expressed by δεδωρέω
is entirely gratis, or of grace; it is the act of God, who is
also the subject of the following statements. The conjunction ὡς is not in place of καθώς, so that in verse 5 we
would have to supply οὕτως; it belongs to the genitive absolute, making that subjective; not the fact alone of the
granting is brought out, but also our apprehension and
perception of it: "seeing that" *etc.*; or: "convinced, considering that" *etc.* By δύναμις we must not understand
omnipotent or absolute power, which is not the attribute
God employs in his kingdom of grace in dealing with souls,
but the **power** of God's mercy and grace in Christ Jesus;
it is that power which wrought out our redemption and
deliverance, and which is now busy in ruling and blessing
the church and bringing it to glory. The modifier θείας in
addition to αὐτοῦ is not a pleonasm, but emphatic and
stronger than δυνάμεως αὐτοῦ or τοῦ θεοῦ, just as ἰδίᾳ δόξῃ καὶ
ἀρετῇ. It is **divine** power indeed, for none other could have
wrought out our redemption, or can now provide for the
members of the church what they need for life and godliness. Πάντα is all-embracing and placed at the head of
the sentence for emphasis. Positively **all things** have been
granted us for our spiritual welfare. "Blessed be the God
and Father of our Lord Jesus Christ, who hath blessed us
with every spiritual blessing in the heavenly places in
Christ." Eph. 1, 3. "He that spared not his own Son,
but delivered him up for us all, how shall he not also
with him freely give us all things, τὰ πάντα." Rom. 8, 32.
Spiritual blessings are meant, τὰ πρὸς ζωὴν καὶ εὐσέβειαν,
namely those for **life and godliness.** The "life," which is
enkindled in us by regeneration through the power of the
Holy Ghost in the means of grace, is the essential thing.

3

Here the continuance of that life is meant, our being spiritually alive day by day. Not the granting of this life as such is referred to, but the granting of all that it needs for its existence and continuance. God sustains our spiritual life as he sustains our natural life. "Godliness" is a comprehensive term for the activity of this "life;" it is the "walk in newness of life," Rom. 6, 4. "If we live by the Spirit, by the Spirit let us also walk." Gal. 5, 25. Reverence and all godly actions are embraced in εὐσέβειαν, the very opposite of "the corruption that is in the world by lust."

Through the knowledge of him that called us by his own glory and virtue. The term ἐπίγνωσις is not merely stronger than γνῶσις, as indicating a stronger activity of the subject, but is constantly used of a **knowledge** which reacts very strongly upon the religious life; it is the knowledge which penetrates and moves the heart in the right direction, *i. e.* the active knowledge of faith. **Through** this knowledge God's divine power grants us all things for life and godliness, it is the medium. Knowledge points to the Word; this is·what we must know, it is the stream which flows to us from above both nourishing our life and giving it power to act. The Word itself, however, is not mentioned, but he who is its sum and substance: knowledge **of him that called us,** τοῦ καλέσαντος ἡμᾶς. This is God, as the Scriptures constantly declare, 1 Pet. 2, 9; successful calling is meant. It is our knowledge of God who has so called us and made us his own which constitutes the means for our receiving all other spiritual blessings. We know a gracious God indeed, one who has called us, and hence will not leave his work in us unfinished; and the better we know him the wider open are our hearts to receive all that he grants us. Peter, however, does not write that God called us by his grace, or some such attribute. Grace, love for the totally unworthy, unmerited love, would suggest on our part gratitude; so whatever attribute of God is put forward in speaking of his calling. Peter aims at the right Christian life on our part, therefore he brings forward the glory and virtue of him who has called us: **by his own glory and virtue** (ἰδίᾳ is added by some good MSS.). "With his own δόξα and ἀρετή God executed our call, in sending his Son, the ἀπαύγασμα τῆς δόξης αὐτοῦ (Heb. 1, 3), whose μεγαλειότης Peter beheld (2 Pet. 1, 16-18), as our Savior to make us partakers of the divine nature." Keil. Some distinguish δόξα = *das Sein;* ἀρετή = *die Wirksamkeit.* But both terms are closely related and synonymous; δόξα includes not only what God is, but also what he shows himself to be, the "glory" always shines forth in splendor. The glory by which God called us is his mercy in Jesus Christ, Rom. 6, 4; this shows his highest excellence. The ἀρετή is the efficiency of God, including its exercise and therefore the honor and credit due him. It is not "virtue" in the common sense of the word (see below, on verse 5). It goes well with "glory;" in calling and bringing us into his kingdom God has put forth and manifested the highest and most wonderful ἀρετή, for if it was a great work to create a living soul, it is equally great to re-create it, as it were, by the implantation of a new life. And now we who are called "by his own glory and virtue" are bound to let this glory and virtue manifest itself fully and adequately in us, which is done when our faith unfolds itself in all Christian virtues and graces. We must not darken the δόξα that has called us, by a wicked life, nor nullify the efficient ἀρετή by an unfruitful, useless, good-for-nothing life. In our good works, as fruits of Christian virtues, God must be glorified; men must see them, "and glorify your Father which is in heaven." Matth. 5, 16.

Whereby he hath granted unto us his precious and exceeding great promises. There is considerable difference of opinion as to what δι' ὧν refers to. Keil makes it correspond to διὰ τῆς ἐπιγνώσεως; others refer it even to πάντα, or to ζωὴ καὶ εὐσέβεια. There is no reason why we should not take δόξα καὶ ἀρετή as the antedents of ὧν; Keil's objection that these are not two concepts to which a plural relative may be applied falls to the ground when we ask: Why not? would a singular relative do? Moreover a di-

vine giving is spoken of in this clause (δεδώρηται) a giving
of the highest kind of gifts (ἐπαγγέλματα), and this requires
a divine source and medium. As we are called διὰ δόξης καὶ
ἀρετῆς, so he has granted us his special promises διὰ δόξης καὶ
ἀρετῆς; the two διά one following hard upon the other belong together. Another gracious giving is here brought in,
and the same verb is used as before. We need not trouble
ourselves whether the gift of πάντα above also includes what
now is mentioned as a gift, τὰ ἐπαγγέλματα, or whether these
promises are viewed by themselves. For the object Peter
has in mind they deserve especial mention. Having such
promises we are bound to let our faith shine out in Christian virtues and graces. Why there should be any debate
concerning the **promises** is hard to see. They have been
granted unto us by God's glory and virtue, that is enough;
whether through the prophets, through Jesus' own word,
or through the apostles, makes no difference, for all alike
voice the promises of God. The word ἐπαγγέλματα, things
promised, points to the future, to what we still expect as
promised us by God's glory and virtue. Of course, this
dare not be disconnected from the things promised and already fulfilled in the redemptive work of Christ and the
sanctifying work of the Spirit. The things that we, together with the first readers of Peter's Epistle, still look
forward to are the crown of all that has preceded. In
2 Pet. 3, 4 and 9 we read of ἡ ἐπαγγελία, which is the act of
promising, but here Peter plainly states what the contents
of the promise is: the παρουσία; and he at once adds to his
vivid and striking description (3, 10): "Seeing that these
things are thus all to be dissolved, what manner of persons
ought ye to be in all holy living and godliness," *etc.* In our
text the "promises" are mentioned for the same reason, and
hence we take them to be exactly the same. They deserve to
be called **precious,** for they bring us the highest treasures,
which we ought to prize above all else; and **exceeding
great,** or the greatest, for they open to us the portals of
eternal glory at the consummation of the world, and there
is nothing greater possible for us. "Precious and exceed-

ing great" are words to transplant into our hearts, for we must so account these promises, else they will not be effective in our lives.

That through these ye may become partakers of the divine nature, having escaped from the corruption that is in the world by lust. These promises are part of the Gospel, in fact its crown and culmination. Their purpose is therefore identical with that of the Gospel in general, to separate us from the world which lies in wickedness and perishes, to make us new creatures who shall live in holiness and righteousness with God forever. This view disposes of the idea that the promises here signify the fulfilled promises in Christ's redemption, since by faith in these we are made partakers of the divine nature in regeneration. What is thus restricted to redemption is true of every part of the Gospel promises: they all have saving power, and not in the least those crowning promises of the παρουσία yet to be fulfilled which rest on the redemptive and sanctifying promises already fulfilled and still in the act of fulfillment. Their saving effect is expressed in a striking way, ἵνα γένησθε θείας κοινωνοὶ φύσεως, in order that ye may become partakers of the divine nature. The aorist γένησθε follows the perfect δεδώρηται and indicates what is to follow a past completed action. We are now already, and not merely at the end of the world, to become partakers of the divine nature; this is also indicated by the aorist participle ἀποφυγόντες. Yet it would be a mistake to exclude altogether the glorification which shall be ours when our bodies are raised from the dust at the final return of Christ. Then our becoming partakers of the divine nature will be completely realized, according to the purposes of God. **Partakers of the divine nature,** Besser writes, Let us speak of this great thing modestly and soberly, and in harmony with the analogy of faith. The spirit of error has stolen this passage and used it as a foreign feather wherewith to decorate itself. As Adam before the fall in his knowledge of God, in righteousness and holiness, was a partaker of the divine nature and yet was not himself God, but a man after the image of God, so we by the grace of God and the power of his precious Gospel promises are again to share in the life and blessings of God, as new creatures, renewed in knowledge after the image of him who created us, in holiness and righteousness. Just as a foreigner is naturalized, we are to be transplanted fully into God's kingdom and naturalized in it, so that all that is in this kingdom becomes properly ours. We are to be children of God in the full sense of the word, John 1, 12; having been begotten again, not of corruptible seed, but of incorruptible, through the Word of God which liveth and abideth, 1 Pet. 1, 23, partakers of his holiness, Heb. 12, 10. "He calls the divine nature that which produces the divine presence in us, *i. e.* our conformity to God, or the image of God, which is reproduced in us through the divine presence in us." Hemming. Φύσις here indicates not the *substantia,* but the *qualitas,* yet more than *imitatio divinae bonitatis.* — The aorist participle ἀποφυγόντες, **having escaped,** does not express a condition present or future (Luther: *so ihr fliehet*), but ·an action prior to the aorist γένησθε or at least simultaneous with it. Nor is it merely the negative side of the participation in the divine nature as something positive; as an action on our part it cannot be the correlative (negative) of a condition (positive) into which we are brought. We must take ἀποφυγόντες as the condition which always accompanies participation in the divine nature. In this respect it is like the "knowledge" in verse 3, and like the implied reception of the divine promises in verse 4: the granting in these verses involves such knowledge and reception, and so the possession of the divine nature involves our fleeing from "the corruption that is in the world by lust." These are two opposites: φύσις θεία, and φθορὰ ἐν τῷ κόσμῳ, **the corruption that is in the world.** To attain the one we must flee the other. They are as wide apart as the poles, as conflicting as fire and water, as exclusive of each other as life and death. What the φθορά looks like we see in 2 Pet. 2, 12-19. "He that soweth unto his own flesh shall of the flesh reap corruption." Gal. 6, 8.

Φθορά == the corruption, decay, destruction, perdition whose
climax is eternal death. The place where this "corruption"
rules and works itself out is "the world," and the means
lust, all the desires of sin in man. But "all that is in the
world, the lust of the flesh, and the lust of the eyes, and the
pride of life, is not of the Father, but is of the world.
And the world passeth away, and the lust thereof." 1 John
2 16-17. The world is the devil's pleasure-garden, and is
full of plants which are not planted by the heavenly Father
and shall be uprooted. To flee away or escape suggests a
power which endeavors to catch and enslave or imprison
us, and such indeed is this "corruption;" lust is the snare
with which it operates.

In these preliminary clauses St. Peter has laid a perfect
foundation for the admonition now to follow. We have
all things that pertain unto life and godliness, and certainly
ought to use them in living a godly life; we have the great
promises of the Parousia, participation in the divine nature,
and escape from the destructive lust of the world, hence we
have the completest call, together with the full ability, to
live the new life for the glory of God.

The admonition to add every Christian grace to faith.

**Yea, and for this very cause adding on your part all
diligence, in your faith supply virtue.** We do not begin
a new sentence with verse 5, but read it as the main clause
of the entire period, verses 3-7. Καί is not "yea," but:
"also." In αὐτὸ τοῦτο we have an adverbial accusative:
this very thing. The δέ following is mildly adversative, an
indication that something different is now to follow.* The
sense is perfectly plain in spite of the somewhat unusual
turn given this beginning of the main clause: the divine
power having granted us so much and of such a kind,
the great thing now is that our faith produce its full fruit.

* Hofmann has a peculiar construction of his own, which Keil
in his *Commentar,* 218 etc. shows to be untenable. We need not
enter upon the argument for our purpose.

Adding on your part all diligence, supply, *etc.;* or, as we would most likely express it: Add on your part all diligence and supply (using two imperatives). Peter presupposes power to do this on our part, which idea lies also in the verb "supply;" he may well do so, addressing believers. "As soon as the Holy Ghost through the Word and holy Sacraments has begun in us his work of regeneration and renewal, it is certain that through the power of the Holy Ghost we can and should co-operate, although still in great weakness. But this does not occur from our fleshly natural powers, but from the new powers and gifts which the Holy Ghost has begun in us in conversion, as St. Paul expressly and earnestly exhorts that 'as workers together' we 'receive not the grace of God in vain' (2 Cor. 6, 1). This then is nothing else, and should thus be understood, than that the converted man does good to such an extent and so long as God, by his Holy Spirit rules, guides and leads him, and that as soon as God would withdraw from him his gracious hand, he could not continue for a moment in obedience to God. But if this would be understood thus, that the converted man co-works with the Holy Ghost in the manner as two horses together draw a wagon, this can in no way be conceded without prejudice to the divine truth." *Formula of Concord,* Jacobs' translation, p. 565, 65-66. "You have a goodly inheritance and field; see to it that you do not permit thistles and weeds to grow therein." Luther. Besser narrates that when he was driving through the rich fields of grain with a Pommeranian peasant and remarked that we should grow spiritually in the same rich manner, the peasant replied: "Yes, the ground is of the right kind!" Ἐπιχορηγήσατε **supply,** is the counterpart to δεδώρηται above; it means, etymologically, to furnish the price of a χόρος, but is used generally in the sense of furnish, provide, supply. We must indeed employ our gift, and not remain unfruitful, unprofitable servants, and lose again what we have. Supply **in your faith,** ἐν τῇ πίστει ὑμῶν, not *to* your faith, or *in addition to* it, but *in* it as belonging to it and naturally growing out of it. Faith is *mater et radix bonorum operum*

(Augustine); it is its very nature to produce Christian virtue and the corresponding works. When then we are bidden on our part to use all diligence and in answer to God's granting to make a return for his honor, the appeal means simply to let our God-given faith bring forth its natural fruit. Whatever we supply in our faith is acceptable to God, whatever we supply in our flesh is an abomination to him, Rom. 14, 23.

The fruit of faith here displayed is sevenfold. No sequence as to time is meant; no gradual development of one grace out of the other. All of them lie in faith as a cluster of buds; and each manifests itself as the occasion requires. The order here is not generic in the sense as if no other grouping were natural. Peter groups these graces with an eye to the false prophets whose teaching and practice ran in the very opposite direction; and he binds one grace to another, making each following one the needed complement for the one foregoing. So the seven form a chain. — In your faith supply **virtue,** *strenuus animae tonus ac vigor,* Bengel; moral strength, Meyer; manliness, manly activity, Daechsel. Having πίστις, see that it lacks not ἀρετή. Not that the latter is something new or entirely different; it is the nature of faith to have and manifest ἀρετή. If faith is not dead, a mere sham, an empty lip-profession, the apostle's injunction will be obeyed: "Watch ye, stand fast in the faith, quit you like men, be strong." 1 Cor. 16, 13. 'Αρετή is used in this sense of moral strength only here in the New Testament; in profane Greek the word has too much the flavor of mere human virtue and the credit resulting from that, and was not adopted by the sacred writers as a standard term. Here, as something that must accompany faith if the latter be real and full of vitality, its meaning is plain and entirely Christian.— **And in** *your* **virtue knowledge.** If strength, excellence, and vigor is to keep in the right channel, and not strike out blindly and foolishly; if it is always to strive for the right objects in the right manner and at the right time, then in our vigor we must supply knowledge derived from

the Word of God. Paul prays: "that ye may be filled
with the knowledge of his will in all spiritual wisdom
and understanding, to walk worthily of the Lord unto
all pleasing, bearing fruit in every good work, and increasing in the knowledge of God," Col. 1, 9-10. "Wherefore be ye not foolish, but understand what the will of
the Lord is." Eph. 5, 17. There was a zeal among the
Jews, "but not according to knowledge," Rom. 10, 2,
and it is not yet extinct in the Christian Church. Knowledge is the driver which guides the reins of every other
virtue. It is the eye of all virtues. Peter might have
used another word, wisdom or understanding; he uses
γνῶσις, because there was a false γνῶσις which men of proud
minds boasted of, even as now yet men are proud of their
vain philosophies and scorn the knowledge which is light
and life. He holds fast the word itself and its Christian
meaning, as the precious fruit of faith. — But even Scripture
knowledge may be abused. Knowing for instance that
we are free, we may turn our liberty into license, and
use our very knowledge to excuse and defend a wrong
course. Hence supply **in** *your* **knowledge temperance,**
self-control, self-denial, a right mastery in all things, *"Mass
in allem Wesen und Wandel, Worten. Werken und
Geberden,"* Luther. There must be κράτος in us (ἐγκράτεια)
to hold in check every appetite and desire, lest it slip
beyond safe bounds. The word is sometimes used of
chastity. Acts 24, 25; Gal. 5, 22. This temperance does
not abolish the use, but the abuse of our appetites and
God's gifts. · There is a "temperance" falsely so-called,
a legalistic total abstinence, which condemns what God
has not condemned, while it permits other things not in
harmony with the Spirit of God. True temperance is
disliked, both by the world which loves intemperance of
all fleshly kinds, and by legalists who set up false standards
for Christians. — For this very reason supply also **in** *your*
temperance patience, firm endurance. Temperance and
patience are akin, the one· holds self with a masterful
hand, so that his own desires shall not draw him into a

wrong course; the other holds self with a firm and steady
hand, so that attacks, persecutions and all the trials of
faith shall not turn him from his goal. Besser combines
both in his reference to the Latin proverb, *Abstine, sustine!*
abstain, sustain. Patience is not stoic endurance, which
sternly bears its fate; nor unfeeling resignation, which
has no hope and is akin to despair. Patience is like the
limb of a verdant tree, it bends with the tempest blast, while
the dry, lifeless branch breaks. — In order, however, to
keep its vitality we must supply **in** our **patience godliness,**
He whose heart is reverently turned to God and who walks
in God's ways will willingly for God's and conscience sake
endure what God lays upon him. The heart and strength
of Christian patience is godliness; mere human patience
is built on reasonable arguments and human training. In
their essential qualities the two differ greatly, whatever
the outward appearance may seem. — But while each is
thus concerned about himself, let him not vitiate all his
graces by lack of love to the brethren: supply **in** *your* **godliness, love of the brethren,** φιλαδελφία. 1 John 4, 20-21:
"If a man say, I love God, and hateth his brother, he is
a liar: for he that loveth not his brother whom he hath
seen, cannot love God whom he hath not seen. And this
commandment have we from him, that he who loveth God
love his brother also." Love of the brethren is the complement of love to God or godliness. In giving my heart
to God I give it to God's children, the brethren, likewise,
and *vice versa.* Our communion of faith must reveal itself in our communion of love. And this even if my
brother show many a fault. 1 Pet. 4, 8; 1 Cor. 13, 7.
History tells us how the heathens were impressed by the
love of the early Christians one to another, exclaiming
in wonder: "See, how they love each other!" It tells
equally, and down to the present day, how many Christians
have failed to supply unto their godliness brotherly
love, and so have lost both. — Yet love dare not restrict
itself to this narrow circle. In our brethren indeed the
saving love of God has realized itself, and we are all chil-

dren of God and hence one family, Matth. 23, 8; yet the
love of God has gone out to all men, and is ever endeavoring to bring the others also into possession of his blessings in Christ Jesus. Therefore supply **in** *your* **love of
the brethren love,** τὴν ἀγάπην, the higher love of the spirit
of Christ, not merely φιλία (affection) as distinguished
from ἀγάπη, and certainly not mere humanitarian love, so
much lauded and prized to-day by those whose unitarian
creed is "the fatherhood of God and the brotherhood of
man," whose one aim is the material betterment of earthly
and bodily conditions; but ἀγάπη, the fruit of the Spirit, the
specific Christian virtue, which, while it neglects not the
body, looks ever first to the soul and man's eternal welfare.
Ἀγάπη signifies the love which is not a characteristic of
humanity, but of divinity; in the Christian it is the product
of the Spirit of God: εἰς ἀλλήλους καὶ εἰς πάντας. 1 Thess.
3, 12; Rom. 13, 10.

The golden chain began with faith and ends in love.
Hope shines out in verse 11, and thus the heavenly trio is
complete in our text. All these graces are like a flower,
one row of petals within another, the whole a perfect
blossom of heavenly odor for the honor of our God. While
the Christian is thus adorned, the worldling adds to unbelief vice, to vice blindness, to blindness intemperance, to
intemperance impatience, to impatience ungodliness, to
ungodliness hatred of God's children, to hatred of God's
children all manner of hate, contention and strife. His
course is from iniquity to iniquity. Rom. 6, 19.

**The blessed consequences of using the divine grace
in adding all Christian graces to our faith.**

These are described both negatively (8-9) and positively (10-11).

**For if these things are yours and abound, they make
you to be not idle and unfruitful unto the knowledge of
our Lord Jesus Christ.** ταῦτα ὑμῖν ὑπάρχοντα καὶ πλεονάζοντα
= these things (the graces just spoken of) being present
with you and abounding. The participles are conditional;

Peter is dealing with two possibilities: the presence, and
that abundant, of these things, and their absence ("he that
lacketh these things"). Πλεονάζειν may mean either *abund-
dare* or *crescere*. Some prefer the former. The essential
thing is to have life and its spiritual manifestations; but we
cannot be satisfied to be just alive and no more, we must
have life and its manifestations in full strength. "I came
that they may have life, and may have it abundantly,"
John 10, 10. Others give preference to the meaning
crescere, which also is acceptable. For homiletical purposes both meanings are good. Faith naturally sets fruit,
if it is real, living faith at all; and this fruit is both to be
abundant and to grow and increase. The abundance as well
as the increase of each grace shows the vitality of faith.
If there be paucity of Christian graces, or if there be cessation of growth, the tree itself is dying, either a blight having
fallen upon it, or a worm eating at its heart. — **They make
you to be,** ταῦτα καθίστησιν with accusative; not merely:
they show or make you appear, but they really put you into
a certain class, since you really are such. The question in
spiritual things is always what you are, not merely what
you appear. Too many, as in earthly things, are content
with appearances; all self-deception in this regard is exceedingly dangerous. — The negatives οὐκ and οὐδέ belong to
the adjectives: **not idle nor unfruitful.** The personal
object is not expressed, as the statement is general; we may
supply ἀνθρώπους (compare the following relative ᾧ). "Not
idle" refers back to "all diligence," verse 5, and forward to
"more diligence," verse 10. Faith is power for work and
for good works. "Nor unfruitful" brings in the beautiful
image of a tree or field. Not merely the lack of fruit, fruit-
less, is meant, but unfruitful, the actual condition with the
lack of power for fruit-bearing implied. This terrible condition results when Christian graces are absent, and this is
what we escape when we add to our faith what Peter here
urges upon us. — We rather expect the apostle to say: your
knowledge will produce fruit; but he reverses the two: not
idle nor unfruitful **unto the knowledge of our Lord Jesus**

Christ, *i. e.* by your Christian graces you will be furthered
in the direction of knowledge: "Walk worthily of the Lord
unto all pleasing, bearing fruit in every good work, and
increasing in the knowledge of God." Col. 1, 10. Christian knowledge is not a theoretical, but a practical thing.
Our experience in faith, Christian virtues and works does
not indeed originally produce, but it extends our knowledge
in a thoroughly practical manner: living the Christian life
we know it ever more fully, and thus also him who has
called us unto it, "our Lord Jesus Christ."

**For he that lacketh these things is blind, seeing only
what is near, having forgotten the cleansing from his
old sins.** A reason is advanced, γάρ; not merely the
counterpart of verse 8, which would require δέ. The direct
reference to the readers of the Epistle (ὑμεῖς) is dropped;
ᾧ takes up a concrete case, specializing and illustrating the
general truth. Preachers do well to paint such concrete
pictures in their sermons. "To whom these things are lacking," ταῦτα, the same as ταῦτα at the head of the previous
verse; μὴ (not οὐ) πάρεστιν, for Peter is thinking of a case,
not speaking of one actually existing. — **Is blind,** but in a
certain way; **seeing only what is near,** and **having forgotten;** μυωπάζων = being a μύωψ, a near-sighted person;
λήθην λαβών = having received lethe, forgetfulness. Luther
and others have the interpretative translation: *tappet mit
der Hand;* that indeed is what such a person will be likely
to do. The R. V. offers the margin: *closing his eyes,*
which of course must be understood of one lacking good
sight and suffering with myopia. This eye-disease is a
dangerous thing for a Christian: becoming myopathic,
near-sighted, he sees only "what is near," his earthly, not
his spiritual interest; the dollar in the hand, not the treasure
in the field; the pleasures of this life, not the glory beyond.
Λαβών, second aorist participle, indicates action prior to
μυωπάζων, present participle. The real cause of the blindness, therefore, must be sought not in the lack of Christian
virtues, but in the root from which they spring, in faith
itself: "Remember Jesus Christ, risen from the dead, of

the seed of David, according to my Gospel!" 2 Tim. 2, 8.
To forget him is fatal. — **The cleansing from his old sins**
he has forgotten, and has thus become blind; the cleansing
in Baptism and justification when faith first apprehended
the cleansing merits of Christ; αὐτοῦ points to the personal
appropriation of the blood of Jesus Christ, his Son, which
cleanseth us from all sin, 1 John 1, 8. To forget that means
the death of faith, and hence the death of the fruits that
grow from faith. This blindness then is the opposite of the
ἐπίγνωσις, the opposite of the constant saving knowledge of
what Christ has done for us in delivering us from sin,
death, hell, and the devil, regenerating, justifying, renewing
us by his grace and Spirit, so that we escape the lust and
destruction of the world, and live in newness of life for
his glory and honor. Hence, to go diligently forward in
this life means to continue and increase in this saving
knowledge; to cease, means to fall into the old night of
blindness and death.

What has thus been expressed in various negative
terms is now amplified in positive statements, prefaced
by a new form of the admonition in verse 5. **Wherefore, brethren, give the more diligence to make your
calling and election sure.** Διὸ μᾶλλον = "wherefore the
more," *i. e.*, the more because of the considerations just
adduced; not "rather give diligence" (μᾶλλον drawn to
σπουδάσατε), as if instead of being blind, *etc.*, a better
course were now urged. Peter assumes that his readers
have been living the Christian life and exercising Christian
virtues, but he has just offered reasons why they should
do this more than ever. In both of his Epistles Peter
uses the address **brethren** only here; that makes the appeal stong — ἀδελφοί joins Peter and his readers into one,
and separates both from the teachers of the gospel of loose
living. That separation still holds good. In σπουδάσατε,
give diligence, Peter takes up again σπουδὴν πᾶσαν, "all
diligence," of verse 5. The mark of the living Christian
is diligence; but this must not be understood merely of
outward works, but first of all of the spiritual life itself.

The garden of the soul must be set with the flowers of Christian virtues. The object of this diligence Peter here puts in a striking way; he does not name again the virtues we are to exercise, or any duty incumbent upon us as Christians, he takes the result of all this and makes that the object of our diligence. If we add every virtue to faith, as Peter has urged, we shall make our calling and election sure. That result Peter sets before us as the object of σπουδάσατε: give the more diligence **to make your calling and election sure.** The verb is an aorist, not a present imperative; giving diligence is conceived as one act, however much it embraces and however long it may continue. **Your calling,** ὑμῶν ἡ κλῆσις cannot mean here merely the invitation of the Gospel. How could that be made sure? It is always sure in itself. Here the efficacious calling is meant, which actually brought Peter's first readers into Christ's kingdom. That indeed can be made sure. The article combines the calling and election: ὑμῶν τὴν κλῆσιν καὶ ἐκλογήν. Various commentators make the ἐκλογή dependent on the κλῆσις. Keil may serve as an example: "The κλῆσις is extended in the proclamation of the Gospel," namely as an invitation, "and in the reception of this proclamation by faith the ἐκλογή results, that is the segregation of those called from out the world, and their transfer into the kingdom of grace, the *regnum gratiæ* whose members are the ἐκλεκτοί, 1 Pet. 1. 1." This interpretation makes the whole matter very simple, too simple in fact. In the first place, it is a mistake to reduce the meaning of both the κλῆσις and the ἐκλογή in this fashion in order to secure such simplicity. The κλῆσις is the effective calling. which of itself transfers into the kingdom. The ἐκλογή is the standard term for eternal election, so also in 1 Pet. 1, 1 (ἐκλεκτοί). This old Lutheran interpretation cannot be brushed aside by the superficial objection that what is eternally fixed cannot be made sure. Certainly, it cannot be made sure as far as God is concerned; but Peter is not speaking of this. It can indeed be made sure as far as we are concerned, and this

is exactly what Peter is speaking of: we are to make our
calling and election sure as regards ourselves. Besser
puts it thus: "I know that the God of all mercy has called
me to his eternal glory, unto which he chose me in Christ
Jesus before the foundation of the world, and I am certain that he will keep me firm unto the end, unto the
entrance into the eternal kingdom of our Lord Jesus
Christ. Whence comes this blessed firmness and certainty
for me? From some special revelation concerning God's
secret counsel? No; but from the common revelation of
the divine will of grace in the Gospel of Jesus Christ in
whom I believe. Because I know in whom I believe, namely
in the God who has saved me and called me with a holy
calling according to his own purpose and grace, therefore I am persuaded that he is able to guard that which
I have committed unto him against that day, 2 Tim. 2,
9-12. When the God of all grace perfects, establishes,
strengthens me in faith, 1 Pet. 5, 10, then is my calling
and election made sure." And John Gerhard write: "As
certain as you are of your faith and perseverance, so certain are you of your election." — But this already explains what it means **to make sure,** or firm, reliable, namely
to place our calling and election beyond doubt as far as
we are concerned. And of course, here our election must
be taken together with our calling; we cannot have certainty of the former without the latter, although our calling took place in time, and our election in eternity. To
make our calling and election sure as regards ourselves,
is to have the certainty of eternal salvation. This certainty is beyond doubt for us, if we follow Peter's injunctions in our text. But that does not mean an unconditional, *absolute* certainty, in the Calvinistic sense of a
secret unalterable decree, for which Christ and his redemption, or for which faith and the way of salvation is
only the mode of realization; but a *conditioned, ordinate*
certainty, as revealed in the Scriptures, conditioned on
Christ, the means of grace, and the order of salvation. *"If*

4

ye abide in my word, then are ye truly my disciples,"
ἐκλεκτοί, John 8, 32. "That the good work which he has
begun in them he would strenghten, increase and support
to the end, *if* they observe God's Word, pray diligently,
abide in God's goodness and faithfully use the gifts received." *F. C.,* Jacobs' transl., 653, 21.

For if ye do these things, ye shall never stumble.
This is another reason (γάρ). Ταῦτα ποιοῦντες takes up the
preceding ποιεῖσθαι: if you do this, *i. e.* make your calling
and election sure. **Ye shall never stumble,** οὐ μή, the
double negative, strong in itself: "in no way," is fortified
by ποτέ : "in no way ever." Πταίειν, intransitive, means to
stumble; metaphorically, to offend (James 2, 10; 3, 2);
here in the pregnant meaning of Rom. 11, 11, to stumble so
as to fall and lose salvation. Peter is not content with the
indifferent stand of so many who indeed after a fashion
wish to escape hell, and yet neglect to make quite certain of
heaven. He sees either right progress in faith (diligence),
or a retrogression into idleness, unfruitfulness, blindness,
forgetfulness, or, as it is here expressed, a stumbling that
is fatal. His admonition is accordingly. The Christian
indeed sins daily, even when his calling and election is as
sure to him in the Gospel manner as was that of Peter and
of Paul, but this, while it reminds him constantly of his
danger, is not a fatal stumbling; holding fast his former
cleansing he has the daily forgiveness of his sins. — Now
the final reason is urged upon the readers (γάρ), the
abundant entrance into the eternal kingdom; it is final, for
beyond it Peter cannot adduce another. **For thus shall be
richly supplied unto you the entrance into the eternal
kingdom of our Lord and Savior Jesus Christ.**
The adverb οὕτως takes up the entire previous consideration; ἐπιχορηγηθήσεται, **shall be supplied,** answers to the
ἐπιχορηγήσατε in verse 5, and it is well to note how finely
the words are chosen and balanced. "Thus" — not as a
reward for your work or merit or virtue, but as a result
of God's gracious working out of his purpose successfully
in us. The σπουδὴ πᾶσα in verse 5 is here balanced by

πλουσίως, **richly,** with ample fulness, and it refers to the verb "shall be supplied," not to "the entrance," nor to what follows after (such as a higher degree of glory in heaven for the faithful). God offers and bestows his grace upon us, and then bids us use it; and when we do use it, he pours out richly his blessings upon us, even also the last, eternal blessedness. The connection of εἴσοδος with ἐπιχορηγηθήσεται is unusual, and hence striking. Not the objective entrance or way shall be richly supplied to us, but **the entrance** subjectively, our entering in, the act itself and whatever is required for that. It shall be "supplied to us," that means as a gracious gift, unmerited by any works of ours; and "richly supplied," even as God's grace is rich and exceedingly abundant. "The eternal kingdom" is the kingdom of glory, into which Christ will lead us triumphantly when he returns; over its portals is the signature shining with eternal grace: τοῦ κυρίου ἡμῶν καὶ σωτῆρος Ἰησοῦ Χριστοῦ.

HOMILETICAL HINTS.

Peter's words coincide with Christ's. When he writes that God has "granted us all things that pertain unto life and godliness, through the knowledge of him that called us by his own glory and virtue," we hear the echo of Christ's reply to the imprisoned Baptist's messengers: "Go your way and tell John the things which ye do hear and see: the blind receive their sight, and the lame walk, the lepers are cleansed, and the deaf hear, and the dead are raised up, and the poor have good tidings preached unto them." Matt. 11, 4-5. To-day the voices of jubilant men made whole spiritually are ready to vie with each other, proclaiming Christ's praise and his power to a world lying in bondage. Behold me, the first would exclaim, I was blind, my eyes extinguished and shut, unable to penetrate this darkness of problems and doubts. But his divine power offered me the right salve for my eyes, I received sight, and now I behold in his despised Gospel the key of all riddles. And look at me, another would cry, for I was lame, unable and unfit to walk God's narrow way, which leads unto life, until his divine power gently touched me with its help, so that now I walk the path of peace. O hear also me, his neighbor would immediately beg. Leprosy was my disease, I was lost, cursed, given

over to death in the nauseous corruption of my sin. But his divine
power cleansed me, made me free and strong to forsake my sin
and to serve God with a new life, in obedience unto righteousness,
without fear, and in godliness. But consider me also, another
would say, for I was deaf, my ears closed for the voice of God in
conscience and the law. But his divine power caused me to hear
what the Spirit saith unto the churches, and to heed the voice of
God my Lord. Me the Savior has made rich by the divine power
of his gracious lips, still another would proclaim to the multitude
of the redeemed, for I was too miserable and poor ever to be called
his child, but his Gospel has sought me in my misery and has
brought me into the blessed kingdom of heaven. But I am the
richest of all, one more would magnify and bless, for I was dead,
inwardly atrophied, like the whited sepulchers, outwardly fair, but
inwardly full of corruption and dead men's bones. But he caused
a new world to open within me, new life, faith, hope, love; and
now I praise his name as long as I have breath. Thus there is
not one who has experienced the divine power of the Savior, but
what must bless his name, and all unite in the one confession:
That which now we live unto God, its origin and content, its
form and manifestation, is all due to our Savior alone! And do
you ask, how it all came about, there is but the one answer:
"Through the knowledge of him that called us by his own glory
and virtue." Rump.

Through the land of Egypt there flows the broad stream of
the Nile. Like no other stream this great river sheds blessings
upon the land through which it sends its flood. Without the Nile
Egypt would be a vast desert. Hundreds of canals have been dug
to send the river's waters with their fructifying power as far as
possible. This Advent season shows us another stream, one that
flows through the great world of men, and a thousand canals have
been dug to send its waters into the deserts of heathendom. And
wherever these waters touch the soil there blossom forth life and
spiritual glory. Jesus is the river of blessing for all the world
of mankind. Riemer.

Of all things that pertain unto life and godliness the forgiveness of sin is first. As many as receive Christ to them God gives
the power to become sons of God, or as Peter here says, "to become partakers of the divine nature."—"His divine power" is the
saving and gracious power of Christ crucified and risen. It is
effective in every one who knows Jesus as his Savior by faith;
and this is "the knowledge of him that called us by his own
glory and virtue." — His power and virtue is manifest and operative
in his Word. In this it goes forth to win ever new victories.

"What is the divine nature? It is eternal truth, rightousness,
wisdom, eternal life, peace, joy and pleasure, and whatever is

called good. He who is made partaker of the divine nature, receives all this, so that he lives eternally and has eternal peace, joy and pleasure, and becomes pure, righteous and almighty against the devil, sin, and death." Luther.

Let him who has escaped from the corruption that is in the world by lust, continue to escape daily.

The root of all that is beautiful is faith.. To be sure, the root of a tree is not beautiful, but it produces all the beauty that grows above the surface. So faith is the mother of all Christian excellence. — Virtue: "Watch ye, stand fast in the faith, quit you like men, be strong." 1 Cor. 16, 13. No painted Christianity. But the real power all from God alone. — Knowledge: "That ye may be filled with the knowledge of his will in all spiritual wisdom and understanding, to walk worthily of the Lord unto all pleasing." Col. 1, 9-10. Blind Samson had strength, but no light whereby to guide and use it. — Temperance: "And every man that striveth in the games is temperate in all things." 1 Cor. 9, 25. It is like the bark which protects the tree and every limb, or like the burr which shields the nut within. It avoids all offense. — Patience: Judas desecrates the sacred lips of Jesus with a traitor's kiss, and Jesus bears it in patience. Peter denies him and adds blasphemies to his lying, and Jesus bears it in patience. Pilate derides him, Herod mocks him, he remains patient. "Alway patient and lowly, howe'er vile scoffers offended." — Godliness: "Fear God." 1 Pet. 2, 17. — Love of the brethren: that which I give them they are to return to me — what wealth! To be loveless, to be alone, how dark and cheerless. — Love: which is the fulfilling of the Law, the glory of the Gospel. Love to all men, to God. — Abound: like a tree laden with choicest fruit. God gives us of the great abundance of his grace, and looks for abundance of fruit. John 15, 8.

It is impossible to separate works from faith, even as it is impossible to separate heat and light from fire. Where there are no works, there is no faith to produce them. And this is to be blind and to forget the cleansing from old sins, *i. e.* justification. — There are two kinds of blindness, one that never saw, one that follows former seeing. And the latter is worse than the former. So there are two kinds of lack of forgiveness, one where faith never existed, one where faith has gone out. And the latter is worse than the former. It is a well that has run dry, a treasure-house which the enemy has rifled.

A Christian must be able to say: I know that the God of all grace has called me to his eternal glory, to which also he has chosen me in Christ Jesus before the foundation of the world was laid; and I am sure that he will keep me firm and faithful to the end, unto my entrance into the eternal kingdom of my Lord and Savior Jesus Christ. Besser. This certainty is based

on no private revelation, but on the Word of God which shows
me God's will of grace in Christ Jesus. Where faith in this Word
is found, there this certainty must appear. And the stronger and
more active the faith, the greater, the more joyful, and confident
this certainty will be.

Faith is the oil of works, and works the flame of faith, which
draws the oil and keeps up its flow. — The sevenfold supply of
Christian graces will meet a sevenfold supply of glory in the
kingdom of Jesus Christ, whose riches are unsearchable. Just as
one opens both wings of the front portal when a welcome guest
arrives with a numerous following, so an abundant entrance shall
be vouchsafed to those who come with the following of works
of faith. Rev. 14, 13. He that hath, to him shall be given, so
that he shall have more abundantly, even also at that day, when
we shall appear at the portal of our Savior's everlasting kingdom.

The Abundant Entrance Into the Everlasting Kingdom of Our Lord and Savior Jesus Christ.

I. *Let Christ's abundant gifts to you*
II. *Produce abundant graces in you,*
III. *And thus provide the abundant entrance unto you.*

Peter's Advent Admonition Unto Holiness.

I. *Its only source.*
II. *Its true manifestation.*
III. *Its glorious advantage.*

C. C. Hein.

How Will I Attain the Abundant Entrance Into the Eternal Kingdom of the Lord?

Two conditions must be fulfilled:

I. *I must partake of the Lord's grace.*
II. *The Lord's grace must become fruitful in me.*

Riemer.

The Advent call:

Make Your Calling and Election Sure!

I. *By faith,* which takes all that the divine power grants
unto us.
II. *By zeal,* which uses all that faith receives.
III. *By hope,* which joyfully goes forward to all that faith is
promised (verses 4 and 11).

Partakers of the Divine Nature.

As such we are

   I. *Freed from sin.*
  II. *Covered with grace.*
 III. *Growing in holiness.*
 IV. *Assured of glory.*

———

The Shining Path of the Christian's Life.

It is made radiant by

  I. *The gifts of grace.*
 II. *The fruits of grace.*
III. *The promises of grace.*

———

THE THIRD SUNDAY IN ADVENT.

2 Tim. 4, 5-8.

This is indeed an appropriate text for the Third Sunday in Advent, a close parallel to the old gospel text; and let us remember, the gospel texts are the ones which give character to the different Sundays in the church year. Faithful John the Baptist (Matth. 11, 2-10) is seconded here by faithful Paul the Apostle and faithful Timothy the Evangelist. The former, as well as John the Baptist, gave his life for his work. The old epistle (1 Cor. 4, 1-5) follows the same general trend: Paul as a faithful steward of the mysteries of God is sure of the divine approval, to which, as it shall be rendered at the last great day, he makes his appeal over against any untimely judgment of men. Both epistle texts mention "that day," and thus stand out as true Advent texts. — The relation of this text to the two epistolary texts preceding it is equally plain: here the close of life is emphasized, a close such as every life should have — note the last clause in the text: *"all* them that have loved his appearing." — Paul and Timothy, as well as John the Baptist (old gospel) and Paul judged by the Corinthians (old epistle) and John the Baptist announcing the kingdom (Eisenach gospel), are incumbents of the office of the holy ministry. This feature may be emphasized, especially if there be circumstances in the congregation making such emphasis necessary. Paul and Timothy are "ensamples to the flock" (1 Pet. 5, 3), "an ensample to them that believe, in word, in manner of life, in faith, in purity" (1 Tim. 4, 12); so every Christian pastor should be. While this special responsibility rests upon them, we must hold fast that the way of salvation is the same for pastor and people; both

56

must be faithful unto death, then shall they receive the
crown of life. Our text, therefore, properly summed up,
sets before us: *The close of a faithful Christian life, to
which the Advent season once more mightily impels us.*
Or, if we prefer to lift out one controlling thought from
the text: *The crown of righteousness which is laid up
for all who have loved the Savior's appearing.* The text
itself falls naturally into two parts, the one introduced by
the emphatic σὺ δέ, "but thou," and the other by ἐγώ, "I."

Paul's admonition to Timothy.

The entire admonition addressed to Timothy is stamped
with the solemnity of the great judgment which Paul
and Timothy alike shall come to face: "I charge thee
in the sight of God, and of Christ Jesus, who shall judge
the quick and the dead, and by his appearing and his
kingdom," 4, 1; comp. 4, 8. These solemn opening words
of our chapter are followed by a prophetic and explanatory
statement showing how wickedly and foolishly people will
act in the days to come: "They will not endure the
sound doctrine; but having itching ears, will heap to themselves teachers after their own lusts; and will turn away
their ears from the truth, and turn aside unto fables."
Timothy is to conduct himself and his office in a manner
altogether opposite to these people: **But be thou sober
in all things, suffer hardship, do the work of an evangelist, fulfil thy ministry.** It is the nature of the entire
Epistle, the tone of which is altogether personal, that the
emphatic pronouns "I" and "thou" should frequently appear; see σὺ οὖν, 2, 1, and σὺ δέ, 3, 10, also σὺ, ὦ ἄνθρωπε
θεοῦ, 1 Tim. 6, 11, and in our text: **But thou.** What the
exact nature of this opposition is, marked by such an emphatic turn, we may gather either from the characterization of the perverted people described in the foregoing
verse, or from the admonition which urges Timothy to
meet such conduct as a Christian pastor should, verse 5.
Where men despise "sound doctrine," Timothy is ever
to proclaim it as an evangelist; where they show "itch-

ing ears," longing for teaching which will permit and
justify their lusts, Timothy is to preach only the Word
with its condemnation of sin and its inculcation of righteousness, whether men will hear or whether they forbear;
where they are in love with "fables," Timothy is to offer
nothing but the everlasting facts of salvation. All this
lies in the four imperatives: **Be sober, . . . suffer
hardship, do the work of an evangelist, fulfil thy
ministry.** They stand out as a tower of strength against
the incoming flood of heresy, fanaticism, and religious perversions and follies generally. "The time will come," we
read in verse 3; Timothy will get his taste of it, and we
know that ever anew these times come, and as the end
of the world draws nearer, their character is more pronounced, and the danger connected with them ever more
grave. "Be sober," νῆφε, pres. imperative denotes continuous action; Timothy is never to lose his head, to
be swept from his course, to lose a right judgment in
things spiritual, to become intemperate in his teaching
or his practice, to grow intoxicated by allowing any false
notion room in his heart and mind. "Let us watch and
be sober," 1 Thess. 5, 6; "Be ye therefore of a sound
mind (σωφρονήσατε) and be sober unto prayer," 1 Pet.
4, 7. Soberness is one of the cardinal and characteristic
Christian virtues; see, besides the passages quoted, 2 Tim.
2, 26; 1 Cor. 15, 34; 1 Tim. 3, 2 and 11; Tit. 2, 2; 1 Pet.
1, 13; 5, 8. The admonition here is a comprehensive one:
in all things, all questions which may arise in doctrine,
or in practice, in the public ministry, or in private life.
This soberness can be maintained only by abiding by the
revealed Word; it alone gives soundness, balance, temperate judgment, safety, that a man stumble not nor fall
by going too far to the one or to the other side. In our
land especially, the paradise of sects and of all manner
of religious extravagance, Paul's admonition must be
heeded. No folly is put forth from some pulpit or church
platform to-day but what some men, and often many, ap-
plaud and adopt it as the quintessence of truth. Think

of Eddyism, Dowie's dreams, Russell's prophecies and sub-
versions of all Christian truth, the revivalism, legalism,
dislike and evasion of hundreds of Scripture teachings
found in sectarian churches, to say nothing of the papal
fables and arrogance, and all the inimical forces outside
the church. Every one of them runs counter to the sober
Word of God. Stellhorn interprets and applies our text
in a fine manner: "Experience teaches, how the tendencies of the day usually carry everything along with
irresistible force, so that often those are swept into the
current who knew and stood for what was right, and
how difficult it is to swim against the stream, especially
for young and comparatively inexperienced men. Therefore Paul is justified in admonishing his young assistant,
and together with him all Christians and particularly all
pastors, to resist with all their might any such tendencies,
and to maintain the Christian and theological presence of
mind amid the universal intoxication and giddiness which
distinguished a Paul, and after him above all others a
Luther, and which through him has become a characteristic and an adornment of the church bearing his name.
But this soberness and balanced judgment must manifest
itself 'in all things' and extend to all questions and occurrences; for a lack of soberness, balance, and caution
in *one* point has frequently become the cause of a mighty
defection in doctrine and in life. All heresy has its origin
in a one-sided, ill-considered emphasis of some truth,
pressed beyond its proper bounds and relations." *Pastoralbriefe* II, p. 57.

The following three imperatives: "suffer hardship, do
the work of an evangelist, fulfil thy ministry," κακοπάθησον,
ποίησον, πληροφόρησον, are aorists (while νῆφε is present tense)
and indicate simple action, referring thus either to individual occurrences, as these may arise from time to time:
"suffer hardship" whenever hardship comes (see 1, 8; 2,
3); "do the work of an evangelist" in every case requiring
such work; "fulfil thy ministry" as now this service or that
is needed; or, summing up the entire conduct of Timothy

in each of the three directions, combining each set of
actions into one point (see Robertson, *Kurzgefasste Grammatik d. Neustest. Griechisch*, p. 190). — **Suffer hardship,**
as a good soldier of Jesus Christ, 2, 3. Timothy is engaged
in a campaign, blows and wounds will be inflicted upon
him, for men "will not endure sound doctrine," 4, 3. They
will resent its preaching by antagonizing the preacher. Try
it; you will soon run against some painful κακόν or evil
which hatred will inflict upon you. Take it as a matter of
course, it is a badge of honor for the true soldier of the
Lord; the veteran — and Paul was one — is justly proud
of his battle-scars. Especially painful are the blows which
come from those who should be our companions in arms,
but who compromise with some error of the day, and then
turn against us when we strike them with the testimony of
the Word. Reylaender's opinion that κακοπαθεῖν here refers
only to the ordinary disagreeable experiences connected
with the ministry in a Christian congregation, is entirely too
colorless and pays no attention to the context. Timothy
may have been somewhat timid, and may have needed the
reminder: "God gave us not a spirit of fearfulness," 1, 7;
but his soldierly courage and endurance was certainly tested
by many special hardships resulting from the stand he had
to take against the delusions and errors that rose one after
another against him. — **Do the work of an evangelist,**
εὐαγγελιστοῦ, which Bengel calls *vocabulum grande*. This
designation applied to Timothy cannot mean an especial
office like that of Philip (Acts 21, 8), distinguished from
that of an apostle, a pastor or teacher (Eph. 4, 11), for
Timothy was not a travelling missionary, but the head-
pastor at Ephesus; he was therefore an evangelist in the
wider sense of the term, as every preacher of the Gospel is
such, a Paul as well as a local preacher of to-day. The
claim that the word is not so used in the New Testament
is refuted by this very passage. Luther's translation is
therefore to the point: *Tue das Werk eines evangelischen
Predigers.* Ἔργον is without the article, but is made definite by the appended genitive εὐαγγελιστοῦ; his activity is

dignified by the term "work" (comp. similar expressions
1 Tim. 3, 1; 1 Cor. 16, 10; Eph. 4, 12), an activity, as
Reylaender puts it, "worthy of the sweat of the noblest."
The work of an evangelist is preaching the Gospel, the very
thing to counteract the μύθοι or fables of the errorists, the
great antidote for all religious follies. Put the eternal
Gospel facts in place of the foolish and pernicious fancies
of men. Evangelical preaching is to-day a crying need, just
as in the days that came for Timothy. — **Fulfil thy ministry.** Ἡ διακονία is wider than τὸ ἔργον εὐαγγελιστοῦ, it embraces every part of Timothy's office, and speaks of it as a
grand whole. Διακονία is the service which is rendered for
the benefit of others, "ministry" in the true sense of the
word, to which Timothy was officially called, which was his
life's work (see 1 Tim. 1, 12; Acts 20, 24; etc.). The verb
πληροφορεῖν, "fulfil," execute, *ausrichten* (Luther), or
better: *vollstaendig ausrichten,* fits the object exactly.   A
minister of the Gospel has many things to do in the service
of his people and of others whom he is able to reach. In
an evil age his duties will include many kinds of special
service. To meet the errors of the coming time Timothy,
for one thing, had to preach the Gospel, but this was not
enough, he had to add whatever else was necessary to lead
and shield the flock commended to his trust, as Paul also
in his two letters shows to him in detail. He must not be
remiss in any single point, lest the enemy secure a hold.
Paul's admonition runs counter to all those views which
offer one's energy, the zealous work, and the success in
one direction as an excuse for dilatoriness, neglect, and
failure in some other direction.   The Gospel minister
especially, and the man of God generally, must be "complete, furnished completely unto every good work" (3, 17).
We must cultivate assiduously not merely the duties we like,
and to which we naturally incline, but even more assiduously the duties which are hard for us, and in the performance of which we at first take less pleasure. If the question
arises: "Who is sufficient for these things?" 2 Cor. 2, 16,
the answer is ready: "As of God, in the sight of God,

speak we in Christ," verse 17; and: "I can do all things in him that strengtheneth me," Phil. 4, 13. Daechsel is wrong when he asserts that *non omnia possumus omnes* applies here, and that each man has a right to search out his strongest abilities and work in the line of these. Paul contradicts these ideas by declaring: "I am become all things to all men, that I may by all means save some. And I do all things for the Gospel's sake, that I may be a joint partaker thereof." 1 Cor. 9, 22-23.

Paul's example a reenforcement of his admonition.

For I am already being offered, and the time of my departure is come. The emphatic ἐγώ is parallel with σὺ δέ in verse 4, moreover the two are intimately related since Timothy was doing Paul's work as his assistant in Ephesus. This ἐγώ is devoid of egotism and altogether in harmony with Christian humility; it was written for Timothy's sake, to inspire him with faithfulness, courage, hope, and joy. Its effect on us is to be the same. Paul asks Timothy to do no more than he has already done himself. But there is here a deeper and more tender touch: Paul has reason to conclude that he is near the end of his apostolic service; death may bring to a ·quick close the work in which Timothy had become his loyal associate. As Paul must relinquish his own activity, he places the work on Timothy's shoulders and urges him to carry it forward with all faithfulness. **I am already being offered,** writes Paul, σπένδομαι, *poured out as a drink offering* (margin). He does not say θύομαι, I am being sacrificed, as thought he likened his anticipated martyrdom to a sacrifice. The figure employed is much finer. His bloody death he compares only to the pouring out of a drink-offering ʹ(Numb. 15, 1-10), the libation which was added to the sacrifice proper and formed the last act of the sacrificial ceremony. Paul looks at his entire .ministry as an offering to God (Rom. 15, 16; Phil. 2, 17), and his death by martyrdom as the last appropriate act in that offering. He uses the present tense, σπένδομαι, not so

much because his actual death is close at hand and he
looks at it as so certain as if he were already undergoing it now, but rather because his imprisonment, trial at
Rome, *etc.*, were already the beginning of the last sacrificial act; therefore ἤδη σπένδομαι, I am already being offered up. However long his actual life might yet continue, he was now looking death in the face and contemplating his service as finished. — In a parallel sentence
Paul repeats and thus emphasizes what he has just said:
and the time of my departure is come. He now uses no
figure, for while ἀνάλυσις (and the verb ἀναλύειν) is properly
derived from the language of sailors: lifting the anchor,
the term is a common one denoting simple departure like
the German *Aufbruch* (*aufbrechen*). The Vulgate translates: *dissolutio*, which might be admitted, yet "departure"
is far more preferable. The verb ἐφέστηκεν, "is come,"
pref. from ἐφίστημι, *herantreten*, expresses the same
thought as the previous sentence, namely that the time
for his departure is now here, and that therefore he is
even now engaged in the preliminaries of departing. When
Timothy read these words there may well have been a
film of tears in his eyes. The γάρ, at the head of the verse,
really takes in all that follows (6-8), although in the
reading, before one passes to verse 7-8, the thought of
verse 6 alone justifies γάρ: Paul about to end his labors,
urges Timothy, his assistant, to continue them for this
very reason with all faithfulness.

But this thought grows at once into a greater when
the next sentences are added: Paul's life of faithful service, now about to be crowned by the righteous
judge, must act as a stimulus and an inspiration to
Timothy, to follow his principal's footsteps. There is no
trace of regret or sadness in these words of the apotle;
on the contrary, as the figures of speech, the balance of
phrase and clause, and the uplift in the entire imagery
show, a radiant joy, a holy satisfaction, a triumphant
hope on the eve of realization. **I have fought the good
fight, I have finished the course, I have kept the faith.**

The object is put first for emphasis: The good fight have I fought; ἀγών in the sense of contest in general for a prize in the games of the stadium (not battle against foes, nor even gladiatorial combat). "I have fought," ἠγώνισμαι, perf. tense, = it is ended, and I stand now as the victor about to receive the prize (1 Tim. 6, 12: "Fight the good fight of faith"). While it is not improper in the interpretation to refer to the devil, the world, and the flesh as those against whom the contest was made (Stellhorn), the idea conveyed here by Paul's figure is really not of a battle against deadly enemies, but of a striving for a prize which could be secured only by the utmost effort and mastery in the contest. There is reference in the figure, as here employed, to defeated contestants. The article τόν must not be overlooked; it points to the one definite contest to which every Christian is called (see πᾶσιν, verse 8), a Paul indeed in the foremost rank, but we all with him. And this contest is a beautiful, honorable one, καλός; Bengel: *bonum illum agonem.* Together with the article this adjective marks the contest as one especially distinguished, namely the spiritual contest for the heavenly prize appointed by the Lord for all his followers, whereby they are to show their faith and faithfulness; it is the same as "the high calling of God in Christ Jesus," Phil. 3, 14, where also the goal and the prize are mentioned; "the holy calling," 2 Tim. 1, 9; "a heavenly calling" in which we are "partakers," Heb. 3, 1. — The ἀγών which Paul has in mind especially is the δρόμος: **I have finished the course,** namely the race, and that as a victor. The object, τὸν δρόμον, is again put forward for emphasis and made definite by the article. Paul's figure here might be restricted to his apostolic course, as in Acts 20, 24; Gal. 2, 2; but verse 8 leads us to include more: his whole Christian life, including, of course, the work of his great office: 1 Cor. 9, 24-26: "Know ye not that they which run in a race run all, but one receiveth the prize. Even so run that ye may attain . . . . I therefore run, as not uncertainly . . . . lest by any means after that I have preached

to others, I myself should be rejected." Every Christian
has his race to run in the place where God put him, with
certain gifts, sometimes in certain offices, always however
in the individual setting his life may have. Let every
man finish his course as a victor. — What the images place
before us with their peculiar beauty is now stated with
simple directness, in a terse climax: **I have kept the faith.**
Here πίστις is not faithfulness in adhering to the rules of
the games, and thus a continuation of the figure, but πίστις
in the Pauline sense: the saving faith in the heart, such
as not only an apostle, but every Christian must have and
keep to the end. Paul had to "keep" his faith; he too then
might have lost it, as we know Judas actually did. Let
us not imagine that pastors and leaders in the church are
exempt from spiritual temptations and dangers; above all
let them not themselves give such ideas room. In fact, we
of the ministry have our own special tests of faithfulness
to undergo, and these generally involve others, often many
others; for which reason also these Pastoral Epistles were
given to the church, with their injunctions and promises
not only as regards our official work, but also as regards
our private Christian life and conduct. 1 Tim. 6, 20;
Rev. 3, 11.

From the arena where the contests are fought out
Paul now takes Timothy and all his readers to the
stand of the judge who will presenty award the prize.
**Henceforth there is laid up for me the crown of right-
eousness, which the Lord, the righteous judge, shall
give to me at that day.** "Henceforth," λοιπόν, really: as
to the rest; as to what remains, all else being finished.
Paul must yet endure his martyrdom, but he gives no
thought to that; to him it is as if it were already endured;
his mind is perfectly at rest, looking at the glorious things
to come. What attracts his gaze, and what he wants Timothy to behold, is **the crown of righteousness** awaiting
him. Paul uses δικαιοσύνη for the imputed righteousness
which is ours by faith, and also for the inherent righteous-

5

ness which is ours by living the Christian life. Both
meanings may here be joined together. The genitive τῆς
δικαιοσύνης = which belongs to righteousness (gen. of possession), not: the crown which consists in righteousness
(*Luth. Com.*, making it gen. of apposition); compare Gal.
5, 5: ἐλπὶς δικαιοσύνης, hope which belongs to righteousness,
to which it has a right, not righteousness as the substance
of hope. "The crown of life," James 1, 12, and "the crown
of glory," 1 Pet. 5, 4, are not true parallels, although they
sound so (against Meyer, ed. 1866), for the simple reason
that the Scriptures speak indeed of "life" and "glory" as
the reward of faith in the life to come, but they never
speak so of righteousness. "Crown of life" = crown
which itself consists of life; but "crown of righteousness"
is not crown which consists of righteousness, but which
belongs to righteousness as its reward. The **crown** στέφανος,
really: the wreath, belongs to the victor; στέφανος ἄφθαρτος,
1 Cor. 9, 25; ἀμαράντινος, 1 Pet. 5, 4. Both the R. and the
A. V. have followed Luther in translating στέφανος with
"crown" instead of wreath; Reylaender remarks that there
is something enduring about the word "crown" which we
appreciate in this connection. — **There is laid up for me,**
ἀπόκειταί μοι, in form pres. tense, but in sense perfect, used
so for the verb ἀποτίθημι; the crown is ready for the apostle,
is has been laid aside for him (so the perf. pass. sense).
The implication is that precently his name shall be announced, the judge will then reach for the crown and place
it on the victor's brow. — **Which the Lord, the righteous
judge, shall give to me at that day.** Ἀποδώσει is placed
before its subject, lending it emphasis: Paul sees the glorious act as it shall occur, and his heart is filled with joy. The
idea of grace, of lack of merit is not conveyed in the
verb "shall give" in this connection, for the giver is
the Lord, Christ, to whom all judgment is committed,
the righteous judge, who "shall render unto every man according to his deeds," Matth. 16, 27; Rom. 2, 6 *etc.*; 2 Cor.
5, 10; 2 Thess. 1, 6 *etc.* Grace precedes justice; now Christ
is ready to pardon and forgive, but at that day he will fol-

low justice alone. He who now rejects pardon will look for it in vain at that day. The adjective δίκαιος corresponds to δικαιοσύνη: the judge deals righteously: to the righteous he gives the crown of righteousness. Christ is our righteousness now by faith in his saving merits, and at the last day he will acknowledge and honor such righteousness in all who have accepted it by faith and shown the power of it in a righteous life. This judge now makes himself our debtor by his gracious promises, and as a righteous judge he will redeem every one of those promises at the last day. — **At that day** = the great day of judgment; Bengel calls it *dies novissimus pantocriticus;* the day when Christ returns in glory. Paul thinks of no special resurrection and judgment for himself and some preferred class (error of the so-called "first resurrection"), but, as the next words indicate, of the universal judgment of all nations and men. — **And not only to me, but also to all them that have loved his appearing.** Οὐ μόνον δὲ . . . καί, while it distinguishes between Paul and all others, at the same time it connects and joins them together. Paul's joy is not in standing alone and receiving a crown all by himself, but in being joined by "all them that have loved his appearing," who all will receive the same honors. We must not forget Timothy among these "all," whom Paul is urging to be faithful in his Christian life and office: Paul's crowning is to stimulate Timothy, but it can do this only when a similar crowning lies in prospect for him; and so with us all. Paul does not emphasize this faithfulness by pointing to its fruits, namely faithful works; he does not say the crown of righteousness is for all them that have been faithful and diligent in righteous works. He does a far finer thing, he points not to the fruits, but to the root of this faithfulness: *love* — "all them that **have loved** his appearing." This is a master-stroke. It at once suggests the question: Does Timothy love the Lord? do we? If so, there will be a faithfulness full of rich fruits in all his life, in ours likewise, after the pattern of the faithfulness Paul has just described in himself. The perfect tense in the participle ἠγαπηκότες might refer to the present (who have loved, and therefore are now loving — Meyer), but is far better explained as written from the standpoint of "that day," and thus referring to all Christ's faithful ones who "have loved" his appearing. Paul does not write simply αὐτόν, him, the Lord, although he certainly means also our love for the Lord; he writes τὴν ἐπιφάνειαν αὐτοῦ, **his appearing.** This cannot be the appearing in the flesh (2 Tim. 1, 10), as has been occasionally interpreted, but must be the appearing unto judgment spoken of in verse 1: "Christ Jesus, who shall judge the quick and the dead," so the great majority of interpreters. Paul has exactly the view of Christ's return which Jesus enjoined upon his disciples: it shall be like the coming of beautiful springtime, Luke 21, 29-30; Matth. 24, 32-33, and our hearts should greet it with loving and joyful anticipation. He loves Christ aright who loves his appearing and sings with the Spirit and the bride, saying: "Come!" Rev. 22, 17. "Amen: come, Lord Jesus," 20.

HOMILETICAL HINTS.

Here Paul turns to Timothy, the man of age to the man of youth, the man grown weary to him who is bright and fresh, the prisoner to the man at liberty, the man who is facing death to him who looks forward to a long life of service; but this is not complaining old age, unable to understand youth, nor is it the old pharisaic manner of a former pharisaic pupil, heaping burdens upon others, whilst unwilling to lay a finger to them himself, or placing a yoke upon others which he, the apostle himself, has never borne. He is not preaching to another, and himself becoming a castaway. The counsel and command he gives here is the sum of his own life's experience, tested and proved in many a hard hour, old gold, precious for every Advent time and all Advent pilgrims.—Matthes.

Live as, when you die, you would wish to have lived. — He who is able to face God in death, need not worry about facing the world. — A Christian is always in the making, hence his fight is never finished. It is a mistake to imagine that here we can reach a period when we shall be wholly at peace and need not strike another blow. One battle is bound to be followed by another; every victory is to help us gain one more. As the Christian looks back he sees only a long line of battles and victories. But these lead to peace and triumph at last: "I have fought the good fight."

The situation of Timothy was not essentially different from our situation to-day. On the one hand he was met by stern legalism, on the other by rank liberalism. Besides Jewish hate and pagen hostility the young church was rent by various sects. One opinion clashed with another, one show of wisdom followed another. Who does not see the resemblance to our own age? What has Paul to say to his son Timothy in this trying situation? This one thing: "Be thou sober in all things." The momentary success of restless fanatics is not to disturb, or mislead, or blind and deceive him. The opposition of men is never to move him from his adherence to the truth. These all shall pass like a shadow, but the Word of God shall abide forever, and they with it who calmly, soberly, steadily, sensibly adhere to it in faith. And it is still so to-day. It will cost a conflict indeed, perhaps many a conflict; but we are called with Paul and Timothy to "suffer hardship," to "fight the good fight of faith," and of the victory there is no doubt.

There is no compromise possible between the vagaries of our time and the eternal truth of God. "Suffer hardship!" — It makes no difference whether ours was a fine career, full of fame and honor, or 'lowly and despised, so we be found faithful at last. — The best earthly advantage is the crown of righteousness in the end.

The sober bread of life is not intended to tickle the perverted palate of our time. They who have found all the wisdom of men to be but apples of ashes, will rejoice to find the true nourishment of the soul in the Word of Jesus Christ. Let us abide by the heavenly manna, nor even think of mixing it with the poisonous spices which every age offers us anew.

Before the sacrifice was slain a drink offering was poured out. Paul's long sufferings in prison were to him the drops of that drink offering slowly poured out; his expected martyr death the final sacrifice.

Let us keep the faith — the faith we confess with all true believers, the heavenly truth committed to our trust. Let us keep the faith — the faith which trusts the Savior and his Word. Let us keep it in our daily life, whatever betide. Let us keep it in love, pitying all who assail our Lord. Let us keep it in battle, fighting in the strength of the Spirit. Let us keep it to the end. The Lord will make us faithful.

The prize of victory in the old Greek contests was highly esteemed. Yet it consisted of no golden reward, no crown set with sparkling jewels, it was nothing but a wreath of pine twigs, or a circlet of olive leaves, and any day any man might pluck for himself the very same kind of twigs and leaves and weave a crown like that. After all it was but a fading reward, well symbolized by what it was made of. But ours is an eternal crown which shall never fade or pass from us.

What a day that shall be when the Lord's "appearing" which we have loved shall actually take place! How will they greet it who have despised his Gospel, betrayed his church, and lifted themselves in the pride of unbelief? How will they meet it who have given rein to their flesh, cast aside the restraints of godliness, and revelled in the liberty which is license? Where will their haughty seats of learning be, and the idle theories they have propounded? Where their temples of pleasures where they brought the sacrifices of sin? And we — where shall we be on that day, and our faith, our service, our hope? It shall shine forever, decked with the crown of righteousness, which the Lord, the righteous judge, shall give us at that day.

The open portal of salvation — the abundant entrance — and now the goal attained at last.

Let This Advent Season Set Before Us the Crown of Righteousness at That Day.

I. *To keep us faithful to the last.*
1. Like Timothy, with so much of his life and labor still before him.
   a) He had to watch and be sober in all things, because of so many false teachers and foolish hearers.
   b) He had to endure affliction, such as was incident to his position and work.
   c) He had to make full proof of his ministry and perform faithfully all the duties of his calling.
2. Like Paul, with his course nearly finished.
   a) He had kept the faith (fought the good fight; finished the course).
   b) He was ready to depart (to be offered up). These are our examples. Let us follow them; so shall the crown be ours.

II. *To fill us with joy in advance.*
1. Joy amid every difficulty, trial, *etc.*
2. Joy ever brighter as the end approaches.
3. Joy unspeakably great when that day as last arrives.

For God and With God in the New Church Year.

I. *In faithful service.*
II. *In valiant conflict.*
III. *In final triumph.*

Slightly altered from Rump.

The Lord's Eternal Advent.

I. *How shall we meet it?*
II. *What shall it bring us?*

Riemer.

Fulfil Thy Ministry!

I. *The faithful administration of the office of the ministry which is full of blessing for a Christian congregation.*
II. *The gracious reward which the faithful minister shall receive at the Lord's hands.*

C. C. Hein.

Follow Paul!

I. *In constant faith.*
II. *In evangelical soberness.*
III. *In ceaseless zeal.*
IV. *In triumphant hope.*

They Who Love the Lord's Appearing

know that

I. *Their position is trying;*
II. *Their weapons are good;*
III. *Their victory is sure.*

Caspari.

THE FOURTH SUNDAY IN ADVENT.

1 John 1, 1-4.

As the last three texts evidently belong together, treating of the fundamentals, the development, and the glorious close of the Christian life, so the next three texts, the Fourth Sunday in Advent, Christmas Day, and Second Christmas Day, also belong together: all three set Christ himself before us, the first as the Word of life, the second as the Remover of our sin, the third as the eternal Son of God; and all three speak of his becoming manifest, the first two using this very term, and the third a similar term, "God hath spoken unto us." — Comparing our text with the one for Christmas we will see that really both are Christmas texts, for in both shines the full light of Christmas joy. The Fourth Sunday in Advent is thus drawn to the Christmas festival, even as it frequently falls very near to that joyous celebration. We may therefore sum up the contents of our text in the great theme, which already has a Christmas ring to it: *The Word of life was manifested for our joy.* In the gospel lesson of the Eisenach selection we have a text from the introduction of John's Gospel (John 1, 15-18), showing us Christ in his grace and truth; for the epistle we have the introduction to the First Epistle of John, showing us Christ the Word of life. Our text is all one grand sentence and hence admits of no division in the usual manner. Yet we may divide the thought: there is first of all the manifestation of the Word of life to the first witnesses, and secondly their testimony and declaration to us; yet these two chief thoughts are closely twined together and interlock in the second and third verse.

72

The Word of Life manifested to the first witnesses.

John's First Epistle does not open like a letter; it lacks the usual form of the address, the author's name, the name of the person or persons addressed, and the words of greeting. It is the same with the close of the Epistle, there are no greetings to individuals or churches, in fact there is no closing word at all. Some, accordingly, have called this a short treatise rather than a letter, yet its epistolary tone is pronounced throughout, so that we are bound to read it as a letter — to be sure, a letter so exalted in its contents and tone as to have only one real parallel, the Epistle to the Hebrews. Daechsel solves the absence of any formal address, *etc.*, by dating the Epistle in the time of the apostle's exile, and this exile he fixes as having occurred between the years 54-68 under Nero (instead of 81-96 under Domitian). He argues that the Roman authorities wanted to separate John from his congregations, and that therefore he dared not address a formal letter to them, but was able to write only "a booklet." The conjecture is ingenious and offers some explanation where otherwise there is really none at hand. Instead of the usual form for the opening of a letter John begins with an introduction, and this so exalted and in general of such a character as to remind us of the Prologue to his Gospel. It is all one sentence, with the object placed first and expanded at length, followed by the main verb with its subject in verse 3: "declare we," *etc.* The construction of this great sentence is unusual, although the sense is as clear as crystal. John's way of using the very simplest words and sentences to express the loftiest thoughts is apparent here also, although his thoughts crowd one another and flow in such abundance as to strain the grammar and intertwine with each other in a unique manner. — **That which was from the beginning, that which we have heard, that which we have seen with our eyes, that which we beheld, and our hands handled . . . declare we unto you.** John here states the grand subject of all

apostolic preaching; and — we may add here at once — in
verses 3 and 4, in the clauses beginning with ἵνα, the purpose of this preaching. His Gospel begins in the same
way, only the purpose is expressed historically and in
general in John 1, 12, and personally at the end in John
20, 31. In both compositions the subject rises before
John's spirit in its divine grandeur; it transcends time
and shines forth from all eternity: ὃ ἦν ἀπ' ἀρχῆς, **that which
was from the beginning.** John uses the neuter ὅ, not the
masculine ὅς. Some of the old exegetes understand it to
mean "the mystery of God, that Christ appeared in the
flesh; Socinus thinks "the Gospel of Jesus Christ" is meant,
not his person; others: the life that appeared in Christ
(not Christ himself); the person of Christ and all his
history included; Christ's pre-existence and his historical
appearance; a statement merely in general of the subject
John wishes to treat; not the Savior himself, but what
constitutes his essence. Some of these ideas are entirely
wide of the mark, as a mere glance shows, others approach
it somewhat. The entire introduction, like the Prologue
to the Gospel, makes it plain that John does mean Christ
himself in these opening clauses; to eliminate his person
in any way empties out the chief part of John's subject
and testimony. Besser puts it finely: *That which* was
from the beginning was *He; that which* we have heard,
seen with our eyes, beheld, handled, was *He.* John, however, has in mind not the person merely by itself, but the
person in respect to all that he was and is for him and
for us all. Always then the person must be understood,
but always also, as the appended verbs indicate ("we have
heard;" "we have seen;" "we beheld;" "our hands
handled;" see also verse 3), the grace, power, salvation,
gifts, and influence connected with the person. The ὅ is
thus wider and more inclusive than ὅς would be. A similar
use of the neuter, plainly referring to persons, we have
in John 4, 22; 6, 37; 17, 2; 1 Cor. 1, 27; Col. 1, 20; Eph.
1, 10. Christ cannot be separated from what he was and
is for us; both belong together as the glory of the sun

and its glow. The theme of John's writing in both the
Gospel and the First Epistle, the theme of all apostolic
testimony and preaching is the Incarnate Son and all he
was and is for men; and in the Epistle this may be specified
more closely: what he is and must be for our Christian
life. — *That which was* **from the beginning,** ἀπ' ἀρχῆς,
beyond question, while not identical with, yet very similar
to ἐν ἀρχῇ, John 1, 1; πρὸ καταβολῆς κόσμου, Eph. 1, 4; ἀπὸ
τῶν αἰώνων, Eph. 3, 9; and in verse 2 of our text explained
ἥτις ἦν πρὸς τὸν πατέρα. In John 1, 1 the great truth to be
emphasized is that the Word existed before the Creation:
in the beginning already the Word *was;* here, in the Epistle,
the truth to be held fast is that the Word was before the
Incarnation: from the beginning already the Word was,
not merely from the day of his earthly manifestation. The
eternal power and godhead of Christ is asserted both times.
And the verb ἦν by no means states that the existence of
the Son reaches back only to "the beginning;" on the contrary, he who *was* before John and his fellow apostles
heard, saw, beheld, handled him and the treasures of his
grace, even *from the beginning,* by this very form of expression is shown not to have *become* then, but to have
existed from all eternity. Meyer is wrong when he asserts,
ἀρχή cannot mean "beginning," but must mean that which
precedes the beginning; we must not strain the word, ἀρχή
is "beginning." But from then the Word "was," altogether
before the glorious manifestation in the fulness of time —
which is the point John here makes; how long before the ·
ἀρχή is not said here, other Scriptures tell us that, only ἦν
here leaves all eternity open.

**That which we have heard, that which we have seen
with our eyes, that which we beheld, and our hands
handled.** No ἐστίν is to be supplied before these relatives, as if the sense were: "That which was from the
beginning *is* that which we have heard," *etc.* The antecedent of ὅ in these four clauses is the same. Their coordi-
nation means to declare that he who revealed himself so
abundantly in the fulness of time is positively the same as

he who was from the beginning. The identity of the λόγος
ἔνσαρκος with the λόγος ἄσαρκος is thus brought out vividly.
To refer the relatives of these clauses to different anteced-
ents, simply on the strength of the different verbs, is guess-
work, with no foundation in the text, cheapens the thought
and makes it quite superficial, and at the same time loses
the all-important truth John is here concerned about: the
incarnate Christ is identical with the eternal Son' of God.
We reject the notion of Ebrard, Grotius, and others, who
would make these clauses read: that which we have heard
(the words of Christ), that which we have seen with
our eyes (the miracles of Christ), that which we beheld
(the glory of Christ), and our hands handled (the resurrection-body of Christ). — There is a gradation in the
verbs; *gradatim crescit oratio:* To see is more than to
hear, to behold more than to see, to handle more than
to behold. The second and the fourth is strengthened:
to see "with our eyes" is as much as to see with one's
own eyes; that which *our* hands handled includes a similar
emphasis. John by these four verbs means to say that
in every possible way he and his fellow apostles received
proof of the reality of the divine and eternal Christ and
all his blessings. He and his fellows were to be Christ's
chosen witnesses for all men and all time; and here John
declares himself such a witness indeed, and that his testi-
money is based on the completest foundation. — **We** is not
the majestic plural, but the combining of all the apostles
into one body of witnesses. John does not lift himself
above the rest; the force of his own individual apostolic
testimony is heightened by that of all the other apostles.
John survived them all, but whether he wrote this letter
after the death of all the rest, or earlier while some were
still alive, he claims no superior revelation for himself.
The one revelation made to all is what we are to believe,
that is ample and perfect; all who came after John claiming a special revelation, all who come thus now, stand
condemned by this "we" and what it implies. — The two
perfects: **have heard, have seen,** ἀκηκόαμεν, ἑωράκαμεν, evi-

dently belong together, and must be distinguished from the two aorists following, ἐθεασάμεθα, ἐψηλάφησαν. All four verbs deal with the past, but the perfects state continued action completed in the past, the aorists simple action. The best interpretation is, that all along during Christ's intercourse with his apostles they saw and heard what he showed unto them concerning himself; and besides this, single cases occurred in which they beheld and even handled the Savior. Moreover, the first two verbs (see and hear) point to more or less involuntary action: Christ set himself and his glory before them, and the sound and vision fell upon their senses; while the next two verbs (behold and handle) denote voluntary action: they themselves with great earnestness, *etc.*, looked and beheld, stretched forth their hands and touched. Examples for these two actions come readily to mind: John 2, 11; 4, 53; 6, 68; 20, 27 and 29; Acts 10, 41; Luke 24, 39. Seeing and hearing might take place without faith, although in the case of the apostles faith was not absent; beholding and handling could take place only with faith (John 1, 14).

Concerning the Word of Life (the margin offers: *word*, without the capital letter), περὶ τοῦ λόγου τῆς ζωῆς, does not belong as a modifier to any of the previous verbs, but is an appositional phrase, coordinate with the preceding relative clauses, and defining more closely what these contain. John does not write the simple accusative τὸν λόγον τῆς ζωῆς, for this could have meant the Gospel, which is properly called "the word of life;" by means of the preposition περί he excludes that meaning of ὁ λόγος completely, for the office of the apostles was not to declare *concerning* the word of life, but to declare that word itself. The term Logos here is the special personal designation of Christ, used exactly as in John's Gospel and in the Apocalypse (19, 13), and stands for the second person of the Godhead, who appeared in the world in human flesh, as the full and complete declaration and utterance of God regarding his thoughts concerning the world. Therefore is he called "Faithful and True," Rev. 19, 11; "the faithful witness," Rev. 1, 5. Christ in himself is the Word, God's living Word to the world, John 1, 18: "The only begotten Son . . . he hath declared him." That includes all Christ's words and works; through them all God speaks continuously to the world. Nor can we ever hope for any fuller, completer, higher, more effective Word of God to mankind; in the Son God himself came to us, and there is none higher who can come. "The Word became flesh, and dwelt among us," John 1, 14; or as our text has it: "the life was manifested;" but before this incarnation and manifestation of the Word of life occurred in the fulness of time, that Word was not inactive. Zahn and his followers are mistaken when they restrict the name and with the name the activity of the Logos to the New Testament, and deny its application to anything found in the Old. While Christ is the Mediator of the new covenant, the entire old covenant was a prophecy and promise of the new, and in this prophecy and promise we have not a different word of God from the Word of God, but the same Word in his preliminary and preparatory work. In fact John 1, 1 goes back to eternity and the beginning, even as John 1, 1 does, and declares: "In the beginning was the Word," and adds: "all things were made by him; and without him was not anything made that was made," verse 3, which our text seconds in verse 2: "the eternal life, which was with the Father." Our old exegetes and dogmaticians were perfectly right in distinguishing between ὁ λόγος ἄσαρκος and ὁ λόγος ἔνσαρκος, however late the actual name λόγος came to be used for the Son who became incarnate. They rightfully interpret Gen. 1, 4: "God *said*, Let there be light;" 26: "God *said*, Let *us* make man in *our* image, after *our* likeness;" Heb. 11, 3: "Through faith we understand that the worlds were framed by *the word of God;*" Ps. 33, 6 and 9: "By *the word of the Lord* were the heavens made . . . . For he *spake*, and it was done; he *commanded*, and it stood fast;" Ps. 107, 20; 147, 15, of the Word. Hofmann's idea, and Luthardt's adaptation of it, that the Word is the Gospel whose content is Christ in his divine person, is an inferior conception of the great name.

"The Word is the living God as he reveals himself, Is. 8, 25; Heb. 1, 1-2." Besser. He is the Angel of Jehovah, who meets us all through the Old Testament from Genesis to Malachi, even "the Angel of the Presence," Is. 63, 9; the image of the invisible God, the firstborn of every creature: for by him were all things created, that are in heaven, and that are in earth, visible and invisible, whether they be thrones, or dominious, or principalities, or powers: all things were created by him, and for him: and he is before all things, and by him all things consist. And he is the head of the body, the church: who is the beginning, the firstborn from the dead; that in all things he might have the preeminence. For it pleased the Father, that in him should all fulness dwell." Col. 1, 15-19. In the face of all this, especially also the latter passage, it is utterly in vain for Zahn to exclude the Logos conception from the Old Testament and to make of the old Lutheran teaching on this point mere Christian speculation carried from the New Testament into the Old. See Zahn, *Das Evangelium des Johannes ausgelegt*, p. 98 *etc.* All this disposes also of the idea that the New Testament Logos conception was derived from the Jewish-Alexandrine philosophy as represented by Philo, and was adopted to satisfy and answer such Jewish and besides them gnostic pagan thinkers. The logos of Philo is not a person at all, but an abstraction, not the personal Word of God, but the impersonal reason of God; a middle link between God and the world, the world-idea, which God formed as an artist makes a model embodying his thought; something subordinate to God, and though personified in speaking of it at times, yet never a true person, as is the eternal Son of God; a pantheistic, impersonal thing, of which it is impossible to say that the logos "became flesh." See my *Eisenach Gospel Selections*, I, p. 108 *etc.* The name Logos was indeed not used by Christ himself, and was formed as a terse and comprehensive designation for God's final personal revelation to the world; yet the name was not invented by human wisdom, but given by divine inspiration. They who decline to admit

this naturally fall into explanations like that of Zahn, or
others inferior even to that: Zahn, however, is right when
he points to passages like 1 Cor. 1, 19 *etc.;* Col. 1, 27; 2,
2-3; 1 Tim. 3, 16; Matth. 11, 27; 16, 17, as containing the
substance of what the name Logos expresses, while the
name itself is not yet introduced. In due time the name
itself was revealed, and now stands as one of the most
significant, divinely inspired designations of the Son our
Savior. — The genitive: **of life** is appositive: "In him was
life," John 1, 4; "This is the true God and eternal life," 1
John 5, 20; "I am . . . the life," John 14, 6; "the
resurrection and the life," 11, 25. Absolutely and in himself, irrespective of us and all creatures, he is the
Word of Life, and therefore the Word of life; and this
life is not a mere idea, an abstraction, such as we get by in-
duction or deduction in studying living creatures; it is the
divine essence itself in the person of the Son. While this
must be said as regards the Son himself, our concern is
with him as the Word of life *for us:* **and the life was
manifested,** namely in its full saving power for mankind.
"The Word was made flesh," that is how, "the life was
manifested;" "when the fulness of the time came, God sent
forth his Son, born of a woman, born under the law, that
he might redeem them which were under the law, that we
might receive the adoption of sons," Gal. 4, 4-5: Thus "the
Word of life" became *"the bread* of life," so that he that
cometh to Christ shall not hunger, and he that believeth on
him shall never thirst, John 6, 35; likewise *"the light* of
life," so that whoever followeth him shall not walk in darkness, 8, 12. Indeed, "herein was the love of God manifested in us, that God hath sent his only begotten Son into
the world, that *we might live* through him." 1 John 4, 9;
and become partakers of the divine nature, 2 Pet. 1, 5. —
The word **the life,** ἡ ζωή, is repeated three times in close
succession, and by its very prominence controls John's entire introductory statement. Ὁ λόγος τῆς ζωῆς — ἡ ζωή —
and ἡ ζωὴ ἡ αἰώνιος all stand for the same person, the Son revealed from heaven, as himself the essential Life, and the

bearer of life to us who were dead in trespasses and sins. In the aorist passive ἐφανερώθη we have one definite act in the past, emanating from the entire Trinity, and the effect of this act is at once added: **and we have seen,** which unites into one what above was expressed by four verbs. God's manifestation of the Life was not in vain, it lacked nothing in fulness, power, or efficacy. The Baptist saw and believed, John 1, 33-34; the apostles likewise, John 2, 11 and again and again in ever greater perfection. And all who thus saw the Life with eyes of faith had life in his name.

The Life declared unto others.

We make our division at this point because the thought permits it, disregarding the grammatical construction. Two thoughts stand out clearly in John's introduction, as the centers about which all else is grouped: the revelation to the apostles; their proclamation to others. . And to the second of these the text now turns. — **And bear witness, and declare unto you the life, the eternal** *life.* The object τὴν ζωὴν τὴν αἰώνιον belongs to all three verbs, ἑωράκαμεν καὶ μαρτυροῦμεν καὶ ἀπαγγέλλομεν, nothing indicates that it is drawn only to the one, or to the last two and not the first. **Life** here has the same significance as before; but the important attribute of eternity is added. Although the Life was manifested in time and John and his fellow apostles beheld it, the Life itself was not changed, did not become a thing of time, but, being ἀπ' ἀρχῆς, it remained superior to time, namely αἰώνιος. Ἡ ζωὴ ἡ αἰώνιος generally signifies "eternal life" as bestowed by Christ upon believers, and we now constantly use the expression in this sense; but here the preceding statements utterly exclude that signification. — Two more modifiers are added in the form of a double relative clause. Instead of repeating ὁ ἦν ἀπ' ἀρχῆς, the apostle writes ἥτις ἦν πρὸς τὸν πατέρα, **which was with the Father,** reminding us at once of the πρὸς τὸν θεόν in John 1, 1. The preposition πρός with the accusative occurs occa-

6

sionally (Math. 13, 56; 26, 55) where we might expect the
dative, or παρά with the dative, which is familiar to John;
but πρός with the accusative, while we translate it in English "with," like the dative, means more than rest and a
being with the Father, namely an inclination towards the
Father and thus a communion with him. The πρός thus
offers a glimpse of the relation of the divine persons to
each other. Together with the adjective "eternal" this first
relative clause declares the divinity of Christ in a most
forceful way: it is the eternal Son who is in communion
with the Father, whom John has seen. A second relative
clause, attached with καί counterbalances the first: **and
was manifested unto us.** He "was" with the Father — he
"was manifested" to us; again, he was "with the Father" —
and he was manifested "to us," *i. e.* the apostles. The
wonderful thing lies in the juxtaposition of these two
thoughts: that the eternal Son in interpersonal communion
with the Father — that he should have appeared here on
earth and be manifested unto men! Just before John uses
ἐφανερώθη, here he repeats it in the emphatic contrast just
shown and with the emphatic dative ἡμῖν. — **And we bear
witness and announce unto you,** that expresses the second
pivotal thought of the introduction. Two verbs are used:
μαρτυρεῖν, referring to the relation of the apostles to Christ,
they being his chosen μάρτυρες; and ἀπαγγέλλειν, referring to
ὑμεῖς, the people to whom they were to be heralds and messengers. In the former verb there lies also the thought of
personal experience and contact with that concerning which
testimony is given; while the second verb is general. Both
are meant to convey one great thought: they who were with
Christ as his chosen witnesses, to whom he fully revealed
himself, and who personally received this revelation, as
such witnesses declare and announce for us to hear and
receive in faith.

The entire second verse is parenthetical, yet by no
means loosely inserted, for it is an intregal part of the
interlocking progress of thought. In the third verse John,
therefore, does not simply continue what he began in the

first, but with one comprehensive sweep ties together all that he has said in both preceding verses, and thus continues. **That which we have seen and heard declare we unto you also;** here is the summing up. The object is again in the neuter, ὅ, "that which," as in verse 1, although now all the explanation that was added must be borne in mind. Seeing is placed before hearing now, but only because ἐφανερώθη immediately precedes and more readily suggests seeing than hearing. "To you also" might imply that the apostles had announced this manifestion to others first, and now come with it to the readers of this Epistle; and the present tense ἀπαγγέλλομεν would harmonize with that. But the fact is that the readers of this Epistle were Christians when the Epistle was written to them, and it addresses them throughout as Christians. The ἀπαγγέλλομεν therefore includes the entire announcement of the Gospel as the apostles made it unto these people, and as John was still continuing in his letter. Hence καὶ ὑμῖν stands in contrast to the apostles: the Word of life was manifested to them, but far from keeping it for themselves — as so many Christians now are content to do, careless even of their own children and grand-children — as true and faithful witnesses they announce it καὶ ὑμῖν. — But the weight of the sentence is in the purpose clause: **that ye also may have fellowship with us,** κοινωνίαν, communion, a joining together which makes him who joins like them to whom he is joined, and at the same time enables him to receive and enjoy what they possess. This is a communion in faith, 1 John 5, 10; in light, 1, 7; in righteousness, 2, 29; 3, 7; 5, 3; in love, 4, 7; 11; 21; in hope, 3, 3; in confidence and joy, 4, 15; 1, 5. Καὶ ὑμεῖς follows hard upon καὶ ὑμῖν; both therefore must imply the same relation: as the apostles do not keep the glad tidings to themselves, but announce them καὶ ὑμῖν, so also the purpose of this announcement is not that the apostles alone form a κοινωνία, but καὶ ὑμεῖς with them. John prefers μετά to σύν, and therefore uses the former more frequently. He says: that also you may have communion **with us,** and

thereby brings out the peculiar, exalted position of the
apostles. The Word of life was manifested, but we, together with John's Gentile and Jewish Christian readers,
receive the blessings of that manifestation only through
the apostles. "Being built upon the foundation of the
apostles and prophets, Christ Jesus himself being the chief
corner stone," Eph. 2, 20. Always, after Christ, the
apostles come first: "And he gave some to be apostles;
and some, prophets; and some, evangelists; and some.
pastors and teachers," Eph. 4, 11; and the latter could
not be without the former, for their work, and hence all
Christian believing, rests upon the apostolic work and
testimony. To be in fellowship with the apostles is to
be a member of the Church. "He that heareth you heareth
me; and he that rejecteth you rejecteth me; and he that
rejecteth me rejected him that sent me," Luke 10, 16,
applies fully and directly to the apostles, and that for all
time as regards their inspired written testimony, and applies to Christian preachers and witnesses now only in
so far as they draw their testimony from that of the
apostles. — But John dares not stop with the "fellowship
with us;" he at once adds: **yea, and our fellowship is with
the Father, and with his Son Jesus Christ.** Καί coordinates, δέ adds a contrasting feature. The sentence is
not to be read: and our fellowship is fellowship with the
Father *etc;* nor is ᾖ, "may be," to be supplied instead of
ἐστίν, as if this second clause also depended on ἵνα; the
R. V. does not even print "is" in Italics, considering it so
self-evidently a part of the sentence. "Our fellowship" =
that of the apostles with God. So two fellowships are
placed side by side: the fellowship of believers with the
apostles, and the apostles' fellowship with God (μετὰ τοῦ
πατρός κτλ. corresponding to μεθ᾽ ἡμῶν). But the two are
so linked together that one fellowship results; for fellowship here is what John writes of in John 1, 12: "As many
as received him, to them gave he the right to become children of God, even to them that believe on his name."
Both the divine persons are plainly named, especially the

Son, to whom John referred above as "the Word of life," and "life eternal." Similarly in the Gospel the name Jesus Christ is withheld till the eighteenth verse, and then solemnly and emphatically introduced. **Father,** as in the second verse, is used with reference to the Son, hence also fully: **his Son Jesus Christ,** showing the essential oneness of the incarnate Son with the Father: "I and the Father are one," John 10, 30; "He that beholdeth me beholdeth him that sent me," 12, 45; 14, 9. John does not say that the Father is our Father in Christ Jesus, but he does say what is equivalent to it, namely that having fellowship with the apostles we have fellowship with the Father and the Son: "If a man love me, he will keep my word: and my Father will love him, and we will come unto him, and make our abode with him," John 14, 23. Our fellowship with the Father and the Son is brought about by the Gospel or apostolic testimony as the means of grace ("the power of God unto salvation," Rom. 1, 16), John 8, 31; 14, 23; Rom. 10, 7; it consists in faith, 1 John 5, 1 and 10 and 13; *etc.*; it embraces all that belongs to the Christian life, culminating here in the *unio mystica* and hereafter in the *glorificatio.* For this fellowship man was originally created, it is the supreme purpose of his being; sin destroyed it; God through the manifestation of his Son restores it.

And these things we write, that our joy may be fulfilled. The R. V. cancels "unto you" after the first clause, and prefers "our joy" to the reading of many authorities "your joy." "And" joins "we write" to the previous "we declare," connecting the specific with the generic, the oral preaching and teaching of the apostles with their inspired writing. **These things** some would restrict to the introductory words just written, others to the contents of this Epistle; Zahn correctly says it includes the entire New Testament literature, which began to be written in the sixties of the first century, directly or indirectly by the eyewitnesses of the Gospel events, and to which John was in the act of contributing. The ἡμεῖς is not the majestic plural, but signifies John and his fellow witnesses, a continuation of the first person plural throughout these introductory verses. Let us note well this formal and positive declaration of John: **these things** we write, which brands as utterly false all the speculations of higher critics whereby they substitute uninspired later authors for the inspired μάρτυρες chosen by Christ himself. — **That our joy may be fulfilled** has its parallel in 3 John 4: "Greater joy have I none than this, to hear of my children walking in the truth." The apostles rejoiced to do their Lord's work. "Woe is unto me, if I preach not the Gospel," writes Paul, 1 Cor. 9, 16. In this they were like their Master, whose meat it was to do his Father's will, John 4,. 34. Their preaching and teaching, in spite of persecution and opposition, was bound to succeed; and this added to their joy. And part of their work was to "write these things," to put them into a permanent record for all time. Thus to crown and complete their work was for them the full measure of joy. The writing is a transmission to others; by means of this the φανέρωσις vouchsafed to the apostles, which in itself filled them with joy, is to produce a πλήρωσις of joy for them. While the reading: "our joy" must stand in place of "your joy," this latter lies very close to the former; for if the apostles rejoiced in receiving the manifestation of the Word of life, in declaring it and writing it for the benefit of others, in fulfilling their glorious calling and serving their Lord, shall not we rejoice, yea, have our joy fulfilled when we receive the fruits of their labor, read the sacred pages, enter their fellowship which is the fellowship of the Father and his Son Jesus Christ, and thus receive all the blessings of the divine grace? The season for which this text is set makes this joy especially attractive; but let a good part of it be like that of John and the other apostles in whose name he writes, let it be our joy to minister the Advent and Christmas blessing, the manifestation of the Word of life unto others.

HOMILETICAL HINTS.

A recent commentator compares our text to Corregio's picture of the Christchild in the manger. All the light in the picture emanates from the holy Child Jesus and illuminates the faces of Mary and Joseph. So all the light in this text shines out from this great fact: *the Life was manifested,* and every other word is made glorious thereby. Whatever theme, then, the preacher chooses, whether he looks back to faithful Paul and Timothy in the previous text, and shows now what all true preachers of the Gospel must proclaim; or whether he looks forward to the Christmas festival already at hand, and in its light reads this text concerning "the Word of life," "the eternal life, which was with the Father, and was manifested unto us;" or whether he concentrates himself upon this text alone, seeking only to reach its rich heart and treasured wealth: always, there will be one central thought, and the picture of Corregio illustrates it.

God has highly honored the human ear, eye, and hand by using them as instruments of testimony for certifying to us the eternal good. Let the Docetists invent a Logos who did not appear in real flesh, but assumed only its appearance as a sham. We will bless the hand of the holy apostle, and kiss it in heaven, for having touched the Lord Jesus our heavenly Savior, and then writing this record for us to read. — O incomprehensible Word of Life, stooping so lowly in order to lift us up to Thee, permitting Thyself to be apprehended by all the senses of man, to be heard and seen and touched and handled by Thine own creatures, simply that they might learn to love and trust Thee, and thus obtain Thine infinite treasures to their eternal enrichment. (After Spener.)

The word is the mirror of the soul, and at the same time the means for imparting to others what transpires in the soul. So Christ in his own person is the mirror of God's inmost thoughts, and in him stand revealed and proclaimed to all the world all the gracious, saving purposes of God. (C. C. Hein.)

The natural life which we have in common with plants and animals does not deserve the name, because it is a gradual dying. The true life is not ours by nature, as though we possessed in our souls an inexhaustible power of vitality. Only God has imperishable, eternal life, and eternal life in Christ Jesus is his gift. For this reason eternal life for us is bound up with Christ, and we must have part in his life, then is our fellowship with the Father and his Son Jesus Christ. And this is called eternal life, not because it is of endless duration, but because in its very essence it is fellowship with the eternal God.

Only where life is can there be joy. With the coming of death sorrow enters. Every increase of life hightens joy. When the billow of life rises high, there is joy; when it recedes, sorrow prevails. We may write it in the form of an equation: joy = the winning and augmentation of life; sorrow = the decline and loss of life.

The church is like a great ambulance which God takes across the battle-field of this world to rescue the wounded and deliver them from certain death. If I have been lifted into this ambulance, I may indeed still die on the road, namely if I refuse to take the medicines offered, the Word and Sacraments, tear away the bandages which stanch my wounds, or I may be thrown out of the ambulance again, namely through unbelief and wickedness on my part; yet the ambulance itself is indestructible, and its course is beyond hindering; it will not stick fast in the mire of this world, and the dust whirled up by its wheels may hide, but cannot swallow it; the devil cannot destroy or stop it, and no other foe can do as much as he. Therefore all who remain on this ambulance and accept the ministrations for which it is designed, will escape alive, will be freed from every wound and pain, and will presently be seated upon the great triumphal car which takes the blessed into the city of eternal peace. (Adapted from Besser.)

There is no communion with the great Head of the Church except that which takes place through his chosen members, the apostles. Ever there have been false apostles, teachers of fables, spirits of error, who endeavor to persuade the members of the church to exchange their communion with the true apostles for communion with the false, and sneer at all who cling to the Church as the institution of God for our salvation, the chosen servant for the dispensation of his invisible gifts. Especially do they hate the Lutheran name, but we readily perceive, as Luther himself declared, their intent is not so much to destroy Luther, as it is to overthrow Luther's doctrine, and on this account they demand to know of you whether you are a Lutheran. Here it is in place to answer with words stronger than rushes, namely with the bold confession of Christ, no matter whether a John or a George have preached it. The man is nothing, the doctrine you must confess and adhere to.

Where St. John abides, there will we abide, and then we bide well.

Lutherans are Christians whose joy is fulfilled because they rejoice in their obedience to the complete truth of the divine Word.

The brightening dawn: the entrance — the abundant entrance — the crown of righteousness — the Son of God our Savior himself!

Joy to the World, the Lord Has Come!

I. *See him as the Word of life.*
  1. Jesus *the Word* (explain) from the beginning, now and ever more.
  2. Jesus *the Word of life*, the essential Life; manifested in a world of sin and death, to bestow life upon us.

II. *Hear the testimony concerning him.*
  1. From the divinely chosen witnesses who heard, saw, beheld, handled.
  2. From the inspired record which transmits their testimony perfectly to us.

III. *Enter into fellowship with him.*
  1. Believe him who is the Word.
  2. Receive him who is the Life.
  3. Let the incarnate Savior lift you from sin and death, regenerate and renew you, enrich you with all the blessings of his grace.
  4. Use the testimony of Scripture ever to keep you with the Father and the Son, to make you live more and more in all things divine.

IV. *Let your joy in him be full.*
  1. Joy in receiving him and all his gifts.
  2. Joy in transferring him and his gifts to others.
  3. A double joy, not put beside worldly joy, but completely superseding it, and growing into the divinely intended fulness.

St. John's Testimony Concerning Christ, the Word of Life.

I. *It rests on the divine manifestation he has received.*
II. *It is proclaimed by his inspired utterance in word and writing.*
III. *It fills him and us all with fulness of joy.*

The Testimony Concerning Christ, as the Office of the Ministry Must Render It.

I. *Its wonderful contents.*
II. *Its trustworthy certification.*
III. *Its glorious purpose.*

C. C. Hein.

How Christ, the Word of Life, Becomes Our Joy.

Three acts are essential:
  I. *The divine Manifestation.*
 II. *The apostolic Declaration.*
III. *The resulting Fellowship.*

Christmas Fellowship With the Father and His Son Jesus Christ.

  I. *Gather at the manger where the Word of Life was first manifested.*
 II. *Listen to the holy apostles who saw and handled the blessed Lord.*
III. *Read the sacred record which brings the Savior to us now.*
 IV. *Let your hearts take in the fulness of the proffered joy.*

St. John Shows Us the Cause of Our Christmas Joy:

  I. *The Life was manifested.*
  I. *We have fellowship with God.*

Riemer.

CHRISTMAS.

---

1 John 3, 1-5.

Our epistolary text for Christmas follows very closely the lines of thought of the old epistolary text for the day, Tit. 2, 11-14. There is first of all the great historical fact itself, set before us in our text by the words: "He was manifested," and in the old text by the words: "For the grace of God hath appeared, bringing salvation to all men." There is secondly a survey of the saving purpose and effects of this historical fact: He was manifested "to take away sins" — "that we should be called the children of God: and such we are" — "we shall" (eventually) "be like him, for we shall see him as he is." The old text has the parallel thoughts: "Who gave himself for us that he might redeem us from all iniquity" — make us "his own possession, zealous of good works" — "looking for the blessed hope and appearing of the glory of our great God and Savior Jesus Christ." There is finally an admonition, implied in the one case: "And every one that hath this hope set on him purifieth himself, even as he is pure;" plainly expressed in the other: "Denying ungodliness and worldly lusts, we should live soberly and righteously in this present world." Each text, of course, has its own peculiar setting, specification of thought, and imagery; that makes the new text different from the old and gives it a value for the pulpit all its own. — The opening sentence has a jubilant ring, which ought to echo through the entire sermon: "Behold what manner of love the Father hath bestowed upon us" *etc.* Christmas must bring us Christ and salvation — nothing else will do, even in an epistle. That is why the Fourth Sunday in Advent already sounded that theme, and now, with Christmas fully come, we must hear it in all its fulness and power. Summing up the contents of our text with this in mind, we have as our subject: *Christ, the sinless Son of God, was manifested in human flesh for our eternal salvation;* or,, more briefly, but still the same: *Christ manifested for our salvation.* The sequence of thought in the text, which, of course, need not be the sequence in the pulpit presentation of it, places the cardinal fact of the manifestation at the end; thus, for our exegesis, we have the following: We are the children of God; we shall be wholly like him; we must purify ourselves: and all this because he was manifested to take away our sins.

Behold, we are the children of God!

John begins this section of his letter with an exclamation which interrupts the calm and lofty flight of his thought and draws marked attention to what he is now saying. It is not, however, something new or strange, not found elsewhere, but something he himself has already said a number of times and implied still more often, something the other apostles have likewise stated, with the same frequency. In the sentence immediately preceding John says that every one that doeth righteousness ἐξ αὐτοῦ γεγέννηται, is begotten of Christ. Here John's exclamation sets in: **Behold!** We often read and say it without much thought or appreciation, this thing which is wonderful in the extreme, namely "that we should be called the children of God." John focuses attention upon it; and as he does so, what rays of light stream out in every direction, and what still more glorious and blessed radiance rises to view behind it, namely the Son's manifestation in human flesh, on which all human sonship of God here and hereafter depends. John really sees it all in its wonderful connection at one glance: **what manner of love the Father hath bestowed upon us.** Ποταπός is a later form for ποδαπός, the same as ποῖος, used in the N. T. in indirect questions; really = *qualis* (Luke 1, 29; 2 Pet. 3, 11), as both English versions have it: "what manner of," but used frequently also of something great and glorious (Matth. 8, 27; Mark 13, 1; Luke 7, 39) and

thus closely approaching *quantus*. Both the character and
the amount of the Father's love deserve attention. — **Love,**
ἀγάπη, here embraces both the mighty power in God himself, and all that it has wrought for us, its entire efficacious
manifestation whereby we have become the children of
God. This love in all its comprehensiveness is a gift to us
(δέδωκεν). More than just the evidence of love hath been
bestowed upon us; not only the Son, in whom the love of
God shines forth so abundantly ("Herein is love, not that
we loved God, but that he loved us, and sent his Son," 1
John 4, 10), but this Son, and in fact every other evidence of
love that can be named, is given us as the all-sufficient basis
of the Father's love itself. — This is the gift he **hath bestowed upon us,** in one long, continued and completed act
(δέδωκεν, perf. tense), so that now this love is our own
possession. John includes himself (ἡμῖν), since the highest
glory even of an apostle consists in the possession of this
love. Luther's *gegeben* (up to 1527) is better than the
present German translation, *erzeiget*. Both ἀγάπη and
δέδωκεν shut out completely all merit of our own, which, in
fact, is the case with the entire statement. — Since John
here speaks of "children," we might presume that he uses
the name **Father** on that account, so that it would be equivalent to "our Father"; but the context John 3, 23-24, and
in fact the entire Epistle, shows that when John employs
this name without further specification he means the Father
in relation to the Son. This gives us a deeper thought
than the other use of the name would; it indicates, as
Haupt points out, the way in which this gift of God's love
comes to us; comp. John 3, 16. It is the Father of the
eternal Son our Savior who has given us his love. Like a
mighty diamond the great gift glistens with its many facets,
here Bethlehem and the angel voices, there Golgatha and
the signs by which God spoke, and here the open tomb with
angel messengers, and there the open heavens with our
ascending Lord. — **That we should be called children of
God,** a purpose clause, ἵνα with the subj. God's intention
and aim in giving us his love was this very thing, which

now also has been realized; he wanted this, and he has attained it. There is no reason to take ἵνα, as Meyer tries to do, in a modified sense; moreover the sense is not: we *are to be* called, as if we are not yet called by this name but shall be at the last day (Daechsel). "That we should be called," ἵνα κληθῶμεν, shows God's purpose and aim in making his gift, and this has already been realized, for we are now — right in this Epistle, in the Scriptures generally, and in the church of the right faith — actually and properly called children of God. — **To be called** is substantially the same as ἐξουσίαν ἔχειν γενέσθαι, John 1, 12, although the thought deals with the εἶναι instead of the γενέσθαι. Καλεῖσθαι here is not the opposite of εἶναι, as if it referred to an *inanis titulus* (Calvin), but — properly so called, with the reality corresponding fully to the title; as Besser puts it: Whenever God bestows the name, he also bestows the thing the name stands for. Yet in κληθῶμεν the emphasis is on the name we have, because this name reveals and makes known the reality which is so precious "It is not enough that we become children of God, we must also be named by that name before the face of God and the Angels." (Luther) — **children of God** in John's writing usually means children by regeneration and the new birth (see the previous verse, 2, 29: γεγέννηται ; 3, 9-10; 4, 4; 5, 1), whereas Paul so frequently bases the appellation on justification, making us children by adoption. In both cases we are children of God by faith, justified and regenerated by faith. "Because faith makes sons of God, it also makes co-heirs with Christ . . . because faith justifies us and renders God propitious" (Apology, Jacobs' transl., 116, 75). *"Das ewige Leben gehoert denenen, die Gott gerecht schaetzet, und wenn sie sind gerecht geschaetzet, sind sie damit Gottes Kinder und Christi Miterben worden"* (Mueller, 143). "The word 'regeneration' is employed so as to comprise at the same time the forgiveness of sins alone for Christ's sake, and the succeeding renewal which the Holy Ghost works in those who are justified by faith. Again, it is restricted to the remission of sins and adoption as sons of God.

And in the latter sense the word is much and often used in the Apology, where it is written: 'Justification is regeneration,' although St. Paul has fixed a distinction between these words (Tit. 3, 5). . . . As also the word 'vivification' has sometimes been used in a like sense. For if a man is justified through faith . . . this is truly' a regeneration, because from a child of wrath he becomes a child of God, and thus is transferred from death to life" *etc.*, 573, 19-20. John does not write τέκνα αὐτοῦ or ἑαυτοῦ, *i. e.* of the Father, but τέκνα θεοῦ, giving the actual title and fully justifying the exclamation at the beginning. — **And** such **we are** is omitted in the text Luther translated, but should be restored in the German translation as undoubtedly genuine. Καί ἐσμεν is not governed by ἵνα, and *simus* in the Vulgate is wrong. The sense is not: in order that we should be called the children of God and be such. What the κληθῶμεν implies, the ἐσμέν states as a positive fact: we *are* children of God; there is no doubt about it. The evidence John furnishes in other places, here he merely asserts the grand and blessed fact: behold it! While in the καλεῖσθαι the εἶναι must be included, this in itself is so important and essential that it deserves emphatic mention.

But the world denies it; and, in fact, we ourselves are not as fully conscious of it as we should be. Both of these thoughts John at once takes up and gives us the one answer we need. First as to the world: **For this cause the world knoweth us not, because it knew him not.** Διὰ τοῦτο might be taken as referring to ὅτι οὐκ ἔγνω αὐτόν, *i. e.*, for this cause, namely because it does not know him. But this makes too great a gap between the former statement, and the one now made. Διὰ τοῦτο refers to καί ἐσμεν: on this very account, because we are the children of God, the world does not know us. — Ὁ κόσμος = **the world** of men fallen from God and hostile to him, together with all for which they live and strive; here especially those who refuse the love of God and continue in their evil course; the world ἐν τῷ πονηρῷ, 1 John 5, 19. An abstract definition of "the world" will cause difficulty with the verb γινώσκειν, hence we do not define with Luther and Calvin *die Gottlosigkeit;* and a materialistic definition instead of an ethical one is certainly beside the mark. John uses ὁ κόσμος as the opposite of τὰ τέκνα θεοῦ, and he deals with this opposition at some length. — There is no reason to take γινώσκειν in a modified sense; it means **know**, really know, understand and comprehend the nature of the person or thing; an intellectual activity, John 14, 17. Of course, such knowledge includes various consequences which naturally follow, and which the writer may even have in mind, but the verb itself does not include them; hence we do not read: *agnoscere pro suis,* or μισεῖν, or something else. All that lies in the name and reality of divine sonship is a foreign thing, not only to the heart and affection, but even to the mind and intellect of the world, a veritable *terra incognita.* 1 Cor. 2, 14; 2 Cor. 6, 9. — And this for the simple reason, **because it knew him not.** Here the verb is the same and has the same meaning; it did not even *know* him, to say nothing more; it had not even taken the first step toward communion with him. The tense is the aorist, which states a simple fact in the past: "To begin with," we may say, "the world did not know him, closed mind and heart against God and the love he offered in Christ Jesus; and the result is, it does not know now God's children, *i. e.* their real character and being as reborn men." In John 1, 10, καὶ ὁ κόσμος αὐτὸν οὐκ ἔγνω, the αὐτόν refers to Christ; in our text it refers to God, yet to him as the Father who offers his wonderful love to men in the Son for their salvation. So the two are closely related; comp. also John 14, 16; 15, 19 and 21; 16, 3. The world is indeed proud of what it calls its knowledge, but the one thing needful to know it does not know. The mystery of regeneration is foolishness in its eyes, and those who claim childhood with God in Christ Jesus it considers as suffering a form of delusion. Its own idea of a universal fatherhood of God and a universal brotherhood of men, without redemption and regeneration, is for it the hight of

wisdom. Let no man count on recognition for his spiritual
life on the part of the world; the names of God's greatest
saints are not engraved on the tablets of the world's temple
of fame and honor. And this cannot be otherwise; if
it were, either the world would no longer be world, or
we would no longer be children of God. The fact that
the world does not know us for what we really are is
proof positive that we are no longer of the world, but
have become foreign to it, otherwise the world would indeed know us.

We shall at last be like him.

The second part of our text also starts with an
exclamatory word, the address **Beloved,** ἀγαπητοί, followers of ὁ υἱὸς ὁ ἀγαπητός, Matth. 3, 17 (the same as
ἠγαπημένος, Eph. 1, 6). The word does not show whether
John addresses his readers as beloved of God, or as beloved of himself (see also 2, 7), as no genitive follows;
but in an Epistle the latter significance is preferable, although, following τέκνα θεοῦ, something may be said for
the former. "Beloved" has come to be the usual form
of pulpit address; it has, as we see, Scripture foundation.
Besser says, John uses it of "his little children." — **Now are
we children of God. and it is not yet made manifest what
we shall be.** Here John describes our present condition,
as to its inward reality, and as to its outward appearance
and manifestation. Νῦν is not in contrast to οὔπω, as some
would take it, but co-ordinate with it: νῦν . . . καὶ
οὔπω; which is better than to, read, as those others prefer:
now, although the world knows us not. Stellhorn, *Schrift-
beweiss,* p. 390: *jetzt (schon) sind wir Gottes Kinder.* —
The repetition: **we are children of God**, is decidedly emphatic; it bespeaks the strongest and most positive certainty. Nor dare we minimize the words to read: we are
children of God as far as our intention, our conviction,
our effort goes, such in idea; no, we *are* in full inward
reality. "Ye are (ἐστέ) sons of God, through faith, in

7

Christ Jesus," Gal. 3, 27. This is the certainty of faith; faith, planted into our hearts by the Spirit through the Word, knows itself and says of itself what it is: I believe! or: I am a child of God! — But the "now" leads us to look into the future, and there we are shown a great difference. Not indeed that we shall ever be more in reality than we now are — no man can climb higher than childhood with God. The difference is not as to reality, but as to appearance and manifestation. As far as "now," the present, is concerned we must say: **and it is not yet made manifest what we shall be.** John has in mind a revelation of the reality, not a mere making known or intellectual apprehension, for we know what we shall be, namely: "we shall be like him." Τί ἐσόμεθα — our glorification at the last day; "an inheritance incorruptible, and undefiled, and that fadeth not away, reserved in heaven for you," 1 Pet. 1, 4; 2 Cor. 5, 4. This glorification is not yet made manifest: nobody sees us in the white robe of Christ's righteousness, which now already is ours, but hidden; nobody beholds the crown of hope upon our brow, the diamond of faith upon our hearts, the pearls of love upon our hands. The imperfections of the flesh both hide the glory we now have, and at the same time darken our eyes so that they cannot see; and in a sinful world with a mortal nature we plod wearily on. A child of God here is like a diamond indeed, all crystal white within, but uncut, and with no light to reflect and blaze out from it. — Over against the present John puts the future: **We know that, if he shall be manifested, we shall be like him.** "We know" is more than so-called Christian conviction, as some commentators make it; divine revelation is behind and in that οἴδαμεν, else it would be an empty claim like the proud: We know! of many a scientist who, when it comes to the ultimate test, must nevertheless admit: *Ignoramus ignorabimus!* "We know," as John writes it for himself and his brethren, is stronger than a mathematical demonstration, more reliable than the evidence of sense, and more certain than the united testimony of any number of men in secular affairs. — And this is what we know, although it still lies in the future: **that, if he shall be manifested, we shall be like him;** a vivid future conditional sentence (*ἐάν* with the subj., followed by the fut. indicative). It is as if John already saw this glorious thing coming to pass; there is no doubt in the *ἐάν*. The subject of the sentence is hidden in *φανερωθῇ*. In order to determine what it is we must look not only to the immediate context, *i. e.* to what precedes, but also to what follows, especially the significance of *αὐτός* and *ἐκεῖνος* in these clauses. It will thus be seen that the interpretative translation of both English versions: "he shall be manifested" is decidedly to be preferred. Yet this is not so absolute for *φανερωθῇ*, mainly because of the preceding *ἐφανερώθη*, that the possibility of an impersonal subject being intended need be denied; hence we have in the margin: *it = τί ἐσόμεθα.* — **We shall be like him,** *ὅμοιοι*, not *ἴσοι*, identical with. We shall always be children of God, we can be no more; but whereas we are now children of God in humiliation, then we shall be children of God in glorification. — **For,** *ὅτι*, introduces a reason, and one which holds up the effect to show that the cause must be there: **we shall see him even as he is.** If we shall see him thus, our eyes must be according, *i. e.* they must be glorified eyes. The possession of such eyes is proved by their seeing him as he is. It is not that seeing him first makes us like him, for before the seeing can take place we must be like him. — Who is meant by *αὐτῷ* and *αὐτόν*, which includes also *ἐπ' αὐτῷ* in verse 3? Many commentators answer without hesitation: God, pointing to *θεοῦ* as proof. These then refer the *ἐκεῖνος* which follows to Christ, remarking that it is John's way thus to refer to the Savior without especially naming him. Now one thing is certain: *ἐκεῖνος* both in verses 3 and 5 must mean Christ; in this all are agreed. Moreover, no special doctrinal or homiletical difference results when some refer *αὐτῷ* and *αὐτόν* to God, and others, especially also our two English versions, refer it, like *ἐκεῖνος*, to Christ. Daechsel cannot be supported when he argues on the basis of 1 Tim. 6, 16 for the invisibility of God, and thus makes "we shall see him even as he is" refer to Christ. Matth. 5, 8: "Blessed are the pure in heart: for they shall *see* God;" and Ps. 17, 15: "As for me, I will behold thy face in righteousness," amply prove the *visio Dei*. So also ὅμοιοι αὐτῷ, "like him;" doctrinally and homiletically both are good: like God, and: like Christ, for both give us the *imago Dei*, holiness and righteousness, Eph. 4, 24, including the *glorificatio*. The question must be decided on other grounds. There are three points which induce us to follow our two English versions in interpreting not only ἐκεῖνος, but also the preceding αὐτῷ and αὐτόν of Christ, the apparent antecedent θεός in the previous sentence notwithstanding. First, in verse 5 we have ἐκεῖνος ἐφανερώθη ἵνα τὰς ἁμαρτίας ἄρῃ, which all agree refers to Christ: Christ was manifested to take away our sins. Comparing this with ἐὰν φανερωθῇ ὅμοιοι αὐτῷ ἐσόμεθα, ὅτι ὀψόμεθα αὐτὸν καθώς ἐστιν, and noting the correspondence between the two verbs φανερωθῇ and ὀψόμεθα (be manifested and see), the conclusion is justified, that the subject of φανερωθῇ (which might be the same as ἐφανερώθη preceding) is also Christ: "if he shall be manifested," giving us for the following: "we shall be like him," Christ, "for we shall see him," Christ, "even as he is," glorified. Secondly, the change from αὐτός to ἐκεῖνος, if Christ is meant throughout, is entirely natural, as αὐτός would hardly be used in the nominative here; see the same change between the oblique cases of αὐτός and the nominative ἐκεῖνος in John 5, 39. There is no question: if ἐκεῖνος ἁγνός ἐστιν (verse 3) refers to the same person as the preceding αὐτῷ and αὐτόν, ἐκεῖνος is the word to use. Finally, by taking Christ as the subject of ἐὰν φανερωθῇ and as the antecedent of αὐτῷ etc. and ἐκεῖνος, we get one uniform line of thought, we escape the break which the change of persons in ἐκεῖνος would otherwise introduce, and the thought throughout is perfectly smooth. The old exegesis is thus amply justified, and there is no call to revise it either in our Catechism or devotional literature. "We shall see him" = sight where now we walk by faith, the evidence of things not seen. Yet "we shall see," not as now we are able to see, with a vision darkened by sin, which so many trust as superior to Christian faith, the evidence of things not seen, but with that glorified vision by which we shall see "face to face," and "know even as I am known," 1 Cor. 13, 12.

We must purify ourselves.

And every one that hath this hope *set* **on him purifieth himself, even as he is pure.** Hope and purity belong together, 2 Cor. 6, 18 — 17, 1; 2 Pet. 3, 13-14. No one can look forward with desire and longing to the time when he will be like Christ (or God, if that interpretation be preferred), and at the same time go on indifferently and carelessly in sin. "Every one" — a rule without an exception. By **this hope** the one just referred to is meant, when we shall be like Christ and see him "even as he is" in all his divine glory and majesty; Ebrard thinks that ἐλπίς = the objective treasure itself for which we look, and the word is so used in Scripture, but equally often, as here, for the sure and certain expectation in our hearts of the great glory to come. This hope is described as *set* **on him,** ἐπ' αὐτῷ, and the dative after the preposition indicates rest. He is the foundation, the everlasting rock; and on him the hope is built, like the house on the rock. All men have more or less of hope in their hearts, but all such hopes lack the ἐπ' αὐτῷ, have none but human foundation, a bit of shaky human morality perhaps, or a little pile of the sand of human philosophy. Such hopes have no power to draw us out of sin into a new life, for their foundation is not high enough. — **Purifieth himself.** Bengel reads it: "preserves himself pure;" that is included, but also a forward and upward movement, an increase in holiness. Ἀγνίζειν includes καθαρίζειν and ἀγιάζειν. By purification we become more and more Christlike, godlike, yet this likeness must be distinguished from that which John calls our hope. The most Christlike saint on earth is not yet like Christ glorified in heaven, or like the all-glorious Father. The ἁγνίζων is not to be performed "by our unaided strength;" it is the activity of the new man in Christ Jesus, the one who has this living hope. He works with new spiritual powers, is aided by the Holy Spirit, and receives constant strength through the means of grace. Total purification, and a sinless condition (the so-called "second blessing" taught by some) is not John's thought (see 1 John 1, 10; Phil. 3, 12; Ps. 143, 2; *etc.*); but a purification which puts off the sins which we can see and know and gives full play to every Christian virtue. Our Confessions have much to say concerning the self-made holiness of the Romanists: "the shocking presumption of those desperate saints, who dare to invent a higher and better life and condition than the Ten Commandments teach" (*Book of Concord*, Jacobs' transl., p. 435); "this semblance of wisdom and righteousness," from which "infinite evils follow" (p. 222; *etc.*), which still flourishes to-day and has many Protestant imitators. Christ in the first place must purify us by His holy blood from the *guilt* of sin; this purification he alone can perform. At the same time he must break the *power* of sin within us by giving us the new life; this also he alone can do. Then only with his help can we crush out more and more the remaining evil *desire* in us, and in this we indeed cannot be too zealous and active (ἁγνίζει ἑαυτόν, present tense for continuous and constant activity). There is no question that herein many of our people fall short, and therefore need the truth here stated to brace them for their high and blessed calling. — **Even as he is pure,** *i. e.* absolutely, and thus for all time and in every way our model (ἐστίν, not ἦν). Ἁγνός ἐστιν denotes a fixed condition, ἁγνίζει a progression; Christ did not "purify himself," there was no sin or stain in him. His purity reaches back to his conception and birth:

> "Now praise we Christ, the Holy One,
> The spotless virgin Mary's Son."

We purify ourselves even as he is pure, when we follow
Paul: "I have been crucified with Christ; yet I live; and
yet no longer I, but Christ liveth in me: and that life which
I now live in the flesh I live in faith, the faith which is in
the Son of God, who loved me, and gave himself up for
me." Gal. 2, 20.

Every one that doeth sin doeth also lawlessness.
Again a rule without an exception. If we are to purify
ourselves, we must know what impurity is and what it includes, and this the more since many false and lax views
obtain; it was so in John's day, and is still the same. This
"every one" is the contrast to the former "every one;" and
there are only these two classes. **Sin,** ἡ ἁμαρτία, with the
article, signifies: that which is sin, the actual thing (not the
concept, or idea merely); it is more than the quality of an
act, it is the principle itself which expresses itself in action.
— **Doeth sin** is the opposite of "doeth righteousness," τὴν
δικαιοσύνην, verse 7. The manner of the doing is not mentioned, it is the doing itself in its proper sense of which
John speaks, a doing in which sin is the real thing; to do
sin — to realize sin in one's action. The present participle
indicates continuation; the man who "does sin" is under the
dominion of sin, does sin as the servant thereof, John 8, 34.
— **Doeth also lawlessness,** i: e. in doing the sin he does the
lawlessness, and this means that he places himself in direct
opposition to the law of God and thus to God himself; and
this is the opposite of purifying oneself and becoming like
God (which in its heavenly completeness is our hope). —
The first axiomatic statement John at once clinches with
another, although in his peculiar manner he attaches it by
means of the simple καί : **and sin is lawlessness.** The
predicate has the article (ἡ ἀνομία) to show that it is
identical in extent with the subject: "Sin" is not a species
of which we predicate "lawlessness" as to genus; the two
are one and the same thing, so that we can reverse the
sentence: lawlessness is sin, and have it equally true. Here
then John brings out the true character of sin, which many
commit so lightly, in which they go on and live so securely:

it is the very opposite of God and all that is God's; it makes absolutely unlike him, leads away from him, and entails all the consequences this involves. John's statement has become the classic dogmatic and catechetical definition of sin. With the true character of sin revealed, do you turn a deaf ear to all who excuse and condone prevalent sins and follow sinful practices themselves with callous consciences.

He was manifested to take away our sins.

One has well said, verse 4 was written for careless Christians, to arouse them to the danger of sin, and should bear the title: "It is hard to be a Christian." And verse 5 was written for the troubled Christian, worried about his faultiness and sin, and should have the heading: "It is easy to be a Christian." The climax of our text is reached in the words: καὶ οἴδατε ὅτι ἐκεῖνος ἐφανερώθη. John appeals to his hearers: **Ye know.** The facts he mentions are so fundamental to Christian faith and life that there can be no question of their knowing. But knowledge is often a dormant thing and not the "power" it ought to be. John wants to quicken that knowledge and get the proper results from it. Ye know **that he was manifested** — the word we have met twice before and find again in verse 8, a glorious word: like the sun rising over the earth and dispelling the darkness; like the plant sprouting out of the earth and spreading itself upward and outward into a magnificent tree. Ἐκεῖνος ἐφανερώθη, this brief sentence contains the essence of the Gospel; in it is all the light of our Christmas joy. If these words were stricken from the Bible, the whole structure of our salvation would lie in ruins. Christ's manifestation in the flesh is meant, his conception and birth of the virgin Mary, but at the same time all that followed and made him known as the Redeemer of men. That is what makes this a fine Christmas text, enabling the preacher to dwell on the Christmas story itself, as he must on this day, and at the same time unfold all that lies in this story. "He was manifested" includes that he was hidden before that; not till the fulness of the time came did God send forth his Son, born of a woman (Gal. 4, 4). Before that the Son existed in the glory of the divine nature together with the Father and the Holy Spirit, and whatever revelation he made of himself was only preparatory. At last ἐκεῖνος ἐφανερώθη, and the angels sang to the shepherds, and the Magi came from afar, and they who beheld his grace and truth believed on him. These two, "he was manifested," and "ye know," agree together; so every believer knows, for the light of his manifestation still shines through the world to light the hearts of men. — He was manifested **to take away sins,** a purpose clause, brief, as John loves to put it, and at the same time comprehensive and powerful. The manifestation was altogether one of grace and mercy, John 3, 17; and this is the heart of our joy to-day. Instead of the singular as before, we now have the plural τὰς ἁμαρτίας, Matth. 1, 21, each and every single sin; thus John unfolds what lies in ἡ ἁμαρτία. There is no sin of any kind for which Christ did not die and make full reparation; and no man has so many sins that Christ did not atone for them all. The A. V. adds "our," which the best texts omit, leaving the universality of redemption in all its grandeur. We may indeed say, he took away "our sins," but only because "he taketh away the sin of the world," John 1, 29. "To take away," αἴρειν, may mean simply to take up and bear (hence the margin: *bear*), or: to take or carry away, to remove altogether. Plain examples of the latter meaning are found John 11, 48; 15, 2; 17, 15; 19, 31 and 38; and there is no reason to restrict the meaning here in any way. The purpose of Christ's manifestation certainly was to remove and rid us of sin altogether. — This too is the thought which John's whole argument requires: we are children of God; godlikeness is our hope; hence we must purify ourselves; the law requires this, for sin is lawlessness; and the Gospel requires it, namely both the work of Christ (he was manifested to take away sins), and the person of Christ (in him is no sin). **In him is no sin** is joined to the foregoing by a simple καί. Christ indeed was able to be our sin-bearer because as the Son of God in human flesh there is no sin in him, but John is not con-

cerned about this thought (2 Cor. 5, 21); he simply coordinates the two: Christ's person and Christ's work; both
show that we must not be indifferent to sin, but must purify
ourselves.   The sinlessness of our Savior is here asserted by
divine inspiration, as also in verse 3; 2 Cor. 5, 21; John 8,
29 and 46; *etc.* 'Αμαρτία is in the singular and without the
article; that means more than that in him no single sin of
any kind is found, it means that what the concept "sin" contains, in the widest possible sense, in no way inheres in him:
he is absolutely sinless.   Therefore also ἐστίν, although the
previous clause has ἐφανερώθη: "is" in the absolute sense,
from the beginning of his manifestation even to all eternity.
And the preacher has cause to emphasize Christ's sinlessness
when he proclaims the blessed Savior's birth (see the author's *Eisenach Gospel Selections,* text for Christmas, vol.
I, p. 88 *etc.*).   In these days when the virgin birth is denied, together with the resurrection and the divine Sonship,
the pulpit has an important work to do, and must realize
it and perform it with thoroughness and power.

HOMILETICAL HINTS.

When missionary Ziegenbalg came to translate 1 John 3, 1, that
we should be called children of God, the Malabar school-master who
assisted him refused to put down the words, and suggested instead:
"God has granted us to kiss his feet."

Three friends sat together in conversation, and their talk
drifted to the subject Christmas. Two of them were believing
Christians, the third called himself a doubter. The latter asked of
the others, whether they considered the Christmas story to be true.
They replied, that they indeed believed it. Then the doubter said:
"You cannot possibly believe it. For if you really believed it, you
could not speak of it so calmly; it would give you no rest, until
all the world knew and believed that God had so loved the world."

Here is something the world cannot understand. The natural
man has an entirely different picture of the love of God. He would
imagine that the love of God at one stroke would transform the
earth into a paradise full of outward glory and fleshly delights. He
would picture the Savior of the world making his entry into the
world by scattering good fortune, glory, and riches on every side.

In his train there would shine magnificent power and compelling majesty, and all his adherents would bask in the royal favor as their immediate reward. That is why the world to-day cannot content itself with a simple Christian celebration of the festival of Christ's birth, it must deck the festival in its own gaudy splendor. In the same way the world fails to understand the true joy of God's children at this time, many of whom praise the love of God amid poverty and misfortune, on beds of sickness and in the face of death. The simple Christmas story is for us not only a history of the appearance of God's Son on earth, but at the same time a history of all God's children on earth. Do we mean to claim more than the child Jesus had on earth? We learn to seek the love of God not in outward earthly things, we behold it and are certain of it when everything in our earthly lives seems to speak against it. The world does not know God and his love; hence it does not understand the children of God, and how he leads those whom he loves. We learn it from the Christmas story: Just as he, Jesus, was in the world, so are we. And therefore even in distress and in spite of scoffings heaped upon us for Christ's sake we hold fast the assurance, that we are the beloved children of God. This remains for us the glad message of God's Father-love in Christ Jesus, which ever anew we draw from the blessed Christmas story. (Riemer.)

How should the world know the children when it does not know the Father? the nature of adoption when the Spirit of adoption is foreign to it? Lacking the annointing of the Spirit, it knows nothing of things spiritual. 1 Cor. 2, 14.

Matth. 6, 22: the eye is not only an organ whereby we behold the light that is without, but at the same time a means whereby this light enters within us and fills us with its radiance ($\mathring{o}\psi\acute{o}\mu\epsilon\theta a$). — As the rose is contained in the undeveloped bud, so the future glory and blessedness of the child of God is contained in his faith. — They who despise and revile us do not know who we are, citizens of heaven, children of the eternal fatherland, companions of the cherubim; but they shall know on the great day of judgment, when in astonishment and grief they will exclaim: These are they whom we derided and despised! and now they are numbered among the children of God, and their inheritance is with the saints of God. (Chrysostom.)

"We shall see him even as he is." Imagine a man — I do not know whether you have ever met such a one — in whose seriousness, prayerfulness, peace of soul, unselfishness, yea, and also joyfulness you realize: This is how a Christian must look! Imagine this man as your neighbor at your side, and yourself constantly under the discipline of his consecrated eyes — would not a stream of constant light, peace, and sanctifying influence emanate from him and enter your life? And yet he would only be a sinful man. Now imagine the Lord himself at your side, illuminated with the glory of the Father, and your own poor eyes opened to perceive the sea of light and love flowing about him: O, how every part of your being would bend to receive of this holiness and love! The hungering, thirsting human heart would be filled and satisfied with the stream of divine life. Seeing him thus even as he is, the apostle's word would be fulfilled: "We know that, if he shall be manifested, we shall be like him." (Dryander.)

Just as the eye is unable to endure a particle of dust and weeps until it be cleansed, so the eye of hope, looking up to yonder glory, will not endure the dust of worldliness; and should a particle be blown into it, the eye would quiver at the slightest touch, and the Lord would make repentant tears to flow, to wash the dust away. (Besser.)

In secret, like the dew of the morning, children of God are born, and with the secret mamma they are nourished and fed; but the glory of their sonship shall shine out publicly at last, to the joy of the angels and the consternation of the world. (Besser.)

It is God alone who purifies us. But he purifies no unwilling one. Thou purifiest thyself, but not through thyself, but through him who comes to dwell in thee. (Augustine.)

Sin's damnation and destruction is in its opposition to the eternal, all-holy, almighty, all-merciful God who has spoken the doom of sin in the Law as well as in the Gospel.

God's children still wear the uniform of misery here on earth; they are princes traveling incognito. Did not the eternal Son of God, from Bethlehem to Golgatha, mark out for us this path as the only one that leads on high?

Our Christmas Joy:

Ye Know That He Was Manifested:

I. *The Son—that we might be made sons.*
II. *The Sinless One — that he might take away our sins.*
III. *The Pure One — that we might be made pure.*
IV. *The now Glorious One — that we might be made like unto him.*

(The reader will note that this outline puts forward Christ himself, whose grace and truth should shine forth from the sermon with fullest splendor, undimmed even by lengthy efforts at admonition and application. Christmas = Christ and appropriation.)

The Christmas Message of the Father's Love.

See what that Love has prepared for us:

I. *In the Christmas at Bethlehem;*
II. *In the Christmas of to-day;*
III. *In the eternal Christmas to come.*

The Father's Love in Christ Our Christmas Gift.

I. *Come, see it!* ("He was manifested.")
II. *Come, take it!* ("Now are we the children of God.")
III. *Come, thank him for it!* ("And every one that hath this hope set on him purifieth himself.")

God's Son Born a Child,

so that we may be

I. *Happy as the children of God;*
II. *Full of hope as the children of God;*
III. *Godly as the children of God.*

We Are Called the Children of God.

I. *The wonder of God's love;*
II. *The dignity of our position;*
III. *The loftiness of our duty;*

C. C. Hein.

The Christchild Makes Us To Be Children of God.

I. *What love;*
II. *What exaltation;*
III. *What a calling!*

Rump.

God's Gifts With the Christmas Light Upon Them.

I. *Behold what manner of love the Father hath bestowed on us.*
II. *Behold what manner of glory the Highest hath prepared*
II. *for us.*
III. *Behold what manner of blessedness the God of grace hath granted us.*

In part from Matthes.

THE DAY AFTER CHRISTMAS.

Heb. 1, 1-6.

All Lutheran pericope systems furnish two texts for the great festivals, one for the festival proper, and one for the day following, which continues the celebration. Our hasty age passes over the great facts of our salvation far too rapidly; two days are all too few for the proper celebration of the Savior's birth. — There can be no doubt as to the purpose of our text for this day: it proclaims *the incomparable glory of him who was born in Bethlehem.* In one majestic sweep it reveals to us what is meant by the divinity of him who rightly bears the name Son. Here indeed is a text to illumine, strengthen, and satisfy our faith; and this must ever be the great purpose of every festival text.

The Son and the prophets.

Like a pent-up stream the writer of the Epistle to the Hebrews, whose identity is not established, allows his thought to burst out and rush forward in a grand introductory statement, which in no way resembles the usual opening of a letter (but comp. 1 John). Verses 1-4 state, in a comprehensive manner, the theme of the entire Epistle, and in the verses immediately following the first great part of that theme is elaborated. The body of the Epistle resembles a sermon: there are doctrinal expositions, on which are based earnest and powerful admonitions. That the whole after all is an epistle the closing sections show beyond a doubt. — **God, having of old time spoken unto the fathers in the prophets by divers portions and in divers manners, hath at the end of these days spoken unto us in** *his* **Son.** The two clauses of this sentence are

110

finely balanced: having spoken by divers portions and in
divers manners — God hath spoken (absolutely); of old
time — at the end of these days; in the prophets — in his
Son. **By divers portions,** πολυμερῶς == now one part or
fragment, now another and thus many (hence the A. V.:
"at sundry times"). The reference is to quantity: God
revealed the truth little by little in the O. T., giving to each
prophet his special measure of truth to convey. The word
suggests diversity as to time, parts, and persons (not:
threats, rebukes, promises, *etc.*). **And in divers manners,**
πολυτρόπως == now in one, now in another manner, as it
suited each time and stage in the kingdom. The reference
is to quality, and the words suggest manifoldness of contents and form (symbols, types, direct prophecies, *etc*).
Some deny and others maintain that these two adverbs are
used to indicate the incompletness of the O. T. revelation.
They do indicate this: for the many parts still lacked the
final and essential part, the revelation in the Son; the
many forms were adapted to the varying conditions as they
arose, and the ultimate and final form was yet to come
in Christ. There was indeed a relative completeness for
God's people at each period, but the absolute completeness
for all men and all times still lay in the future. — In πάλαι,
of old time, the entire ante-Messianic dispensation is embraced; it is contrasted with "the end of these days;" and
this agrees with λαλήσας and ἐλάλησεν, the aorist participle
indicating time prior to the definite past action of the aorist
main verb, really: "after God had spoken . . . he did
speak." — **God** is the speaker in each case, and the same
verb λάλειν, (**having spoken . . . hath spoken**) is
used both times, a favorite expression of the author for
divine revelation. It includes here not merely the verbal
or written utterances of the prophets, but the entire revelation of God in whatever form (πολυτρόπως) bestowed.
Here we have a powerful proof for the inspiration of the
Old Testament, as well as the New, both as to contents
and to form. In every kind and part of this revelation
God spoke, he and none other, and in the prophets just as

in the Son. Whoever touches λαλήσας, overthrows at the same time ἐλάλησεν. — **To the fathers,** the members of the O. T. people of God, yet not as the ancestors of the Jews of the writer's time, but as the "fathers" of spiritual descendants in the days of Christ and thereafter (ἡμῖν). — **In the prophets** means prophets in the widest sense of the word, not one excepted in whom God in any way spoke (whether by what he wrought or uttered or wrote as the agent of God; all are meant, because the Son's superiority to them all is here to be set forth. The ἐν is significant, and must not be reduced to διά, "through" (Luther and others), by means of a Hebraism or otherwise, for the author uses διά where this is his meaning, verse 2; 2, 2, etc. Ἐν denotes that for the fathers the prophets were the bearers and mediators of what God spoke in them by means of a spiritual impartation; it includes an indwelling, and makes of inspiration something far other than the mechanical operation pictured by the minds of those critics whose efforts are put forth solely to overthrow this fundamental doctrine of Scripture. — **At the end of these days** might in itself mean the end of certain days the author has in mind and here refers to, *i. e.* the final days of the O. T. dispensation; but the phrase ἐπ' ἐσχάτου (or ἐσχάτων) τῶν ἡμερῶν is a standing eschatologic expression for the times of the new dispensation, from the coming of Christ to his return. This then is the period referred to, and τούτων, "these," is added, not to change the sense of the phrase, but to indicate that the writer and his readers were living in this time. — **Hath spoken,** ἐλάλησεν, aorist, comprehends the entire revelation in Christ and through Christ as one finished act of God: God "did speak," and this revelation of his stands forever. **Unto us,** not the Hebrews alone, nor only those living at the writer's time, but all men generally who live in the end of days. — **In** *his* **Son,** note again ἐν, and how it links together the work of the prophets and that of the Son. Ἐν υἱῷ lacks the article, and some on this account read "Son" in a predicative sense: "in One who is Son;" but, in the first place, the Greek article is not needed since

"Son" is definite enough (Robertson, *Kurzgef. Grammatik d. Neustest. Griechisch*, 111: "The Greek article is placed wherever a word with a definite reference would not be sufficiently defined without it"); and secondly, as Keil urges, υἱός is here followed by relative clauses which make it definite beyond question. In our English manner of speaking we would most likely use "his Son," as also both English versions have it, or "the Son" (hardly, as the margin reads: *a Son*, which, because indefinite, is contrary to the sense of the Greek). The whole sentence culminates in the word **Son.** God can speak in none greater to us; hence in the Son we have the ultimate and complete revelation of God, for which all other revelation was but the preparation. There is something close and intimate in the statement: God hath spoken to us in his Son. So wondrously he condescends, so wondrously he lifted us up and honored us. And *in* his Son, behold, what he said, for instance there at Bethlehem, or on Golgatha, or at Joseph's tomb: he spoke love, grace, mercy, pardon, peace, blessedness, eternal salvation. He had spoken so before, but never with such might and light, never with such finality and completeness.

The glory of the Son our Savior.

Two relative clauses state an action of God regarding the Son, and a third, greatly amplified, states an activity of the Son himself. This. helps to clear up the question: Does the appointment of the Son as heir of all things refer to a divine act in eternity, or to a divine act in time? The former is meant, in spite of the arguments of Keil, Zoeckler, and others. "God did speak to us in his Son" — that he did in time. Now the great question is raised by the writer of Hebrews: Who is this Son? And he answers, summing it all up: The Greatest of all! But what is the proof? First, his person and work before his incarnation; secondly, his work as the incarnate Son, culminating in his session on the right hand of the Majesty on high. And of all

8

the statements used to present these mighty things to us it has truly been said: *Tot verba, tot pondera.*

Whom he appointed heir of all things, refers to υἱός, a name which belongs to him equally before and after the incarnation. Sonship and heirship belong together, and normally the one is contained in the other, and that from the beginning. So it is said of us, the moment we become children of God: "and if a son, then an heir through God," Gal. 4, 7; and of Christ and us: "heirs of God, and joint-heirs with Christ," Rom. 8, 17. "All" is more than the church; yet the lordship of the church is always united with the rule over all things, Eph. 1, 22-23; Ps. 2, especially 6 and 8-9; comp. John 13, 3; Matth. 11, 27; John 3, 35; 17, 2; Matth. 28, 18. Whenever we thus read that God gave all things unto Christ, we have the execution of the eternal purpose of God when he made the Son the heir of all things, even his human nature participating in this divine prerogative. But in picturing this to our minds we must not confuse the actual position of the Son as heir and lord of all, with his plans and purposes as the Savior, which are now going forward and in which he endeavors to subject men to him in faith. Christ is now heir of all things and in full possession, ruling unrestrictedly among his enemies, and he has been such from the beginning. And this makes it the more wonderful, when we glance at Bethlehem, that God should have sent the Heir himself to humble himself and bear our sins, Matth. 21, 37-38. — **Through whom also he made the worlds:** "All things were made by him, δ' αὐτοῦ; and without him was not anything made that hath been made," John 1, 3. The Son, then, existed from all eternity, prior to the making of the worlds. The full meaning of διά is hidden from our minds, we cannot fathom this working of the one person of the Godhead through the other. Yet note that δ' οὗ is different from ἐν υἱῷ and could not be exchanged for ἐν ᾧ. Sonship, heirship, and partnership in the creative act, all go together, and all reveal the true character of the Son, one in essence, power, and glory with the Father. The καί before ἐποίησεν

ranges this act alongside of the other expressed in ἔθηκεν,
so that where this is mentioned the other is added as belonging with it. Ποιεῖν is the same as *barah*, Gen. 1, 1:
call into being; πάντα ἐγένετο, οτ ὁ κόσμος δι' αὐτοῦ ἐγένετο;
call from non-existence into existence, and thus "create"
in the full sense of the word. For **the worlds** the margin
offers the *ages*, which is the first meaning of οἱ αἰῶνες, *viz.*
world periods; but like the later Hebrew plural *olamim* it
has received a metonymic meaning: *complexus eorum, quae
temporibus continentur*, the world, in the sense of the ages
with all that transpires in them.

   **Who being the effulgence of his glory, and the very
image of his substance, and upholding all things by the
word of his power, when he had made purification of
sins, sat down on the right hand of the Majesty on high.**
The subject of this second and extensive relative clause is
the Son in whom God spoke to us; and of him it is said,
that he sat down on the right hand of the Majesty on high.
This, of course, refers to the exaltation of the human
nature of Christ, wherefore the subject of this relative
clause is the incarnate Son. Three participial clauses
modify the subject: 1) "who being the effulgence" *etc.*
(the Son's relation to God); 2) "and upholding all things"
etc. (the Son's relation to the world); 3) "when he had
made purification" *etc.* (the work of redemption). The
main verb, ἐκάθισεν, is an aorist and hence denotes one
definite act in the past: "he sat down;" the aorist participle
ποιησάμενος denotes simple action prior to that of the main
verb, hence: "had made;" ὤν and φέρων, two present participles, denote continuous condition and action, simultaneous
with the main verb, hence have the force of imperfects.—**Being the effulgence of his glory** is here predicated of the incarnate Son, but not as a description of what the incarnation is; it means to reveal to us the eternal and divine glory
of this Son who in the fulness of time appeared in the flesh.
Ἀπαύγασμα is the result of ἀπαυγάζειν, the effect of sending
out the αὐγή; the word occurs only here in the N. T.
Chrysostom defines it as φῶς ἐκ φωτός, a sun produced

from the original Light, participating in its essence, yet
viewed by itself. The eternal generation of the Son lies
behind this thought. **Effulgence** — the radiation itself or
the luster caused by it (yet not like light falling on some
medium and reflected from it, as the sun's light is reflected
from the moon). The hidden and inscrutable glory of
God is made manifest in the Son, who is the effulgence of
that glory. **Glory,** δόξα, — not merely one divine attribute
among others, but the unfolding of them all (the αὐτοῦ after
ὑποστάσεως must be attached also to δόξα). The Son as the
effulgence of God's glory is God in essence with every attribute, and this not veiled and hidden, but shining forth.
As we cannot see the sun without the light and radiance
which it sends forth, so God is hidden from us as to his
real essence and attributes without the Son, the effulgence
of his glory. — **And the very image of his substance**
rounds out and completes the statement just made; for
the Son is not a temporary, passing effulgence of God's
glory, but the very image of God's substance or being.
"Effulgence" corresponds to "image;" "glory" to "substance;" and "image" is related to "substance" as effulgence" is to "glory." All the divine attributes shine
forth in the Son because he is the image of God's substance.
Substance, ὑπόστασις, here signifies the real nature or being
which supports its form (μορφή) and properties. The word
is used in many ways in Scripture, but here, employed of
God, it designates his essential and absolute being. The
theological use of the word for "person" is considerably later
and must not be introduced here (as some have done, reading it in the sense of the person of the Father). **The very
image,** χαρακτήρ (margin: *impress*), predicates of the Son
that he is the complete and adequate expression of the
divine being. All that God is the Son is, and this in a
manner so that it can be seen, known, apprehended. The
expressive χαρακτήρ is from χαράσσειν, to engrave or inscribe,
and means both the tool for such work, and the impress or image made by the tool (especially the latter).
Col. 1, 15; Phil. 2, 6; John 14, 9; 20, 28. — Language

fairly groans with the weight of thought here piled upon
it. Our poor human tongue and mind, occupied so much
with the things beneath us, must strain to rise unto these
blessed higher regions. But let no one imagine that he
may pass by the great things here stated by the Spirit of
God; they are the very rock bottom of our faith, and as
the passages cited will show — many others might be added
— the very essence of many a sweet Gospel statement. —
The next clause is added by means of τε (not καί) because of the self-evident and very close connection: **and
upholding all things by the word of his power.** Here we
have the Son's relation to the world (τὰ πάντα = οἱ αἰῶνες,
verse 2). Keil urges that φέρειν = *bear* in the sense of
administer, *i. e.* rule; so that the clause would say: he administers, governs, rules all things with the word of his
power. Others take it in the sense of *sustain* (*praeservatio*).
There seems to be no reason why the one meaning should
exclude the other, especialy since φέρειν includes motion.
The Son is not an Atlas with the world as a dead weight
upon his shoulders, merely keeping all things from sinking into nothingness; he bears all things so that his will
and purpose is fulfilled. Hence **the word of his power,**
which is a stronger expression than "the powerful word;"
ῥῆμα = the word uttered, the expressed will of the Son,
hence not the Gospel-word, but the word of his omnipotent
power: He speaks, and it is done; he commands, and it
stands fast. What is predicated of God, Col. 1, 17, is
here predicated of the Son; and this is the Son who "sat
down on the right hand of the Majesty on high," the incarnate Son; he was not destitute or deprived of the divine
power when he assumed our flesh, for did he not use **the**
word of his power in miracle after miracle?

When he had made purification of sins is closely connected, because of its aorist participle ποιησάμενος, with the
aorist main verb, and thus needs no conjunction to join it to
the present participles preceding. The A. V. adds δι' ἑαυτοῦ,
"by himself," which the best texts omit; but the middle
voice of ποιησάμενος gives a similar thought. The genitive

τῶν ἁμαρτιῶν after καθαρισμός is not unusual, especially since καθαρός and its derivatives have the genitive about as often as the preposition ἀπό. The Son in dealing with the world encountered sin. What did he do with it? One comprehensive statement furnishes the answer: he made purification of sins. The expression as well as the thought itself recalls the work of the Jewish high priest on the great day of atonement: "For on that day shall the priest make an atonement for you, to cleanse you, that you may be clean from all your sins before the Lord," Lev. 17, 30; the expression really speaks of Christ as the High Priest (comp. 2, 17: "to make propitiation for the sins of the people"). Only the middle voice indicates that the act was reflected in some manner on himself; we know why: he made the purifying by means of his own blood. The incarnation is taken for granted in this statement, in fact its real purpose is here brought out — to enable the Son to accomplish this purification by the shedding of his blood and by his sacrificial death. The purification meant here is the objective atonement for sin, rendered for all the world (hence: "of sins," without a restrictive modifier), which each sinner must now appropriate unto himself in faith.

Sat down on the right hand of the Majesty on high, in one solemn, formal, all-glorious act. We rightly distinguish with the Apostle's Creed and all our dogmaticians between the Ascension which the eyes of the apostles beheld, as one act, and the enthronization or *sessio ad dextram Dei* in the invisible world as another. The right hand of God is not a circumscribed locality in heaven, as Zwingli, Calvin and others teach in the interest of their doctrine of the Lord's Supper, when they deny the possibility of the true body and blood of Christ being in, with, and under the sacramental bread and wine; this is plainly shown here by the phrase ἐν δεξιᾷ τῆς μεγαλωσύνης; the abstract μεγαλωσύνη has no locally circumscribed "right hand," or left hand. The right hand of God (Ps. 77, 10; 118, 16; Ex. 15, 6; Is. 48, 13; Matth. 26, 64) is the infinite power and majesty of

God, whereby he works, governs, and fills all things; and to sit at the right hand of majesty signifies to exercise dominion over all things with divine power and majesty. The phrase in our text ἐκάθισεν ἐν δεξιᾷ is taken from Ps. 110, 1: "Sit thou at my right hand until I make Thine enemies Thy footstool." A biblical description is found Eph. 1, 20-22. **On high** is the same as ἐν τοῖς οὐρανοῖς, and modifies the verb "sat down," not "the Majesty," which would require τῆς ἐν ὑψηλοῖς. Our Confessions carefully note that this exaltation refers to Christ's human nature: "That God's right hand is everywhere; at which Christ is in deed and in truth placed according to his human nature, being present, rules, and has in his hands and beneath his feet everything that is in heaven and on earth; there no man else, or angel, but only the Son of Mary is placed." Book of Concord, Jacob's transl., 512, 12. The reason for this is stated 518, 15: "because he was assumed into God when he was conceived of the Holy Ghost in his mother's womb, and his human nature was personally united with the Son of the Highest." This includes that the human nature of Christ "received, over and beyond its natural, essential, permanent properties, also special, high, great, supernatural, inscrutable, ineffable, heavenly prerogatives and excellencies in majesty, glory, power and might above everything that can be named, not only in this world, but also in that which is to come." 633, 51. Hence, "that he also, according to his assumed human nature and with the same, can be and is present where he will, and especially that in his Church and congregation on earth, as Mediator, Head, King and High Priest, he is not half present or there is only the half present, but the entire Christ is present, to which two natures belong, the divine and the human . . . For the certain assurance and confirmation of this he has instituted his Holy Supper, that also according to our nature, by which he has flesh and blood, he will be with us, and in us dwell, work, and be efficacious." 640, 78.

Better than the angels.

In a very simple manner, by means of a concluding participial clause, the masterly writer of Hebrews turns his grand opening sentence so as to merge into the first part of the great theme he has set for himself, the superiority of Christ over the angel mediators of the old dispensation. These are connected with the work of Moses, which is accounted the most glorious period of Israelitish history, in part because of this angelic ministration, to which the N. T. makes emphatic reference in Gal. 3, 19; Acts 7, 53; Heb. 2, 2. It was necessary then, especially for Hebrews, to show the Mediator of the new covenant in every way superior also to the angels. **Having become by so much better than the angels, as he hath inherited a more excellent name than they** (far better than: *being made*, A. V.) The aorist participle γενόμενος refers to the time of Christ's enthronization just mentioned (ἐκάθισεν). If he became better than the angels, he must have been lower; and he was, during the days of his humiliation: "But we behold him who hath been made a little lower than the angels, even Jesus, because of the suffering of death crowned with glory and honor," Heb. 2, 9. During his humiliation Christ ordinarily did not use his divine power and glory, but appeared in the form of a servant (Phil. 2, 6-8), assumed many of the infirmities of our nature, and lowered himself even unto the terrible death of the cross. But all this changed, he became better than the angels, κρείττων, in dignity, glory, and all that belongs to his exalted state. And this already during the 40 days preceding his ascension. By how much better is directly stated: **by so much, as he hath inherited a more excellent name than they.** This name is not the one which no man's tongue can utter (Rev. 19, 12), but the name already recorded: υἱός, "Son". Τοσούτῳ . . . ὅσῳ is never used by Paul, but occurs several times in Hebrews; and κρείττων is used only rarely by Paul, and then in the neuter and adverbially, while Hebrews has it 13 times, and Peter also. Διάφορος already expresses comparison, and this is intensified by the comparative διαφώτερος; originally it meant "different," and this conception still marked the word in its later use; hence here: "more excellent" ═ with an excellence different altogether from that of the angels. Παρά after the comparative, frequently in Hebrews, ═ beside or in comparison with. The inheritance of the more excellent name "Son" Christ had according to his human nature, to which the entire exaltation refers, from his conception and birth on: "He shall be great, and shall be called the Son of the Most High," Luke 1, 32. Now the name "sons of God" is bestowed also upon the angels (Job. 1, 6; 2, 1; Ps. 29, 1; 89, 7), but only in a generic way; and Israel is called a son Ex. 4, 22; Hos. 11, 1; Deut. 14, 1; Solomon likewise, 2 Sam. 7, 12-14; and we are "all sons of God, through faith, in Christ Jesus," Gal. 3, 27. But the name "Son" belongs to Christ in a way altogether different and superior to that of any creature, namely by an inheritance, *i. e.* by virtue of the personal union of his human nature to the divine. The only begotten Son was the Son in human flesh also, and now, exalted on high according to his human nature, sits as the Son on the right hand of the Majesty on high.

Our text includes three quotations from the O. T. here introduced to show Christ in every way superior to the angels. In general we must say that the writer of Hebrews, without further ceremony uses the Messianic meaning of the O. T. passages he introduces. This is neither rabbinical refinement on his part, nor the introduction of a foreign meaning into these passages, but the very contrary, a penetration into the real, full meaning they contain. And this because of divine inspiration, on the one hand of the original passages, and on the other hand of the mind and pen of the N. T. writers. The Holy Spirit thus himself reveals what the types and prophecies of the O. T. contain according to God's intention, even if the original writers and readers did not perceive this. Speaking through the N. T. writers he uses a masterful and never a timid or slavish manner in dealing with O. T. utterances. In what way to quote, what passages perhaps to combine, what new words to use in re-

stating his meaning in the fuller N. T. light, is the prerogative of the Spirit who speaks in both Testaments.   And it is
for us to bow before his authority and accept what he says.
In many quotations all is perfectly clear, the type or the
prophecy is plain; in others, where we, like the O. T. readers, would not have perceived the Messianic or prophetic
reference, we learn and accept it from the N. T. statements
themselves. — **For unto which of the angels said he**
(God) **at any time,**
    Thou art my Son,
    This day have I begotten thee?
The rhetorical question expresses a strong negative; ποτέ,
"at any time," demands the answer: οὔποτε, "at no time
ever."   Ps. 2, 7 is quoted from the Septuagint which
agrees with the original Hebrew.   The entire Psalm is Messianic.   Referring to David's installation as king of Israel,
it speaks in language fitting him only whom David typified.
To this eternal Messianic King God gives the name **Son,**
and predicates of him the essential of sonship: **This day**
have I begotten thee; something that never could be, and
never was, said of any single angel.   Commentators divide
as to the time meant by σήμερον, **this day,** some thinking of
the generation in eternity (contrary to the context); others
of the conception of the Holy Ghost (which is in no way
indicated); Zoeckler even denies any specification as to
time.   A reference to Acts 13, 33: "God   .   .   . raised
up Jesus, as also it is written in the second psalm, Thou art
my Son, this day have I begotten thee;" and Rom. 1, 4:
who was declared to be the Son of God with power,   .   .
.   .   .   by the resurrection of the dead," shows that a
specific time and act is meant, namely the glorification of
Christ.   Not as though the sonship began then and did not
exist before; yet in a real way the resurrection is called,
and compared with, the act of begetting, for he who died
for our sins was raised up and thus begotten into a new
ever-glorious life by the glory of the Father.   Keil and
others point to the ascension as the time when Christ entered into his full royal power.   Matth. 28, 18.

At once the second proof is advanced: **and again,**
I will be to him a Father,
And he shall be to me a Son?
The question continues: "and" to which of the angels said
he at any time "again," followed by a quotation from 2 Sam.
7, 14. There the person immediately concerned was Solomon who instead of his father David was to build God a
temple. But in promising to be a Father to Solomon and
naming him a son, God looked far beyond David's immediate heir, namely to the eternal Solomon, the Messiah, in
whom alone could be fulfilled the promise: "And thine
house and thy kingdom shall be established forever before
thee: thy throne shall be established for ever," 2 Sam. 7,
16; Ps. 89, 28 *etc.* To this eternal King God gave the name
"Son" in its full meaning; to no one else did God ever thus
give it.

And when he again bringeth in the firstborn into the
world he saith, And let all the angels of God worship
him. The margin: *And again, when he bringeth in,* cannot
be accepted, because this would require πάλιν δὲ ὅταν, like
our English (comp. 2, 13; 4, 5; 10, 30); to speak of πάλιν
being "carelessly placed," as some have ventured to do, is
to condemn one's self. Between verses 5 and 6 δέ indicates an antithesis; we might translate: "But when" *etc.*
Verse 5 refers to the first Advent of Christ, verse 6 to the
second. Πάλιν goes with εἰσαγάγῃ (comp. 5, 12; 6, 1 and 2):
When he again, *i. e.* a second time, bringeth in the firstborn
etc. Here again Christ's superiority over the angels is
plainly shown by the O. T. Scriptures. He is called **the**
firstborn because of his brethren, who are also born of God
(1 Pet. 1, 3 and 23; James 1, 18); and are also called "sons
of God" (2, 10). He who came into the world as the Son
will return again as the firstborn, because in the meantime
many will have been born after of God (Hofmann). Rom.
8, 29 furnishes a true parallel expression: πρωτότοκος ἐκ
πολλοῖς ἀδελφοῖς, the firstborn of many brethren. **Into the**
world (not κόσμος. but οἰκουμένη) is really: *into the inhabited*
earth, which also the margin offers. We frequently use

"world" in the same sense, namely the world of men, the same into which Christ first came. — The quotation is taken from the Septuagint Deut. 32, 43; the words are not in our Hebrew text. The codex Vaticanus has them almost as here quoted, while the codex Alexandrinus has "sons" instead of "angels," yet has "angels" in the version of the Song of Moses which is repeated at the end of Psalms (see Keil, also Meyer). Ps. 97, 7; Is. 44, 23 show that the thought is certainly scriptural. The problem is a textual and not a homilitical one, and need not occupy us here. — **Him** = Jehovah; our text rightly refers this to the Son. His superiority is now demonstrated not by his name, but by the homage paid him: **let all the angels of God worship him** — πάντες, not even Gabriel, Michael, the archangels, the cherubim and seraphim excepted. Worship, προσκυνεῖν, kiss the feet, fall down upon their faces at his feet, indicated the most humble form of worship; and for the angels to render it to Christ it so acknowledge and know him as God. The quotation is especially appropriate, being from the song of triumph over the enemies of Israel, and here quoted in connection with Christ's return to judgment when all his enemies shall meet their final doom. Then indeed his glory shall shine forth, and all things in heaven and earth and under the earth shall bow the knee before him and proclaim him Lord to the glory of God the Father.

HOMILETICAL HINTS.

Poverty and need is the outward picture that meets our eyes in the Christmas story concerning the Child Jesus. Yet we know that in this picture there lies hidden from the eyes of the world a divine glory. Luther sings of it: "In our poor flesh and blood is clothed now the eternal Good." The simple Christmas story itself would have but a poor message for us, if we should refuse to behold in it this hidden radiance. But in order to perceive it we must go beyond the outward picture which the history presents. What is there shown as a part of the history of the world and our race, we must comprehend as part of eternity itself and of the history of God. The moment this is done, poverty and need becomes greatness and glory, and the weak Child in the manger the eternal King of heaven and earth. Our text lifts the veil, and permits us to see what lies behind the outward events. There we behold: *The Divine Glory of the Child Jesus.* (Riemer's introduction and theme.)

"And when he again bringeth in the firstborn into the world he saith, And let all the angels of God worship him." That was done when God brought in the firstborn for the first time: the multitude of the heavenly host appeared and sang Glory to God in the highest. That song is hushed, only a few on earth heard it. But that same angel host is waiting for Christ's return in glory. Then shall we all see them as they bow before the throne of our exalted Redeemer and give utteranc to their adoration and praise. And we ourselves shall join them and take up their heavenly words to pour out our eternal adoration to the Son of God.

One word constitutes the theme of Hebrews, and we have it already in our text: κρείττων, BETTER.—Jesus the man is the favorite theme in many pulpits of to-day; the mystery of the virgin birth is denied; Arian conceptions are put forward as the true teaching of the Gospel; instead of a Redeemer we are shown only a model which we are to copy in our own strength. Here is a text which takes issue with these revamped errors and shows us the blessed truth concerning Jesus in all its fulnes and glory. Our people need this very teaching. — "Unto you is born this day in the city of David a Savior, which is Christ the Lord," and Christendom makes answer to this announcement: Yea, and has made purification of sins! In speaking of this purification the Christmas thought must not be exchanged for the thought of Good Friday.

See what a high person was necessary to be our Savior and to take away the sins of the world: God's own Son, who is the effulgence of his glory and the very image of his substance. See what power this person had, and had to have: through him the worlds were made, and he upholds all things and governs them by the word of his power. See what glory and majesty is his now, in order that the purification he has wrought may reach its eternal results: he sits at the right hand of the Majesty on high, and all the angels of God shall worship him even as they have worshipped him. Can sin then be a small thing to remove? Can we broken, helpless creatures put away even one single sin so that it shall not destroy us? Impossible. Yet thousands of men imagine themselves fully able to cope with all the sins that lie upon them and with the death and damnation that are contained in these sins.

Luther has a Christmas sermon on Heb. 1, 1-12, and ex-

plains the text section by section (*Erlangen Ausg.,* 7, 190-218).
Verse 3: These words are to be understood more with the heart,
than explained with tongues and pens. They are clearer in themselves than any explanation, and the more they are explained, the
darker they become. This is the sum of them: In Christ is the
entire Godhead, and to him all honor belongs, as to God; yet
so that he has this not of himself, but of the Father: that is to
say: two persons, one God . . . . Here faith is needed, and not
a great deal of sharp speculation, the words are clear, certain, and
strong enough. — As the fathers believed the servants, how much
more should we believe the Lord himself. And if we believe not
the Lord, how much less would we have believed the servants.

The Divine Glory of the Christ Jesus.

We see it

I.   *In his divine Being;*
II. *In his divine Work;*
III. *In his divine Honor.*   M. Riemer.

What Think Ye of the Christchild in Bethlehem?

I.   *Of his relation to God?*
II. *Of his relation to the angels?*
III. *Of his relation to the world?*
IV. *Of his relation to man?*

Shall All the Angels of God Worship Him

and we fail   (1.)   *To see his glory;*
             (II.) *To prize his work;*
             (III.) *To join in his praise?*

The folly of men when they estimate what kind of a Savior
they need. The wisdom and glory of God in the Savior he thought
we needed, and whom he actually sent to accomplish our salvation.

God's Son, the Effulgence of God's Glory, the Very Image of His Substance — Our Savior.

I.   *He alone could make the final revelation.*
II. *He alone could accomplish the real purification.* .
III. *He alone could rule at the right hand of Majesty.*

The Gift in Bethlehem.

I. *A Child.*
II. *A Son.*
III. *A King.*
IV. *A Servant.*

"God Hath Spoken Unto Us in His Son."

I. *In his person* (of the infinite love that sent him).
II. *In his work* (of the blessed way of salvation he has prepared).

THE SUNDAY AFTER CHRISTMAS.

2 Cor. 5, 1-9.

Three texts deal with the great Christmas fact, those for the Fourth Sunday in Advent, for Christmas, and for the Day after Christmas, similarly three texts now deal with the change of the year, those for the Sunday after Christmas, for New Year's Day, and for the Sunday after New Year. They resemble three circles, the second drawn within the first, the third within the second. Our text for the last Sunday of the old year deals with the end, both the end of earthly life and the end of all earthly things. Philippi, *Gloubenslehre,* 6, 29, calls our text the *locus classicus* for the Christian hope that the redeemed soul at once after the death of the body attains to the communion with God, to the vision of God, and to the glory of heaven. The text for New Year's Day speaks of *the future in general,* and what the believer is assured of in the entire course of his life up to and including its glorious conclusion. The third text, for the Sunday after New Year, speaks of *the immediate future,* namely of the way the believer proceeds step by step in his earthly life. The three together form a whole, and deal with subjects worthy of every man's, and certainly also of the Christian's, fullest attention. Where the worldling goes on blindly, the Christian's life is like a shining pathway lit up by the splendor of divine grace and leading into eternal glory. In order to utilize all three texts the preacher may take the one for the Day after Christmas for the Sunday after Christmas, and our present text for the last evening of the old year, Sylvester-eve, for which no special text is assigned in the present selections. — Our text, as to its contents, may be divided as follows: 1) our eternal house in the heavens, verse 1; 2)

128

our longing to be clothed upon, verses 2-4; 3) our good
courage while waiting, verses 5-8; 4) our aim to be well-
pleasing to him, verse 9.

Our eternal house in the heavens.

Our text continues the line of thought in the previous
chapter. Amid presecutions and trials Paul and his co-
workers keep the great Christian hope before their eyes:
"Knowing that he which raised up the Lord Jesus shall
raise up us also, and shall present us with you" (4, 14). So
he faints not (16), considers only the eternal weight of
glory (17), and looks at the eternal things that are not
seen (18). Here our text takes up the thought and gives
the reason for this proceeding of the apostle; it is this: We
know the great Christian hope is ours. — **For we know
that if the earthly house of our tabernacle be dissolved,
we have a building from God, a house not made with
hands, eternal, in the heavens.** This knowledege is personal, hence the apostle speaks here for himself; yet it is
not peculiar to a certain preferred few, hence Paul includes
all other faithful Christians with himself. In this "we
know," written to the Corinthians, there is a call for them
to bethink themselves of the great hope they had learned
to know. This knowledge is based on divine revelation
alone, and it is held by the heart in faith; without this
knowledge men may talk of hope, but it is all idle dreaming
— they do not *know*. — **If the house . . . be dissolved,** ἐάν with the subj. καταλυθῇ == "if it shall have been
dissolved" (comp. 1 John 3, 2, Christmas; Heb. 1, 6, Day
after Christmas); and this should normally be followed by
the future: "we shall have". But Paul writes: **we have,**
ἔχομεν, because this future treasure is already a present possession. Some call ἔχομεν "a logical future," but it is better
to take it exactly as it stands, a present tense, but one that
will never disappoint us in the hereafter, as all self-made
hopes must disappoint. — **The earthly house of our tabernacle** is rendered in the margin: the earthly house of our

9

bodily frame, because σκῆνος is the philosophical designation used for the body as a dwelling-place of the soul. But we prefer not to attribute this philosophical meaning to the tent-maker Paul; "tabernacle," or tent, is amply sufficient, especially from him, and certainly better than "bodily frame." Many commentators are satisfied to understand by the entire phrase: our earthly bodies. Now, the body may indeed be compared with an earthly house, or a tabernacle (the gen. σκήνους is appositive). But Stosch, *Apostol. Sendschreiben,* II, 147, points out that the difficulties adhering to this interpretation have not been sufficiently considered. He is right; one cannot help but note how these commentators stretch words and strain doctrine to get through with Paul's beautiful metaphors and really, after all, simple meaning. For if simply the earthly body is meant here, its heavenly counterpart would have to be the resurrection-body, or even the glorified body of Christ. Besser even combines the two and makes a mosaic of his interpretation entirely unworthy of so fine a commentator. But when we die the incontestable fact is that the resurrection-body is not yet extant. It is in vain to talk of its existing "ideally;" ἔχομεν must not be tampered with, it is the key in the arch. Some, like Olshausen, in order to help out, imagine a temporary, ethereal, spiritual body for the interval between death and the resurrection, but this is simply a theosophic figment, unscriptural and militating against the doctrine of the resurrection of the body. And as far as Christ's glorified body is concerned, he does call this a temple, but he never speaks of it as the abode of believers after death. Besser's reference to believers as "members" of Christ's body is the unwarranted introduction of another figure, used for an entirely different thought, and simply shows to what a pass he, and others, are brought in making something of Paul's words. — The case becomes considerably better, both exegetically and doctrinally, when a number of commentators, while like the others they make "the earthly house of our tabernacle" mean our natural earthly bodies, interpret "the house not made with hands" to mean *heaven* (instead of resurrection-body, or the temple of Christ's glorified body). But even so the two are not true counterparts, and the result is that Paul's figure and thought is made to limp on one side. Stosch obviates all this trouble by taking "the earthly house of our tabernacle" to signify: our earthly existence, *i. e.* our earthly life as a transient thing, marked as such by our bodies dwelling in structures made by poor human hands. The true counterpart of this is **a building from God, a house not made with hands, eternal, in the heavens.** When our transitory earthly existence shall be **dissolved,** taken down and removed like a tent, the blessed, glorious, eternal existence is ours, the heavenly home. And this indeed, without any stretching or straining at either end, is the Christian's true hope. Note the balance in the terms Paul uses: the one is **earthly,** marked with the character of earth in its sinful condition; the other is **in the heavens,** marked by the exalted character of the abode of God. The one is a **house** indeed (οἰκία), yet after all only a **tabernacle,** a mere tent; the other, a **house** also (οἰκία), for we shall live there, but far different from a transient tent, **a building** (οἰκοδομή), an enduring structure. One camps in a tent for a brief time, but he needs a permanent house for continuous residence; how much more for eternal dwelling hereafter. One is **our** tabernacle, *i. e.* the earthly existence as we have made it by sin and its results; the other is **from God, not made with hands, eternal,** the perfect and permanent work of God's omnipotence and glory (Heb. 11, 10; 9, 11). What a contrast! Against the dull background of our poor earthly life how gloriously the great hope of the life to come looms up! Here a poor tent for a day; but when this is folded in death, there the many mansions in the Father's house. Here a poor earthly sojourn with all the evils that oppress us and from which we daily pray to be delivered; there the sojourn amid the eternal joys of heaven. — Note also that Paul writes **if,** ἐάν, vividly picturing death, but not shutting out absolutely the possibility of living till Christ returns. Paul was in the same position as we are: he did not know exactly

when Christ would come. To press his words, as some
have done, making him say in one place that he has abandoned the expectation of seeing Christ's return, and in
another place that he is certain he will not die but see that
return, is a shameful abuse of his words; and one can only
be sorry that so many commentators are guilty of it.

Our longing to be clothed upon.

Paul amplifies his figure by adding to it another, that
of being clothed with something, making the one metaphor
melt into the other as it were. Again he succeeds in
puzzling many of his commentators, especially with the
third verse, some of them even abandoning the analogy
of faith and resorting to extreme means, without apprehending the sense of his words. The chief point in
this section is Paul's longing for the fulfillment of the
great hope shining in his heart. This he expresses in a
figurative way indeed, and — master of language that he
is and with a full stream of thought ever flowing through
his heart — he turns his figure in various ways, but ever
so that it fits a well-balanced Christian heart yearning for
the glory to come. In following his words we must keep
the same balance, and not sail off on the wings of imagery
alone and what this might otherwise suggest. — **For verily
in this we groan, longing to be clothed upon with our
habitation which is from heaven.** Καὶ γάρ = "for also,"
or (making the "also" strong): **for verily.** Paul says:
We look at the things eternal, first, because we know
we have a house eternal in the heavens; secondly,
because we groan in longing for this house. Ἐν τούτῳ is
read by most commentators as referring to σκῆνος: **in this**
tabernacle. The meaning is: now already, not only when
our dissolution approaches. Luther has: *ueber diesem;*
and others: *propterea; unter solchen Umstaenden.* These
refer ἐν τούτῳ back: on this account, because the earthly
house of our tabernacle is to be dissolved; or they refer it
to what follows: we groan on this account (in this regard), namely longing to be clothed upon *etc.* But the

parallel in verse 4: "For indeed we that are *in this tabernacle* do groan, being burdened," taking up once more the
groaning and showing another side of it, settles the reference of ἐν τούτῳ to σκῆνος: in this (tabernacle) **we groan.**
— This groaning is the outward expression of the earnest
longing and desire in the heart; this is so strong that it
cannot remain silent (Rom. 8, 23). We hear this groaning in many an earnest Christian prayer, and especially
in many beautiful Christian hymns:

> "Safe into the haven guide;
> O receive my soul at last."
>
>   (C. Wesley.)

> "Jerusalem the golden,
> Shall I e'er see thy face?
> O sweet and pleasant city,
> Shall I e'er win thy grace?
> I have the hope within me
> To comfort and to bless;
> Shall I e'er win the glory?
> O my Redeemer, yes!"
>
>   (De Morlai.)

> Jerusalem, thou city fair and high,
> Would God I were in thee!
> My longing heart fain, fain to thee would fly,
> It will not stay with me;
> Far over vale and mountain,
> Far over field and plain,
> It hastes to seek its Fountain,
> And quit this world of pain."
>
>   (Mayfarth.)

We must hold fast that the groaning thus expressed is
not the longing to be rid of the earthly life and its crosses,
but the desire to reach the blessedness of heaven: "longing to be clothed upon with our habitation which is from
heaven." Paul writes ἐπενδύσασθαι, **to be clothed upon,**
to have a garment put on over something. Here he adds
the figure of a garment to that of the tent and house, blend-
ing the two together. Stosch prefers for ἐπενδύσασθαι *mit
Verlangen eingehen,* but this is not essentially different

from the other meaning, both being given for the Greek word; and this shows the relationship between Paul's two figures and how he comes to combine them. — **With our habitation which is from heaven** brings the new word τὸ οἰκητήριον, where before we had οἰκοδομή; it is descriptive of the οἰκία or house adding the thought of dwelling, hence the translation **habitation,** permanent place of residence or dwelling (where οἰκοδομή above added the idea of building a permanent structure). "Our habitation which is from heaven" is identical with "a building from God, a house not made with hands, eternal, in the heavens;" only where the latter views our heavenly home as a permanent structure, the former views it as a permanent residence. Those who see in this "building" and "habitation" the resurrection-body or the so-called transformation-body point to ἐξ οὐρανοῦ, and say that "from heaven" cannot mean heaven itself (which no one asserts, for it is "our habitation which is from heaven" which is "heaven" itself). But if they urge the local sense of "*from* heaven," will this fit the resurrection or transformation-body? It surely is not a body kept in heaven and sent down from there. The resurrection or transformation-body is in reality our own natural body glorified and nothing more. Ἐξ οὐρανοῦ simply describes the origin and character of the "habitation;" it is heavenly, as opposed to earthly (see 1 Cor. 15, 47: ἐκ γῆς; "not of this building," Heb. 9, 11). — These exegetes also urge the term ἐπενδύσασθαι, **to be clothed upon,** in the sense of not merely putting a garment on, but of putting it on over another garment. They attribute to Paul a *Todesscheu,* a fear of death, on the face of it a grave injustice to Paul's faith and courage. Next they attribute to him the desire not to die, but to live till Christ's return and then to be transformed without passing through death (1 Cor. 15, 51-54; 1 Thess. 4, 15-17). This makes Paul think and say something out of keeping with the entire context. Verse 1 shows that he is speaking of his death (if the earthly house of our tabernacle be *dissolved*), and in regard to this, as pertaining to himself and Christian believers generally, he is voicing the blessed hope of heaven which he and they with him have. Worst of all, however, the transformation-body cannot be called a garment to be put on *over* the garment of the natural body. The entire idea is preposterous, simply because there are not two bodies; and to talk of the natural body "disappearing" when the transformation-body is put on over it, shows to what lengths these exegetes permit their imagination to run when they get upon a wrong track. Over against these imaginings we set Paul's thought in all its simplicity and hold fast to that; he says: We know we have a heavenly home, and for this reason we groan and long to enter it. Or, more fully: In our present habitation, which is a transient one, subject to death and dissolution, we, on this account, and because we are destined for a blessed eternity, long to be clothed upon with our heavenly home. Compound verbs in Greek are commonly used in the same sense as corresponding simple ones, the compound form being somewhat stronger. 1 Cor. 15, 53 and 54, where Paul speaks of the resurrection and the transformation of those living at his second coming, he uses the simple form ἐνδύσασθαι, showing that he means the same thing with both forms of the verb: to be clothed upon; to have put upon us as a garment.

If so be that being clothed we shall not be found naked. Few passages have caused interpreters so much trouble as these few words; some have even ventured to say that the apostle might have omitted them. The trouble generally is that any wrong ideas inserted into the previous verses cause double confusion when this verse is reached. For εἴ γε καί a few texts read εἴπερ καί. This we may pass by at once: εἴ γε καί is the proper reading, and it expresses a condition coupled with certainty ("since also"; "if so be also", as indeed it shall be); εἴπερ would express doubt ("provided"). Another difference in reading deserves notice: some texts have ἐκδυσάμενοι instead of ἐνδυσάμενοι, which would simplify the sense. But here too the case is

plain; we must follow the best authorities and read
ἐνδυσάμενοι. — There is one interpretation which homiletically
would be very valuable, but which exegetically cannot be
held: "if so be that being clothed (with the garment of
Christ's righteousness) we shall not be found naked (destitute of the right to enter heaven). Calvin, Calov, Philippi,
Daechsel, and Besser have it, and the thought, taken by
itself, is certainly Pauline. One sees at a glance how the
preacher may use it to introduce the strongest warnings.
But he must abandon it, for nothing in the text or context
indicates that **clothed,** ἐνδυσάμενοι, is taken in a new sense.
We cannot have "clothed" in verse 2 and "unclothed" in
verse 4 referring to one kind of garment, and "clothed" in
verse 3 referring to a different kind of garment, unless
something positive and plain marks the difference. And
there is nothing of that sort in the text, hence we yield to
the rule that words in the same sentence and connection
must have the same meaning. Moreover, Paul's entire
thought is occupied with himself and his fellow believers,
who all share one hope, and not in any way with unbelievers
who lack that hope (note the constant "we"). A second
interpretation operates with γυμνός in the sense of bodiless
spirits, and we are told that the Greeks so regarded the
souls in hades and dreaded this state. This interpretation
hangs together with the notions of the resurrection and
transformation-body already rejected above. Sometimes
the intermediate state between death and Christ's return is
brought in and a sort of ethereal body imagined for that
state. This is theosophic speculation, entirely without
Scripture foundation, and militates against the doctrine of
the resurrection of the body. — The correct interpretation
holds firmly to the thought Paul expresses in this entire
section. He and we desire to be invested with the heavenly
home, "since also (καί) being clothed with this home, we
shall not be found naked, *i. e.* without a true home." The
objection that this is too simple and self-evident a thought
for Paul to express (so Meyer), is refuted by the greatness
of the hope with which the apostle here deals. To him and

us all in our faith, labors, and trials the heavenly home is everything; to be certain of that is comfort indeed, to be without it is to be found naked and destitute in all eternity. Εὑρεθησόμεθα, fut. pass., refers to the time when the earthly house of our tabernacle shall have been dissolved; οὐ, in Greek with γυμνοί, is read in English with the verb; ἐνδυσάμενοι, aor. part., indicates a definite act preceding the main verb which is future. Stosch: Naked in the sense of the Greek word means destitute of what one needs, and this according to whatever the context may imply; here: destitute of the *Heimatsrecht* (James 2, 15, destitute of appropriate clothing; in battle, destitute of weapons; Rev. 3, 17, destitute of true righteousness; Rev. 16, 15, destitute of watchfulness).

For indeed we that are in this tabernacle do groan, being burdened; not for that we would be unclothed, but that we would be clothed upon, that what is mortal may be swallowed up of life. Καὶ γάρ adds an explanation. Paul does not wish to be misunderstood; his expression of longing must not be read as if he were unmanly and his great desire were to shake off the burden of this life. **We that are in this tabernacle,** οἱ ὄντες, is not: "whilst we are" *etc.,* which would omit οἱ; ἐν τῷ σκήνει "in *this* tabernacle," the one already indicated, our earthly existence. Paul means himself and his fellow believers as they still live this transient earthly life and go forward on their earthly pilgrimage. Again he says, **we do groan,** but qualifies with a different participle, not "longing" now, but βαρούμενοι, **being burdened** (pres. tense: continuously). The question arises as to what we are burdened with. To this the margin offers an answer in the way it reads the text and injects an intrepretation: *being burdened, in that we would not be unclothed, but would be clothed upon.* This means, that upon Paul and his fellow believers there lies, while they live this life, the burden of desire not to pass through death, but to live till Christ's return and then to be changed in a moment. This marginal reading takes ἐφ' ᾧ in the sense of

"because that": "we groan because that we do not wish
to be unclothed" *etc*. But the reverse is true: Paul did
not shrink from death; he had the desire to depart and
be with Christ (Phil. 1, 23); he was willing "to be absent
from the body," verse 8; he faced death joyfully a hundred
times. Again, the interpretation contained in the margin
takes ἐπενδύσασθαι in the sense rejected as unwarranted in
verse 2: to put the transformation-body on over the
natural body. It makes Paul say: We groan, being burdened, in this that we would not put off this body, but
put on over it the transformation-body. Instead of the
margin we take the text of the R. V. with its semicolon
after "burdened." The burdens of believers need not be
defined anew here by the apostle; read 4, 8-12: "we are
pressed on every side" *etc*. That is altogether plain. But
Paul, like all true believers who know their calling and
their hope, was neither *kreuzesscheu* nor *todesscheu*, he
shrank neither from affliction nor from death, Rom. 5, 3-5;
8, 37-39. And so he writes here concerning death: We
do groan, being burdened; not **for that** (ἐφ' ᾧ) **we would
be unclothed;** or: wherefore (on which account) we do
not want to be removed from this life. We groan indeed under our burden, but the motive of our hope is not
negative, to escape the trials set for us by the Lord (much
less to secure exemption from death). There are some
who tire of life and its burdens, but theirs is a morbid
state, which they ought to conquer. Some too quail at
the thought of death, but this too is not the normal Christian attitude. In place of all such negative thoughts Paul
puts something entirely different: **but that we would be
clothed upon,** *i. e.* "to depart and be with Christ; for it is
very far better." Phil. 1, 23. **That what is mortal may
be swallowed up of life,** 1 Cor. 15, 53-56: this is the climax
of the entire statement, the last and highest summing up
of the apostle's wish (θέλομεν). The right desire to depart
is not to get out of life, but really to live. For, after
all, all earthly life (not merely the body) is τὸ θνητόν, and
this, if life is truly to be reached, must "be swallowed up

by life." It is a paradox: Christians wish to die because
they wish to live. Here we have Paul's own description
of what he means by being clothed upon with the heavenly
home: to have all that is mortal swallowed up by death-
less, immortal life.

Our good courage while waiting.

"It was something very heroic and grand for a poor,
persecuted man to stand thus erect in the presence of his
enemies and in the immediate prospect of death, and avow
such superiority to all suffering, and such confidence of a
glorious immortality. The apostle, therefore, adds that
neither the elevated feelings which he expressed, nor his
preparation for the exalted state of existence which he
so confidently expected, was due to himself." Hodge.
**Now he that wrought us for this very thing is God,
who gave unto us the earnest of the Spirit.** "This very
thing," A. V. : "the self-same thing" = being clothed upon
so that what is mortal shall be swallowed up of life. And
this is not something that is ours by nature, nor by human
effort and merit, it is the work of God: he made us fit for
this, accomplished it in us by giving us the requisite quali-
fications. Instead of saying how God did this, Paul tells us
who this God is that did it: **who gave unto us the earnest
of the Spirit.** By this gift of the Spirit he wrought us for
this very thing. **The earnest,** ὁ ἀρραβών, from the Hebrew
erabon, is a first-payment or pledge, assuring full payment
and complete fulfillment of a promise. The earnest **of the
Spirit** (appositive gen.) = the earnest which consists of
the Spirit; and we receive this earnest when the Spirit is
given us in Baptism and by the Word and Sacraments generally, working Christian faith and all things spiritual in us.
These means (objectively) and our faith and Christian life
(subjectively) assure us that we are in possession of "the
earnest," and thus give us the certainty and joyfulness of
Paul's hope. See 2 Cor. 1, 22; Eph. 1, 13-14; Rom. 5, 5;
8, 16. In Rom. 8, 11 the Spirit is a pledge for the resurrection of our bodies (1 Cor. 6, 19); in our text he is a

pledge for the soul's entering heaven and its glory immediately after death. The two belong together, but the latter has its own peculiar value.

Οὖν, **therefore,** introduces the results, and these are of such a kind that they flow from all Paul has here said of the Christian hope and its earnest of fulfillment. The sentence following is an anacoluthon, begun in one way, but not finished as begun. Paul evidently started to write: "Being therefore of good courage and knowing . . . we are willing rather" *etc*. Instead he wrote as the text shows. **Being always of good courage,** no matter what may happen, 4, 17, is the tremendous advantage of every one who has Paul's blessed hope. There is a self-made courage of men amid dangers and misfortunes, which may indeed carry them with head erect and flying colors into the jaws of death, but they face eternity blindly and have no divine hand behind them to crown them with victory in the hour of final strife. Paul's and his fellow believers' good courage is a different thing entirely. It is not for strong men alone, but a child may have and show it, a weak woman, a man with all earthly prospects shattered. It is the fruit of the Spirit, and a mystery to those who themselves have it not. — **And knowing that, whilst we are at home in the body, we are absent from the Lord,** coordinates this piece of knowledge with our being of good courage; καί is not "although," or "because." The hopeful Christian realizes the situation completely, he knows exactly where he stands with his hope and courage. Ἐνδημοῦντες is set over against ἐκδημοῦμεν; he dwells in the body as his present home, and he is thus absent from visible union and communion with the Lord; the time of trial is still present. His courage is not an idle condition of the heart, there is ample use for its exercise: he is of good courage, and knows there is room for its display. Why? **For we walk by faith, not by sight.** There is no question, εἶδος is not the activity of seeing, but objective, the thing seen, the form, the visible appearance, the reality as we actually behold it; and to this we must add the negative οὐ : not by things actually seen. Faith, πίστις, is usually taken subjectively, believing as an activity of the heart; but as such it would not be an actual contrast to εἶδος. Either we must allow this inequality to remain, or we must make both "faith" and "sight" subjective, or both objective. Many do the former, but the latter is certainly preferable, because the word πίστις is regularly used to express objectively that which is believed, *i. e.* the doctrine, confession or word, while εἶδος is not used subjectively for ὄψις. So we may say of faith with Calvin: *Loco rei verbo aquiescimus.* The entire mark of our walk now is διὰ πίστεως; we look at the things not seen, τὰ μὴ βλεπόμενα, 4, 18; we are governed by what we believe, the Word. We do not walk διὰ εἶδους, in the light of the things actually beheld; that will not take place until we reach our heavenly home. So we have need of good courage, and of knowing exactly what our situation is and what we may expect. — Paul now takes up his original sentence again, but repeats the thought and makes a fresh start: **We are of good courage, I say.** Δέ may be translated as here the R. V. does, "I say," resuming the original thought, or adversatively: "we walk by faith and not by sight, yet we are of good courage." When the longing for the home above and the burdening presses his heart he "groans;" but when he looks at God who has made him ready, and at the earnest of the Spirit, he is of good courage. Death does not trouble him, in fact he welcomes it, just as he wrote the Philippians: "For me to live is Christ, and to die is gain," 1, 21. So here: **and are willing rather to be absent from the body, and to be at home with the Lord.** To be absent from the body is the condition of death, when the body lies in the grave and the soul is separated from it; this is what "unclothed" means in verse 4. To be at home with the Lord is the dwelling of the disembodied soul in the glory of heaven with the Lord Jesus Christ; and this is what "clothed upon" in verses 2 and 4 signifies. This latter, with courage and confidence, Paul as every good Christian prefers. Their song upon the pilgrimage long or short is ever: "Heaven is my home." "The

Christian's heaven is to be with Christ for we shall be like
him when we see him as he is. Into his presence the believer passes as soon as he is absent from the body, and into
his likeness the soul is at death immediately transformed;
and when at the resurrection, the body is made like unto
his glorious body, the work of redemption is consummated.
Awaiting this consummation, it is an inestimable blessing
to be assured that believers, as soon as they are absent from
the body, are present with the Lord." Hodge.

Our aim to be well-pleasing unto him.

Wherefore also we make it our aim, φιλοτιμούμεθα,
are ambitious (margin), **whether at home or absent, to
be well-pleasing unto him.** Those who have this hope
purify themselves, even as he is pure, 1 John 3, 3. The
A. V. has: "we labor," but the word means to make a thing
a point of honor, to set one's honor in doing or attaining
something. A nobility, a sort of holy heroism and devotion
is implanted in the heart by the Christian hope. It is personal, inspired by the love of Christ, with whom the soul
would dwell "at home." The thought of approaching
nearer and nearer to him every day makes us ashamed to
do anything displeasing unto him, and spurs us on to do
everything well-pleasing to him. **Whether at home** (in the
body), **or absent** (from the body) = whether living or
dying. "For whether we live, we live unto the Lord; or
whether we die, we die unto the Lord; whether we live
therefore, or die, we are the Lord's." Rom. 14, 8. "Whether
we wake or sleep, we should live together with him." 1
Thess. 5, 10. It is also possible to supply: **Whether at
home** (with the Lord), **or absent** (from the Lord), which
in substance gives the same sense; but the former is to
be preferred because it puts this life first and then mentions what follows. But Paul loses sight of the special
reference, having used the verbs ἐνδημεῖν and ἐκδημεῖν now
in one order, now in another. So here, combining them
once more, he means to say: no matter in what condition
we find ourselves, our hope holds us true: we want to be

well-pleasing to the Lord. In what way we accomplish this is not said; the fact, and not the manner is here the chief thing. He who knows the Lord and has the hope of being eternally with him will readily find the manner in his Word.

HOMILETICAL HINTS.

How do these two agree — Christmas with its jubilation, and now the thought of death, the grave, eternity? The world cannot understand it, but surely we do. Christmas festivity and the dull hush of death are as widely apart as the poles for the children of this world, but never for us. For did not the Christ-child come from heaven for the very purpose of conducting us into heaven? Did not the Babe of Bethlehem come to celebrate Christmas here below with us, in order that we might be brought to celebrate Christmas above with him? And how can this be done except we put off the garment of this earthly life and by death pass into his glorious presence? And indeed, there is our true home. The Child in the manger has made us children of God, and if we are true children of the Father in heaven, our place is in heaven, our Father's house. That is our true home, and thither the Savior would lead us by means of death. And, beloved, is not our desire to go home? If we Christians are Christians indeed, Paul's words will repeat themselves in our hearts: We are willing rather to be absent from the body, and to be at home with the Lord. — C. C. Hein, from the introduction, Sunday after Christmas.

When the weary traveler has plodded along for hours, perhaps days, and then finally reaches some elevated spot from which he can look far ahead into the distance, he strains his eyes to catch a glimpse, if possible, of his goal, at least some mark or sign by which he can tell how near the end he has come. So we stand upon the height of the year now, the last evening of 365 days. We have come far, and now, standing at the place where two years meet, we cannot help but look ahead. Are we in sight of the goal? How far are we yet to go? Perhaps just beyond that next elevation, or down in the valley where the road turns out of sight, is the blessed end of all our efforts — home, *home,* HOME! — From the introduction, Sylvester-eve.

The great truth embodied in this text is the Christian hope and assurance, that the moment our earthly life is ended, our souls enter the house not made with hands, eternal, in the heavens —

our heavenly home. In other words: the moment the soul is
absent from the body it is present, or at home, with the Lord. So
Jesus said to the malefactor dying on the cross: "To-day shalt
thou be with me in Paradise," Luke 23, 43. So Stephen dying
prayed: "Lord Jesus, receive my spirit," Acts 7, 59. In no way
must the preacher allow this great and shining hope to be darkened
in his own heart by any exegetical or theological problems his
books may offer him — and some such difficulties are unnecessarily
introduced into this very text. And in no way dare the preacher
becloud or even dim this shining hope in his sermon on this text.
Not that he dare think one thing concerning the intermediate state,
either speculatively, or "theologically," while he preaches another,
namely the old Christian hope. He never dare be a hypocrite on
any theme, least of all on one so vital as this theme. No, he must
be established once and for all in the fundamentals of the Christian hope, proof against every objection speculator or critic may
raise, because the *sedes* of this great doctrine are clear and convincing beyond shadow of doubt, and with this firm, triumphant
conviction in his heart, he must preach the great Christian hope.

How can the house "in the heavens" be heaven itself? Calov
has answered that question finely: Heaven is τοῦ *commune Elec-
torum*, an abode in common for the elect; and οἰκία, *cujusvis
proprium* τοῦ *in coelis*, the personal place of each individual. So
Jesus speaks of "the eternal tabernacles," Luke 16, 9; and of the
"many mansions," John 14, 2; comp. Jude 6; Acts 1, 25.

"Longing to be clothed upon" — like the heir who for a time
must wear the livery of a servant and do his menial work; but he
knows that he is the heir, and while he does his Father's will in
the servant's coat, yet ever longs for the hour when he shall put
on the garments which belong to him as a royal prince and heir
of his Father's glory. Was the change great when the prodigal
son received the son's best robe instead of the swine-herd's filthy
rags, shoes for his bare feet, a ring upon his hand, and a festive
repast in his honor, greater still shall be the change when we who
are sons of God by faith in Christ Jesus shall be decked with
eternal glory and sit at the heavenly table together with the
patriarchs of old, the apostles, and all God's saints.

Nowhere in this text does Paul voice any shrinking from
death, any reluctance to leave the body. There is no room here
to introduce descriptions of how unnatural the separation of soul
and body seems to us in death, to elaborate, as Besser does, on our
"right to a sacred resentment against death." Paul, with his
heart full of triumphant hope, is far beyond that. Death itself,
the process and act of dying, with whatever pertains to that, is
not in his mind; only two things occupy him, and he sets them in
glaring contrast to each other: the poor tent of our earthly life

— the heavenly home God has prepared for us and in which Christ dwells. And his heart is all filled with hope.

On the gift of the Spirit Luther writes, adding however what the Scriptures otherwise tell us concerning the body: "Since our soul has already spiritually obtained its portion, and by faith already lives in a new, eternal, heavenly life, and cannot die and be buried, therefore we have nothing to expect but that this poor hut and the old pelt shall also be made new and imperishable, since the best part is above and cannot leave us behind. And as he who is called *Resurrexit* is gone away out of death and the grave, he who says *Credo* and clings to him must go after; for he preceded us for this very reason that we should follow him, and has already made a beginning of it in that by the Word and Baptism we daily rise in him."

We are absent from the Lord, Calov says, does not mean that the Lord is absent now from us, because he dwells in the believer, John 14, 23; 2 Cor. 6, 16, and is with us alway even unto the end of the world, Matth. 28, 20. Nor does it mean that we are absent from the Lord, in whom we live and move and have our being, Act. 17, 28, by nature; and in whom we also live by faith spiritually, Gal. 2, 20; John 14, 20. But we are without the visible presence of God as strangers and pilgrims here, and have not the direct vision of God; nor are we with the Lord so that we behold his glory, John 17, 24, wherefore Paul also desires to depart and be with Christ, Phil 1, 23, and the maefactor also received the promise that to-day he would be with Christ in Paradise, Luke 23, 43.

Now we walk by faith, we have Christ in his Word; presently we shall walk by sight, Christ shall stand before us as he is, and we shall see him face to face.

The Christian's Desire to be at Home With the Lord.

I. *A fervent longing.*
II. *A patient waiting.*
III. *An earnest striving.*   C. C. Hein.

Our Confidence as We Pass from the Old Year Into the New.

I. *We have the home awaiting us above.*
II. *We have the Spirit now leading us to our home.*

Blessed are the homesick, for they shall reach home. (Jung-Stilling.)

10

Our Precious Christian Hope.

Precious indeed, for

I. *Its foundation is sure* ("we know," by the Word of God).
II. *Its possession is justified* ("we have the earnest of the Spirit").
III. *Its contents is glorious* ("a building from God" *etc.* — "at home with the Lord," at once when the soul leaves the body).
V. *Its power is effective* (an earnest desire and groaning in us — good courage — the aim to be well-pleasing).

The Homesickness of God's Children.

I. *Its source;* II. *Its power;* III. *Its blessing.*

Walking with Paul in the Light of Christian Hope.

This light illumines for us

I. *The great beyond.*
   1. The house not made with hands.
   2. At home with the Lord.
II. *The hour of death.*
   1. The tent and old garment of this life laid aside.
   2. Clothed upon with the habitation which is from heaven.
   3. That which is mortal swallowed up of life.
III. *Our whole earthly pathway.*
   1. We see for what God prepares us.
   2. Hope and good courage cheer us.
   3. Our aim to be well-pleasing to the Lord remains stead fast.

Our Good Courage as We Pass Through Life.

I. *We indeed groan* (verse 2);
II. *Yet we know* (verse 1);
III. *And we walk by faith* (verse 7);
IV. *And set our aim right* (verse 9);
V. *Thus we cannot fail.*

NEW YEAR'S DAY.

Rom. 8, 24-32.

Our text is from that section of the eighth chapter of Romans which deals with the sufferings of this present time (verse 18), thoroughly explains the conditions under which we live as believers, and administers the most effective comfort. The text is admirably suited for the opening of the new year. It looks into the future: "For by hope were we saved," and hope looks to a coming realization; "all things work together for good, even to them that are called according to his purpose," and that means day by day in the time to come; and "how shall he not also with him (Christ) freely give us all things," as we may have need in our future lives. But this *assured and comforting outlook into the future* is here shown to rest on an equally assured and comforting past and present: God has foreknown, foreordained and called us according to his purpose; even now the Spirit is ours and all his help and grace. A future so fortified is glorious and blessed indeed. The text itself may be divided as follows: 1) by hope were we saved; 2) the Spirit helpeth our infirmities; 3) God's gracious purpose is wrought out in salvation; 4) with Christ all things are ours.

By hope were we saved.

The first sentence of our text carries forward the thought just preceding it, that we are "waiting for our adoption, to wit, the redemption of our body." This present time is full of suffering (verse 18, *etc.*); the creation generally groans and travails in pain together, even as we do (22); we have not yet reached our heavenly goal (23). This whole situation is explained and summed up in the

147

brief opening word of our text: **For by hope were we saved.** One thing is incontrovertible: ἐσώθημεν, **we were saved.** The aorist states a definite past act, and says nothing of any continuance; nor does it need to: he who was perishing, and then was rescued by a saving hand, is saved and safe still. God did so rescue us poor sinners who now believe in him; he did it by one definite past act, and here we are now, safe and sound. For this reason the A. V. has the interpretative translation: "We *are* saved." What that act was whereby we were saved is beyond doubt: justification, the act of God whereby, of pure mercy, for the sake of the merits of Christ, he pronounces a poor sinner, who truly believes in Christ free from guilt and declares him just. That was a real rescue (ἐσώθημεν) from sin, death, and damnation, a translation into God's kingdom of grace. To explain the aorist ἐσώθημεν, as Stoeckhardt does, of the fulness of future salvation as ours now already, is to lose sight both of the verb σώζειν, to save or rescue, and the tense here used. — But **by hope** were we saved; and this word is put emphatically forward as the real point of the statement. Some make ἐλπίδι the dative of means or instrument (Hofmann, Zahn), and therefore take "hope" objectively, the thing hoped for. The sense would then be: We were saved by something hoped for. But the point here is not the kind of instrument or means which wrought our salvation; if that were to be named, it would certainly not be designated as something hoped for, but as something actually there when the saving took place. The point here is the kind of saving we have experienced. Ἐλπίδι is to explain the "waiting" in the previous sentence: Why, since we were saved, do we yet wait for our adoption, to wit, the redemption of our body? Answer: For *by hope* were we saved (ἐλπίδι, *dat. non medii, sed modi,* Bengel); *hoffnungsweise,* Philippi. In the same way Paul says: "We walk by faith, and not by sight," 2 Cor. 5, 7. All that our salvation contains is not yet ours to see, handle, and enjoy. We own and possess it all, but like an heir who at some future time shall enter upon his inheritance. The difference between faith and hope may here be noted: faith embraces salvation as it is present; hope reaches out and holds salvation as it includes a wealth of future treasures and blessings; but hope always builds upon faith, and faith always bears with it hope. Melanchthon says, faith accepts in the present the remission of sins, hope looks for future liberation. — **But hope that is seen is not hope.** An ἐλπὶς βλεπομένη is really a *contradictio in adjecto;* for if it is "seen" it could not be "hope," and if it is "hope," it could not be "seen." Here hope is used objectively, "in the energetic manner in which all languages designate the object itself of my hope as my hope" (1 Tim. 1, 1; Col. 1, 5; Heb. 6, 18); and thus hope cannot be seen. Whatever is visible and present to the senses is apprehended in some other way than by hope on our part. — **For who hopeth for that which he seeth?** (Note the varied reading in the margin.) This rhetorical question answers itself: No one; for no one can; hoping and seeing do not go together; this is our universal experience. — **But if we hope for that which we see not,** *then* **do we with patience wait for it.** This draws the conclusion from the admitted premises, a conclusion for us all to bear in mind and take to heart in this connection. We Christians do hope for what we as yet do not see; we do not doubt or deny the promises of the Gospel which are yet to be fulfilled. Well and good: then certainly we do not expect to see now, and enjoy now, all that is contained in our salvation — **then do we with patience wait for it** (ἀπεκδεχόμεθα, the same verb as in verse 23, ἀπεκδεχόμενοι). Hope means waiting; the two cannot be separated. But the right kind of Christian waiting is **with patience,** that is with steadfastness and endurance. For hope is the unshaken conviction that certain blessed things will come to pass just as God has promised in Christ Jesus, and so it naturally includes and justifies patience, the steadfastness of the soul which waits for those blessings, no matter how long the time or how trying the experiences that intervene.

This patience is the opposite of discouragement and despair. How necessary, as we stand at the beginning of another year of our earthly life, to be reminded of the kind of salvation that is ours, one with its full fruition lying in the future, hence to be held with hope and patience! Let us go forward then confidently, courageously, joyfully, and all that we hope for will in due time appear.

The Spirit helpeth our infirmity.

And in like manner adds (καί) something different (δέ) corresponding to what precedes (ὡσαύτως): "but also in like manner." Either: just as we wait in patience, so also the Spirit helps our infirmity; or: as we ourselves groan (verse 23), so also the Spirit helps our infirmity. The closer connection is preferable. To connect as some do: the creature groans; the Christian groans; and in like manner the Spirit groans (Luthhardt, Stoeckhardt, Reylaender) is to substitute for the grammatical connection a parallel discovered in the general contents of verses 18-29. It is not true that the Spirit groans "in like manner" as we do, for the manner is described, and is very different from that of the creature or of the Christian. Moreover, the sentence to be connected is not the one which speaks of the Spirit's "groanings," but the one which says: **the Spirit also helpeth our infirmity.** — Τὸ πνεῦμα is the Holy Spirit, our other Paraclete, John 14, 16. — What is meant by **our infirmity, ἡ ἀσθένεια ἡμῶν?** That infirmity (note the article) or lack of strength which is implied in all that has been said in the previous verses from the 18th on; the infirmity due to "the bondage of corruption," manifested by our "groaning," necessarily connected with our "waiting" "for the redemption of our body." Some commentators restrict ἡ ἀσθένεια to infirmity in prayer, and Stoeckhardt goes still farther and restricts it to infirmity in praying for eternal blessedness, claiming that this latter is what the section deals with. But both are wrong. Prayer is our general means of obtaining help in all cases of need, and so it is spoken of when here our infirmity is mentioned. It is true,

the ultimate goal of our hope is eternal blessedness, but this
very hope includes that we be patient and wait day by day.
Here is where our infirmity at once appears: we do not
wait as we should; we are not as patient as we should be:
we do not suffer as we should; we do not hope as we
should; and — worst of all, we do not even exercise our
means of getting help in all these conditions as we should,
that is, we do not pray as we should. Such is our infirmity,
and the connection of hope and prayer with it. — But where
we are infirm and lack proper strength, we have one that
helpeth, συναντιλαμβάνεται, who helps us by laying hand to
the work. The idea is that where we come to a standstill
for lack of strength, the Holy Spirit steps in with his
strength. He "helpeth our infirmity" (dat. after σύν) =
he helps us in our infirmity, and that by supplying of the
abundance of his infinite grace. — **For we know not how
to pray as we ought.** This, as already shown, is more
than an example of our infirmity; it is that part of our infirmity, which, if left unrelieved, would prevent us obtaining the help we must have to reach the goal of our hope.
And that is why the Holy Ghost "helpeth" us especially at
this point; by doing so here he helps all our infirmity in
every part. — The expression **to pray as we ought** includes
all prayer uttered and attempted on our part. There is no
reason whatever to restrict it with Stoeckhardt to the special
prayer for eternal blessedness. — **As we ought,** καθὸ δεῖ, is
best construed with προσευξώμεθα, as our English versions
also have it: "how to pray as we ought." Some read it: "we
do not know as we ought." The sense is practically the
same; if we do not know properly, we will not pray properly; and if we do not pray properly, it is because we do
not know properly. By placing the article τό before the
indirect question τί προσευξώμεθα, this is put into the form of
a noun in the objective case, the object of οἴδαμεν. We do
not know how to pray as we ought includes that we do pray,
and also that we know how to pray aright in a certain
measure; it states, however, that we fall grievously short.
— **But the Spirit himself maketh intercession for** *us*

with groanings which cannot be uttered. The Spirit
dwells in us and we are led by him as sons of God (verse
14). Christ promised him as "another Comforter," Advocate, or Paraclete, and here we learn part of his blessed
work. — **Maketh intercession for us;** ὑπερεντυγχάνει stands
alone (without ὑπὲρ ἡμῶν which some manuscripts add), and
the context shows sufficiently that he makes this intercession
with God, and for us, or in our behalf. Luther adds: *aufs
beste,* but ὑπέρ in the verb does not indicate a degree. The
verb itself indicates that as a true Advocate and Paraclete
the Holy Spirit takes our part and speaks for us and in our
behalf, when we are unable because of our infirmity to
speak for ourselves. Besides the intercession of Jesus
there is then also an intercession of the Holy Spirit. —
This is described as taking place **with groanings which
cannot be uttered;** στεναγμοῖς ἀλαλήτοις, not ἀλάλοις un-
uttered, *i. e.* dumb and silent, but: "unutterable," with no
language or words in which we can utter them. Besser's
idea that some of these groanings were uttered for us all in
the Psalms is untenable; if they were thus uttered, they
would not be unutterable. In trying to understand this intercession of the Spirit with unutterable groanings we must
hold fast: 1) that the Spirit himself intercedes; 2) that he
does this in us, as dwelling in us (Christ's intercession is
outside of us, apart from his indwelling); 3) that he uses
unutterable groanings. The old dogmaticians generally
hold that this intercession of the Spirit with unutterable
groanings signifies that he causes us to pray and groan,
teaches us what to pray for aright, and forms our prayers
aright. Quenstedt III, 259. But this would contradict the
ἀλαλήτοις, and greatly modify ὑπερεντυγχάνειν. The groanings
are unutterable, and the intercession does not furnish them
with words, but uses them as they are (dat. of means).
Two possibilities are left open: either the Spirit himself
groans in a way not to be put into words; or, when words
fail us, we groan, and the Holy Spirit as our Paraclete uses
these groanings and himself puts meaning into them for us.
Of these two the latter is decidedly to be preferred.

Philippi voices the idea of our old dogmaticians, when they declined to admit groanings put forth by the Holy Spirit himself: "To assume that the Spirit groans without using our own spirits is devoid of sense and of Scripture analogy." In this the old dogmaticians are evidently right. We must hold fast as they do, that the "groanings" come from our own hearts ("he that searcheth the hearts," verse 27), produced in us, like all other spiritual *motus* and *actus,* by the Holy Spirit; but — and here we cannot follow the old dogmaticians — there are no words for these "groanings" to give them any meaning we could express, nor does the Holy Spirit give them human or other words of prayer, they remain "groanings which cannot be uttered;" the Holy Spirit, however, uses them in making his intercession for us, he puts his own meaning into them ("the mind of the Spirit," 27) and so sends them up to God. To speak as Stoeckhardt does of groanings of the Spirit which we are able to distinguish within us from groanings of our own, is mere imagination, in no way substantiated by Christian experience, and liable to lead into dangerous mysticism (spirit voices, and the like). With Luthardt we reject the parallel which Meyer and Zahn here introduce between these "groanings" and the speaking unintelligibly with tongues. The chief difference between the intercession of Christ and that of the Spirit is, that the former takes place outside of us in Christ himself and is based on Christ's own merit, the latter takes place in us and rests in the merit of Christ. — **And he that searcheth the hearts** is the omniscient God, frequently designated in this manner; but the reference to our "hearts" here indicates, as already shown above, that the "groanings which cannot be uttered" emanate from our "hearts." Our hearts are not the place where the Spirit groans, but the agents who groan. If the "groanings" were the activity proper of the Spirit, Paul should have written, not "he that searcheth *the hearts,*" but "he that searcheth the deep things of the Spirit." — **Knoweth what is the mind of the Spirit,** τὸ φρόνημα, his intercessory thought, intention, purpose; not then any language or words

bestowed upon the groanings to give them utterance and
intelligibility. Together with Meyer Stoeckhardt urges that
if God is to understand "the mind of the Spirit," the "groanings" must be the Spirit's own and not ours; but this does
not follow necessarily. God knows the mind of the Spirit
equally as well when he takes up our groanings and adds his
intercessory meaning to them. And it is upon this φρόνημα
that everything depends. — **Because he maketh intercession for the saints according to** *the will of* **God.** Ὅτι may
be read either "because," or "that." Philippi keeps the former, like our two English versions: God knows because he is
omniscient, and because the Spirit maketh intercession κατὰ
θεόν. But this second reason for knowing seems hardly adequate, since God in his omniscience knows also what is οὐ
κατὰ θεόν. It is better, therefore, to read: The omniscient
God knows what is the mind of the Spirit, namely that he
maketh intercession κατὰ θεόν. And κατὰ θεόν is put forward
for emphasis; it means: in a divine manner, one comporting
with God· hence θεόν, and not merely αὐτόν, *gottgemaess,*
over against κατὰ ἄνθρωπον, such as would have place with us
only. Here again it may be noted that this implies a use of
our groanings on the part of the Spirit; for any activity of
the Spirit alone in groaning could not be otherwise than
κατὰ θεόν, since he is true God; but here he uses what comes
from poor human hearts, caused indeed by himself, yet
after all human, and of this it is important to know that he
makes use of it "according to the will of God." This is
additional comfort for us in our infirmity. — The objects of
the intercession, not mentioned directly in verse 26, are
now named: **the saints,** ἅγιοι (Philippi: ἡγιασμένοι ἐν Χριστῷ
Ἰησοῦ), made holy by the atoning merits of Christ. There is
no article in Greek: "for saints," *i. e.* such as are saints;
and this in spite of all infirmity yet adhering to them.

God's gracious purpose is wrought out in our salva-tion.

We have just seen that the Christians need not fear,
even in their infirmity; they have the intercession of the

Spirit. But they also need not fear as to any happening in their lives: God according to an eternal purpose has already given them the highest gift, he will add all others as needed. And so the eternal goal will certainly be reached. **And we know,** namely by divine revelation in the Word (compare the story of Joseph), that is with the knowledge of faith, not of intellectual investigation and demonstration merely. Δέ moves forward to something new, hence here translated "and." — **That to them that love God all things work together for good.** The ἀγαπῶντες τὸν θεόν are the same as the ἅγιοι in the previous verse. Why the change in designating them? Many commentators pass this question by in silence, others like Zahn find an unsatisfactory answer. Zahn's is that in verse 26 "infirmity" was mentioned, and that makes it necessary now to indicate that after all love is left in the heart. Zahn overlooks entirely the name ἅγιοι at the end of verse 27. Though troubled with "infirmity" Christians are still God's "saints" because washed in the blood of the Lamb, and the Spirit intercedes for them. The new name ἀγαπῶντες τὸν θεόν does not refer back to "infirmity," in fact it does not refer back to anything at all. It goes together with what now is said of the Christians. A glance at 1 Cor. 2, 9 and at James 1, 12; 2, 5 shows that when the bestowal of God's gifts is mentioned, the relation of love is wont to be emphasized. We see the same thing in Christ's description of the last judgment, where he pictures the works of love as the decisive thing. So here in our passage the thought is simple and appropriate: God's loving providence takes care of those that love him. The idea is just as natural as that a Father should take care of his children. Of course, love is born of faith; the love is there, because we are children of God by faith in Christ Jesus; and the love does not earn the divine care, which is all the gift of grace. — **All things,** πάντα, is general and without any restriction: it purposely includes every kind of painful experience in our Christian lives, every strange and startling thing that may come upon us. What things were

present to Paul's mind when he wrote may in fact be
gathered from verse 38-39. Gess writes: "Whoever is
to mature unto heavenly glory needs now humiliation, now
encouragement, now a spurring on to haste, now a holding back to silence and sitting in quiet, now one effect,
now another entirely different; and so divers things must
combine, in order that each at the proper time may lend
its special aid." — In συνεργεῖ, **work together,** the σύν does
not indicate a combination of the single elements embraced
in πάντα, as if these worked in unison, but σύν refers to
the persons: all things work in their interest, for their
benefit; συνεργεῖ is as much as βοηθεῖ, help. — **For good** is
alsa general, in *heilsamer, foerderlicher Weise* (Philippi).
This ἀγαθόν is not eternal salvation directly, but it is evidently included; all "good" in the true sense of the word
looks to salvation, and Bengel's remark is exactly to the
point: *In bonum, ad glorificationem usque.* — The persons
already designated as ἅγιοι and as ἀγαπῶντες τὸν θεόν are
now still further described: **to them that are called according to his purpose,** τοῖς κατὰ πρόθεσιν κλητοῖς οὖσιν, i. e.
to those who are the called (τοῖς is drawn to οὖσιν, with
κλητοῖς as the predicate). Here the real reason why all
things work together for good to certain persons is stated:
God has called them according to a purpose; the reason
is not something on their part (their love), but something
on God's part (God's gracious call which has made them
his own). By οἱ κλητοί true believers are meant, in whose
case the call was not in vain. The designation is a standing term for true Christians, just like πιστοί, ἅγιοι, ἀγαπητοί,
ἐκλεκτοί; it describes them in a peculiar way, as people
who have accepted the gracious and efficacious call of God
extended in the Gospel. In Matth. 20, 16; 22, 14 all who
simply hear the call, whether they heed it or not, are designated as κλητοί; but very generally in the letters of the
apostles the term is used in the pregnant sense already
described. Not that κλητός itself signifies acceptance, this
idea is added by the context and general sense of the
passages in which it occurs; comp. 1 Cor. 1, 9; 1 Pet. 2, 9.

— **According to** *his* **purpose,** καταὰ πρόθεσιν, really: "according to a purpose." Calvin's idea that there is a difference
in the call of God to men generally, that in the case of
some it is a call καταὰ πρόθεσιν, and in the case of the rest not
καταὰ πρόθεσιν, is an unwarranted deduction which overthrows the universality of grace. A call not "according to
his purpose" is no call, but a sham and deception which it
is blasphemy to attribute to God. Stoeckhardt reduces καταὰ
πρόθεσιν to mean merely "purposely," the opposite of acci-
dentally, in this peculiar way: God has called efficaciously
those *whom he intended to call in this way.* He explains
what he means by saying: "This eternal purpose is substantially identical with eternal election," and by "election"
he means the unconditional selection of a certain fixed
number of persons from the *massa perdita.* There would
then, after all, be two calls, one which would rest on this
"purpose" ("election" in Stoeckhardt's sense), and one
which would not. The assurance and comfort here offered
to the Romans would be that their call is of the former kind.
The question how Paul could know this of the call of the
Romans would, of course, remain unanswered. He had
no special revelation on this point. But this entire view,
advocated by Stoeckhardt and the Synodical Conference
in general, is at heart Calvinistic. In the first place, there
is no "election" such as Stoeckhardt imagines, namely an
unconditional selection of a certain number of individuals
from the *massa perdita* unto eternal salvation in Christ
Jesus. And in the second place, there is no warrant whatever in Scripture for limiting the πρόθεσις to what is
properly called election in the narrow sense of the word,
i. e. the *discretio personarum* on the basis of the universal
plan of salvation. There is no particular or limited "purpose" behind the "call" of any Christian; if there is, then
all who do not receive this kind of a call are absolutely
shut out from salvation. — To be called καταὰ πρόθεσιν is, of
course, to be called purposely of God, but purposely in the
sense of God's gracious and universal Gospel call (John 3,
16; Mark 16, 16). There is but one such call, the one

extended to all men alike (Matth. 28, 19; 1 Tim. 2, 4; Mark 16, 15). This, and no other the first readers of Paul's letter had accepted, as we have likewise done to-day. And this call is κατὰ πρόθεσιν. All who reject it reject not merely a call, or a call without God's purpose behind it, but the call κατὰ πρόθεσιν; they reject the "purpose" as well as the "call," and so remain in their lost condition. The πρόθεσις or **purpose** according to which God calls is "not according to our works, but according to his own purpose of grace which was given us in Christ Jesus before the world began," 2 Tim. 2, 9. This "purpose" our dogmaticians sometimes term predestination, but always in the wider sense of the word as God's "counsel, *purpose*, and ordination" by which "he prepared *salvation* not only *in general,* but in grace considered and *chose to salvation each and every person of the elect* . . . *All this,* according to the Scriptures, is comprised in the doctrine concerning the eternal election of God to adoption and eternal salvation," *etc. F. C.,* Jacobs, 653, 23-24. Luthardt writes: "The πρόθεσις is not the predestination of individual persons" (Calvin, Stoeckhardt), "but the divine purpose of salvation in general." Beck: "The divine πρόθεσις belongs to the divine world plan as the universal counsel of salvation, and does not merely contain a pre-determination of single persons to salvation." Calov writes that the πρόθεσις is *"non quidem absoluto decreto, sed certo mediorum τάξει definito.* Meyer: it is "the free decree formed of God in eternity to save the believers in Christ." And Philippi: "The eternal counsel founded not on our works, but in the free will of God, and formed in Jesus Christ, has . . . for its content and aim our σωτηρία, and has not only been accomplished objectively in general for humanity as a whole in the person and work of Jesus Christ, but it is carried out subjectively and specifically in all separate individuals who actually attain the σωτηρία."

For, ὅτι, really "because," introduces the reason and explanation why all things work together for good to them that are called according to his purpose. It unfolds

what lies in this "purpose" for those who have accepted
the Gospel call, and what they must bear in mind for their
comfort when now strange afflictions come upon them. It
is this: **whom he foreknew, he also foreordained** *to be*
conformed to the image of his Son, etc. Οὕς is general,
but really embraces the very class just mentioned: "them
that love God," "that are called according to his purpose."
They are the ones whom God "foreknew," and consequently
"foreordained" (A. V.: *predestinated*) to be conformed
to the image of his Son. Being thus established in the
saving grace of God, all things cannot help but work together for their good. And for them to realize this is to
enjoy the strongest kind of comfort. — **Whom he fore-**
knew, οὓς προέγνω (2nd aor., a definite past act) our old
exegetes translate *quos praescivit* and supply, not grammatically, but exegetically as correctly elucidating the sense,
credituros esse. B. Weiss supplies: whom he foreknew as
ἀγαπῶντες τὸν θεόν. Meyer looks at what follows, and supplies: whom he foreknew as following the order of salvation and being conformed to the image of his Son. If anything is to be supplied, the reading of Weiss is grammatically
the best, although all the readings mentioned agree in substance. Faith cannot be without love, and both are essential
in conforming to the image of the Son. But προγινώσκειν as
here used really needs no predicate at all; its meaning is
complete in itself: to foreknow as one's own. This is clearly
shown where the simple form of the verb is used: "I never
knew (ἔγνων) you: depart from me," Matth. 7, 23. The
idea is not: I never had any knowledge of you; but: I
never recognized you as my own. A similar meaning is
required in John 10, 14-15; Gal. 4, 9; 1 Cor. 8, 3; 13, 12;
2 Tim. 2, 19. "To know" in these passages means to recognize and acknowledge in love; it is the *noscere cum affectu*
et effectu of the old dogmaticians. But always the act of
the intellect, the knowing, is the fundamental thing; the
emotion of love, where this is implied as present, is always
superadded. And it is the same with προγινώσκειν, which
is used in the New Testament only here in Rom. 11, 2,

although the noun πρόγνωσις occurs more frequently. It
means "to know before;" or, in the pregnant sense just indicates: "to recognize and acknowledge before." In our
passage the πρό goes back to eternity. As long as the
emphasis in this verb is on the intellect, the act of knowing,
even though this is strongly *cum affectu et effectu,* our
passage will stand as a *sedis doctrinae* for the Lutheran
doctrine of predestination *intuitu fidei* as opposed to Calvinism, *i. e.* the doctrine that God elected from all eternity
unto everlasting salvation all those in whom he foresaw the
merit of Christ apprehended by faith. — Calvin, of course,
could not possibly admit this natural meaning of προγινώσκω;
he writes: "The foreknowledge of God, to which Paul
here refers, is not a mere knowing beforehand, as certain
inexperienced people foolishly imagine, but it is an adoption
to the estate of children whereby he has separated us forever from the rejected. In this sense Peter writes that the
believers are elect according to the foreknowledge of God
the Father, through sanctification of the Spirit. It is an
absurd ratiocination that God has only elected them of
whom he knew before that they would be worthy of his
grace." The verb προγινώσκω has played an important part
in the controversy concerning predestination. The essential
point is, first, whether the word means chiefly an activity
of the intellect, or one of the will; and secondly, whether
God's mind restricted itself to behold the persons here
spoken of only as they lay in their lost condition exactly
like all other lost men, or whether he beheld also his purpose of grace operating successfully upon them, while other
men hardened themselves against it. Here is the fork in
the road where Lutheranism and Calvinism divide. The
latter, with Calvin, eliminates the activity of the intellect
and declares the word cannot mean "foreknow." Thus
Stoeckhardt, and with him the Synodical Conference, declares: *Gewiss, das nicht naeher bestimmte προέγνω bezeich-
net einen Willensakt Gottes, einen goettlichen Ratschluss.*
He endeavors to substantiate this by pressing the words
of the commentators who dwell on the pregnant meaning

of γινώσκειν and προγινώσκειν. Hofmann defines, quite correctly: *im voraus zum Gegenstand eines Erkennens, wie
man das Verwandte und Gleichartige erkennt, machen;* this
Stoeckhardt alters completely: *den Erkenntnisgegenstand
dem erkennenden Subjekt gleichartig und verwandt machen.*
Where Hofman conceives God as beholding and *knowing*
us in advance as people already related to him and like him,
Stoeckhardt says, God (beholding and knowing us as
altogether unlike him and unrelated to him) *makes* us like
him — that this is what προγινώσκειν means. Thus to eliminate the native meaning of a word, and to substitute for
it a meaning demanded by the doctrine one advocates, is
to put human opinion in the place of God's Word. Even
Zahn, although he declines to accept the interpretation of
our old dogmaticians, practically admits that they are right,
for he explains that what the apostle really says is this:
God "makes the Christians who love him an object of his
loving thought already ere they existed." Thus οὓς προέγνω
will always mean: **whom he foreknew,** or in the pregnant
sense here apparent from the lack of any modifying word:
whom he lovingly foreknew, or recognized in advance, as
his own. And any doctrine which finds iself compelled to
alter this native meaning of the word stands condemned
by the very word thus altered.

Whom he foreknew, **he also foreordained.** Προορίζειν
is the biblical word for "predestinate," as also the A. V.
translates it. This is an act of God's will, and by it, in
all eternity (πρό), he determined what those whom be foreknew in love as his own should eventually be: **conformed
to the image of his Son.** Συμμόρφους is the predicative accusative, and may be followed either by the genitive as
here, or by the dative as in Phil. 3, 21. It signifies: to have
the same form as another, and that together with the. essentials to which the form belongs. We are "conformed to
the image of his Son," when we are altogether Christlike.
This is attained in us when the work of grace is done, and
we at last stand in the presence of Christ and see him

11

even as he is, 1 John 3, 2; 1 Cor. 15, 49; 2 Cor. 3, 18; Phil. 3, 21. Not till we reach the state of glory will we have the υἱοθεσία for which we still wait (verse 23). There is indeed a *conformitas crucis* which we reach already in this life; but verse 30 shows beyond question that the *conformitas gloriae* is meant. And this complete and final conformity to the image of the Son is what Paul points the Christians to as their assured hope, for their comfort amid trial and affliction. — **That he might be the firstborn among many brethren** shows that God's principal concern is his Son, and our salvation in so far as this tends to the glorification of his Son. He is before all, and the head of the body (Col. 1, 17-18), the firstborn, with many other sons as brethren (Heb. 1, 6; 2, 10-11). He is the **firstborn,** not merely because he is the Son from all eternity, but also as *princeps et dux* (ἀρχηγός, Heb. 2, 10; Ps. 84, 27; Col. 1, 18; Rev. 1, 5), and because he is by nature and in himself what we can be only by adoption and through him. He is "over all, God blessed forever" (9, 5), θεάνθρωπος (1 Tim. 2, 5), we only ἄνθρωποι θεοῦ (1 Tim. 6, 11; 2 Tim. 3, 17). This then is the great purpose of God's predestination, to surround his Son in heavenly glory with all the host of sons made glorious like him through his grace and merit. This shall certainly be achieved, and we are now to comfort ourselves with the certainty, for it is the consummation of the divine πρόθεσις, and the heavenly fulfilment of the divine προορισμός. So also the F. C. uses this great statement of Paul, showing first of all, that "we should accustom ourselves not to speculate concerning the mere, secret, concealed, inscrutable foreknowledge of God, but how the counsel, purpose, and ordination of God in Christ Jesus, who is the true book of life, has been revealed to us through the Word, *viz.* that the entire doctrine concerning the purpose. counsel, will, and ordination of God pertaining to our redemption, call, righteousness, and salvation should be taken together; as Paul has treated and explained this article (Rom. 8, 29, *etc.;* Eph. 1, 4, *etc.*), as also Christ in the parable (Matth. 22, 1, *etc.*)" *etc.* Jacobs,

652, 13 *etc.* Secondly, "this doctrine affords also the excellent, glorious consolation that God was so solicitous concerning the conversion, righteousness, and salvation of every Christian, and so faithfully provided therefor, that before the foundation of the world was laid he deliberated concerning it, and in his purpose ordained how he would bring me thereto and preserve me therein. Also, that he wished to secure my salvation so well and certainly that since, through the weakness and wickedness of our flesh, it could easily be lost from our hands, or through craft and might of the devil and the world be torn and removed therefrom, in his eternal purpose, which cannot fail or be overthrown, he ordained it, and placed it for preservation in the almighty hand of our Savior Jesus Christ, from which no one can pluck us (John 10, 28). Hence Paul also says (Rom. 8, 28 and 39): Because we have been called according to the purpose of God, who will separate us from the love of God in Christ?" Jacobs, 657, 45, *etc.* — The word **brethren** elevates us very highly, and, meaning here our future state of perfection and glory in communion with our greatest Brother, Christ, is indeed full of comfort. The risen Christ called his disciples "brethren" (John 20, 17), and they were such by justification, but here to all the blessedness, grace, and honor that lies in justification is added also that last and highest measure, future glory, when Christ shall acknowledge us as his brethren before the face of God and all his angels.

And whom he foreordained, them he also called: and whom he called, them he also justified: and whom he justified, them he also glorified. These three terse and comprehensive statements set forth how the eternal predestination of God, resting on his foreknowledge, is carried into effect in time. There are three essential acts, the calling, the justifying, the glorifying. Οὒς . . . τούτους, those very ones of whom Paul speaks from verse 28 on God called. It is best to take καλεῖν in the pregnant sense of κλητοί in verse 28: **he called** them, as indeed he calls all men, but these accept the call in the obedience of

faith. Actually many men reject the call and the purpose
of grace that is in it, but Paul does not speak of them, he
deals only with those whom God foreknew as his own;
they accept the call. But do not some accept the call only
for a time, and in the hour of temptation fall away. These
are also excluded here, and counted, because of their ultimate unfaithfulness, as belonging together with those who
spurn the call generally. Philippi rightly cautions us, not
to break the connection of Paul's line of thought, for only
in that line as it stands are Paul's statements true. — Whom
he called **them he also justified;** δικαιοῦν in the N. T.
almost always combined with a personal object as here =
to pronounce or declare just; as does a judge in court when
the claims of justice are satisfied. See the definition given
above. There is no salvation without justification. We
might expect Paul to add also sanctification, but, although
he has dwelt on it at length (6, 1-8, 13), he makes no separate mention of it here, for it does not stand on a level
with justification as a *causa* of salvation, but is only the
via by which glorification is reached. — And whom he justified, **them he also glorified,** as the crowning and completion
of the work. Because of the aorist ἐδόξασεν Luthardt considers this act also already completed, like the calling and
the justification; hence he interprets the δόξα ideally, "in
Christ." But our conformity to the Son's image in glorification must be viewed as taking place at the last day
with soul and body reunited in the glory of the life to
come. The aorist therefore is proleptic; Paul speaks of
our coming glorification as if it had already occurred. It
is so certain that he does not change the tense, but uses
the aorist as in the preceding verbs. It is a bold thing to
do, but very much like Paul. Bengel: *Paulus docet, Deum,
quantum in ipso est, a gradu ad gradum perducere suos.*
The certainty of eternal salvation and glorification here
taught by the apostle is full of comfort and cheer for every
afflicted Christian: nothing can prevent the saving purpose
and work of God from attaining its glorious goal. Yet
Calvin is wrong when he attempts to make this certainty

absolute, by basing it on an absolute predestinatory act of God. Stoeckhardt does the same thing, resting the certainty of salvation on a predestination *dem Begriff wie dem Wesen nach verschieden von dem Ratschluss der Erloesung oder der Feststellung des Heilswegs, sowie von dem allgemeinen Gnadenwillen.* It is a fearful mistake to presume that the purpose of redemption, or the way of salvation, or the universal will of grace is not sufficient ground for our certainty of salvation, but that we must seek some act of God outside of and apart from these. There is no such ground, and to imagine it, and base our certainty of salvation on what we imagine, is deplorable beyond expression. Our comforting and joyful certainty is wholly conditioned on the universal purpose of grace, on the great way of salvation here described by Paul. When this gracious purpose carries us forward step by step, then indeed are we certain of salvation, and then alone; for this purpose is sure and cannot fail. To scorn this purpose, to run counter to its gracious and blessed provisions, is to lose both the certainty and the salvation itself.

With Christ all things are ours.

Paul has reached the climax of his argument, and his diction rises accordingly. Erasmus exclaims: *Quid usquam Cicero dixit grandiloquentius?* Paul draws the glorious conclusions from what he has just presented, and our text closes with the first of these. **What then shall we say to these things?** πρὸς ταῦτα, with these things before us as unquestionably true, namely God's foreknowledge and predestination, his call, justification, and glorification? Can we still stand and lament, as if ours were a sad lot, full of sufferings and bare of joy? Must we not rather be ashamed of our unbelief, murmuring, dissatisfaction, doubt, *etc.* What we ought to say to these things Paul himself sets forth: **If God *is* for us, who *is* against us?** This **if** introduces a condition fulfilled; it does not balance between: Perhaps he is for us; and: Perhaps he is not for us. He *is* for us, and there is no shadow of doubt about it! For

us, says Paul, and shows us what he meant all along in verses 28-30. Luther remarks, that if we could decline well the pronoun *nos* and *nobis,* we would be able to conjugate *Deus,* and make a verb out of the noun: *Deus dixit et dictus est,* God has spoken and is himself spoken in the Word. Ὁ θεὸς ὑπὲρ ἡμῶν sums up into a single expression all the gracious saving acts of God (the true God, hence the article) just set forth by Paul. With this established, **who is against us?** (A. V.: "who can be against us?") The answer is self-evident: all the world, a thousand foes, unnumbered ills may indeed oppose us, they cannot prevail — God is greater, mightier than they, and he is on our side, even from his eternal purpose on. — Paul now singles out the very heart of what lies in the general and comprehensive statement that "God is for us," namely that he delivered up his Son for us. **He that spared not his own Son, but delivered him up for us all, how shall he not also with him freely give us all things?** The γε is lost in the English; *quippo qui, der ja.* The wording "spared not" vividly recalls Gen. 22, 16 ("hast not withheld thy son, thine only son;" Septuagint: οὐκ ἐφείσω τοῦ υἱοῦ σου), and no doubt is meant to do so. Meyer indeed denies that, saying the expression is quite common, but there is a double correspondence here, namely of both the word and the fact, and that in the writing of one thoroughly versed in the Old Test. What God acknowledges as the highest proof of love in Abraham he himself has furnished unto us: he has actually delivered up **his own Son** for us (ἴδιος υἱός emphatic). "Picture well to yourself this dear own Son," writes Luther, "then you will feel intimately the flow of divine love. If you had a son, who was not only your own bodily son, but also your only son, an intelligent, wise, sensible, pious, good, and very dear son: and for the sake of a miserable strange servant, who in addition was your debtor, you now spared not this son, but you send and let him go on and endure even death, just in order to redeem that servant. Would you allow the ingratitude of such a servant, supposing that he would fail to appreciate and would despise

the great love you and your son had borne him in counting
him worth so much, would you allow it to go unpunished,
and with patient silence say nothing about it? How much
less should you expect such a thing of God and God's Son!"
— The negative "he spared not" is followed by the positive:
but delivered him up; which is Paul's favorite way of impressing a thing strongly and making it very emphatic.
Ὃς παρέδωκεν αὐτόν, *sc.* εἰς θάνατον, into death (Is. 53, 12), is
paralleled by Χριστὸς παρέδωκεν ἑαυτόν, Gal. 2, 20; Eph. 5, 2;
also 1 Tim. 2, 6; Tit. 2, 14. The will of the Father and of
the Son agree in the sacrifice made on the cross. — **For us,**
ὑπὲρ ἡμῶν, in our behalf, and thus in our stead. **Us all =**
every single Christian, not one excepted. This in no way
limits the atonement; Christ died for all men alike. But
many spurn his sacrifice and remain without its saving
effect. Here Paul deals only with those who accept Christ's
atonement by faith, and he wants to comfort every one of
them and cheer and fortify them against any affliction;
hence he says ὑπὲρ ἡμῶν πάντων. If one has the supreme gift
of God's saving grace, the Son, he may rest easy as to everything else. — And this is the argument of Paul, *a majorem
ad minus,* from the greater (and here the supreme) to the
less: **how shall he not also with him freely give us all
things?** Καί is best drawn to πῶς οὐχί instead of to σὺν αὐτῷ,
as Meyer would have it, like the Latin *quidni etiam.* **Freely
give us** is one word, χαρίσεται; a gracious giving, one that is
gratis and asks no price or reward. By implication Christ
is here represented as such a gift: **with him,** just as he has
already given us "him," so also he will continue to give us
τὰ πάντα, all those things we may need. The sweep of this
assurance is great indeed: it reaches through all our earthly
life, and will at no time permit us to be destitute of what
we need; and it reaches into all eternity, for all the glory
that awaits us there. But, however, great τὰ πάντα may
seem to us, "all things" as compared here with Christ,
whom we already have, are like a handful or two thrown in
for good measure when one makes a purchase. It is simply
impossible that God should deny us a single thing that we

really need and that is necessary to complete his work in us, after he has given us his Son and we have received him by faith. To have this blessed assurance is to be fortified at all points in all our coming life. And in all the world, with all its power, wealth, and pleasure there is no assurance like this; let us take it with all the gratitude we are capable of, and so enter upon the new year.

HOMILETICAL HINTS.

As often as the world numbers a new year and utters its wish of good fortune for the days to come, the church holds up the name of Jesus to men and points to the mercy-seat of Christ in his blood first shed for us in his circumcision. May God help us that we may begin every year of our pilgrimage with the acceptance of the gift of eternity, and amid all fear and anxiety close it with the victorious question of Christian faith: "How shall he not also with him freely give us all things?" Besser. In this text time and eternity are blended together, and eternity sheds its heavenly light upon the Christian's entire pathway through time.

Hope and faith are not the same and do not look to the same thing, but they hang together, as Luther says, and can never be separated; the one always looks toward the other, as the cherubim upon the mercy-seat. — Likewise Luther ascribes to hope especially the Christian's courageous manliness. — Sight deposes hope and destroys its office; God will indeed at the last day thus depose hope, and whoever usurps that prerogative of his now will come to hurt. Besser. — He also writes: "If you are determined to have a church whose holiness and power, wealth and honor, foundation and authority are apparent to the eye, the Christian Church cannot be your hope, for Christ's kingdom is not of this world.

Besser describes our infirmity: We hate sin, and yet we sin: we are not of the world, and yet the lust of the world contaminates us; we have overcome the evil one, and yet we feel his fiery darts; we believe Christ is risen, and yet we are afraid of death; there is now no more condemnation in us, and yet we tremble at the thought of hell; we have received an eternal kingdom, and yet we often worry even to utter discouragement concerning the church of our almighty Lord, and are afraid of the threats of those who can kill only the body; we know our calling unto suffering in hope, and yet we shrink from the cross, seek ease, are given to earthly-mindedness, and our souls are weary. Nothing but infirmity on every side! But thanks be to God, the Spirit also helpeth our infirmity. He extends to the child that stands on its weak feet, his own strong hand, until the dread is past.

The promise that the Spirit helpeth our infirmity applies only to those who have the Spirit. And our greatest infirmity comes when we are plunged into such perplexities, or overwhelmed with such grief and anguish, or so at a loss to comprehend the ways of the Lord in dealing with us, or in sickness and in the hour of death so weak in body and mind as not to be able to utter a word. Then the Spirit dwelling in us takes our groans, inarticulate cries, and puts his blessed meaning into them and sends them as acceptable prayer to the Father's throne. — Even the arms of Moses grew weak and had to be upheld. Elijah was faint and ready to give up under the juniper-tree. What did Joseph pray in prison as the months lengthened into a year, and a second year followed the first? God sent them all the support they needed, and so he will do for us in all the years to come. We have the Spirit within us, and our very sighs and groanings shall be heard.

Our times of anxiety are to be turned into times of blessing by means of childlike prayer. And yet how miserable often are our prayers at such times! Afflicted from within and tempted from without we poor creatures are so distressed concerning ourselves that we are scarcely able to fold our hands. In times of conflict we are so occupied with our own defense that we can scarcely collect our thoughts in order to cry for help. Yea, under the pressure of the cross, amid pains and plagues our mind grows confused, we lose our heads, and simply cannot ask at the moment what we really need, however apparent that may actually be. Who of us has never experienced such times of disturbance, when all our thoughts clashed against each other in impenetrable darkness, when body and soul were completely exhausted, and the spirit could find no words to cry unto God! And who of us, when he recalls such moments of crushing, exhaustion, and utter fainting of the inward man, is not frightened at the thought, how will it be if in this coming year we are thrown again into such turmoil. To-day all our worry is to find its answer and lose its deadly sting: The Spirit also helpeth our infirmity, *etc.* Rump.

God is so good that he would permit no evil, if he were not so mighty as to be able to bring good out of every evil. Augustine.

Centuries ago Chysostom lived at the court of the emperor in Constantinople. When on one occasion he had rebuked the sins of the court without fear or favor, the empress sent him a message of displeasure, and threatened him with deposition from his office as bishop, imprisonment, and execution, unless he altered his preaching. But the messenger said to the empress: What is the use of this against a man who has no fear, except the fear of sin? Matthes.

God has called us from eternity unto his grace. This grace protects us. Older than our enemies, greater than their power is the purpose of God, who will have all men to be saved, especially those who love him. No effort of human power is able to nullify this purpose or to bring it to nought. Rump.

Besser warns us against any Calvinistic perversion of Paul's thought, when he says that we must never insert an "if" into the clause: "To them that are called according to his purpose," so that it would read: *if* they are called according to his purpose.

Do you know the greatness of God's grace? It goes back to all eternity before the world was, or a single human being had been created. Then the eyes of God already beheld us, and not merely as creatures of his, like the countless creatures great and small about us, not merely as fallen creatures who through the fault of one had been drawn into sin and death, but as creatures of his reached by his great purpose of salvation in Christ Jesus. He saw that purpose as it touched our souls one by one, and by its blessed power won us to be his own. And with his eyes thus upon us, beholding us as his own, he foreordained, he predestinated us. In a mighty decree, infinitely gracious and blessed, and reaching into all the eternity to come, he declared that we should be made like unto his Son our glorious Savior. "Whom he foreknew he also foreordained to be conformed to the image of his Son, that he might be the firstborn among many brethren." Even now the purpose and predestination of God is being carried out: we behold it in every one who is called by the Gospel and won for God; in every one who is justified and by faith rejoices in the pardon through Jesus' blood; in every one who finishes his earthly pilgrimage in faithfulness to the end and enters into the glory beyond. Are you one of this number? You are, as surely as this work is proceeding in you. You are not, as surely as you persist in rejecting God's purpose of grace and continue to go on in sin and guilt to your doom. But O the blessedness of God's love and protection for all who are his own! All things must bring them some good — even pain, sorrow, persecution, dark and inexplicable occurrences. God will keep, bless, and guide safely home all his own.

The real calamity in life is when God is against us. To have God against us means eternal destruction. We here see what is at stake, and what is more necessary than daily bread. Everything depends on this one thing that God be for us. . . . God is for us and with us in Christ. Riemer.

God's Children Entering the New Year.

I. *Hope before us.*
II. *The Spirit within us.*
III. *A sure and blessed Providence over us.*

When Columbus, the discoverer of America first stepped upon the strange land, he fell upon his knees, thanked God, dedicated the land to him and raised the banner of the cross. When Gustavus Adolphus stepped on the shores of Germany in his campaign to deliver the Lutherans of Luther's country from their Romish enemies, he too fell upon his knees, thanked God, and prayed that he would aid his work. As we to-day step upon the unknown land of a new year, to fight on in the battle of faith for the heavenly prize against many a foe, let us fall on our knees, raise the banner of the cross, and lift up our eyes to the hills whence our help cometh.

The Light of Grace That Illumines the Portal of the New Year.

I. *The hope of salvation in Christ Jesus.*
II. *The intercession of the Holy Spirit.*
III. *The foreordination of our heavenly Father.*

Adapted from Wunderlich.

God Is For Us — Who Can Be Against Us?

I. *He has foreknown us.*
II. *He has foreordained us.*
III. *He has called us.*
IV. *He has justified us.*
V. *He has given us his Spirit.*
VI. *He has promised to make all things work together for our good.*
VII. *He has assured us of final glory.*

The Christian Enters the New Year with the Blessed Certainty of Salvation.

I. *That certainty rests on the saving purpose of God.*
From the Word

    1. I am certain that God purposes to save all men, hence also me.

2. I am certain that God has redeemed all men in Christ, hence also me.

3. I am certain that every believer now actually has salvation, hence I also have it by faith.

4. I am certain that God will leave nothing undone to bring every bĕliever to glory, hence also me.

5. I am certain that God from all eternity knew the triumph of his purpose and grace in every believer, hence also in me.

II. *That certainty is experienced in the saving acts of God.*

1. I experience it in that God calls me by the Gospel, and I now hear and accept his gracious offer.

2. I experience it in that God justifies me, and I now hear and accept his pardoning declaration.

3. I experience it in that God promises me eternal glory, and I now hear his promise and rejoice in its sure and certain fulfillment.

III. *That certainty triumphs in the constant help of God.*

1. I know that the Spirit helps my infirmity by his intercession whenever. I need it.

2. I know that alľ things work together for my good, no matter what may happen to me in this coming year.

3. I know that with God for me nothing can be against me.

4. I know that together with his Son the Father gives me all things.

All Things Work Together For My Good.

I. *God's saving purpose declares it.*
1. He wants to save me.
2. He sent his Son for me.
3. He has called and justified me.
4. He has promised heaven to me.

II. *God's gracious providence performs it.*

1. He sees that I get whatever I need.

2. He will let no foe prevail against me.

3. He brings some blessing for me even out of the most painful experience.

4. He makes the Spirit my intercessor in the hour of greatest need.

THE SUNDAY AFTER EASTER.

James 4, 13-17.

To the words of Paul in the previous text we now add those of James. After the eternal counsel of God, which comprehends our whole life and eternal salvation, has been expounded to us, we are now shown also the practical side of the Christian's life, how he is guided day by day, and step by step, in all his business and work, by the will of God. We need the towering truths which Paul sets forth in Rom. 8, the certainty that reaches back to eternity and forward to eternity and beholds in its full sweep the unspeakable grace of God toward us poor sinners; but we need besides that the working program which James furnishes us for our every-day lives and labors, the reminder that all our earthly plans are subject to the providence and will of God. Our text deals with *the Christian's immediate future,* and shows first of all the folly of planning without God, and secondly the wisdom of planning with God.

The folly of planning without God.

Go to now; ye that say, To-day or to-morrow we will go into this city, and spend a year there, and trade, and get gain. ῎Αγε is used almost like an interjection. The added νῦν makes it more direct and pointed. In the classics it usually introduces an imperative either in the singular or in the plural; in the New Testament it appears only here and in 5, 1, where the imperative κλαύσατε follows in the regular way. Some think that James had this κλαύσατε in mind from the beginning, but the two are too widely apart for that, introducing two distinct paragraphs and addressed to two classes of people who are

173

by no means necessarily identical. The conclusion is unwarranted that they who planned (or who now plan) their
business operations as described in our text, are always
also people who are guilty of the wickedness depicted by
James in 5, 1-6. It is enough to assume that some people
in the congregations of the Christians forget God too much
in their business and life plans generally. These the
apostle addresses in a dramatic way: **Go to now,** or:
Come now! Nothing needs to be supplied. **Ye that say,**
οἱ λέγοντες, is vocative, and the participle is predicative:
who think and say as a regular thing what now follows.
The reading varies: **To-day or to-morrow;** or: to-day and
to-morrow. The former may indicate an uncertainty in
the minds of the speakers, as if the trip intended may be
taken either on the one day or on the other. The other
reading makes the thing certain: the trip will take exactly
to-day and to-morrow, two days, and everything is fully
settled in their minds. If the choice were between these
two meanings, the latter reading would be decidedly preferable, since the people here described are so sure of
themselves and their own movements. But the "or" may
indicate diversity; either that now they say: To-day we
will go! and another time they will fix the date for to-
morrow. Or some of them will plan to go on one day
(to-day), others on another day (to-morrow). And this
is how we prefer to understand their words, leaving intact
their certainty and assurance. — **We will go into this city,**
εἰς τήνδε τὴν πόλιν, the demonstrative adjective indicating the
particular city had in mind. **We will go** = it is fixed and
settled; there is no further if about it. It is the same
with the three other future tenses. *Deo volente* has fallen
from the minds of these people; *nobis volentibus* has taken
its place. — **And spend a year there, and trade, and get
gain.** Everything is planned out with complete assurance.
There is no thought of how much is thus assumed as
altogether certain, concerning which no man can in the
least be certain. Ἐνιαυτός is any fixed and complete period
of time, and is frequently used in the sense of a year. Here

ἐνιαυτόν is simply the object of ποιήσομεν. Much may happen in a year, but all such possibilities are here overlooked. Life, health, and strength, a thousand other favorable conditions, even success in business ventures, are all taken for granted. James gives us a picture of business men when he sets forth this particular kind of folly which forgets God. The Jews were (and, for that matter, still are) great traders, and no doubt there were merchants enough to whom the apostle's description applied. But this is not a folly restricted to one class or profession. Pleasures and all sorts of occupations are planned just as these traders planned their traveling and trading.

Whereas ye know not what shall be on the morrow, οἵτινες οὐκ ἐπίστασθε τῆς αὔριον. This the usual reading and division of the sentence is stronger and preferable to the other which extends the sentence to include also the following words οἵτινες οὐκ ἐπίστασθε τῆς αὔριον ποία ἡ ζωὴ ὑμῶν, "who do not know of what sort your life of the morrow will be." Meyer rightly remarks that the former reading leaves in doubt whether these men will at all live on the morrow; while the latter grants that they will live, and restricts the doubt to the condition they will be in. Some also read: τὰ τῆς αὔριον, "the things of to-morrow," which furnishes a direct object for ἐπίστασθε, instead of the elliptical genitive τῆς (supply ἡμέρας) αὔριον, which the A. and R. V. both render: "what shall be on the morrow." "Boast not thyself of to-morrow; for thou knowest not what a day may bring forth." Ps. 27, 1. An example in point is the rich fool who planned to build his barns greater, when that very night his soul was required of him. What folly to make plans for a whole year ahead, when we really do not know what a single day may bring forth! — We see that James has this very uncertainty of human life in mind by what he at once adds: **What is your life?** ποία, *qualis,* of what kind. Its very quality is transitoriness and uncertainty. **For ye are a vapor, that appeareth for a little time, and then vanisheth away.** By adding "for," γάρ, the answer is turned into a proof for the thought that underlies the

question, namely that our life is very transient. It is
that indeed, because "ye are a vapor" — ἐστέ stronger than
ἐστί, namely our life. We ourselves are but a vapor. Ἀτμίς is
really "breath;" Acts 2, 19 has the phrase "vapor of smoke."
In the O. T. it is used in the sense of smoke, and Luther
translates *Dampf* in our text, others *Dunst*. In 1, 10 James
uses another figure for the same thought, "the flower of
the grass." Ἀτμίς alone would be enough, but the apostle
adds the further description: **that appeareth for a little
time, and then vanisheth away.** That is the real characteristic of ἀτμίς; it appears indeed, but only πρὸς ὀλίγον,
a brief instant, and then also (καί) is gone forever. What
an impressive picture of ourselves? Not a man among us
knows whether he shall live through the year just begun,
or even through any considerable part of it. Ps. 39, 4-6.

The wisdom of planning with God.

**For that ye ought to say, If the Lord will, we shall
both live, and do this or that.** The marginal translation:
Instead of your saying, is a fine and close rendering of the
Greek construction: ἀντὶ τοῦ λέγειν ὑμᾶς. This prepositional
phrase reaches back to οἱ λέγοντες: "ye that say . . .
instead of your saying," making the intervening question
and answer parenthetical. Over against what these people
actually say James now places what instead they ought to
say. The reading: ἐὰν ὁ κύριος θέλῃ (or the aor. subj.
θελήσῃ), followed by two future indicatives, καὶ ζήσομεν καὶ
ποιήσομεν, is in every way to be preferred. There is only
one condition, one in which all others are necessarily involved: **If the Lord will.** Our life and every movement
depend on his will. Ps. 31, 15: "My times are in Thy
hand." Without the Father not a sparrow shall fall to the
ground, Matth. 10, 29-30. Accordingly also Paul makes his
promise to return to Ephesus, Acts 18, 21, conditional, "if
God will." We see the same thing 1 Cor. 4, 19; 16, 7 with
the variation "if the Lord permit;" Heb. 6, 3. These are
not empty phrases, nor must they become such when we
use them; they must express the real attitude of our hearts,

our constant dependence on God and the hand of divine providence. — With two future indicatives following, the sentence continues: **we shall both live, and do this or that.** James too would have us use the positive future ζήσομεν, ποιήσομεν, but only in connection with the condition just mentioned. He, however, introduces what these foolish merchants utterly forgot to insert: **we shall live.** They took that, like everything else, for granted: "we shall go and spend a year there." The intelligent Christian knows that he cannot even live without God's willing it, to say nothing of carrying out any special undertakings. He daily and hourly thanks God for life and health, and receives both as a gift from the hand of God. After the important ζήσομεν James adds καὶ ποιήσομεν τοῦτο ἢ ἐκεῖνο: **we shall do this or that,** *i. e.* whatever God may permit or grant us to do. Nothing is said about trading and getting gain; James takes in much more than mere business and money-getting, showing that his mention of certain traders in the beginning was only by way of example. The Lord, indeed, grants his people also earthly success and profit by means of fair and reputable dealings, but our every work and every form of success depends on his will. And sometimes he sends us failures, because these too are necessary in our lives, to keep us humble, and in general to give us the discipline we need. — Instead of the two future indicatives some read ζήσωμεν and ποιήσωμεν, two subjunctives; or ζήσωμεν and ποιήσομεν, one subjunctive and a future indicative. These are transalted respectively: "If the Lord will and we live, let us also do this or that;" or: "we will also do this or that." But the double condition is hardly acceptable, for the simple reason that the Lord's will must refer not only to our doing this or that, but also to our living at all. So also the hortative subjunctive, "let us do this or that," does not match the preceding condition (ἐάν with the subjunctive) as well as the indicative future.

But now ye glory in your vauntings: all such glory-ing is evil. Νῦν δέ once more introduces the reality which

12

is in glaring contrast to what should be (comp. Luke 19, 42; 1 Cor. 5, 11; 14, 6). James calls the unconditional planning of these merchants ἀλαζονείαι, **vauntings.** ʼΑλαζονεύεσθαι is to make false pretensions; and that is exactly what these people do. Their talk is both false and pretentious, a boasting utterly vain, since they cannot live even for a moment, or do a single thing, without the will of God, and yet talk and act as if they could and did. The plural ἀλαζονείαι is used to embrace all boastings like the sample furnished in verse 13. James does not say merely that they utter such "vauntings," but that they **glory** in them, καυχᾶσθε. The verb signifies loud, prideful talking. Counting on themselves, their ability, experience, skill, they give loud utterance to their lofty ideas. Their previous success has made them sure of themselves, and so they go on with new plans, expecting still greater success. But: **all such glorying is evil.** Whatever satisfaction they may have derived from following their own will and wisdom in life, the result is πονηρός, bad, worthless, harmful, detrimental. It is offensive to God, who certainly cannot · bless their undertakings, but must visit his displeasure upon such haughty boasters; and in itself it is hurtful for men to harbor foolish ideas and to take satisfaction in expressing them. Πᾶσα καύχησις τοιαύτη signifies all glorying of this kind, having this character; no matter to what it refers, or in what way it comes out. There is nothing good or beneficial in any of it. — But some of these boasters may plead that by speaking as they did, they really did not intend to ignore God and his providence in their lives. They may claim that they merely omitted to mention what in reality they know, namely that all their life and plans are in the hands of God. James meets them on this point: **To him therefore that knoweth to do good, and doeth it not, to him it is sin.** Οὖν draws a conclusion. Some commentators think it reaches back through all the previous admonitions of the Epistle; but, if it includes that much, there is no apparent reason why it should not have been reserved for the closing section of the entire Epistle, thus including also the admonitions in chapter five. Nor is there any explanation forthcoming why the first four chapters should thus be summed up by a general ethical statement on sins of omission. On the other hand, verses 13-17 constitute a unit in a marked way. Here a sin of omission is described in a concrete and detailed way. After the character of this sin has been made plain, and the opposite right conduct of a Christian, the apostle concludes with the general ethical law or principle which embraces the case in hand: "To him that knoweth to do good, and doeth it not, to him it is sin." Surely, every man must know that God is over him. If then in his thinking and planning he fails to take note of that, as James has shown in the case of the merchants he characterizes, he is committing a grave sin of omission. And if, in order to excuse himself, he admits that he knows what yet he fails to take proper account of in his plans, his very excuse becomes his own condemnation; for to know good, and yet not to do it, is beyond question sin. De Wette rightly remarks, to omit doing the καλόν is equal to doing the πονηρόν. The fact that the principle which James states is a general one, while the sin he describes is a specific act, need not trouble us in the least. All the commandments of God are general, and yet they cover the specific transgressions of which we are guilty, cover them all just because they are general. So also the Gospel principles which rule the believer's life; they are general, and he must apply them to every individual thought, word, and deed. Verse 17 then is rightly used to cover all sins of omission; and for this very reason is introduced here where a signal sin of this kind is treated. Καλὸν ποιεῖν refers to any and every good; εἰδότι and μὴ ποιοῦντι are likewise altogether general. Both nature and the Word of God furnish the knowledge here involved, especially the latter, which the men here addressed on a particular point had in abundant measure. Nevertheless, these men acted contrary to this better knowledge. Hence their action to them is sin, ἁμαρτία, a missing of the mark, just as in every case when better knowledge is not followed. This is especially true of every man who

claims to be a Christian believer. Let us mark it well, now
that we have entered upon a new year, and in every case
where we have been remiss confess our sin, and by the help
of the Savior follow the blessed knowledge he has given us.

HOMILETICAL HINTS.

Ps. 31, 14-15: "But I trusted in thee, O Lord: I said, Thou
art my God. My times are in thy hand." — Prov. 27, 1: "Boast
not thyself of to-morrow; for thou knowest not what a day may
bring forth." Comp. Luke 12, 19-20. — Eph. 5, 15-16: "Look therefore carefully how ye walk, not as unwise, but as wise; redeem-
ing the time, because the days are evil." — Job. 10, 12: "Thou
hast granted me life and favor, and thy visitation hath preserved
my spirit." — Is. 40, 29-31: "He giveth power to the faint; and
to them that have no might he increaseth strength. Even the
youths shall faint and be weary, and the young men shall utterly
fall: but they that wait upon the Lord shall renew their strength;
they shall mount up with wings as eagles; they shall run, and not
be weary; and they shall walk, and not faint." — 1 Pet. 5, 5:
"God resisteth the proud, but giveth grace to the humble." — Luke
12, 47-48: "And that servant, which knew his lord's will, and
made not ready, nor did according to his will, shall be beaten
with many stripes . . . And to whomsoever much is given, of
him shall much be required: and to whom they commit much, of
him will they ask the more." — John 9, 41: "Jesus said unto
them, If ye were blind, ye would have no sin: but now ye say,
We see: your sin remaineth." — These passages have been used
effectively in the sermons by Johann Rump, A. Matthes, and others.

When this Sunday occurs in the church year it comes one
or more days after New Year. Our hearers, then, have already
entered upon the new year, and many of them have made special
plans for the year, and perhaps are already carrying them out.
Have they made these plans subject to the will of God? — In the
same way, for business or for pleasure, we determine on this or
that course; we build, we buy, we move, we establish ourselves
anew. Do we think as we should of the Lord's will? — A mother
sits at the cradle of her child and dreams fondly of its future.
A young man starts out in life to make his fortune; he counts
on many years of life, and means to rise to great heights. A
young couple begin their married life under fair auspices; they
see a path of roses before them, with only an occasional thorn.

Every one of these needs the lesson of our text. If we can and must commit our immortal souls and their eternal welfare to the hands of God, shall we think of withholding from him the guidance of our poor earthly lives?

"We shall trade, and get gain!" This is the one thought of the great majority of men. How the mind springs forward at the thought of gain; the journey may be hard and long, but it is cheerfully undertaken; many difficulties may block the road to success, but there is no hesitation about seeking ways and means to overcome them. The scent of gain draws man with unfailing certainty, and too often so that his heart forgets God, his governance of human life, and the higher tasks he has set for us in this earthly life of ours. Earthly business may claim days, months, a whole year of our lives, the Lord's work in many instances must not claim more than a few moments at a time. In pursuit of gain, or for our own pleasure, we spend freely, willingly, and ever anew, but when the work of the Lord calls, we close our hearts and purses and complain that collections never end. To serve the Lord is the greatest gain, but our eyes are so trained to see the dollar in the ordinary business deal, that we cannot see the divine blessing in the opportunities for doing good which the Lord graciously puts into our way. What plans have you made for this year? only business plans, labor plans, pleasure plans, in a word secular plans? Have you planned nothing of what you would do in building the kingdom of God, in aiding your own congregation and its work, in helping the poor and needy, in a word in utilizing your spiritual opportunities? All these will of themselves make you think of God and keep you in touch with him and his will, whereas all mere worldly plans lead the heart away from God.

It was a heathen emperor who one evening realized, that the day had passed without his having granted a favor to any-one, and then exclaimed: I have lost a day! But a Christian's duty extends much farther: he must do good in every direction known to him. For him to see the opportunity and not to use it, is sin. But it would be a mistake for us now to strain after single instances of doing good, now this act, now that one, with the fear that one might escape us. Our hearts must belong to Christ so completely that we naturally hear and obey his voice in all things; even as Luther describes faith — it is so active and devoted that before the command is given it has already performed the work and is ready for the next.

"All such glorying is evil." The patience of God may bear with us. Even though we do not thank him he may continue to give us life, health, strength, and allow us to use them for our own purpose. But the whole course is evil and leads to no good results. Our glorying in our own independence, wisdom, and success is hollow after all. Many things will occur to show us that after all we are not independent, that we make many foolish decisions, that our desired success proves a disappointment in the end, or a failure in spite of our skill and effort. But the worst of it all is that such glorying leaves the poor soul naked and wretched, deceives it miserably while life lasts, and when its brief breath is about to vanish sends the soul into eternity empty of all true treasure and abiding possession. — Therefore let our prayer and desire be that of the Psalmist: "Remember me, O Lord, with the favor that thou bearest unto thy people: O visit me with thy salvation; that I may see the good of thy chosen, that I may rejoice in the gladness of thy nation, that *I may glory with thine inheritance.*" Ps. 106, 4-5. "Glory ye in his holy name." Ps. 105, 3. So also the prophet calls to us: "Thus saith the Lord, Let not the wise man glory in his wisdom, neither let the mighty man glory in his might, let not the rich man glory in his riches: but let him that glorieth glory in this, that he understandeth and knoweth me, that I am the Lord which exercise loving kindness, judgment, and righteousness, in the earth: for in these things I delight, saith the Lord." Jer. 9, 23-24. And the apostle likewise: "He that glorieth, let him glory in the Lord." 1 Cor. 1, 31; 2 Cor. 10, 17. "But far be it from me to glory, save in the cross of our Lord Jesus Christ, through which the world hath been crucified unto me and I unto the world." Gal. 6, 14.

The Lord and the Course of our Earthly Life.

I. *If the Lord will* (humbly).
II. *As the Lord will* (courageously).
III. *What the Lord will* (devotedly).

Adapted from Rump.

Our Motto for the New Year: If the Lord Will.

I. *An admonition against pride in ourselves.*
II. *A consolation in resignation to God.*
III. *An inspiration for courage in all good works.*

Adapted from A. Matthes

The Resolutions that Lie in The Word: If the Lord Will.

I. *Let us realize humbly our helplessness.*
II. *Let us learn wholly to depend on God.*
III *Let us strive earnestly to do the Lord's will.*

"Ye Are a Vapor."

I. *It is true.*
II. *It must kill our pride.*
III. *It ought to turn our hearts unto God.*   (Ps. 103, 13-18.)

Make a Prayer of the Word, If the Lord Will.

I. *Lord, since thou wilt.*
II. *Lord, as long as thou wilt.*
III. *Lord, only what thou wilt.*

Caspari.

Your Net Gain in the New Year.

I. *If you depend on yourself.*
II. *If you depend on the Lord.*

THE EPIPHANY CYCLE.

THE EPIPHANY CYCLE.

The Epiphany Festival to Sixth Sunday after Epiphany.

The Eisenach gospels for the Epiphany cycle present the ancient Epiphany theme, namely *Jesus showing himself as the divine Savior*. For further details see the author's *Eisenach Gospel Selections*, vol. 1, p. 192 etc. This general theme of the gospel lessons is utilized also for the Epistle lessons, as the controlling text, the one for the Epiphany festival, clearly shows. Here Paul declares: We preach *Christ Jesus as Lord, i. e.* as the Savior, not ourselves. But this general theme is necessarily modified in the epistle texts after the manner of the epistolary writings of the apostles. No special historical incidents are presented showing us the way in which Christ manifested himself as the Savior; this is altogether the part of the gospels. But Christ is revealed as the divine Savior in the general way in which this revelation takes place now since he has ascended on high and sent forth his Gospel for the salvation of men. A glance at the Epiphany festival text shows this; Paul writes of "the light of the gospel of the glory of Christ, who is the image of God," and declares: "We preach" this Christ as Lord, and testifies that God "shined in our hearts, to give the light of the knowledge of the glory of God in the face of Jesus Christ." *The Epiphany of Christ as it proceeds now in the hearts of men through his Word* is therefore the epistolary theme of our cycle.

In seven luminous rays this great theme is unfolded. The central one is the text for the Epiphany festival itself, which is most like the gospel texts in that it rivets our attention in a marked manner upon Christ himself. The general theme of the text is: *The Epiphany light, Christ in his glorious Gospel, shines in the hearts of believers.*

This is followed by a text which shows us that they who have received the Epiphany light must ever be separated from the darkness of Belial and unbelief. The figure of Christ still stands in the foreground, and all in whose hearts he shines are described as the people of God, his sons and daughters, who cannot be joined together with unbelievers. The general theme of this text in the Epiphany series is: *All they who have seen the Epiphany light are separated from the darkness of this world.*

The third text speaks of wisdom instead of light, "even the wisdom that hath been hidden, which God foreordained before the worlds unto our glory." It centers in the crucified Lord of glory, and is revealed unto us through the Spirit. Here too the objective and the subjective elements go hand in hand. We may formulate as the general theme of the text: *All they who have seen the Epiphany light have received the eternal saving wisdom of God.*

The central thought of the fourth text is evidently the declaration that the Gospel is the power of God unto salvation, since therein is revealed the righteousness of God by faith unto faith. Or, in briefer form: "The just shall live by faith." The text otherwise speaks of Jews, Greeks, and barbarians, and shows the latter two especially as sunken altogether in unrighteousness, and without excuse. So we sum up this text in the statement: *All who have seen the Epiphany light have found the righteousness that delivers from sin and condemnation.*

The fifth text deals with the law and its mission to reveal sin and makes it exceedingly sinful and intolerable for the sinner. It describes the painful experience of the apostle Paul in detail, so as to show us what our experience must be to-day. This text, at first glance, seems least like an Epiphany text, but we see its importance and bearing when we note that: *All who have seen the Epiphany light have experienced the painful work of the law.*

The sixth text is an evident companion to the fifth, taken from the very next chapter of Romans. It shows the believer free from condemnation, walking not after the flesh, but after the spirit. It is a fine text on the essentials of sanctification (in the narrower sense). It proclaims: *All who have seen the Epiphany light, walk in the spirit.*

The final text sets before us the hope that is ours who have no veil before our faces, but reflect as a mirror the glory of the Lord. *All who have seen the Epiphany light are transformed from glory to glory.*

In preaching on these texts it is imperative that we keep in mind their definite trend, and hold fast throughout the Epiphany idea. Christ is revealing himself now as the Savior, and he does this in us. He shines in our hearts by the light of the Gospel, and does for us all that these texts say. In the measure in which this is accomplished in us we now have what once they had who beheld Christ's Epiphany in the days of his flesh.

THE EPIPHANY FESTIVAL.

2 Cor. 4, 3-6.

· The Epiphany features of this text are so marked that the preacher must see them at once. We are told of "the light of the gospel of the glory of Christ, who is the image of God," of the apostles who "preach Christ Jesus as Lord," and of God "that said, Light shall shine out of darkness, who shined in our hearts, to give the light of the knowledge of the glory of God in the face of Jesus Christ." All this imagery of light, shining, and glory, and its counterpart, gospel, preaching, and knowledge, is highly befitting the day. As in the beginning God said: Let there be light! so now in this Epiphany festival and season the saving light that has appeared in Jesus Christ breaks forth and shines in full radiance amid the darkness. Some, indeed, do not see it, they who are "blinded," and will not let the light heal them. The preacher, however, will not put them forward unduly on this day. Light, shining, glory, as also Gospel, preaching, and knowledge imply darkness, shadow, shame, and conditions which require the saving power which Christ brings, and these the sermon must treat; but it will suffice to touch but briefly those who harden themselves in unbelief and thus perish eternally.

The text is quite brief, comprising not even one entire paragraph. There are three general thoughts, according to the three subjects of the main sentences: the first concerning those who perish because of blindness and unbelief; the second concerning the apostles and their preaching of Christ; the third concerning God and the light he bids shine in our hearts.

190

Concerning those who perish because of blindness and unbelief.

St. Paul comes to speak to those who reject his preaching and the Gospel of Christ, because the objection was raised, that when he called the Gospel "the manifestation of the truth," it could not be such a manifestation (φανέρωσις), since many failed to see it. This argument is still used today. The heathen may say to the missionary: If your Gospel is really such a good thing, why do not all your own people accept it? Skeptics and unbelievers object: The number of those who see nothing in the Gospel is greater than of those who see everything in it; hence the claim of St. Paul and other Gospel preachers is unfounded. Here our text makes direct and telling answer: **But and if our gospel is veiled, it is veiled in them that are perishing.** The fact that the Gospel is veiled to many is fully admitted; for this reason ἐστίν is put forward. The sense is: If our gospel is veiled, and it is indeed veiled (namely in certain people). The Gospel here signifies Paul's entire preaching of Christ as the Savior of the world. He calls it τό εὐαγγέλιον ἡμῶν, not because of any special form or peculiarity of his own preaching, a so-called Pauline type of Gospel, but because of his possessing the ministry to which the preaching of the Gospel was committed. He is dealing with his own work of preaching, and the rejection which he himself has experienced. And his experience is, of course, shared by every preacher of the Gospel: some hearers always reject this message. — He says that his Gospel is **veiled,** κεκαλυμμένον (perfect participle). The word implies that the Gospel is really a light sending forth strong radiance; nothing has happened to the light itself, it is not dimmed, it has not lost any of its radiant power. But a veil has been interposed between it and certain people. And the image of the veil is used because of what Paul has just written in the previous chapter (3, 12-16), namely that he and his fellow preachers are not like Moses who veiled his countenance, but they speak forth with boldness, in an

unveiled way; only the Jews always have a veil lying upon
their hearts when they read the Gospel words of Moses and
the O. T.   What Paul thus said of the Jews he extends
now to the rejecters of the Gospel generally: the light of the
Gospel is shut out from them by an evil veil. — Who are
these people?   **They that are perishing;** ἐν τοῖς ἀπολλυμένοις
ἐστὶν κεκαλυμμένον.   The preposition ἐν means "among."   What
a pitiable lot of people these ἀπολλύμενοι, the perishing, are,
they who are in that act now, going to eternal perdition.
Paul would say: Indeed, some do reject the Gospel, but
do you see who they are, the most pitiable people on earth,
the perishing? think of that before you say anything more.
— But he makes further explanation, where this veil of
the perishing comes from.   It is not placed before their
hearts by God.   There is no mysterious will or decree of
God which shuts some men out from the light of the Gospel.   Nor is the Gospel a two-faced thing, coming with
saving power to some, and coming to others without that
power, only as an empty sound.   In a way all men by nature
are in the way of perishing, because all are sinners, and the
wages of sin is eternal death.   But Paul thinks here only
of those who, by rejecting the divine rescue and salvation
offered in the Gospel, actually do reach eternal perdition.
His explanation is in regard to them alone, and he declares
their destruction to be due to the devil: **in whom the god
of this world hath blinded the minds of the unbelieving.**
Ἐν οἷς parallels ἐν τοῖς ἀπολλυμένοις; no ὅτι, because, or anything else, need be supplied. · Paul states a simple fact,
namely that Satan blinded their minds; this fact is, of
course, a reason and meant as such, but it is stated only in
the form of a fact, and is thus very effective for the reader.
The god of this world is Satan, "the prince of this world,"
John 12, 31; 14, 30, *simia Dei* (Calov), the chief of the
κοσμόκραται, "the world-rulers," Eph. 6, 12.   Αἰών is "age",
or "world" in respect to the time of its duration.   **This
world,** ὁ αἰὼν οὗτος, as distinguished from the world to come,
is always viewed in its ungodliness and opposition to God.
And in this sense Satan is called "the god of this world,"

as he is the author of all the ungodliness and evil that is in it, and directs it as the supreme ruler of all evil. One of the worst of these evil works of his is here described, namely his blinding the minds of men. It is not necessary that one should consciously consent to his control and realize what it signifies and involves; it is enough that he does actually rule, and that one obey him. And we must understand fully and hold fast what is thus stated, for deception in this matter is exceedingly great. Men will deny the existence of the devil the while they are ruled by him; or they imagine themselves their own masters, while they are nothing but Satan's dupes and slaves. Let all men know: they who reject the Gospel reject God and accept the devil — there is no middle way. — His activity is here described as a blinding: ἐτύφλωσεν τὰ νοήματα τῶν ἀπίστων, **hath blinded the minds of the unbelieving.** "This control of Satan over the human mind, although so effectual, is analogous to the influence of one created intellect over another in other cases, and therefore is perfectly consistent with free agency and responsibility. It should, however, make us feel our danger and need of divine assistance, seeing that we have to contend not only against the influence of evil men, but against the far more powerful influence of the rulers of darkness, the pantocrators of the world. Eph. 6, 12." Hodge. The blinding here spoken of takes place when the Gospel comes to men in order to enlighten them unto salvation. It is then that the devil tries in every way to put a veil between their "minds" (or *thoughts* — margin) and the Gospel light; so that they either conceive Christ in a false way altogether and empty his work of that which really saves, or that they reject him altogether because of some vain philosophy of their own or because of worldly considerations. In the verb τυφλοῦν the figure of the veil is intensified; now the eyes themselves lose the power of sight. By nature all indeed are blind, but the Gospel is the eye-salve to give sight to the blind. The devil's work is to fill the mind with lies and deceptions of one kind or another,

13

so as permanently to counteract this eye-salve and prevent it from exerting its salutary effects; and this is the blinding here spoken of. — In whom he hath blinded the minds **of the unbelieving** is a pleonasm grammatically, the sentence appearing to be complete without the added genitive. Τῶν ἀπίστων is not an apposition to ἐν οἷς, although the common explanation treats it as virtually such. Meyer thinks the ἄπιστοι are more numerous than the ἀπολλύμενοι, and that the blinding work which Satan does in all the unbelieving reaches its fatal effect only in the perishing, while the rest of the ἄπιστοι finally come to faith. But the entire weight of Paul's argument requires the identity of the perishing with those in whom the Gospel is veiled and who are blinded by Satan, *i. e.* the ἄπιστοι. It is best then to acknowledge the grammatical peculiarity. Paul's meaning is entirely clear. Ἐν οἷς merely refers back to the ἀπολλύμενοι without in any way characterizing these people. This characterization the added genitive supplies: they are "unbelieving." In them Satan indeed has full sway, to blind them with his deceptions and thus to work their destruction. The question has been raised, which is first, the blinding or the unbelief? As to the perishing there is no doubt; that follows unbelief: "He that disbelieveth shall be condemned," Mark 16, 16; "hath been judged already, because he hath not believed on the name of the only begotten Son of God," John 3, 18. As between the blinding and the unbelief, it is best to take the former as the cause of the whole evil: the blinding of the devil makes unbelievers who finally perish. The aorist ἐτύφλωσεν describes Satan's work as one complete past act, whatever stages it may have had; his victims have been fatally blinded, rendered unresponsive even to the sight-giving power of the Gospel, and are now become miserable ἀπολλύμενοι, men in the act of perishing. — **That the light of the gospel of the glory of Christ, who is the image of God, should not dawn** *upon them.* Εἰς τό expresses both the purpose and the result, or the purpose attained. The devil's purpose was that the light of the Gospel should not penetrate

his victims' hearts, and this he achieved. — It is best to read
τὸν φωτισμόν as the subject of αὐγάσαι, and not as the object,
which latter would require αὐτούς to be supplied in thought
as the subject. The reference has been to the minds of the
unbelieving, and αὐγάζειν in its transitive meaning (*bestrah-
len*, to let radiance fall upon) is less fitting in this connection
than the intransitive meaning (*strahlen*, to shine, to dawn)
with the light of the Gospel as the subject. Luther indeed
translates: *dass sie nicht sehen das helle Licht des Evan-
gelii;* and the margin translates: *that they should not see the
light.* But the text of the A. as well as of the R. V. is best.
Ὁ φωτισμός is **light,** radiance, *illumination* (margin), used
only here in the N. T., but a word that goes exceedingly well
with **the gospel of the glory of Christ.** The Gospel indeed
has a glory, and this glory has light and radiance which
shines forth. By the glory of the Gospel is meant "the sum
of all the divine and human excellence which is centered in
Christ's person, and makes him the radiant point in the
universe, the clearest manifestation of God to his creatures,
the object of supreme admiration, adoration, and love, to all
intelligent beings, and especially to his saints." Hodge. The
light of this Gospel can, of course, never be dimmed; the
devil cannot hurt the Gospel itself or rob it of one bit of its
glory or one ray of its light. But he can prevent this light
from dawning, *i. e.* from spreading itself in the minds of
certain men. And this he has done and does in all those who
perish. They remain in darkness, while the light is there and
God desires that they too should be enlightened thereby.
That these men fail to be enlightened is nothing to the dis-
credit either of the Gospel or of the preachers of the Gospel
(Paul here, and others also). To think so, or to argue so,
as did some of Paul's opponents, is to cast reproach upon
God and Christ himself. — For Paul reminds us that Christ
is the image of God. He means what Jesus said, John
14, 9: "He that hath seen me hath seen the Father;" and
John 12, 45: "He that beholdeth me beholdeth him that sent
me." Christ is in the form of God and equal with God,
Phil. 2, 6, "the effulgence of his glory, and the very image

of his substance," Heb. 1, 3.   The word **image** here refers
to the exalted Christ; the Godman on the throne of glory is
the essential image of the Father.   In him now shines forth
forever all the Father's love for us, and in him we behold
all that that love hath wrought for our salvation.   To have
the light of his Gospel dawn in our hearts (by faith) is to be
saved.   God created man in his own image and after his likeness (*i. e.* in true holiness and righteousness), but Christ is
that image himself, equal with the Father and yet revealing
him to men.   The medium for this is the Gospel, hence called
properly "the gospel of the glory of Christ."   To be shut
out from that is to be eternally lost.

Concerning the apostles and their preaching of Christ.

Paul has spoken in verse 3 of "our gospel," which
some assailed, and he has set forth the true excellence of
that Gospel as "the gospel of the glory of Christ, who
is the image of God."   Now he combines both and emphasizes the combination: Whoever rejects his preaching, rejects the blessed and glorious Christ himself:
For we preach not ourselves, but Christ Jesus as Lord.
No doubt Paul's opponents insinuated that he preached
himself, which means that his preaching had for its real
purpose his own personal interest, honor, influence, *etc.*
This he emphatically denies; also 1 Cor. 10, 33: "not seeking mine own profit."   There were in Corinth "certain that
commend themselves," 2 Cor. 10, 12.   There are some
such to-day.   At bottom in all their ministry they are concerned about their own standing, welfare, advancement,
social position, financial profit, *etc.*   They so shape their
Gospel that all men may speak well of them; they are
afraid to offend, and omit unpopular doctrines, or modify
them to suit public opinion; even when they do preach
Christ their message is warped and emasculated.   This
danger of looking to ourselves threatens all preachers to
some extent.   We are all liable to consider too much our
personal interest, to attach people too much to ourselves,

to make their attachment to the preacher the criterion of their attachment to Christ. Let us take warning lest in some subtle way we preach ourselves. According to the context ἑαυτοὺς κηρύσσομεν might be taken in the sense of ἑαυτοὺς κυρίους κηρύσσομεν, but the statement is entirely general and not thus to be modified. — Not ourselves do we preach, **but Christ Jesus as Lord.** That was the sum and substance of all apostolic preaching. The statement is a pregnant one, like 1 Cor. 1, 23: "We preach Christ crucified;" and 1 Cor. 2, 2: "For I determined not to know anything among you save Jesus Christ, and him crucified." Κύριον might be a simple apposition to Χριστὸν Ἰησοῦν (so Bachmann), but the R. V. makes it a predicative accusative: **as Lord,** which is decidedly preferable. To read "Christ Jesus the Lord" distributes the emphasis over the entire phrase; to read: "Christ Jesus as Lord (= that he is Lord) centers the emphasis on the final word "Lord." This is more in line with Paul's argument, in which he has already referred to Christ as the center of the Gospel. Now he declares that he preaches this Christ, and preaches him "as Lord," *i. e.* in all his saving power and grace. The term is used here in its widest sense; Meyer: *Ist in seiner ganzen Allgemeinheit zu belassen.* This commentator sees "the entire majesty of Christ" in it. Following the Scriptures themselves we may combine the following elements as belonging to Christ's Lordship: "He is Lord of all," Acts 10, 36; "the Lord of glory," 1 Cor. 2, 8; "the Lord our righteousness," Jer. 23, 6; "the lord of the sabbath," Matth. 12, 8. Paul's preaching too is not a mere saying. "Lord, Lord," Matth. 7, 21, so that while he says it, he "does not the things which I (the Lord) say," Luke 6, 46, or allows others to ignore the Lord's commands. He preached Christ as the Lord in all faith, in sincerity and truth, proclaiming "the whole counsel of God" unto human salvation. To preach Christ as Lord means then to proclaim him as the Messiah of God, the divine Savior, the ruler of the Kingdom. Here Paul shows the greatness and glory of his office, and all preachers of the Gospel share

it with him. Let us thank God who has counted us worthy
to be heralds (κηρύσσομεν) of the "Lord." — But Paul has
referred to himself, and so he is led to place beside the
negative statement already made the positive one: **and**
(we preach in a certain sense) **ourselves** (namely) **as your
servants for Jesus' sake.** The thing cannot be avoided.
Whoever brings the Lord to others, in and by that very
act brings himself to them in a certain manner; he makes
himself their servant (*bondservant,* margin) for Jesus'
sake. This true position of himself as an apostle and
preacher Paul gladly acknowledged; in fact, he emphasized
it frequently, so that people might know and receive him
accordingly: "For though I was free from all men, I
brought myself under bondage to all, that I might gain
the more," 1 Cor. 9, 19. "Not that we have lordship over
your faith, but are helpers of your joy," 2 Cor. 1, 24.
"Servants of Christ Jesus," δοῦλοι, Phil. 1, 1; Tit. 1, 1.
The term δοῦλος here corresponds to the preceding κύριος;
it is very strong, signifying complete servitude. In the first
place Paul, and every preacher, is a servant of Christ or
God; but for that very reason also a servant of others,
δοῦλος ὑμῶν, "a debtor both to Greeks and to Barbarians,
both to the wise and to the foolish," Rom. 1, 14. The connection between this double servitude Paul expresses by
the phrase: **for Jesus' sake,** διὰ Ἰησοῦν, not; *through Jesus,*
διὰ Ἰησοῦ (margin), which is less well authenticated. "For
Jesus' sake" = because we are wholly devoted to him in
love and service. This is the mainspring of every true
preacher's work, which moves him to face unflinchingly
whatever hardship, sacrifice, or suffering his office may
entail. The designation "servant" (minister) is not to
the liking of worldly men who prefer grand (even if
empty) titles, pomp, power, and honor. And there have
been little popes even in the church, who, instead of serving,
tried to make themselves lords of other men's faith, 2 Cor.
1, 24, lording it over the charge allotted unto them, 1 Pet.
5, 3. But Paul was far from such notions. Having so
grand a Master, he could, and did indeed, assert himself

and his authority in the servant position assigned to him, lest the Master's interests suffer; and yet in this as in all else he faithfully kept to his office and work as a δοῦλος, both κυρίου and ὑμῶν.

Concerning God and the light that shines in our hearts.

The sixth verse is the climax of our Epiphany text and contains the heart of the Epiphany message: ὁ θεὸς . . . ἔλαμψεν ἐν ταῖς καρδίαις ἡμῶν. The negative thought of the preceding verses when the unbelieving were spoken of, now becomes gloriously positive since believers form the topic. **Seeing it is God, that said, Light shall shine out of darkness, who shined in our hearts, to give the light of the knowledge of the glory of God in the face of Jesus Christ.** Paul furnishes a reason for what he has just said before: ὅτι, *etc.* But hardly for the secondary thought that he and his fellow laborers are servants of the Corinthians. Greater matters are under discussion, to which this thought is merely incidental, namely that Paul preaches the Gospel which some do not believe, that he and others with him preach Jesus Christ as Lord. For this he now furnishes an all-sufficient reason: "God shined in our hearts." And this reason is the more noteworthy and striking, because it shows that the very God and Gospel whose light some repel through the influence of the devil have actually performed their beneficent work in others, namely Paul and his fellow believers. Their hearts are bright with the knowledge of the glory of God in the face of Jesus Christ, where others have preferred darkness; and they, having experienced this divine enlightenment, are proclaiming this Christ to others. The subject ὁ θεός has no verb, and the sentence appears unfinished. 'Εστί is supplied: **Seeing it is God, etc.** To put the verb in this place (which makes the smoothest rendering in English) tends to place the emphasis on God, as if Paul meant that he and no other has done this. Yet the emphasis, we must observe, really rests on the relative clause: "who shined in our hearts," and we must so read the translation. The A. V. cancels the relative pronoun ὅς, for which there is no justification, although the general sense of the sentence is not changed thereby. — Paul draws a parallel between the first great act of creation and this second creative work of God. The parallel is the more wonderful since the second creative act is here spoken of as just as great as the first, or even greater. What a blow to those who despise the light of, Christ and the Gospel! **God, that said, Light shall shine out of darkness** restates the words of Moses, Gen. 1, 3. We must read λάμψει, future indicative, not as in the A. V. λάμψαι, aorist infinitive. "Out of darkness" vividly pictures the first blazing forth of light from the darkness that covered the face of the deep. All at once in its very heart there was a mighty radiance spreading afar in every direction, making day where night had been. This was no gradual evolution, requiring ages for its accomplishment, but an instantaneous act; there are no possible gradations between the σκότος and the φῶς. — As on the first day of creation, so now: it is God who **shined in our hearts.** We too were utter darkness and night, "a people that walked in darkness . . . that dwell in the land of the shadow of death," Is. 9, 2. "For ye were once darkness, but are now light in the Lord," Eph. 5, 8. But here too, in this higher realm of the spirit and soul of man, the stupendous miracle was wrought: the light shone forth — and God was the light. "Thou art the health of my countenance, and my God," Ps. 42, 11. If it is wondrous beyond human conception that the night brooding over chaos should suddenly be rent asunder by the bursting forth of light, it is more wondrous still that the spiritual night of sin and death should be hurled back by the breaking forth of spiritual light. And yet it is not wondrous — for God is here, and he himself fills our hearts, and thus they shine with light. Luther finely expounds our text and refutes all synergistic notions of self-illumination on man's part: "We believe in the God who is an almighty Creator, able to make everything out of nothing, good out

of what is evil, salvation and blessedness out of what is
utterly corrupt and lost. Even as in Rom. 4, 17, this is
ascribed to him, where Paul says: 'He calleth the things
that are not, as though they were;' and 2 Cor. 4, 6: 'God
that said, Light shall shine out of darkness.' He does not
say, a spark from the coal, but light out of darkness. Even
so he is able to bring forth life out of death, righteousness
out of sin, and the kingdom of heaven and the liberty of
the children of God out of the servitude of the devil and
hell." Yet the Calvinists err when they argue for an
irresistible grace, declaring: just as little as chaos could
prevent the bursting forth of light, so little can he whom
God means to save prevent the creation of faith in his
heart. Paul has just shown that men can and do remain
in blindness, and perish, through the devil's work and their
own fault. "O Israel, thou hast destroyed thyself; but in
me is thine help," Hos. 13, 9. "God does not force man
to become godly, for those who resist the Holy Ghost and
persistently oppose the known truth, as Stephen says of
the hardened Jews, Acts 7, 51, will not be converted; yet
God the Lord draws the man whom he wishes to convert,
and draws him, too, in such a way that his understanding,
in place of being darkened, becomes enlightened, and his
will, in place of perverse, becomes obedient. And the
Scriptures call this 'creating a new heart', Ps. 51, 10."
Formula of Concord, 564, 60. In regard to the creation
of light on the first day and the creation of spiritual light
in conversion Calov writes: "The power is the same in
both instances, but the mode of its operation is not the
same. Man who is to be converted is fleshly and dead because he lacks the good ability of cooperating in his conversion, not because of any lack of evil ability to resist
the converting will of God." And we must add: the
irrational creature yields to God's power without a will
of its own, but man yields when God by his grace has
wrought a change in his will. — **To give light,** πρὸς φωτισμόν,
really reads in the Greek: "unto illumination." And it is
not the **knowledge** that is illuminated: πρὸς φωτισμόν τῆς

γνώσεως; but the illumination is the knowledge itself. Φωτισμός is not transitive, as if Paul meant to say: God shined in our hearts πρὸς φωτισμόν, *i. e.* in order through us to illumine others (so Luther's translation; Meyer, and some others). All believers attain light in the same way: ὁ θεὸς . . . ἔλαμψεν ἐν ταῖς καρδίαις, God shined in their hearts. Φωτισμός is intransitive, and πρός indicates in what God's shining in their hearts results, namely in "light," or illumination of knowledge. And this word γῶσις, **knowledge,** points distinctly to the means by which God comes to shine in our hearts, namely by the Gospel which gives us the knowledge that saves; and this knowledge is faith, since it is the knowledge **of the glory of God in the face of Jesus Christ.** By the "glory of God" which our hearts apprehend by the heavenly knowledge of faith, is meant all his excellence, especially his grace, mercy, and love "in the face of Jesus Christ," *i. e.* as manifested in Christ. For this reason God by the Gospel shines in our hearts, that our hearts may be filled with this knowledge of his excellencies as they were revealed in Jesus and all his work. The heaped-up genitives: "of the knowledge of the glory of God," have a heavy sound, as Meyer states, but exhibit something grand and majestic. The parallel between the creation of the natural and that of the spiritual light extends even to the divine means by which both are accomplished. God said, Let there be light! It is also by his Word that the light of salvation radiates in the soul. "All things were made by him" (the Word); "and without him was not anything made that hath been made," John 1, 3. Likewise as regards our hearts and salvation: "There was the true light," namely Jesus, "even the light which lighteth every man," John 1, 9. "And in none other is there salvation: for neither is there any other name under heaven, that is given among men, wherein we must be saved," Acts 4, 12.

HOMILETICAL HINTS.

The celebration of Christ's birth at Christmas time is followed by the Epiphany festival which draws attention to his earthly sojourn, when he revealed his divine glory to men for their salvation. This is the revelation our text sets before us, making the central thought of the entire Epiphany season the shining forth of Christ's glory as the Savior of mankind.

Johann Rump preaches in Bremen, Germany, a city notorious for its ultra liberal preachers who have completely destroyed the heart of the Gospel in all their teaching. In his festival sermon on our text Rump raises the pertinent questions: What about this Gospel that we hold fast with so much opposition in our own city? What is there in it that causes so much divergence of thought, so much conflict and contention? Are we not perhaps after all mistaken as to its value? They number ten thousands in our own city who smile at this Gospel as a useless thing, and only a few thousands praise it thankfully as the power of God. What have we to say to this numerical comparison, except that we must abandon our position and give up this Gospel? Majorities have immense weight in our day when the masses rule. What about the Gospel in the human heart? This last question is Rump's theme and he answers it from the words of St. Paul, much like this apostle met the very same ideas among the people at Corinth almost 1900 years ago.

Who has the most enemies to-day? We all agree as to the answer — Jesus, our Redeemer. — The Gospel is veiled and hidden for those who are on the road to perdition and determined not to forsake it. — Enmity against the Gospel of Christ is by no means a modern achievement, the result of tremendous progress in a modern age, the fruit of the latest scientific knowledge which has left previous ages far behind. This notion is a vain delusion intended to impress the ignorant who neither read their Bibles nor know the records of history. Enmity against God and his Word is as old as God's Word itself, and the first and greatest representative of this enmity is the devil who is a liar and murderer from the beginning. — It has been reserved for our time, with its elevation of man to the highest degree of culture, to degrade him morally to the level of the beast. Our age is busy cancelling one moral law of God after another. Follow your own nature, however depraved, is the wisdom that is now preached by philosophy and science. And the result is that many of the old heathen vices are again receiving public endorsement, and corruption is rampant in all departments of society.

Yes, the Gospel is veiled for those who are carried away by the spirit of our age. It is veiled by its "miracles," which our science and philosophy cannot see its way to admit; by its blood-atonement which modern superficial views of sin resent; by its great doctrines of the Trinity, the two natures of Christ, regeneration, and justification, the sacramental mysteries, and other great teachings, which our rationalizing age cannot comprehend, and therefore derides and spurns. The Christ which the lying Rabbis in Corinth and elsewhere in Paul's mission fields preached to their deluded followers was much more comprehensible and acceptable to them than this Christ which Paul proclaimed. And to-day the empty theology of many a pulpit has likewise invented a Christ of its own, stripped of the divine nature, decked out with ideal human excellencies, turned into a mere moral teacher, a great reformer, a model for our following. And this Christ is more agreeable to many than Immanuel, the Virgin's son, in whom we see the Father, more believable than the Lamb of God, the heavenly ransom for the world's sin, more adorable than the Conqueror of death, the grave, and hell, sitting at God's right hand as King of kings and Lord of lords. And so the Gospel is hid, for they have taken all the Savior glories away from Christ, and covered him with the filthy rags of their own imaginings. — The simple Gospel does not satisfy the sensational cravings of many, and so they pronounce judgment upon it. Indeed, a judgment is in order, but upon these blind judges who crown falsehood and exile truth.— Dare the blind accuse the sun that it lacks light?

"Arise, shine; for thy light is come, and the glory of the Lord is risen upon thee. For, behold, the darkness shall cover the earth, and gross darkness the people; but the Lord shall rise upon thee, and his glory shall be seen upon thee. And the Gentiles shall come to thy light, and kings to the brightness of thy rising." What is our text but a glorious New Testament repetition of this old Epiphany epistle from Isaiah's pen. Indeed, the light is come: God hath shined in our hearts through Jesus Christ.

We preach Christ Jesus as Lord, nothing self-invented, self-chosen, skillfully designed and fabricated by our wisdom. We preach him whom Paul gladly followed till he met a martyr's death, whom John worshipped and glorified through all his long life, whom Luther proclaimed anew amid the papal night, whom thousands of faithful confessors, both small and great, have carried in their hearts, whom now the souls of just men made perfect honor on his heavenly throne, before whom at last every knee shall bow, and every tongue confess that Jesus Christ is Lord, to the glory of God the Father. — Not in a thousand years has a single man found peace and hope for his immortal soul save in Jesus Christ our Lord. — Against the wanton enticements of sin and the octopus tentacles of doubt there is no power of rescue, save the power of Jesus Christ.

"The Church is above the ministers." Smalcald Articles, 340, 11. — They are in the office of love, which makes them every man's servants for Jesus' sake. Worldly wisdom makes its bearers and promulgators lords of others. The desire to rule and the claim to superior honor are found in every department of intellectual activity when men of special talents appear. But the greatest preachers of the Gospel have put away all thought of self-aggrandizement and have made themselves the servants of others.

Hunnius writes: In Christ the unfathomable mercy of God has revealed itself to us, and through Christ the divine wisdom of God has completed and realized the adorable counsel of salvation.

Some admonitions naturally attach themselves · to our text. Thus one preacher writes: Words are but short sermons. Deeds make an impression and exert an influence. Let men see in our words and deeds what the Gospel is to us. — And another: Whenever faith and discipline suffer, let us withdraw. Where scoffers sit and mocking words are spoken we must forego association and friendship.

No society, no undertaking, which tends to alienate from God and faith, dare receive our support or even our silent approval. No desire to please men and cowardly consideration of self dare move us to assent to anything that will hurt the souls of others. — Someone has well said: I cannot hear your (fair) words for the noise you make by your (evil) deeds!

The Great Epiphany Light: Christ in His Glorious Gospel.

I. *It is the light indeed.*

    1) God sent Christ as the Sun of Righteousness.

    2) Christ is the light of salvation for the sinful world.

    3) In the Gospel the radiance of this light shines forth.

II. *It shines in our hearts.*

    1) The Gospel has wrought faith in our hearts.

    2) We have become the children of light.

    3) We rejoice in the blessed change.

    4) Nor can we ever turn to darkness again.

III. *It is kept out of some only because they love darkness more.*

    1) We would expect all men to fly to the light and drink it in, but many do not.

    2) The god of this world has blinded their minds, and they wilfully resist the power of the light.

3) They perish, but without God's or the Gospel's fault.
4) Warning and admonition: the devil has not given us up, but seeks to throw us into darkness again; God does not give up the lovers of darkness until his last effort is made, nor must we cease shedding forth the Gospel light.

"Let all the house of Israel therefore know assuredly, that God hath made him *both Lord and Christ,* this Jesus whom ye crucified." Acts 2, 36.

"The word which he sent unto the children of Israel, preaching good tidings of peace by *Jesus Christ (he is Lord of all)*— that saying ye yourselves know." Acts 10, 36.

"Wherefore I give you to understand, that no man speaking in the Spirit of God saith, Jesus is anathema; and no man can say, *Jesus is Lord,* but in the Holy Spirit." 1 Cor. 12, 3.

We Preach Christ Jesus As Lord.

I. *The light of his glory shines in the Gospel.* (Whether men believe it or not. Verse 4.)
II. *The light of the knowledge of his glory shines in our hearts.* (By faith. Verse 6.)

How Jesus, the Epiphany Light, Illumines the World.

I. *God sent forth his Son, and there was light.*
II. *God gave the light into the hearts of chosen witnesses, and these were bearers of the light.*
III. *God blessed the work of his chosen witnesses, and there was a kingdom of light.*

The Bright Radiance of the Gospel.

I. *It emanates from God.*
  a) The creation miracle, Gen. 1, 3.
  b) The redemption miracle, John 1, 9.

II. *It enters our hearts.*
  a) As the morning, Is. 58, 8.
  b) As the full noon-day, in the face of Jesus Christ, verse 6 of the text.

III. *It encompasses the world.*
  a) The apostolic mission.
  b) The mission work to-day.

Boy.

The Epiphany Fiat: Let There Be Light!

I. *Christ shines forth.*
II. *The darkness is dispelled.*
III. *Thousands walk in the light.*

The Light of the Knowledge of the Glory of God in the Face of Jesus Christ.

I. *It is the light of faith.*
II. *It reveals the glory of God.*
III. *It radiates from the person and work of Jesus Christ.*

THE FIRST SUNDAY AFTER EPIPHANY.

2 Cor. 6, 14 — 7, 1.

In the most natural way the text for this Sunday links itself to the text for the Epiphany festival. If our hearts are illumined by Christ and his Gospel, then there is but one thing for us to do, namely turn ever and always away from the devil's darkness. "Come out from among them, and be ye separate, saith the Lord." It is the thought of the first part of the old epistle for this day: "Be not fashioned according to this world: but be ye transformed by the renewing of your mind," Rom. 12, 2. Our text elaborates this injunction with a wealth of detail and in a dramatic manner which makes it very telling and effective. The divine promise which is woven into the text: "I will dwell with them," etc.; "I will be to you a Father," etc., enriches it with the full Gospel wealth, and makes the call to turn away from everything ungodly exceedingly sweet and attractive. The general theme of the text, especially in its setting in our Epiphany cycle, lies as it were on the surface: *They who have seen the Epiphany light must ever be separate from the darkness and defilement of the world.* — When no service is held on the Epiphany festival proper, the author's advice is to take the festival text itself for the First Sunday after Epiphany, and to shift the remaining text accordingly.* — Our text naturally divides into three sections, coinciding with the three grand sentences of which it is composed. Paul urges all true Christians to be *separate;* he makes them see, that it cannot be otherwise; that it ought not be otherwise; and resolve, that it shall not be otherwise.

*Any Epiphany texts not used for Sunday mornings may be worked, perhaps, for the evening services.

Christians must be separate — it cannot be otherwise.

Paul's questions are highly dramatic, but at the same time they are so many incontrovertible arguments for the great ethical truth he is enunciating, namely that believers must be separate. The argument in these questions is, that being what they are it is impossible for them to live in communion with unbelievers. This separation pertains to everything which concerns the faith. It does not extend to business, political and other secular relations, except when our faith is jeopardized in such relations; then too the interests of our faith must be safeguarded, which may require that we sunder even such relations. **Be not unequally yoked together with unbelievers.** Μὴ γίνεσθε with a participle does not merely emphasize the action indicated in the latter, but expresses also the beginning of that action or the tendency toward it: Do not begin or incline to be unequally yoked together with unbelievers. "Unequally" hardly does justice to the thought of ἑτεροζυγοῦντες, which means yoked together heterogeneously, *viz:* with people alien to us and altogether different from us. The reference here is to Deut. 22, 10, which forbade harnessing up an ox and an ass together to the plow, a clean and an unclean beast. The believer has been cleansed, while the unbeliever has not, and it is wrong to put them together as if this tremendous difference between them did not exist. The verb occurs only here, but its meaning is perfectly plain; ἑτερόζυγος is found in the Septuagint Lev. 19, 19, although there can hardly be a reference here to what this passage forbids. **With unbelievers,** the simple dative ἀπίστοις, is peculiar. The idea expressed is: Do not help unbelievers draw their yoke which is altogether foreign to you. Some call it an ethical dative, and Meyer points out that in this dative the real danger that threatens believers is indicated. They are liable to help others draw a yoke which they should abominate. There is no article with ἀπίστοις, for certain ones are not meant, but unbelievers in general as unbelievers. To think only of

14

heathen people is unwarranted, since in Paul's day the majority of the Jews were just as adverse to Christ and the Gospel as any heathen could be. For the Corinthians there were special dangers in forming wrong associations and cultivating compromising intercourse with the heathen unbelievers surrounding them on all sides; note the reference to "idols" in verse 16. But Paul's injunction is general, applying to unbelievers as unbelievers, no matter who they may be. In applying Paul's command to-day it is simplest and best to consider the varying forms of worldliness of our day and immediate surroundings, all of which are glaringly incompatible with faith and the Christian life. There are so many and such grave and enticing dangers in this regard that the remoter reference to certain false doctrines and practices of erring Christians may well be reserved for treatment under other texts applying to them more directly. Besser, however, introduces here an extensive warning against unionism. Bachmann's translation is very fine: *Tretet nicht in (wesensfremde) Verkoppelung mit Unglaeubigen.*

Already in ἑτεροζυγοῦντες a convincing argument is put forward why believers must be separate; they can be joined together with unbelievers only by becoming ἑτεροζυγοῦντες, people yoked up to a foreign yoke. But the thing is so vitally important for Christians that Paul showers the most destructive blows upon any such unnatural, abnormal, and highly dangerous union. He does this by means of repeated questions whose answers are self-evident. In each of the questions a new and penetrating light is cast upon the ungodly union which would bind together what is really as wide apart as heaven and hell, God and the devil. **For what fellowship have righteousness and iniquity? or what communion hath light with darkness?** The first pair of questions deals with the qualities and powers involved, the second pair with the persons, the governing ones first, and then those governed. In the first question *the inner quality and character* of both believers and unbelievers are placed side by side in glaring contrast. On the one hand there is **righteousness,** δικαιοσύνη, on the other hand "iniquity" ("unrighteousness," A. V.). Some commentators make the latter term the one which marks the distinction, and thus define "righteousness" merely as the opposite of "iniquity." They conclude thus that it is a general ethical concept, referring to the believer's life and conduct. But why go backwards, and why make the negative term the controlling one? The apostle speaks of believers in contrast to unbelievers, and here the distinction "righteousness" marks the Christian's essential characteristic. This righteousness is deeper than action and conduct; it is something objective, as Cremer states; it includes and starts with the imputed righteousness which Paul preached so mightily, and from which alone acquired righteousness (in life and conduct) grows. Thus Paul writes in chapter 5, 21: "That we might become the righteousness of God in him" (Christ). This righteousness of God which we have "become" is here put into opposition to the iniquity of unbelievers. It is, as Besser says, the Christian's chief possession, his regal dignity in God's kingdom. — Unbelievers, on the other hand, are marked by **iniquity,** ἀνομία. Ps. 5, 5: "Thou hatest all workers of iniquity." Opposition to God's law and all that this includes is the shame, the guilt, the doom of unbelievers. Not only are they without Christ's gift of righteousness, which is also the source of all our own righteousness, but the opposite is in them, the evil wellspring of sin and all the stream of bitterness that flows from it. "The mind of the flesh is enmity against God; for it is not subject to the law of God, neither indeed can it be: and they that are in the flesh cannot please God." Rom. 8, 7-8. Any show of righteousness which they may have is nothing but filthy rags (Is. 64, 6), and does not count with God. Civil righteousness, common morality and virtue are ever full of ἀνομία, "without fear of God, without trust in him, and with fleshly appetite," *Augsb. Conf.* II. "Man's will hath some liberty to work a civil righteousness, and to choose such things as reason can reach unto; but it hath no power to work the righteousness of God, or a spiritual righteousness, without the Spirit of God." Art. XVIII. "Ignorance of God, contempt for God, the being destitute of fear and confidence in God, inability to love God. These are the chief faults of human nature, conflicting especially with the first table of the Decalogue," *Apology,* 78, 14, hence the very worst ἀνομία. It is further described (79, 26) as: "The not being able to believe God, the not being able to fear and love God; and, likewise, the having concupiscence which seeks carnal things contrary to God's Word, *i. e.* seeks not only the pleasure of the body, but also carnal wisdom and righteousness, and, contemning God, trusts in these as good things." — These two then, righteousness and iniquity, are as wide apart as the antipodes. Hence they can have no **fellowship,** μετοχή (μετά and ἔχω, to have together with some one). The word occurs only here in the N. T., but we have μέτοχος Heb. 1, 9 and Luke 5, 7. There is no element in righteousness which occurs also in iniquity, or *vice versa;* they mutually exclude each other. And because they do (γάρ), therefore believers and unbelievers must always be separate.

It is the same when we consider what lies back of these two attributes just named, *the powers which produce* righteousness and iniquity: **or what communion hath light with darkness.** The one is light, φῶς. God himself is light, and in him is no darkness at all, 1 John 1, 5; Christ is the true light, John 1, 9, the light of the world, John 8, 12; and his Word is the light of life. This light-power has entered the believer and makes him a child of light, Matth. 5, 14; John 12, 36; Eph. 5, 8, and so the believer walks in the light, John 12, 35-36; 1 John 1, 7, although there is still some darkness in him because his old nature has not been wholly put off. He is also a "partaker of the inheritance of the saints in light," Col. 1, 12. — **Darkness,** σκότος, is the opposite of this light-power. In the beginning God separated the light from the darkness, Gen. 1, 4, and this separation is typical for the spiritual, saving light also. "Ye were once darkness, but are now light in the Lord." Eph. 5, 8. "Have no fellowship with the unfruitful works of darkness, but

rather reprove them." Eph. 5, 11. The devil and his angels
are "the rulers of the darkness of this world." Eph. 6, 12.
All his followers walk in darkness, John 3, 19, and shall at
last be cast into outer darkness. Matth. 22, 13; 25, 30; 2 Pet.
2, 17. Out of this spiritual darkness God has called the believers, 1 Pet. 2, 9, and delivered them from it, Col. 1, 13.
Hence there can be no **communion,** κοινωνία πρός between
light and darkness, no association of the one (φωτί, dative)
with the other (πρὸς σκότος). They are forever separate,
hostile, at war, without any turning on the part of the light
toward the darkness in any form of companionship. In the
believer the power of light is ever active and thus excludes
the darkness, without any possibility of changing this an-
tagonism.

The next step brings in *the personal authors* of light and
darkness: **And what concord hath Christ with Belial?**
It is in vain that Bachmann denies the soteriological significance of light and darkness here, for the apostle mentions
the σωτήρ himself in the very next breath. **Christ** has
obtained righteousness for us, was made unto us
righteousness, 1 Cor. 1, 30, and is our everlasting
light, Rev. 21, 23. As Christ, the Anointed, he is our
Prophet, High Priest, and King, the author of our salvation,
Heb. 12, 2. — **Belial,** or rather Beliar, is the personal name
of the devil, and signifies worthlessness, or wickedness. The
Septuagint has the word as a common noun in the sense of
transgressor, impious, foolish, pest (Vincent), and Milton
describes Belial as a sensual profligate. He is the author of
sin, the seducer of our race, the prince of darkness. — Can
there be any **concord** between Christ and Belial? Συμφώνησις
(only here in the N. T.) = harmony of sound. Can any
utterance of these two in any way harmonize? It is impossible that the discordant notes of hell's inhabitants should
ever symphonize with the sweet music of the angels and
saints about the heavenly throne of Christ.

The second pair of questions deals with the persons involved, and the apostle therefore adds: **or what portion
hath a believer with an unbeliever?** This question is a

continuation of the argument, and not merely a statement of the point to be proved, as some think. Paul is not arguing general principles merely, but, as his opening injunction shows, things which pertain most intimately to every individual reader. So, after he has dealt with the qualities concerned and the powers producing them, he brings in their personal authors, and in connection with them *the personal subjects themselves.* All that he has said thus far runs to a focus in the believer himself, and in the unbeliever. The righteousness, light, and Christ, however in themselves divided forever from iniquity, darkness, and Belial, are here considered as pertaining to human individuals. The **believer** is one who is justified by faith, Rom. 3, 28, and thus the bearer of the highest blessing, Rom. 4, 6-7, at peace with God, Rom. 5, 1, and assured of eternal salvation, Mark 16, 16. The light of the knowledge of the glory of God in the face of Jesus Christ has shined in his heart, 2 Cor. 4, 6; he walks no longer as the Gentiles in the vanity of his mind, with an understanding darkened, Eph. 4, 17; and presses forward toward the prize of his high calling in Christ Jesus, Phil. 3, 14.— On the other hand the **unbeliever** ("infidel," A. V., but not in the special sense of a disbeliever in the existence of God) is the very opposite of all this. "He hath been judged already," John 3, 18; he "shall not see life," 3, 18; he is not one of Christ's sheep, John 10, 26; he shall not enter into God's rest, Heb. 3, 18-19; yea, he shall be damned, Mark 16, 16, and cast into the lake of fire, Rev. 20, 15. — **What portion** then hath a believer with an unbeliever? The words are without articles, simply πιστός and ἄπιστος, referring thus to every believer inasmuch as he is a believer, and to every unbeliever likewise. Has the former in his character as a believer any "portion" in common with the unbeliever in his character? Absolutely he has not. The unbeliever has no righteousness, no pardon, no spiritual life and light, no faith, no hope of salvation, no place in heaven. At all essential points the believer and the unbeliever diverge. What the one has, the other has not; what the one strives for, hopes for, and finally secures, the other spurns, seeking something else, and realizing what is wholly opposite. And this is the proof-point in the fourth question, bringing the matter down into the very experience of each individual Christian. He must realize that not only righteousness, light, and Christ as such are utterly at variance and contradictory to iniquity, darkness, and Belial, but that all these meet in his own heart as a believer and shut him out from yoke-fellowship with the unbeliever completely and forever.

Christians must be separate — it ought not be otherwise.

The personal side of the great subject reached in the last question is further developed by the final question with its appended explanation and admonition. It deals with *the highest side of the personal subjects* here concerned, namely with believers as the temple of the living God. **And what agreement hath a temple of God with idols? for we are a temple of the living God.** The climax reached in this question, in so far as it goes beyond the others, is not to be sought in the idea of God, as if no question could ask anything beyond God, and no opposition and contradiction could involve anything superior to him (so Bachmann). The subject here is not God but **a temple of God,** and we ourselves as that temple, *i. e.* the indwelling of God in us. The fifth question thus builds directly on the fourth, and thereby proves once more that the fourth is a true link in the upward climbing argument. The apostle is not satisfied when he reaches the believer as such and drives the point of his proof home to him in his own person as a believer. There is one step more, a mighty and yet perfectly well-known fact: believers have God dwelling in them. This once more and with utmost power establishes the contention, now about to be turned into an admonition, that believers must be separate. — **A temple of God,** ναός (*sanctuary,* margin), without the article, does not refer especially to the well-known temple at Jerusalem, but to any place dedicated to God for him to dwell

there and be worshiped there. **Idols** likewise has no article
and thus refers to any or all of them. The Corinthians
were perfectly right in thinking of all the false gods they
had worshiped before their conversion. The point of Paul's
question is missed when an ellipsis is assumed and ναοῦ is
supplied before εἰδώλων, as if the apostle were asking:
"What agreement hath a temple of God with a temple of
idols?" The **agreement** here mentioned is not between
temples, but between temples and worshiped beings.
"Agreement," συνκατάθεσις (comp. Luke 23, 51) = *Ueberein-
kommen,* as when two cast the same vote, each assenting
to the other. There is such a perfect assent or agreement
of the temple of God with God, but never of a temple of
God with any idol. God's temple is wholly arranged for
him, for his honor, service, worship; all its distinctive features proclaim and indicate that. There is no place there
for any idol or anything that pertains to an idol. In fact
all this is positively and most radically excluded. "I am
the Lord thy God; thou shalt have no other gods before
me." To introduce another god is to desecrate God's
temple; this was the crime Ahaz and other kings of Judah
committed; compare also 2 Thess. 2, 4. One lie may admit
beside it another lie, for there is a basic agreement between the two; but truth excludes and condemns every
lie in its very essence.

Paul's question as here asked is simple and of a kind
that any Christian will at once furnish the right answer.
The more effective, therefore, is the thought the apostle
has in mind in asking it: **for we are a temple of the living
God.** By the ready answer that the temple of God and
idols certainly can have no agreement, the very thing Paul
is driving home is fully established, for it is also beyond
question that every true believer is indeed a temple of God.
Text critics differ as to the reading ἡμεῖς and ὑμεῖς (A. V.):
homiletically there is no important difference, since in either
case the preacher must make the application to the believers
he has before him. God is a **living God,** hence he can do
what no idol is able to do, make our hearts his temple and

abode. It is the mystic union which Paul here asserts, of which Christ speaks John 14, 20 and 23: "Ye in me, and I in you . . . If a man love me, he will keep my word: and my Father will love him, and we will come unto him, and make our abode with him." What the old Jewish temple foreshadowed is thus fulfilled in the most blessed reality in every Christian's heart: God dwells in him as in a temple. There is no essential difference whether the individual Christian is here named by himself, or the whole body of believers, "the church of the living God," 1 Tit. 3, 15, as in Eph. 2, 21: "a holy temple in the Lord . . . a habitation of God in the Spirit;" or 1 Pet. 2, 5: "a spiritual house." — But Paul furnishes his own proof for the fact that we are indeed a temple of the living God: **even as God said, I will dwell in them, and walk in them; and I will be their God, and they shall be my people.** What Moses and the prophets wrote, God said. The real speaker is God and none other. This is one of the strong incidental proofs, scattered through the Bible, which establish the verbal inspiration of the Scriptures. The words here brought in as proof by the apostle are not an exact verbal repetition of an O. T. utterance, but a free repetition of Lev. 26, 11-12: "And I will set my tabernacle among you . . . and I will walk among you, and will be your God, and ye shall be my people." So also Ezek. 27, 27: "My tabernacle also shall be with them: yea, I will be their God, and they shall be my people." The latter statement is one that occurs repeatedly: Hos. 2, 23; Jer. 24, 7; 30, 22; 31, 33; 32, 38; *etc.* Besser interprets "I will walk in them," as signifying that God shows his presence and working in his church by the gifts, offices, and powers he bestows, 1 Cor. 12, 4 *etc.* The whole blessedness of this union of God with his people is not understood until we see how this was his intention from the very beginning, and how it realized itself step by step, when God dwelt with the patriarchs of old, travelled with his people through the desert in the pillar of fire and in the cloud, manifested his presence in the tabernacle and in the temple, in the words of his prophets, finally in his own Son incarnate and in the Spirit shed abroad on Pentecost; all which shall reach its climax when St. John's vision shall be fulfilled, Rev. 21, 1-3: "And I saw a new heaven and a new earth: for the first heaven and the first earth are passed away; and the sea is no more. And I saw the holy city, new Jerusalem, coming down out of heaven from God, made ready as a bride adorned for her husband. And I heard a great voice out of the throne saying, Behold, the tabernacle of God is with men, and he shall dwell with them, and they shall be his peoples, and God himself shall be with them, and be their God."

On the foundation thus laid Paul now once more makes his appeal. He puts it into the shape of a conclusion or deduction: **Wherefore,**. But he clothes it in words gathered from the O. T., as if God himself were directly addressing the readers; "doing this according to the riches of his spirit, melting together many passages into one heap, and forming from them a text furnished by the entire Scriptures, and one in which the sense of the entire Scriptures appears." Luther.

Come out from among them, and be ye separate, saith the Lord,
   And touch no unclean thing;
   And I will receive you,
   And will be to you a Father,
   And ye shall be to me sons and daughters,
saith the Lord Almighty.

Here is first of all an adaptation of Is. 52, 11: "Depart ye, depart ye, go ye out from thence, touch no unclean thing; go ye out of the midst of her; be ye clean, that bear the vessels of the Lord." Verse 12 adds: "And the God of Israel will be your rereward," or exactly: "will gather you," hence Paul's thought: "will receive you." Compare also Ez. 20, 34: "and I will bring you out from the people, and will gather you" *etc.;* 11, 17; Zech. 10, 8. The great propriety of Paul's allusion to these passages lies in the fact that, just as he now is urging the Corinthians to forsake everything idolatrous and heathenish, so God exhorted Israel

of old, and that after his severe dealing with them in the
Babylonish captivity. The application of this mighty admonition, voiced as it were out of the heart of the whole
Bible, from the lips of "the Lord Almighty" himself, must
extend to all the forms of worldliness prevalent to-day, in
the seeking of pleasure tainted by the flesh and so capti-
vating to an evil generation, in godless business methods,
godless learning, godless associations generally; it must include every connection with Christless altars, ideas of salvation, prayers, brotherhoods; likewise all fellowship with
doctrines that run counter to the revealed Word of God, and
all altars established on them. Paul's words must destroy
in us the evil spirit of indifference which is so fatal to many
professing Christians and makes them touch carelessly
many an "unclean thing." — They who heed this admonition shall have as their "rearward" (Is. 52, 12,
R. V.) **the Lord Almighty,** who will be unto them
a Father, and they shall be unto him **sons and
daughters.** *Ex hac appellatione perspicitur magnitudo
promissionum,* Bengel; and as Meyer adds, the certainty of
their fulfillment. This name of God, he who is mighty in
all things, occurs repeatedly in Revelations, and is used by
the Septuagint in 2 Sam. 7, 8. The promise itself is a free
rendering of 2 Sam. 7, 14, repeated in various forms in
other passages. Besser reminds us, however, that *Meiden*
and *Leiden* here go together, and that the very greatness
and might of God must make us shrink from offending and
insulting him: "Or do we provoke the Lord to jealousy?
are we stronger than he?" 1 Cor. 10, 22.

Christians must be separate — it shall not be other-wise.

The last verse of our text is still in the form of an
admonition, but it is now one which enlists the inmost desire
of the Christians themselves and their willing cooperation
with God. Hence we use the caption with an expression of
this desire and the determination that goes with it on our
part: We will be separate — it shall not be otherwise.

Having therefore these promises refers to the ones just stated so effectively; they are the inward motive power in our hearts. We have these promises in faith, and thus they are already fulfilled for us; and we have them in another way in hope, namely so that we yet await and confidently expect their still greater fulfillment. — **Beloved,** Paul addresses his readers with fervent affection, the more to move them to agreeable action. — His appeal is both negative and positive: **Let us cleanse ourselves from all defilement of flesh and spirit, perfecting holiness in the fear of God.** This cleansing is like that spoken of by Christ in John 15, 2-3, where he says of the disciples: "Ye are clean because of the word which I have spoken unto you," and yet states that the Father "cleanseth" every branch, "that it may bear more fruit." There is indeed "now no condemnation to them that are in Christ Jesus," Rom. 8, 1; they are blessed "whose iniquities are forgiven, and whose sins are covered . . . to whom the Lord will not reckon sin," Rom. 4, 7-8. "But ye were washed, but ye were sanctified, but ye were justified in the name of the Lord Jesus Christ, and in the Spirit of our God." 1 Cor. 6, 11. We are clean, and yet we must cleanse ourselves. "He that is bathed needeth not save to wash his feet," John 13, 10, yet this he needs, else he will have "no part with me" (Christ). The Corinthians are an example how Christians are still subject to defilement in their contact with the world, and because of their own evil nature still adhering to them. "For we daily sin much, and indeed deserve nothing but punishment," Luther, *Smaller Catechism.* — This cleansing must be **from all defilement of flesh and spirit;** outer and inner defilement, or all that proceeds from outside and enters in, and all that from within proceeds outward. **Flesh** as here set beside "spirit" signifies the outer man with his bodily senses and members; **spirit,** the mind and heart of man, his inner being. **Defilement** may occur in either, affecting, of course, the entire man. Sin invades the senses and draws our bodily members into its power, as when "ye present your members as servants to uncleanness and to iniquity unto iniquity,"

Rom. 6, 19. Again sin occurs in the "spirit," in unholy thoughts and inflaming desires, in passions and secret lusts, in doubts, hypocrisies, secret unbelief, in selfishness, pride, and other evil inward motions. If this defilement is allowed to remain, God cannot continue to dwell in us, and we lose our first cleansing and adoption. Righteousness and iniquity cannot be wedded together. Καθαρίσωμεν ἑαυτούς, **let us cleanse ourselves,** by repentance, and by overcoming all solicitations of sin from without and stirrings of sin within. Cleansing is spoken of as an activity of God exercised upon us, Acts 15, 9; Eph. 5, 26; 1 John 1, 9: "He is faithful and righteous to forgive us our sins, and to cleanse as from all iniquity." Christians, however, are also bidden to cleanse themselves, since the Spirit dwells in them and gives them spiritual power. This they are to exercise with might, and the very Word which bids them do this stimulates and renews this power within them. — **Perfecting holiness in the fear of God,** Paul adds. Luther translates ἐπιτελοῦντες (ἐπί and τέλος): *fortfahrend,* proceeding forward with. The word indicates that a start has been made and that now the goal is to be reached. **Holiness** is to be perfected, *die Heiligkeit ist vollstaendig zu erweisen* (Cremer); we are to practice every necessary part of it, so that nothing may be missing. All that belongs to the Christian holiness of life is meant, every virtue, every good work. — And this **in the fear of God,** in that fear which goes hand in hand with love, which always looks with childlike reverence and awe to the great God and Father above and dreads to disobey and offend him. Meyer rightly retains the native sense of ἐν as indicating the ethical sphere in which this perfecting of holiness is to go forward. The all-seeing eyes of "the Lord Almighty" are ever upon us; his presence and power are ever with us; and thus we must always walk before him in holy fear. Like an armor of steel it is to protect and shield us, and keep us safe with him.

HOMILETICAL HINTS.

We must bear many a yoke in this life; many a burden is laid upon us, and others too we willingly assume. But there is one yoke to which our necks dare never bow, from which Christ has freed us, the yoke of unbelievers. Let us not be entangled again in the yoke of this bondage. Gal. 5, 1. — Where there is union with God in Christ, there must be separation from all that is ungodly and Christless. Separation means decided, conscious, positive, definite dedication to God and consecration to our calling as God's children. Absalom was the son of David and fought against his own father; not so we.

Paul's five questions strike home in every Christian's conscience. — Will you love companionships which cost you the love of God? — "Take my yoke upon you," says Christ, "for my yoke is easy, and my burden is light." And Paul adds: "Be not unequally yoked together with unbelievers." One yoke we must bear, it is a question which one we will have.

Although we still have sin in us, and the darkness still assails us, yet we are not to walk in darkness, but in fellowship with God by virtue of the cleansing blood of Jesus Christ his Son. 1 John 1, 6. — Where the Word of God is taught in its truth and purity, and we as the children of God also lead a holy life according to it," only the righteousness, light, and Christ prevail, and iniquity, darkness, and Belial are overcome. — It is not "opportune" in the eyes of many to be really separate. They see many advantages in taking "a middle course." They dread to be called "extremists." But Paul's questions snatch the mask from all such self-deception and the danger that lurks in it. It was "opportune" for Peter to make a frank confession of his Lord in the court of the highpriest's palace. But he failed to do it, yet when he saw how he had yoked himself to the foes of Christ, he withdrew his neck from the evil yoke by repentance unto tears, and returned to his Lord.

What God hath joined together, let no man put asunder — ever. What God hath put asunder, let no man attempt to join together — ever. — "Whoever says he loves the Savior, and yet does not hate what he rejects, or forsake what he abominates, is in reality a liar, and a child of darkness. He who howls with the wolves must not be surprised to be counted a wolf." Matthes.

However infirm our faith may look, we are never to count as anything small and inferior our separation from the world which we have obtained by faith in Jesus our Lord and by the Spirit of God. Rieger. — "Sons and daughters." Then was this promise fulfilled when over the plains of Bethlehem the heavenly hosts sang of glory to God, peace on earth, and good will to men; when God showed indeed that he so loved the world that he gave his only begotten Son; when that Son became our Brother, fulfilled all righteousness, took the burden of the world's sin as the Lamb of God, and finished our redemption on the cross; when his love went forth in his precious message of pardon and peace and drew men to him everywhere. And so we now are separate from sin and death and made one with God in sonship in his kingdom of light and life.

"This dwelling and walking of God in us is accomplished when, in addition to man's first believing and holding to the Word, God also rules in him by his divine power and operation, so that he is enlightened more and more, becomes richer and stronger in spiritual understanding and wisdom; and, following that, increases daily and continues in life and good works, and becomes a kind, meek, patient man, of service to God and man." Luther.

Sins of the flesh are bodily uncleanness, intemperance, incontinence, *etc.;* sins of the spirit, pride, ambition, envy, domination, *etc.* But sins of the flesh and sins of the spirit do not exclude each other, but touch and cross at many points; the more need to battle alike against both. — The brighter the light of the Lord shines, the more clearly the stains and faults appear in us; the more his love has entered our hearts, the more it will impel us to put away whatever displeases him. — Our Christianity is no possession settled and fixed once for all, but a constant watching and guarding of a precious treasure. Not an outfit to be worn for life without further attention, but a beautiful white robe which must be kept spotless and whole with constant care. — Real holiness consists not in crying with the loudest voice: "Lord, Lord!" in speaking or even preaching of him with the greatest fervor, in knowing the Bible doctrines concerning him with superior knowledge, and in having the strongest conviction of their truth; but in doing the Father's will, in practicing what we rightly preach, in using our knowledge in faith and our convictions in faithfulness.

The fear of God is our fortress and protection. Let us not be lured away from this shelter by presumptuousness. 2 Pet. 3, 17. Rieger.

The Epiphany Call:
Be Ye Separate!

I. *Learn once for all that there is no communion between Christ and Belial.*

a) Consider: they themselves and their kingdoms are absolutely against each other; so also the powers they represent (light, darkness); so also the effects they produce (righteousness, inquity); so also the followers they secure (believers, unbelievers); so also the worship they establish (temple of God, idols).

b) Apply: in the Corinthian church Christian worship and the sacramental feast, and over against this idol feasts; Christian faith and virtue, and over against it heathen vileness in all its abominable forms; Christian truth and knowledge, and over against it the vain pagan philosophies, without help and hope. —In our day: God's people, and the world; our assembly about the Word and Sacrament, and theirs with the Sunday newspaper, some pleasure resort, *etc.*, far from God and his saving Gospel; here the light of Christ and the cross, there Christless altars, prayers, associations, or a mere human Christ and a human gospel; here faith and Christian zeal, there self-righteousness, worldly views and notions, shifting opinions, all manner of errors and delusions, and lives according; here worship and praise, there the dance, the theater with its vileness, the service of the flesh and the corruption that leads to hell.

Behold the gulf! Let no lie of the devil spread a fog over it to deceive you.

II. *Embrace once for all the communion with God and his promises.*

a) Temples of God, dedicated to him in Christ Jesus through living faith, separated from idolatry of all kinds forever.

b) Sons and daughters of the Father through Christ Jesus, in constant association with the Father and the things of his house, separated from the world and the things of this world.

c) Cleansing both flesh and spirit from every defilement that would turn us away from the Savior; perfecting holiness in every virtue and good work, in the fear of God.

Behold the blessedness of this communion! Let no deception of the devil ever dim its riches and glories in your eyes.

———

Suppose St. Paul, the apostle of Jesus, would appear in the church of the present day and repeat the admonition he once addressed to the Corinthians in the words of our text, to come out from among the children of unbelief and be separate — what would people say? I know what the world would say, the children of darkness and unbelief. They would sneer at him, denounce and even persecute him, as once they did nearly 2,000 years ago when he proclaimed the Gospel of Jesus, which was a stumbling block and offense to the world. — But what would the so-called Christians do, the members of the various churches of the present day, if St. Paul would demand in person of them, in so forcible and eloquent a manner, complete and total separation from all who do not share the Christian faith? It seems to me we are able to answer that question. Ours is the age of unionism. The great majority of Christians is altogether indifferent to matters of doctrine and faith. At any time they are ready to set aside all difference and fellowship anyone who leads a moral life, even such as deny the very fundamentals of our faith, the Holy Trinity, the divinity of Christ, *etc.*, and join with them in the so-called work of the church. They will tell you that it is foolish to quarrel about matters of faith, that it shows a spirit of arrogance and self-conceit to refuse fellowship to those who are not of our faith. That this is the spirit of the Middle Ages, not that of our advanced age. Thank God, they will say, the church realizes. that her strength does not lie in doctrines and creeds, but rather in charity and deeds. If St. Paul then would appear again with his ringing call to be separate, I am sure they would denounce him as a fanatic, a man of antiquated views, one who did not know the spirit of Christ, one who had failed to perceive that Christianity is the great religion of tolerance and love. . . . But we know that what St. Paul demands is the very will and Word of God. . . . And because so many run counter and act contrary to it, therefore the more we must give ear to this Epiphany call:

"Come Out From Among Them, And Be Ye Separate!"

Let us understand well:
I. *Why this is necessary.*
II. *How this is to be done.*

C. C. Hein.

Decisive Christianity.

I. *Decisive for faith.*
II. *Decisive against unbelief.*

Conrad.

15

Ye Are the Temple of the Living God.

I. *Glory in your temple's consecration.*
II. *Beware of your temple's desecration.*

Faber.

On Into the Light!

I. *Away from the darkness that surrounds us.*
II. *Casting out the darkness that still lingers in us.*
III. *Rising completely to the divine light that invites us.*

Christ's Epiphany in the Hearts of His People.

I. *The curse it removes.*
II. *The blessedness it brings.*
III. *The glory to which it leads.*

THE SECOND SUNDAY AFTER [EPIPHANY.

1 Cor. 2, 6-16.

The general subject of this text is entirely plain, it describes the Gospel of Christ as divine wisdom, a wisdom hidden from men, but revealed by the Spirit, and apprehended in a spiritual way. The Epiphany character of this text is equally plain, for Christ, the Lord of glory is the center of this wisdom, and the text thus shows us how he comes to the hearts of men and is apprehended by them. This is the chief thing in the text, this and the fact that he has thus become known and apprehended by us. — We may note also the connection with the previous text and the step forward now taken. That text showed us the great gulf between the children of God and the world, and here again we meet "the rulers of this world" who in their blind wickedness slew the Lord of glory himself. But our text does not stop with this opposition; it goes on and shows how the Gospel or wisdom of God is brought to us by the Spirit and delivers us from the world and its fatal blindness, so that now we possess this greatest and most comprehensive blessing: the Lord of glory rules in our hearts, we have the mind of Christ. And this is the general theme for this text on this day: *We have the Epiphany light, namely the eternal saving wisdom of God.* — The text sets forth first the character of this wisdom, secondly the way it has come to us, and finally the manner in which we receive and possess it.

The character of God's saving wisdom.

In the first chapter of our Epistle Paul has exposed the folly of mere human wisdom when it comes to saving souls. That wisdom God has brought to nought, and saves

227

men by the foolishness of preaching. Accordingly Paul
came to the Corinthians "not with excellency of speech or
of (human) wisdom;" his preaching was "not in persua-
sive words of (human) wisdom", and the faith of the
Corinthians was not made to "stand in the wisdom of
men." He had determined to know nothing among them
save Christ and him crucified, and their faith was made to
stand thus wholly on the power of God. Suddenly now
Paul reverses his line of argument: while the Gospel of
Christ may indeed look like foolishness to the vain wisdom
of men, in reality it is the highest and most wonderful
WISDOM of all, infinitely transcending all wisdom and
philosophy of men. **Howbeit we speak wisdom among
the perfect.** The former assertion stands unmodified,
Paul and his fellow workers do not teach and preach
human wisdom and philosophy, and yet they teach wisdom, something which deserves the name far more than
what is usually so called. **Among the perfect** means in
their midst, ἐν in the natural local sense; not "for the
perfect," or "in their judgment." The question is whom
does Paul mean by οἱ τέλειοι ? Some answer, the mature
Christians as distinguished from the babes in Christ
(νήπιοι). Consequently they restrict σοφία to mean the
higher mysteries of the Christian faith, the hidden things
of the future, the most difficult doctrines, and the like.
The marginal translation seems to favor this interpretation: *fullgrown*. A τέλειος is one who has reached the
τέλος or goal, and it is left to the context to define what
that goal is, in other words what special meaning the designation contains. Now the entire context here shows only
two kinds of people: such as accept the Gospel in faith,
and such as despise it and prefer their own wisdom. There
has not been, and is not in this section (6-16), a single
reference to undeveloped believers in contrast to fully developed believers, whatever there may be elsewhere. Moreover, Paul himself prevents us from understanding by σοφία
some special difficult doctrine, prophecy, or superior mystery connected with the Gospel, for he calls his preaching

of Christ crucified, this very center and heart of the Gospel, "the power of God and *the wisdom* of God," 1, 24; and throughout our text he intimates no change in this definition. The Gospel itself is **wisdom,** the "wisdom of God" as distinguished from "the wisdom of men," verse 5. To modify this meaning, as the commentators referred to propose, is to destroy the force of Paul's presentation in all that follows. Meyer's attempt to state what special mysteries are embraced in "wisdom," outside and beyond the common substance of Paul's Gospel, introduces subjects entirely foreign to these chapters; the same is true of the varying attempts of others. The τέλειοι are those who have reached the goal Christ crucified, in faith. Paul's great aim everywhere was to teach "every man in all wisdom, that we may present every man perfect (τέλειον) in Christ," Col. 1, 28. Of course, it was a question whether those among the Corinthians who hankered after a different wisdom belonged to the τέλειοι. — To **speak,** λάλειν, means simply to give utterance. Paul was simply the mouth-piece of God in sounding forth the Gospel.

Yet a wisdom not of this world, nor of the rulers of this world, which are coming to nought. This is that other wisdom, the vanity of which is set forth so effectively in the first chapter of our Epistle. It is **of this world,** or *age* (margin), belongs wholly to it; and a stream cannot rise above its source, nor can it carry anyone above it. **The rulers of this world** (compare verse 8) are the men of influence, whether for their wisdom, power, or birth; they who lead and rule others. If any one expects more of them in the line of "wisdom" than of men generally, he will be disappointed; in spiritual things their superiority otherwise, counts for nought. Some interpret the designation of angels, but in verse 8 the same term occurs and must there mean men, namely the Jewish authorities and Pilate; in our verse any and every such ruler is meant, "the wise," "the scribe," "the disputer of this world," 1, 20; "the mighty," "the noble," 1, 26. — **Which are coming to nought,** 1, 28. Their entire wisdom is leading them to

nought; it can produce no other result, no matter what
they themselves expect. "Already in this world one card-
castle of human wisdom after another falls to pieces, and
finally the sentence of destruction uttered against all
worldly things will be executed in the judgment to come."
Besser. — Paul follows up his negative statement on the
character of the wisdom he speaks, with a positive one:
but we speak God's wisdom in a mystery, *even* **the** *wis-*
dom **that hath been hidden, which God foreordained**
before the worlds unto our glory. He uses the strong
adversative ἀλλά, and he repeats both λαλοῦμεν and σοφίαν,
thus putting a deep solemnity into his declaration. **God's**
wisdom, with the emphasis all on the word set in front,
contrasts this wisdom strongly with σοφία ἀνθρώπων in verse
5. The genitive denotes that the wisdom is altogether
God's, as to origin, nature, and contents, and therefore
infinitely superior to all the wisdom of men. Let all the
world's wise men note it well! — **Wisdom in a mystery**
troubles the grammarians because of its construction.
Some draw the modifying phrase "in a mystery" to the
following participle (ἀποκεκρυμμένην), but this participle
itself is the explanation of what is meant by "mystery."
Others, like Meyer, connect with λαλοῦμεν, but this makes
a strange thought: We speak in a mystery. What kind
of speaking could that be? We decidedly prefer the construction σοφίαν ἐν μυστηρίῳ, "wisdom in a mystery," either
supplying in thought οὖσαν (as many do), or dispensing
with this, since ἐν with an object is frequently attached to
nouns or pronouns, which Meyer and others overlook.
Compare Rom. 16, 3, also in verses 8-13; in 11 the participle is found, showing the constructions to be practically
equal; 1 Cor. 5, 17; Eph. 2, 13; Phil. 4, 21; 1 Thess. 4, 16;
Philemon 23. Luther translates freely: *Wir reden von der*
heimlichen . . . *Weisheit Gottes,* which conveys the
general sense. God's wisdom is in very truth "wisdom in
a mystery;" the entire sphere in which it exists is a mystery
for us, for it is altogether beyond mere human power to
penetrate. This is further brought out by the addition:

even **the** *wisdom* **that hath been hidden,** namely in the secret counsels of God, into which no one could look, not even the angels of God (1 Pet. 1, 12). There is only one way in which this wisdom could be discovered by men, namely by God's revealing it himself and showing us that God was in Christ reconciling the world unto himself, 2 Cor. 5, 19. This wisdom is a mystery still, but now a revealed mystery, which we too know, but which is still hidden from the world. "And so the Gospel and knowledge of Christ remains a secret, hidden thing; not that it is not proclaimed to all the world publicly enough, and placed clearly into the light, but that the world despises it and considers it as compared with its wisdom folly and offense, and is believed only by the simple, who are not offended by the unattractive picture of the cross of Christ, and by this faith learn and experience consolation, power, victory, life and salvation." Luther. — Paul therefore adds: **which God foreordained before the worlds unto our glory.** Here we have the plan and determination of God laid openly before us. "Before the worlds," or *ages* (margin), that is in all eternity, before ever man was formed or the first phospor-light of his little wisdom began to glow, God's wisdom was complete and his decision as to its object and result. That wisdom, namely his wonderful plan of salvation in Christ Jesus, was to be εἰς δόξαν ἡμῶν, causing and bringing it to pass. **Glory** is the final goal, to which God determined to bring us, that blessed state when we shall see the Lord of glory as he is and be made like unto him. What, pray, is all human wisdom compared with this wisdom of God's grace, which reaches from eternity to eternity, and is full of divine power to lift man from sin, corruption, and death to everlasting glory in heaven. — Such is God's wisdom, a wisdom evidently "not of this world, nor of the rulers of this world," verse 6; but also one **which none of the rulers of this world knoweth.** It is not only not theirs to begin with, originating far higher, and sweeping on its course far above their puny thoughts; rulers though they are, none of them, not one, even

knoweth this wisdom, ἔγνωκεν (Am. Com.: *hath known;* A.
V.: "knew"), *i. e.* has attained it, appropriated it intellectually and spiritually, when it came to them and was offered to them. — Conclusive proof is offered for this fact
(γάρ) : **for had they known it, they would not have crucified the Lord of glory** (εἰ ἔγνωσαν, οὐκ ἂν ἐσταύρωσαν, regular
past condition non-fulfilled). The crucifixion of Christ is
the final demonstration that the world's highest representatives did not, and do not, know God's wisdom; here all
their guilty and fatal ignorance comes to the surface, John
18, 38; Luke 23, 34; Acts 3, 17; 13, 27. The Jewish and
Gentile authorities in Christ's day are typical in this respect. Besser remarks: "World is world; wherever the
world lets out its real self in its leaders, there Christ is
killed in Jerusalem and in Rome, everywhere always."
Note the tremendous contrast between "crucify" and "Lord
of glory;" the one stands for the deepest disgrace and
shame, and the other for the highest exaltation and
majesty (Phil. 2, 6 and 8; "in the form of God," "even
unto death, yea, the death of the cross"). During his
whole earthly life, and while nailed to the cross Jesus was
the Lord of glory; God indeed purchased us with his own
blood, Acts 20, 28. The person is here designated according to his divine nature, while the thing predicated of him
refers to his human nature. This establishes the *com-
municatio idiomatum* of Lutheran theology. "Zwingli calls
it an *allœosis* when anything is ascribed to the divinity of
Christ which nevertheless belongs to the humanity of
Christ . . . Beware, beware, I say, of the allœosis;
for it is a mask of the devil, as it at last forms such a
Christ after which I certainly would not be a Christian.
For its design is that henceforth Christ should be no more,
and do no more with his sufferings and life, than another
mere saint. . . . If the old sorceress, Dame Reason,
the grandmother of the allœosis should say, Yea, divinity
can neither suffer nor die; you should reply, That is true;
yet, because in Christ divinity and humanity are one person, Scripture, on account of this personal union, ascribes

also to divinity everything that occurs to the humanity, and the reverse. And thus, indeed it is in truth. For this must certainly be said, *viz.* the person suffers and dies. Now the person is true God; therefore it is rightly said: The Son of God suffers. For although the one part, *viz.* the divinity, does not suffer, yet the person, which is God, suffers in the other part, *viz.* in his humanity; for in truth God's Son has been crucified for us, *i. e.* the person which is God. For the person, the person, I say, was crucified according to the humanity." Luther, quoted in the *Formula of Concord*, 631, 39 *etc.* An allœosis is a rhetorical figure, merely putting one term in place of another; others have called it a synecdoche, a placing of the whole (the person) for a part (the mere humanity). All such explanations entail the consequences pointed out by Luther, and empty the words of Scripture of their full meaning. **Glory** here is the sum of the divine attributes which belong to Christ.

> **But as it is written,**
> **Things which eye saw not, and ear heard not,**
> **And** *which* **entered not into the heart of man,**
> **Whatsoever things God prepared for them that love**
> **him.**

The adversative ἀλλά refers to the previous negatives, over against which a positive statement is now set in the form of a quotation. The grammatical construction is quite free. Some consider the sentence purposely unfinished; Hofmann construes "things," *etc.*, as the object of the verb "revealed" in verse 10, which is not acceptable for various reasons; we prefer to make the quotation depend on the emphatic main verb λαλοῦμεν twice repeated in verses 6 and 7. — **As it is written** is regularly used by Paul in quoting from the O. T. canon. Here Isaiah 64, 4 is freely used by the apostle. Some ancient writers thought that the words are from the Apocalypse of Elias, a spurious composition now lost; on the critical questions involved see J. Weiss, ninth edition of Meyer's *Kommentar*. The general sense is perfectly clear: God's wisdom is utterly beyond

the ability of men to discover for themselves, for it consists of "things which eye saw not," *etc.* **The eye** and the
ear are the ordinary senses by which men discover things,
and the **heart** here is the source of human thought. By
none of these means could man discover **whatsoever
things God prepared for them that love him.** These
things refer to the present as well as to the future, namely,
to all that God made ready for us in Christ Jesus our
Savior: pardon, sonship, peace *etc.*, and finally everlasting
glory. The passage is quoted by us very often, and this
reference to present as well as future blessings must not
be overlooked. Isaiah wrote: "for him that waiteth for
him," really: "for one waiting for him" (Hebrew verse 3),
for which Paul uses τοῖς ἀγαπῶσιν αὐτόν, **for them that love
him.** The idea of waiting is not altogether lost, for, however much we may already have and enjoy of God's saving
gifts, more shall yet be revealed to us in the heavenly future.
It is not that our loving God merits these divine gifts,
for by them God himself enkindles our faith and creates
love in our hearts; but only they in whom this is done can
receive, own, and enjoy these gifts. He who will not let
the love of God enkindle love in his own heart cannot have
God's gifts of love. In this sense these gifts are prepared
only for "them that love him."

The way in which God's saving wisdom has come to us (through the apostles).

God's wisdom is in a mystery, hidden, above the reach
of the world's wisest men. This Paul has set forth
mightily. How then shall any man ever know this divine
wisdom? Here is the answer: **But unto us God revealed**
them **through the Spirit.** "To us," ἡμῖν, is set emphatically forward, and stands for the apostles, as the
context shows (verses 6-7 and 13-14), over against "the
rulers of this world." The great Revelator is **God** himself ὁ θεός, the true God, he of whom Paul has been speaking all along; and the only way in which his thoughts and
plans could become known to men is by his revealing them.

Natural religious evolution among men is a figment of "the rulers of this world." God **revealed,** and so he imparted the saving Gospel to the minds and hearts of men. God began this work already in the garden of Eden, Gen. 3, 15. The complete revelation was made by Christ in the fulness of time (John 1, 18: ἐξηγήσατο) and by his Spirit (John 14, 26; 16, 13). Our text mentions especially the activity of the Spirit, who was promised to the apostles in an extraordinary degree: **through the Spirit.** The apostles were his last instruments, completing what the prophets of old had prepared. By the Spirit's inspiration they recorded the Word of God, so that the Scriptures are now God's revelation to all men and all times, and we to-day as believers are built upon the foundation of the apostles and prophets, Jesus Christ himself being the chief cornerstone, Eph. 2, 20. What God revealed is not explicitly stated in this sentence; we are left to supply the object of ἀπεκάλυψεν from the foregoing sentence (ἅ, and before that σοφίαν θεοῦ).

Infinitely above the natural capacity of man is the wisdom of God. Hence God alone can bring us into possession of it, and this he did by his Spirit. But Paul wants his readers to understand that this act required divine powers and activities utterly beyond man. For not only is the wisdom itself a divine thing, but the revealing of it to us is a divine act, possible only to God. God reveals his will through the Spirit: **for the Spirit searcheth all things, yea, the deep things of God.** By ἐραυνᾷν (Alexandrine for ἐρευνᾷν) is not meant a process of investigation, as when one goes from one thing to another, or penetrates into a thing step by step, but a result, namely full, profound, adequate comprehension (Ps. 139, 1 and 7). The Spirit of God is God himself, and he alone sounds the depths of **all things** in heaven and on earth, millions of them beyond even our knowledge of their existence, positively also including **the deep things of God,** those of his essence and attributes, as well as of his thoughts, purposes, plans, and providence (Rom. 11, 33).

And let us remember that the cross of Christ, which appears as foolishness to men, belongs to these deep things, for us at the same time the most exalted and the most blessed wisdom. There is here no thought of setting the Spirit over against the other two persons of the Godhead, as if he alone searched the deep things of God; for in essence the three persons are one, and the third person is named here because it is his especial office to make revelation unto men. — To make this entire matter clearer to his readers Paul introduces an analogy: **For who among men knoweth the things of a man, save the spirit of the man, which is in him? even so the things of God none knoweth, save the Spirit of God.** The inner emotions, feelings, motives, thoughts *etc.* of any individual man (τὰ τοῦ ἀνθρώπου) only the spirit of that man (τὸ πνεῦμα τοῦ ἀνθρώπου) knows (Prov. 20, 27); to all other men they are hidden. It is the same in this respect with God: "the things of God," these in general, and among them his gracious saving wisdom for us, "none knoweth, save the Spirit of God." The similarity between the power of man's spirit and that of God's Spirit here brought out refers only to the one point described, and we must not draw other parallels from these words of Paul, thus perhaps gravely misleading ourselves. One difference between the spirit of man and the Spirit of God, Paul himself indicates, when he says of the former that it "is in him," but does not say this of the Spirit in regard to God.

But we received, not the spirit of the world, but the spirit which is of God (Am. Com.: *from God*). The main question is: How do **we** get the divine wisdom? *i. e.* Paul and his fellow apostles who convey this wisdom to others. Verse 10 has said: by revelation; verse 12 now adds: by receiving the spirit which is of God. But first a negative is introduced, to bring out once more the opposition which runs through our entire text: We received, **not the spirit of the world.** What is meant? The spirit that fills, controls, and animates the world, *i. e.* the children of this world as alien to and opposed to the Spirit of God;

the spirit which produces the wisdom of this world and manifests itself especially in the rulers of this world who are coming to nought, verse 6. In reality it is the spirit that is produced in men's hearts by the devil who rules the world (2 Cor. 4, 4; Eph. 6, 11; *etc.*), although Paul does not say this directly. It is a spirit which is "received" (ἐλάβομεν), hence not merely natural reason ("the spirit of the man, which is in him"), for this we do not receive by any special act, but have by nature as creatures of God. Besser improves this last idea, by pointing out that natural reason is "impoverished and emptied of God," which is true, but still does not bring out directly the force of the genitive τοῦ κόσμου. In verse 6 the difference is between the temporal wisdom "of this age" and the eternal wisdom "foreordained before the ages to our glory;" here the difference is of quality: "of the world" and "of God," or "from God" (origin). — God's wisdom is in the possession of Paul and his fellow workers because they have received not the spirit of the world, but **the spirit which is of God.** Both English versions rightly translate "spirit," not "Spirit", although the article· τὸ πνεῦμα τὸ ἐκ τοῦ θεοῦ refers back; but ἐκ τοῦ θεοῦ is not the same as τοῦ θεοῦ, and designates, not the Holy Spirit as he proceeds from God, but the spirit wrought in us by God's Spirit. It is the spirit of faith, obedience, knowledge, love, and all godly motives, the true opposite of the spirit which dwells in the hearts of the children of this world. This spirit Paul received in his conversion; and we receive it in the same way. It alone enabled the apostles to grasp the divine wisdom; and because the world lacks it, it remains in the darkness of its own speculation. — The purpose for which the apostles received the spirit of God is now expressly stated: **that we might know the things that are freely given to us by God;** or, as the Am. Com. prefers to translate χαρισθέντα: *the things that were freely given us of God.* The wisdom of God is meant, which the world could not grasp and know; the things which eye saw not, and ear heard not, but which God revealed to the apostles. They themselves were to **know** these things, and, of course, by this knowledge possess and enjoys them to their own salvation, and at the same time convey them to others. They were freely given, a gratitous gift in the full sense of the word, a gift of grace. And as they were given to the apostles, so now through them they are given to us, in the same gracious way. The entire context shows that Paul is speaking of the Gospel, the· blessed wisdom of God, for the transmission of which to men generally the apostles were the divinely chosen agents; hence those commentators who interpret χαρισθέντα of the inward spiritual blessings of believers generally, or of the future blessings of the saints, fail to follow Paul's thought and argument.

This appears very clearly from the statement which now follows. In verse 6 and 7 Paul asserted: "We speak wisdom . . . we speak God's wisdom." He has added many important explanations, and now winds up again with "we speak" (λαλοῦμεν), showing now both what he and his fellow apostles speak and the character of the words they use in speaking. **Which things also we speak, not in words which man's wisdom teacheth, but which the Spirit teacheth.** A simple relative connects this sentence with the foregoing. "The things freely given us of God" by his divine revelation, which constitute the heavenly saving wisdom of God, are the things which the apostles not only know, but also utter, that others may know them. **We speak,** thus carrying out the command to teach all nations and to preach the Gospel to every creature. And the apostles still · speak through their written word. As in the previous verse, so here both a negative and a positive statement is introduced: **not in words which man's wisdom teacheth.** In no way, not even as to the λόγοι, is God's wisdom dependent on the world's wisdom; not even the λόγοι of the latter are exalted enough to serve in uttering the former. The philosophers, dialecticians and rhetoricians of the world formed and employed many concepts or "thought words" (Vincent) to express their worldly reasoning, but the apostles did not adopt them in their utterance of the divine wisdom. They could not, for they would not do for this work. Διδακτοῖς ἀνθρωπίνης σοφίας ═ "taught of human wisdom," and this suggests the great teachers of those days and the followers who adopted their reasoning, their μαθηταί. There are similar teachers to-day who wield a tremendous influence in the learned world. They are animated by "the spirit of the world" (verse 12), and their λόγοι are valueless for God's wisdom; and one of the greatest follies of some Christians is their effort to shape the wisdom of the Gospel so that it will fit these foreign forms of thought and language. Not the words which man's wisdom teacheth, **but which the Spirit teacheth,** did the apostles use. "Through the Spirit" (verse 10) God "revealed" not only the general ideas he wanted them to know and proclaim, but also the words necessary for their proper utterance. In fact, the two cannot be separated; for to leave the "words" to human selection would invite all manner of improper, inadequate, and wrong statement, altering and thus nullifying the divine wisdom. Here then we have proof positive for the doctrine of verbal inspiration, which is otherwise also extensively taught in Holy Scripture. The Spirit of God controlled completely the choice of words which the apostles employed in communicating the divine truth. This has been stigmatized as "the mechanical theory of inspiration," as degrading the sacred penman into mere automatons and machines. The diversity of style between the individual writers of the sacred books has been adduced as overthrowing any such verbal inspiration. But the impartation of the λόγοι by the Spirit is no more a mechanical operation than the impartation of the thought itself, since both normally go together, and we still teach truth by means of words fitted to convey it. Note the expression: words which the Spirit **teacheth,** διδακτοί; this eliminates everything mechanical, for teaching divine wisdom by means of divine words is a highly spiritual operation. And so little did the Spirit make automatons of the sacred writers that he left to each his individual style, and used it with its peculiarities for his exalted purpose, yet in each case controlling every word so completely that, with all the variety remaining, not one writer utters a false note, uses a false word or phrase, or contradicts in a single statement in his style what another has expressed in a different style. — Paul rounds out what he has said by adding three words: πνευματικοῖς πνευματικὰ συνκρίνοντες, **comparing spiritual things with spiritual.** Notice in passing the striking paromasia, which our translation cannot imitate: πνεύματος, πνευματικοῖς πνευματικά. The margin offers instead of the dative πνευματικῶς, and Luther's translation reflects this: *und richten geistliche Sachen geistlich;* but the adverb is not as well authenticated as the dative. The English margin offers: *interpreting spiritual things to spiritual men.* This makes πνευματικοῖς masculine, and πνευματικά neuter, and uses the modified meaning of the participle found in the Septuagint (Gen. 40, 8). A number of exegetes choose this rendering. But it is rightly objected that it anticipates verse 15, and does not fit the context closely enough. Paul has not been speaking of men; this he does in what follows; here he is speaking of the form of apostolic utterance. J. Weiss argues that Paul speaks negatively of men in verse 14, and this requires that a positive statement concerning men precede; but he overlooks that in verse 12 as well as in verse 13 Paul puts the negative first, and that he does exactly the same thing in speaking of men in verse 14-15. By far the best rendering, harmonizing completely with the context, is to make πνευματικοῖς refer to λόγοις, which immediately precedes, and πνευματικά to ἅ: *combining spiritual words with spiritual things.* Συγκρίνειν = *zusammensichten,* to combine with discrimination, to separate from other matter and compound anew, to compound, to combine. In a very terse way Paul sums up what he said at greater length: he unites spiritual words with spiritual things. Thus the doctrine of verbal inspiration is greatly strengthened; and we may also take to heart Besser's admonition, not to treat of spiritual things in words of human wisdom, as if they needed such a dressing up in foreign garments. The wool of our own wisdom does not harmonize with the pure linen of God's truth (Lev. 19, 19).

The way in which God's saving wisdom is received by us.

After describing the character of the divine wisdom which the apostles speak, and how it came to them by divine revelation, Paul treats of the reception of the divinely inspired apostolic utterance among men. He again begins with a negative, and then follows with a positive statement. **Now the natural man receiveth not the things of the Spirit of God.** In the very first word of this sentence (ψυχικός) we have a vivid example of how even the words of God's wisdom are derived from the Spirit. Paul takes the word which the later Greek literature "constantly employed in praise as the noblest part of man" (Trench), and reduces it to its proper level. For him ψυχικός is no longer a word of honor, but together with σαρκικός designates man as under the dominion of sin. Both these terms are opposites of πνευματικός. The former designates a person who has only the ψυχὴ ζῶσα, and not the πνεῦμα of divine regeneration, one therefore who has only the natural powers of the ψυχή and is moved and controlled only by them; and since these are altogether corrupt through sin, every activity of his soul and mind will be darkened and tainted accordingly. A σαρκικός is one who is fleshly and follows all the promptings of his sinful bodily nature. We have no exact equivalent for ψυχικός in English, and **natural,** or *unspiritual* (margin), is as close as we can come; Jude 19 describes the ψυχικοί as "having not the Spirit." — The natural man **receiveth not the things of the Spirit of God,** that is when these things are brought to him by the speaking of the apostles or other messengers of God, he does not admit them to his heart and make them his own. The reason is plain: **for they are foolishness unto him,** something insipid, tasteless, absurd. In his pride he often calls them fables, fit only for children,

16

etc. They do not agree with his own perverted ideas and desires, but run counter to them, condemn them, and work to root them out. Hence his opposition. And not only that he does not receive the things of the Spirit : **he cannot know them, because they are spiritually judged,** or *examined* (margin), *i. e.* so that the examination brings out their real value. **Know** is the equivalent of "receive" just used, it means to discern and apprehend truly. For spiritual things this requires nothing less than spiritual powers of discernment, and these the natural man as he is constituted has not. It is therefore not merely that he will not, or does not, but literally that he cannot discern and apprehend them. He has nothing but the organ of purely human cognition, and this does not reach into the spiritual realm. Just as a blind man cannot see the sun, so the unspiritual man cannot see the radiance of heavenly wisdom; just as a deaf man cannot hear the sweetest music, so the natural man cannot take in the sweet tones of the Gospel message. Only he that is of God heareth God's Word, John 8, 47. "In worldly and external affairs, which pertain to the livelihood and maintenance of the body, man is intelligent, reasonable, and very active, but in spiritual and divine things, which pertain to the salvation of the soul, man is like a pillar of salt, like Lot's wife, yea, like a log and stone, like a lifeless statue, which uses neither eyes nor mouth, neither sense nor heart. For man neither sees nor perceives the fierce and terrible wrath of God on account of sin and death, but he continues even knowingly and willingly in his security, and thereby falls into a thousand dangers, and finally into eternal death and damnation; and no prayers, no supplications, no admonitions, yea, also no threats, no reprimands are of any avail; yea, all teaching and preaching are lost upon him until he is enlightened, converted, and regenerated by the Holy Ghost." *Formula of Concord,* quotation from Luther, 556, 20-21. The conversion of man, the implanting of the spiritual nature in him, is therefore altogether and in every part the work of God himself, and no synergism of man's natural powers is possible in this work. This work God performs through the Word and Sacraments, his means of grace, which not only offer the heavenly treasure of wisdom to man in his helpless condition (collative power of the Word), but at the same time work faith and acceptance in him (efficacious or operative power of the Word).

Paul is not dealing here with the doctrine of conversion, but with the character of the Gospel and wisdom of God which lifts it altogether above the powers of the natural man and makes it accessible only to the spiritual man. **But he that is spiritual judgeth all things.** John said the same thing, 2, 20: "And ye have an anointing from the Holy One, and ye know all things." Paul himself was spiritual, but he speaks generally here of any and every one who is reborn through the Spirit. Such a person **judgeth all things.** The verb ἀνακρίνειν really means examine, investigate (follow up, ἀνά, a series of points, in order to distinguish, κρίνειν), and so inferentially to judge. Πάντα, "all things," is a surprise; Paul here goes far beyond the bounds of the Gospel as such. A moment's thought shows how right he is: the natural man does not judge aright even the things of this life, he does not see their true nature, purpose, relation, *etc.,* and hence he makes such a wrong use even of earthly things. The spiritual man has new eyes to see, a new mind to examine and estimate, and the true standard whereby to measure. Often indeed he does not exercise as he should his new powers, and falls back into the follies of his old nature; hence he must be admonished: "Be renewed in the spirit of your mind," Eph, 4, 23. But Paul here describes the exalted condition of the spiritual man, and lifts his head in holy pride above all the foolish wisdom of the world and its rulers. Hence he adds of the spiritual man: **and he himself is judged of no man,** namely of those who are without the Spirit. None of these has the ability to examine him aright; for just as the natural man does not and cannot know the things of the Spirit, so he cannot know aright and judge aright the man who has made the things of the Spirit the center of his life and being. Let no Christian ever worry about the judgment of worldly men. In their eyes we will always be pitiable fools. — **For who hath known the mind of the Lord, that he should instruct him?** Paul here quotes Is. 40, 13, as he does in Rom. 11, 34. And he adds: **But we have the mind of Christ.** He thus establishes what he has just said, namely that the spiritual man is judged of no one. The argument is a syllogism with a self-evident conclusion which needed not to be stated in so many words. No one can instruct the Lord (Christ). We have the mind of the Lord. Therefore no one can instruct or judge us. What folly for those who have not even the ability to receive the things of the Spirit of God, to sit in judgment on these things and on the people who glory in their possession? Do they mean to instruct Christ? will they attempt an impossible, presumptuous, blasphemous thing like that? Isaiah spoke of Jehovah, and Paul rightly refers this to Christ, for he is God, and the wisdom of God has its source in the entire Trinity. To have "the spirit which is of God," verse 12, is not identical with having **the mind of Christ.** "The spirit" includes more than "the mind;" the latter is restricted to the believer's understanding of Christ's blessed teaching. Christ dwells in them, and so the mind of Christ is their mind; his thoughts have become theirs and control their entire understanding, their judgment, and decisions. Walking thus in the light of divine wisdom, they who with the apostle have the mind of Christ are a puzzle to the world. But let its criticism never disturb you; rather test yourself constantly that you may never deviate from the mind of Christ and its divine saving wisdom.

HOMILETICAL HINTS.

The motto of every Lutheran pulpit is, and must be: "We speak God's wisdom!" The Epiphany season is intended to bring the full meaning of this assertion home to us anew, for it shows us the glory of the Gospel of Christ and of him who forms its

center. — Our motto is a challenge to all those pulpits in our land
which have discarded the Gospel and its blessed doctrines, and have
substituted something else in their stead. Alas, there are many
of these! They undertake to deal with the questions of the day,
civic and social needs, all manner of reforms and human remedies
in the world of labor, commerce, civil administration, and society
in general, progressive scientific theories, and a host of other matters. St. Paul sums up all the preaching of this kind in the one
phrase: "Wisdom of this world, and of the rulers of this world."—
It is bad enough that there are thousands of pulpits devoted to
the promulgation of this wisdom, but it is worse that some of
our own people are attracted by this false message, and imagine
their own church is not sufficiently up-to-date and progressive
since it everlastingly adheres to the old doctrine of salvation in
Christ Jesus. Therefore, it is doubly necessary that the wisdom
of God be shown us once more in all its divine greatness and
power, and in its tremendous contrast to the sham wisdom of
this world, that is of this transient passing age, the adherents of
which, however great they may appear for a time, shall all miserably
come to nought.

"The perfect" are not a select class, the finest of the entire
body of Christians, but all those Christians who are what their
name signifies, "spiritual" (verse 15), anointed with the Holy
Spirit. Phil. 3, 15: "Let us therefore, as many as be perfect, be
thus minded." Besser. — The rulers of this world never saw the
Christmas glory of the Christ child in Bethlehem, nor the Epiphany
glory of the Servant of God; but the humble shepherds on Bethlehem's fields saw it, and the devout here and there in the land,
longing for the light to break, beheld its radiance and bowed in
adoration.

One of the wisest of the ancient Greeks refused the high title
his contemporaries bestowed upon him, declaring it presumptuous
to call himself wise, and claiming to be only a friend of wisdom.
— Another of that nation, when it had risen to its highest power,
said of himself: "I know only this one thing, that I know nothing."
— And these confessions have been reiterated again and again.
One exclaimed: "I see only this, that we can know nothing, and
it almost consumes my heart." A famous scientist of to-day con-
fesses: "*Ignoramus; ignorabimus* — we do not know; we shall
not know." Many have called themselves agnostics, that is men
who do not know. What is light; electricity; gravity; matter;
force; life; Spirit — *i. e.* what is the real essence of these things?
No man knows. If the mind of man in studying the things of
nature arrives again and again at a blank wall beyond which no
human power is able to go, how shall the unregenerate mind of
man know him who made all these things, or penetrate his eternal

thoughts, plans and purposes? If human wisdom comes to nought in earthly things, how shall it ever attain to those that are heavenly? — World-wisdom desires world-power. But when its tower of Babel is almost finished, it breaks down, and the great tower turns into a desolate ruin. — The old weapons of human science, once turned against the Word, are consumed by rust; what was yesterday proclaimed as the liberating word of truth, crushing once and for all the old story of the cross, is discarded to-day as a garment out of fashion, and one with a different cut, but just as transient, takes its place. But the Word of God abides forever.

For fear of the lord at Rome Pilate had the Lord of glory crucified. For fear the Romans would take their last trace of power away, the Jewish rulers brought to the cross him to whom all power was given in heaven and on earth. This is the wisdom of the rulers of this world, and its mark is total blindness, extravagant folly, and desperate failure.

Revelation — necessary; possible; worthy of God; alone adequate to bring his wisdom to men! God's wisdom was a mystery, but it is God's wonderful work to make known the hidden things by his Spirit. God's wisdom comprised the heavenly purposes and plans of his love, but it is the glory of the Highest to condescend to his fallen creatures and unfold these exalted plans to them by his Spirit. Revelation is a gift, a light, heavenly wealth, divine power unto salvation. Angels sing its praises; babes rejoice in its possession; the mightiest men of God cannot comprehend it all. It is the heavens opened, and the angels of God ascending and descending. — God himself is the Revealer. He who searches even the deep things of God, prepared a way to shed the saving light into the hearts of men. It is a wondrous way. He spoke through chosen men by inspiration, and fixed their words in written form whereby to speak to all men everywhere.

In their wise conceit even some who are Christians would limit the power of God's Spirit and debar him from choosing the language and words best fitted to convey his heavenly thought. More than 2,000 times the Spirit declares in one form or other. "Thus saith the Lord!" and yet they doubt whether he really has said thus, and find here a flaw and there an error, which after all are only evidences of their own misunderstandings and ignorance. In our hypercritical age let us hold fast the divine assertion that the Spirit combines his own spiritual words with his own spiritual thoughts.

"I believe that I cannot by my own reason or strength believe in Jesus Christ, my Lord, or come to him; but the Holy Ghost has called me by the Gospel, enlightened me with his gifts." Luther says further: "The natural man is the man without grace, with all his reason, art, senses, and ability in the best form." — This is the wonder that God's Spirit by his Word turns the natural man into a spiritual man; plants life, where death was, light where darkness reigned, wisdom where folly sat enthroned, and salvation where damnation had set its seal. He makes kings and princes of us poor worms, and sets us to judge the world. Yea, he gives us the mind of Christ, "who was made unto us wisdom from God, and righteousness and sanctification, and redemption: that, according as it is written, He that glorieth, let him glory in the Lord." 1 Cor. 1, 30; Jer. 9, 23.

Has God's Wonderful Wisdom of Salvation Been Revealed Unto You?

I. *The hidden wisdom which God ordained before the world;*
II. *The heavenly wisdom which he revealed by His Spirit;*
III. *The blessed wisdom which brings us salvation in Christ Jesus:*
IV. *The spiritual wisdom which gives us the mind of Christ?*

The Gospel of Christ, the Supreme Wisdom.

For it is
I. *Not a wisdom of this world, but of God.*
II. *Not a wisdom discovered by men, but revealed by the Spirit of God.*
III. *Not a wisdom for the natural man, but for the man made spiritual by the grace of God.*

C. C. Hein.

Jesus Christ, the Treasure of Eternal Wisdom.

I. *Hidden from the world.*
II. *Revealed by the Spirit.*
III. *Appropriated by faith.*

God's Saving Wisdom Brought Unto Men.

I. *By revelation.*
II. *By inspiration.*
III. *By spiritualisation.*

The Holy Scriptures Our Highest Treasure.

I. *They are God's revelation;*
II. *Given by inspiration;*
III. *Imparting to us the mind of Christ.*

The Things that God Hath Prepared for those that Love Him.

I. *Glory through the crucified Lord of glory.*
II. *Wisdom through the revelation of his Spirit.*

THE THIRD SUNDAY AFTER EPIPHANY.

Rom. 1, 13-20.

The wisdom of God, which centers in the crucified Lord of glory, "God *revealed* through the Spirit," 1 Cor. 2, 10. That was the message of the previous text, and it is now followed up by the declaration that in the Gospel "is *revealed* a rightousness of God by faith unto faith." Again a revelation, and again one that centers in Christ and thus forms a fine Epiphany theme: *They who have seen the Epiphany light have found the righteousness that delivers from sin and condemnation.* The text really speaks of two revelations: the revelation of God's righteousness, and the revelation of his wrath against all ungodliness and unrighteousness of men. Our joy is that we know not only of this latter, but also, and very fully, of the former. The Gospel of this righteousness is for all men, Jew and Gentile alike; this too is a fine Epiphany thought, especially when we add the feeling of duty that ought to pervade our hearts, as it did Paul's when he wrote himself a debtor to the Gentiles. But God's righteousness is "by faith unto faith," and no Epiphany can take place in any sinner's heart who does not believe. Here again the sharp line of separation meets us which we have noted before: for those who reject the saving revelation of righteousness in God's mercy and Christ's merits there remains nothing but the revelation of God's wrath. — Our text contains two distinct sections, which for our purpose we may summarize briefly as: the Gospel of God's saving righteousness; the only Gospel for those who are unrighteous.

The Gospel of God's saving righteousness.

In advance of his coming personally to Rome and as a substitute for his personal presence the apostle Paul

writes to the Christians in the great world-capital, set
ting forth unto them at full length the central doctrine
of the Gospel of Jesus Christ. He tells them of his
earnest desire in the past to make the journey to Rome,
so that he might preach there also, in the very heart of·
the great Empire, the Gospel of salvation, and thus win
additional souls for the Savior. **And I would not have
you ignorant, brethren, that oftentimes I purposed to
come unto you (and was hindered hitherto), that I
might have some fruit in you also, even as in the rest of
the Gentiles.** The phrase **I would not have you ignorant**
is frequent with Paul, and always introduces a matter of
importance to his readers; so also here. He calls the Christians at Rome **brethren,** for this is the relationship that
unites all believers in Christ into one, the humblest and
weakest as well as the most prominent and influential. He
finds no necessity, either in his introduction to the Epistle,
or at this point when he is about to mention the great theme
he intends to elaborate, for emphasizing his official authority as an apostle. Having spoken of his longing to see the
brethren at Rome personally, he now assures them furthermore, **that oftentimes I purposed to come unto you.**
From chapter 15, 23 we learn that this desire had been in
Paul's heart these many years. At various times it had
crystallized into the definite purpose to start on the journey,
but always something interfered: **and was hindered
hitherto;** a parenthetic explanation. No details are offered,
and none are needed for us who know the apostle's abun
dant labors and severe trials. The reason for his desire
finally also to reach Rome is stated in the purpose clause:
**that I might have some fruit in you also, even as in the
rest of the Gentiles.** Jesus himself had used the figurative term **fruit,** καρπός, John 4, 36; 15, 8 and 16; and Paul
too liked to compare his work and its results with those of
a husbandman, a vine-dresser, or a gardener. Men won
for Christ are the apostle's "fruit," just as is still the case
with faithful preachers of the Gospel. That this is Paul's
meaning we see by his placing side by side **in you** and **in**

the rest of the Gentiles. The fruit he had gained among the other Gentiles, the people in other localities (ἔθνος), consisted of men brought to faith, and in the same manner (καθώς) he earnestly desired to reap fruit ἐν ὑμῖν, in Rome, speaking of the Christians there as part of the entire population. **Some** fruit is Paul's humble desire, whatever the Lord might grant him to gather in.

The apostle's desire to secure some fruit in Rome was not a mere personal wish on his part, but a natural result of his obligation as an apostle of the Gentiles, 1 Tim. 2, 7; Gal. 2, 7; 2 Tim. 1, 11. **I am debtor both to Greeks and to Barbarians, both to the wise and to the foolish.** His debt is to the Gentile world, not to the Jews, for the Lord himself had obligated him, saying: "Depart: for I will send thee forth far hence unto the Gentiles," Acts 22, 21. This was more than a mere national obligation, such as Paul might have felt toward the Jews as his native people. The greatest office in the world had been committed unto him, so that he himself declared: "Necessity is laid upon me, for woe is unto me if I preach not the gospel . . . I have a stewardship intrusted to me," 1 Cor. 9, 16-17. In making applications from Paul's statements to-day, this definite meaning must not be overlooked. We too have our obligation from the Lord; not indeed an apostolic commission like Paul's to go out personally to all the Gentile world, but a general commission nevertheless laying upon us all the duty to evangelize the world. And like Paul we should feel that we are debtors. — **Greeks and Barbarians** include the entire Gentile world, naming its two grand sections after the fashion of the Hellenists of that day; those who possessed the Greek language and culture were classed as Greeks, and all others were lumped as Barbarians. Besides this pair, indicated as such by τὲ καί, another is placed, including the same people: **the wise and the foolish,** but now not according to national cultural standing, but according to individual educational attainment; the σοφοί were men of Greek philosophical training, and the ἀνόητοι were the multitudes, who

knew nothing of such schooling. Many of the Romans, no
doubt, classed themselves among the former. To them all,
whatever their national standing or their individual culture
and education, Paul felt himself a debtor. For "the wise"
especially the foolishness of preaching was the medicine
to heal the hurt of worldly wisdom and pride, and to "the
foolish" the Gospel brought the heavenly light which makes
wise the simple. In the same way all men still need the
Gospel, those who now are puffed up by the attainment of
science and cultural advance, and those who lack education
and the worldly refinement it brings. The dark picture
which Paul drew of the proud Greek and Roman world of
his day (verse 18 and the following) has its counterpart in
the ungodliness and the moral corruption found to-day
among the puffed-up possessors of twentieth century education and progress.

    So, the apostle concludes, **as much as in me is, I am
ready to preach the gospel to you also that are in Rome.**
The construction is peculiar. It is best to take τὸ κατ' ἐμὲ
πρόθυμον as belonging together, supply ἐστί: "Thus
there is readiness on my part." Κατ' ἐμέ is equivalent to
the genitive, and τὸ πρόθυμον to ἡ προθυμία : "my readiness
is thus to preach" *etc.* This is better than to combine τὸ
κατ' ἐμέ and make πρόθυμον the predicate with ἐστί supplied.
The emphasis is on κατ' ἐμέ. Paul's desire together with
his feeling of obligation to "Greeks and Barbarians" made
him ready to preach the Gospel also to those in Rome. This
readiness to go where duty calls is the mark of every true
Gospel preacher. Paul stood anxiously awaiting the opportunity to go to Rome — not an easy place to labor in by
any means, but, judging from his experience in other great
cities, the hardest place of all. Yet he had absolute confidence in the Gospel, and even the mighty capital of the
world had no wisdom which would make him feel ashamed
and fear defeat.

    Accordingly Paul continues by stating why he is
ready to preach also in Rome: **For I am not ashamed of
the gospel.** Some authorities, and with them the A. V.,

read: "gospel of Christ." Zahn points out that in writing
to the Romans Paul refers to educational distinctions in a
manner more marked than in any of his other letters, and
that there is indeed a temptation for the preacher in the
cultural attainments of his hearers, making him easily
ashamed of the Gospel as not in line with their advanced
ideas, with the result that he either hesitates to speak out
freely, or attempts to accommodate the Gospel to their intellectual notions. Here the example of Paul must fill every
preacher, no matter how humble his earthly position, with
courage and holy pride. Christ himself warned his followers, Mark 8, 38, not to be ashamed of him and of his
words in an adulterous and sinful generation, lest the Son
of man be ashamed of them when he comes in the glory
of his Father with the holy angels. Paul accordingly declared: "I am not ashamed of the gospel;" he also urged
Timothy: "Be not ashamed therefore of the testimony of
our Lord," 2 Tim. 1, 8; yea, he actually gloried in the cross
of our Lord Jesus Christ, Gal. 6, 14, and suffered gladly
any reproach of men, glorying even in tribulation, Rom.
5, 3. — There is the strongest reason in the world why
Paul should not be ashamed of the Gospel: **for it is the
power of God unto salvation to every one that believeth;
to the Jew first, and also to the Greek.** The personal
bearing of these words, in furnishing a reason for Paul's
attitude toward the proudest culture of his day, is overshadowed by the general importance of what they express.
We really have here a definition of the Gospel, and immediately following it an additional statement which rounds
out and completes the definition. And this constitutes the
great theme of the entire Epistle which Paul is writing, to
which theme he addresses himself without any further
reference to his own person. — The **gospel,** εὐαγγέλιον, is a
glad message; the word is regularly used for that specific
message which Christ commissioned his disciples to carry
to all nations, namely that whosoever believes and is baptized shall be saved. The Gospel thus is an announcement
by a herald, but it differs from all mere human messages

in that it consists of more than so many words and the
natural sense connected with them; it is **the power of God.**
The genitive denotes more than origin, it signifies God's
power, one in which God himself is constantly active. "The
word of the cross is to them that are perishing foolishness; but unto us which are being saved it is the power of
God," 1 Cor. 1, 18; "the sword of the Spirit, which is the
word of God," Eph. 6, 17, the vehicle of the Spirit. and
thus power (Philippi); it "also worketh in you that believe," 1 Thess. 2, 14. "For the word of God is living, and
active, and sharper than any two-edged sword, and piercing
even to the dividing of soul and spirit, of both joints and
marrow, and quick to discern the thoughts and intents of
the heart." Heb. 4, 12. Therefore the Formula of Concord
warns us (654, 29) not to consider the preaching of the
Gospel a *Spiegelfechten,* a sham fencing; and Bengel notes
two of its divine attributes: *magna et gloriosa,* for which
Winer especially commends him. Every preacher, as he
faces his people with the Gospel, must have the fullest conviction in his soul that the Gospel is not merely a powerful
thing, but the divine energy itself. But the Gospel is not
God's omnipotence, the absolute and irresistible energy of
his will, but that distinct energy of his love or saving will
which works only in one peculiar way, according to one
fixed order, and for one specific end. This lies already in
εὐαγγέλιον, glad tidings, for the power is identified with the
message, and is not apart from it. It appears furthermore
from the modifiers **unto salvation** and "to every one that
believeth." The law too is a power of God, but the law
condemns; the Gospel saves. "Receive with meekness the
implanted word, which is able to save your souls," James 1,
21. **Salvation** is rescue from mortal danger. It includes
deliverance from sins, Matth. 1, 21; from the hand of our
enemies, Luke 1, 74; from death, 1 Cor. 15, 55; from perdition, Phil. 1, 28; from the wrath to come, 1 Thess. 1, 10.
Positively it includes justification, Rom. 3, 28; peace, 5, 1;
blessedness, 4, 7-8; eternal life, 5, 21; 6, 23. Salvation is
often spoken of as present, Luke 19, 9; 2 Cor. 6, 2; yet

salvation is also future, in heaven, 1 Pet. 1, 5 and 9; Heb.
1, 14. In our passage salvation is taken in the latter sense,
as is shown by the future tense "shall live" in verse 17, and
by 5, 21 where Paul summarizes all his previous elaboration. — **To every one that believeth,** παντὶ τῷ πιστεύοντι, is
the correlative of εὐαγγέλιον, for the glad tidings are intended both to produce faith and to be held fast by faith.
And in every case where faith occurs there salvation is the
unquestionable result. Thus παντί is full of comfort for
every troubled heart, since it mightily establishes the universality of the saving power of the Gospel. This is further
brought out by the apposition: **to the Jew first, and also to
the Greek.** The priority thus ascribed to "the Jew" is
based on the position of his nation in God's plan of sending
salvation to all men; "the Greek" is mentioned as the representative of the Gentile world. Zahn urges various
reasons against this established explanation, and himself
draws πρῶτον to both the Jew and the Greek, reading: "to
the Jew and also to the Greek first," on the plea that as yet
the Gospel had not wrought among Barbarians. This
thought, however, may be found in Paul's words also when
πρῶτον is construed in the usual way; for in verse 14 he
mentions the Barbarians beside the Greeks, but omits them
here, so that we may well say he is not speaking theoretically of the Gospel, but practically, referring his Roman
readers to the actual results achieved by the Gospel among
both Jews and Greeks. In every case the universality of the
saving power of the Gospel must be held fast. Our Greek
text encloses πρῶτον in brackets, yet the best manuscripts
contain the word, and it cannot be cancelled.

Why the Gospel is such a power is now stated: **For
therein is revealed a righteousness of God by faith unto
faith.** Note that **a righteousness,** δικαιοσύνη, is placed first
for emphasis; there is no article, and the omission suggests,
not the well-known divine attribute of justice, but a special
righteousness, one which, as the context shows, saves the
believer. Δικαιοσύνη is the quality or condition of one who
is δίκαιος, who satisfies the claims of δίκη, the norm of right;

here, of one who is as God would have him. Δικαιοσύνη is
the opposite of ἀνομία or lawlessness, of ἁμαρτία or sin, and
of ἀκαθαρσία or impurity. Now man is by nature and in his
whole life altogether opposed to the divine law, sinful, and
impure, without true righteousness, and without ways and
means of removing his sinfulness and guilt and securing
true righteousness. The wisest of the wise, whether in
Rome in Paul's time, or in any of the ages since, has never
discovered a way to turn a guilty, sinful soul into a righteous one. But this wonderful thing, utterly beyond human
ability, is brought to us by the Gospel which reveals unto
us **a righteousness** leading unto life and salvation. This
is not a human righteousness, but one that is **of God.** The
genitive θεοῦ must not be restricted to the idea of origin:
derived from God. This too lies in the word (Phil. 3, 9:
ἐκ θεοῦ), but there is more: it is a righteousness which is divine, therefore satisfactory to God, meeting all his requirements. Luther brings out this sense finely in his interpretative translation: *die vor Gott gilt,* which avails before God.
— Paul speaks of the Gospel: **therein is revealed,** he says,
this saving righteousness of God. It is unveiled there;
whoever hears the Gospel aright, when it is preached, beholds this blessed righteousness. But not as something
afar off, like the righteousness existing in the holy angels,
but as a quality and condition for the hearer himself, extended to him, and efficaciously offered to him. In his
Epistle to the Romans Paul tells all about this righteousness, and makes this the great theme of his letter. Just how
this righteousness came to be we are not told here in the
brief statement of the theme; that we find in Rom. 3, 25:
it results from Christ's propitiatory work. In that and the
following chapter the essential feature of this righteousness is elaborately set forth: it is a righteousness by divine
imputation, *justitia imputata;* for Paul writes: "We reckon
therefore that a man is justified by faith apart from the
works of the law (3, 28) . . . . Blessed is the man to
whom the Lord will not reckon sin" (4, 8).— In our text
we have the summary statement: **by faith unto faith.**

Philippi construes ἐκ πίστεως εἰς πίστιν with δικαιοσύνη, supplying οὖσα; like Rom. 3, 22: δικαιοσύνη διὰ πίστεως. Thus
this saving righteousness is one proceeding out of faith
as its condition, unto faith as the organ for its apprehension. Grammatically and according to the order of the
words it is better to construe ἐκ πίστεως εἰς πίστιν with the
verb ἀποκαλύπτεται, as most modern commentators do: this
righteousness is revealed out of faith unto faith. While it
shines forth in the Gospel, it is not seen except by faith, so
that the revelation is always in the Gospel out of faith, and
at the same time unto faith. The revelation is not complete unless faith is wrought by the Gospel and thus the
righteousness is seen by faith apprehending it. Substantially there is no difference between the two constructions; for to see by faith the righteousness revealed in the
Gospel is to have it under the condition of faith; and again,
for this revelation to be intended for faith is equal to saying that faith is the organ for apprehending it. Koegel
(Cremer: *Woerterbuch der Neutest. Graezitaet,* 10th ed.)
remarks that Paul's words must be referred to the experience of faith, *i. e.* to what is inwardly revealed to faith (ἐκ
πίστεως) and thus leads to faith and deepens it (εἰς πίστιν), in
the sense that in the Gospel there is the revelation of a
righteousness of God *aus Glauben heraus zum Glauben.*
Indeed, Paul is not ashamed of the Gospel, and in stating
the reason brings forward no abstract doctrinal proposition,
but one out of his own personal experience as a believer
himself and as a preacher who has caused many others to
believe. — **By faith unto faith** is not to be taken in the
sense of a progress of faith, either from O. T. faith to N.
T. faith (Bengel), or from a lower degree of faith to a
higher; for the apostle is not speaking of the growth,
progress, or development of faith. He is simply showing
the place and importance of faith in the revelation of God's
righteousness; *fides est prora et puppis* (Bengel). Nothing
whatever is required of us, when the Gospel brings its
revelation of righteousness to us, or at any time thereafter,

17

except faith, and this the Gospel itself works in the hearer's
heart by its efficacious power. — Zahn and Stoeckhardt
both lay stress on **revealed,** and argue from the principle
of mere common-sense that a thing must exist before it can
be revealed to anyone. Hence the former finds this righteousness existing in Christ, who was made unto us righteousness, I Cor. I, 30; and the latter finds it existing in a sentence of forgiveness pronounced by God upon the entire
world of sinners declaring them all to be righteous. Now
Christ is indeed our righteousness, namely Christ in his
atoning merits; but Paul does not indicate this treasure
(*Gut*, Zahn) in our text, as Koegel also points out; and
in I Cor. I, 30 the apostle does not speak of Christ our
righteousness objectively, but as he is apprehended by the
faith of believers: "But of him are ye" (Corinthians) "in
Christ Jesus, who was made unto us . . . righteousness," when we received him by faith. Likewise it is true
that God accepted Christ's merits as sufficient for the
whole world of sinners, and mightily declared this by raising the crucified Christ from the dead; but this likewise our
text does not refer to, nor is this an actual forgiving of the
sins of all the sinful world in the sense of Stoeckhardt.
The righteousness here spoken of is the δικαιοσύνη
ἀποκαλύπτεται ἐκ πίστεως εἰς πίστιν, that is the righteousness
which God graciously and for the sake of Christ's merits
imputes by a special divine act to every individual sinner
who truly believes in Christ, thus forgiving him all his sins
and pronouncing him free from guilt and in God's eyes
just, Rom. 3, 22 and 26; 4, 4 and 8; Ohio Synod Catechism,
239. It is the righteousness which consists of the forgiveness of sins or justification as you and I and every believer
have it. "Therefore," with our entire Lutheran Church,
"we believe, teach, and confess that our righteousness before God is, that God forgives us our sins out of pure
grace, without any work, merit, or worthiness of ours preceding, attending or following." *Formula of Concord,* 501,
4. This is the righteousness which forms the great subject
of Paul's Epistle, which none of the world's wise men ever

dreamed of in their philosophy, the preaching of which is still foolishness to the natural man and his reasonings, but which the believer contemplates as his dearest treasure and highest joy. — Paul substantiates this interpretation by the quotation from Hab. 2, 4: **as it is written, But the righteous shall live by faith.** The tiphcha accent in the Hebrew puts the emphasis on "by his faith," which Keil defines as *firma fiducia* and *fides.* The apostle omits the possessive "his," for which the Septuagint placed "my," bringing out the full, deep sense of the prophet's words in using them as a basis for the doctrine of justification by faith. "By faith" must be construed with the verb **shall live:** the righteous man shall live out of (ἐκ) faith. Whatever else he may possess in moral qualities, is of no avail; faith alone will preserve him from perishing: by faith he shall live. Not as though faith either merits or of itself produces this life; any such view is a gross perversion of faith; but it is the divinely wrought means by which God makes us partakers of life. To live here is the same as to have the σωτηρία, verse 16. And Luther has well said that wherever there is forgiveness of sins (righteousness out of faith), there is also life and salvation; the reverse is equally true.

The only Gospel for those who are unrighteous.

Launching out now into his theme Paul proves at length and convincingly that all men are utterly lost in sin and have no possible way of attaining righteousness by any ability or effort of their own. The conclusion then is evident, nothing but God's righteousness can save them. The Gospel of this righteousness is the only one for those who are lost in unrighteousness. **For the wrath of God is revealed from heaven against all ungodliness and unrighteousness of men, who hold down the truth in unrighteousness.** The righteous shall live by faith, for (γάρ) outside of this righteousness of God which is by faith, there is no hope or help, nothing but unrighteousness and the wrath of God. Both ἀποκαλύπτεται and ὀργή θεοῦ are counterparts of ἀποκαλύπτεται and δικαιοσύνη θεοῦ in the previous verse, only the verb is put first this time, and has ἀπ' οὐρανοῦ with it instead of ἐν αὐτῷ (εὐαγγελίῳ). These two revelations therefore are parallel and yet in marked contrast; in the one there is life, in the other death. **Is revealed** writes the apostle, so exactly like the word in verse 17 that we cannot refer it only or even chiefly, as Philippi and Stoeckhardt do, to the revelation of wrath at the end of the world. A present revelation is meant, one which men now, in the course of their lives, are able to see and do see. **From heaven** is added to show both the origin and the nature of this revelation; it is "from heaven," not in the sense of the visible heavens, but in the sense of the seat of God's ommipotence and majesty. "From heaven" belongs to the verb, not to the subject. A constant revelation of **the wrath of God** (margin, more exactly: *a wrath*) is in progress. God's wrath is the displeasure of his will against everything contrary to it; it is the activity of his holiness and righteousness in dealing with sin. This wrath is no fiction or figure of speech, but a dread reality, as all the Scriptures testify, corroborated by every other evidence accessible to man. Its first revelation coincides with the first sin, which cost the sinners Paradise and made them subject to death; and so at every step it has followed sin in countless ways, and made its terrors known to every sinner, sometimes blazing forth with the most awful intensity. Its final manifestation is reserved for the last great day. God's wrath is directed **against all ungodliness and unrighteousness of men,** taking in the two sides of sin, and this completely: any and every form of irreligion and of immorality; every transgression of the first as well as the second table of the law. There is no article with ἀνθρώπων so that all men generally are meant. The entire expression is comprehensive in the widest manner; there is no kind or instance of ungodliness or of immorality in any man anywhere but what the divine wrath goes out against it. Men may laugh at certain sins, may count them venial, excusable, unavoidable, merely natural, and the like; not so God. "Here Paul lumps all men into one mass, and concludes, they are all godless and unrighteous, ignorant of the righteousness that avails before God, the righteousness of faith." Luther. The worst feature in man's sinfulness is brought out by the addition: **who hold down the truth in unrighteousness.** The A. V. and the margin of the R. read: *who hold the truth,* which necessitates an explanation amounting in substance to the other translation; to hold the truth in unrighteousness is to hinder or repress it, κατέχειν, to hold it down. **Truth** here is not the Gospel, but the truth of God as nature reveals it to rational creatures, as also the apostle explains in the next clause. The truth demands proper recognition in man's heart and conduct, but men **hold down** the truth, refuse to obey it and yield to it, and this by means of **unrighteousness,** ἀδικίᾳ, the immorality just mentioned as the companion of irreligion. Bengel: *Veritas nititur in mente et urget, sed homo impedit eam.* He dethrones truth and will not let it reign in his heart and members, allowing his immoral desires to triumph in rebellion. He overrides the promptings of conscience, disregards the voice of duty, puts away the thought of God and the retribution of divine justice. In other words, he sins knowingly, again and again, against the light of truth God has placed in his heart; and this is what makes men's sins so exceedingly heinous in God's eyes.

Paul substantiates it: **because that which may be known of God is manifest in them; for God manifested it unto them.** Διότι = διὰ τοῦτο ὅτι, *propterea quod,* **because,** introducing the explanation concerning "the truth" which men hold down in unrighteousness. In the classics τὸ γνωστόν is **that which may be known,** and both English versions as well as prominent commentators retain this meaning here, the latter because they think the other meaning of the word would introduce a tautology: "that which is known is manifest in them." But the N. T., as Philippi shows, uses τὸ γνωστόν in every other case to express: "that

which is known," and this alone would be almost conclusive
here. The classic meaning, however, is too wide, for many
things which may be known of God are not actually
known and manifest to men. In addition we find no
reason here why the knowable things of God should be
distinguished from the unknowable, the mysteries beyond
comprehension. Nor need a tautology result, for Paul states
that what is known of God **is manifest,** or clear, **in them,**
in men generally, their hearts and consciences. Though
it is manifest or clear "in them," they refuse to obey it.
For God manifested it unto them — "God," put forward
emphatically: God himself, we might say. By the whole
work of creation, by a thousand beneficent providences and
retributive inflictions, as well as by the workings of man's
own mind and conscience, God manifested himself unto
men: Acts 14, 17; Ps. 65, 8-13; Matth. 5, 45; Rom. 2, 15.
All this manifestation from God himself to men, "that they
should seek God, if haply they might feel after him, and
find him," Acts 17, 27, man's unrighteousness held down and
frustrated in its purpose. — But Paul is even more explicit:
**For the invisible things of him since the creation of the
world are clearly seen, being perceived through the
things that are made,** *even* **his everlasting power and divinity.** This explains more fully what has just been said
concerning God's manifestation. "The invisible things are
clearly seen," τὰ ἀόρατα καθορᾶται is an oxymoron, a paradox;
for how can invisible things be seen at all, to say nothing
of being seen clearly? The solution of this apparent contradiction is indicated by the addition: "being perceived
through the things that are made." Paul uses the plural:
the invisible things, for he refers to the divine attributes,
two of which he mentions in the close of the sentence, the
power and the divinity. These, invisible in themselves,
are nevertheless **clearly seen** (καθορᾶν a strengthened ὁρᾶν),
and that generally by men, not merely by a few gifted
with unusual powers of vision or insight. **Being perceived
through the things that are made** means that they are
apprehended by the νοῦς, man's reason and mind, by which

he is distinguished from all other earthly creatures. The
word νοούμενα, from νοεῖν is especially fine and expressive,
as it fits exactly a perception obtained by means of the
senses and man's reasoning powers combined. The eye,
ear, *etc.*, brings to the mind the wonders of **the things that
are made** by God's creative power and wisdom, and the
mind perceives their true meaning and significance. The
heavens declare the glory of God, and the earth showeth
his handiwork, Ps. 19, 1. Behind the veil of created things
the great Creator himself stands, and man's eyes, even
though dimmed by sin, are fully able to behold him. And
this **since the creation of the world,** since the beginning
of time; ἀπό is not "from" in the sense of means. Ever
since all things were created, and man himself with his
powers of reason, he perceived the power and divinity of
the Creator as this was constantly manifested to him.
What he did with this perception and how he perverted
and misused it, and how he still tries to evade and even
deny it, Paul in part shows in the following sentences. We
must note especially the comprehensiveness of his statement: "since the creation of the world," from Adam on,
all men through all the ages, whoever had eyes to see
and a mind to think. The invisible things of God which
were clearly seen are designated as **his everlasting power
and divinity.** "Everlasting," ἀΐδιος (from ἀεί, ever), is
that power which never ceases, declines, fades, or grows
old and weak, as do all the powers of the creatures. "Thy
years are throughout all generations. Of old hast thou
laid the foundation of the earth: and the heavens are the
work of thy hands. They shall perish, but thou shalt endure: yea, all of them shall wax old like a garment; as
a vesture shalt thou change them, and they shall be changed:
but thou art the same, and thy years shall have no end."
Ps. 102, 24-27. The **power** of God is his omnipotence manifested in the creation, preservation, and government of the
universe. **Divinity,** θειότης, is Godhood not θεότης, Godhead,
as the A. V. translates it; it really signifies the sum-total
of the divine attributes, all God's perfections in one. The

glory, majesty, wisdom, and beneficence of God all shine
forth beside his omnipotence in the works of his hands.
The apostle places this comprehensive term beside the narrower one in order to bring out in one brief statement the
full extent of what God manifests concerning himself in
creation. His entire elaboration shows that he utterly re-
pudiates any view of the world, scientific or otherwise,
which assumes that matter is eternal, that the world came
into being of itself, that nature brought forth herself the
wonders and varieties we see, *etc.* — Is εἰς τὸ εἶναι αὐτοὺς
ἀναπολογήτους a purpose clause, as the R. V. translates it:
that they may be without excuse, or a result clause, as
the margin and also the A. V. has it? Commentators are
divided, some saying positively it cannot be the latter. 2
Cor. 8, 6 shows that εἰς with the infinitive can express
simple result, although it is usually used to express purpose. Here a result clause is evidently simplest, and
Philippi notes that the apostle's following statements in
no way take up the thought of purpose. Paul is reporting simple facts: God manifested himself; men saw his
omnipotence and divinity; and now he adds: they are without excuse. They cannot plead ignorance of God, because
his manifestation was constantly before their eyes; nor
inability to perceive that manifestation, because they all
did see it, but held down the truth in unrighteousness and
followed their own evil inclinations. That this is God's
purpose also in his manifestation of himself is not to be
denied, although certainly not his only purpose, but, as
Zahn states, his purpose in regard to those who will not use
the truth for their own good. — Here our text breaks off.
It gives enough of Paul's argument to show that all men
are utterly lost in unrighteousness, and that the Gospel
with its revelations of God's righteousness is their only
hope. What a blessed Epiphany that God revealed his
righteousness in the Gospel amid this world full of unrighteousness and sin! We who are utterly unjust in ourselves can become righteous and live through faith in Jesus
Christ.

HOMILETICAL HINTS.

The King's banner ever goes forward. There is never a command to surrender or retreat. The cross ever leads on to the crown, and the very blood of the martyrs is the seed of the church. The kingdom of heaven is never won by the half-hearted. Many a victor has passed over the black basalt pavements of Rome's thoroughfares to place his triumphant banners in the shrine of some pagan temple on the heights. Now comes one in spirit greater than all these. His victories are greater; the power that achieved them is greater; the spoils are greater. In place of the Emperor's eagles he unfurls the banner of the cross. And no sneer that he is but a provincial can make him ashamed in the great metropolis, for the power of the Gospel has won and will ever continue to win triumphs which utterly outdo all the achievements of earthly weapons and wisdom. All the world is my debtor was the imperial claim, which exacted tribute from every corner of the world, Greek and Barbarian alike. But Paul comes with mighty acknowledgment of duty and love: I am debtor to all the world, Greek and Barbarian alike, and by the untold, exhaustless riches of God's saving Gospel he will pay that debt and enrich Rome and the world with eternal possessions.

> "Ashamed of Jesus! yes I may
> When I've no guilt to wash away,
> No tear to wipe, no good to crave,
> No fears to quell, no soul to save.

> "Till then—nor is my boasting vain—
> Till then I boast a Savior slain!
> And, oh, may this my glory be,
> That Christ is not ashamed of me!"—J. Grigg.

The purpose of the Gospel is the rescue of those who are in mortal danger and would utterly perish if God would not extend unto them this powerful means of rescue. . . . The apparent or real unreasonableness of the Gospel might make not only the hearer whom it would convert, but also the preacher who is to proclaim it suspicious. But the power that conquers all such suspicion lies on an altogether different plane. He who is fighting for his life amid storm-tossed billows never thinks of asking whether the life-saving appliance carried out to him is constructed according to the laws of reason; despairingly he grasps at a straw, and much more at a mighty cable which, he sees, others around him are grasping and are saved beyond question from destruction. Zahn.

Faith saves. Every believer has that experience. It does not make one happy in the shallow, superficial sense of the word; it does not make one joyous after the fashion of those who want to be gay and amuse themselves; it does not bring the fulfillment of wishes for this life, as many dream that fulfillment, wishes for ease and comfort; it drives Paul across land and sea, brings him to Jerusalem into prison, bonds, and suffering, holds him confined in Cæsarea for years, plunges him into the deeps of the sea in the shipwreck on his journey, locks him fast to a soldier-guard in Rome, and finally lays his head on the block for the sake of Jesus' name — but it saves him, so that he exclaims: Nothing shall be able to separate us from the love of God which is in Christ Jesus! Matthes.

Though we proudly call ourselves sons of the 20th Christian century, three dread powers hold us in talon grasp, three frightful shadows block our way, a bar to our haughty onward course. One of them is from yesterday, and follows us with a voice of lamentation, or rather of accusation, whithersoever we flee. It is the power of our guilt, the voice of a conscience raising its testimony ever against us, from which there is no escape. Our own past damns us. All of us! Never an exception! Not only the criminal in his bare cell behind grated bars! We all carry our conscience with us. It mocks at all our efforts to hush it. You cannot kill it by speech or by silence, by tears or by laughter. And what shall deliver us from the second, born of to-day? It is the power of helplessness in moral bankruptcy. The present enmeshes us with its unforeseen assaults, its unexpected temptations. Before our will assents we are already lost. We no longer know what we do; we no longer do what we will; we no longer will what we ought. Called into being by the Creator to be rulers of the earth, we are not even masters of ourselves. In our own sins we perish, strive as we may. What shall free us from this shadow? And what, finally, from that other which is born of to-morrow, and also blocks our path? It is the power of our blind uncertainty concerning our eternal destiny. What about life and about death? Does it pay at all to live? Is it safe at all to die? Painful was our coming into life, dreadful will be our exit from it. And what then? Only a little dust? The odor of decay? Instead of being, dissolution? And meanwhile pains and plagues, burdens and cries, offenses and fears? And for this all our loving and suffering, our striving and battling? What will help us and arm us against these impenetrable shadows of our own perishableness? Rump.

To speak of God's wrath is little relished in our day. The word sounds harsh to the weak nerves of our race. Is God a man that he should be angry as we are? Is not God love, alto-

gether love? As though we ever intended to deny that! But let
us beware lest we draw God down into our human limitations. In
religious things we dare never make assertions simply to quiet
weak, nervous systems. Truth must ever be supreme, lest we
belong to those who hold down the truth in unrighteousness.
Nothing will deliver us from God's wrath, as long as we close our
eyes to the truth. . . . One of the fundamental errors of our
time is the idea that religion has developed from crude beginnings
to a clearer and purer knowledge of God. On account of our
guilt the very reverse has taken place, and still takes place this
very day. . . All these ideas are a unit in assuming that God's
righteousness is our well-earned merit. It is due to ourselves if
our lives finally meet God's approval. How strange it sounds to
men when the Gospel proclaims an entirely different righteousness
to them! We can well understand the hatred of the Pharisees
against Jesus for daring to place above a Pharisee a miserable publican who could do nothing but pray, God be merciful to me a sinner,
and declaring that this man went down to his house justified rather
than the other. Is that righteousness? It certainly is according to
the Scriptures which declare that God resisteth the proud and
giveth grace to the humble. This righteousness was fully brought
to light by the Gospel of Christ. For according to the preaching of
this Gospel, undoubtedly this is revealed as the righteousness of
God, that every believer in Christ is accounted righteous and
acceptable in the sight of God. Riemer.

Luther writes concerning the word "righteousness" in Rom.
1, 17: There I sought long, and knocked again and again; for the
word *Justitia Dei*, the righteousness of God, lay in my way, since
common usage gave it the interpretation: God's righteousness is
the virtue whereby he is righteous in himself and damns the
sinner. Thus all the doctors, Augustine excepted, had interpreted
this passage, saying: The righteousness of God is the wrath of
God. As often then as I read this passage, I ever wished God
had never revealed the Gospel. For who could love a God who is
wroth, judges, and damns? Until finally by the Holy Spirit's
enlightenment I considered more diligently the word of the prophet
Habakkuk: "But the righteous shall live by faith." From this I
drew the conclusion that life must come out of faith and thus I
turned the abstract into the concrete (as they say in the schools),
that is, I turned the word "righteousness" into the word "righteous."
namely that a man becomes righteous in God's sight through faith.
Then the entire sacred Scriptures, and heaven itself, were opened
unto me. — And a year before his death he wrote: Then at once I
felt as if I were born anew, and had found a wide open door to go
into Paradise itself; and the Scriptures also now appeared unto me
in an entirely different light than heretofore, and I ran through the

entire Bible, as I could remember it, and gathered also in other words its interpretation according to this rule. . . . Just as hitherto I had earnestly hated this word: "God's righteousness," I began now to count it precious and esteem it as my dearest and most comforting word; and this passage in St. Paul was in truth to me the real portal of Paradise. — Not in Rome, but in Romans, did Luther find the forgiveness of sins.

The Revelation of God's Saving Righteousness:

I. *Shining forth in the Gospel.*
II. *Justifying every believer.*
III. *Bestowing life eternal.*

Salvation in God's Righteousness.

For

I. *This is righteousness indeed,* and
II. *This righteousness brings salvation indeed.*

The Fundamental Revelations God has Made unto Man.

He has revealed:

I. *His power and divinity.*
II. *His righteous wrath.*
III. *His pardoning grace.*

Be Not Ashamed of the Gospel of Christ!

I. *Miserable he who lacks it.*
II. *Lost he who spurns it.*
III. *Blessed he who believes it.*
IV. *Honored he who proclaims it.*

Langsdorff.

The Gospel a Power of God.

I. *Because of what it gives.*
II. *Because of what it works.*

C. C. Hein.

The Righteous Shall Live by Faith.

I. *The perfection of his righteousness.*
II. *The power of his faith.*
III. *The blessedness of his life.*

THE FOURTH SUNDAY AFTER EPIPHANY.

Rom. 7, 7-16.

This text deals with the law and its work. It does this not theoretically, but practically, describing the actual experience of the apostle Paul. And this is by no means exceptional, but a vivid exhibition of our experience generally. The office and work of the law is to produce the knowledge of sin, first with a view to contrition and conversion, and after that with a view to constant repentance in the Christian life. So our text forms an important link in the chain of Epiphany texts in the Eisenach selections. Hitherto we have studied the blessed work of the Gospel; but this would not be complete unless we also understood the painful work of the law. Christ's Epiphany in our hearts will thus be more clearly set forth. *All who have experienced this Epiphany have experienced likewise the painful effects of the law.* Our text belongs together with the following one, which is taken from the very next chapter of Romans. In preaching on our text it will be necessary to refer to the saving work of the Gospel already so fully explained in the previous texts; in other words, we must rightly divide the Word, separate and correlate law and Gospel, and thus do full justice to our text as part of the series in which it appears.

There are two clearly distinguished sections: the first shows the work of the law before regeneration (verses 7-14); the second, the work of the law after regeneration (verses 15-16).

The work of the law before regeneration.

In the sections preceding our text Paul declares that Christians have been made free from sin (verses 18 and

22), and likewise that they have been delivered or dis-
charged from the law. This places side by side deliverance from the servitude of the law and deliverance
from the servitude of sin. There is danger here of
drawing a false conclusion, of classing the two together.
What shall we say then? Is the law sin? Ὁ νόμος
ἁμαρτία? The question is not concerning a possible
identity of the two, which would require ἡ ἁμαρτία with
the article in the predicate; and such a question would be
foolish on the face of it. Nor does the apostle ask whether
the law is the origin of sin. His meaning is simply: Is
the law something sinful, *per se pravum et vitiosum?* This
is the conclusion Paul's readers might draw from his statement that we are delivered by the Gospel both from the
bondage of sin and of the law. But: **God forbid,** μὴ
γένοιτο! This would be utterly to misunderstand the law
and its relation to sin. — Paul sets the matter right:
Howbeit, I had not known sin, except through the law.
He uses the strong adversative ἀλλά, which the R. V.
translates with the concessive **howbeit.** The A. V. uses
nay, which is better; it is the German *sondern,* "on the contrary." Here for the first time since chapter 1, 16 Paul
speaks in the first person. He does it not because of his
own person, but in order, by describing his personal experience, the better to set forth the work and purpose of
the law. His own experience is typical of the experience
of men generally when they come under the power of the
law. He has already summed the matter up previously
(3, 20) in the statement: "For through the law cometh
the knowledge of sin." To **know sin** is really to understand its character as ἀνομία and ἀσέβεια, opposition to God,
the divine Giver of the law. Men sin, and talk of sin,
before they come under the hand of the law, but they consider their wickedness only as something light and excusable, a natural weakness. Even crimes are thus ex-
tenuated, as countless examples in our court trials and in
public opinion concerning certain misdeeds still testify.
But all this changes in the face of the **law,** which Luther

and the Formula of Concord (592, 17) define as follows: "Everything that reproves sin is and belongs to
the law, whose peculiar office it is to reprove sin
and lead to the knowledge of sins." Nobody knows
what sin is until the law brings it home to him. —
Paul proves and explains it by adding an example:
**for I had not known coveting, except the law had said,
Thou shalt not covet.** The τέ corresponds to the following δέ in the next sentence (on the one hand . . . on
the other). In the apodosis οὐκ ᾔδειν the ἄν is omitted, as
is sometimes done, making the statement more positive.
The future: "Thou wilt not covet!" is used in an imperative sense, which also follows the regular Hebrew way of
expressing legal commands, Paul here quoting Ex. 20, 17;
Deut. 5, 21. The apostle combines the last two commandments of the Decalog for his illustration. He says he
would not have known **coveting,** that is as sin and offense
to God, if the law had not come and positively forbidden it.
Men generally do not think of calling coveting, or *lust* (so
the margin), or the depraved desires of their hearts (the
παθήματα, verse 5; the ἐπιθυμίαι, Mark 4, 19), sin in the
sense of a breaking of the law, of an insult to God. Philippi
says the ethics of the Bible are the opposite of Kant's doctrine of morality, and we may add, the opposite of all
worldly ideas of what is moral and what immoral. Coveting or lust is the first stirring of sin in the heart, as we
see in the very first sin in Eden, Gen. 3, 6; and from it
spring countless wicked acts (compare Ahab coveting
Naboth's vineyard). But even before a single outward
act results, and if none ever results, the lust in the heart
is an offense to God, a rebellion against his law. And
that is what the law showed to Paul when he came in
contact with it, just as the law now repeats this operation for others. — It did another thing for the apostle:
**but sin, finding occasion, wrought in me through the
commandment all manner of coveting.** Ἀφορμή is from
ἀφορμάω (ἀπό and ὁρμάω), to make a start from a place,
and expresses the origin, cause, **occasion,** pretext of an

act. So **sin,** "the sin which dwelleth in me" (7, 17 and 20),
"the potency of sin," "the principle of sin," original sin,
or the inborn perversion and depravity of our nature, took
the law as an occasion, a pretext, a point to start from in
its evil work. Sin is always looking for an occasion to
break out. Temptation does not need to invite it very long.
And on the other hand, since sin in its nature is rebellion
against God, the divine law does not need to utter its
prohibitions very long, until sin answers in its wicked way,
deliberately challenging the commandment by a flood of
evil deeds. The R. V. translates λαβοῦσα with **finding;**
sin is eager to find an occasion, its evil eyes constantly
seek pretexts, and greedily grasp them. The Greek uses
λαμβάνειν ἐκ, παρά, or ἀπό, but not διά; on this account, and
because of the position of the phrase **through the commandment** in the sentence, the R. V. connects it with the
main verb: "wrought in me through the commandment all
manner of coveting." The A. V. translates: "Sin, taking
occasion by the commandment." Some commentators
justify the latter because they think the apostle is bound
to indicate what constitutes the occasion. And he does indicate it, without forcing his language; for if sin, finding
occasion, works through the commandment all manner of
coveting, the occasion is undoubtedly that very commandment of which sin runs foul. With the commandment to
incite the wickedness sin **wrought** in Paul, κατειργάσατο,
wrought thoroughly so as to produce its effect; it actually
accomplished **all manner of coveting,** lust of every sort
(1, 29), now this, now that evil desire. And thus the
result of the law's coming to Paul was twofold: he now
knew sin, coveting for instance, in its true character as
opposition to God, and he now found sin putting out one
lawless expression after another. Luther writes: "Whenever by the law there is made known to a man sin, death,
wrath, God's judgment, hell, *etc.*, he cannot but be im-
patient, murmur, and hate God and God's will." And
again: "Now when he learns to know sin and death, he
would rather there were no God. So the law makes him

hate God exceedingly, which means not only that by the law one sees and knows sin, but also that by knowing it sin is increased, fanned to a flame, kindled, and .made great." This effect of the law upon the sinner and his sin is due to the vicious nature of sin. Sin is always the *causa efficiens,* when new outbreaks occur. They are the effect of the law only *per accidens,* as the dogmaticians put it. Godet says that "sin takes advantage of the law" to blaze forth the more. — Paul himself adds in explanation: **for apart from the law sin** *is* **dead.** "Is" must be supplied, not "was," which, if this were the sense, could not have been omitted. The proposition is entirely general. Sin is like a stream, flowing calmly on, until the law interposes a dam; then it boils up and grows into a flood. 1 Cor. 15, 56. Sin sleeps like a wild beast in its lair; the moment the voice of the law is heard, it rouses up, gnashes its fangs, and rages forth.

The apostle goes on now to tell more particularly of his experience with the law before his regeneration. **And I was alive apart from the law once: but when the commandment came, sin revived, and I died.** There was a time when the sin that was in him since his birth caused no special disturbance. It was when he was **apart from the law,** before it met him with its full condemning force. Paul says of this time: **I was alive once.** Both the ἐγώ and ἔζων have emphasis. After stating in general: "Apart from the law sin is dead," Paul now makes this personal; he says: I have myself had such a time apart from the law, when I and my sin went securely on, and no messenger cried halt. Of this time and condition he says: "I was alive once." What time does Paul · refer to, and what sort of life was this? Our dogmaticians are helpful here with their distinction of three states, the *status securitatis,* the *status sub lege,* and the *status regenerationis.* Paul is speaking of the first when he says that at a certain time he was apart from the law and thus alive. With all his sinfulness and sin he never recognized his

18

terrible condition. He was "alive" because the death-blow
of the law had not struck him down. He sat secure in
the house of his own righteousness and ignorance, as
though all were well, never dreaming that it rested on
nothing but sand. Most commentators take it that Paul
is speaking here of his childhood days, the sunny period
before religious questions troubled him; some even designate the twelfth year as the limit of this period, since
Jewish boys at this age were held to observe the outward requirements of the law. But such fixing of time is
a mistake, the greater because it fails to understand fully
what Paul is describing. His days of false security went
on far beyond his childhood. Besser is right when he says
that they continued more or less through the entire time
when he was in the flesh; and Philippi adds that all through
this period, whenever the law came to disturb Paul, he
ever and ever worked back again to his old security. And
that is exactly the situation with men to-day. Before they
have come in contact with the condemnation and terrors
of the law they are filled with security. They have little
trouble with their worldly ideas of morality; their consciences are easily hushed, if now and then they awake.
And even after the thunders of God's law strike them,
they often succeed in stopping their ears again and getting
away from that law and the resentment it arouses in them.
— But Paul's fine life of security was destined to extinc-
tion. **The commandment came,** that is the law in its
specific commandment, as Paul has just instanced one. It
met him squarely with its prohibition as from God: Thou
shalt' not! and with its requirement: Thou shalt! When
this occurred for the first time in Paul's experience, so
that it struck home in his heart, we are not told. Moreover, we must not assume that this happened just once,
with the full effect resulting at one stroke. No doubt the
commandment forbidding coveting was the one that first
took hold of Paul's sinful heart; whereupon **sin revived,**
and blazed forth in resentment and rebellion, as has been
shown above. So other of God's commandments pierce

the armor now of this, now of that sinful, secure heart; and always "sin revives" and shows its real opposition to God. Paul says ἀνέζησεν *revixit*, became alive again. The verb has no other meaning, as Philippi shows conclusively over against those who would make it mean "came to life," after the analogy of other compounds with ἀνά. The exceptional meaning is urged here, because in Paul the individual sin did not live before, then die, and finally under the law revive. But Bengel already points out that Paul looks beyond the individual: sin was first alive in the open disobedience of Adam, then is dead in men who live in security apart from the law, and thus revives, becomes alive again, every time the law makes itself felt. But the first stroke of the law in Paul's pharisaic heart was not enough. He rallied and felt secure again, until again the strife between his sin and the law broke out. The two states of security and of rebellion against the law alternated. The same thing is witnessed in men to-day similarly placed. Nor can this wavering come to an end, unless the law is utterly repudiated and cast off, or despair with its dread consequences sets in under the lashings of the law, or the grace of God in Christ Jesus leads the stricken soul to true peace and life. — Concurrent with the effect just described is the other, put into the striking words: **and I died.** "The sting of death is sin; and the power of sin is the law," 1 Cor. 15, 56. Under the law sin showed its power and revived but in this very act it showed what it had held hidden in its sheath — death: Paul felt in himself the sting of spiritual death. His being alive was robbed of its mask, he realized that he was in the talons of death. No doubt he battled against the thought, and succeeded in snatching back longer or shorter periods of the old security, until at last the climax of the *status legalis* was reached in the vision on the way to Damascus and the three days of blindness which followed. Then Paul died indeed: dead in his sin under the law he knew it, and was raised to life by that power which is greater than the law, mightier than sin, the Gospel of pardon in the Redeemer's blood. — So this strange thing happened — and it happens again and again to-day: **the commandment, which** (according to the divine intention) *was* **unto life, this** (very commandment) **I found** *to be* **unto death.** Meyer would have us note the tragic emphasis of these words. Lev. 18, 5: "Ye shall therefore keep my statutes, and my judgments: which if a man do, he shall live in them." Luke 10, 28: "This do, and thou shalt live." But alas: "There is not a just man upon earth, that doeth good and sinneth not." Eccl. 7, 20. And so the law works nothing but death, for: "Cursed is everyone which continueth not in all things that are written in the book of the law, to do them," Gal. 3, 10. — But let us ever place the blame where alone it belongs, upon sin, never upon the law (which would place it also upon God): **for sin, finding occasion, through the commandment beguiled me, and through it slew me.** Here again the R. V. construes more correctly than the A. V. Sin, looking for an occasion, found one and skillfully, cunningly used it. The very commandment which was given to Adam and Eve to safeguard them, the treacherous tempter used in order to beguile them: "Yea, hath God said, Ye shall not eat of every tree of the garden?" "For God doth know that in the day ye eat thereof, then your eyes shall be opened, and ye shall be as gods, knowing good and evil." Gen. 3, 1 and 5. And so sin slew them. How much more readily is the process repeated in those who by nature are already under the dominion of sin! Forbidden fruit is sweet. Even the heathen with only the light of nature to guide them have recognized it. Ovid writes: "The permitted is unpleasing; the forbidden consumes us fiercely." Again: "We strive against the forbidden, and ever desire what is denied." Philippi remarks that the deception extends farther: after man has committed the sin, he imagines he can escape the results by efforts of his own, expiation by his own sufferings, or attempts to lead a more moral life. And so sin slays him again and again, and he is altogether lost in the meshes of death. — Yet it is sin that does this; Paul positively asserts: **So that the law is holy, and the commandment holy, and righteous, and good.** This conclusion stands because nothing contrary to it can be found in the connection of law with sin. The entire **law** of God **is holy,** because it is the expression of God's holy will. "Ye shall be holy: for I the Lord your God am holy," Lev. 19, 2. And so is every **commandment** of which the law is composed. The commandment is mentioned especially because of the one commandment which first took hold of Paul, and because it is generally by means of one of its specific commandments that the law strikes the sinner's heart. It is **holy,** just as is the law of which it is a part; moreover, it is **righteous,** requiring nothing but what is in harmony with the divine norm of right; and it is **good,** ethically excellent and precious, which is even more than merely wholesome and beneficial, although it includes this. — But again one might be puzzled: **Did then that which is good become death unto me?** The good law and the evil sin coming into contact with each other might confuse a careless thinker. For a good thing can certainly not become evil to me, or work evil in me, to say nothing of working the greatest evil of all, death, temporal, spiritual, and eternal. This reasoning is as specious as that above when the law was regarded as sin, because we are delivered alike from both by the grace of God. So here too Paul interposes an energetic **God forbid.** And then he sets the matter right: not the law, **but sin** is become death unto me. Ἀλλὰ ἡ ἁμαρτία is elliptical, and we must supply from the previous sentence ἐμοὶ ἐγένετο θάνατος. The evil is wholly in sin. But men do not recognize it. So God sends them the law to show them what sin is, namely a death-dealing thing. He touches it with the law, and at once all its death-dealing qualities and activities appear. **That it might be shown to be sin** expresses this divine intention, God wants us to recognize sin as what it really is. Note that ἁμαρτία here lacks the article and must be read as the predicate, and not the subject of φανῇ. And sin is shown to be sin

by working death to me through that which is good;
it is so deadly that it takes even the good law of God
and uses, or rather abuses, it for my destruction. Just
how it does that Paul has shown above; he refers to it
here, because this shows up sin as God wants us to see
it. — A second purpose clause brings out more fully
God's intention in sending the law to the sinner. The
second *ἵνα* takes up the first and amplifies the thought:
**that through the commandment sin might become ex-
ceeding sinful.** The law does not add to sin more sin,
or new sinful qualities, but it exposes the sinfulness of
sin by meeting it with the divine: Thou shalt, and: Thou
shalt not! which sin then, true to its wicked nature, fla-
grantly, rebelliously transgresses and tramples under foot.
So sin "through the commandment" comes out in its real
nature, becomes exceedingly sinful, shows how exceedingly far it misses the mark. In all which the law remains absolutely good, without a single blemish. What the
ultimate intention of God is in thus showing us the wickedness and deadliness of sin, Paul does not state here; God
means to deliver us from sin, that was his purpose in
Paul, which also was graciously accomplished. And the
Romans understood the apostle well, for they too had been
delivered from sin's terrors and dominion (6, 18 and 22).

The work of the law after regeneration.

When the apostle now continues the narration of his
personal experience with the law, the question arises
whether he still speaks of his former unregenerate state
as before, or whether, with the marked change of the verbs
from the past to the present tense, he now tells us what
occurred after his regeneration. The old Greek fathers
thought that he continues describing his former unregenerate state. Augustine at first had the same view, but
changed it when the controversy with Pelagius impelled
him to examine the question more closely. In this he was
followed by our theologians, while most of the Romanists,
and also the Socinians and Arminians followed the exegesis

of the Greek fathers. Our Confessions quote this section of Romans repeatedly, and use it as a proof passage for the doctrine that the flesh still adheres to the regenerate. "Nevertheless the old Adam always clings to them (the believers) in their nature and all its internal and external powers. Of this the apostle has written, Rom. 7, 18; also 7, 16." Repentance therefore must ever continue: "This repentance in Christians continues until death, because through the entire life it contends with sin remaining in the flesh, as Paul (Rom. 7, 14-25) shows, that he wars with the law in his members, *etc."* The older Calvinists agree with this interpretation. But the Pietists went back to the other, and were followed by the Rationalists and others. Most of the best later commentators abide by the Lutheran exegesis. A full discussion of the history of the exegesis is found in the commentaries by Tholuck, Philippi, and Luthardt.

The work of the law continues and must continue even after regeneration because of the sin which still remains in our nature. Paul has defended the law against two possible aspersions. It cannot be classed with sin, nor is its nature to produce death. Why not? **For we know that the law is spiritual.** This reason covers also the other truth Paul has set forth, namely that the law brings out the sinfulness of sin. This too it does and is bound to do because it is spiritual. **We know** means that we Christians or believers have this knowledge; all others are blind to the real nature of the law, which they so generally show by trying to satisfy it by mere outward works. Semler conjectured that Paul wrote οἶδα μέν instead of οἴδαμεν, and Zahn agrees with him. The manuscripts are positively against this reading; moreover, if Paul had used the singular, the μέν could not stand with οἶδα, but would have to stand in the following clause: ὁ μὲν νόμος. Paul does not say: "I know," but: "we know," we who have received the Spirit of Christ and are able thus to judge aright of spiritual things. Of the law we know that it is **spiritual.** Usually this is explained by pointing out that the law is an expression of God's will, and must therefore be spiritual; πνευματικός, to agree with the divine πνεῦμα. Calvin points to "the celestial and angelic righteousness" which it requires, as evidence of its spiritual quality, and others to still other manifestation of its spirituality. All this is quite correct, although Paul does not dwell on these details of origin, connection with God, character of its precepts, rewards, *etc.*, but speaks of our experience with the law, by which we know that it is altogether spiritual. This is the thought that runs through his whole argument. We who have had full experience of the law, we know that it is spiritual. "If the law were a bodily matter, we could satisfy it by outward works; but since it is spiritual, no one can satisfy it, unless he do from the bottom of his heart all that he does. But such a heart is the gift only of the Holy Ghost." Luther. Men without Christ do not realize this, but "imagine that by outward works they can fulfil the law . . . Hence Christ takes the law into his own hands, and explains it spiritually from Matth. 5, 21 *etc.*; Rom. 7, 14; and 1, 18." *Formula of Concord*, 591, 10. — Here, however, is where the trouble results: The law is indeed spiritual: **but I am carnal, sold under sin.** Paul might have continued in the plural: We are carnal *etc.;* but, as before, he prefers to use himself and his own experience as an illustration of the condition of believers. The ἐγώ is emphatic: "I, apostle though I am, I am carnal." He uses the present tense: **I am;** but he does not contrast this with what he formerly was. His present condition is connected with the past, as also the γάρ plainly indicates, it is the outgrowth of the past. Certainly it is not something that has set in with his regeneration, or after it. I am **carnal,** he writes. The best texts all have σάρκινος, *carneus*, which means "of flesh," and denotes the substance, σὰρξ ὤν; whereas σαρκικός, *carnalis*, means "fleshly," denoting the quality, κατὰ σάρκα ὤν. Σάρξ, when contrasted with πνεῦμα (here πνευματικός), signifies our sinful human nature. Paul says: "The law is spiritual, but I am of flesh." Born of flesh he is still flesh, although reborn. Nor does this conflict with the statement in the next chapter, 8, 9: "Ye are not in the flesh, but in the spirit." "The new spiritual insight communicated in regeneration, and increasing with santification, enables him more and more to see the real nature of the indwelling corruption that pervades and underlies all that he does and thinks. A few drops of aniline or of blood color a large amount of water and render it impure by penetrating every atom. The more deeply spiritual the believer, the more delicate is his sense of sin, and the more vivid his consciousness of its presence. . . . Just to the degree then that he recognizes himself as carnal, has he begun to be spiritual." Jacobs. — The apostle defines more closely what he means and to what point he especially refers, by adding: **sold under sin.** The image is that of a slave driven to do his master's will. It is deeply humiliating, and we must not overlook the sadness with which Paul writes these words, nor the longing which fills his heart to be fully and completely free from this servitude (verse 24). In so far as he is still flesh sin exerts its mastery. "I know that in me, that is, in my flesh, dwelleth no good thing," verse 18, and this comes out when the flesh wars against the spirit: "I see a different law in my members, warring against the law of my mind, and bringing me into captivity under the law of sin which is in my members," verse 23. By σάρκινος Paul means this law of sin in his members; and by his being sold under sin he means his being brought into captivity to this law, which occurs every time he sins and sinful stirrings mar his good works. — Very vividly Paul describes his condition as a slave and prisoner of sin: **for that which I do I know not: for not what I would, that do I practice; but what I hate, that I do.** So he is not free; his spiritual life cannot unfold itself as it would and as indeed it should. **That which I do,** ὃ κατεργάζομαι, means what I carry out and accomplish, and refers to Paul's actual deeds. These, he says, **I know not,** which cannot mean: I do not *allow*, in the sense of "approve,"

as the A. V. translates, since γινώσκειν never has this meaning. Neither does the apostle say that he acts blindly,
involuntarily, without being conscious of what he does. His
sins are indeed sins of weakness, and into many of them,
no doubt, he is hurried and does not fully realize their
import at the moment; he does not sin deliberately and wilfully, which would mean the loss of regeneration. But this is
hardly what οὐ γινώσκω means to convey; for he continues:
not what I would, that do I practice, showing that it is
the opposite of his will, or desire, or of that in which he
delights (verse 22), and hence that he knows and is conscious enough of his sinful acts. And again he says:
what I hate, that I do, and hating it he evidently knows
both the sinful act and its character. All three verbs:
κατεργάζομαι, πράττω, and ποιῶ are in the present tense, indicating what is done repeatedly. By οὐ γινώσκω Paul denies
none of this actual knowledge; what he denies is that other
knowledge which is always combined with affection and appropriation, as when we know what we love and hold it as
our own, the *nosse cum affectu et effectu.* The sinful things
he finds himself doing look strange to him; he indeed sees
them in himself, and knows that he is guilty of them, and
yet they look to him as if another were doing them. And
this is what makes him feel like a slave, under compulsion;
a foreign power has hold of him. It is needless to say that
only a regenerate man is able to feel and speak thus concerning himself. The unregenerate sins with full purpose and
intent. When, however, Paul says that **not what I would,
that do I practice; but what I hate, that I do,** we must
not suppose that his sins are altogether involuntary, performed apart from his will as a person, or done under complete compulsion. Sin has its real seat in the will, and
whoever sins, sins willingly, else his deeds would not be
sins. But the will of the regenerate man, while dominated
by the spirit, is not free from the influence and sway of
the flesh; and whenever in any measure it yields to the flesh,
sin results. Yet the regenerate man can and must always say
of such sin: What I hate (according to the spirit), that I

do (provoked thereunto by the flesh). And now the apostle returns again to the law and adds a concluding statement: **But if what I would not, that I do, I consent unto the law that it is good;** in other words, I concur that it is morally excellent (καλός), and I second the righteousness which it requires and hate the sin which it forbids. Again, only the regenerate man can say this of his will. And as long as he does, the result for him is bound to be daily contrition and repentance, combined with the gracious pardon of the Holy Spirit, who "daily and richly forgives all sins to me and all believers." To help produce this blessed result is the purpose of the law in the regenerate. *Formula of Concord*, 509, 4; 596, 7-8 and 14.

HOMILETICAL HINTS.

"Everything that reproves sin is and belongs to the preaching of the law." *Formula of Concord*, 506, 4.

God's thoughts concerning what is holy, right, and good, are the only correct thoughts; and these are the thoughts he expresses in the law. Therefore the law is the only mirror that does not deceive us when in it we view ourselves in regard to our sins; it shows us our sin in all its sinfulness, making it appear utterly hateful, abominable, and naked in its wickedness. It is God's purpose that it should; and we should use it for that very purpose. — Is it the mirror's fault when it reflects nothing but stains and spots as you look into it? Will you remove a single blemish by breaking the mirror?

Thou shalt not covet is the sum of the entire law on its negative side. Its positive side is love to God above all things.

Absolutely the worst evil lust is that with which sin turns against God himself when the commandment condemns it; it is the enmity against God who forbids what I love, and commands what I dislike. Besser.

Sin is like the fire in a hot iron, showing itself very effective the moment water is cast upon it. So a mighty commotion results when the law comes into contact with the sin in us. — Place the flint and the tinder side by side: they will remain thus indefinitely. But let the steel strike the flint, the sparks will fly and the tinder be caught in a blaze. Let the hard steel of the law strike the stony heart of man, and lust will flash out and burn fiercely in sin. Matthes.

See how necessary is the work of the law! If a mother sees her child playing at the mouth of an open well, will she allow it to play on unconscious of its danger, because she is loath to disturb the child? If a traveler is picking his way over cliffs and treacherous rocks, will he wish that the bright sunlight may cease, so that he shall not see the dangers besetting his course and be frightened thereby? And the sailor at sea, is he anxious that the fog may blot out his vision, and the noises of the vessel occupy his ears, so that he shall not see and hear the boom of the surf upon the reef? Is ignorance of our danger the same as safety? This, too, is the folly of sin that under its sway the sinner never welcomes the law, but rebels against it with all his might. Is the law our enemy? No, but the sinner is the enemy of God.

To stand condemned and utterly helpless, hopeless, and lost before the condemnation of the law — that is to die, *i. e.* to feel and realize the death in which because of our sins we lie. Luther says that this knowledge of sin and self is like our descent into hell, which must precede if we are to ascend with Christ in his grace and pardon to heaven. — To be sold as a slave is worse than to be born a slave; and man was sold, for God never made him a slave when he created him. Bengel. — How many of us live in full security and satisfied with ourselves, content with our empty show of righteousness and the shielding conviction that we are certainly as good as others, until the commandment steps forth and with the sharp scythe of its condemnation cuts down the foolish flower of our flesh and turns it into dead hay.

As the drop of blood tinges the water red, so the flesh stains all our best works, Christians though we are. — How strange some brother looks to you and me when the evil that still slumbers in him is stirred up, and we see him saying and doing what is wrong before God and man. And that is how we look, when our flesh comes to the surface. People hardly recognize in us the quiet, kind, pious persons we formerly appeared to be. And we must look strange to ourselves when with eyes enlightened by the Spirit of God we view the stirrings and deeds of our fleshly nature.

Thank God, that Paul has told us so much concerning his own distressful experience. It shields us against becoming presumptuous and against tormenting ourselves. We are still carnal, and therefore dare not become secure. The old lusts and passions still slumber in us, and look for an opportunity to break forth; and sometimes they take unexpected forms. So we must crucify again and again our selfishness, our pride, our angry thoughts, our impure imaginings, our love of pleasure, our unbelief and lack of obedience. Contrition and repentance dare never leave us, else we are lost.

Presumption and security must ever be shattered and destroyed. And likewise all pietistic martyrdom of self which leads to discouragement and despair. Let the devil, if he will, paint the Christian all in glossy colors of perfect saintliness and then demonstrate to me that I am not and can never be such a Christian. My refuge is in Romans seven, where the Spirit of God shows me the picture of Paul, one of God's real Christians, one of the grandest of them all. With many a sin he bows repentant under the law, and his only hope is the Gospel of grace and pardon. So will I bow low, and, having tasted the grace of my Lord, I will go courageously, joyfully on, until Christ shall sweep out of my heart the last trace of the flesh and translate me into the kingdom of his glory.

Why do so many pass the Gospel by? They fail to see the supreme need of the remedy it offers. They are satisfied to put a plaster on the boil, and do not see that the entire system is full of poison. They try a little morality preaching, a little outward reformation, and do not see that the whole heart must be made new. Let God's law undeceive us.

Face God's Holy Law!

   I. *Unless you do, you will slumber on in sin.*
  II. *When you do, you will find sin revives.*
 III. *Not until you do, will you see the sinfulness of sin.*
 IV. *After you do, you will embrace the Savior and hold him fast.*

What Does the Law Do in Order that the Gospel May Exercise its Power?

   I. *It revives sin.*
  II. *It slays the sinner.*

C. C. Hein.

The Exposure of Sin by the Law.

   I. *In the unregenerate.*
  II. *In the regenerate.*

What Experience Have You Had with the Law?

I. *Has it destroyed your security?*
II. *Has it exposed your sinfulness?*
III. *Has it made you feel your death?*
IV. *Has it driven you to Christ?*
V. *Has it kept you in constant repentance?*

The Terrors of the Divine Law.

I. *God condemns our sin.*
II. *All our rebellion is vain.*
III. *Christ is our only deliverance.*

THE FIFTH SUNDAY AFTER EPIPHANY.

Rom. 8, 1-9.

The former text moves mightily to daily contrition and repentance. This is the right basis for a life and walk, not after the flesh, but after the spirit. Our present text proceeds with this subject. The Epiphany thought of Christ's revelation in us is still retained; for with Christ shining in our hearts we certainly will not mind the things of the flesh, but ever the things of the spirit. Hence the theme: *All who have seen the Epiphany light walk after the spirit.*

The new power.

"The apostle now shows the other side of the life of the regenerate. He has pictured the distress caused by the sin still constantly present; now he pictures the power and glory of the new life-principle, of the gift of grace and the spirit, possessed by the believers in Christ Jesus." Philippi. **There is therefore no condemnation to them that are in Christ Jesus.** Οὐδέν is put forward for emphasis: "Not one" (condemnation). Luther understands κατάκριμα in the sense of that which condemns, *nichts Verdammliches,* and the forms in μα frequently signify that which causes or produces a thing. But the fact is that the regenerate have something worthy of condemnation in their lives, as the entire seventh chapter shows. Their sin is certainly not an indifferent thing even though they are in Christ Jesus and have God's pardon through his sacrifice. The usual meaning of the word is **condemnation,** judgment, *i. e.* the act or sentence which condemns or adjudges guilty, *Verurteilung, Verdammung.* Paul states that there is not a single sentence of condemna-

tion for those in Christ Jesus. If it be asked whether there
are several such sentences, we may reply, first, that every
sin really deserves such a sentence, and secondly, that God
utters repeated condemnation upon the ungodly, in this
life, at the end of life, and at the last great day; but for
the believer, never a one. And Paul concludes this from
what he has just said in the preceding sentence: ἄρα,
therefore, consequently; νῦν, **now,** temporal, not in the
sense of οὖν. The believer serves the law of sin only with
the flesh, with the mind he serves the law of God (8, 25).
As long as this is the case, his sins are at once pardoned in
Christ and not condemned. — When Paul described the
work of the law and his contest with the flesh in chapter
seven, he used himself as an illustration and employed the
personal pronoun "I," now that he pictures the blessed
life of freedom he uses that pronoun only once more, preferring terms which at once include all believers: No condemnation **to them that are in Christ Jesus;** supply:
ἐστίν, "there is." The ἐν denotes the most intimate communion of faith and spiritual life. We need supply nothing
with τοῖς ἐν Χριστῷ Ἰησοῦ, as the article makes a substantive
out of the phrase. "They that are in Christ Jesus" are the
accepted in the Beloved, the branches of the Vine, the
members of the one great Head, the stones built upon the
foundation of which Christ is the chief corner stone, the
chickens gathered by the hen under her wings, the sheep
in the keeping and care of the Good Shepherd. It is impossible that there should be condemnation for them, John
4, 24; wherefore also this passage has been full of the
strongest comfort for true believers at all times, a very
bulwark against doubt, fear, and the accusations that arise
from within and from without. — And it is easy to see why
this should be so: **For the law of the Spirit of life in
Christ Jesus made me free from the law of sin and of
death.** The term **law,** νόμος, is here used in the special
sense of a regulative principle or power. Both the Holy
Spirit and **sin and death** have such a "law," which they
put in operation wherever they rule. The term "law" is

used because it denotes control and, on the part of those in whom this law is established, obedience and subservience. It is incorrect for Stoeckhardt to identify this "law" in the one case with the Spirit, and in the other with sin and death; the possessives "of the Spirit" and "of sin and of death" show that a "law" emanates from each and belongs to each. And the contrast between these two laws or principles is brought out by the amplification: Spirit **of life in Christ Jesus,** which we construe together, instead of drawing "in Christ Jesus" to the verb as a good many do. Paul is not speaking of the essential, divine life of the Spirit, but of the saving life which appeared in Christ Jesus for us sinners and is now transmitted to us by the Spirit through faith. This is the life which is the opposite of **death,** the result and companion of **sin.** Where sin and death have sway with their destructive law, there condemnation is found, John 3, 36; but where the law of the Spirit of life in Christ Jesus prevails, there condemnation, past, present, and future, is abolished. This takes place in a signal act: **made me free,** an aorist: ἠλευθέρωσεν, a definite past act, John 8, 36. Some texts read "thee" instead of "me;" practically there is no difference. The liberating act takes place in justification, or, which is the same, in regeneration, when the law of the Spirit of life in Christ first establishes itself in the sinner's heart. Then the guilt is removed, and the power of sin and death shattered.

Another **for** explains still farther. **For what the law could not do, in that it was weak through the flesh, God sending his own Son in the likeness of sinful flesh and** *as an offering* **for sin, condemned sin in the flesh.** The sentence begins with an absolute nominative, in apposition with the divine act now described. Τὸ ἀδύνατον τοῦ νόμου, the impossible (thing) of the law, *i. e.* what is impossible for the law, that God performed in a different way. Here the Mosaic **law** is meant, the operation of which the apostle has so vividly described in his own case

19

in the previous chapter. This law, while in itself good, righteous, holy, and spiritual (7, 12 and 14), was rendered inefficient in the case of the sinner, as far as aiding him against sin is concerned, because (ἐν ᾧ, **in that**) of his condition: **in that it was weak through the flesh.** By **flesh** our inborn corrupt and sinful nature is meant, John 3, 6. This rendered the law weak and helpless, as far as aiding us is concerned; ἠσθένει, an imperfect, denotes continuous past action or condition. Acting upon man in his fleshly condition the law could only condemn him, it could not rid him of sin. — Then **God** stepped in, **sending his own Son in the likeness of sinful flesh,** and working a deliverance indeed. Τὸν ἑαυτοῦ υἱόν is placed emphatically before πέμψας. His own, like ἴδιος in 8, 32, points to the divine nature of the Son, and the participle **sending** indicates his preexistence and personality. **In the likeness of sinful flesh,** or, margin: **flesh of sin,** is one of those exact phrases of Scripture which admit of no change. "The likeness of flesh" would be Docetism, Christ would then have been without real flesh; "the flesh of sin" would be Ebionitism, Christ would then have had sinful flesh; but "the likeness of sinful flesh" is Gospel doctrine, Christ assumed our flesh, yet not its sinfulness. The apostle has just used the term "flesh" (the law was weak through the flesh); if he had gone on and written that God sent his Son in the "flesh," the sense would have been that the Son appeared in our corrupt, sinful nature. This he avoids by the phrase: "in the likeness of the flesh of sin." Our flesh is our corrupt nature, properly called "flesh of sin;" Christ came not in this, but in the likeness of it. The likeness of the flesh of sin is the flesh without sin, John 1, 14. — The purpose of the sending is briefly added: καὶ περὶ ἁμαρτίας, which the A. V. and the margin of the R. V. translate exactly: **and for sin,** omitting the interpolation of the R. V.: *as an offering* (θυσίαν) **for sin.** On account of, or concerning, sin God sent his Son; the preposition embraces the whole relation of the mission of Christ respecting sin, all that he was to do concerning it. "For sin" recalls pas

sages like Gal. 1, 4; 1 Pet. 3, 18; Heb. 5, 3, and others in
our Epistle, 3, 24-25; 5, 11 and 18, which state that Christ's
mission regarding sin was to atone for it, to remove it, and
to free us completely from it. — Sending his own Son for
sin, God **condemned sin,** does not mean that the sending
itself was already the condemning, but that it was the
necessary prerequisite for such condemnation of sin. There
were two distinct acts, the sending for sin, and the condemning of sin; the second rests upon the first, and is its
culmination. God **condemned** sin in the flesh, and this condemnation (κατέκρινε) explains why now there is no condemnation (κατάκριμα) to them that are in Christ Jesus.
Christ bore the condemnation for us, and so we are free.
Κατέκρινε (aorist) refers to a definite past act of God regarding his Son. Philippi is right when he points to the death
of Christ on the cross as the signal act whereby God condemned sin so that we might escape its condemnation and
power. The sending of the Son in general, and his life and
deeds in general can hardly be considered a specific act of
God whereby he condemned sin; but the death of Christ
can be so considered in an eminent manner. Then, when
Christ was slain for the sins of the world, the divine sentence upon sin was both pronounced and executed once for
all. — The question is raised whether **in the flesh** modifies
the verb: "condemned in the flesh;" or the object: "sin in
the flesh" (which is in the flesh). Grammatically both are
possible, although to place the latter beyond doubt would
require: τὴν ἁμαρτίαν τὴν ἐν σαρκί. Commentators are badly
divided. In forming our decision we keep close to the
apostle's line of thought. He tells us that it was the flesh
which rendered the law weak and helpless, and that therefore God sent his own Son into the flesh (but without sin)
and in this way overcame sin, namely by condemning it in
the flesh. The entire argument turns on the word flesh.
Where the law was at a fatal disadvantage because of the
flesh, God in his mercy found a way to get the better of the
flesh: he sent his Son in the likeness of sinful flesh, and
thus in the very flesh which baffled the law smote sin with

a death-blow. But this was possible only through the sinless flesh of God's incarnate Son. It is a mistake to claim that then the apostle should have written: "in *his* flesh." He keeps in mind the connection of Christ's (sinless) flesh with our (sinful) flesh. Besser asks: "In which flesh did God condemn sin? Evidently in the flesh of his Son, but for this very reason in all flesh. God sat in judgment on the sin of the flesh of the whole world (John 12, 31) when he executed the judgment of condemnation on the sinless flesh of him whom he made to be sin on our behalf (2 Cor. 5, 21) and a curse for us (Gal. 3, 13)." — All this God did: **that the ordinance of the law might be fulfilled in us, who walk not after the flesh, but after the spirit.** Δικαίωμα τοῦ νόμου is here the righteous *requirement* (margin) of the law, that which it declares to be right and thus demands or requires; A. V.: "the righteousness of the law." Δικαίωμα cannot mean justification here, as Philippi urges, for justification is not a function of the law, but the heart of the Gospel, and the verb "fulfilled" likewise excludes this meaning. God's intention in sending his Son and condemning sin in his death on the cross was "that the requirement of the law might be fulfilled in us." The old exegetes think that this fulfillment occurs in us through the imputation of Christ's righteousness and merits, but the modifiers: "who walk not after the flesh, but after the spirit," show that the apostle is not writing of justification, but of sanctification. Paul has dealt with the former in previous sections, here he shows that the divine intention in sending his Son and condemning sin in his death was our sanctification. Not only the old guilt of our sin was to be removed, but also the old power of sin. "Our human nature, hitherto subject to sin and death, was to become the dwelling-place and the instrument of a life just and pleasing to God." Zahn. **In us,** not by us, the requirement of the law is to be fulfilled, because this entire fulfillment is a work of grace, not of our achievement or merit. The passive πληρωθῇ points to God as the agent. Really the divine intention of grace extends to all men, as also the law and the Gospel

pertain to all alike; here, however, the apostle considers
those in whom God's intention is realized: **us, who walk
not after the flesh, but after the spirit.** In these the flesh,
which proved such a hindrance to the law when it came
alone, has been dethroned by the spirit, planted in them
through the gracious work of God in Jesus Christ. While
sin still clings to them, because they are not fully free from
the flesh, yet the law of their lives is the spirit, not the flesh;
and they earnestly strive to fulfil the requirements of the
law of God, and in the power of the Spirit succeed. The
apostle indicates this intention and striving by using the
subjective negative μή, not the objective οὐ. Τοῖς περιπατοῦσιν,
who walk, refers to the outward conduct and life; its inner
motive is the spirit, not the flesh. **After the flesh,** κατὰ
σάρκα, means after or according to flesh in general; just as
flesh walks. **After the spirit,** κατὰ πνεῦμα, just as spirit
walks. Bengel is right when he points to the opposition of
flesh and spirit as evidence that πνεῦμα here means not the
Holy Spirit, but the renewed spirit of man, enlightened and
energized by the grace of God's Spirit. The A. V. as also
some commentators translate "Spirit." Materially no difference results, as the two norms "after the spirit" and
"after the Spirit" are identical, God's Spirit governing the
regenerated spirit of man in all things.

The new glory.

After describing *the new power* by means of which the
Christian escapes condemnation, is freed from the law of
sin and death, enabled to fulfil the requirement of the law,
and to walk after the spirit, the apostle proceeds to show
the new glory of the life which thus results. He does this
by contrasting the product of the flesh with that of the
Spirit, first in a general way, speaking in the third person,
verses 5-8, then applying this directly to his readers, using
the second person in verse 9, with which our text ends, and
the following.

It is the manner of St. Paul now and then to introduce
a thought incidentally, and then to use it as a theme for

fuller elaboration. So here the participial clause: "who walk not after the flesh, but after the spirit," leads him to explain fully what is involved in these two kinds of conduct. **For they that are after the flesh do mind the things of the flesh.** The **for** furnishes both proof and explanation. All they who walk after the flesh do so because they **are after the flesh;** their conduct is only an evidence of their condition, an outgrowth of their nature, a mark of their actual character. Their very being is fashioned and formed κατὰ σάρκα, after the flesh, and they are properly characterized as flesh, Jno. 3, 6. This involves that they **do mind the things of the flesh,** φρονοῦσιν, consider and concern themselves about the interests, objects, and affairs of the flesh, of course so as to realize them: wealth, ease, pleasure, honor, this or that form of earthly happiness, the satisfaction of this or that craving, lust, passion, *etc.* Being of the flesh their whole occupation is with the things of the flesh, and they rise to nothing higher. And this condition and mind always underlies the conduct which the apostle has just referred to in verse 4: "walking after the flesh." — On the other hand (δέ), **they that are after the spirit** (do mind) **the things of the spirit;** their very nature is spiritual, and so their thoughts and concerns are spiritual. And this condition and mind always underlies spiritual conduct and action, verse 4. The A. V. and the American Committee of translators in the R. V. translate πνεῦμα throughout these verses with "Spirit," while the text of the R. V. offers "spirit," as at the end of verse 4. Materially, as already stated, there is no difference; Bengel's principle for deciding the question applies here as well as in the foregoing verse. — The apostle continues with another explanatory "for:" **For the mind of the flesh is death,** τὸ φρόνημα, the mind itself, not that which it thinks, but that which thinks and all its thinking and striving. "The imagination of man's heart is evil from his youth," Gen. 8, 21. And this **is death,** spiritual death, separation from all true life; now already, not merely in the future, although, of course, as it progresses it leads to nothing else in the end; spiritual death results in eternal death. Generally the person governed by the flesh is unconscious of his condition of death; he thinks he lives and by his efforts is securing an augmentation of life, but he merely deceives himself. At times, however, something of the truth dawns upon him, when he feels the emptiness, the hollowness, the vanity of all his attainments. But in himself he is utterly powerless against this death and the flesh in which it dwells. — On the other hand (δέ), **the mind of the spirit is life and peace;** the mind itself and its very thought and action is the opposite of that of the flesh, namely **life,** true spiritual life wrought by the Spirit of God, and in present possession, the antecedent of eternal life hereafter. The apostle adds a second term: **and peace,** paving the way, as Bengel points out, for the further characterization of the mind of the flesh as "enmity against God." "Life" includes "peace," which is the harmony of the spiritual mind with God. All the activity of the spiritual mind is spiritual life; the more this activity increases and unfolds, the richer, fuller, sweeter will be the spiritual life with which it is identified. In the same way, the spiritual mind is peace, harmony, friendship, communion, and agreement with God; and the more this mind asserts itself, the fuller, stronger, sweeter will this harmony and agreement be.

The reason why the mind of the flesh is death is given at length: **because** (διότι, from διὰ τοῦτο ὅτι, *propter hoc quod*) **the mind of the flesh is enmity against God,** ἔχθρα, the opposite of peace, harmony, and union. But God is the source of all true life, therefore to hate and oppose him is to reject life and fall into death. Like the mind of the flesh, so also the friendship of the world is enmity against God, Jam. 4, 4. This fatal enmity is explained: **for it is not subject to the law of God,** οὐχ ὑποτάσσεται, it will not arrange itself under this law, in obedience to God; it rebels against every command that interferes with its plans and lusts. Worse still: **neither indeed can it be,** its very nature forbids that. The law of God and our sinful flesh are utterly opposed, and, as Philippi states,

for each there is an ἀδυναμία; the law cannot conquer the
flesh, it can only arouse and inflame it to more and greater
sin, and the flesh cannot be subject to the law, it can only
hate, oppose, and trample it under foot. And this mind
of the flesh cannot be converted or altered; even in the
regenerate the flesh that remains is wicked and hostile to
God and must be crucified, mortified, and thus destroyed.
— The conclusion then is plain: **and they that are in the
flesh cannot please God.** It is impossible; their ἔχθρα is
and must be answered by his ὀργή. Not for one instant
can God consent to deny his law, to abrogate his life, to
justify their enmity, and to agree to their wickedness and
sin. The fact that the flesh cannot but oppose God, that
such opposition is its very nature, is not only no excuse
for its action, but only makes the case worse. Just because the flesh cannot be subject to God's law, it cannot
please God. There is no real difference between ἐν σαρκί
ὄντες and κατὰ σάρκα ὄντες; the former indicates the sphere,
the latter the norm or rule. — Rom. 8, 7 is one of the
proof passages for the utter inability of the natural man
in spiritual things. On the strength of this and similar
passages the Formula of Concord denies to the natural
man the *liberum arbitrium.* "We believe, teach, and confess that the will of unregenerate man is not only turned
away from God, but also has become an enemy of God, so
that it has inclination and desire for that which is evil and
contrary to God, as it is written Gen. 8, 21 .   .   .   Also
Rom. 8, 7." 497, 3. "Likewise Rom. 8, 7-8: .   .   .
These testimonies are so manifest that, to use the words
of Augustine which he employed in this case, they do not
need an acute understanding, but only an attentive hearer.
If the carnal mind is enmity against God, the flesh certainly
does not love God; if it cannot be subject to the law of
God, it cannot love God. If the carnal mind is enmity
against God, the flesh sins, even when we do external civil
works. If it cannot be subject to the law of God, it certainly sins, even when, according to human judgment, it
possesses deeds that are excellent and worthy of praise."

89, 33. The deduction therefore is beyond question: "The Scriptures deny to the understanding, heart, and will of the natural man all aptness, skill, capacity, and ability in spiritual things, to think, to understand, begin, will, undertake, do, work, or concur in working anything good and right, as of himself." 554. 12. And especially as regards conversion: "Hence it is manifest that the free will, from its own natural powers, not only cannot work or co-work as to anything for its own conversion, righteousness, and salvation, or follow, believe, or assent to the Holy Ghost, who throught the Gospel offers him grace and salvation, but rather from its innate, wicked, perverse nature it hostilely resists God and his will, unless it be enlightened and controlled by God's Spirit." 555, 18. All synergism is therefore to be rejected in conversion; conversion is *in toto* the gracious work of God, wrought by the means of grace, Word and Sacrament.

The apostle now turns directly to his readers, without stopping to unfold the other side of his thought, namely that the mind of the spirit is life and peace because it is friendship with God. **But ye,** he says, **are not in the flesh, but in the spirit, if so be that the Spirit of God dwelleth in you.** The personal turn puts ὑμεῖς forward with emphasis. The strong adversative ἀλλά separates the phrases put in contrast. **In the spirit,** in the sphere that belongs to the renewed nature, is the opposite of **in the flesh;** the two exclude each other, although they who are in the spirit still battle with the flesh. It is significant that the apostle does not stop with this positive assertion: "Ye are in the spirit," but adds the condition: **if so be that the Spirit of God dwelleth in you.** The εἴπερ expresses no positive doubt, yet it raises the question for the persons addressed: "if so be, as I assume and hope." It would induce the readers to examine themselves, for there are some who claim to be in the spirit and yet are in the flesh, deceiving themselves with an outward show of spirituality. The essential thing is that the Spirit of God dwell in us, with his saving and regenerating grace. — **But if any man hath not the Spirit of Christ, he is none of his.** This is the cardinal truth to which the condition just mentioned refers. It is expressed in a negative form to bring out fully the danger at which the preceding conditions hint. · The apostle writes οὐκ ἔχει, and not μή, because the negative refers to the verb alone. Everything depends on our possessing the Holy Spirit, because it is he to whom the work of regeneration and sanctification especially belongs. In the preceding sentence he is called "the Spirit of God" because there the reference is to the law of God. He is thereupon called **the Spirit of Christ** because reference is had to our belonging to Christ as the Redeemer in whom alone is salvation. The two designations side by side furnish a proof for the *Filioque* of the Nicene Creed. Bengel also points out that the designation "Spirit of Christ" implies that Christ is God, and that thus we have here a *testimonium illustre de S. Trinitate.* To **have** the Spirit of Christ is the same as saying that the Spirit dwells in us; when he takes possession of our hearts in regeneration, then we "have" him. The consequence is that then we are **his,** namely Christ's, his sheep, his disciples indeed. 1 John 4, 13. And all who are Christ's through the Spirit are free from condemnation and the law of sin and death, and in the power of the Spirit who fills their hearts they walk after the spirit, and please God.

HOMILETICAL HINTS.

If a tree is to flourish, it must be set into the right soil; so we must be planted "in Christ Jesus." Whoever would be free must found his life upon Christ, must be rooted and grounded in him. This is the secret of inward liberty. Planted in him your life will be replenished by his life.

The vessel which Moses pilots with his staff through the storms of life will be wrecked, the skiff of our own righteousness springs ever a new and desperate leak, and the life-lines which others would cast out for our deliverance tear in our hands. And through the roar of the tempest and the tossing billows comes ·

the despairing cry: Lost! What we need is nothing less than everything. Rescue is impossible. The will may be ever so good, the power is utterly absent. No man ever yet caught himself by the locks and drew himself out of the engulfing mire; the more he struggled, the deeper he sank. And this is the descent into hell for the natural man. Matthes.

Who can harmonize these contradictory statements, that there should be sin in us, and yet not harm us; that one should merit damnation, and yet not be damned; that one should be rejected in God's eyes, and yet be a dear child of his; that one should deserve God's wrath and eternal death, and nevertheless go unpunished by them? Christ, the one Mediator between God and man, he harmonizes these contradictions, as St. Paul declares: No condemnation to them that are in Christ Jesus. Luther.

When the law strikes a man in his sins he is broken and shattered, but in the death of Christ sin itself and all its power of condemnation was broken and shattered: So now everyone who is in Christ is delivered from sin and made free from the condemnation of the law.

Men are exceedingly cunning. They evade the law of God by making themselves law-makers and reducing the divine requirements to such dimensions as suit their own desires and wisdom. One simple step, and they laugh at God's law and are happy in their self-invented religion. Alas, their dreams are quickly dispelled! The moment they step into the presence of the true Law-Giver, the terrors of death take hold of them.

God condemned sin by a judgment from which the Christ whom he judged came forth victorious, taking with him unjudged all who are in him.

Although we cannot kill the old man in us at once, yet we are to plague him with so many blows, scourgings and thorns, and pierce him with nails, that finally he bows his head and expires. For they that are of Christ Jesus have crucified the flesh with the passions and lusts thereof. Gal. 5, 24. Luther.

As the flower turns to the sunlight, so they that are after the spirit turn their hearts and minds to God and his Spirit, and he fills them with grace and strength to grow and mature in holiness.

Many great and wonderful things they that are after the flesh are able to do. Some of them, as among the ancient Romans, attain the fame of heroes and benefactors of the fatherland; others, as Saul among the Jews, achieve the glory of pharisaic righteousness and observance of the law. But one thing none of them are able by all their efforts to attain: they cannot please God. Though they please all the world of men, and their names be blazoned through all the ages of the world on the pages of fame, yet all is in vain, as long as God's pleasure is not attained.

There are only two classes of men on earth, just as there will be only two classes in the hereafter: the dead and alive; they who are of the flesh, and they who are of the Spirit; they in whom the Spirit of God dwells, and they in whom the devil rules; they who are Christ's, and they whom he never knew. All efforts to wipe out, cover up, ignore, deny this division are utterly in vain. Hence the question of supreme importance will always be, whether the Spirit of God really dwelleth in us. And our highest happiness and joy must ever be, to know of a certainty that we are indeed Christ's own.

A Glorious Hymn on the Christian's Deliverance:

I. *Deliverance from the guilt of sin—righteousness.*
II. *Deliverance from the power of sin—sanctification.*
III. *Deliverance from the penalty of sin—blessedness.*

No Condemnation for Us.

I. *We are in Christ.*
II. *The Spirit of Christ is in us.*

The Joy of Living After the Spirit.

It is supreme joy

I. *To shake off the power of sin.*
II. *To escape the clutch of death.*
III. *To feel the pulse of the new life.*
IV. *To know that we please God.*
V. *To experience the Spirit's help.*
VI. *To be Christ's own forevermore.*

The Supreme Question: Have We the Spirit of Christ?

We can tell by testing:

I. *Whether we are in Christ by faith.*
II. *Whether we walk after the spirit.*

They That Are After the Flesh and They That Are After the Spirit.

What a tremendous difference:

  I. *In their nature.*
 II. *In their possessions.*
III. *In their minds.*
 IV. *In their walk.*
  V. *In their end.*

The One Way to Please God.

 I. *Accept Christ.*
II. *Receive the Spirit of Christ.*

THE SIXTH SUNDAY AFTER EPIPHANY.

2 Cor. 3, 12-18.

The real climax of the entire Epiphany cycle appears in the last verse of this text: "We all with unveiled face reflecting as in a mirror the glory of the Lord, are transformed into the same image from glory to glory." This is the highest result of all Christ's Epiphany in and through the Gospel; there is nothing beyond the glory of eternal blessedness. And so the cycle closes with the theme: *They who have seen the Epiphany light shall pass from glory to glory.*

The unveiled clearness of the Gospel.

Having therefore such a hope, we use great boldness of speech. The participal clause is causal: "Since, or because, we have such a hope." What the apostle means by **such a hope** we gather from what he has just said, namely that the Gospel and its ministry were, and would prove themselves, superior to the law and the ministry of Moses. "Hope" points to the results yet to be expected in the progress of the Gospel and its proclamation, and this "hope" is not merely a subjective expectation on the part of the apostle, but an objective assurance wrought by the New Testament Gospel itself, the nature and power of which Paul had come to know fully. Like him every true preacher and every true believer of the Gospel rejoices in the firm assurance that God's plan of salvation as now revealed, and all the provisions of his grace as now made in Jesus Christ, are superior to anything that has ever been in the world, and will stand superior to the end of time. — As a result of such a hope, Paul says: **we use great boldness of speech,** $\pi\alpha\rho\rho\eta\sigma\iota\alpha$, openness, outspokenness,

302

withholding and veiling nothing in our preaching and teaching. And indeed there is no need for any resistance or stopping short because the Gospel of the apostles is not, like the message of the prophets of old and of Moses, only preparatory, or something partial, or a message only for a certain time and people, but the complete manifestation of God's grace and salvation for all men and all time. Its very nature requires that it should be proclaimed without the slightest reserve. In this it differs not only from the O. T. which left many things for future unfolding, but also from heathen religions which all had their esoteric doctrines carefully guarded and reserved for the initiated few. Rome to. this day keeps its people in ignorance, and tells them it is enough for the priests to have the Scriptures, they bear the responsibility, and all the people need do is follow their bidding and leading. — Paul dwells at length on the contrast between the O. T. and the N. T. ministrations in this regard, using an illustration from the conduct of Moses, to which he had already referred in verse 7: **and are not as Moses, who put a veil upon his face, that the children of Israel should not look steadfastly on the end of that which was passing away.** The A. V. in Ex. 34, 30-35 makes Moses put the veil on his face "till" he had done speaking with the children of Israel; but the Hebrew. as well as the Septuagint state simply: "Moses ceased to speak with them, and put a veil over his face." So with unveiled face, shining with the glory that still emanated from it from his having been in God's own presence, Moses appeared before the Israelites and announced his message from God to them. In verse 7 Paul writes that they could not look steadfastly upon the face of Moses for the glory of his face. They must then have dropped their eyes, or shielded them with hands or arms. But not till the message was finished did Moses place the veil over his head. And Paul now informs us of the purpose of this act; it was **that the children of Israel should not look steadfastly on the end of that which was passing away.** Πρός with the infinitive here denotes purpose or intention; but the intention of Moses is evidently due to the intention of God himself. The glory on Moses' face lasted only a certain time, then it faded away or vanished slowly. This Paul calls τὸ τέλος, **the end,** and τὸ τέλος τοῦ καταργουμένου, **the end of that which was passing away,** namely of the glory of Moses' countenance, verse 7. Some commentators have puzzled about this action of Moses, its motive and its purpose arguing even the question of deception on his part. The matter is not nearly as complicated as they make it. Whenever Moses brought a message to the Israelites from God he had to do this with unveiled face, with the glory shining forth from it upon the people, that they might recognize in him the representative of the all-glorious God. And this periodic glory made the ministry of Moses glorious, verses 7-11. But the glory was only for the time of the announcement; after the message was spoken, the face of Moses was covered, and beneath the cover the glory disappeared unseen. The people were thus to connect the message from God with the glory on the messenger's face as he uttered it. Beyond that they were not to see how the glory faded away, ἀτενίζειν (τείνω with a *intensivum*), to stare intently in watching it diminish slowly or go out suddenly, whichever may have been the case. There is no hint that they imagined the glory on Moses' face continued indefinitely, for ere long they beheld him again with ordinary countenance. Much less is the idea of Paul that Moses by veiling his face tried to keep up the delusion in the minds of the Israelites that the shining of his face continued indefinitely. The apostle simply contrasts the message of the two covenants and the manner which the respective messengers employ: Moses had only brief periods in which to bring God's word to the people, then came the veil and silence for him; but the apostles, having the ever-glorious Gospel of grace in Jesus Christ to proclaim, know of no veil, no silence, no restriction of any kind, but use ever "great boldness of speech." Both ministries thus were glorious (verse 9), also the manner of the messengers of both; but the manner which the apostles were able to employ greatly excelled the manner proper for Moses.

Although the glory of Moses' countenance was transient, and the Israelites saw it only while he delivered his message to them, yet one would suppose that these messages were received ón their part in a way to match the manner of their deliverance unto them, *i. e.* with a ready and believing heart, especially as to the Gospel features in them. Instead Paul is compelled to write: **but their minds were hardened,** ἐπωρώθη, made hard or callous. Νοήματα, the result of νόειν, are thoughts, and then derivatively the minds themselves. Paul states a sad historical fact (aorist). In no way was this fact due to the way God's Word was brought to the Israelites by Moses. Paul does not hint at anything of the kind; on the contrary, the way he describes the glory of Moses' ministry shows us that this adverse action of the Israelites is due to their own perverseness. — As proof for the historical fact just stated Paul points to the condition of the Jews of his day, using in a new way the reference to Moses' veil which he had just employed in comparing his own work with that of Moses: **for until this very day at the reading of the old covenant the same veil remaineth unlifted.** The old covenant was put in written form by Moses and so was read by the Jews; some assume a metonomy, making ἡ παλαιὰ διαθήκη stand for the books of the old covenant, but this is not necessary. With their hearts hardened the Jews never comprehended the true meaning of that covenant. It was as if **the same veil** which Moses put over his face after speaking the divine words of that covenant to them, was now upon the hearts of the Israelites themselves, preventing them from seeing Christ in the old covenant. — As between the two possible constructions **the same veil remaineth unlifted; which** *veil* **is done away in Christ,** and that offered in the margin: *the same veil remaineth, it not being revealed that it is done away in Christ,* we agree with Schnedermann (Strack u. Zoeckler: *Kommentar*) that the former is

20

altogether the most natural, κάλυμμα and ἀνακαλυπτόμενον being in grammatical agreement and even forming a paronomia. But the best texts read ὅτι, "because," and not ὅ τι **which**. Paul says: "The same veil remaineth unlifted, because in Christ it is done away." Paul speaks of the veil throughout, and a veil may both be lifted and done away. The underlying thought is that since the Israelites failed to see Christ in the old covenant, they read it as under an unlifted veil; if they had seen Christ in it from the beginning, they would have understood the old covenant, for **in Christ** the veil is not only lifted up, but καταργεῖται entirely taken away, so that everything is plain. There is no real reason why καταργεῖσθαι may not be employed with κάλυμμα; the fact that presently (verse 16) the apostle employs περιαιρεῖσθαι is certainly no valid objection. — **But unto this day, whenever Moses is read, a veil lieth upon their heart.** To read **Moses** is to read the old covenant, and the Pentateuch was diligently read by the Jews in their synagogues, the entire five books being divided into sections or pericopes, called *paraschas*, for reading at the Sabbath services. But ever **a veil,** something which hid the true meaning of Moses, **lieth upon their heart,** ἐπὶ τὴν καρδίαν αὐτῶν, spread out over it, so that they fail to see Christ and believe in him as the Redeemer. What this veil really is the apostle does not say. Hodge even thinks of two veils, one over the O. T. itself, and one over the hearts of the Israelites; but this multiplication is unnecessary. The entire idea in Paul's figurative use of the veil of Moses is misapprehended when Bachmann and others conceive of it as a symbol which the Jews did not comprehend, namely that the old covenant with its glory should pass away. Paul first compares the boldness of speech justified by the new covenant with the veiled and silent lips of Moses when he had finished speaking to the people with glorified countenance. This illustration plainly shows that the new covenant is vastly superior, for its glory shines uninterruptedly in Christ, there is far more than periodic bursts of glory. In the next place Paul likens the hardness of Israel's heart to the veil over Moses' face. Instead of believing in the Christ of which Moses testified with shining face, they remained blind and obdurate, as if under the veil beneath which the glory vanished. What made them so, and what thus constituted the veil over their faces, is evidently their clinging to their own righteousness and rejecting that of Christ. So Paul says that in Christ the veil is completely done away with, and adds a second statement even more clear: **But whensoever it shall turn to the Lord, the veil is taken away.** The subject of ἐπιστρέψῃ is not expressed and must be supplied from the context. The margin offers: *a man,* but the context does not suggest it. Some suggest "heart" from the preceding sentence, which is acceptable. The R. V. follows the A. V. in supplying **it,** namely Israel, from the general context; which is also good. Materially there is no difference between the latter two. **Lord** must mean Christ, who has just been mentioned; and to **turn to the Lord** signifies conversion, a turning to Christ in faith. This, of course, means that **the veil** of hardness **is taken away,** and that the true glory of the Gospel is seen and apprehended. Some are inclined to interpret what Paul here writes of Israel turning to the Lord, of a general conversion of the Jewish nation to Christ in the last days; but such a doctrine is without Scripture warrant. Our text is remarkable in this sudden change from the plural to the singular (ἐπιστρέψῃ) when the subject of Jewish conversion is touched; it is as if the apostle had in mind each individual person as he comes to faith in the true Redeemer. The key to the entire O. T., or Moses, is Christ; whenever he is recognized as the Jehovah or Lord, who appeared to Moses in the mount, and whose glory made the face of Moses shine so wonderfully, then the veil is removed forever, in fact, as the apostle now sets forth, the believer himself reflects the glory of the Lord and is transformed into the same image from glory to glory.

The glorious work of the unveiled Gospel.

The apostle has finished with Moses and the veil, and
now places over against this human mediator of the old
covenant the divine Mediator, and shows what results when
he is seen with the eye of faith. Therefore the δέ, which
introduces a contrast, and not γάρ, is used, which would
be required if the apostle meant only to introduce a reason or
an explanation. **Now,** as over against Moses and the "letter"
(verse 6), **the Lord is the Spirit: and where the Spirit of
the Lord is,** *there* **is liberty.** Paul describes **the Lord** as
absolutely superior to Moses, and at the same time in a way
to show what great results must follow if we turn to him.
The early fathers read "the Spirit" as the subject and "the
Lord" as the predicate, but the context positively requires
that ὁ κύριος be the subject, since he has already been mentioned in the previous verse (therefore the article). For
this reason also "the Lord" means Christ, as in verse
16, and not merely his doctrine, his Gospel, or anything
else. So also τὸ πνεῦμα, **the Spirit** designates the Holy
Spirit, **the Spirit of the Lord,** as both English versions indicate by capitalizing. The A. V. reads: "that Spirit," as if
it referred the word back to verse 6, where "the letter" is
contrasted with "the spirit," yet it does not capitalize the
word in verse 6. We may indeed connect the two, although
they are not identical: the spirit which giveth life is born of
the Holy Spirit. Paul does not assert the personal identity
of Christ and the Spirit, but their identity in essence and in
work. Where Christ is there is his Spirit, and where his
Spirit is there is Christ, because the divine essence is one.
But here the apostle's concern is the work of Christ and his
Spirit (liberty and transformation). The Lord who is one
in essence with the Spirit works through the Spirit, and the
Spirit's work is to glorify the Lord by taking the things of
the Lord and showing them unto us, John 16, 14. The
Spirit thus stands in the same relation to the Son as to the
Father, and is therefore called **the Spirit of the Lord,** as
in Rom. 8, 9 "the Spirit of Christ," and in Gal. 4, 6 "the
Spirit of his Son," whom the Son sends and gives, John

16, 7. In this designation the fact that the Lord and the Spirit are two divine persons is brought out. Also we see why the identity of essence was first emphasized: the Lord works through the Spirit; it is "the Spirit of the Lord" who works liberty, that Spirit with whom he is one, yet in and by whom he comes to us and works in us. — And here it is **liberty** which the Spirit of the Lord bestows wherever he is present; οὖ, relative pronoun used adverbially of place, **where**, like ὅπου. The context always shows what the term "liberty" includes; and for this reason it will not do to identify the liberty spoken of in one context with that mentioned in another, the two may be very different. Here the context refers to the "boldness" which the apostle was able to use as a servant of the new covenant in Christ. Accordingly the "liberty" wrought by the Spirit of the Lord is the inward and outward freedom from the restrictions, limitations, and obscurities of the old covenant. Paul and all Christian ministers enjoy a spiritual freedom in the possession and proclamation of the full truth in Jesus Christ, which was utterly out of the question for Moses and the O. T. priesthood. But verse 18 shows that the apostle is thinking not only of Moses, but also of the hardened Israelites. By "liberty" then he means that blessed condition when we are free from the veil of hardness, the joyous liberty of the true knowledge of Christ, and of the faith and the spiritual life in him. This comprehensive spiritual liberty is found wherever the Spirit of the Lord is, and he is where men turn to the Lord (16).

The blessed truth which the apostle has just stated in general terms he now applies specifically to his readers and all Christians, at the same time unfolding what it contains, thus showing concretely the work of Christ through his Spirit and Gospel. **But we all, with unveiled face reflecting as a mirror the glory of the Lord, are transformed into the same image from glory to glory, even as from the Lord the Spirit.** The connecting particle is the transitional δέ; ἡμεῖς is emphatic, **but we all,** namely Paul and the Corinthian Christians, and thus

Christians generally, in contrast, not indeed with Moses as
one, which would emphasize πάντες, but with all the hardened
Israelites. — A second emphasis rests on ἀνακεκαλυμμένῳ
προσώπῳ, **with unveiled face,** as its position shows, and the
implied contrast with the veiled faces of the Israelites, the
veil being the hardening.. For us who have turned to Christ,
Paul would say, the veil has been taken away, so that with
the eyes of faith we now see Christ fully and clearly both in
the old covenant and in the apostolic preaching of the
new. — The participle κατοπτριζόμενοι is properly translated:
reflecting as in a mirror, and not as the Am. Com. prefers:
beholding as in a mirror (margin). The word occurs only
here in the N. T. and both translators as well as commentators are divided as to its meaning. Bachmann gives the most
recent and satisfactory statement of the case, according to
which the Greek fathers understood the word to mean: "to
reflect" as silver reflects the rays .of the sun, while the meaning "to behold" lacks attestation; moreover, if "beholding"
the glory of the Lord were intended, the context would
require that this be direct, as Moses beheld the glory of the
Lord, and not indirect, merely in a mirror. Hodge thinks,
the contrast to the veil which blinded the Israelites requires
for the Christians a "beholding" with unveiled face; not a
reflecting; but the apostle here has in mind more than
Hodge notes, namely a contrast which combines into one
what he has said regarding Moses and regarding the
Israelites, and he even adds something new and striking on
top of that. Our faces, Paul would say, are not veiled like
those of the hardened Israelites, but with unveiled face, like
Moses, we both see the glory of the Lord and reflect that
glory as in a mirror, not of course outwardly, but inwardly,
spiritually. Yea, we exceed Moses with the glorious reflection on his face, which faded away, in that by our reflecting
the Lord's glory we are actually transformed into his
image, so that the reflection and glory ever remains and
even increases. — **The glory of the Lord** spiritually reflected in us is the divine excellence of the Godman who is
the Head of the church, the Dispenser of heavenly gifts, the

Judge of the world, the Conqueror of all his foes, the Intercessor for his believers, in a word the Bearer of the entire
divine majesty, which makes him Lord and King over all
(Meyer). — The sense is, that *by* reflecting this glory we
are transformed into the same image from glory to
With μεταμορφούμεθα we might expect εἰς or κατά, but the
simple accusative is also used. The present tense denotes
that this transformation is occurring now, so that now we
are all turned into the image of our glorious Lord; "that ye
may become partakers of the divine nature," 1 Pet. 1, 4;
"until Christ be formed in you," Gal. 4, 19; "Christ liveth in
me," 2, 20. Yet Calov adds significantly that this metamor-
phosis is not *essentialis*, as the fanatics would have it, but
mystica et spiritualis. Its ultimate result is, of course, the
heavenly glory. — **From glory to glory** means from one
step to another, in constant upward progress of holiness
in this life. This is a better interpretation than: "from the
glory of the Lord to the glory in us," or other even less acceptable ideas. — **Even as from the Lord the Spirit,** even
as one might expect from such an author or agent. The
work corresponds to the workman. Paul does not introduce
the cause here for our spiritual glorification, but rather the
fountain and source from which it proceeds (ἀπό). — And
this is **the Lord the Spirit,** *i. e.* the Lord who is the Spirit.
The reference is evidently to what was said in verse 17, and
this excludes the interpretation: Lord of the Spirit or
Spirit of the Lord. Our conversion, our sanctification, and
inward spiritual glorification is wrought by the Lord who is
one with the Holy Spirit, sends him, is present with him,
and ever works in us by and through him. And the work
thus accomplished is the very highest and most glorious this
side of eternity. The Epiphany of the Lord thus works a
spiritual Epiphany in us, with corresponding eternal results.

HOMILETICAL HINTS.

Jesus said he would tell his disciples "plainly," John 16, 25;
in the same way his messengers use great boldness of speech

now. — So great, so abundant is this boldness that it has been called the resplendent dawn of eternity, the early morning radiance of eternal light. Besser.

"But the Comforter, even the Holy Spirit, whom the Father will send in my name, he shall teach you all things, and bring to your remembrance all that I have said unto you," John 14, 26. "The permanent glory is one that needs no veil." Luth. Com.

"The light shineth in the darkness; and the darkness comprehended it not," John 1, 5. "He came unto his own, and they that were his own received him not," John 1, 9. This was because of the veil over their hearts. For the entire Old Testament testifies of Christ. Do you wish to hear its Advent message, then read Ps. 24: "Lift up your heads, O ye gates; and be ye lift up, ye everlasting doors; and the King of glory shall come in." Do you desire to behold the Christmas miracle, then turn to Micah 5 with its word on Bethlehem little among the thousands of Judah; and to Isaiah 7 with its word on the virgin's son, and to Isaiah 9, where the names of the child that is born unto us are written. Would you study the mysteries of Good Friday? Turn to Ps. 22 with its prayer: "My God, my God, why hast thou forsaken me?" and its plain reference to the crucifixion: "They have pierced my hands and my feet." It even tells us what happened with the clothing of Christ: "They part my garments among them, and cast lots upon my vesture." It describes the very mockery of the Jews: "He trusted on the Lord that he would deliver him: let him deliver him, seeing he delighted in him." Or do you require the Easter message, then study the great Easter Psalm 118: "The stone which the builders refused is become the head stone of the corner. This is the Lord's doing; it is marvelous in our eyes."— How could Israel read all this, we ask amazed, and not recognize its Savior? But Israel is not the only one who reads the Scriptures through a thick veil.

How many educated and intelligent men there are who do not know what to do with the Scriptures. To some it is a book of fables and myths, venerable because of its age, but hardly of service for our advanced times. To others it is an ancient document by means of which, if we combine here and transpose there, ages long past can again be brought to view, like buried cities of old uncovered by the excavator's spade. But whenever thus we would make something out of the Scriptures we forget what is far more important, that they should make something out of us. Riemer.

"In thy light shall we see light," Ps. 36, 9. Away then with the veils of prejudice, habit, dependence, tradition and hardness of heart! Is some such veil over your eyes? "The hypocrites make a veil for themselves, namely the presumption of their works and external holiness; they have no desire to look fairly into the eyes of the law, and come to know that such righteousness amounts to naught." Luther.

Worldly men think of liberty only as the ability to do just as they please; and this is the height of slavery. A man is truly free when he is able in all things to be and to do exactly what his Creator intended. To be like Christ is to be free; to trample the flesh under foot and serve Christ in holiness and righteousness is to be free. And this is the liberty found where the Spirit of Christ dwells and rules in a heart.

Rump writes that a slave of mammon bears a different imprint than a slave of lust; every sin has its seal which it impresses upon its victim. In the same way the Spirit of Christ, in making his glorious impression upon the soul of man, puts something ennobling into his very countenance. — Some think of the Gospel as the mirror in which we are to behold Christ; but the Gospel is more than a mirror and offers us more than a reflected picture of Christ. The Gospel is the means by which Christ himself shines upon us; it is a sun shining, not a mirror reflecting. You and I are to be the mirror, and we are to reflect the glory of the Lord that shines upon us, not out of heaven, but out of the Gospel.

In the Eisenach texts as first published the committee which selected the texts underscored the words: "the glory of the Lord."

The Glory of the Lord in His Congregation.

I. *Proclaimed without a veil.*

II. *Seen with believing hearts.*

III. *Reflected in Christlike lives.*

The Sunlight of Christ's Saving Grace.

I. *It fills the whole Bible.*

    a) The dawn in the Old Testament.

    b) The full splendor in the New.

II. *It shines upon men.*

    a) Some shut it out by a veil.

    b) Others turn to it in faith.

III. *It glorifies all who believe.*

    a) By transforming them into Christ's image.

    b) By glorifying them in ever increasing measure.

Our Glory in Christ Jesus.

I. *Its openness.*
II. *Its spirituality.*
III. *Its growth.*

The Great Purpose of the Bible.

I. *To show us Christ.*
II. *To make us Christlike.*

What do You See in the Scriptures?

I. *If you use a veil.*

A law — works — fables and myths — history — morality.

II. *If you discard all veils.*

Christ — liberty from works, or salvation — a power that transforms us into the image of Christ — the way to spiritual glory here and heavenly glory hereafter.

What About Christianity?

It is the religion
I. *Of clearness.*
II. *Of liberty.*
III. *Of glory and perfection.*

THE LENTEN CYCLE.

THE LENTEN CYCLE.

Septuagesima to Good Friday.

The subject of the lenten cycle is always the Passion of our Lord and Savior. This subject is treated in one way by the gospel texts, and in another by the epistles. A perusal of the author's introduction to the lenten cycle of the *Eisenach Gospel Selections* will be helpful in showing just how the gospel texts are intended to treat the lenten theme. In brief, we repeat, that they do not actually tell the passion story, which is reserved for the special lenten services during the week-days, for which the proper texts are also provided in the Eisenach series of gospel texts. In the Sunday morning gospel texts we have *Christ himself showing himself to us in his passion* — an incomparable theme, and presented in the individual texts in the most effective way. The one thing to hold fast in the gospel texts is Christ in his passion. In all these texts there are other valuable elements, but all of them, even when extensive and inviting, are secondary, and should not tempt the preacher to lose sight of the great central thought of the texts. The lenten epistles follow a course which might almost be called the opposite. Here too the passion of Christ remains the great theme, yet this is not elaborated so as to bring out the different features of the passion. That is the proper function of the gospels. The epistles deal with *the fruits and results of the passion*. This includes even the epistle for Good Friday, in which if in any we might look for a description of the crucifixion or of some feature of the death of Christ; instead we find that the grand text set for that solemn festival, while it mentions the death of Christ, sets forth the reconciliation or atonement effected by that death. So, in general, we will find that in

317

the gospels throughout Christ himself shows himself to us
in his passion; but in the epistles the apostles show us:
the saving effects of the passion of Christ upon men.
In some of these texts the cross of Christ, his suffering,
death, *etc.*, are mentioned directly; yet even where this
occurs we must remember that these parts of the texts belong to the general foundation upon which all the lenten
texts rest, even those in which no specific reference to
some part of the passion occurs. Throughout them all the
emphasis rests on the saving effects or fruits of the passion. This is the golden thread upon which the precious
epistle pearls are strung. That must not be misunderstood
to mean that the preacher is to neglect the special reference
to Christ's passion which an individual lenten text may
contain; quite the contrary, he must utilize such parts of
his texts fully, and must even reach back to the passion
in those lenten texts which do not make mention of it in
so many words. His warrant for the latter is the sacred
season of the church year which every one of the texts
provided for him is to interpret in its special way. Yet,
as it is the business of the epistolary writings of the apostles
in general to set forth on the basis of the great Gospel
facts the salvation which rests on them, so it is the specific
function of the lenten epistle texts, as distinguished from
the lenten gospel texts, to present to us now this and again
that individual feature of that great salvation, and in this
lenten season those features which are intimately connected
with the Savior's passion.

With this general function of the epistle tests clearly
apprehended, it will not be difficult to follow the path which
step by step is marked out for us in the Eisenach lenten
epistles. There are eleven texts in all, the two for
Septuagesima and Sexagesima of an introductory and more
general character, and the last two, for Maundy Thursday
and for Good Friday, setting forth the special significance of
these two church festivals. The seven lenten texts proper
unfold the great lenten theme as such.

The text for Septuagesima bids us, with one heart and

mind walk worthy of the Gospel in faith and even in suffering for Christ. With our faces set towards Calvary this inclusive admonition receives a specific coloring. We may summarize its great wealth in the general theme suggested by its opening sentence: *All they who stand beneath the cross of Christ must walk worthy of the Gospel.* — The text for Sexagesima reminds us of the old epistle pericope for this day, which also deals with the personal experience of St. Paul. It is the apostle's earnest desire that Christ be magnified in his body, whether by life or by death, and this he brings out with striking effect in the memorable statement: "For to me to live is Christ, and to die is gain." Here the preacher finds his theme ready to hand. On the threshold of Lent it will follow some line like this: *All they who stand beneath the cross of Christ count it Christ to live and count it gain to die.*

Quinquagesima or Estomihi, even in the old gospel pericopes, is used to open up the lenten series proper, although Lent does not actually begin until the Wednesday after. A glance at the old gospel text will make this plain: "Behold, we go up to Jerusalem." Luke 18, 21. The same arrangement is observed in both the Eisenach gospel and epistle for this Sunday. The latter mentions directly "Christ crucified," and describes him in his saving grace as "the power of God and the wisdom of God," Christ Jesus "made unto us wisdom from God, and righteousness, and sanctification, and redemption." All the other thoughts of this text are evidently subordinate to the one which we employ in the theme: *All they who stand beneath the cross receive Christ as the power of God and the wisdom of God.* In substance there would be no difference if we insert instead of power and wisdom the contents of the last verse, namely wisdom, righteousness sanctification, and redemption.

The brief text for Invocavit mentions Christ as our "high priest" and his having passed through temptation like our own; it then draws the conclusion which points to the theme: *All they who stand beneath the cross approach the throne of grace with boldness.*

The text for Reminiscere does not mention the passion of Christ directly, although it does refer to the forgiveness of sins "for his name's sake." The climax of the text is in the extended admonition not to love the world, which receives a solemn emphasis when uttered during the season which commemorates Christ's passion. *All they who stand beneath the cross turn from the love of the world.*

The brief word of Peter selected for Oculi is very plain in its message for a lenten Sunday. The preceding context mentions the sufferings of Christ and the glories that should follow them, but this can hardly be utilized in the text as it stands. Yet the admonition during Lent will of itself turn our hearts to him who died for us upon the cross: *All they who stand beneath the cross strive after holiness.*

Laetare brings us a subject which Lent dare not lack, namely repentance. The preacher will readily see the fitness of the theme: *All they who stand beneath the cross rejoice in godly sorrow.*

The text for Judica, 1 Pet. 1, 17-25, may at first puzzle the student of this cycle. Here indeed we find the fullest and richest direct reference to Christ's passion: his precious blood as the Lamb without blemish and without spot, foreknown from eternity and manifested at the end of time for our sakes. The purpose of the text becomes clear as soon as we note that all the apostle here says centers in the two admonitions: to pass the time of our sojourning in fear, and to love one another from the heart fervently. These two admonitions Peter builds on the mighty foundation of Christ's precious blood, our redemption, and our regeneration, and we must do the same: *All they who stand beneath the cross continue in fear and love.*

Palm Sunday has an especially fine text, Heb. 12, 1-6, very appropriate also for the confirmation of catechumens which in so many of our churches, and very properly, takes place on this Sunday. Here is a direct mention of Christ who endured the cross and despised the shame, willingly passing through both, to sit now at the right hand of God. He is the Author and Finisher of our faith, to whom we as

sons of God are to look in running our race and enduring
our chastening. Every part of this text is rich with meaning for the day and for the ceremony that graces it. We
sum it all up in one word: *All they who stand beneath the
cross must persevere.*

On Maundy Thursday Christ instituted his holy Supper; hence the text 1 Cor. 10, 16-17. It is an excellent practice to celebrate the Lord's Supper on this day or on the
evening of it. Once at least in every church year this sacrament in all its blessedness should be set before our hearers
from the pulpit. If this cannot be done on the very day or
evening when the supper was instituted, some other suitable
time certainly ought to be found. The theme will always be:
*All they who stand beneath the cross are made one by the
communion of Christ's body and blood.*

Good Friday, even in the epistle, 2 Cor. 5, 14-21, paints
the cross before our eyes: "One died for all." At the same
time, in the regular way of the Epistles, this text shows us
the fruit of the cross, the reconcilation and atonement which
it accomplished, and how, embracing this by faith, we now
should live for him who died for us and rose again. There
is but one theme, however we may formulate it: *The Cross
of Christ which wrought our reconcilation.*

Glancing back over the texts thus outlined, we will find
that the seven from Quinquagesima to Palm Sunday follow
a clearly marked line. Omitting all beauty of statement and
giving the bare thought in each text, we trace the following
fruits of Christ's passion for and in men: 1) redemption; 2)
pardon; 3) separation from the world; 4) union with God
in holiness;)5 constant sorrow for sin, or repentance; 6)
the general Christian graces or virtues, fear, love, *etc.;* 7)
perseverance. Each text is thus found in its proper place,
and each subject a vital link in the lenten chain. And the
whole lenten series adding the two introductory texts, and
the two festival texts in which the series culminates, constitutes as fine a cycle for this section of the church year as
has ever been gathered from the epistolary writings of the
apostles.

21

SEPTUAGESIMA.

Phil. 1, 27-2, 4.

The texts for Septuagesima and Sexagesima are both taken from the first part of the Epistle to the Philippians. They constitute a pair, like two pillars between which we enter the portals of the sacred lenten season. We may say that the first of these treats of the Christian's life as such, and the second of the inner motive, or motive-power, which should animate that life. The first bids us walk worthy of the Gospel of Christ, first as regards those without who oppose us: we are to stand fast and strive for the faith ot the Gospel, to be unafraid of our adversaries, and to count it an honor to suffer for Christ; secondly as regards those within who are our brethren: we are to live in unity and love with them. The following text then brings out the spirit which must animate us in this Christian life: "For me to live is Christ, and to die gain." Phil. 1, 21. Our theme for Septuagesima is simple and plain: As now once more we turn our faces to Calvary, *let us walk worthy of the Gospel of Christ,* both as regards the opponents of our faith, and as regards the brethren in the faith.

As regards the opponents of our faith.

In the 25th verse the apostle expresses his assurance that he shall not yet meet death and thus be removed from the Philippians, but that he shall be released from his imprisonment in Rome and "shall abide, yea, and abide with you all, for your progress and joy in the faith." In the 26th verse he even speaks directly of "my presence with you again," namely of his actually coming to his beloved Philippians again. Then he continues: **Only let your manner of life be worthy of the gospel of Christ.** How-

322

ever things may turn out with Paul, for the Philippians **only** this one thing is needful. In stating it the apostle uses the verb πολιτεύεσθε, **let your manner of life be,** or as the margin prefers: *behave as citizens.* The latter clings more closely to the etymological meaning of the word, while the former takes it in the broader sense in which it naturally came to be used; the A. V. has: "let your conversation be." The more general meaning is preferable here, since the apostle makes no use of the idea of a πόλις or city in the entire connection, but uses altogether different imagery ("stand fast," "striving," "affrighted," "conflict"). The only citizenship which the word could imply, if we should prefer to follow the etymology closely, is that of the Christian commonwealth. — **Worthy of the gospel** means so as to grace the Gospel which has made the Philippians Christians and children of God; so that the Gospel they believe will be honored by their conduct and life. This Gospel is the glad tidings that Jesus Christ has saved us from our sins and through faith makes us forever blessed. It is the doctrine of salvation in Christ with all that it contains. It is called **the gospel of Christ,** or "Christ's gospel," because it is his, emanating from him, which makes it both salutary and heavenly in its character. So the "only" of St. Paul is by no means a small thing; it really embraces in one all the requirements of the Christian life. And yet this "only" must be demanded of every believer. If we are Christians, we must show it by living the Gospel we believe. The great trouble is that many subtract heavily from this "only" and yet profess adherence to Christ's Gospel; they walk unworthy of it and dishonor it, whether they eliminate some of its blessed doctrinal contents and pay no attention to these parts, or set aside some of its moral precepts and absolve themselves from obedience to them.

Paul's purpose in reminding the Philippians of their general Christian obligation is a personal one: **that, whether I come and see you or be absent, I may hear of your state, etc,** He writes as a loving pastor, and a solicitous father and friend. He might have put the injunction on

higher ground, namely that Christ himself might be pleased
with their walk and conversation. This, of course, he does
not mean to eliminate. Still, the personal touch is always
a powerful thing. The thought of a dear father, or mother,
or pastor, or some other person bound to us by the holy
ties in Christ has often wrought wonders; and Paul's appeal here touches the tender bond that unites him with the
Philippians. The construction in this purpose clause has
frequently been found fault with by exegetes as not quite
regular, but without good reason; for ἵνα followed by the
subjunctive ἀκούω is entirely regular, and the arrangement
of two participles, ἐλθὼν καὶ ἰδών, with the first parenthetical
εἴτε, and only one, ἀπών, with the second, is altogether ad-
missable. It is unnecessary to urge that the verb "I may
hear" really matches only the last participle "be absent"
and not the first two "come and see you." In either case
the verb "hear" may well apply; for if Paul should come
and see the Philippians, he would certainly at once inquire
of them how they had been conducting themselves, just
as he would inquire if, while away from them, he would
meet someone who had been in Philippi. — While Paul in
the 25th verse expresses the assurance that he will again
meet the Philippians, he does not know how soon this will
be; he may **come and see** them in a short time, or he may
be absent from them for a long while, busy with other
work. But in either case he wants to **hear** τὰ περὶ ὑμῶν,
the things concerning you, **of your state.** And what he
desires to hear he at once elaborates at some length: ὅτι
στήκετε . . . συναθλοῦντες . . . μὴ πτυρόμενοι . . .
ἔχοντες (verse 30), **that ye stand fast, etc.** The apostle
wants to hear good things of the Philippians, and he is
sure that he will. In telling them what these good things
are he virtually urges them to strive after them, so as not
to disappoint the apostle. — The expressions he uses refer
to a contest with opponents, in which the Philippians are
to prove themselves victors. **That ye stand fast** means that
they show themselves firm and unyielding in maintaining
their faith. This firm stand they are to hold **in one spirit,**

in unity of conviction, mind and will. There is no indication here that ἐν πνεύματι means the Holy Spirit, as Ewald
thinks; nor can it mean the higher side of the soul, the
spiritual part of the believer, since all the Philippians together are to manifest the "one spirit," and this oneness
can exist only where there are many persons bound together and acting as a unit. — The same thing is true of
μιᾷ ψυχῇ, **with one soul,** which modifies the following participle. The two phrases are not identical, although they are
as closely related as soul is to spirit. The Philippians are
to stand firmly together as if "one spirit" controlled them,
and they are to do this by striving as if "one soul" animated
them. Just as their convictions, thoughts, and wills were
to be one in this matter, so also their affections, desires,
and sympathies. — Their firm stand is to be maintained by
striving for the faith of the gospel. The σύν in συναθλοῦντες
does not refer to their association with each other in the
strife or with Paul as their companion in arms, but to the
dative τῇ πίστει: they are to strive **for the faith,** to maintain
and uphold it against the opposition they are bound to meet.
The faith of the gospel, then, is the blessed doctrine which
they have come to believe through Paul's preaching. This
as a precious possession of their hearts, they are to contend
for. "Beloved . . . I was constrained to write unto
you, exhorting you to contend earnestly for the faith which
was once delivered unto the saints." Jude 3. The verb
which Paul uses (συναθλεῖν) reminds us of the athletic contests which called forth the best efforts of the contestants
in striving against their respective opponents. In the same
way the Christians of each congregation are to stand as
a unit and with one soul overcome triumphantly everything
that would deprive them of the truth of the Gospel and
of their adherence thereto. — The image which the apostle
has in mind he carries one step farther: **and in nothing
affrighted by the adversaries.** The verb πτύρεσθαι originally refers to the shying of startled and terrified horses,
and then is used in a general way of startling fear or a
panicky condition. **In nothing** are the Philippians to be-

come startled, upset, affrighted, and thus driven to let go their precious treasure, no matter what **the adversaries** may say or do. They are to keep their heads and be fully assured at all times, even as Paul himself had showed them when he first visited Philippi and went cheerfully to prison and had his feet laid in the stocks, while he and Silas sang joyful praises unto God. The adversaries tried a good deal on Paul at that time, but in nothing could they affright him. The same conduct Paul now expects the Philippians to maintain. What a pity that Christians who have every reason to feel sure of their faith and the Word of God in which it is anchored, should ever be startled by hostile attacks! Let unbelieving men bring forth the latest weapons of reason — all of them have been tried and shattered long ago. Let them ridicule this or that doctrine of the Gospel as contrary to science and advanced knowledge — God's truth is eternal and smiles at the puny ridicule of men, which cannot make even one of its foolish boasts good. Let them injure and attack us for our confidence in the Gospel and its doctrines — we can afford to suffer with God as our supporter and friend, and no persecution of believers has ever altered a particle of the divine truth they have held fast. — By a kind of parenthesis the apostle shows how little reason the Philippians have to be upset at anything their foes may attempt: **which is for them an evident token of perdition, but of your salvation, and that from God.** The feminine ἥτις stands for ὅ τι by attraction to the following ἔνδειξις, and refers to what the apostle has just said, namely the action of the believing Philippians in being unafraid. This actually **is**, objectively, whether the adversaries realize it or not, **for them an evident token,** something which points out, a demonstration, or proof, first **of perdition,** namely as far as they themselves are concerned in their wicked opposition to the Gospel and its believers, **but of your salvation,** namely as people true to the Gospel. **And that,** the apostle adds, namely the double significance of the token, **from God,** who lends this significance to the token, and who sets this and other signals of warning in the path of his adversaries. Lightfoot connects this with the imagery of the contest: "The Christian gladiator does not anxiously await the signal of life or death from the fickle crowd. The great Director of the contest himself has given him a sure token of deliverance." The text, however, while it tells the Philippians of the token, describes this as one for the adversaries (αὐτοῖς). Perdition awaits all who fight against the Gospel and the church, salvation all who hold fast the truth of salvation courageously, and our very faith and courage wrought by God is an evidence of this, which at least we ought to realize for our encouragement, and which it would be well for our adversaries to realize also, as it is especially intended for them, that they may yet escape from the danger into which they are plunging. — How the firm faith of the Philippians can be such a token is shown by the appended reason : **because to you it hath been granted in the behalf of Christ, not only to believe on him, but also to suffer in his behalf.** Your faith, and on top of that your suffering, is a gracious gift to you, and therefore to those who make you suffer a token as described. The ὑμῖν is emphatic; let all who believe and suffer rejoice: "Blessed are they that have been persecuted for rightousness' sake," Matth. 5, 10. The verb signifies that an unmerited gift has been bestowed, and this a twofold one: **to believe on him** (πιστεύειν here construed with εἰς) and **to suffer.** The **not only . . . but also** lifts the second above the first, as a special honor and distinction. Yet believing is the fundamental thing, therefore also here inserted in front of suffering. Without true faith the suffering that is a gracious gift of honor could not even occur. Both the faith and the suffering the apostle wants us to view alike as a gift from our gracious God. The suffering is especially qualified as **in behalf of Christ,** a phrase which the apostle repeats since he thrusts in the thought of believing: to suffer **in his behalf.** This duplication increases the emphasis. The Christian's suffering. due to persecutions of one kind or another, whether small or great, is constantly viewed in Scripture as undergone "for Christ's sake." That is the distinctive mark of this suffering, separating it from all other and making it precious in the eyes of God. Peter even speaks of it as a partaking of Christ's sufferings, 1 Pet. 4, 13. Frequently we Christians view the hardships, losses, and hurts that come upon us from a wicked world as a kind of calamity from which we must make every possible effort to escape. Paul teaches us the true view: our sufferings are marks of distinction, badges of honor, a special grace and gift of God. Gladly then we ought to suffer in Christ's behalf; rejoice in the honor conferred upon us; expect it at the hand of God; and bear the marks of it in triumph. Let those who will lament, we, like Paul and Silas one time in the Philippian prison, will sing praise unto God. — The closing participial clause, **having the same conflict which ye saw in me, and now hear to be in me,** has the nominative ἔχοντες, which Westcott and Hort connect, like the other participles συναθλοῦντες and πτυρόμενοι, with the original main verb στήκετε (27); others construe it loosely with the dative ὑμῖν (29) as implying a nominative ὑμεῖς, Ewald even making an absolute nominative, simply appended to the sentence in general. We prefer the first of these constructions because it is simplest grammatically. Paul's conflict the Philippians **saw** while he was at Philippi, Acts 16, 16 *etc.;* 1 Thess. 2, 2, and the messenger, Epaphroditus, who carried this Epistle to them, no doubt made a full report by word of mouth concerning Paul's present state, in connection with what the apostle here writes himself, so that they could **now hear.** The fact that **the same conflict** as in Paul was also theirs must have been a great encouragement to the Philippians: "Rejoice, and be exceeding glad: for great is your reward in heaven: for so persecuted they the prophets which were before you," Matth. 5, 12. Suffering for the cause of Christ makes us companions of the greatest saints of the kingdom of our Savior.

As regards the brethren in the faith.

From the thought of adversaries and a contest the apostle now turns to the thought of brethren and their fraternal relation to each other. **If there is therefore any comfort in Christ, if any consolation in love, if any fellowship of the Spirit, if any tender mercies and compassions, fulfil, etc.** The **therefore** refers back to what he has said of the duty of the Philippians regarding their adversaries; this duty requires what now he elaborates at length, a manifold duty also towards each other. The crux in these opening statements is the τις before σπλάγχνα. Some have ventured the correction τινα; others have accepted the intolerable solecism, or have dared to call it a *lapsus calami* on the part of the apostle himself. The fact is that the reading τις is overwhelmingly attested, and that therefore both the translator and the interpreter is bound to meet it in a satisfactory way. Yet both the A. and the R. V. translate as if the Greek had τινα; this simply will not do. Besides the Greek wording, a second difficulty arises when the thought expressed in the four "if" sentences is to be combined with the thought in the conclusion: "fulfil ye my joy, *etc.*" This fourfold condition, especially its last member, does not fit the conclusion, even if we substitute τινα for τις. It will not do simply to ignore these difficulties and make what we can of the case with the difficulties unsolved. Accordingly the best commentators have labored to find a satisfactory explanation without violating the attested Greek text or forcing the thought into unnatural combinations. The efforts of Hofmann and of Meyer have been carried a good step farther by Ewald, who puts us on the right track. Instead of a fourfold condition followed by a conclusion, as given in the English translations, we have here four separate coordinate conditional sentences standing by themselves. And an entirely new sentence begins with πληρώσατε: "Fulfil ye, *etc.*" Accordingly we read: "If there is any comfort in Christ" so that "in Christ" becomes the predicate: "If there is any comfort, it is in Christ." Likewise the following: "If any consolation, it is of love; if any fellowship, it is of the Spirit." In the last member we supply as follows: εἰ τις (κοινωνία), σπλάγχνα καὶ οἰκτιρμοί, and read: "If any (fellowship), it is tender mercies and compassions." The four sentences, however, are hortatory, and so we may read each one after this pattern: "If there is any comfort, *let it be* in Christ." The last pair is combined by having the same subject and condition. An independent sentence follows in verse 2: "Fulfil ye, *etc.*" — **If there is any comfort,** or as the American Committee prefers: *any exhortation,* let is be **in Christ.** The verb παρακαλεῖν means to call to one's side; παράκλησις the action of calling one to one's side, and in the modified sense a request, an urging, or an *exhortation.* This may be, and often is, of a comforting nature, hence the translation **comfort,** or as others suggest: *encouragement.* We must not trench on παραμύθιον, the synonym, in the next sentence. The apostle is speaking of the duties of the Philippians to each other as brethren. Among them is the duty of exhortation or encouragement to each other, especially also amid the trials and difficulties that arise because of the attacks of their adversaries. Now all such exhortation must be **in Christ.** In him they all stand by faith, and any word of one brother to another, encouraging and strengthening him, must remain in this circle. Paul himself illustrates his meaning when frequently he urges his brethren for Christ's sake to do this or that. So every exhortation must grow out of faith in Christ, be inspired by our connection with him, and rest on his will and Word. Then it will be of the right kind, and will find the right response in the believer's heart. — **If any consolation,** let it be **of love,** the kind that love offers, *i. e.* the love born of Christ or faith in him; not a consolation offered by mere sentimentality or mere humanitarian love, or, worse yet, officious intrusion. Παραμύθιον (παρά, beside, and μῦθος, speech or word) means incentive, and thus also **consolation.** This is exactly what true love offers the brethren, especially when in any contest for Christ they need it especially.

So also Paul writes: "Ye know how we dealt with each
one of you, as a father with his own children, exhorting
you (παρακαλοῦντες) and encouraging you (παραμυθούμενοι)".
1 Thess. 2, 11. Where faith in Christ, and faithfulness
to Christ, is, there love will be also. — **If any fellowship,**
let it be **of the Spirit,** for he is the author of Christian
communion and fellowship, and all our brotherly relation
and intercourse must be **of the Spirit,** produced, governed,
and made faithful by him. Paul speaks first of the author
and source of the κοινωνία, the Holy Spirit, then he adds
a description of its manifestation: **If any** fellowship, let
it be **tender mercies and compassions.** The σπλάγχνα
are really the nobler viscera, which were considered the
seat of the feelings and affections. So we now speak of
the heart; hence the metaphorical rendering **tender**
mercies, *Herzlichkeit.* To this the apostle adds οἰκτιρμοί
(from οἶκος, pity), **compassions,** expressions of pity toward any brother in trouble or distress. These tender
mercies and expressions of pity and compassion describe
very finely one side of Christian fellowship. It may be
that the apostle thought of his own need when he penned
these words, at least he appreciated the evidences of fellowship which the brethren showed him in sending him help
and comfort; and we know how kind he was to others. —
Of the four conditional sentences thus grouped together
the first and the third correspond (Christ, the Spirit), and
the second and the fourth (love, heartfelt compassions).
All four belong to those who would walk worthy of the
Gospel of Christ (verse 27).

    Fulfil ye my joy, that ye be of the same mind, the
apostle writes, bringing in a personal note. He implies
that already the Philippians have filled the cup of his joy
to a considerable degree, and he now urges that they fill
it completely full. His **joy** is his delight in seeing the
Gospel produce its blessed fruits in the believers. So every
true pastor delights in the progress of his flock. "Greater
joy have I none than this, to hear of my children walking
in the truth." 3 John 4. — **That ye be of the same mind**

means unity of mind and thought. On ἵνα after verbs of request, *etc.*, see Winer, 44, 8. The apostle elucidates at length what he means by this unity of mind, adding one participial clause after another: ἔχοντες . . . φρονοῦντες . . . ἡγούμενοι . . . σκοποῦντες. — He adds first: **having the same love,** in the one heart as in the other, wrought by the same Spirit, burning with the same desire, striving for the same objects and ends. — Some read as belonging together: σύνψυχοι τὸ ἓν φρονοῦντες: "with one accord of one mind." Our translators "chop off," as Ewald says, the σύνψυχοι and translate it as a separate member in these elucidating clauses: **being of one accord,** adding as the third member: **of one mind.** This makes τὸ αὐτὸ φρονῆτε and τὸ ἓν φρονοῦντες tautological, for to think the same thing and to think on thing is identical. Some endeavor to evade this by making τὸ ἕν mean "the one thing needful." yet the entire run of Paul's thought is foreign to such a turn. Paul wants the Philippians to think the same thing by thinking this one thing as σύνψυχοι, as people whose souls are united. The emphasis is on σύνψυχοι; and τὸ ἕν with its article refers back to τὸ αὐτό. — The apostle thus brings out in two ways the roots of Christian like-mindedness: having the same love, our minds and thoughts will be one; having our souls joined together, one thing will occupy our minds and thoughts. If one man loves the world, and another Christ, they will diverge fundamentally in their thinking; likewise, if some are only outwardly attached to the church, while others have given their souls to Christ and become spiritually one with their brethren.

The next additions are negative: *doing* **nothing through faction or through vainglory.** Really we need not supply *doing,* as Paul's energetic manner purposely omits a verb form. Moreover, if a verb is needed for these emphatic statements the context would offer φρονοῦντες from the previous clause. Ἐριθεία means originally to serve for hire, then to seek gain, or to strive for advantage in a selfish, scheming, intriguing manner. Thus **a faction** is a party within a party, selfishly seeking its own advantage, disregarding the general good. This, of course, would be the death of like-mindedness, and it often is in congregations rent by the factional spirit. The worst of all is when the pastor himself succumbs to factionalism and seeks his own personal advantage, perhaps even under the cloak of service to Christ, gathering about him his special friends whom he views as being "on his side." — In James 3, 14 "bitter jealousy" is joined to "faction," but here the apostle adds **vainglory,** κενοδοξία (κενός, vain, and δόξα, opinion, good opinion, and thus glory). To think or do anything **through,** κατά, according to, faction and vainglory is to make these the principle or mainspring of our thoughts and actions. "Let us not be vainglorious, provoking one another, envying one another." Gal. 5, 26. Any glory or credit we may get by securing our own selfish advantage among the brethren is vain. Selfishness always defeats itself by securing merely what after all is vain, empty, disappointing. — Over against (ἀλλά) these disrupting passions the apostle outlines the right course for unity with our brethren: **but in lowliness of mind each counting other better than himself.** This ends vainglory. Paul uses the article τῇ ταπεινοφροσύνῃ, which indicates as much as "due lowliness of mind," that which ought to grace the Christian. This **lowliness of mind** is the same as humility, and its characteristic action is to see things praiseworthy in others, so that without envy or resentment it delights in their being honored, yea, it counts others **better than self.** "In honor preferring one another." Rom. 12, 10. — Another opposite of faction and vainglory is added: **not looking each of you to his own things, but each of you also to the things of others.** The second ἕκαστοι is drawn by some to the following sentence. If added to our sentence, by its repetition it renders the admonition the more impressive. The plural ἕκαστοι is rare in the N. T., some texts show the singular in our passage. The idea in σκοπεῖν τά τινος is to desire to secure someone's advantage. The world always "looks out for it-

self," but those who walk worthy of the Gospel of Christ are
equally concerned about the welfare of others. In contrasting **his own things** with **the things of others** Paul
adds an "also" to the adversative: **but also,** indicating that
the Christian is indeed to care for himself in all the affairs
of this life, but never to the exclusion of others. God's
law is that you love your neighbor as yourself, which certainly includes our brethren in the faith. In the spirit of
Christ and by the aid of the Holy Spirit (verse 1) the
Christian is to live according to this law. How he is to
do this as regards earthly property Luther has indicated
in connection with the seventh commandment: "Help and
protect his property and business." Ex. 23, 4. See also
the ninth commandment. "By love serve one another."
Gal. 5, 13. The greed of worldly men, especially in business, has always been in evidence, crushing out small
dealers, forcing prices up so as to create great want among
the poor, piling up vast fortunes while thousands starve.
The spirit of the Gospel follows the opposite course, and
this especially as regards those who are one with us in the
faith.

Paul goes on in the following verses and shows us the
mind that ought to be in us by outlining the example of
our Savior; but our text is sufficiently rounded out, setting
before us the double line of conduct which we must follow,
both as regards our adversaries and as regards our
brethren, if we would walk worthy of the Savior's precious
Gospel.

HOMILETICAL HINTS.

In its general contents this epistle harmonizes with the old
gospel lesson concerning the laborers in the vineyard, and also
with the old epistle for the day concerning the race to be run
and the prize to be won; yet withal this text for Septuagesima has
a character all its own.

We are citizens of an earthly commonwealth, writes Rump,
and are loyal to our native land, and especially do we work for

the best interests of our own community. To do otherwise is to be a traitor and to deserve the execration reserved for all such. But we have another citizenship, infinitely higher than that of our home-land. In this world we are yet not of this world, but translated into the kingdom of our Lord and Savior Jesus Christ. And in this spiritual home-land of ours, dare we be anything but loyal, faithful, and true? That will mean two things especially: we must join hands in fighting every foe, we must again join hands in supporting every fellow citizen. — Who are the greatest foes of our country? Those of foreign lands who marshal their arms against it? No; these we have often conquered, and can conquer again. Our worst foes are those within, who undermine our liberties and institutions, who subvert the very principles on which our country rests. Who are the worst foes of our spiritual home-land, the church of Jesus Christ? Blatant unbelievers who marshal their attacks against the Bible and our Lord, who ridicule our faith and sneer at our professions of loyalty to Christ? No: he that sitteth in the heavens shall laugh; the Lord shall have them in derision. Their worst assaults have always failed, and shall ever fail. Their mightiest weapons are straws which break before they are used. Our worst foes are within, who are inwardly disloyal to the Lord, their King, whose doubts undermine the faith of their very brethren, whose love of the world opens the door to the great enemy and makes the love of many turn cold. Against these we must stand and fight the good fight under the banner of the Lord.

"Think not that I came to send peace on the earth: I came not to send peace, but a sword." Matt. 10, 84. — "Fight the good fight of faith." 1 Tim. 6, 12. — "And if also a man contend in the games, he is not crowned, except he have contended lawfully." 2 Tim. 2, 5. — "Let us patiently run the race that is set before us, looking unto Jesus the author and perfecter of our faith." Heb. 12, 2.

"The strength of the adversaries with whom we have to do is deception, a stratagem and sham, intended to hide their real weakness. When we hear them cry out to-day with such assurance: Christian faith is a thing out of date; there have never been any miracles: Christ could not rise from the dead! this may impress the foolish multitude. We read in their hatred against things truly Christian the signs of their own weakness. Nobody thinks of hating what is long out of date and with no prospect for the future. Hatred is often, and here also, the sign of a bad conscience, and a verdict of condemnation upon itself." Riemer.

In this fight you need no sword of steel, no armies, no state laws, no mere human power and might. You need the weapons of the Spirit of God.

Can one healed of lameness by the almighty Word of the
Lord Jesus, live and not move his limbs? Can he who has been
freed from the power of sin go on bound to its yoke as before?—
If we walk unworthy of the Gospel we are like a store whose
flaring sign may attract some customers, but when they see the
kind of goods that are offered for sale, they decline to buy.

No greater honor can come to a Christian than to suffer for
Christ and the Gospel's sake. — In contending for the faith we become companions in arms with Jesus himself. — It is the fire that
tries the gold. — Where are your scars, my comrade, honorable
scars won in the fight? No Christian is without them. He who
flees the fight, who surrenders in every fight, has no scars to
show, but only the fetters of the captive. — The wounds of Jesus
are his trophies of victory. By them even doubting Thomas knew
him after his resurrection.

Without war, without peace. — Through the garden of the
Christian church there flows a blessed stream; its waters are
comfort, consolation, fellowship, tender mercies and compassions.
Its source is Christ and the Spirit.

In earthly matters opinions always differ more or less, but in
the things of the Spirit, in that which is highest and best, our common faith and love must join our hearts and minds in one.

Do you know the wild boars that break into the Lord's vineyard and root up and destroy the precious vines and trample the
sweet fruit in the mire? Paul names two of them here: strife
and vainglory. Do you ever mean to open the gate to them that
they may enter in?

The apostle writes as if he were addressing our congregations
of to-day and knew of their coldness, indifference to one another,
their strifes and envyings. How easily one or the other becomes
offended or hurt; and how little some care whether they really
do offend and hurt others. In honor preferring myself, is the
motto of many a life. The lowly tasks are shunned, nobody cares
to stoop; but the offices and positions of honor are selfishly
sought. Many boast greatly of the few small things they have
done, and never credit those who have done far more. Yes, there
are many dark lines in the picture; we will not draw them all.

But is Paul's picture not too ideal? Is it possible to have
all this consolation and love and tender mercy and concord and
lowliness and unselfishness? It is not, if we look only to ourselves; but where the Spirit of the crucified Christ is allowed
full play, there miracles are wrought. — Do we miss much of what
the holy apostle here requires of Christ's followers? Then let us
bow our heads in repentance and shame. The way to the hights of
strong faith and fervent love leads ever through the lowly portal
of contrition. Bow down at the foot of Christ's cross; the drops

that trickle there wash away our stains and bring new life into
our arid hearts.

Let Your Conversation Be as Becometh the Gospel of Christ.

Graced by
I. *Courageous contending.*
II. *Patient suffering.*
III. *Fervent loving.*
IV. *Humble serving.*

Adapted from Matthes.

All in All for One.

I. *As companions in faith.*
II. *As companions in suffering.*
III. *As companions in love.*

Stand in One Spirit!

I. *In the one faith against all adversaries.*
II. *In the one love towards all brethren.*

Worthy Gospel Christians:

Have
I. *One spirit in the same contest.*
II. *One mind. in the same love.*

The Kind of Conversation that is Worthy of the Gospel of Christ.

It is that which is full of
I. *Gospel faith.*
II. *Gospel loyalty.*
III. *Gospel love.*
IV. *Gospel lowliness.*
V. *Gospel service.*

When will our Christian Life Impress the World?

I. *When we fight without fear.*
II. *When we suffer without complaint.*
III. *When we love without dissimulation.*
IV. *When we serve without reward.*

22

SEXAGESIMA.

Phil. 1, 12-21.

The real motive, the inner spirit and principle of St. Paul's life is set before us in a comprehensive manner in this selection from the Epistle to the Philippians. He reports to his readers the joyful fact that the turn which his affairs as a prisoner in Rome awaiting trial at the Emperor's hands have taken of late is one which furthers the Gospel, even encouraging most of the brethren to speak the Word of God more boldly than before; he rejoices that Christ is proclaimed also by others, even if the motives of some are not entirely pure; and of one thing especially he is certain, namely that Christ shall be magnified in him whether he lives or dies. So Paul's motive is clear; it is Christ to whom he is entirely devoted in life and in death, Christ who is his joy while he lives and his gain when he dies. In this Paul is a fine example for us all who in the previous text were urged to live worthy of the Gospel, and we see how these two texts fit finely together. What was the apostle's motive and life-principle must be ours likewise. Therefore, as now again our faith looks to the cross on Calvary, *let Christ be our heart's desire whether in life or in death.* — Paul writes the words of our text as "the prisoner in the Lord" (Eph. 4, 1), as one who bears the cross for Christ's sake, and even faces death for his faith and testimony. This is a special element which may be utilized in preaching on this text. Beneath the cross, and in the face of death, the true spirit of the Christian's whole life is to manifest itself in a marked degree. In this feature our text resembles the old epistle pericope to some extent; there Paul gives an extended catalog of his sufferings for Christ's sake, and in connection with them all praises the grace of God which is

338

sufficient for him. — In living and dying for Christ the great apostle's desire as here outlined, and ours likewise, is that the cause of Christ may prosper, that the Gospel of Christ may be proclaimed, and that the name of Christ may be magnified.

Paul's desire that the cause of Christ may prosper.

After a number of introductory statements Paul writes as follows concerning his own situation and affairs in Rome: **Now I would have you know brethren, that the things** *which happened* **unto me have fallen out rather unto the progress of the gospel.** He employs a phrase common in one form or another in the letter-writing of his day in imparting special information (comp. Rom. 1, 13): **I would have you know.** The implication is that they did not yet know. Paul addresses his readers as **brethren,** showing thus for one thing the closeness of their spiritual relation, and for another the strong interest they must have felt in his affairs, an interest which their brother Paul reciprocated. — It is good news which the apostle imparts thus early in his letter: "the things which happened unto me have fallen out rather unto the progress of the gospel." By τὰ κατ' ἐμέ, my affairs (comp. Rom. 1, 15), the apostle refers to certain special and recent occurrences in his captive life. What these were he does not state or even hint, the Philippians, no doubt, understanding exactly to what he referred, fearing what the outcome might be, especially for Paul personally. As far as we can judge, the situation was this: after two years of waiting as a prisoner under guard in his own rented house, Paul had finally been remanded for trial, and the first hearing had taken place. No doubt, his friends, and also those in Philippi, who knew what was impending, were filled with deep concern. The first hearing was entirely favorable to Paul, as we gather from his own words in this Epistle, and, though his case was by no means finished, and the possibility of danger was not removed, he rejoices to report to the Philippians, not indeed concerning his own individual interests, but concerning the favorable outcome in the interest of the Gospel. By inserting μᾶλλον, **rather,** he hints at what so many had feared, namely hindrance for the Gospel, quite the contrary of which had actually resulted. And the perfect tense ἐλήλυθεν (singular verb with a neuter plural subject), **have fallen out,** instead of the aorist, shows that the good result is a fixed thing for the present; even while the apostle was writing **the progress of the gospel** continued. What he means by this "progress" he at once states, showing very strikingly what he was chiefly concerned about, and taking for granted in a significant way that his readers shared his feelings in this respect. His one great desire was the progress or furtherance of the Gospel. Anything that put the Gospel forward in a marked way was news which he delighted to impart to his friends. — The Gospel was advantaged in two ways, first of all, **so that my bonds became manifest in Christ throughout the whole prætorian guard, and to all the rest.** The A. V. construes "in Christ" as modifying "my bonds:" "my bonds in Christ," Hofmann likewise; but there is no reason for separating "in Christ" from its natural and nearest connection and joining it to a word farther removed. Paul says that **my bonds,** his being a prisoner under accusation and on trial before the Emperor himself, **became manifest in Christ,** *i. e.* that men saw he was no ordinary prisoner, committed for this or that crime against the laws of the state, but that he was in bonds for being connected with (ἐν) Christ. His brethren, and perhaps a few others, had known this from the start, but now everybody else knew it likewise. — The translation of the A. V.: "in all the palace and in all other places," making ἐν ὅλῳ τῷ πραιτωρίῳ καὶ τοῖς λοιποῖς πᾶσιν refer to localities, is incorrect. The palace where the Emperor resided was never termed τὸ πραιτώριον; the latter is the name for the barracks where the Emperor's guard was stationed in Rome, or, as here, for this guard itself. The prætorian guard consisted of a picked body of men, 10,000 in number, and all of Italian birth, especially attached to the Emperor as his body-guard, first organized by Augustus, and usually called *praetoriae cohortes.* They received double pay and enjoyed special privileges, every soldier ranking with the centurions in the regular legions. The entire guard was not always stationed in Rome, certain divisions being at times posted in the adjacent towns. Because of its numbers and position the prætorian guard wielded a powerful influence in the state; the Emperor often courted its favor and on his accession bestowed upon it liberal donations. Paul was in the keeping of the commander of the prætorians from the start, a soldier being regularly detailed to guard him. By means of a coupling-chain (Eph. 6, 20) the prisoner was fastened to his guard, but he was free to move about with him and was even allowed to live "in his own hired dwelling" (Acts 28, 30). Some of the prætorians thus became acquainted with Paul as a prisoner for the Gospel of Christ, but certainly only a limited number. Now, however, the apostle reports that **the whole prætorian guard,** the entire body of 10,000, came to know of him as a man in bonds for Christ's sake. This was no small piece of news by any means; really, it was a matter of tremendous importance. It could not have been brought about gradually through the individual soldiers who had been guarding Paul these two years, as some commentators suppose; Paul's reference to "the things which happened unto me," *i. e.* recently, since the Philippians last had news of him, shows that something especial had happened, and this, as far as we are able to judge, could only be the beginning of his actual trial before the Emperor. His case, so entirely different from those usually reviewed by the Emperor, had attracted the attention of the entire cohort. — We may read τοῖς λοιποῖς as a simple dative depending on φανεροὺς γένεσθαι, **and to all the rest,** or, as seems preferable, an object, co-ordinate with ὅλῳ τῷ πραιτωρίῳ, depending on ἐν; "became manifest among the whole prætorian guard and all the rest." Knowing the size of the prætorian guard, the whole of which now knew Paul's case, "all the rest" here cannot mean the few officials who handled Paul's case when now it came to trial, but must mean all the people of Rome in addition to the prætorians. Paul was

discussed by all Rome, as one who was suffering affliction
and bonds because of his apostolic connection with Christ.
Mighty news indeed the apostle thus sends to Phillippi; his
heart is filled with elation, and the joyful note in this entire
Epistle is, beyond question, due in large measure to this unexpected and promising "furtherance of the Gospel." The
general interest which all Rome took in Paul's case was
evidently favorable to him, and thus in a degree to the
cause he represented, at least it opened a door for more
extended preaching of the Gospel. — This is the second advantage which Paul reports to the Philippians:
**and that most of the brethren in the Lord, being confi-
dent through my bonds, are more abundantly bold to
speak the word of God without fear.** Καί merely adds
this favorable result to the one already stated, yet evidently
the two are intimately connected. The fact that Paul's
bonds were manifest in Christ to all the people in Rome
furnished opportunity and encouragement for the brethren
to speak more freely and courageously the Word of God
concerning Christ. The apostle writes: **most of the
brethren;** literally: the more, the greater number, or more
than before, only a few holding back timidly for some
reason or other. He calls them brethren **in the Lord,** in
joint communion with the Lord, one faith connecting both
Paul and them with Jesus Christ and thus making them
"brethren in the Lord." Because "brethren in the Lord"
occurs nowhere else in the N. T., some commentators prefer
to connect "in the Lord" with the following participle:
"being confident in the Lord *etc.*" Yet in Col. 1, 2 we have
"brethren in Christ," and this too as the only case of the
kind in the N. T. Some add that to attach "in the Lord"
to "brethren" makes "in the Lord" a mere phrase; but this
is gratuitous. — Paul's brethren in Rome certainly never
doubted him and his cause; they knew he was innocent of
any crime, and merely in bonds for Christ's sake. Yet as
long as the outcome of his trial was altogether in doubt,
some of the brethren showed timidity in speaking the Word
of God. They were not all as brave as they might have

been. If the great apostle should be condemned by the Emperor and perhaps even lose his life, they feared for themselves, especially for those who had made themselves conspicuous in preaching the Gospel in the capital. So some at first held back. This changed when the first critical stage of the apostle's trial took such a favorable turn. — There was still doubt as to the final outcome, and so a few were still very cautious; yet more of them than hitherto, as Paul writes, are now **confident through my bonds,** or as the margin has it: *trusting in my bonds* (comp. for the construction with the dative Philem. 21; 2 Cor. 10, 7), relying on them as "manifest in Christ" to men generally, promising a vindication of their bearer, and not an unjust condemnation, which might involve the Christians in Rome generally, and especially their preachers. — In this confidence the brethren **are more abundantly bold,** περισσοτέρως τολμᾶν, or courageous, which implies a certain degree of boldness and courage even before this; **to speak the word of God without fear,** *i. e.* fearlessly to utter it (λαλεῖν) in their missionary activity among the Gentile Romans. Nothing could please Paul more than to see others take heart and help spread the **word of God,** the precious Gospel of Christ, which was God's own saving message to all men, in the very heart of the Empire through the provinces of which he had travelled as a messenger of God these many days. The progress of the Gospel must become our passion, our supreme desire in the same way. Our highest personal interest must ever be that poor sinners may hear of Christ, and our delight to see many others just as zealous and devoted as ourselves. Therefore, we must bless with Paul every leading of providence which gives the Gospel wider range and opens the door for increased missionary activity.

Paul's desire that the Gospel of Christ may be proclaimed.

While most of the apostle's brethren in the Lord were now courageously speaking the Word of God, there was nevertheless a difference: **Some indeed**

preach Christ even of envy and strife; and some also of good will. Can the first of these be included in the πλείονες whom Paul calls "brethren in the Lord" made "confident through my bonds"? Meyer and Ewald think this is out of the question, and that the apostle must mean a minority different from the πλείονες; they find it impossible to harmonize "in the Lord" and "confident in my bonds" with "envy and strife" over against the apostle. But these commentators do not give sufficient weight to Paul's statement: Some indeed **preach Christ,** *i. e.* the true Gospel with Christ as its center; and nowhere does the apostle charge these preachers with false doctrine. The apostle even declares that in this their preaching of Christ he rejoices and will rejoice, verse 18. Moreover, when in verse 14 he writes πλείονας λαλεῖν, the λαλεῖν suggests that the minority was silent, gave no utterance at all to the Word of God in a public way. The solution then is that τινὲς μέν, while indeed moved in part by wrong motives, were not so utterly controlled by them as to lose their faith and Christianity altogether; they were foolish and sinful brethren and preachers, but still brethren in the Lord and preachers of Christ. They do preach Christ, and that is good; but **even of envy,** namely because of the apostle's prominence, influence, and success, and that is not good; and their envy produces **strife,** personal contention and dispute with the apostle, which also helps to spoil their work. There are often such envious brethren in the ministry who cannot feel satisfied that God should give greater gifts and higher and more influential positions to other men. They feel themselves thrust into the background and their authority and following greatly reduced, hence they cause strife and personal contention. That there should be preachers of this stripe in Rome is not strange, when we remember how Paul came to the capital and soon had a large following, and now was talked of in the whole city. They resented all this, objected to their hearers always going to Paul and quoting his authority, and claimed that. they, and not he, were the rightful pastors in Rome. As

far as doctrine was concerned Paul finds no fault with
them; they were not legalists or Judaizers, as some have
thought; they merely opposed Paul's personal standing in
Rome from selfish motives. — While a few acted in this
manner, there were others, probably the greater number,
of whom the apostle could write: **and some also of good
will,** namely "good will" toward the person and position
of Paul as an apostle and a man of power in the church. —
The one *do it* **of love, knowing that I am set for the
defense of the gospel.** The A. V. transposes verses 16
and 17, but the best texts are followed by the R. V. We
may read: **the one,** οἱ μέν alone, and so also οἱ δέ alone, as
the subject; or οἱ may be read as the article in both cases,
joined in the one instance with ἐξ ἀγάπης as the substantive,
and in the other with ἐξ ἐριθείας. The latter is the preference of the American Committee of translators: *they that
are moved by love* do it etc. . . . *but they that are
factious etc.* The construction and translation in the regular text of the R. V. is simplest, and therefore best. The
one class do their preaching of Christ **of love,** out of that
Christian love which embraces also the apostle as their most
notable and highly honored brother. They did not let
selfish personal considerations blind their eyes: **knowing
that I am set for the defense of the gospel,** to defend
it by my preaching and teaching, and thus to help spread it
among men. They recognize his divine office and the efficiency of his defense of the Gospel over against the objec-
tions of Jews and Gentiles. — **But the other proclaim
Christ of faction.** Paul puts the two: "Christ" and "faction," so close together in order to bring out the incongruity.
To proclaim Christ ought to eliminate all faction, but these
men ·combine the two. They have had many followers in
one way or the other. Let every preacher see that his
heart is pure, cleansed by the love of Christ from all
wrong, narrow, selfish, personal, pettish motives. On "faction" see the previous text, Phil. 2, 3. — To proclaim Christ
of faction is to proclaim him and his precious Gosepl οὐχ
ἁγνῶς, **not sincerely,** not with a heart made chate and pure

by the power of what they proclaim. — So these envious
preachers in Rome lacked even pity for the apostle in his
bondage: **thinking to raise up affliction for me in my
bonds.** They tried to make his bonds press more heavily
upon him; θλίψις is pressure, hence **affliction.** Imagining
Paul to be actuated by motives and thoughts like their own,
they supposed that any special success on their part would
make him envious of them, and would make him chafe
under his bonds which prevented him from competing fully
with them, as otherwise he might. In a fine manner Paul
thus brings out the ingratitude of these men, who on the
one hand were made more bold and fearless in their preaching of Christ by the very bonds of the apostle, and yet
reward this aid in their work by making those bonds (as
they supposed and meant it) more galling. — But they little
understood the nobleness and grandness of the man whom
thus they meant to afflict. **What then? only that in
every way, whether by pretense or in truth, Christ is
proclaimed.** We may read τί γάρ as a question by itself:
What then? what of it? *i. e.* as far as I and my personal
feelings are concerned; or we may join the interrogative
to what follows: "What then except that *etc.*" The sense
is plain in either case: Paul is not concerned about his
own person at all, all he desires is: **that in every way . . .
Christ is proclaimed.** For him this overshadowed everything else, and utterly dwarfed any personal considerations.
— **Whether in pretense or in truth** once more brings out
the difference Paul is discussing and states that difference
in the tersest way. There is a false appearance, a certain
sham about these envious preachers, since beneath their
fine words about Christ and his spirit they hide their
miserable feeling of envy. The others, who obey the
promptings of love in their conduct toward the imprisoned
apostle, thereby preach Christ in truth; the words of their
preaching and the feelings of their hearts correspond.
What a lesson for us preachers all! How much envy, ill-
feeling, contention, strife, selfish desire, fleshly ambition

still enters the pulpits covertly every Sunday! How much
pretense spoils our fine words on love, fellowship, kindness toward each other, and the like! That means that
we preach the Gospel, and yet are not heart and soul concerned about the Gospel, but place our personal earthly
ambition and interest above it. Brethren, this ought not
so to be! — A wrong application is sometimes made of
what Paul here says when the brethren who preach Christ
of envy and strife are thought to b'e errorists whose doctrine still includes Christ, but is mingled with sectarian
follies. In regard to such we should not say, because Paul
does not say it, here or elsewhere: "Only that in every
way Christ is proclaimed!" None of the apostles rejoice
in the preaching of error. The thing they are willing to
bear, hoping that after all the Gospel itself and their own
love and integrity will overcome it, is the sinful personal
dislike of some of their brethren. In this sense Paul writes
of all the preaching of Christ in Rome: **and therein I
rejoice, yea, and will rejoice.** His grand and noble heart
rose to the height which every preacher should attain, above
personalities of all kinds, centering itself completely upon
Christ and the precious work of the Gospel. When Paul
adds the future tense: **I will rejoice,** he means to say: "No
matter what may come personally to me!" His joy is fixed,
and nothing shall dim it. Would that Christ and his
Gospel meant so much to us that the sound of it going
forth on every hand through our brethren might lift us in
satisfaction and joy above the little things that now so
often vex us and fill us with disagreeable thoughts!

Paul's desire that the name of Christ may be magni-fied.

This desire is the climax of Paul's thought as embraced
in our text; the words in which he summarizes his lofty
assurance and deep joy have found an echo in all true
Christian hearts throughout the ages, and even the poet has
clothed them in metrical form:

"For me to live is Jesus,
For me to die is gain;
To Christ I gladly yield me,
And pass where he has lain."

The last words of verse 18: ἀλλὰ καὶ χαρήσομαι, "but I shall also rejoice," are drawn by some to what follows, which in the Greek they indicate by the punctuation. The commentators who choose this reading must, of course, show another cause of rejoicing, and since the future tense here, following immediately upon the present (χαίρω . . χαρήσομαι), is decidedly emphatic, a cause for rejoicing greater even than the one first named, namely the apostle's joy in the preaching of Christ far and wide. The only cause for joy that could thus be named would have to lie in the words: ὅτι τοῦτό μοι ἀποβήσεται εἰς σωτηρίαν, "that this shall turn to my salvation," *i. e.* to my good. But the apostle never puts his personal benefit above Christ and the proclamation of his name. It would be altogether unlike him to say that he rejoices in the extensive proclamation of Christ, and then to add emphatically that he rejoices in knowing that things shall turn to his own salvation or good. The fact is that Paul so delights in the advance of Christian preaching all through Rome that he expresses his joy in two words, one dealing with the present, which lifts him above the despite he now suffers, and the other with the future, which shall lift him above any other despite he may yet have to suffer. After thus most emphatically stating his joy, he goes on to speak of what concerns himself and the Philippians in a personal way. — **For I know that this shall turn to my salvation, through your supplication and the supply of the Spirit of Jesus Christ, according to my earnest expectation and hope, that in nothing shall I be put to shame, but *that* with all boldness, as always, *so* now also Christ shall be magnified in my body, whether by life, or by death.** He writes that he rejoices and shall rejoice in the proclamation of Christ, and adds that this joy of his shall not be disturbed by anything that may happen to him personally in his trial, **for I**

know, he says, that whatever happens to me, my expectation and hope shall not be disappointed, since Christ shall be magnified in my body, no matter whether I remain alive or go to my death. — In saying this he appropriates the words of Job 13, 16: **This shall turn to my salvation,** much as we are wont to insert an apt and pertinent quotation or allusion in our utterances. Read the section from Job in its whole setting. This will show at once that τοῦτο can refer only to Paul's bondage and affliction. Paul is sure, just as Job was in his severe trials, that all **this** is in God's hands and must turn out μοι εἰς σωτηρίαν, "for me to salvation," *i. e.* **to my salvation.** In the quotation "salvation" does not mean eternal blessedness, — as some would interpret Paul's words, — but salvation in the general sense of the word, just as in Job's case, namely his welfare and good. The context, and especially also verse 25, shows that Paul meant this in the sense of acquittal at his trial. Yet, while he feels assured of his coming release, he still keeps in mind the other eventuality, possible banishment, or even death. He is entirely ready for this too, and if this should actually come, even it would not dim his joy. We have here a fine example of how a Christian should look into the future when in the midst of trials; even when he feels certain of approaching relief, he must not altogether dismiss the thought of further trial and even death. That is the fine thing about true faith and trust: it makes us ready in every way. — **Through your supplication** refers to the prayer of the Philippians. We can easily guess what the burden of that desire or petition was, namely that, if it be God's will, the apostle should be spared unto them and the church generally. The "salvation" which Paul expects is thus viewed as an answer to the prayer of his devoted Philippians. — **And the supply of the Spirit of Jesus Christ** signifies the supply or assistance which the Holy Spirit will certainly render to Paul. The addition to Spirit, **of Jesus Christ,** reminds us of the promise Jesus gave to his disciples (Matth. 10, 19-20; Luke 12, 12) that in their trials before human judges the Spirit would supply them with what they should answer in making their defense. Perhaps the Philippians had included in their supplication the request to Jesus to fulfil this promise abundantly in the apostle's case. — **According to my earnest expectation and hope** also modifies the clause: "this shall turn to my salvation." "Earnest expectation," ἀποκαραδοκία (ἀπό — κάρα — δοκεύω), means watching for something with head stretched forward; "hope," added to this, strengthens the thought of a favorable outcome. Paul's bonds shall turn out for his good according to what he has earnestly looked and hoped for, namely **that in nothing shall I be put to shame.** In not a single thing (οὐδενί) of importance in what shall happen to Paul, will he be made to feel ashamed. "'Hope putteth not to shame." Rom. 5, 5. Some think here of Paul's own conduct, *i. e.* that he shall not act in any single point so as afterwards to feel ashamed of what he has done. But this twists the apostle's thought. He has in mind the fulfillment of hope which God shall grant him; and he says here that he shall not be disappointed, and thus ashamed, of what God will do for him, no, not in a single point. God never makes us ashamed of having hoped and trusted in him, if only we would not come short so often in our hope and trust. — This negative statement is made clearer by a positive one, which also mentions fully what the apostle expects: **but** *that* **with all boldness, as always,** *so* **now also Christ shall be magnified in my body, whether by life, or by death.** "Boldness" cannot well mean in this connection the free, open, frank conduct of the apostle, but rather openness in general, publicity before the eyes of all. This sense harmonizes best with the passive μεγαλυνθήσεται, which implies that the agent is not Paul at all, he furnishing only the instrument, the σῶμα, but God. **As always,** *so* **now also** connects the past and present with what the apostle expects in the future. Openly, publicly in all his ministry, and in his past trials Christ has been magnified; and this shall be the case in the future. **Christ shall be magnified** means that the Savior shall be made glorious and great in the eyes of men by whatever God permits to occur in Paul's trial. He writes: **in my body,** instead of: "in me," because of the two things he has in mind: **whether by life, or by death,** whether by his acquittal, or by his martyrdom for the Gospel. In the former case all that Paul has endured for the Gospel's sake by the help of God's supporting grace will magnify Christ and the grace and help he has vouchsafed to his servant. The same would be true in the case of the apostle's death. In either instance all Christians would see the greatness of Christ and his power and grace, and would praise and extol his name; and also before others that greatness would shine, to attract and win them for their Savior. Here again we see how Paul's heart is centered wholly in Christ, and that not in a narrow and selfish way. Rejoicing in his grace and help for his own person at every step, he ever views that grace and help in its magnitude and extension to others also, yea, to all men. And so his joy reaches that pure and holy height, that nothing delights him more than to serve as a humble instrument, in whatever capacity it may please Christ, to bring out before the eyes of as many men as possible the greatness of his divine Savior. Where other men seek their own exaltation, Paul lays his body and life humbly at the Savior's feet, that he may use it to make known his divine and gracious exaltation to those who may be helped thereby.

In elucidation of what he has just said the apostle adds a pregnant statement, so expressive of all true Christian faith: **For to me to live is Christ, and to die gain.** **To me** is decidedly emphatic, standing at the head of the sentence — "to me" as over against others who are indifferent, unconcerned about Christ and his Gospel, and the magnifying of his name. For me **to live,** what I count life, real actual, true life, is something entirely different from what men generally count life. It is **Christ,** the divine Savior, who himself is life, John 14, 6, so that all who have him have life, John 1, 4. Luther makes "Christ" the subject: *Christus ist mein Leben,* but it is best to follow the simplest order of the words, and make the infinitive the subject; so also in the next part of the sentence. We must note that τὸ ζῆν (or ζῆν) is not, what preachers often make it without due study of the original, continuance of earthly life, as if Paul meant to say that if he should continue in life he would do so with Christ entirely ruling his life and filling it with himself and his grace; or, still less correctly, as if the apostle said, he would be entirely devoted to Christ, entirely given to his service. The apostle does speak of his continuance in this earthly life, but only in what follows: "to live in the flesh," verse 22, "to abide in the flesh," verse 24, and he also intimates what this would mean for the Philippians (and thus also for himself): it is "more needful for your sakes," namely that he might serve them. But here Paul is dealing with a deeper thought altogether. He is not thinking of the character of his earthly life, of anything he can use his earthly life for, or of any service or honor he can render on his part in his earthly sojourn to Christ; he is thinking of his spiritual life, of the very essence of what life and living is, of that life which is infinitely superior to mere earthly existence, of the gift of life which God has given him, of Christ in so far as he is the believer's true life. And in his argument he is giving the one great reason why Christ would be magnified in the poor body of the apostle, no matter whether that body lived or died. The all-sufficient reason for that is that he has a life which thousands of others know nothing about, namely Christ. He uses the infinitive τὸ ζῆν to match the following τὸ ἀποθανεῖν, and the present infinitive ζῆν denotes the continued flow and activity of spiritual life, while the second aorist ἀποθανεῖν indicates the single, momentary act of dying. — The usual ideas which men connect with life and death do not apply in the apostle's case, since for him "to live" is Christ, and, co-ordinate with that, for him **to die,** to lose his bodily life, if such should be God's will now soon, or at any future time, is **gain.** Men count death a tremendous loss, an irreparable calamity. Hence they shrink from dying and use all possible means to ward off death. What will not a man give for his life? since that is the only life he has. But as Paul's life is really a different thing from what men ordinarily call life, so also his death is different; it is **gain** for him, since it merely transfers him into a heavenly state of existence, into eternal glory and blessedness, where he will be completely and forever united with his glorified Savior Christ. — The apostle has thus opened up for us in a wonderful way the inner principle of the Christian life, which in his own case stood out so strongly and prominently. His whole being was bound up with the Gospel, the fullest proclamation of Christ, the magnifying of his name. In these rested his highest joy and satisfaction, lifting him far above the afflictions he here undergoes, whether in the bonds his Jewish and Gentile opponents have brought upon him, or in the ill-will which his own brethren turn against him. The principle and controlling power of our lives must be the same; and this will be the case when for us too, wholly and completely, Christ is our life now and evermore.

HOMILETICAL HINTS.

Many a prisoner may have been in Rome in the days when Paul was there chained to his soldier guard, but not another like this man Paul. Here there was one discouraged, despairing, there another sullen and silent. On the brow of this one and that one you might have seen the brand of Cain, stamped there by sin and crime, while his lips were framing falsehood to hide his guilt and deceive his judges. In the eyes of others there lurked the gleam of cunning, planning escape and a return to their former evil life. And in the bearing of still others there stood out the tragic elements of a broken life, the utter hopelessness of mending again what was shattered and lost so completely by the working of sin. But here was this solitary exception with joy filling his heart and shining in his countenance; a strange nobility and exaltation in his whole bearing; no recriminations, falsehood, excuses on his lips, but words of love and a message of salvation and peace in his words. His very guards were attracted to him and loved him while they attended to their stern duties. What was the secret of this remarkable prisoner? What made him so utterly

23

exceptional? Why was a man like this in bonds, and how could he bear them as he did? One word explains it all: Christ — "For me to live is Christ, to die gain."

The captive is a conqueror; he who is bound to a soldier of the Emperor's guard, binds this very guard perhaps, and others, to the yoke of Christ, the King of kings; he who bears the fetters of men and the shame that they imply, has found and enjoys the liberty which alone deserves the name, and on his brow rests the crown of a hope that glistens with immortal glory.

Envy and jealousy are noxious weeds; where they occupy the soil, green grass and flowers cannot thrive. — There is a selfish competition, even among preachers, which belies the Gospel of fraternal love which they proclaim. Likewise, there is a selfish desire for honor, attention, and distinction, even among the followers of Christ, which belies the Gospel of humility and generous love to others which they believe.— God's cause does not always progress when our own cause seems to advance. Nor does His cause depend upon our own strength and skill, as we so often suppose. We sometimes serve God best, when our own natural desires come to naught. God finds us useful in His work, after He has taught us that really all our excellence amounts to nothing. No man is indispensable in the work of God.

The main word in our entire text is Christ; and the words next in value are those immediately connected with Christ: his Gospel; proclaiming him; magnifying him. These must constitute the heart of the sermon. Tell something about Paul, but tell more about Christ and the things here mentioned as connected with him; and what you tell of Paul, formulate it so that it will reflect Christ through Paul.

It is not enough that Christ should be something to you, he must be everything. Riemer.

Watch the swinging pendulum. It is in constant motion, now to the right, now to the left. Yet the one fundamental, perpendicular line governs all its motion. This is the line to which it ever returns, and in this line will all its motion finally come to rest. Nor would it swing out to either side, and then return, if the dominating line of gravity did not hold and control it with the secret power. So let your Christian life be full of activity to right and left; but let one perfect, perpendicular line form the center of it all, one line, pointing — not down, as in the pendulum, but — straight up, in which at last you come to rest. That line is Christ, your Savior on the throne of glory. Riemer.

Men diverge in every direction, just as do their ideas of what life really is. Some pile up money, some devote themselves to one whom they love, some want adventure, some glory in power; and so the list goes on. Yet in none of these things has ever been found what would justify such men in saying: To die is gain. As much as they all diverge, in one essential respect they are all alike: when death sums up their possessions, it is not gain, but everlasting loss.

Many of us believe in Christ, at least to a degree; we love Christ, at least somewhat; we serve him, at least in some ways; we honor him, at least on occasion. But our Christian life never fully develops, never fully reaches the power, purity, elevation, and completeness which it should. Christ is not altogether our life. Our supreme joy is not yet the furtherance of the Gospel, the proclamation of his name, the magnifying of his grace among men. And yet these are and must be the supreme things for us all, if for us really to live is Christ. The example of one in whom these things stand out so gloriously ought to be held up to us all with power and effectiveness, so that the inner motive of our spiritual being may cast off all obstructions and put forth in our lives in rich abundance these necessary fruits.

How Does St. Paul Show that Christ is His Life?

He rejoices

I. *To see the doors open for the progress of the Gospel of Christ.*
II. *To know that his brethren more fearlessly proclaim salvation in Christ.*
III. *To find in himself opportunity to magnify the name of Christ.*

We step into a prison; we behold a man fettered to his guard. Ours is a natural feeling of gloom and sadness. — We go about and talk with the Christians in Rome; we find a divided sentiment, some dislike and envy St. Paul. Again we feel depressed and sad. — We talk with the guard who has St. Paul in charge; we learn that, however favorable the outlook is at present, there is still danger that St. Paul may be condemned. Again we feel discouraged and sad.

But let us talk to St. Paul himself. Here we have his words: not a trace of discouragement, sadness, or gloom; his heart overflows with joy, confidence, and hope.

And do not misfortune, ill-will of men, the shadow of death in some form or other come to you? Is there not many a cloud of discouragement, depressing sadness, dismal gloom trying to settle its chilling folds upon you? Would you not like to know the secret of the apostle's confident joy? He tells us what it is:

"For Me To Live Is Christ."

That means:

I. *To have Christ.*
II. *To work for Christ.*
III. *To suffer with Christ.*
IV. *To die in Christ.*

"Only let your conversation be as becometh the Gospel." — We must discover the real motive power behind such a conversation, or:

The Real Secret of the True Christian's Life.

I. *Christ has become his true life.*
II. *Christ's cause has become his chief love.*
III. *Christ glory has become his one aim.*

Christian conversation requires Christian character.

The Greatness of Character Which the Grace of Christ is Able to Produce.

I. *Joyous faith* — "I shall not be put to shame."
II. *Glowing devotion* — "The things which happened unto me have fallen out rather unto the progress of the Gospel."
III. *Tender friendship* — "Brethren;" "through your supplication."
IV. *Noble unselfishness* — "Only that in every way Christ is proclaimed."
V.. *Absolute fearlessness* — "to die is gain."

The Glorious Results that Must Follow if Christ be Our Life.

I. *Our lives must magnify Christ.*
   a) By doing his work with sincerity and love.
   b) By suffering in his cause with patience and trust.
   c) By dying in hope.
II. *Christ will bless and glorify our lives.*
   a) By lifting us above selfish and worldly things.
   b) By making us a help and support for others.
   c) By governing all things for our good.
   d) By translating us at last into eternal glory.

Adapted from Latrille.

QUINQUAGESIMA OR ESTOMIHI.

1 Cor. 1, 21-31.

"We preach Christ crucified . . . the power of God, and the wisdom of God . . . Christ Jesus, who was made unto us wisdom from God, and righteousness and sanctification, and redemption." That is the heart of our text, and there is no need to explain why, or to show how to appropriate this is to the Sunday which opens the portals for Lent. We cannot get a mightier or richer theme than: *Christ crucified, the power of God, and the wisdom of God;* or, some summary statement which combines the contents of verse 30. — The text itself evidently divides into two sections: verses 21-25 contain God's power and wisdom as exhibited by the foolishness of preaching; and verses 26-31, this power and wisdom as corroborated by the experience of the Corinthians.

Christ crucified, the power of God and the wisdom of God: exhibited as such by the foolishness of preaching.

In the entire section 1, 18 to 2, 16 Paul sets forth "the word of the cross," namely the Gospel which he preached. He does it in a manner so masterly, so crushing to the false wisdom of his day, so triumphantly convincing for the faith of all true believers of the Gospel, that his words have echoed and re-echoed through the church of all subsequent ages. With words full of power and wisdom the power and wisdom of God is here announced. Let the preacher read the entire section repeatedly and receive the full, glorious impression of the apostle's statements, and then when he feels the elevation and grandness of "the word of the cross," let him begin his sermon on the section which constitutes our text.

357

As far as substance is concerned our text might just as well as not begin with the opening verse (18) of the paragraph. Paul starts by announcing that "the word of the cross" is "foolishness" to certain people, but "the power of God" to others. He proves this by a quotation from the O. T., to which he adds a number of dramatic questions: "Where is the wise? where is the scribe? where is the disputer of this world? hath not God made foolish the wisdom of the world?" The answer is self-evident: "These proud men are nowhere; God has made their wisdom foolish." Here our text sets in with γάρ, **for,** furnishing the proof for the answer just implied. **For seeing that in the wisdom of God the world through its wisdom knew not God, it was God's good pleasure through the foolishness of the preaching to save them that believe.** In the N. T. ἐπειδή is usually not temporal, but causal: since, inasmuch, because, or, as here well rendered: **seeing that.** It introduces the reason why God selected the foolishness of preaching for the saving of believers: "in the wisdom of God (*in media luce,* Calvin) the world in its wisdom knew not God." **In the wisdom of God** is emphatic by position, and this is augmented by the repetition of the word "wisdom," by the strong contrast in "foolishness," and by the fact that "wisdom" (σοφία) was the classic term with which all the philosophers of the day charmed their disciples and attracted followers. — **The wisdom of God** was spread out before men in all the works of creation and providence, in the course of history, in the wonderful constitution of man himself, and for the Jews in the O. T. revelation in addition. The result should have been, as the apostle implies, that **the world** of men should have known God, τὸν θεόν, *the* God, *i. e.* the true God. But sad to say: "the world **through its wisdom** knew not God." Man's σοφία is really the correlative to the divine σοφία, his reason, that which elevates him above the brute, the organ for which the manifestations of the divine wisdom are intended, that it may receive and perceive them. But sin has so ruined the soul of man that even his reason fails to see what is so clearly put before it, or seeing it perverts it in false speculation or by other abuse. So the wisdom of God and what the world counts wisdom, *i. e.* the product of its reasoning, no longer agree. While the everlasting power and divinity of God are clearly seen, being perceived through the things that are made, so that man is without excuse, if he does not see them and know God, Rom. I, 20, the fact is that in the midst of all this light he is not enlightened. The revelation of God was faultless, it was divine wisdom, but men did not want to retain God in their knowledge, Rom. I, 28. Even the Jews, with all the special revelation granted them, kept falling into the idolatries of the Gentiles, and when they did not do this, they still failed to see the principal thing in that revelation, the grace of God in the promised Messiah. The reason for all this inexcusable result on the part of the world is **its wisdom,** which ever goes off in its own proud, self-sufficient, self-glorifying paths. It does this to this very day, after all these years of N. T. light and grace. The haughty astronomer gazes for years at the stars and then tells us with an air of finality, he has found no God. The natural scientist discards the Bible and follows his own speculation, and then announces that the ape is his ancestor, and that all life has evolved in countless ages from a tiny cell in the primordial slime. The Christian Scientist even takes the name of Christ to decorate his "wisdom" and haughtily repeats the old lie of pantheism: God is all, and all is God. And so the catalog lengthens with what the "world" in its "wisdom" has done with "the wisdom of God." Ever and ever it **knew not God** (ἔγνω, 2nd aorist), not even intellectually, as he revealed himself to all the world, to say nothing of spiritual and saving knowledge.

> "All our knowledge, sense, and sight
> Lie in deepest darkness shrouded,
> Till Thy Spirit breaks our night
> With the beams of light unclouded."
> Claussnitzer (Winkworth).

Because of the condition thus summarily described **it was God's good pleasure through the foolishness of the preaching to save them that believe.** Εὐδόκησεν ὁ θεός expresses the free determination of God. That which really impelled him was his infinite love for the world; but in fixing his gracious plans he took into account the condition of the world as Paul here describes it, and this is the force of the ἐπειδή at the head of the sentence. Διὰ τῆς μωρίας, **through the foolishness** of the preaching, is the emphatic parallel to διὰ τῆς σοφίας. But **foolishness** here, like its parallel σοφία, is used from the standpoint of the world; in the wisdom of God this "foolishness" is also the most glorious and profound wisdom (verse 23; 2, 6). The foolishness **of the preaching** (note the article: τοῦ κηρύγματος) is not the act of public proclamation (κηρύσσειν) or teaching, but the substance of the message announced, "Christ crucified." To announce as the Savior one who died the vile death of a criminal on the cross is the acme of foolishness, the climax of absurdity to the wisdom of the world. How can one who died **save**, rescue, man eternally from sin, death, and all their destructive power? How can one who himself suffered the greatest earthly shame possible, the death of the cross, lift man to eternal honor and glory? To the world it seems preposterous. The solution of the riddle lies in πιστεύοντας, **them that believe,** that rely in faith upon this Savior sent of God. There is a fine correlation in the first place between κηρύσσειν and ζητεῖν and αἰτεῖν, and in the second between κήρυγμα and πιστεύειν, preaching and believing. Both acts lie in an entirely different domain from the wisdom of "the wise," "the scribe," and "the disputer of this world," in the higher domain of spiritual contact, wrought by the Spirit through the Gospel as a means of grace. We must not imagine that God tried first one way, and when that failed another way, to accomplish his end. "The good pleasure of God" goes back to all eternity (2, 7; Eph. 1, 4). So also, while the foolishness of preaching was inaugurated for all nations in the N. T. dispensation, this foolishness is already a mark of the O. T., even down to the patriarchs of old (Is. 61, 1; Ps. 40, 9; 2 Pet. 2, 5). In reality the foolishness of preaching has been the means of salvation for all who have been saved; they all have believed the κήρυγμα, which in one of its many ways had reached them.

A second ἐπειδή introduces a parallel to the previous sentence, but one elaborated with fuller explanations: **Seeing that Jews ask for signs, and Greeks seek after wisdom: but we preach Christ crucified, unto Jews a stumblingblock, and unto Gentiles foolishness; but unto them that are called, both Jews and Greeks, Christ the power of God, and the wisdom of God.** We now see that Paul meant both **Jews** and **Greeks** (the chief representatives of the Gentiles), when he wrote κόσμος before. Both names lack the article: Jews as a class, Greeks likewise. Paul also shows what he had in mind when he said that the world "knew not God:" "Jews **ask for signs,** and Greeks seek after wisdom." Jesus wrought many signs during his ministry, and the last and greatest was his resurrection from the dead, "the sign of Jonah," Matth. 16, 4. He even pleaded with the Jews: "Believe the works," John 10, 38; "Believe me for the very works' sake," John 14, 11; but all in vain. Then already they sought other signs according to their fleshly wisdom; and so also after Christ's exaltation to heaven they kept on asking for astounding signs, such as would befit the Messiah they had in mind. The old Jewish clamor is still heard in many variations. Some want the church to heal all social evils and thus establish its divinity. Some demand the sign of an imposing outward ecclesiastical organization, and cannot imagine salvation without it. Some expect a millennium of signs, a visible earthly kingdom of triumph, and cannot imagine that the course of the Gospel can end with anything less. — And the Greeks **seek after wisdom;** they are speculative philosophers, searchers who hope to find. How vain their efforts are we see in the question of Pilate who had tested this wisdom: "What is truth?" They demanded principles, chains of reasonings, systems with new and striking conclusions; they laughed at Paul when he spoke of Christ's resurrection. All these centuries have passed, and the men of reason and philosophy are still seeking, seeking, seeking, with the goal as far off as ever. The poor instrument they work with will never attain it. Both Jews and Greeks, however they differ and antagonize each other, are really one in setting up their own wisdom and being guided by that alone.

In sharp contrast to both Paul writes: **but we preach Christ crucified.** In the two words: **Christ crucified** (*a Messiah crucified,* margin) he sums up the entire Gospel. This Christ the world passes by as foolishness. He is **unto Jews a stumblingblock,** σκάνδαλον (the later form for σκανδάληθρον, the stick in a trap to which the bait is affixed and by which the trap is sprung), metaphorically an offense, a scandal, an insult, "a stone of stumbling and a rock of offense," Rom. 9, 33; 1 Pet. 2, 8. The offense to the Jews is not merely the crucifixion, but in addition the Christian abrogation of the Mosaic laws, and the Gospel's refusal to furnish the signs demanded. The Jews still spit at Christ's name in execration. — **And unto Gentiles foolishness;** here ἔθνεσιν is synonymous with the Ἕλλησιν used before; the apostle means all others outside of Jews, chief of which were the Hellenes, the men who had enjoyed all the advantages of Greek culture. To them Christ crucified is μωρία, **foolishness.** They scoff at the cross and the idea that Christ's blood can remove sin and procure salvation. To this very day the modern successors of those ancient scoffers deride the atonement and delude many followers of Christ to discard this "blood theology," and to make of Christ a mere ethical Savior, an ideal man to inspire us, whose death was that of a martyr. — Over against the Jews and the Gentiles who comprise "the world" and reject Christ, the apostle now places again the third class already mentioned and describes it: **but unto them that are called, both Jews and Greeks, Christ the power of God, and the wisdom of God.** These also are **both Jews and Greeks** as far as nationality is con-

cerned, yet they differ radically from all their national
brethren in that they are the κλητοί, those **that are called.**
The ending τος, in κλητός, gives the word a passive meaning,
and thus points to one who has called these Jews and Greeks,
namely God. In the Epistles κλητοί is the regular designation for those who have been called effectually, that is for
those in whom the divine Gospel call has wrought living
faith. The κλητοί are thus identical with the πιστεύοντες in
verse 21, and with the σωζόμενοι of verse 18. The apostle
uses these and similar terms, also ἐκλεκτοί, interchangeably
for true Christians. Lange points out that σωζόμενοι has
reference to the divine blessings which Christians enjoy,
namely salvation; πιστεύοντες, to their subjective character;
and κλητοί to the divine agency which wrought in them. But
this agency is implied also in the passive form of σωζόμενοι,
for God alone saves; and πιστεύοντες hints at the means of
salvation, the Word which is believed; and κλητοί likewise
refers to the call of the Gospel which proved efficacious in
those who heard it. When Hodge says: "There is a twofold
call of the Gospel; the one external by the Word; and
the other internal by the Spirit," he is offering us Calvin's
doctrine. The Word and the Spirit are always united;
where the one is there is also the other; the Spirit never
works apart from the Word in calling. When Christ says
in Matth. 22, 14, that many are called (εἰσιν κλητοί), he
has in mind the *invitati,* all who in any way hear the call,
whether they accept it or not; but the use of the word for
only those effectively called is very marked in the Epistles,
and has the force of a fixed term. — To all of these
Christ crucified is **the power of God, and the wisdom of
God,** *i. e.* to them subjectively; they have found him to be
this by their own experience. When Paul writes that Christ
is the **power of God, and the wisdom of God** to "both
Jews and Greeks," he means to say that both alike have
found in Christ, in the fullest and truest sense of the word,
what on the one hand only the unbelieving Jews had demanded, and on the other the unbelieving Greeks. In the
person and work of Christ there is the highest manifesta-

tion of both the power and wisdom of God, and this the called have not merely seen in an outward way, but have discovered in their own experience, namely when the saving effects emanating from Christ were realized in their souls. By a most wonderful divine power, and according to a most wonderful divine plan of salvation they have been delivered from sin and death. Just as "the power of God" is something objective and outside of the called, coming to them from above and working in them, so also is "the wisdom of God." Yet this power is not omnipotence, as Stoeckhardt makes it in explaining Ephesians 1, 19 and other passages, but the saving power of God's grace. Bengel, however, adds that *experientia potentiae prior est, sapientiae sequitur.* And we must say that while this double experience in a way matches the demands and the seeking of the unbelieving Jews and Greeks of all ages, it does this in its own way, and not as arrogant unbelief prescribes, but as God in his love and wisdom designs. For the most stupendous sign in the heavens could not save a single Jew who may clamor for it, and the most marvelous development of philosophy could not save the most intellectual Greek who keenly seeks such a result; yet the power and wisdom of God in Christ does this very thing and by doing it abolishes once for all the wrong requirements in which blind unbelief persists. — Paul adds a striking proof for his statement concerning "the called:" **Because the foolishness of God is wiser than men; and the weakness of God is stronger than men.** He uses the neuters τὸ μωρόν and τὸ ἀσθενές, instead of simple abstract terms, because he means "the foolish thing" and "the weak thing" which God employs for our salvation; according to the context this is the crucifixion of Christ: "For he was crucified through weakness, yet he liveth through the power of God;" and the apostle adds: "For we also are weak in him, but we shall live with him through the power of God toward you." 2 Cor. 13, 4. Foolish and weak this divine means for saving us seems, of course, only in the estimation of unbelieving men, whose ideas of

strength and wisdom are different from God's, and who
pride themselves on their own great measure of both.
But God's means for our deliverance is infinitely **wiser**
and infinitely **stronger than men,** *i. e.* than men themselves in all their capacities, whatever they may boast of,
even outside of wisdom and strength. "I thank thee, O
Father, Lord of heaven and earth, that thou didst hide
these things from the wise and understanding, and didst reveal them unto babes; yea, Father, for so it was well-
pleasing in thy sight." Matth. 11, 25-26.

**Christ crucified, the power of God and the wisdom
of God: corroborated by the experience of the Corinthians.**

After discussing "the foolishness of preaching" to
show what God thinks of the wisdom of the world, the
apostle points to the Corinthians themselves as further
evidence in the same line: **For behold your calling,
brethren, how that not many wise after the flesh, not
many mighty, not many noble,** *are called.* When Paul
addresses the Corinthians as **brethren,** he makes himself
one of them. We may read βλέπετε either as an imperative:
behold, which seems to harmonize best with the forceful
form of Paul's words here, or as an indicative: *ye see*
(A. V), or: *ye behold* (margin); the substance of the
thought remains unchanged. By the **calling** is meant the
divine call of the Word and Spirit; κλῆσις is not used for
mode of life, profession, or station. The pronoun **your**
refers to the membership of the church at Corinth, but that
of all future ages is in harmony with the Corinthian type.
— **The wise after the flesh** are men of secular and
human learning, as distinguished from the spiritual wisdom
of the Gospel. 2 Cor. 1, 12; James 3, 15; John 3, 6. The
mighty are men of power in the world, such as Caiaphas
Pilate, Felix, Nero, and others. The **noble** are the well-
born, εὐγενεῖς, of distinguished lineage, of "blue blood"
perhaps. **Not many** of these were found among the Corinthian Christians, not many — but, let us not forget, some:

for instance Crispus, Acts 18, 18; I Cor. I, 14. In Rome
there was Erastus, Rom. 16, 23; and here and there some in
the other churches founded by Paul. So there have always
been some, and often men of great note, yet the vast
majority of the classes named by the apostle have rejected
the Gospel. Paul omits the verb in the sentence, and
we may supply either: *there are* not many; or, not many
are called; or, *have part therein* (margin), namely in the
calling. The fact which Paul here adduces is not accidental,
but a result of God's plans in offering salvation through
the crucified Christ. God is bound to reject what men
count great, wise, and high, because this has always shown
itself as unable to "know God," verse 21. It always tends
to make men self-sufficient, arrogant, haughty, even before
the Gospel comes near them, when they have only the
light of nature or some preparatory revelation of God.
Therefore the wisdom of God in his good pleasure discards
the foolish greatness of men and makes its saving appeal
from a different side entirely. — **But God chose the
foolish things of the world, that he might put to shame
them that are wise; and God chose the weak things of
the world, that he might put to shame the things that
are strong; and the base things of the world, and the
things that are despised, did God choose,** *yea* **and the
things that are not, that he might bring to nought the
things that are: that no flesh should glory before God.**
In contrast to what God did not and could not choose the
apostle places what God did choose. At some length he
describes the great principle which it pleased God to follow
in the work of salvation, of which the Corinthians had a
living exhibition in themselves. The description is in the
form of a climax, the apostle piles up one term after another to show how God chose the opposite of what men
esteem in their blind unregenerate state, ending with
τὰ μὴ ὄντα, the things that men do not even take notice of.
The neuters are used throughout: τὰ μωρά, τὰ ἀσθενῆ, τὰ
ἀγενῆ, τὰ ἐξουθενημένα, τὰ ὄντα, although the reference throughout is to persons, because Paul desires to make his

statements as general as possible (Winer, 27, 5); these neuters indicate the categories or classes to which those chosen of God belong. — **The foolish things of the world** constitute the general class whose mark is foolishness, lack of worldly wisdom, men without worldly culture and education. The genitive "of the world" merely implies that they belonged to the world and were part of it, when God chose them, beholding them in eternity in his omniscience, and hence that they were morally and spiritually no better than the rest. **The weak things of the world** are the general class which lacks power, authority, and influence in the world, ordinary men in the ordinary walks of life. **The base things of the world and the despised** are even a step lower: that class which is the opposite of "the noble" mentioned above, without any prerogative of birth, socially or otherwise, and therefore ἐξουθενημένα, "counted nothing" and left out of the reckoning entirely. To the last two designations the apostle adds by way of apposition the still stronger term: **the things that are not,** τὰ μὴ ὄντα, the class that is considered (note the subjective negative μή) as not even having existence. God chose not only common people, but even such as were held in contempt, yea, and those below contempt, too insignificant to be noticed at all, completely ignored as if they did not even exist. — These **God chose,** ἐξελέξατο, selected and elected for himself by one definite act; and this statement is emphatically repeated three times in detailed opposition to the "wise," the "mighty," and the "noble" mentioned before. An eternal act, prior to the κλῆσις or calling in time, is meant, one, in fact, on which the κλῆσις rests and from which it grows. This choosing of God is a free act of his infinite mercy; that God chose at all, and chose as he did, is due solely to himself. Yet his elective act is not arbitrary or blind, for he chose according to certain fixed and definite principles which are here revealed to us. God elected the foolish, and weak, and despised things of the world. Yet not because in men of this class there was anything meritorious or deserving above others. How can foolishness be a merit, or lack of culture and education, or baseness of birth and social position? The election of God is in every way an act of divine grace, and the condition of those whom he elected proves it. — But we are told the purpose God had in mind in making the choice he did: he chose the foolish, **that he might put to shame them that are wise;** and the weak, **that he might put to shame the things that are strong;** and the things that are not, **that he might bring to nought the things that are.** These neuters likewise refer to men and designate the categories or classes to which they belong. A man is **put to shame** when the very things he prides himself on and boasts of are rejected as good for nothing. And this was the very intention and purpose of God in choosing the persons he did for his kingdom. The wisdom, power, and glory of the world and its children is good for nothing in his kingdom; he cannot take it into his kingdom because it is fleshly, worldly, sinful, and they who will not let go the idea of their own superiority, value, and merit by this very thing block the gracious intention of God concerning them and the work of grace by which alone he makes men fit for his kingdom. Therefore, instead of choosing such, he puts them to shame and brings them to nought by discarding them; he cannot do otherwise. The verb καταργεῖν is stronger than καταισχύνειν, it means to make useless, vain, of no effect, as regards his spiritual kingdom. And this he does with τὰ ὄντα, **the things that are,** the class that makes its presence felt and is therefore reckoned with by the world and esteemed accordingly. There is, however, something gracious in this act of God, for if any of the wise, strong, and noble of the world allow themselves to be brought to shame and to nought by the wisdom of God as he manifests it in his Word and church — and there are always some who do — these will also have been chosen of God in his omniscience, and will have his blessed purpose and grace to thank eternally for their deliverance from the world. — The divine purpose is summarized once more in conclusion: **that no flesh**

should glory before God. By **no flesh** is meant no man. The Greek: ὅπως μὴ καυχήσηται πᾶσα σάρξ, really: that all flesh should not glory *etc.* For this meaning of flesh compare 1 Pet. 1, 24; Acts 2, 17. Not a single man is to rise **before God,** in his presence, and boast of himself or any attainment or excellence of his own. There is not one who has a single thing he could thus boast of with any real reason, for all have come completely short of the glory of God, and if they are saved at all are saved by the unmerited grace of God.

The counterpart to all that is thus said concerning the wise, powerful, and noble now follows in a grand concrete statement concerning the Corinthians themselves as true believers; and they stand as examples for us all: **But of him are ye in Christ Jesus, who was made unto us wisdom from God, and righteousness and sanctification, and redemption: that, according as it is written, He that glorieth, let him glory in the Lord.** There is a kind of contrast between τὰ ὄντα, the things that are in the estimation of the world, and what Paul writes of the Corinthians: ὑμεῖς ἐστέ, **ye are,** namely in Christ Jesus. What they are, however, is wholly due to God: ἐξ αὐτοῦ, **of him** are ye *etc.*; and this completely, for of themselves they are altogether nothing, and if they ever thought themselves anything, this has been put to shame and brought to nothing in their case. All that we as Christians are and have is ἐξ αὐτοῦ, or as we read Eph. 2, 8: οὐχ ἐξ ὑμῶν, θεοῦ τὸ δῶρον; not one particle is of ourselves, but all is of God's pure grace and giving. — Some commentators would combine: ἐξ αὐτοῦ δὲ ὑμεῖς ἐστέ, and have this modified by ἐν Χριστῷ Ἰησοῦ; but the simplest and most natural reading is: "Ye are in Christ Jesus," and this is "of him," due wholly to God. **Ye,** whom God has chosen, who are now the opposite of the world, ye **are in Christ Jesus,** in spiritual union and communion with him, through faith. And this is God's work, "of him." — Now follows a description of what Christians have in Christ Jesus, which contrasts tremen-

24

dously, first with the poor things of which the world in its pride boasts, and secondly with the original emptiness and poverty of those whom God has chosen: **who was made unto us wisdom from God, and righteousness and sanctification, and redemption.** Ἐγενήθη is the later form used for ἐγένετο, **was made,** really "became." Paul suddenly puts in the first person plural: became **unto us,** where a moment before he used the second person; he thus markedly includes himself, and some think he includes besides all true Christians. — Once more the divine authorship of our salvation and of all its foundation and treasures is here emphatically ascribed to God: "who was made unto us **from God** wisdom" *etc.* That we have these infinitely precious gifts in Christ has come "from God" and from his grace alone. — In harmony with all that precedes Paul puts forward **wisdom,** but he at once defines this by adding two other gifts: *both righteousness and sanctification* (so combined in the marginal reading in a close translation of δικαιοσύνη τε καὶ ἁγιασμός), *and redemption.* The entire thought deals with what Christ actually is for believers (ὑμεῖς, ἡμῖν), not only with what Christ is objectively for all men, although this lies back of our subjective possession. The Corinthians and Paul, and so we all, have in Christ "wisdom," that highest, most blessed, and glorious wisdom which makes us wise unto salvation. Christ is the soul and center, the sum and substance of the Gospel, and this Gospel is ours by faith, the heavenly wisdom of God's efficacious thoughts and plans concerning us, enlightening our hearts in living possession. — To have this "wisdom" is to have, either in and with it (if we read "righteousness, *etc.*" as an apposition to "wisdom"), or in addition to it (if we read three co-ordinate members: first, wisdom; secondly, righteousness and sanctification; thirdly, redemption): **righteousness and sanctification.** Christ is our righteousness; by his merits, embraced by faith, we are justified before God. And in addition to this we are sanctified and rendered holy in the eyes of God, are made "a holy temple in the Lord," Eph. 2, 21; Eph. 5, 25-27. Christ himself dwells in us, together with the Father and the Son, and so we are sanctified. We indeed still sin daily, but our sins are daily and richly forgiven, and so we do not lose Christ and his indwelling sanctifying grace. — In addition Christ has become unto us **redemption,** which some understand in the general sense of objective redemption wrought by Christ in his death on the cross; but which should here be understood, as following righteousness and sanctification, of the subjective possession of the final deliverance from all evil which is ours in Christ. It can indeed be said of Christ that he has already become our deliverance in this sense, though we have not yet been translated into glory, because, like all future blessings, this one also is ours now already through the sure and certain promises of God. Righteousness thus corresponds to faith, sanctification to love, and redemption to hope; the first points to the past when first we were justified and pardoned, the second to the present in which our sanctification is to appear more and more, and the third to the future, when we shall see the glory of our eternal deliverance. — The apostle closes this statement with a purpose clause parallel to the former one, at the end of verse 28. There we have the negative: "that no flesh should glory before God;" here we have the positive which exactly corresponds: **that, according as it is written, He that glorieth, let him glory in the Lord.** The construction is broken, as is often the case when the apostle introduces a quotation and retains the construction of the original. In the regular way he would have written: "that he that glorieth should glory in the Lord." The apostle summarizes the Septuagint translation of Jeremiah 9, 23-24: "Thus saith the Lord, Let not the wise man glory in his wisdom, neither let the mighty man glory in his might, let not the rich man glory in his riches: but let him that glorieth glory in this, that he understandeth and knoweth me, that I am the Lord which exercise loving kindness, judgment, and righteousness, in the earth: for in these things I delight, saith the Lord." So Paul shows himself a close student of Jeremiah, as Schnedermann puts it; in

fact, the apostle's entire elaboration is a N. T. exposition
of this O. T. word.   Receiving everything from God
through Christ we can indeed **glory,** and God bids us do so.
We have whereof to glory and lift up our heads in holy and
thankful pride; but only **in the Lord,** in God, the fountain
of all our blessings.   An example is given us in the
Smalcald Articles, section thirteen, where both our righteousness and our sanctification is referred to Christ: "By
faith we acquire a new and clean heart, and God accounts
and will account us righteous and holy for the sake of
Christ, our Mediator.   And although sin in the flesh has
not been altogether removed and become dead, yet he will
not punish or regard this.   For good works follow this
faith, renewal, and forgiveness of sins.   And that in them
which is still sinful and imperfect is not accounted as sin
and defect, even for Christ's sake; but the entire man,
both as to his person and his works, is and is called just
and holy, from pure grace and mercy, shed upon us and
displayed by Christ.   Wherefore we cannot boast of our
merit and works, if they be viewed apart from grace and
mercy, but as it is written: He that glorieth, let him glory
in the Lord, *viz.* that he has a gracious God."   335, 1-3.

HOMILETICAL HINTS.

    "Behold, we go up to Jerusalem!" is the message with which
this Sunday ushers in the coming season of Lent.   More than at
other times the passion of Christ is to occupy our thoughts and
devotions.   How many will go with us on the sacred journey?   Who
will care to bow the head in sacred sorrow at Gethsemane and
on Golgotha?   Who will want the holy influences of the cross
once more to fill his heart and life with all their power?   Thousands stand aside, and turn a hostile ear to the Gospel of the
crucified Christ.   Some scoff at it as so much folly and delusion,
and some hate it with a bitter hatred, as if the Christ of God
had done them an enormous wrong with his sacrifice and love.
And now, as we once more set out for our journey toward Jerusalem, we pause to ask, why this should be so.   Many intelligent
and sensible people seem to be altogether unattracted by the

preaching of Christ crucified; people in many respects honorable and estimable turn a deaf ear when you approach them on the subject of attendance at church, prayer, the Word of God, and faith in the crucified Redeemer. Why is. this? We cannot lightly pass the question by when now once more we mean to lay our hearts at the foot of the cross. And the answer is at hand in the words of our present text. Here God himself tells us: *He can use only people who have grown utterly small in their own sight.* M. Riemer's introduction.

"Wisdom" was the word with which the proud Greeks of ancient times conjured, "wisdom" in the sense of philosophy and learned speculation. Anything new, startling, promising in this line was bound to attract and hold them — at least for a time. "Science" is the magic word to-day. Anything unscientific is bound to be passed by as undeserving of serious attention. Even religion is asked to wear this strange modern coat, and there are thousands who accept for their souls only what has passed through the crucible of modern scientific tests, however meager may be the results of actual spiritual and divine truth. Shall we also pay homage to this twentieth century idol? Shall we also kneel at the altar of these latter-day Greeks and sacrifice thereon our most precious soul-treasures?

Humanity has never saved a single soul; divinity alone can do that. The beauties of art, the discoveries of science, the charms of music, the attractions of the drama, the speculations of philosophy — none of these has ever brought true peace to a single sinner's soul. Not in all the ages that have passed. Only one thing can do that: the foolishness of the preaching of the cross of Christ.

All the wisdom of God is poured out in the preaching of his Gospel. And there is only one possible way of receiving and appropriating it unto salvation: by faith. In both respects God's proceeding directly contradicts the haughty ways of men, who like the Jews demand the marvels of material satisfaction, or like the Greeks the wisdom of intellectual satisfaction. Yet ever the one need of the sinner is the Savior, and to accept God's Savior is faith.

A prominent lady once accosted Superintendent Bengel: "I hear that you are a prophet; will you not tell me whether there are reserved seats in heaven for people of quality?" Bengel replied: "I certainly am not a prophet, but I cannot deny that God has given me some insight into his revealed Word. And so I can say to you that there are indeed special seats for the people you speak of, but these, as you will discover from Matth. 19, 24 and 1 Cor. 1, 26, are covered with dust."

Among the foolish, the weak, the base and despised who stand out as great in the kingdom of God, the very pages of Holy Writ telling the church of all ages of them and even recording many of their names, are the shepherds at Bethlehem, old Simeon and Anna, the Galilean fishermen, Matthew the publican, Onesimus the slave, Aquila and Priscilla, and others like these. The names and deeds of countless emperors, generals, and great men of all kinds have been utterly forgotten or live only in the dusty pages of ancient history; but these who were made noble by the blood of the cross will shine to all eternity.

On two things the world is blind: sin and grace. And yet the world is full of sin, and the Gospel of grace is proclaimed from the housetops to all the nations. Edison has discovered many of the mysteries of electricity, but he has not found out that the inwardness of sin is death, and that eternal damnation can be warded off only by the grace of God in Christ Jesus.

There are fashions in dress and in manners; there are also fashions in thought. Fashion is the imitation of others, and fashion acts as an authority. The idea of evolution has long been fashionable; the idea that the church must really be an institution for humanitarian purposes and the betterment of material social conditions is becoming more and more popular. Doctrine and dogma are not fashionable, nor the cleansing power of Christ's blood, nor the justifying grace of God in Christ Jesus, nor the inspiration of God's Word. Let not the fashion of human notions catch you in its whirlpool grasp.

Christ became nothing at all through men, but men can become everything through Christ. The hosannas of the multitude never made Christ a king, he was King by the power of God. He is our wisdom, our righteousness and sanctification, and our redemption; but no wisdom or power of man added one particle to this greatness of his. And to have him and his blessedness as our own we must throw aside all that we have hitherto esteemed in ourselves.

Ours is an erring race, despite all the wisdom it boasts of. Nothing can put us right save the wisdom of God in Christ. Ours is a guilty race, despite all the excuses we frame for ourselves, and all our schemes for betterment. Only the righteousness of God in Christ Jesus can cleanse our souls. Ours is an ever falling race, a prey of all the devil's temptations, despite every effort at reformation and moral and ethical culture. Only the sanctification of God in Christ Jesus can make us triumphant in the battle against sin and keep us in the way of peace and purity. Ours is a weeping and dying race, plunging from one misery into another until the brink of a lightless eternity is reached; and this in spite of all the phantom joys we chase and all the false comforts we apply to make ourselves forget. Only the redemption of God in Christ Jesus can wipe away our tears, give us songs for sighing, and deliver us from every evil.

Nowhere is our helplessness made more apparent than before the judgment-seat of God. Nowhere is the power of the cross of Christ made more apparent than before that very judgment-seat, when we shall be accepted through the blood of the Lamb.

"We Preach Christ Crucified":

I. *The wisdom of God, to deliver from the folly of sin.*
II. *The righteousness of God, to deliver from the guilt of sin.*
III. *The sanctification of God, to deliver from the power of sin.*
IV. *The redemption of God, to deliver from the evils of sin.*

Christ, the Power of God, and the Wisdom of God.

I. *In the Gospel of salvation.*
II. *In the congregation of the saved.*

The Saving Sign of the Cross:

I. *The stamp of our faith.*
II. *The badge of our life.*
III. *The seal of our hope.*

Why Did God Choose the Foolishness of Preaching?

Because our salvation could be wrought only by:

I. *Divine wisdom.*
II. *Divine grace.*
III. *Divinely wrought faith.*

The Miracle of the Cross.

I. *Its weakness was might.*
II. *Its foolishness was wisdom.*
III. *Its shame was glory.*

"Let Him That Glorieth Glory in the Lord!"

  I. *In the cross of Christ I glory,*
     Towering o'er the wrecks of time.
  II. *In the gifts of Christ I glory,*
     Crowning me with grace divine.
 III. *In the friends of Christ I glory,*
     Gathering round his throne sublime.

Our Calling and Election in the Light of the Cross.

   Beneath the blessed cross of Christ
  I. *We unhesitatingly acknowledge all our emptiness and un-*
    worthiness.
 II. *We joyfully contemplate all God's grace and gifts.*
III. *We thankfully render to God all the glory and praise.*

·INVOCAVIT.

Heb. 4, 15-16.

The old gospel text for Invocavit describes the three-fold temptation of Christ in the wilderness, yet the old epistle text has no special connection with this great work of our Redeemer. In our present text we have a fine epistolary parallel to the old gospel text, which likewise matches the Eisenach gospel for this Sunday, Matth. 16, 21-26, Christ's temptation through Peter. Our text is especially fine also in fitting so well the place assigned to it in the lenten series. Beside the cross of Christ in the previous text is now placed the throne of grace in heaven; beside the Christ crucified, the High Priest tempted in all points like as we are; beside those who glory in the cross of Christ as their wisdom, righteousness and sanctification, and redemption, Christ's great saving gifts, those who amid weakness and temptation receive Christ's supporting gifts, mercy and grace to help in time of need. In whatever way we may formulate the general theme of our text, we will in one way or another include *our High Priest's throne of grace,* or, putting the subjective element forward more prominently, *our drawing near with boldness to the throne of grace.*

Our High Priest touched with the feeling of our infirmities.

We have already stated that the entire contents of the Epistle to the Hebrews may be summed up in the one word "better," and this applies markedly to the person and office of Christ with which our text deals. In chapters one and two Christ is shown to be better than the angels, in chapters three and four better than Moses,

377

and in chapter five *etc.* better than the Levitical priest-hood. From the transition between the last two of these sections our text is taken. The thought that Christ "hath suffered being tempted," and "is able to succor them that are tempted," has already been expressed at the end of the second chapter; in our text we meet it once more together with an earnest admonition to draw nigh to the throne of grace. **For we have not a high priest that cannot be touched with the feeling of our infirmities; but one that hath been in all points tempted like as** *we are, yet* **without sin.** This statement is used as one of the great reasons (γάρ) for heeding the admonition to "hold fast our confession" (verse 14). The danger to which the Hebrew Christians were exposed from the synagogue was that of allowing themselves to be deterred by persecutions from making an open confession of their faith, or of finally abandoning it altogether. Intimidation has silenced many and driven them at times to an open denial of the faith they once held in secret. Jewish converts of to-day generally have to fight this battle before they come to Baptism, and there are others placed similarly who shrink from openly and fearlessly avowing their convictions in the face of the bitter and at times unscrupulous opposition they must meet. Here all such, and any others who may tremble before the foes of our faith, are fortified and encouraged by being pointed to their High Priest and his victory over all temptation whether of this or another kind. "We have not a **high priest** that cannot be touched by our infirmities" implies, as just stated in the previous verse, that we indeed have "a great high priest." His very greatness, however, his superiority as the Son of God over the angels, Moses, and all other priests, might lead to the thought that he is so far above all our weaknesses, that we practically stand alone in the battle of facing fierce opposition to our confession. The very opposite is the case. Christ is our High Priest, and in his person and office necessarily of divine greatness, for otherwise he could not have made atonement for the sins of the world and made us acceptable to God. But just as he is divine and infinitely above all other servants of God and mediators, so he is also intensely human and exceedingly close to us. — He is not one "that cannot be touched **with the feeling of our infirmities."** Our ἀσθένειαι are our weaknesses, and these are many. Our bodies are weak and naturally shrink from suffering, and our hearts are weak through sin, very susceptible to the threats and allurements of the world, and not ready always to be bravely true to Christ under all conditions. We therefore need divine help. The writer to the Hebrew Christians does not rebuke them for these their weaknesses; he here takes these as a matter of course, and therefore points to the way in which they can be overcome. — And he does this in an exceedingly effective and tender way, which must at once awaken a response in our hearts: Our High Priest can **be touched** by our infirmities. The verb συμπαθῆσαι signifies that he can feel with us, put himself entirely in our position, realize our difficulties by his own experience, and thus sympathize with us and help us. — Although he is divine and now sits on the throne of glory, no gulf separates him from us, **but he is one that hath been tempted like as** *we are.* The reference is to all the temptations through which our High Priest passed working out our salvation on earth, first of all that notable temptation for forty days in the wilderness, and then every other temptation that followed until the sacrifice on the cross was accomplished. Christ was really **tempted,** and this **in all points like as** *we are.* His temptation was no sham, nor was it only a temptation in part, so that in certain points he escaped what we must undergo and thus cannot know from his own experience what we must endure. Κατὰ πάντα καθ᾽ ὁμοιότητα means: "according to all things according to likeness," *i. e.* of us, ἡμῶν, or with us, ἡμῖν, and καθ᾽ ὁμοιότητα is decidedly stronger than the mere adverb ὁμοίως. The reason for this full experience of temptation on the part of Christ is that he was true man; and here his full humanity is strongly emphasized for our consolation and encouragement. Christ knows all about our temptation and can and does feel with us, his poor followers, because by his own experience he thoroughly knows all about temptation. There is not a single temptation that we undergo but what in its essential trying features he has also undergone, and in a degree beyond what is possible for us, for all the unchecked power of the tempter was allowed to vent itself upon him. — But the likeness has one significant exception: **without sin,** χωρὶς ἁμαρτίας (without the article), sin in general. Delitzsch: This "limits the similarity of his temptation and ours in this sense, in order to bring out more clearly the unlimited similarity in all other respects." Not only was Christ without sin in all his temptations, but, being tempted as our High Priest and Mediator, his victory was the victory over our foes won for our deliverance, and thus still more serves to encourage and strengthen us. — In considering the temptation of Christ some have thought that, in order for Christ's temptation to be real and not a mere sham, there must have been a possibility of his falling and sinning. So they interpret χωρὶς ἁμαρτίας only of the actual result, that he did not fall. But "without sin" excludes from the entire temptation of Christ the very thing which makes our temptations so dangerous to us, the liability, propensity, and inclination to sin, which lies in all of us since the fall of Adam, and is not wholly eradicated in this life. Temptation could and did assail Christ only from without, and the evil solicitation never for an instant awakened an affirmative desire and response within him. And yet, though it came from without and found no weakness in Christ, the temptation was directed with all the cunning and power of Satan against the human side of our Savior. It especially showed him an easy way to the crown of Messiahship and the throne of the Kingdom instead of the terrible way of suffering and death under the burden of our sin and damnation. This made the temptation of Christ so severe, so real in its terribleness, beyond anything we could have endured, especially when the last penalty of our sin was about to be laid upon him on Calvary. This caused the bloody sweat in Gethsemane, and to this Hebrews 5. 7 refers in the "prayers and supplications with strong crying and tears." We may say that just as Christ's pain of body and mind was real, although he was true God, so also was his temptation real, although it was the Son of God who bore it. Yet as the Son of God, the .second person of the Godhead, the Savior made higher than the heavens, with the Holy Spirit poured out upon him without measure, he could not fall. With Hoenecke we may compare him to a mighty workman altogether sure of success in the work he has undertaken, yet winning that success only after the hardest kind of effort and labor in body and mind. When the objection is raised that surely the devil would not have wasted his efforts upon Christ if he had known of his impeccability, we point to the crucifixion of Christ and ask in return: If Satan had known that Christ's crucifixion would accomplish the redemption of the world, would he have brought that crucifixion about? It is not safe to argue from the devil's knowledge or ignorance.

Our drawing near with boldness to the throne of grace.

This properly follows the statement just made on the sympathetic character of our High Priest. It also goes together well with the admonition in verse 14: "Let us hold fast our confession." With our great High Priest in heaven we ought to lift our heads fearlessly in the face of opposition; and with a High Priest so closely united to our human needs, we ought to lose all hesitancy and draw near to him and his throne with all assurance of finding the help we need. **Let us therefore draw near with boldness unto the throne of grace, that we may receive mercy, and may find grace to help** *us* **in time of need.** The admonition προσερχώμεθα (subjunctive in exhortation): **Let us draw near,** refers especially to prayer, but includes more than an occasional approach to our High Priest when some particular need drives us. We are to draw near constantly in our constant infirmity and so live in communion with the fountain of all

our help and strength. Προσέρχεσθαι is a favorite term in
Hebrews; it has a liturgical meaning suggesting either the
approach of a priest to the altar (Heb. 10, 22), or, as here,
the approach of those who are levitically pure to the sanctuary of God (Lev. 22, 3). The suggestion is that we are
bidden to a high and holy function, a lofty, precious privilege to which none may lightly aspire. — This is conveyed
also by the addition: **with boldness**, *i. e.* with the assurance
that we will not be cast out or approach in vain. Our boldness, however, is to be based entirely upon the character of
our High Priest; our boldness is to be the answer to his
sympathy. — By **the throne of grace** is meant the heavenly
throne which God's grace in Christ Jesus possesses, the
throne where our High Priest sits exalted, ready to receive
and bless us. The word **throne** implies a King in royal
splendor, and finely associated with it is **grace** as the royal
kindness extended to those who in themselves are utterly
unworthy. We must therefore think of our High Priest
as both King and Priest in one and this brings
out also what lies in the entire description of the
superiority of Christ, our Mediator, in Hebrews. The
royalty of our Priest and the power and splendor
of his gracious throne indicate the all-sufficiency and
abundance of his help when we draw near unto him.
— But this is expressly stated in the purpose clause: **that
we may receive mercy, and may find grace to help *us* in
time of need.** The words are arranged so as to form a
beautiful chiasm: λάβωμεν ἔλεος καὶ χάριν εὕρωμεν, a cross
arrangement, with first the verb and its object, and secondly the object with its verb. While ἵνα, "in order that,"
expresses only the purpose of our drawing near, the verbs
receive and **find** plainly imply that none of us shall draw
near in vain. A promise lies hidden in the purpose thus
attached to the exhortation. — The difference between ἔλεος,
mercy, and χάρις, **grace,** is that the former usually refers
to man's misery and wretchedness, and that the latter refers
to his guilt and sin. "In the divine mind, and in the order
of our salvation as conceived therein, the ἔλεος precedes the

χάρις. God so *loved* the world with a pitying love (herein was the ἔλεος) that he *gave* his only-begotten Son (herein the χάρις) that the world through him might be saved: compare Eph. 2, 4; Luke 1, 78-79. But in the order of the manifestation of God's purposes of salvation the grace must go before the mercy, the χάρις must make way for the ἔλεος. It is true that the same persons are the subjects of both, being at once the guilty and the miserable; yet the righteousness of God, which it is just as necessary should be maintained as his love, demands that the guilt should be done away before the misery can be assuaged; only the forgiven can, or indeed may, be made happy; whom he has pardoned, he heals; men are justified before they are sanctified." Trench, *Synonyms of the New Testament*, I, 226. The two concepts together with their verbs are here combined into one rich thought; "mercy" is put first because temptation distresses us, and "grace" is added to it because none of us deserve the love and help we receive. We are to obtain the merciful grace, or the gracious mercy of God. — And this εἰς εὔκαιρον βοήθειαν, **to help us in time of need,** *i. e.* for timely, seasonable help, when the need is upon us in the hour of temptation and danger. Some turn the word "timely" to refer to the hour of grace, while help may still be had, before the day of grace comes to a close; but this is not in harmony with the thought of our text which hints at no limitation, but offers us the grace of our High Priest at all times. The noun βοήθειαν recalls the βοηθῆναι in 2, 18. Our Confessions use Heb. 4, 14 and 16 to enforce the doctrine "that sins are remitted for the sake of Christ, as Propitiator . . . this Propitiator thus profits us, when by faith we apprehend the mercy promised in him, and present it against the wrath and judgment of God." This the Apology does, 97, 82, by urging that "the apostle bids us to come to God, not with confidence in our own merits, but with confidence in Christ as a High Priest; therefore he requires faith." The 15th verse is likewise used, in the Formula of Concord, 547, 43 (where, however, the reference "Heb. 2, 14" is wrongly given), to show that "the Scriptures testify forcibly that God's Son assumed our human nature without sin, so that he was, in all things, sin excepted, made like us, his brethren, Heb. 2, 14. Hence all the old orthodox teachers have maintained that Christ, according to his assumed humanity, is of one essence with us his brethren; for he has assumed a human nature which in all respects (sin alone excepted) is like our human nature in its essence and all essential attributes, and they have condemned the contrary doctrine as manifest heresy." In our text we are to draw the blessed practical conclusion from this great doctrine of Scripture in confidently drawing near to the throne of our loving High Priest who knows what we need and abundantly grants us his help.

HOMILETICAL HINTS.

The Sunday whose ancient gospel lesson is the history of Christ's temptation in the wilderness bids us look up to him who in all things was tempted like as we are. Just as the passion of Christ was not restricted to the last few days of his life, so also his temptations occupied more than the days in the wilderness or the brief moments on the pinnacle of the temple and on the high mountain from whence he was shown the glory of the world. Luke tells us that after this notable temptation the devil left Christ, but only "for a season," to return again at a more convenient time. And there were many such seasons. Do you remember the earnest face of Peter and the soft human love in his voice when on one occasion he took the Master aside to say to him who had just announced his readiness to go into death for our redemption: "Be it far from thee, Lord; this shall never be unto thee"? and how the Lord had to repel the alluring voice of the tempter who used his own foremost apostle as the instrument of temptation: "Get thee behind me, Satan: thou art a stumblingblock unto me; for thou mindest not the things of God, but the things of men!" How must the heart of Christ have been oppressed when he turned to his little band of disciples with the words: "Did not I choose you the twelve, and one of you is a devil?" And in Gethsemane, when the cup of gall and fire was placed to his holy lips, we hear the stricken heart of our High Priest cry out to the Father in the distress of his trial: "If it be possible, let this cup pass from me!" And even on the cross, as his enemies stormed about him, there came again the same old devilish temptation: "He saved others; let him save himself, if this is the Christ of God, his chosen!" "If·thou art the King of the Jews save thyself!" And so in many ways the waves of temptation burst upon him, now the loving, innocent looking suggestion, now the glory of false hopes and assurances held out to him, now the blind misunderstanding of friends and relatives, now the loud, imperative clamor of his opponents, now the evil one himself with false Scripture and yet supernatural cunning — temptation upon temptation. But through them all Christ went with unfaltering step.

The temptation of Christ was entirely passive: just as his sufferings were temptations for him, so also on the other hand his temptations were only sufferings for him, things that came upon him from without, which he merely endured. Riehm.

Overlook not the addition: "yet without sin." This is what makes the sympathy of Christ so valuable. What will the sympathy of one in the same condemnation benefit us? He, of course, will be ready to pardon and justify the sin of another, because this is what he wants and needs for himself. Criminals always acquit each other, but that is all the good it does. Likewise the consolation of sentimental and so-called tolerant people is valueless. We can be justified only by one who also has the right to judge us. And this is the great and comforting thing in our sympathetic High Priest, that he whose holy life and death is the severest condemnation of our sin, that he who might have rightly despised and condemned us all, nevertheless bore all our sins even unto the criminal's death on the cross. When he who is pure pardons, that has value. When he who is holy stoops to seek the communion of sinners, that has redemptive and rescuing power. Riemer.

To be touched with the feeling of our infirmities is not by any means to consider our sins only as pardonable weaknesses, as is so common in the world. Many have tried to make of Christ such a sentimental apostle of pity, who understands everything about us, and understanding pardons. The Gospel has nothing to do with such false preaching of flabby love, except to condemn it.

Let us beware of the false comfort as though all that our High Priest does is merely to say yea and amen to the pardon which we pronounce upon ourselves! The first Gospel call to sinners on the day of Pentecost was: Repent!

To-day you are invited into the throne-room of Christ, your great High Priest. There are angels and archangels and the

25

eternal glory of God. But look not on these, look at the figure and heart of him who sits exalted thus, and at the multitude of poor sinners who kneel unafraid and happy with heavenly relief before its gracious light.

Our Blessed High Priest's Throne of Grace.

I. *See who sits upon it.*
   a) Not one who is merely all-holy, and from whose presence we poor sinners would flee in terror;
   b) But one who shares our nature and has endured all our temptation in order to save us;
   c) And remained sinless amid them all and victorious in the fight for us;
   d) Who now opens his sympathetic hand to us, extending his mercy, grace and help, and bidding us draw near.
   O blessed vision for every poor sinner's heart!

II. *See who kneels before it.*
   a) Men like us, weak, tempted, fallen, oft in mortal spiritual danger.
   b) Men with eyes open to their sin, temptation, and danger, and to the grace and mercy upon that throne (contrition; faith).
   c) Men who yearn for grace to help in time of need, meaning to employ it to overcome every temptation and win the victory in every battle.
   O blessed vision for every poor sinner's heart!

"O Great High Priest, Forget Not Me!"

I. *I trust thy sympathy.*
II. *I rely on thy grace.*
III. *I come at thy bidding.*

The Infinite Tenderness of Our Great High Priest.

I. *He was tempted as we are.*
II. *He is touched with our infirmities.*
III. *He calls us to draw near.*

Let Us Draw Near to the Throne of Grace!

It invites us
I. *With its highpriestly sacrifice to cleanse.*
II. *With its royal power to protect.*
III. *With its tender grace to strengthen and uplift.*

Christ Our Help in Every Temptation.

I. *He has vanquished the tempter.*
II. *He delivers the tempted.*

The Great Importance of the Lord's Temptation.

I. *As regards himself* — it has made him a perfect High Priest.
II. *As regards us* — it gives us boldness to draw near to the throne of grace.

C. C. Hein.

REMINISCERE.

1 John 2, 12-17.

The most satisfactory way of handling this text homiletically is to follow the natural line of thought which it presents. The apostle John has briefly traced the essentials of the Christian faith and life, and is now about to add a number of admonitions. Before he proceeds with these he reminds his readers of their position and condition as true Christians. As such he writes to them (verses 12-14), and admonishes them first of all not to love the world but the Father (15-17), and then adds other admonitions in what follows our text. The natural culmination of our text is therefore the injunction, that *they who have the forgiveness for Christ's sake love not the world*. The appropriateness of this theme for Lent is apparent without further argument. It is one of the vital admonitions for this holy season. We may note also that the reference to the forgiveness of sins connects our text in the finest manner with the two preceding ones which place before us Christ crucified and our sympathetic High Priest. In and through him we have this forgiveness, and now we certainly ought to show that our lives are changed, that we turn from the world (as this text bids us) and strive after holiness (as we shall find the next text urging us). The division of our text is thus also simple and obvious: there is first the basis for the apostle's admonition, and then the admonition itself.

The basis for the apostle's admonition.

Two great thoughts are twined together in John's First Epistle, one setting forth positively the blessed state of grace in which all true Christians are found, and

388

the other urging them to live up to this state by doing all that its nature demands and by avoiding all that is contrary to it. Both of these thoughts meet in our text. **I write unto you,** *my* **little children, because your sins are forgiven you for his name's sake.** The apostle refers to his entire present Epistle when he states: **I write unto you,** and by τεκνία, the diminutive of τέκνα, **little children,** he means not children in years, but the Christian congregation in its entire membership, the ἀγαπητοί in verse 7; that this must be the meaning is clearly shown by the frequent recurrence of this form of address, 1 John 2, 1; 2, 28; 3, 7 and 18; 4, 4; 5, 21. Jesus himself used it toward his disciples, John 13, 33; but it is so entirely natural, especially as coming from one of great age, that we need not say that the apostle copied it from the Master. Moreover, it fits exceedingly well the tender and loving nature which we know John possessed; he is frequently called the disciple of love. Coming from him then this affectionate word breathes out the tender love and concern of a spiritual father toward the children whom he has begotten in Christ Jesus and to whom he is most deeply attached. And, surely, true children will always hear and heed the loving words of a father. — The ὅτι which follows does not introduce *what* the apostle writes (so Luther translates it), but, as the following sentences and the entire connection show, *why* he writes, *i. e.* writes as he does; hence the correct translation is **because.** This, of course, includes the *fact* thus introduced, namely that the sins of the persons here addressed are forgiven, but John presents the fact here as a *reason*. **Because your sins are forgiven** points to the fundamental blessing of all true Christians, no matter who they may be. The verb ἀφέωνται is the Doric perfect passive from ἀφίημι (Winer 14, 3), "have been sent away," *i. e.* have been removed, and furnishes a fine image of what is really meant by the forgiveness of sins: these sins have been taken away and removed forever, and, of course, all their guilt and punishment has gone with them. The perfect tense indicates that the forgiveness occurred in the past, but continues on and on in the present, which the English **are forgiven you** brings out especially. Our Confessions define the entire Scripture doctrine on forgiveness in the most excellent way in the Formula of Concord: "A poor sinful man is justified before God, *i. e.* absolved and declared free and exempt from all his sins, and from the sentence of well-deserved condemnation, and adopted into sonship and heirship of eternal life, without any merit or worth of his own, also without all preceding, present, or subsequent works, out of pure grace, alone because of the sole merit, complete obedience, bitter suffering, death, and resurrection of our Lord Christ, whose obedience is reckoned to us for righteousness." *Book of Concord*, 571, 9. Again, in the Augsburg Confession: "Men are justified freely for Christ's sake through faith, when they believe that they are received into favor, and their sins are forgiven for Christ's sake, who by his death hath satisfied for our sins." 38, 2-3. — This forgiveness, John says, is **for his name's sake,** διὰ τὸ ὄνομα αὐτοῦ, "on account of his name." John does not need to say whose name; there is but one name under heaven given among men whereby we may be saved. The **name** of Jesus is here referred to because it expresses and reveals who and what he is; the correlative of the "name" is faith: we believe in his name. Meyer is right, therefore, when over against others he insists that John here mentions both the objective and subjective cause of forgiveness in one: Christ embraced by faith. Our Confessions do the same thing when they quote this passage to show *quod propter Christum, non propter nostra opera, fide consequamur remissionem peccatorum.* Mueller, *Symb. Buecher,* 135, 153. The quintessence of salvation is the forgiveness of sins. And the certainty of this forgiveness rests not on any guarantee offered by the church, which is a Romish idea; nor on our own feelings and emotions, which is *schwaermerish* and Methodistic; nor on our own moral efforts or achievements, which is rationalistic, pharisaic, and also Romish; but on the name of Christ, on the divine assurances which we have in the

Word and Sacraments, and this is Scriptural, evangelical, and Lutheran. The difference between the children of God and the children of the world is not that the former have no sins, while the latter have, but that the former have the forgiveness of sins, and the latter have it not. And God's children rejoice in the certainty of this forgiveness, not because they always feel at peace, or because they see a great spiritual uplift and progress in their lives, but because they have the divine assurance of forgiveness in the Word and rest secure and certain in that by faith.

All the τεκνία the apostle now divides into two classes: **I write unto you, fathers, because ye know him that is from the beginning. I write unto you, young men, because ye have overcome the evil one.** All the older members of the church are addressed as πατέρες, **fathers,** and all the younger as νεανίσκοι, **young men.** The effort to spiritualize these designations, making the "fathers" ripe Christians whether old or young, and the "young men" immature Christians whether young in years or old, is a refinement which goes beyond the plain, natural sense of the apostle; moreover, immature Christians are usually called νήπιοι, Matth. 11, 25; Luke 10, 20; Rom. 2, 20; 1 Cor. 3, 1; Heb. 5, 13. John here addresses his readers in a way often employed by pastors in speaking to their people, turning now to those who have had a longer experience of life, and then to those who are in the flower and strength of youth. Jesus himself makes a division as to age, John 21, 15 *etc.* But while age makes the difference, this goes together with many things in the spiritual life naturally pertaining to differences in age; the apostle properly says one thing to the older Christians, another thing to the younger. — I write to you, fathers, he says: **because ye know him which is from the beginning.** Because of this knowledge John writes to the fathers; in what he writes this knowledge is to be used as a premise or basis. The perfect ἐγνώκατε indicates knowledge that began in the past, when the Gospel first came to these older members, and still continues to the present. The kind of knowledge John has in mind we see by referring to verse 3; it is the knowledge of the heart, which has become a living, molding power within. — As the object of this knowledge John designates: **him which is from the beginning.** Compare the explanation on 1 John 1, 1 for the Fourth Sunday in Advent. Christ, the λόγος, is meant, our Savior as the eternal God. In John 1, 1 we read: "*In* the beginning was the Word;" there the apostle places himself at the initial point of time and looks back into eternity, when Christ already "was;" in 1 John 1, 1 he writes of him "who is *from* the beginning," placing himself at the same point of time, but looking forward to all that has occurred since. To the "fathers" John thus attributes a true knowledge of the divinity of Christ, and of all that this means in regard to their own salvation, the forgiveness they possess, their comfort and hope in the Gospel. These fathers, Augustine writes, were lovers of the Everlasting Father (Christ), Is. 9, 6. The idea that all the older Christians knew Jesus from having seen him while on earth, is far from the entire context and irrelevant to the thought. Steinhofer writes: "We know our lesson. It can be put into two words: Our *Jesus* in whom we believe is *the Son of God.* But so many, deep, necessary, unfathomable, blessed things of the divine mystery of our salvation are embraced in it, that we never come to stop, never tire and grow satiated, nor dare to turn to anything else. Our one need is ever to penetrate more deeply into this truth, and pass from one glory to another, in order that our spiritual growth may advance, and we may be prepared for all the fulness of God." — To the young men John writes: **because ye have overcome the evil one.** The devil is meant by ὁ πονηρός, Matth. 13, 19 and 38; John 17, 15; Eph. 6, 16; 1 John 3, 12; 5, 18-19, as the foe who by suggestions from within and allurements from without keeps men bound fast in his power and tries to bring them under it again when once they have escaped. Every young Christian has his fight to wage against this foe, and blessed are they who have conquered and stand secure in their victory. "Youth must ever be in conflicts, theoretical and practical," writes Ebrard. "The glory of young men is their strength," Prov. 20, 29, and all our young people are to use this strength spiritually when the devil sings the siren song: "Come now, let us live merrily while we may, and make use of our body while it is young. Let us not miss the flowers of May; let us wear wreaths of young roses ere they wither." Wisdom of Solomon, 2, 6 *etc.* But this too, as Besser says, is "the devil's envy." We need not describe here the allurements of the evil one which he spreads all about the feet of youth at the present time; our cities reek with the fetid pleasures of the flesh; the garish light of a corrupt and corrupting stage, the hot breath of the dance, the sparkle of the alluring cup, the laughing banter of all sorts of questionable companionships, have proved the undoing of thousands. But there are those who **have overcome,** not without a battle, and some not without deep scars, and yet the victory is theirs through him who for us has destroyed the works of the devil. And because of this victory John writes; to the victors he brings a special message.

Instead of going on now, as one might expect, and introducing the admonitions he has for his readers old and young, John repeats: **I have written unto you, little children, because ye know the Father. I have written unto you, fathers, because ye know him which is from the beginning. I have written unto you, young men, because ye are strong, and the word of God abideth in you, and ye have overcome the evil one.** Where before we had the present tense γράφω three times with the emphasis of this reiteration, we now have in addition to that the aorist ἔγραψα, **I have written unto you,** or *I wrote* (margin), three times in the same way. Commentators have been puzzled a good deal by this repetition and the marked change in the tense. Of the various explanations offered the best are the following two: that John here refers to the Gospel he had written prior to the Epistle (Hofmann, Ebrard, *etc.*); or that γράφω means what John was writing at the moment, and ἔγραψα what he had written in the first paragraphs of this Epistle (Meyer, *etc.*). The former explanation is the more satisfactory when we notice that in substance the three ἔγραψα sentences are identical with the preceding γράφω sentences. John then tells us first why he is writing this Epistle, and then he adds in the same striking and emphatic way why he wrote his Gospel, namely for the same ethical reasons in his hearers. — Another question confronts us in παιδία, **little children** (not again τεκνία as before). Does John mention three classes: fathers, young men, and children, or only two: fathers and young men, and all of them combined in the affectionate τεκνία which is only varied in παιδία? The latter is plainly the case. There can be no doubt that τεκνία in verse 12 signifies all the readers of the Epistle; the word is repeatedly used by the apostle in this letter. That leaves only two classes, the πατέρες and νεανίσκοι, in the three sentences beginning with the present tense γράφω. The next three sentences introduced by ἔγραψα are so strongly parallel that it would be strange indeed to find three classes instead of two addressed in these sentences. It is in vain to appeal to verse 18 for the third reference to "little children," since what John here writes to the παιδία is far beyond the comprehension of "little children." In both cases παιδία is only a variation of the τεκνία in verse 12. — So the apostle says that he wrote his Gospel to all his readers practically for the same reason as now he writes his Epistle to them all: **because ye know the Father,** who is your Father through Jesus Christ. "We are all the sons of God, through faith, in Christ Jesus." Gal. 3, 26. "And this is life eternal, that they should know thee, the only true God, and him whom thou didst send, even Jesus Christ." John 17, 3. God's children always know their Father; that is one of the marks of childhood. They know him as their Father with a very practical knowledge, for he has made them his children and keeps them as such by forgiving them their sins for Christ's sake (verse 12). Because John's readers had this knowledge he wrote his glorious Gospel to them, to deepen and strengthen

and glorify this knowledge in the richest possible way. Old
Bugenhagen wrote of this knowledge:

Si Christum bene scis, satis est, si cetera nescis;
Si Christum nescis, nil est, si cetera discis.—

**I have written unto you, fathers, because ye know him
which is from the beginning.** As to the "fathers" John
does not vary his language at all. The same reason
which now moves him to write his Epistle to them
moved him in the first place to pen his Gospel. They
know the eternal, divine Savior, his true nature, and
therefore the true character of all his saving work.—
**I have written unto you, young men, because ye are
strong, and the word of God abideth in you, and ye have
overcome the evil one.** Here the variation from the
former statements consists of two explanatory clauses.
To overcome the evil one requires strength: **ye are
strong;** this is the spiritual strength of true faith.
But all such strength is the gift of God through the
Word which he implants into the heart, therefore the
addition: **and the word of God abideth in you.** This **word
of God** is the Gospel of Christ which early and careful
teaching had implanted into the hearts of the young men to
whom John wrote, so that it lodged there and wrought its
blessed results: **abideth in you.** "But abide thou" (Timothy) "in the things which thou hast learned and hast been
assured of, knowing of whom thou hast learned them; and
that from a babe thou hast known the sacred writings which
are able to make thee wise unto salvation through faith
which is in Christ Jesus." 2 Tim. 3, 14-15. Here John
indicates to us how we may fortify our young people against
all the wiles of the devil and the world, and all the stirrings
of their own flesh: we must fill their hearts with the Word
of God. Fathers and mothers must train up their children
in the nurture and admonition of the Lord; teachers in
Christian schools must carry on the same blessed work; and

the one aim of the church in its Sunday School, catechetical instruction, and in every church service must be the same. At this season of the year there are always classes of young people in our congregations approaching the end of their preparation for confirmation; John's words to the young men of long ago afford the finest kind of an opportunity for a true pastor to say things of eternal value to the young people under his spiritual care, and to their parents likewise. John was moved to write both his Gospel and Epistle also to such young men, and we see that he had a hundred blessed things to impart to them. One of these now follows in the second section of our text.

The apostle's admonition regarding the world.

Those commentators who over-emphasize the division which John makes among the members of the church, who count three where he only made two, and turn what he says in the first member of his second triad to all Christians into a word addressed only to little children, make the further mistake of applying what now follows principally to young men. But John writes to all the members of the church and twice addresses them all most affectionately as his beloved "little children" (τεκνία and παιδία), distinguishing among them only the fathers and the youths. Therefore the admonitions which now follow in all the rest of the chapter pertain equally and directly to all, and not principally only to the one class, and only secondarily to other classes. To old and young alike John writes: **Love not the world, neither the things that are in the world. If any man love the world, the love of the Father is not in him. For all that is in the world, the lust of the flesh, and the lust of the eyes, and the vainglory of life, is not of the Father, but is of the world. And the world passeth away, and the lust thereof: but he that doeth the will of God abideth for ever.** The basis of this grand admonition is the state of grace of John's readers. It is in vain to urge those who are still of the world not to love the world; we can never hope to pluck figs from thistles, or to gather good fruit from corrupt trees. But where we have people who have overcome the evil one, who know the Father, and have forgiveness for Jesus' sake, there we may and must admonish as John does here: **Love not the world, neither the things that are in the world.** John uses ἀγαπᾶν, the word for love which in the N. T. always refers to the love that indicates a direction of the will or an intelligent choice (Cremer), not φιλεῖν, which is used for the love of natural affection. With μή ἀγαπᾶτε, **love not,** the apostle therefore appeals to the new nature in man, his regenerate will. — The word κόσμος (originally: ornament, order) has a variety of meanings in the N. T.: the universe; the earth; the whole human race; the ungodly who are far from God; and finally — in an ethical sense — all that is opposed to Christ. By world John here means the entire earthly world, not in as far as God made it, but in as far as the devil corrupted it, and it now "lieth in the evil one" and is ruled by him as the prince of this world, and thus constitutes a kingdom opposed to the Father and the kingdom of grace in which Christ rules. As children of God we have been delivered from the world in this sense, and the world hates us, knowing that we are not of it (John 15, 18-19). Luther writes: "To be in the world, to see the world, to feel the world is a different thing from loving the world; just as to have and to feel sin is a different thing from loving sin." — **Neither the things that are in the world** points to the individual deceptive treasures, pleasures, and honors of the world; its wealth, its power, its wisdom, *etc.* There is no prohibition here against admiring, appreciating, working for, and using aright the natural things of this earth, such as relatives, friends, the fatherland, the beauties and grandeur of nature, home, occupation, and the thousand attractive things God has put all around us. But whatever in its connection, tendency, and influence is hostile to Christ and his kingdom, however alluring or attractive it may otherwise be, is a "thing of this world," to which we must be hostile since we belong to Christ and his kingdom. "Ye adulteresses, know ye not that the friendship of the world is enmity with God? Whosoever therefore would be a friend of the world maketh himself an enemy of God." James 4, 4. "Man, who cannot be without love, is either a lover of God or of the world." Leo the Great. "Where the love of God has entered a heart it means to be the sole queen." Besser. And it makes little difference whether the world holds you with a thread or with a chain; as long as it holds you, you belong to it, and not to God. It is very significant that John insists, not only in general that we love not the world, but also in particular that we love not "the things that are in the world;" for we generally love the sinful world by loving some special sinful thing in the world. Thus the apostle insists that every sinful tie be sundered, so that we belong wholly to God. — **If any man love the world, the love of the Father is not in him.** This is the convincing proof for John's admonition. To **love the world,** to have this love as the ruling principle in the heart, is the very opposite of **the love of the Father,** *i. e.* of our love to him. The two are mutually antagonistic and exclusive. You cannot mix fire and water. Whatever love controls us is an evidence of the state of the heart; and no man can accomplish the feat of being at the same time a child of the Father and a child of the world. — Why the two loves are opposed is set forth in the same convincing manner: **For all that is in the world, the lust of the flesh, and the lust of the eyes, and the vainglory of life, is not of the Father, but is of the world.** When the apostle writes πᾶν τὸ ἐν τῷ κόσμῳ he does not mean again τὰ ἐν τῷ κόσμῳ, the things which the world offers, but that which makes the world what it is, its real essence, its inner life, that which determines its character. He at once specifies by adding three appositions showing the main tendencies and forms of all worldliness. Two of them he designates as **lust,** the sinful desire to get something and enjoy it, ἐπιθυμία; and the other as **vainglory,** a sinful proceeding regarding what one already has. — The first is **the lust of the flesh,** the lust or desire which springs from the corrupt nature of man (σάρξ) and reaches out to grasp and enjoy the desired object in sinful pleasure. This lust comes out especially in sensual appetites and gratifications. Besser specifies Phil. 3, 19: "whose god is their belly;" Luke 21, 34: "surfeiting and drunkenness;" 1 Cor. 15, 32: "Let us eat and drink, for to-morrow we die;" 1 Cor. 6, 18: "He that commiteth fornication sinneth against his own body." Already the desire itself for such sinful gratification is true worldliness, even if the actual gratification is not attained. The world ever invites us to its "pleasant, merry companionships," its "innocent amusements," its "good times," and by such euphonious phrases tries to make us forget what the Scriptures say of the lusts of the flesh. O, writes Besser, how many a youth who has at one time experienced the power of the blood of sprinkling has after all at last been drawn into the snare of this lust, and has not realized perhaps until too late "that it is for his life." Sometimes the *secret* worm of this lust eats out the heart and fills even the body with its corrosive poison; many an early grave has closed over the pitiful victim who would not heed the voice of warning. Others go on openly, "as it came to pass in the days of Noah . . . they ate, they drank, they married, they were given in marriage *etc.*" Or as James writes 5, 5: "Ye have lived delicately on the earth, and taken your pleasure; ye have nourished your hearts in a day of slaughter." — The second is **the lust of the eyes,** the sinful desire which seeks and finds delight in the very seeing itself, feasting the eyes upon unseemly sights that the heart may burn with unholy pleasure. The former lust grasps certain things for its desires, but this takes in even those things which it cannot actually grasp, sweeping through the wide world for its food of sin. The old exegetes specified especially the glitter of gold, making this lust include avarice, and in addition the glamor of stage-display. "Every one that looketh on a woman to lust after her hath committed adultery with her already in his heart." Matth. 5, 28. Food for this fiery lust is every vile picture, every "spicy" paper or novel, and every evilly suggestive image that falls under the eye. And when the devil has properly trained such an eye, what all will it not see·to keep the furnace of the imagination constantly aglow? Yet the world calls many of these vicious sights "artistic," "beautifully realistic," and would persuade us that its stage immoralities teach "beautiful moral lessons." — By **the vainglory of life** the apostle designates the pride, boastfulness, and outward display connected with all sorts of earthly possessions. The English *"vainglory"* brings out the suggestion of the vanity and unreality of all such possessions suggested by ἀλαζονία; all this pride and boasting is hollow, and he who is filled with it is a poor self-deluded fool. John uses βίος for **life,** meaning this poor earthly existence, not the ζωή, the true life that really deserves the name; the *vita, quam vivimus,* as distinguished from the *vita, qua vivimus.* "The pride of life" (A. V.) is that haughty, puffed-up arrogance which we meet at every turn in the world. It makes thousands wish to be as great as possible in the eyes of others in food, dress, means, furniture, buildings, lands, attainments, learning, position, honors, *etc.,* and to gratify this wish they resort to much exaggeration and all manner of shams. How many have lived beyond their means until at last the bubble burst; and how many others have been eaten with envy because they could not vie in display with their neighbors. How many whom God did bless with some degree of riches, knowledge, and other advantages, that they might humbly use these gifts for the benefit of their fellow-men, have spoiled his blessings by their vainglory and the prideful use they made of their possessions. These poor fools love nothing better than to talk of themselves, of the great things they have done, the fine treasures they own, the great learning with which they shine, *etc.* But all their vainglory is only glory that is vain. Rom. 12, 16: "Set not your mind on high things, but condescend to things that are lowly." 2 Cor. 10, 17-18: "But he that glorieth, let him glory in the Lord. For not he that commendeth himself is approved, but whom the Lord commendeth." 2 Cor. 11, 30: "If I must needs

glory, I will glory of the things that concern my weakness."
— The fatal defect in "all that is in the world" is that it
is not of the Father, but is of the world. "To be of,"
εἶναι ἐκ, expresses origin. The **Father** and the **world** are
diametrically opposed; whatever is of him, caused and produced by him, is not of the world, and *vice versa.* He is
the source of light, life, salvation, and holiness; and the
world ever brings forth lust, sin, ruin, death. How can a
Christian, realizing this, still love the world: "What I
love, to that my soul clings. What I love is what I live,
what I delight in, and this becomes part of my unconscious
life, of my meditation, my dreaming. What I love becomes
more and more part of my very self. He who loves the
world becomes worldly, a man filled with the world." Dryander. — John speaks first of the source and origin, then
of the effect and result: **And the world passeth away, and
the lust thereof,** the world itself in its ungodliness and opposition to the Father is doomed, and therefore all that is
of it, **the lust thereof,** the lust which belongs to it and
grows from it. Its very nature is that it passes away, because it is far from the author of all true being. The present tense *παράγεται* (compare 2, 7) denotes that the world
is even now in the act of passing away and coming to an
end. Its glory is fading, its flowers are withering, its promises are breaking, its hopes are crumbling. Is. 14, 11. A
thousand wrecks lie strewed along its path, and at last it
shall all be wreck and ruin. 1 Cor. 7, 31. What this implies in regard to the lovers of the world John lets us conclude for ourselves. They will be left naked, wretched,
shattered, doomed. All their treasures and pleasures like
water will have slipped from their fingers, their castles will
all be ashes, their crowns a curse. Their souls, burnt and
blasted by the sins of the world, will have nothing left but
the penalty and the remorse. Does the siren voice of the
world ring in your ears? Hear the word of truth: "The
world passeth away." — In a sudden effective contrast the
apostle adds: **but he that doeth the will of God abideth**

'**forever.** To "do the will of God" is the opposite of worldly lust. 'Ο ποιῶν is one whose heart belongs to God, one in whom his Word abides (14). **The will of God** is his good and gracious will, which is our salvation, our sanctification, and "to do" that will is to accept it by faith and let it rule our lives. — The result always is that he who does this **abideth for ever,** preserved by the grace and power of God. The eternal Father keeps all his children eternally. Whatever they may lose in this life, they are not lost; their real treasure, the Father and the Father's will with which they have identified themselves, keeps them safe and whole to all eternity. "To abide for ever" is to live with God in eternal blessedness. John holds up before our eyes these two: the world and Father; the lust of the world and the will of God; the passing away of the world, and the eternal abiding of the doers of God's will. Every true instinct of our nature as well as every motive of grace must compel us to choose the latter and abide by that choice forever.

HOMILETICAL HINTS.

Forgiveness of sin is the bread by which both great and small, an apostle and a repentant malefactor, king and beggar live in the kingdom of God. A strange "and" joins the fourth and the fifth petition of the Lord's Prayer, connecting the earthly bread with the heavenly.

John does not write: Ye have no sin! If he did that, I would know indeed that he had not written it for me; and you, my friends, would certainly know the same regarding yourselves. Not this distinguishes us from the world that we have never sinned, but this that before God in heaven all our sins are forgiven. — Of this we are certain not because of any feeling of the nearness of God, or of any marked improvement in our conduct, valuable and encouraging as both of these may be; but because the cross of Christ on Golgotha rises before our eyes and His heavenly Word declares unto us and all believers: Your sins are forgiven in Christ's name.

The poor discouraged monk in his cell at Erfurt rose up rejoiced from all his own vain efforts at peace of conscience and hope in God when by His grace he learned to understand the words of the third article of the Creed: "I believe the forgiveness of sins."

Christians are sinners whose sins are forgiven.

An old pagan philosopher wrote the noteworthy word: "Know thyself!" But the apostle of Christ writes: "Ye know him which is from the beginning." And again: "This is life eternal, that they should know Thee the only true God, and him whom thou didst send, even Jesus Christ." John 17, 3.

No; not the growing experience of age makes one strong as over against the world, not the increase of authority in judging the value of things in this life, not the gradual fading out of youthful passions and desires. Perhaps some venerable sire may show these traits — but oh, how much oftener we see the very opposite: old age bound more firmly than ever to the world; that which the soul has fed on all its life long become more and more indispensable as time goes forward. Even the lust of the flesh and the lust of the eyes may continue, the more hideous and abominable, on into old age when the very possibility of gratification has long passed. Even among the aged we meet these hollow forms, internally empty of God, clinging with trembling, palsied hands to the vanity of this passing world, as if it were eternal, at the very portals of death. No; age does not make strong as over against the world; only conversion does that, and faith in him who was from the beginning and in the fulness of time entered our world to unlock for time the portals of eternity and sanctify our poor human lives to be vessels of his own eternal glory. Blessed are the aged who bear in their hearts the image of the Savior. (From Dryander.)

"Do you know also the Lord Jesus?" an old man was asked who was telling of the many famous people he had met in his long life. He grew silent at the question; but he never forgot it, and at the eleventh hour he sought the acquaintance which alone will be inquired after when the portals above are reached.

Brave and great is the conqueror of a world-empire; braver and greater he who has conquered himself.

In a fine introduction to a sermon on this text Matthes speaks of the preparations under way for the young people soon to be confirmed. He points to the change which this will make in many a young life, when now they go forward into the days of youth, into the opening world with its allurements and pitfalls on every side. What would a loving pastor, loving parents and friends impress upon these young hearts to make them strong in their young faith, victorious over the enemy, happy and divinely successful for life? A golden Reminiscere: remember your Savior and his grace; remember your foes and your dangers.

The devil as a roaring lion goeth about, seeking whom he may devour. His pathway is strewn with crushed bones, marking the thousands of victims he has struck down — fair and ruddy youths many of them, sweet and gracious maidens, once the delight and hope of fond parents, the fair center of a fair circle of friends. But they strayed from the Savior's path, they were lost in the jungle of the world, the beast caught them, and their destruction has gone to augment the tale of dread that follows ever in the wake of the evil one. Do you know, young men, this monster lies in wait for you? Do you know how alone you can strike him down and triumph over his power? Take Christ with you — he alone is mightier than the beast of hell; put his Word in your heart — "one little Word o'erthrows him."

Judas was once a fine man, his heart touched with high aspiration, his feet climbing the upward path. He even became one of the Twelve. But the evil one slew him, and you know the weapon he used. — What part of the world is most dangerous for you? You may scorn some of its temptations and lightly kick away some of its snares. But there are others that appeal to you. Ask what they are; know that death lurks in them; and let Christ arm you against these.

Even the fair, the beautiful, the grand things of the world may twine themselves about your heart so as to draw it down into the gulf. If you have time and thought only for these, their very excellence may blind you to your danger. Even the best things of this present world pass away and leave their devotees empty and naked. Do God's will, and live forever.

Last Sunday before the throne in heaven, now in the world with all its attractions about us. If you have gazed aright upon the throne, you will look aright upon the world.

In the World, Yet Not of the World.

I. *Ours is a higher treasure.*
II. *Ours is a higher love.*

Love Not the World!

I. *Because you are sealed with the name of Christ.*
II. *Because you have conquered the evil one.*
III. *Because your delight is the Father's will.*

Little Children, Remember That You Are God's Children!

I. *He has purchased and won you from all sin, from death and the power of the devil.*
II. *He has lifted you up to serve him in his kingdom in everlasting righteousness, innocence, and blessedness.*

Would You Abide Forever?

Then be sure

   I. *That you keep the forgiveness of sins.*
  II. *That you grow in knowledge, and the Word abide in you.*
 III. *That you spurn the love of the world.*
 IV. *That you delight in the will of God.*

The Absolute Folly of Loving the World.

To love the world means:

   I. *To remain under the curse of sin, when we can have the forgiveness of sin.*
  II. *To be bound by the evil one, when we can overcome him.*
 III. *To be cheated by the lusts of the world, when we can be blessed by the Word of God.*
 IV. *To perish at last with the world, when we can abide with God forever.*

Do You know That You Are Writing the Epitaph for Your Tomb?

Let your life spell these three lines:

   I. *He had forgiveness, for he knew the Father.*
  II. *He overcame the evil one, for he loved not the world.*
 III. *He abideth forever, for he did the will of God.*

OCULI.

1 Pet. 1, 13-16.

Both the old epistolary lessons for Reminiscere and for Oculi contains strong admonitions to holiness, amplified by a variety of details. What is there spread over two texts is here combined in one. In our previous epistle text the main emphasis was on the negative injunction not to love the world. The positive side indeed also appeared, but here this positive side receives the eminent emphasis it deserves. In turning from the world we must turn unto holiness. Besides this holiness our text also urges hope, and one might be inclined to make that the central thought of the sermon. In itself this would not be amiss, but the most natural course in the line of thought of these lenten epistles will be to make holiness the chief subject and to group around that all else contained in the text. We who have reaped the benefit of the cross must *strive after holiness in all manner of living.* The one reference to Christ in our text speaks of his revelation at the end of time, which accords well with the admonition to hope, in connection with which we must leave it. Any reference to the cross of Christ or to his passion which may be needed for the sermon must be brought in synthetically, as already explained in the introduction to the lenten cycle. The text is so brief that we treat it as a whole in the exegesis.

The entire body of Peter's First Epistle consists of admonitions, and the first of these constitute our text. Writing, as is generally agreed, from Rome to the Christian congregations in Asia Minor, founded mostly by Paul and afterwards visited by Peter, it is the apostle's endeavor to comfort and strengthen them in the afflictions which have come upon them. He tells his readers

himself (5, 12): "I have written unto you briefly, exhorting
and testifying that this is the grace of God: stand ye fast
therein." Our text is from one of the hortatory sections of
the letter. It is closely connected with the elaborate and
grand introductory statement, verses 3-12, in which the
apostle blesses God for the present and future salvation of
himself and his readers, and testifies to its greatness and
the joy it produces. Having such salvation all Christians
ought to live and act accordingly, as the apostle shows at
length in his entire letter, beginning with the duty of hope
and of holiness.

**Wherefore girding up the loins of your mind, be
sober and set your hope perfectly on the grace that is to
be brought unto you at the revelation of Jesus Christ.**
With διό, **wherefore,** the apostle refers to his entire introductory statement, the central thought of which is the
lively hope of his readers and the end of their faith, namely
the final salvation of their souls. There is nothing to indicate or justify any restriction in this reference, either only
to the greatness and excellence of God's grace (Calvin), or
to the trials through which Christians proceed to their goal
(DeWette). In view of our entire salvation as we now
have it and as it awaits us in glory beyond Peter calls upon
us to gird up our loins and set our hope on the grace to
come. — The main verb is the aorist imperative ἐλπίσατε,
and this is introduced by two participles, the aorist
ἀναζωσάμενοι and the present νήφοντες. The first states the act
or deed necessary for setting our hope on the grace to come,
and the second the condition which thus results and is likewise necessary for such hope. **Girding up the loins of
your mind** is a figurative expression (compare Luke 12,
34-37), referring to the long loose robes worn by the orien-
tals; in order to walk or work energetically these were
drawn up and belted around the waist to give the legs free
play. So Christians are to gird up the loins of their mind,
διάνοια, their thinking, including purpose and will. Besser,
following Luther, calls the girdle faith. Instead of letting
their minds, purposes, and thoughts hang loose and drift

idly hither and thither in careless fashion as momentary
impulse may suggest, they are to gird up their thoughts and
direct them to the one great object set before them. This
girding, with hope for something great to come, suggests a
journey; Christians are going somewhere, they mean to
attain a notable goal. Therefore their thoughts cannot idle
along, or go after this or that attraction, but must be stren-
uously applied to the object of their hope. — The second
participle, νήφοντες (really: "being sober"), also recalling the
passage in Luke, is translated by the imperative: **be sober,**
to make the English smoother; yet this English rendering
retains the suggestion of the Greek (there being no καί between the two participles), that the girding up of the loins
of the mind results in the condition of being sober. The
sobrietas spiritualis is meant, which the Scriptures inculcate
so frequently: 4, 7; 1 Thess. 5, 6 and 8; 2 Tim. 4, 5; Rom.
13, 11; Rev. 3, 3. Soberness is the opposite of infatuation
with the things of this world, a calm, steady state of mind
which weighs and estimates things aright and thus enables
us to make the right choice and abide thereby. Not only
the world with its allurements, but also the various forms of
religious error and delusion intoxicate the mind and sweep
it away. With minds girded we are to remain sober and
sensible. — The adverb τελείως may be drawn either to the
participle νήφοντες or to the main verb ἐλπίσατε, and gives an
excellent meaning either way. Some commentators think
the participle would be too bare without any modifier; but
most of them follow Luther and the English translators,
because the main emphasis is on the imperative, which thus
naturally takes the modifier. We take νήφοντες as rounding
out the sense of ἀναζωσάμενοι, and so connect the adverb with
the imperative: **set your hope perfectly on, etc.** Here
hope, which in verse 3 is described as a great blessing and
perogative of the Christian, is made an admonition. We
who have hope as a gift (objectively) are to exercise hope
as an activity (subjectively). Christian hope is the sure
expectation, longing and looking forward to what God holds
out to us and has promised us for the future. It differs

from all the hope in the hearts of worldly men in this essential regard that they hope and expect where there is nothing forthcoming, while we hope where, even beyond what we are able to picture to ourselves, a real and great treasure awaits us. Moreover, worldly hope is self-made, while Christian hope is produced by God himself in our hearts. Peter uses the aorist ἐλπίσατε, which denotes a single act; but not, as Stoeckhardt explains it, because the apostle combines into one single act all the hoping which extends through the lives of Christians. The aorist imperative is stronger and more mandatory than the present (Winer 43, 4); this is sufficient for our passage. We may add, however, that Peter wants us to set our hope upon the coming grace by one definite act on our part, and then leave our hope thus fixed and settled. The verb ἐλπίζειν is usually used with εἰς, ἐν, ἐπί with the dative, or with ὅτι; ἐπί with the accusative is rarer, and is well translated by: "set your hope *on* the grace *etc.*" — The object of our hope (not merely the reason and ground for it) is **the grace that is to be brought unto you at the revelation of Jesus Christ.** A future grace is meant, namely the unmerited gift of eternal life. But Peter describes this by adding a present participle: τὴν φερομένην ὑμῖν χάριν, "the grace that *is being brought* (margin) to us at the revelation of Jesus Christ." He thus pictures this revelation as occurring now and now fulfilling all the promises of Christ. This is a strong encouragement and incentive to our hope; its fulfilment is as certain as if it were actually taking place now. **The revelation of Jesus Christ** is neither his incarnation nor his gracious revelation in the Gospel; the phrase always refers to the revelation of Christ in glory at the end of the world (compare verse 7). The hope of Christians is ever directed to the great day when he who once hung on the cross and died for our salvation shall return in glory to lead all who have accepted his merits in faith into the eternal kingdom of glory. On this revelation and its eternal gift of grace Peter bids us set our hope perfectly, completely, so that it may never waver.

Hope and holiness lie very close together in the
Scriptures and must not be separated in life. The admonition to the one naturally leads over into an admonition to the other. We have seen this in the
Christmas epistle, 1 John 3, 3: "And every one that
hath this hope set on him purifieth himself, even as he
is pure." We now have it here in that Peter who bids
us set our hope on the grace to come at once adds: **as
children of obedience, not fashioning yourselves according to your former lusts in** *the time of* **your ignorance:
but like as he which called you is holy, be ye yourselves
also holy in all manner of living; because it is written,
Ye shall be holy; for I am holy.** When the apostle calls
his readers **children of obedience** we very properly think
of the opening words of his Epistle, where in verse 3 he
speaks of "God and the Father of our Lord Jesus Christ
who according to his great mercy begat us again unto a
lively hope," and where in verses 1 and 2 he calls them "the
elect" "in sanctification of the Spirit, unto obedience *etc.*"
Childhood and obedience go together. Luther and the A.
V. translate: "as obedient children," but the genitive "of
obedience" is stronger. It describes the peculiar constitution and character of these children which is impressed
upon them in their very birth and belongs to their nature.
In the same way they are called "children of light," Eph. 5,
8; compare also the designations for the ungodly Eph. 2,
2-3; 2 Pet. 2, 14. The **obedience** here meant is obedience
to God's saving will, or to the Gospel, not a mere legal
obedience, or moral life, outside of and apart from the
Gospel; it is the obedience which consists in believing in
Christ and following him in love. "This is the work of
God, that ye believe on him whom he hath sent," John 6,
29. — What we are by virtue of our new spiritual nature
must come out in our life and actions; our obedience must
manifest itself in every way, and this is one vital way:
**not fashioning yourselves according to your former lusts
in** *the time of* **your ignorance.** Συσχηματίζεσθαι signifies to
adopt the σχῆμα which some one has; and σχῆμα (scheme)

is here a certain fashion, form, or design of life, a *habitus*, or scheme of conduct natural to some one. However, instead of pointing to other persons to whose wrong fashion of life Peter's readers are not to conform, as Paul does Rom. 12, 2: "Be not fashioned according to this world," the apostle here points to the wrong fashion of life which his readers formerly had: not fashioning yourselves according **to your former lusts in** (the time of) **your ignorance;** or, translating closely: "according to your lusts formerly in your ignorance." **Formerly,** before they became children of God and of obedience, they lived on **in ignorance** (Eph. 4, 18) of the Gospel, and fashioned their lives accordingly, obeying the sinful impulses or **lusts** and evil desires of their unregenerate hearts. All this is to be done away with now (μή, the negative of exhortation, because of the following imperative γενήθητε); it would be a contradiction of their very nature. The admonition which Peter here uses is a very common one in Scripture, and highly effective: we are shown what the grace of God has made of us, in order that we may willingly, joyfully live in accord therewith and shun whatever is contrary thereto. And the holy writers all use strong and glorious terms in showing God's work of grace in us, thus making their admonitions to holiness the stronger. What business have children of obedience with the fashion and form of disobedience in which they formerly lived, and in which the children of ignorance still live? None whatever! must be the involuntary response of our hearts. — Over against what does not comport with our nature Peter now places, with the strong adversative ἀλλά, what this nature requires: **but like as he which called you is holy, be ye yourselves also holy in all manner of living.** The margin translates more closely: *like the Holy One which called you.* By τὸν ἅγιον God is meant; and the call is his Gospel call of grace which Peter's readers had obeyed in faith. God is here described as "the Holy One" to show what must be the fashion and form of life of all in whom his call is effective. He is holy in that he loves everything that is good and pure, and hates, abominates, and punishes all that is sinful. God is absolutely and immutably holy in himself, from all eternity, and has revealed himself to men without deviation as thus holy. But his revelation was for the purpose of lifting us who had fallen into sin back again into holiness, for God is the source and fountain of holiness. So Peter writes that the Holy One has called us to communion with himself, out of the darkness of ignorance to his own marvelous light (2, 9), out of evil unto blessing (3, 9); out of shame to eternal glory in Christ (5, 10). Besser. — Hence: **be ye yourselves also holy in all manner of living.** The imperative γενήθητε (aorist like ἐλπίσατε) does not mean: "become ye," but "be ye" holy, or "show ye yourselves" as holy; it is commonly used in this sense instead of the rarer imperative of εἶναι. Active holiness is here commanded for the children of God: **in all manner of holy living,** ἐν πάσῃ ἀναστροφῇ. When πᾶς has the article following it denotes a whole; when without the article as here it summarizes a multiplicity; all, or every, manner of living, whether it be business or pleasure, labor or rest, joy or sorrow, difficult situations or easy ones; all are meant. To be holy is our obligation not in the sense of an outward legal requirement laid upon us, for which we must furnish the ability and power, but in the sense of God's call which furnishes us the power and ability. The Gospel call to holiness always includes this, and is therefore efficacious to produce what it requires. The hand that points us to holiness is the hand that extends its grace to us for holiness; in pointing us upward it lifts us upward. Thus the plea is cut off: I am not able to be holy. Every Christian can indeed, and must be, holy, although sin still clings to him in various ways; he can conquer the old lusts and in the strength that God gives do the works that please God. Peter admonishes to holiness in order to spur us on that we may make the fullest possible use of God's help and glorify him and his grace more and more in all manner of holy living. — An O. T. reference is used to strengthen the apostolic word: **because it is written, Ye shall be holy; for I am holy,** Lev. 11, 44; 19, 2; 20, 26. The requirement of holiness is fundamental and essential in both covenants. What God asked of Israel when he made that people his own he now asks, and must ask, of us whom he has called by the Gospel. God does not connive at sin and unholy living now that the forgiveness of sins has come through Jesus Christ. Let no one think he can go on in all manner of unholy living, or in this or that open sinful course, and yet be accounted a child of God. Only the pure in heart shall see God, and without holiness it is impossible to see God. Christ died not to save us in our sins, but from our sins; and this is the very necessary lenten message of our text.

HOMILETICAL HINTS.

When the children of Israel were to leave the land of bondage and start on their journey to the land of promise, they were ordered to eat the Passover with their loins girded and with staves in their hands. We are now travelling to our great land of promise, and our loins must likewise be girded for energetic progress — we cannot tarry by the way. — Ours is a great goal; we can approach it only step by step, and through many a conflict. This is why we must discipline ourselves, not merely outwardly in certain lines of conduct, but also and especially inwardly, that our thoughts, feelings, and volitions may ever respond in the right way to shut out and oppose what would hinder us and to appropriate and use what would help us. There is truth enough and grace enough to help us all onward and upward, if only we would take it and use it as we should.

Who of us does not hope? But do we hope perfectly? How many things cloud our hope and dim its brightness! Every lust that remains and lures us aside, every manner of living that is not as holy and fully devoted to God and our Savior as it should be.

Christians are never to let themselves go, not even in their thoughts. — When multitudes are carried away by some infatuation (in some rampant revival, in some new religious fad, in some popular error of doctrine or morals), our Christian soberness is to preserve us in balance.

A child has far deeper insight into the proceedings of a home than a servant. Yet the servant who knows his master's will and does not do it, shall suffer many stripes. How then about the child that chooses disobedience instead of obedience? — The sins of the world are not as bad as the sins of a Christian. The world does not know better, has always followed its evil course, imagines this is entirely proper or at least natural. This is the ignorance of the world, its blindness and darkness. But a Christian is a child of God, a dweller in God's own house; he knows the power of Christ's atoning blood, he has been justified and regenerated, forgiven and reborn; he knows the Father's will and the blessedness of it, and also the power and grace which enables us poor sinners to do that will. To go counter to all this, to turn from holiness of life to the former lusts, is a sinful proceeding far more terrible than the ignorant and blind godlessness of the world.

Do we hope for the grace that is to be brought unto us at the revelation of Jesus Christ? Do we expect to stand before the throne where the angelic host sings: Holy, holy, holy is the Lord of hosts? Then let the words ring in our ears and hearts now: Ye shall be holy; for I am holy! Be ye perfect as your Father in heaven is perfect! They who will not strive after holiness here, cannot reach the holiness that awaits us there. — There are many who promise to praise God with golden harps, with new tongues, with angelic words when at last they reach heaven. Why do they not try it with their mortal tongues here on earth already, behind the counter, in the office, at the work-bench with saw and plane, behind the anvil with hammer and tongs, when they follow the plow or the drill, or ride the cultivator or the reaper, or whatever their occupation may be? "Whatsoever ye do in word or in deed, do all in the name of the Lord Jesus, giving thanks to God the Father through him." Col. 3, 17. Is it hard at first? — every beginning has its difficulties. Practice makes perfect; practice produces mastery. What if our singing at first be a quaver, our speaking a stammering. He who tries here shall certainly succeed there. All holiness begins on earth; to postpone it for heaven is to postpone it forever.

"Cynics like Diogenes, who would have no house, but lay in a tub, may commend such heathenish holiness. Such examples pertain in no way to Christian perfection. Christian holiness consists in much higher matters than such hypocrisy." *Apology,* 281, 46. — "But the other works claim the astonished attention of men, being aided by their great display, expense, and magnificent buildings, and these they so adorn that everything shines and glitters; they waft incense, they sing and ring bells, they light tapers and candles, so that nothing else can be seen or heard. For it is regarded a most precious work which no one can sufficiently praise if a priest stand there in a surplice embroidered with gilt, or a layman continue all day upon his knees in church. But if a poor girl tend a little child, and faithfully do what she is told, that is nothing; for else what should monks and nuns seek in their cloisters?" *The Large Catechism,* 435, 313. — There is no holiness in fasting or any outward observance. And by no holiness of ours can we win heaven. All such "holiness" is pharisaical, papistical, an abomination of God. Matt. 15, 9. — "For now we are only half pure and holy, so that the Holy Ghost has ever to continue his work in us through the Word, and daily to dispense forgiveness, until we attain to that life where there will be no more forgiveness, but only perfectly pure and holy people, full of godliness and righteousness, delivered and free from sin, from death and all evil, in a new, immortal, and glorified body." 446, 58.

Christ's throne in heaven (Invocavit); the world and its allurements (Reminiscere); now your own soul; search it under the cross. Holiness — unwelcome word to many; yet conscience condemns all sin (unholiness). Many false notions. Christians often compromise, trying to be worldly and holy at the same time. Self-invented and false holiness, superficial, hypocritical. Let us know the truth about holiness.

Our Crucified Savior Calls Us Unto Holiness.

I. *He is holy who calls us.*

a) Perfectly, in himself.

b) But he sent his Son to deliver us from sin and make us holy.

II. *It is holiness as the fruit of faith.*

a) The Law alone with its demand of holiness drives to despair.

b) But the Gospel gives us the new life and power of faith, the normal, natural fruit of which is holiness.

III. *This holiness is the true soundness and elevation of our being.*

a) All unholiness is like a pestilence, a poison, with death in it. Do not touch it, laugh at it, mistake it.

b) To be holy is to be rid of the poison of sin, to grow healthy and sound again in heart and life; to be what God designed us to be, his children, princes, kings, conquerors, not slaves, beggars, outcasts, prisoners in dungeon chains.

IV. *The call to holiness puts new energy into us.*
   a) Minds girded for effort.
   b) Soberness which shuns what is fanatic and fantastic.
   c) Hope to spur us on.
   d) The joy of happy, blessed, childlike obedience.

Oculi: Eyes Illumined by the Cross.

They look:
   I. *Sorrowfully upon past ignorance and sin.*
   II. *Thankfully upon present grace and pardon.*
   III. *Hopefully upon the grace and glory to come.*
   IV. *Soberly, yet zealously upon the Holy One who has called them.*

Ye Shall Be Holy, For I Am Holy!

   I. *By God's grace in Christ Jesus.*
   II. *In all manner of holy living.*

Why Be Holy?

   I. *Because a holy God calls us.*
   II. *Because a holy Savior helps us.*
   III. *Because a holy heaven invites us.*

The Peculiar Character of the Children of Obedience.

   I. *They follow the Father's call.*
   II. *They forsake the fashion of the world.*
   III. *They fulfil the Savior's behest.*

The Blessed Pilgrimage of the Children of Obedience.

   I. *From a world of ignorance and lust,*
   II. *In constant striving for holiness,*
   III. *Their loins girded with earnest endeavor,*
   IV. *They hasten hopefully homeward.*

LAETARE.

2 Cor. 7, 4-10.

Christian repentance is surely one of the great subjects for Lent, and here we have it following a text on holiness. There is no holiness without repentance, and in all our holiness we need constant repentance. Our text records the repentance of a whole congregation. The Corinthians had been involved in a sin largely of omission in that they had allowed unrebuked and undisciplined in their midst a case so glaringly sinful that even among Gentiles its equal was hard to find, namely that a man should have his own stepmother to wife after his father's death. The apostle at once rebuked the Corinthians in the most vigorous manner when the dreadful news reached him, 1 Cor. 5. The result finally was Christian repentance and amendment on the part of the Corinthians; and this so rejoiced the apostle that he writes of it at some length in his second Epistle, some six months after the first, in the section from which our text is taken. Laetare means rejoice, and Paul's words of rejoicing over the godly sorrow of his beloved Corinthians form a text eminently fitting for this very Sunday. Its great subject is clear: *the sorrow of Christian repentance* which all must experience who stand beneath the cross. The apostle sets forth first of all the joy which such repentance brought him on the part of the Corinthians, then he describes the sorrow in which such repentance consists, and finally he points to the salvation to which such repentance leads.

Paul rejoices over it.

Intense feeling marks the first words of the apostle in our text: **Great is my boldness of speech toward you,**

27   417

great is my glorying on your behalf: I am filled with comfort, I overflow with joy in all our affliction. Titus has come to him from Corinth bringing the good news that Paul's first Epistle had thoroughly done its work, especially also in regard to the grave case of discipline which the apostle had treated so emphatically in that letter. His heart, at first full of gravest concern as to how matters would go at Corinth, is now immensely relieved and filled with rejoicing. He writes: **Great is my boldness of speech toward you,** παρρησία, freespokenness, openness, frankness; the word denotes a state of mind in which one feels free to speak with full openness, and hence is sometimes best translated confidence. Paul finds he is not deceived in the Corinthians, they are true to their teaching, and he can use great openness toward them (as, indeed, he had done already in his first Epistle). — Great is **my glorying in your behalf,** when occasion arises to speak to others concerning the Corinthians and how they have acted in this matter. The apostle can boast of them as having shown themselves true. — **I am filled with comfort,** πεπλήρωμαι, "I have been filled," and thus am full of comfort now. The article in τῇ παρακλήσει points definitely to the comfort contained in Titus' good news from Corinth; the dative is instrumental, yet names the thing which fills Paul's heart. **I overflow with joy,** ὑπερπερισσεύομαι, "I abound with" it, I have it in exceeding measure. Note again the article τῇ χαρᾷ. **In all our affliction** belongs to both verbs. The comfort and joy together cheer the apostle in the affliction which he and those with him (he uses the plural ἡμῶν) have recently been undergoing in their work. This was oppressing him (θλῖψις = oppression), and his anxiety concerning Corinth made the pressure greater; but now with the comfort and joy in place of anxiety his affliction was immensely relieved. The great apostle is here permitting us to look into his very heart. He was a man who could be deeply moved and who was not ashamed to let others see it. His words are like waves rolling in, one hard upon the other. Christian pastors may here learn something of the emotions which should rise in their hearts when their church-members awake in repentance and respond to the right teaching of the Gospel. Joy like Paul's will bind their hearts together with ours and make them more faithful than ever.

The apostle now explains what made the report brought by Titus especially comforting to him. Exceedingly desirous to hear from Corinth Paul had gone forward from Troas, where he had started labor, into Macedonia, where Titus could reach him more quickly (2, 12, *etc.*), but even here tribulation beset him. **For even when we were come into Macedonia, our flesh had no relief, but** *we were* **afflicted on every side; without** *were* **fightings, within** *were* **fears.** The apostle speaks of **flesh** because his afflictions were due in part to outward opposition; in 2, 13, where he refers only to his anxiety at the delay of Titus and news from Corinth, he writes: "I had no relief in my spirit." "Flesh" in this connection means the body and soul of Paul, without connoting sin or a sinful and depraved state. Our flesh, he writes, **had no relief,** ἄνεσιν (from ἀνίημι), loosening or relaxation, as when a bow is unbent. **But** *we were* **afflicted on every side; without** *were* **fightings, within** *were* **fears** — which explains why there was no relief or unbending. Paul had been kept on a constant strain; the afflictions from one side augmenting those coming from the other. Two sides are especially mentioned: **without** and **within,** *extra et intra ecclesiam,* as the old commentators have it, but more properly "without" and "within" the writer himself. **Without, fightings,** battles, yet hardly physical combats (for instance, with wild animals, as Reylænder supposes), but sharp clashes and contentions with either Jews or Gentiles, or both, spurning the Gospel and seeking to obstruct it. **Within, fears,** yet hardly because of these battles or their possible outcome; far more likely misgivings and painful apprehensions in regard to the outcome of affairs at Corinth, lest his enemies there should prevail, the congregation be turned against the Gospel, and all his labors in that important center be lost. All these afflictions combined and

caused Paul no little suffering. Troubles often pour in upon
us like a flood, and there is a measure of truth in the old
adage: It never rains but what it pours. The perfect tense
ἔσχηκεν, as well as the present participle θλιβόμενοι, indicates
that all this affliction for a time continued steadily to press
Paul and keep him on a severe strain. There is a slight irregularity in adding the nominative plural θλιβόμενοι to ἡ σάρξ
ἔσχηκεν, which betrays the emotion of the writer; though
he made "the flesh" the subject of his sentence, the
real subject he has in mind all along is ἡμεῖς, we. —
**Nevertheless he that comforteth the lowly, *even* God,
comforted us by the coming of Titus; and not by his
coming only, but also by the comfort wherewith he
was comforted in you, while he told us your longing,
your mourning, your zeal for me; so that I rejoiced yet
more.** Paul puts ὁ παρακαλῶν τοὺς ταπεινούς forward in the
form of a general statement referring to all the lowly, to
comfort whom is thus said to be the characteristic work
and special office of God. In the word **lowly,** ταπεινοί there
is no reference to moral excellence or any merit, nothing
but their depressed and miserable condition. All the
"lowly" may rightfully look to the great Comforter (ὁ
παρακαλῶν) for relief; an invitation to do so is hidden in
the apostle's words. — Himself and those who were partakers of his affliction Paul mentions as belonging to this
great class of the ταπεινοί, when he says of the Comforter:
he **comforted us,** then adding ὁ θεός, *even* **God.** They had
to wait, pray, and exercise patience, but they were greatly
rewarded at last: a rich measure of comfort came: **by the
coming** (margin: *presence*) **of Titus.** Paul's messenger
to Corinth finally returned. What this meant to him and
his friends he tells us in a fine manner: they were comforted already by his mere arrival, which in itself ended the
suspense they had suffered: **and not by his coming only,**
ending the question why he remained so long away,
**but also by the comfort wherewith he was comforted
in you while he told us, etc.** Paul makes Titus not only
the bearer of comfort, but also the recipient, thus in a

beautiful way linking Titus together with those who were waiting for his comforting news in deep concern for the Corinthians. Note the repetition of the word comfort: "God *comforted* us by the *comfort* wherewith Titus was *comforted* while he told us, *etc.*" It is Paul's emphatic way of showing how precious this comfort was to him. Meyer, followed by others, makes Titus experience anew the comfort he had received in Corinth in reporting his good news to the apostle; our English versions do the same: **wherewith he was comforted in you, while he told us, etc.** The aorist παρεκλήθη, with the present participle ἀναγγέλλων, is thus understood of the time of Titus' arrival in Macedonia; and this makes the construction regular, since both properly speak of the same time. Those who try to make the main verb refer to the comfort Titus received in Corinth have difficulty with the participle and assume, unnecessarily it seems to us, an irregularity, and offer various guesses as to what the regular construction should be (Bachmann suggesting a genitive absolute: αὐτοῦ ἀναγγέλλοντος). The apostle vividly pictures to his readers what he saw of the comfort of Titus when he made his report. We may add also that the entire comfort of Titus in this matter centered in the report he made (ἀπαγγέλλων) to Paul, and to be able to make so favorable a report was beyond question a great comfort to him, the same comfort transferring itself, as he spoke, to the apostle and the other listeners. — Three things he tells: **your longing, your mourning, your zeal for me.** The emphatic repetition of ὑμῶν: **your** longing, **your** mourning, **your** zeal for me, suggests that somebody else also experienced these emotions, namely Paul himself when he wrote his first Epistle to the Corinthians; and his great comfort now is that such a response was made by the Corinthians. Their **longing,** or earnest desire, was most likely to see Paul and secure his approbation; their **mourning,** bewailing (Luther: *Weinen*), was because of the sins with which they had offended God and grieved the apostle; **their zeal for me** was their effort to come up to the requirements set them by the apostle.

Note that he now uses the singular and speaks properly of himself alone. The three points reported by Titus bear a strong personal touch, which, of course, will not be misunderstood. The apostle was far from attaching people only to his person, as some preachers selfishly cultivate such personal attachment among their hearers. The devotion of the Corinthians to Paul rested altogether on their devotion to the Gospel and its requirements which he had presented to them in such an effective manner; they were faithful to him because they were faithful to Christ in whose cause he labored so disinterestedly. Wo unto us preachers if we crowd ourselves in ahead of Christ in the hearts of our hearers, and get men to cling to our persons instead of clinging above all to Christ, and to us only for Christ's sake! — The result of Titus' report was: **so that I rejoiced yet the more.** No doubt the others also rejoiced greatly, but Paul rejoiced **the more,** *i. e.* for the feelings the Corinthians now bore to him. The mere report that the Corinthians had heeded his admonitions and rebukes would have made him rejoice; his joy was augmented beyond that by the personal features of the report he received. This explains the μᾶλλον better than to say that he now had joy rather than the sorrow he had before. — For a sermon on Laetare we can find no better joy to preach on than that of Paul over the repentant sinners in Corinth. May a similar joy be spread in all our congregations by their heeding the earnest rebukes and admonitions of faithful pastors! But the apostle does more than rejoice over the sorrow of Christian repentance in Corinth.

Paul points out its godly character.

There is some considerable difference among text-critics, translators, and therefore also commentators, as to the proper way of reading verses 8 and 9. The R. V. gives us the following: **For though I made you sorry with my epistle, I do not regret it, though I did regret; for I see that that epistle made you sorry, though but for a season. Now I rejoice, not that ye**

were made sorry, but that ye were made sorry unto repentance: for ye were made sorry after a godly sort, that ye might suffer loss by us in nothing. But the American Committee prefer that the whole be read as one sentence, and that in the following manner: "For though I made you sorry with my epistle, I do not regret it: though I did regret *it* (for I see that that epistle made you sorry, though but for a season), I now rejoice *etc.*" This was Luther's way of solving the problem of the text, and it is to be preferred as decidedly best. According to the R. V. Paul says that he is not sorry for having made the Corinthians sorry, and then gives us the reason: "for I see that that epistle made you sorry, though but for a season." But these words state no reason at all; moreover the "for" (γάρ) is questionable in the Greek. It is much better to take the sentence: "(for) I see *etc.*," as a parenthetical statement. Besides this the imperfect: εἰ καὶ μετεμελόμην, "though I did regret," stands in evident correlation with the following: νῦν χαίρω, "I now rejoice," and should not be separated from it; at the same time Paul's joy now explains why he does not regret having made the Corinthians sorry, their sorrow proving to be godly sorrow. The apostle's line of thought then is this: he does not regret — he did indeed for a time — he now rejoices, the sorrow of the Corinthians being of a godly character. — The apostle's great joy over the report of Titus that the Corinthians were full of great sorrow makes it decidedly necessary that he explain. How can he be so rejoiced and so comforted to hear of their sorrow? **For though I made you sorry with my epistle, I do not regret it.** Rejoicing as he does, he cannot indeed feel regret at having written them formerly as he did. Yet Paul admits: **though I did regret,** and the imperfect μετεμελόμην signifies that this regret lasted for a time. It was evidently during his time of anxiety while he was waiting for Titus and debating with himself as to the course he had pursued when he wrote his rebukes to the Corinthians. During this time he actually regretted what he had done. Some of the old commentators find a difficulty here. If Paul wrote by inspiration, wrote the very Word of God under the very special influence of the Holy Spirit, how could he have such regret? They try to explain this regret away. But they need not, for Paul was human as we are, and his inspiration did not extend to his thoughts and anxieties in the trying situations in which he was placed. The apostle was in the position of many a pastor who now, when he does what is entirely right in rebuking and disciplining his members, yet worries over his actions and debates whether he has done just the right thing or not, and thus is troubled with misgivings, doubts, and regrets for a time. Paul's admonition may serve as a comfort for us in such situations. — **For I see that that epistle made you sorry.** This is a parenthetical explanation. He sees ($\beta\lambda\epsilon\pi\omega$) it now since Titus has told him; before this he was in the dark and harassed by all manner of conjectures concerning the effect of his former letter. He tenderly adds: **though but for a season,** letting the Corinthians feel how he dislikes to make them sorry; and his present letter will certainly make them feel glad again. Titus too, no doubt, had already administered comfort in advance, though, of course, the Corinthians felt they had to have word from Paul himself. — Twice the apostle here mentions a former **epistle.** This is commonly taken to be the canonical First Epistle to the Corinthians, and together with the old exegetes some of the most prominent N. T. students of recent times adhere to this view (Hofmann, B. Weiss, Zahn, and others). The critical case, then, which caused the apostle so much anxiety, and concerning which he writes in our text, was that of the incestuous man mentioned in 1 Cor. 5. Others assume that the "epistle" here referred to by Paul was an extra-conical letter written some time between our two canonical Epistles, and lost not long after reaching its readers. Besides this letter some assume a visit of Paul to Corinth during this intervening period, either before or after the lost letter. This furnishes material for a variety of combinations and conjectures, all built on slender ground, and all impossible of any adequate measure of proof. Instead of the case of the incestuous man these scholars assume some other flagrant case in Corinth, one connected with most serious personal insult to the apostle; and this, they think, he is dealing with in the text before us. The old view, especially as it is fortified by the more recent N. T. scholars, has such a strong basis of proof, that we certainly cannot think of exchanging it for one of the many newer combinations now offered, resting so largely on mere ingenious conjecture. Least of all could we be satisfied to assume a flagrant case of personal insult to Paul as the subject of his statements in our text; such an assumption would require a different kind of proof than is at present forthcoming.* — Paul's regrets have vanished: **I now rejoice,** he writes, for all is clear to him now. Yet he adds: **not that ye were made sorry;** let them not think for a moment that their pain as such could delight him: **but that ye were made sorry unto repentance.** — Here we meet one of the most important words in the N. T.: μετάνοια, **repentance.** Its meaning in the writings of the apostles and evangelists, and in all Christian usage from the earliest times on, goes far beyond the conceptions of secular writers. The word is used in a wider and in a narrower sense, as our Confessions note: "The term 'repentance' is not employed in the Holy Scriptures in one and the same sense. For in some passages of Holy Scripture it is employed and understood with reference to the entire conversion of man, as Luke 13, 5: 'Except ye repent, ye shall all likewise perish.' And in chapter 15, 7: 'Likewise joy shall be in heaven over one sinner that repenteth.' But in Mark 1, 15, as also elsewhere, where a dis-

---

* The best outline of events regarding Paul and the Corinthian letters is the following: Paul visits Corinth about in the year 54 and during a stay of one and a half years founds a Christian congregation; he writes a letter to Corinth, which has not been preserved to us; he receives a letter from Corinth; he makes a second visit to Corinth, which proves painful; he writes the First Epistle (canonical) from Ephesus about Eastertime, in the year 57; he sends Titus to Corinth and meets him on his return in Macedonia, probably in Philippi; he there writes the Second Epistle, about 6 months after the First.

tinction is made between repentance and faith in Christ (Acts 20, 21) or between repentance and remission of sins (Luke 24, 46-47), repentance means to do nothing else than to truly acknowledge sins, from the heart regret them, and to abstain therefrom. This knowledge proceeds from the Law, but does not suffice for saving conversion to God, if faith in Christ be not added, whose merits the consolatory preaching of the holy Gospel offers to all penitent sinners who are terrified by the preaching of the Law. For the Gospel proclaims the forgiveness of sins, not to coarse and secure hearts, but to the bruised and penitent (Luke 4, 18). And that from repentance or the terrors of the Law despair may not result, the preaching of the Gospel must be added, that it may be repentance to salvation (2 Cor. 7, 10)." 590, 7-9. Repentance then may signify either *contrition* alone, or *contritition and faith* combined. The latter is the case in our text where Paul distinguishes the sorrow in a marked way from repentance: **ye were made sorry,** *i. e.* were grieved and made contrite, **unto repentance,** so that your being grieved leads to what is full and complete repentance. — And the reason why the sorrow of the Corinthians is really unto repentance is: **for ye were made sorry after a godly sort,** κατὰ θεόν, "after a godly manner" (A. V.), in accord with God, his mind and will. When Paul rebuked the Corinthians in his first Epistle, this was "according to God," and when the Corinthians were made sorry by the rebuke, this was likewise "according to God." — In both proceedings there was a divine intention, namely, **that ye might suffer loss by us in nothing.** God did not want the Corinthians damaged or punished in anything coming from the apostle and his helpers (ἐξ ἡμῶν), as some might imagine who did not understand the nature, purpose, and results of godly sorrow (note the subjective negative ἐν μηδενί). The very opposite was the case: the grieving of the Corinthians was to be for their greatest spiritual good. Sorrow like theirs is a blessing; not to have such sorrow is fearful damage and loss.

How this can be is now set forth in an explanation that

applies generally to all godly sorrow: **For godly sorrow worketh repentance unto salvation,** *a repentance* **which bringeth no regret: but the sorrow of the world worketh death.** Paul repeats the phrase κατὰ θεόν, and we see also by what follows that there are two distinct kinds of sorrow for sin, and naturally also two results of such sorrow, one ἡ κατὰ θεόν λύπη, "the sorrow according to God", the other a sorrow apart from God. **Godly sorrow** is not the sorrow, grief, remorse, or despair that sin itself produces when now it brings its dread consequences upon the sinner. There is an abundance of sorrow of this kind among sinners everywhere. Its fearful operation we see in the suicide of Judas Iscariot. There is nothing godly about this kind of sorrow, and it is not according to God's gracious will and intention. "Godly sorrow" (κατὰ θεόν) is always connected with God and produced by him. In godly sorrow the sinner may or may not feel some of the dread consequences of sin, one thing he does realize and feel, that he has offended God, broken his Law, incurred his displeasure and wrath, and it is this that plunges him into grief. So the blessed thing about this sorrow is that it **worketh repentance** (contrition combined with faith) as its proper result. It does this, of course, under the influence of the Law and the Gospel which are brought to bear upon the sinner. Godly sorrow is never apart from the Word of God. And such repentance is **unto salvation** (deliverance from sin, guilt, and the curse of both) through the blessed grace of God. The repentance does not produce or cause the salvation, that is God's work alone, but the salvation takes place only under the condition of repentance. Those who repent are saved, none else. And this applies as well to those who for the first time come to repentance as to those who have repented before, like the Corinthians, and then fallen again into sin. In fact, as Luther says in the first of his 95 Theses, when our Lord and Master Jesus Christ says that we are to repent *etc.,* he desires that the entire life of believers should be a repentance. The Bible furnishes many fine examples of such repentance, for instance David, whose great sins the prophet Nathan reproved; Peter, who denied Christ, but went out and wept bitterly; the malefactor on the cross, who there was brought for the first time to a proper confession of sin and received Christ's pardon. — It is a fine question whether ἀμεταμέλητον, **which bringeth no regret** modifies μετάνοιαν or σωτηρίαν. Its position would indicate the latter: "a salvation which bringeth no regret;" but both English versions, and many commentators, judging that the epithet applies better to repentance, connect accordingly: *a repentance* **which bringeth no regret,** "repentance not to be repented of" (which makes ἀμεταμέλητον = ἀμετανόητον), A. V. The preacher will naturally abide by the latter: repentance may be distressful, but as Paul did not regret having brought such distress upon the Corinthians, and as no preacher ought to regret doing the same thing to-day, so no repentant sinner will ever regret the sorrow of his repentance, because of the infinitely blessed results which follow. regret in this regard is only for those who would not repent. — **But the sorrow of the world worketh death.** Paul heightens the effect of his former statement by this conclusive contrast. There is bound to be sorrow for sin, either godly sorrow, or **the sorrow of the world** apart from God, such as is common among worldly men. This kind of sorrow does not grieve because it offended God, but because its sin is bringing its bitter, burning fruit, terrifying the conscience with its fearful accusations, filling the heart with dread and terror. If God is at all considered in such sorrow, it is only to rebel and rage against him and to make unreasonable and blasphemous demands of him (the impenitent malefactor on the cross!). Such sorrow also **worketh** something, it brings forth what always lies dormant in sin, namely **death,** the opposite of salvation, the very thing God would save us from, an eternal separation from God and life and blessedness. Repentance may be painful, humiliating, crushing, and all that, but it cannot compare with the eternal pain and terror of death. To be delivered from that is salvation indeed. Cain, King Saul, Judas, the impenitent malefactor, Herod (Acts 12, 23), and others furnish examples of the sorrow that worketh death. God grant us ever true repentance, the sorrow that leads to joy, life, and eternal salvation through the pardon in Christ's blood.

HOMILETICAL HINTS.

Rump begins his sermon by dwelling on the following contrasts: "Christianity looked at from a distance certainly appears to be full of contradictions. There is the little child in the manger —and it is called the eternal Son of God, angels singing his cradle-song. There is Jesus on the cross, numbered among transgressors — and yet he is the only righteous One amid all the unrighteous, the only One with a pure white soul in a world full of sinners. There is the Master, in the form of a servant, and with a crown of thorns — and yet he is the King to whom all power in heaven and earth belongs. His followers are ordinary people, men with rough coats, and rough hands, used to toil — and yet they are embassadors of God, a royal nation, like him who sent them. And now: there is stillness in Christian homes, stillness in Christian hearts, pulpit and altar are draped in black, for we are remembering One who died, we enter a death-chamber. And yet in the very midst of Lent, as we reach the height of the sacred season, there rings out, so that it may reach as far as possible, the cry: Laetare — rejoice, rejoice! Is it any wonder that those who stand afar find Christianity a world full of contradictions? — And yet the skilled eye sees how all the varied colors in a painting blend, how all the wandering lines in a Gobelin tapestry follow a hidden law, and finds delight in contemplating their mingling and their crossing. So all the contradictions disappear in the life of our Savior, and unite in the sweetest harmony, where we draw near and look with the eye of faith; and he who is truly keeping Lent in his heart will hear with grateful love and deep understanding the gracious call: Laetare — rejoice!"

Some of us will remember Drummond's book, which for a while became world-famous: "The Best Thing in the World." Many other books followed it, all with titles naming some superlative thing in the world. But here is this old,. old letter of St. Paul to the Corinthians, and it deals with two supreme things: the saddest thing in the world; and the most joyful thing in the world.

Never in all the long course of the world did a sinner of himself come to abominate his sin. Wherever and whenever a sinner did come to loathe his sin, it was God who caused him to do it.

Over against much superficial sorrow for sin it has well been said, a man must be sorry enough to quit. But quitting a certain sin is not yet conclusive evidence that the sorrow is of the right sort. Worldlings also quit, and yet lack Christian repentance.

When parents lose a beloved child, that is certainly sad, but how much sadder when the child lives and is spiritually lost. We understand the grief of the widow and orphan when the lifeless body of a dear father is lowered in the grave; but how much sadder for him to live, neglect and abuse his family, or rear his children in worldliness and ungodliness. We keep thinking that death is the saddest thing in the world, and it is really not death, but the sin which is the sting of death, and without which death would lose its dread. Our Savior wept tears when his friend Lazarus lay dead; but infinitely sadder were the tears which he wept over Jerusalem when he had to say of its people: "Ye would not!" What was the saddest thing Jesus experienced? Was it not the sin of Judas? Dead — O that may say very little. Blessed the poor pilgrim who has entered upon his rest! But if we must say: "Lost!" that indeed is the saddest, saddest thing in all the world. Riemer.

He also writes: Sin knows no mercy; it plunges man into misery until at last there is no escape. And that is the saddest thing in the world.

"There shall be joy in heaven over one sinner that repenteth," Luke 15, 7. "There is joy in the presence of the angels of God over one sinner that repenteth," Luke 7, 10. People who know nothing of true religion imagine repentance to be a terrible thing. Talk of repentance to them, and a secret dread takes hold of them; they see something dark, the death of all the joy and delight of life, the blotting out of all happiness and cheer. That too is one of the devil's deceptions. Repentance means escape from the dark shadow of guilt, deliverance from the fetters of tyranny, release from the dungeon of hopeless effort and despair; repentance saves, makes the heart free, joyous, happy, with a divine happiness that shall never end. Pity him who lives and dies without repenting. You need not bless him who lives and dies repenting — God does that and all the angels of heaven, they bear him up to the golden heights of eternal joy.

True repentance is found beneath the cross alone. No man can repent except the Gospel bring him God's pardon in Christ's blood when the law has struck him down with its curse. What melted the heart of Peter to tears, what but the pitying look of his thorn-crowned Savior? What brought the repentant confession from the malefactor's lips, what but the sight of the Savior hanging by his side, and the sound of the words he had heard from his lips.

The Godly Sorrow of Repentance.

It is
  I. *Wrought by the Word of God.*
  II. *Does the work of God.*
  III. *Attains the salvation of God.*
  IV. *Delights the children of God.*

The Two Kinds of Sorrow for Sin.

They differ:
  I. *In origin.*
    a) The one is due to the knowledge of sin.
    b) The other is due only to the damage caused by sin.
  II. *In manifestation.*
    a) The one grieves at offending God, abhors the wickedness of sin, longs for and seeks pardon.
    b) The other grieves at the hurt of sin, cares nothing for the wickedness of sin, and is unconcerned about pardon.
  III. *In results.*
    a) The one leads to repentance, attains pardon and peace, that is salvation.
    b) The other leads to vain evasions of the consequences of sin, sometimes to open despair, always to eternal death.
            After Dieffenbach.

The Repentance Not to be Repented of.

  I. *Either by him who helps cause it,*
  II. *Or by him in whom it is caused.*

The Joy of Godly Sorrow.

  I. *The sorrow which brings such joy.*
  II. *The joy which springs from such sorrow.*

The Pastor and Christian Discipline.

  I. *He faces the duty of it.*
  II. *He is bowed by the burden of it.*
  III. *He reaps the joy of it.*

How a Christian Congregation Ought to Receive Christian Discipline.

  I. *With due submission to the Word of God.*
  II. *With true repentance for past sins.*
  III. *With earnest amendment of life.*
  IV. *With heartfelt gratitude towards its pastor.*

JUDICA.

1 Pet. 1, 17-25.

After a fine introduction of blessing (verses 3-12) Peter begins the body of his Epistle with a number of positive admonitions (13-25), which he follows up with others of a negative character (2, 1 *etc.*). The first of these (13-16) we have used as a text for Oculi, and the following ones are now to occupy us. But we must note Peter's way of applying admonitions: he erects them upon the strongest kind of foundation, namely upon the saving acts of God. Sometimes the actual admonition is quite brief, while the description of what obligates us in the saving grace and blessings of God is extensive, elaborate, and rich. So here. There are really but two short admonitions, one to fear, and the other to love: "pass the time of your sojourning in fear;" "love one another from the heart fervently." All the rest of the eight verses forms the basis of these admonitions. And one of the divine deeds here described makes this a grand text for Lent, namely our redemption with the precious blood of Christ, so that our theme will be well taken if we say that *all who are redeemed by the precious blood of Christ and trust therein are bound to live in fear and love.* The text itself is divided accordingly.

Peter's lenten admonition to fear.

The admonition to hope in verse 13 and to holiness in verse 15 is followed (καί) by a third, to fear. And this like the others rests on a basis: **And if ye call on him as Father, who without respect of persons judgeth according to each man's work, pass the time of your sojourning in fear.** Peter would say that we have reason to walk in holy fear, if we call upon the great impartial Judge

432

as our Father. The sentence has the conditional form, εἰ
ἐπικαλεῖσθε, **if ye call upon,** but plainly implies that the condition is fulfilled, *i. e.* that Peter's readers do call upon the
Judge as Father, the conditional form being used to make
the words more impressive: "if you really do this, and mean
and understand what you are doing." To **call upon** God
as Father is to assume the position and perform the act of a
child. By praying to God as our Father we on our part
manifest that we are "children of obedience" (14), and our
calling upon God is the answer on our part to God's act in
first calling us (15). Thus Peter weaves together this new
admonition with the foregoing one; only here he emphasizes
something on our part (calling upon God), where first he
emphasized something on God's part (his calling us), the
two, of course, belonging together in this order. To call
upon God **as Father** looks like a reference to the Lord's
Prayer, although we cannot be entirely sure. It means, of
course, that we ask him to do a Father's part and give us
a Father's gifts in all that pertains to our lives. When we
remember that Peter wrote to Christians troubled by affliction, we understand the better why he referred to calling on
God, and what a privilege this meant to his readers. — The
object of ἐπικαλεῖσθε is τὸν ἀπροσωπολήμπτως κρίνοντα κατὰ τὸ
ἑκάστου ἔργον, **him who without respect of persons judgeth
according to each man's work,** and describes God as one
who is just and righteous, not partial, moved by personal
considerations, weakly sentimental, or who cannot be stern
and severe. The adverb ἀπροσωπολήμπτως, **without respect
of persons,** is from πρόσωπον, countenance or person, and
λαμβάνειν, to take or accept, with *a privativum;* personal
relations count a great deal with men, a mere face sometimes decides the entire case, but not so with God. You
may call yourself a child of his and claim special rights, but
this will not influence him. The mere cry, "Lord, Lord!"
will not move him, you must do his will, for, as Peter here
says, he **judgeth according to each man's work,** which
applies to every Christian as well as to every non-Christian.

28

He judges thus now (κρίνοντα, present tense), and always, and will do so at the final judgment on the last great day. — Usually the plural is used, God judges each man's "works;" the singular, **work,** here combines all our works into one, summarizing our lives as it were. God does not pick out a single work here and there, a few fair looking works, or a few faulty ones; he takes the real sum and substance of our lives, which as such is either a doing of his Gospel will or a rejection of it. There is no discrepancy between this judgment according to our work and the doctrine that we are accepted only through faith in Christ Jesus; for our "work" (ἔργον) is the outward expression of what animates the heart, and if faith is there, the life and "work" will be according, if faith is absent, the life or "work" will show it. God himself sees and knows both fully, the "work" and the faith (or its absence), but he pronounces judgment according to the "work," because that is manifest to all, an evidence which all can see and on the basis of which all can and therefore must approve the divine judgment. — But if thus our lives lie open before God and are judged impartially by him, we, who claim to be the children of such a God and ask him to do a Father's part by us, have all reason to do what Peter calls upon us to do: **pass the time of your sojourning in fear** (ἀναστράφητε, passive aorist imperative). **The time of your sojourning** is the time of dwelling here as strangers. We are strangers and pilgrims on earth, our true home is in heaven where we shall dwell as citizens forever. While thus we live on earth in a strange land we must pass the time **in fear,** not indeed the fear of slaves which is cast out by love (1 John 4, 18), nor merely the awe in which the creature must stand of the infinite Creator, but the fear which is the opposite of security and lightness or indifference of the mind, the fear which recognizes that the all-just Judge must condemn evil in whomsoever found. Calvin: *Timor securitati opponitur.* So Peter writes a second time, 2, 17: "Fear God;" and Paul agrees with him: "Let us cleanse ourselves from all defilement of flesh and spirit, perfecting holiness in the

fear of God," 2 Cor. 7, 1. In other words, we must constantly bear in mind whom we are calling Father, lest that
Father, who is an impartial Judge, after all be compelled
to disown and disinherit us. As long as we sojourn as
pilgrims in a strange land, beset with temptations and assailed even by our own flesh, this true and proper fear dare
not leave our hearts. Barnabas, one of the apostolic fathers,
writes: "Let us be careful lest we yield to slothful rest
and go to sleep in our sins, after we have already been
called, so that the evil one may not get us into his power,
awaken us and exclude us from the kingdom of God."
There is a true Christian and evangelical fear which old
Quenstedt describes: "The apostle does not mean that we
are to fear lest we be not in God's grace, but lest we fall
from grace. Fear is the opposite of security, not of joyful
faith, and we do not reject the fear of vigilance and caution
which is afraid of insulting God and falling into the danger
of forsaking him, but we reject the fear that is due to
doubt."

A second motive is added to the first: **knowing that
ye were redeemed, not with corruptible things, with
silver or gold, from your vain manner of life handed
down from your fathers; but with precious blood, as of
a lamb without blemish and without spot,** *even the blood*
of Christ. To catch the force and purpose of these and the
following words we must note that the admonition to fear is
in integral connection with the preceding admonition: Christians should gird up their loins (13), put away former
lusts (14), and walk in holiness and in fear of God, since
they know with what price they have been redeemed. The
substance of what they should fear is thus plain without
further specification, which leaves the more room emphatically to set forth why they should fear. The price of
our redemption requires it; he who falls into security,
careless indifference, or who openly disregards the will of
God, he can do so only by counting his redemption cheap
and not worth while; to value that redemption aright must
mean that we exercise the most earnest care and caution

in preserving what this redemption has brought us. Thus
all that Peter says in regard to the price of our redemption
is connected with the admonition to fear, which is de
cidedly to be preferred to the other connection which some
commentators attempt, namely with the admonition to
brotherly love in verse 22. — **Knowing,** εἰδότες, is in the
sense of: "since ye know," and includes a proper consideration and estimate of the thing known, namely the price of
our redemption. That this was **not with corruptible things**
is put forward for emphasis, and all corruptible things are
meant, two of which are at once mentioned: not **with silver
or gold,** since indeed these are considered very valuable by
men, and are also frequently used in paying a ransom. The
reason why no such price was paid is evidently because it
would never have been accepted, being absolutely insuf-
ficient. This applies even to the Jewish sacrifices which
were offered according to divine arrangement.

> "Not all the blood of beasts,
> On Jewish altars slain,
> Could give the guilty conscience peace,
> Or wash away the stain.
>
> But Christ, the heavenly Lamb,
> Takes all our sins away;
> A sacrifice of nobler name
> And richer blood than they."

The verb **ye were redeemed,** ἐλυτρώθητε, is here used in its
full native meaning, to free by the payment of a λύτρον, a
price or ransom. This is the more apparent since Peter
states plainly both what we were ransomed from, and what
the λύτρον itself was. "The Son of man came . . . to
give his life a ransom for many, λύτρον ἀντὶ πολλῶν;" Titus
2, 14; 1 Tim. 2, 6; Col. 1, 14; Rom. 3, 24. "Ye were bought
with a price," 1 Cor. 6, 20. — This ransom freed us **from
the vain manner of life handed down from your fathers;**
Peter means the life "according to your former lusts in
the time of your ignorance," verse 14. He is addressing
Christians who have not only been redeemed (objectively),

but have actually come into possession of the blessed release and freedom of this redemption (subjectively). The
old manner of life is called **vain,** empty, useless, because it
leads to nothing good.   It comes to us by inheritance,
handed down from your fathers, πατροπαράδοτος, and so
is the opposite of the new birth which brings "an inheritance incorruptible and undefiled and that fadeth not away,"
verses 3-4. Peter does not say in so many words that we
are all born in original sin, but it is evident that we all
follow in the sinful footsteps of our fathers not merely
because of our training, education, and their example, but
because the very nature handed down to us by our fathers
is infected with sin.   This also involves that no man of
himself is able to cast off the bondage and free himself; all
are bound closely together, one generation passes its bondage on to the next.   No wonder that to free us a far greater
and different kind of ransom than "corruptible things" was
required. — We were redeemed, not with corruptible things,
but with precious blood, and the apostle puts the word
forward, thus emphatically stating the ransom paid for us.
The word **blood** in itself already, and certainly because of
what follows, is shed blood, and points to the death of
Christ by violence.   Its preciousness is especially stated,
because this made it a sufficient and effective ransom.
Precious is the blood that redeemed us because it is the
blood **of Christ,** God's own Son who offered himself as our
substitute.   Paul brings this out when he urges the bishops
of Ephesus "to feed the Church of God, which he purchased (acquired) with his own blood," Acts 20, 28.   The
preciousness is in the greatness of the Person who gave
his blood.   When God's Son poured out his blood, a ransom of infinite value was offered.   The genitive Χριστοῦ
modifies τιμίῳ αἵματι, and is amplified by ὡς ἀμνοῦ ἀμώμου καὶ
ἀσπίλου.   Both the mention of blood and of the Lamb as a
means of redemption shows that the ransom was by way of
sacrifice, and therefore a transaction with God.   Shed as a
sacrifice for sinners the blood redeemed us. — **As of a lamb
without blemish and without spot** indicates a likeness

Judica.

divinely intended and typical. In the old covenant the sinner who had broken the law and incurred guilt before God was released by the sacrifice of a lamb that had no blemish, Lev. 19, 22; *etc.* In the same way the Lamb of God, which God himself provided, was slain for all the sinners of the world, and by his holy, precious blood, and his innocent suffering and death all their guilt was cancelled. Peter writes **a lamb,** and thus refers in a general way to the Jewish sacrifice of lambs, including of course the Passover lambs. In the old covenant these were a visible and constantly repeated promise of God, that a blood-ransom, actually able to do what the blood of animals could only typify and picture, would be forthcoming at last; and in the fulness of time this Lamb of God, in the highest and holiest sense "without blemish and without spot," poured out its precious ransoming blood.

Peter adds another feature which helps to show his readers the greatness of the ransom paid for them, and at the same time he connects what Christ did for all men, in a special way with his readers as believers in Christ, thus showing their obligation to walk worthy of their redemption. He says of Christ: **who was foreknown indeed before the foundation of the world, but was manifested at the end of the times for your sake, who through him are believers in God, which raised him from the dead, and gave him glory; so that your faith and hope might be in God.** We have met the verb προγινώσκειν in Rom. 8, 29 in the text for New Year's Day. Here Peter uses the perfect passive participle προεγνωσμένος ("having been foreknown") of Christ, the anointed Redeemer and his sacrifice: **who was foreknown indeed,** namely as such, by the mind of God, **before the foundation of the world,** *i. e.* before the first beginnings of creation. The verb expresses an activity of God's mind, not of his will, although it is often coupled with the thought of affection: "lovingly foreknow." It is a mistake to read into it the idea of predestine, foreordain, decree, or elect, for all which the Scriptures have distinct terms. Peter might indeed have said of Christ that he was predestined or foreordained or elected as the Christ, which would be entirely true. Connected with God's foreknowledge there are necessarily other coördinate activities, especially the decisions of his will. These may precede or they may follow his foreknowledge, as the case may be; but however closely related to it, they are not the foreknowledge itself. In regard to Christ and his sacrifice the foreknowledge of God rested on his gracious decision and decree to send him as our Redeemer; because God so decreed, he foreknew. Yet the two activities are clearly distinct, as Peter himself shows in Acts 2, 23, where he speaks of Christ's deliverance into his sacrificial death "by the determinate counsel and" (resting on this βουλή) "foreknowledge of God." In the same way God's "foreordination" in regard to Christ is spoken of, but without mention of the foreknowledge, Acts 4, 28. Burger points to the selection of the Passover lambs four days in advance of their slaughter, and says that thus Christ was foreknown before his sacrificial death. And Besser remarks that Christ's reconciling sacrifice was seen of God as eternally present. Brenz has the fuller statement: "The eye of God sees history in an entirely different way from the eye of flesh. God's eye sees everything in an instant. If in the eyes of God Christ had not already existed as the One incarnate, dead, and glorified in the time of Adam and Abraham, the patriarchs could never have obtained forgiveness of sins and justification." The foreknowledge of God in regard to Christ is connected with his foreknowledge concerning all who believe in him, although in them the foreordination follows the foreknowledge, while in the former it precedes. — Peter combines and contrasts the foreknowledge on the one hand (μέν) and the manifestation of Christ in time on the other (δέ): **but was manifested at the end of the times.** This manifestation is the visible appearance of the Redeemer to accomplish his redemptive sacrifice. It implies his pre-existence before this appearance, although he became the Messiah and actually rendered the sacrifice only in his manifestation. The adjective ἔσχατον is used as a noun, and **the end of the times** embraces the entire era from the first coming of Christ to his second coming; compare Heb. 1, 1; Acts 2, 17. Surely, the blood of him who was thus foreknown of God and manifested in the fulness of time has a preciousness which outranks utterly that of all corruptible things, and is able to serve as a ransom for our souls. And we who know and consider this properly are bound to prize our redemption so as to walk in fear in order that no fault of ours may make us lose our blessing. — The apostle now connects the manifestation of Christ as the Redeemer with his readers: he was foreknown and manifested **for your sake** (and thus for the sake of us all), **who through him are believers in God.** Christ indeed rendered his sacrifice for all men, but its blessed object is attained only in those who believe, and so it is properly said that for their sake Christ was foreknown and manifested. God's love was thus centered especially upon believers. But those who believe do so only **through him;** he with his saving work has produced in them faith and trust **in God,** and this is the God, **which raised him from the dead, and gave him glory.** The construction πιστοί or πιστεύω εἰς is frequent in the N. T., especially in John's writings. God is here described as the God of salvation by bringing forward those acts by which he set his seal of approval and acceptance upon Christ's sacrificial death. He raised him who for our sins went into the grave from death and lifted him to eternal glory. Heb. 13, 20; 2, 9-10. Both statements refer to the human nature of Christ, and thus rightly mention the agency of God. In both all the grace of God toward us comes out mightily, justifying our faith in him completely and setting before us the most glorious hope. — This the apostle mentions especially: **so that your faith and hope might be in God,** i. e. both combined. But the clause: ὥστε τὴν πίστιν ὑμῶν καὶ ἐλπίδα εἶναι εἰς θεόν, may also be translated: "so that your faith is also hope in God," which Meyer, Besser, and Burger prefer. Stoeckhardt prefers the other rendering, making faith refer to the raising of

Christ and hope to his glorification in a *parallelismus membrorum;* but faith and hope rest alike on Christ's resurrection and glorification, which destroys the supposed parallel. The emphasis is on hope as directed to God, even as our faith rests on him. We are sojourners here, as Peter has said in verse 17, and must walk in fear in order that we may not miss the glorious goal of our hope which Christ by his sacrifice, accepted of God, has set before us in God.

Peter's lenten admonition to love.

Peter closed the admonition to fear with a reference to faith and hope; it is natural that he should also speak of love, especially as this is one of the cardinal Christian virtues. He does it in an elaborate admonition similar to the one on fear, connecting with the admonition itself those vital considerations which move the heart to willing and joyful obedience. **Seeing ye have purified your souls in your obedience to the truth unto unfeigned love of the brethren, love one another from the heart fervently.** The imperative ἀγαπήσατε is preceded by the perfect participle ἡγνικότες: **seeing that ye have purified your souls,** or "'having purified." This purification must precede the love, for love is one of the results of it, and it must be a thing fixed and established once for all (hence the perfect participle, and not the aorist). For us Christians the thing is settled: we have purified our souls through faith in the Redeemer's sacrifice and by means of his cleansing blood. The participle refers to the act of believers who cleanse their souls **in obedience to the truth,** *i. e.* when they become and remain obedient to the saving truth of redemption in Christ's blood; the ἐν denotes the sphere. The truth is a realm of purity; he who has entered there and dwells there in obedience cannot continue in impurity. The A. V. adds: "through the Spirit," who is the author of all sanctification. "Here Peter offers the right remedy, namely obedience of the truth in the Spirit. This is the right help, besides which you will find none that is able to hush all evil thoughts. For when this gets into the heart, all evil inclination soon leaves.

Try it who will, you will always find it so, and they who
have tried it know it well . . . Therefore it is not
enough to preach and hear the Gospel but once, we must
continually impress it; for the Word has this grace. that the
oftener we handle it, the sweeter it becomes; although it is
always one and the same doctrine of faith, one cannot hear it
too often, unless the hearts be presumptuous and coarse."
Luther. — **Unto unfeigned love of the brethren** points
out the special side of the obedience, which Peter has in
mind and recalls the strong admonitions of Christ to love
our fellow disciples. Love of the brethren is one of the
vital points of faith in Christ. But this love must be **unfeigned,** without sham and deception: "My little children,
let us not love in word, neither with the tongue, but in deed
and truth," 1 John 3, 18.— While Christians have indeed
purified their souls and thus love each other, there is still
need of the admonition: **love one another,** for our brotherly
love, once begun, obligates us to continuance, and needs
constant stimulation and exercise, lest it grow slack and fail
to develop properly. The emphasis is therefore on the
modifiers: **from the heart fervently;** our love must come
"from the heart" as the expression of our real being, glowing
with real tenderness and affection toward our brethren; at
the same time it must be earnest, full of strong endeavor and
constant readiness ($\dot{\epsilon}\kappa\tau\epsilon\nu\tilde{\omega}s$, straining itself to constant effort). We must not grow weak in the exercise of love, or
stop at rebuffs, especially when some occasion puts us to
the test, as perhaps when our love is not properly appreciated and no return is made. This strength of love lies also
in the aorist imperative $\dot{\alpha}\gamma\alpha\pi\dot{\eta}\sigma\alpha\tau\epsilon$, which is more emphatic
and imperative than the present tense would be (Winer
43, 4).

A second motive is now added to impress the
apostle's admonition: **having been begotten again, not
of corruptible seed, but of incorruptible, through the
word of God, which liveth and abideth. For,**

All flesh is as grass,
And all the glory thereof as the flower of grass.

**The grass withereth, and the flower falleth:
But the word of the Lord abideth for ever.**
**And this is the word of good tidings which was preached
unto you.** Two things are here emphasized, first, *the
fact* of our regeneration which makes possible and at the
same time requires what Peter asks; secondly, *the means* of
our regeneration, the living Word of God, which produces
a life the very nature of which is to possess and exercise
love. Stoeckhardt therefore rightly says: "We Christians
would forget and deny our very nature, if we withdrew our
love and sympathy from our brethren." Parallel with the
active perfect participle ἡγνικότες in verse 22, referring to an
activity on our part, now comes the perfect passive participle
ἀναγεγεννημένοι, **having been begotten again,** which refers to
the divine activity lying behind the other. Only they have
purified themselves who have been begotten again to the life
which makes them children of God and puts them into communion with God. The natural power, impulse, and inclination of this life is to love those who are one with us in
having the same life, being members of the same spiritual
household and family, with the same Father in Christ Jesus.
And so the requirement must be made of us: "Love one another fervently!" — But the apostle adds in an emphatic
manner: **not of corruptible seed, but of incorruptible.**
Just as we have been redeemed by Christ "not with corruptible things," but with the "precious blood" of Christ, so we
have been regenerated by the Holy Ghost, "not of corruptible seed, but of incorruptible." "Corruptible seed brings
forth flesh unto death; the incorruptible seed of life, in
which the Holy Ghost is active, changes us into its own
kind: we are born again to be children of God through the
Word of God." Besser. This incorruptible seed is **the
word of God,** *i. e.* the Gospel of Jesus Christ, **the word
of good tidings which was preached unto you,** τὸ ῥῆμα τὸ
εὐαγγελισθὲν εἰς ὑμᾶς, announced unto us as good news. Christ
himself calls the Word the seed in his parable of the Sower.
It is seed because when it enters the human heart it brings
forth life there, the spiritual life of faith, which makes man

a new being, a very child of God. — Of this Word Peter says: it **liveth and abideth,** or as the Isaiah quotation has it: "The word of the Lord abideth for ever." The margin offers the translation: through the word of God, *who liveth and abideth,* drawing the adjectives to the word "God," instead of to "the word;" but the quotation following shows that this is not the apostle's intention, for he emphasizes, not that God, but that his Word abideth for ever; and the position of σῶντος before θεοῦ likewise indicates that it does not go with this word, but with λογοῦ before it. Heb. 4, 12 says of the Word that it is "living and active;" and Jesus said: "Heaven and earth shall pass away, but my words shall not pass away," Matth. 24, 35. — The apostle first uses the preposition ἐκ, **of,** or "out of" not corruptible, but incorruptible seed; and then, when he mentions the seed itself, the Word, he uses διά, **through.** In substance there is no difference, only the first preposition expresses the origin of the new life, that out of which it springs, and the second the means by which it is wrought and through which it is enkindled. So the Word itself lives and grows in us and gives its own spiritual and heavenly nature to us; and again it brings forth the new life in us and nourishes and strengthens it. — The abiding nature of the Word (and by implication also of the life which it produces) is emphasized by a quotation from Is. 40, 6-8, following the Septuagint, with a slight deviation. A simple διότι, **for,** introduces the quotation, which the apostle evidently intends as an illustrative proof, a word from the ancient prophet saying identically the same thing that the apostle is here bringing out. By means of a fine simile Isaiah shows the difference between what is corruptible and what is incorruptible. **All flesh is as grass,** and flesh alone is what corruptible seed is able to bring forth, for like always produces like. By **flesh** the prophet means man as he is in his transient condition and life on earth. The comparison is heightened by the parallel statement: **And all the glory thereof,** its excellence and magnificence. or as the Hebrew reads: its "goodliness," beauty, attractiveness, **as the flower of grass.** The life of grass culminates in its tasselled flower; and both it and the grass from which it shoots up — how transient are they. So is . man in his natural condition and all that his life of itself is able to bring forth, its beauty, strength, riches, honor, art, education, learning, virtue, greatness, and the like. **The grass withereth, and the flower falleth,** ἐξηράνθη . . . ἐξέπεσεν (two aorists), "is withered . . . fallen." Not these aorists, as Stoeckhardt thinks, but the entire statements express a universal experience. In this very transitoriness all flesh and its glory are like the grass. Nothing more abiding is corruptible seed able to produce; the grass that grows from such seed teaches us who are like the grass, born also from corruptible seed, a mighty lesson. — But now comes the contrast, a seed that is not corruptible, the seed of which all the children of God are born: **But the word of the Lord,** in the Hebrew and the Septuagint: "the word of God," **abideth for ever.** It is as imperishable, as unchanging, as God himself. "The Word is an eternal divine power. For although the sound and speech of it disappears, its kernel, that is its meaning, its truth, which the voice expresses, remains. Just as when I place a cup containing wine to my lips, I drink the wine down, but I do not plunge the cup down my throat. So also is the Word which the voice conveys, it falls into the heart and becomes living, although the voice remains outside and disappears. Thus indeed it is a divine power. It is God himself." Luther. — In a terse and striking way Peter drives home and applies the chief point in the prophet's words to his readers: **And this is the word of good tidings which was preached unto you,** preached so that it entered your hearts and regenerated you, imparting its life and permanence, overcoming what is corruptible and perishing and must end in eternal death, by placing in its stead what is incorruptible and heavenly and shall dwell with God forever. It is for us then to rejoice in our redemption and in our regeneration, ever to remember the price of the former and the power of the Word in the latter, so that living in fear and exercising our new life in love, all the gracious work of God for us and in us may reach its fullest and most blessed fruition.

HOMILETICAL HINTS.

"We must all be made manifest before the judgment-seat of Christ; that each one may receive the things done in the body, according to what he hath done, whether it be good or bad." 2 Cor. 5, 10. Therefore be on your guard, that you may stand at the day of his appearance. Watch and pray! The spirit is willing, but the flesh is weak!

Fear — this hardly meets our expectation regarding the new life. We generally suppose that fear has been cast out of the hearts that call God Father. But this mark of the new life is connected with the alternations between confidence in ourselves and confidence in God. Peter reminds us how great was the price of our redemption. This is bound to give us serious thoughts. Sin is no small fault, easily to be corrected, to be paid for by silver or gold or a few acts of virtue on our part. The precious blood of Christ had to be poured out for our redemption. The more we value this, the greater will our fear be, lest it be poured out in vain for us, lest it be preached to us in vain and fail of the effect which it ought to produce in our lives. Since God has done such great things for us, we may well dread that most shameful sin, ingratitude. Since the preaching of the cross of Christ has planted into our hearts the tender heavenly plant of a new life, we may well tremble in fear lest we ourselves crush it, or smother it. We fear nothing whatever on God's part, but we do fear everything on our own part, and therefore also for ourselves. This is not the fear of an evil conscience, nor of a cowardly slave, but the fear of an awakened conscience and of a child of grace most deeply concerned for the love of his Father. It is Paul himself, looking back upon his past course and realizing that God works all in all, who for this very reason bids us work out our salvation with fear and trembling; for it is God who worketh in us both to will and to do, according to his good pleasure. It is the new life that makes us really in earnest regarding our confidence in God. Riemer.

Christians can indeed become holy. But not as though some fine day they could be finished saints in whom sins could pro-

duce no more temptation. There are still confused enthusiasts
in our own day who proclaim such a doctrine of perfectionism,
consider themselves sinless, and do not see that in the very
instant when they place the halo of sanctity about their own
brows, they are sinning. No; Christians are not perfect and
complete saints; certainly not. Nevertheless they are saints in
the making. Rump.

To know indeed that we are saved with precious blood, the
blood of the Lamb without blemish and without spot, puts that
into our hearts which from within creates an entirely new life
in us. What is this? Faith.

The new life is not produced by a change in the outward
mode of life, but by a change in the inner direction of life. This
cannot be produced by the simple word of man, nor can it be
caused by the very finest example. Peter calls the Word which
makes this change a living Word. It must be a word full of
Spirit and life. It must penetrate into the innermost heart and
conscience, but not as a sword — that would produce death —
but as a seed that penetrates the ground, strikes root, breaks
the earth's crust and brings forth a new life. — The law is also
God's Word, but it is not like seed, but rather like a plowshare
or a harrow, penetrating indeed deeply, but able to do only the
preparatory work, loosening the soil of the heart and making
it receptive. Riemer.

A poor negro was once bought by a kind Englishman for
twenty pieces of gold on the slave-market and then given his
freedom besides a sum of money with which to buy a piece of
land and establish a home for himself. "Am I really free?" he
cried in great joy, "and may I go where I please?" "Then I
will be your slave, Massa," he declared. You have paid the
price for me, to you I owe everything; please, make me your
slave." The man was deeply touched and took the negro into
his service. He never had a more devoted servant. "But," said
he, "I ought to learn something from this devoted and grateful
servant of mine, something that I have not sufficiently appreciated
hitherto, namely what the apostle means when he writes: Know
that ye were redeemed, not with corruptible silver and gold,
but with the precious blood of Christ."

A slave's child is always only a slave, deprived of its freedom from the first day of its life till the last. And the strange
thing is that they who live in the slave-quarters of sin and constantly hear the rattle of their chains and the crack of their
driver's whip, find nothing surprising in the sounds, nor look
astonished when they see their children in exactly the same con-

dition. The great marvel is that one should come and lay down his own life's blood to make these slaves free and transfer them into a new and blessed existence.

Only God's eternal plan of salvation assures us of the comfort and deliverance we need. If the paschal lamb had to be chosen in advance, here is the Lamb of God that bears the sins of the world, chosen long before the Baptist stretched out his hand and exclaimed: Behold, the Lamb of God! long before Isaiah saw the Lamb led to the slaughter and not opening his mouth, yea, long before God himself in Paradise promised our first parents the seed of the woman who should crush the serpent's head and in doing so suffer his heel to be bruised. Before the foundations of the world were laid, our salvation was complete in the mind of God. This is what makes us feel assured and certain.

New life is found, only where the old life of selfishness is thoroughly overcome. Often the very love of the natural man is the most selfish and loveless thing about him. It flows from an impure heart, because it seeks only its own advantage and enjoyment. These are the admixtures which make it impure. True love of the brethren is to be the mark of the new life in the Christian. But if we arrange our love according to whether a person loves us, or does what pleases us, or wears our party colors, or thanks and rewards us, or what other reasons there may be, then is our love tainted with the evil of worldly loves. The pure love of a Christian heart is always obedient to the truth, prompted by the Word and Spirit of God, doing the works of love for Christ's sake, who first loved us; and loving especially those who with us love him as their Lord and Savior. Let God's Word and true faith meet in a heart, and it will blossom all over with brotherly love, the sweet odor of which will envelop the entire life.

John the Constant, Elector of Saxony had the initial letters of his motto, V. D. M. I. Æ. (*Verbum Domini manet in æternum*) inscribed on his coins and embroidered on the garments of his servants. Whenever misgivings assailed his heart at thought of the great opposition to the true church and the Gospel, he whispered these words to himself. When the Archbishop of Salzburg mocked him, saying that no doubt the Elector thought the Word of the Lord remained in the sleeves (*Aermel*) of his servants, the latter aptly replied: "Your Grace is mistaken; the letters mean: *Verbum diaboli manet in episcopis* — The devil's word abides in the bishops!"

Consider the Precious Price of Your Redemption!

I. *Its value in what it brings you — do not lose it!*
   a) It is more than silver and gold can buy.
   b) It is deliverance from the curse and bondage of your fathers.
   c) It is faith and hope in God as your Father.
   d) Therefore walk in fear, lest the Father who redeemed you through the Son, must condemn you nevertheless.

II. *Its value in what it makes of you — do not hinder it.*
   a) Children of God by redemption.
   b) Partakers of the incorruptible life through the incorruptible Word.
   c) Obedient children of the truth.
   d) Therefore walk in love, that the newness of your life may appear before God and men, and especially also your brethren.

Read in the Precious Blood of the Lamb the Pricelessness of Your Salvation.

I. *Before the foundation of the world God ordained that Lamb and his blood for your salvation.*

II. *In the last times that Lamb without blemish and without spot was offered for your salvation.*

III. *That Lamb and his blood makes the Word of God the incorruptible seed for your salvation.*

IV. *By faith in the blood of the Lamb you are freed from your former vain conversation.*

V. *By faith in the blood of the Lamb you are born again to a life of obedience to the truth.*

VI. *In this faith you must walk in fear and in love, and thus continue in salvation.*

Your Faith in the Triune God of Salvation a Reason for Self-Examination.

I. *You believe in God the Father; therefore I ask you: Do you walk in the fear of God?*

II. *You believe in God the Son; therefore I ask you: Do you walk in the love of Christ and his brethren?*

III. *You believe in God the Holy Spirit; therefore I ask you: Do you walk in obedience to the truth of the Spirit?*

29   C. C. Hein.

The note accompanying our text, as originally selected, reads: "The precious blood of Christ." It may well serve as our theme:

The Precious Blood of Christ.

I. *Divine.*
II. *Redemptive.*
III. *Sanctifying.*

Luther's explanation of each commandment: "We should fear and love God."

The Evangelical Motives of Fear and Love.

I. *Our redemption through the precious blood of Christ.*
II. *Our regeneration through the living Word of the Lord.*

Who Has Redeemed Me, a Lost and Condemned Creature, Purchased and Won Me.

I. *From all sins, from death, and from the power of the devil,*
II. *Not with gold or silver, but with his holy, precious blood, and with his innocent suffering and death,*
III. *That I may be his own, and live under him in his kingdom, and serve him in everlasting righteousness, innocence, and blessedness.*

PALM SUNDAY.

Heb. 12, 1-6.

The homiletical worker will at once see the appropriateness of a text on *perseverance* or steadfastness for Palm Sunday. The subjects treated thus far in our lenten cycle are now rounded out to a symmetrical whole: the boldness of faith, unworldliness, holiness, repentance, fear and love, and now, to complete it, faithfulness to the end. The day itself, devoted throughout the Lutheran Church to the solemn rite of Confirmation, in all its associations requires a subject of this kind. It is offered here in our epistle text which meets these requirements in the very finest way. As in the old gospel text with Jesus riding into Jerusalem, and in the Eisenach gospel text with Jesus anointed at Bethany, so here Jesus stands out prominently as "the author and finisher of our faith," from whom our faithful perseverance must be drawn. His grace gives us strength, and his example furnishes us inspiration. Where the old gospel shows us the fickle multitude, and the Eisenach gospel only one heart with full insight and truth, there we have in our epistle text "a cloud of witnesses," who have all proved steadfast to the end and now point us to the crown of victory which we too may attain. Various fine images lie embedded in the text: we are to run the race, to resist to the blood, to be sons submissive to a father's chastening. A number of fine phrases invite the preacher's skill in formulating the theme and divisions of his sermon; and withal the message of the text is so plain and so pertinent that it cannot but make a deep impression if at all adequately handled. We are bidden first of all to run the race and not grow weary, and secondly not to faint when reproved.

Let us run the race and not grow weary.

The eleventh chapter of Hebrews unrolls before us
the grandest examples of enduring and triumphing faith,
and the opening words of the twelfth chapter connect
the admonitions which now follow most intimately with
that glorious line of examples. **Therefore let us also,
seeing we are compassed about with so great a cloud of
witnesses, lay aside every weight, and the sin which
doth so easily beset us, and let us run with patience the
race that is set before us.** Only twice does the New
Testament use the strong and grand-sounding connective
τοιγαροῦν, **therefore,** here and in 1 Thess. 4, 8. The
eleventh chapter deserves that the strongest kind of an *ergo*
should follow it. The τοι is affirmative of the matter in
hand, γάρ argumentative, and οὖν draws an emphatic conclusion. The καὶ ἡμεῖς, "we also," ranges all the Christian
readers of this Epistle alongside of those glorious, triumphant saints of old, for ours is the same faith, the same
strength, the same conflict, the same crown. The A. V. is
incorrect in translating: "we also are compassed about with
so great a cloud of witnesses," since the holy writer does not
mean that the faithful believers mentioned in chapter
eleven were so encompassed. The correct rendering is:
seeing (or since) **we are compassed about with so great
a cloud of witnesses.** The figure of **a cloud** for a vast
multitude is common among Greek as well as other writers.
By νέφος is meant a mass of cloud covering the heavens,
without outlines, and so differing from νεφέλη, a detached
and sharply outlined cloud. We must note the grandness
connected with the word here used. God's children on
earth are but a "little flock," but God's children through the
ages are a tremendous host indeed. Chapter eleven mentions by name only the most illustrious O. T. believers, then
summarizes, and tells us that there are many more; we know
besides that the N. T. era has been even more prolific of the
very finest examples of faith and faithfulness. The cloud of
witnesses is far greater now than when Hebrews was written. Ἔχοντες περικείμενον is well translated: "are compassed

about," because the two words, while each has its own
grammatical construction, really belong together as expressive of the verb thought. The μάρτυρες are **witnesses,** not of
our faith and actions, but of faith itself, just as we now are
to be witnesses of faith, proving that we indeed are such, by
our faithfulness. In 11, 2; 4; 5 and 39 the passive is used:
they had witness borne to them through their faith. This
idea of the faith still governs when now these believers are
themselves termed witnesses; for we are admonished to run
the race looking to Jesus as the author and finisher τῆς
πίστεως, of the faith. Delitzsch and others make these witnesses "spectators" of our faith, or at least combine this
idea with the other, even picturing the arena in which we are
to run as surrounded like a vast amphitheater with wit-
nessing spectators, or, if heaven is chosen as the place they
occupy, lining closely the ramparts of heaven and leaning
over to watch our running. But these ideas are an importation, and while atttractive and dramatic in a way, harbor
spiritualistic notions, as if the spirits of the dead still hover
over and around us; against everything of this kind we must
be on our guard. The souls of the saints are at rest and no
longer taken up with the trials occurring on earth; the
Scriptures teach that they behold the heavenly glories,
but say nothing of their beholding and watching events
on earth. Speculations in this direction are decidedly
unsafe. — The first participial clause, which is causal
("seeing, or since, we are compassed"), is followed
by a second, which is instrumental: "having laid aside,"
or "by having laid aside," ἀποθέμενοι, aorist: **lay aside every
weight, and the sin which doth so easily beset us.** To run
the race it is certainly necessary that we first put away
every weight, or *all cumbrance* (margin), whatever would
impede or stop our free action in running. The term is entirely general and refers to anything that hinders the Christian's progress of faith. This may be one thing for one person, and another for the next; Bengel thinks of pride, others
of cares, of worldly place and position, of worldly ways, *etc.*
The preacher is free to make whatever application his hear-

ers may especially need. **the sin which doth so easily beset us** is sin in general as outside of us. The qualifying εὐπερίστατον has been variously interpreted, as in all Greek literature the word appears only here (εὖ, readily, deftly; περίστημι, to place itself around, middle voice). Some think of the clinging folds of a garment; compare the marginal translation: *which doth closely cling to us;* but it is better to think of sin as standing in our way to block our course in running. That this sin invites us with its joys, as the second marginal rendering implies: *which is admired of many,* goes beyond the etymology of the word. The holy writer wants us to get rid of two evils: the burden that is upon us, and the hindrance that puts itself into our way. For the latter the translation: "which doth so easily beset us" is excellent, only it does not refer to what is usually understood by "besetting sins," which are the sins that we are very prone to fall into because of our individual weakness, temperament, inclinations, *etc.;* these belong rather to the weight that we ought to throw aside. — Now follows the main verb of the entire sentence, a subjunctive of exhortation, τρέχωμεν: **let us run . . . the race that is set before us.** The writer uses the imagery which Paul so often employs, that of a δρόμος, or race, here ἀγών, contest in games, a wider term, but including the race. Every man who embraces the Christian faith and profession enters the course for the race that is to win him a crown of imperishable glory. Some, like Paul when writing to Timothy, are already near the end and can say: "I have finished the course;" others, like many a young catechumen with a long life before him, have just begun the race and the long track stretches ahead of them. It is the race or contest **that is set before us,** marked and outlined as in the regular athletic contests of the Greeks of old, or for that matter in the modern Olympic games, or in lesser contests. So the course lies before (προκείμενος) the Christian, marked out by the Gospel; and its lines are true and abiding faith with all that this involves. — We are urged to run this race **with patience,** that steadfast endurance which bears the hardships involved and steadily, perseveringly presses on; δι' ὑπομονῆς, "through endurance," with endurance all through, steadfastly maintaining it to the end. "We are not of them that shrink back unto perdition, but of them that have faith unto the saving of the soul," Heb. 10, 39. There are many who start, but not so many who finish; and this is because not a few lack the patience which the believer needs and must attain in order to reach the goal.

A third participial clause is added to show the essential condition of success and to inspire to strenuous and persistent effort: **looking unto Jesus the author and perfecter of** *our* **faith, who for the joy that was set before him endured the cross, despising shame, and hath sat down at the right hand of the throne of God.** We are to run the race and succeed in the effort by **looking unto** the author and finisher of faith, Jesus. By ἀφορῶντες followed by εἰς is meant a looking away from everything else and keeping our eyes only on Jesus. We might see many things to dishearten us and make us give up the race entirely, but keeping our eyes on Jesus, nothing will discourage or stop us. We are to see in him **the author and finisher of** *our* **faith.** Cremer completely disposes of the idea of Delitzsch and others that ἀρχηγός here means the forerunner of faith, who by himself believing leads the way for other believers. Faith as we have it cannot be attributed to Christ. The word means an originator, and when the sense of the statement requires it, an originator who is himself the first partaker of what he originates. But where this is not clearly implied in the statement itself the correct meaning of ἀρχηγός is the one already adopted by all the old exegetes, namely αἴτιος (compare Heb. 5, 9 with 2, 10), an author or cause, yet not a remote one, as αἴτιος might be, but one connected with the beginning of what he causes, which here is **the faith** (τῆς πίστεως), that of believers in general, and so also of *our* faith, as the English versions have it. The margin offers *captain* (Kuebel has: *Herzog*) instead of author, following the Septuagint in using the word for prince or lord; but this is not acceptable since it does not parallel the companion term "finisher of our faith." Jesus is properly called **the author** of our faith, because he has caused it and wrought it by his saving work. This applies also to the faith of the O. T. saints mentioned in the eleventh chapter, for their faith looked to the future work of Christ and thus springs from Christ. — In the same way Jesus is **the finisher** of our faith, in that he brings it to a successful issue, so that we "receive the end of our faith, even the salvation of our souls," 1 Pet. 1, 9. He who has begun the good work will certainly leave nothing undone to carry it to completion. This interpretation of the two terms gives a far richer and stronger meaning than the one which makes Jesus merely the greatest exemplar of faith and thus puts him at the head of all who run the race of faith. We all need much more than a perfect example of faith, we need a divine helper who will do more than merely inspire and encourage us. At the same time this interpretation leaves us free to bring in the idea that Jesus is the great Lord of the contest in which we are engaged, ruling and ordering it, and at last bestowing the crown of victory. — The relative sentence which now follows shows how Christ became the author and finisher of our faith: **who for the joy that was set before him endured the cross, despising shame, and hath sat down at the right hand of the throne of God.** "The joy that was set before him" is the glorification that followed the sufferings of Christ, together with his kingship over all believers. It includes all that his glorious victory attained. The preposition ἀντί is here used as in verse 16: "*for* one mess of meat." Some have thought that this joy refers to the heavenly joy of the Logos prior to his incarnation, or to the joy Christ might have had here on earth if he had refused to suffer; but προκειμένης must refer to what lies before, just as it does in the previous verse, and the meaning of the sentence must run parallel to what has just been said regarding believers, who are to endure the hardships of the race in order to gain eternal joy. All through his humiliation, and especially when foretelling his death on the cross,

Christ referred to his coming resurrection and his return to glory with the Father; on that his eyes were ever fixed, and that is "the joy that was set before him." — And so he **endured the cross, despising shame,** all of it that was connected with the cross and that led up to it. How much Christ endured in all this we know from the Passion History, yet the joy that followed after was even greater. Σταυρός is a post driven into the ground, for the execution of a criminal, and so comes to signify a **cross;** the definite article is missing both before σταυρός and αἰσχύνη, making both terms general: Christ underwent such a death as that of a cross, and such a shame. He **despised** the latter, yet certainly not as being a small matter; for who can measure the awfulness of the dishonor, mockery, blasphemy, and all manner of vileness heaped upon the Son of God? He despised the shame by counting it as nothing compared with the joy he had set himself to reach; he always looked beyond and above the shame, letting his heart remain fixed on that, refusing thus to be influenced by the shame. — **And hath sat down at the right hand of the throne of God** describes the completion of Christ's great work when he attained the joy after the cross and shame. The statement refers to Christ's human nature when this entered upon the full and unrestricted use of the divine glory, majesty, and power. We must note the tenses: ὑπέμεινεν, aorist, endured as a single past act; and κεκάθικεν, perfect, hath sat down, so that ever after he remains seated. The throne of God is his divine majesty, and to be seated at the right hand of the throne is the exercise of the divine majesty of which Christ's human nature was made complete partaker. Our Confessions say "that it was not a mere man who, for us, . . . ascended into heaven, and was raised to the majesty and almighty power of God, but a man whose human nature has such a profound, ineffable union and communion with the Son of God that it is one person with him." 518, 13. The right hand of God "is no fixed place in heaven, as the Sacramentarians assert without any ground in Holy Scriptures, but is nothing else than the almighty power of God, which fills heaven and earth, in which Christ is placed according to his humanity, really, *i. e.* in deed and truth, without confusion and equalizing of the two natures in their essence and essential properties." 629, 28 *etc.* — Two things are involved in this entire description of Christ's action, the first of which especially must not be overlooked or neglected in preaching; this first is Christ's suffering and glorification as the redemptive acts by which he became the author and finisher of our faith, to whom we do not look in vain; and secondly, his suffering and glorification as exemplary acts which we now are to use as our model in running the race set before us. To dwell only on the latter would be a serious mistake.

Let us not faint when reproved.

The second part of the admonition is closely coupled with the first, in fact is but its negative side, with some elaboration. **For consider him that hath endured such gainsaying of sinners against himself** (American Committee), **that we wax not weary, fainting in your souls.** The word for **consider,** ἀναλογίσασθε, implies a reckoning up, a calculation, and the subject of this action is expressed so as to include both the person of our Savior and what he has done. The conclusion which we will thus draw must encourage us greatly, since we will find that our sufferings and hardships are far inferior to his. — We are to consider not merely this or that important truth, which might indeed prove helpful to us, but the foundation of all our help ("looking unto Jesus"): **him that hath endured such gainsaying of sinners.** This repetition of the verb ὑπομένειν (now ὑπομεμενηκότα, the perfect participle, where a moment ago we had ὑπέμεινεν, the aorist) is an effective way of urging upon us that ὑπομονή with which we are to run our race. Trench calls it a noble word, in which there always appears a background of manliness, and he defines it as the *brave* patience which bears the persecutions and evils that come against it. — It was thus that Christ endured the cross, and

such gainsaying of sinners against himself. There is not sufficient reason to read εἰς ἑαυτούς, "against themselves," instead of εἰς ἑαυτόν, against himself, as the American Committee very properly insists. This **gainsaying** is called **such,** not with reference to anything like it which we must bear, since nothing has been mentioned thus far, but with reference to the cross of Christ and the shame; this is the gainsaying Christ had to endure, when Caiaphas rose against him, the Jewish high council, the wicked mob, the mocking soldiers, even the malefactors themselves. It was a gainsaying that did not stop at words, even curses and blasphemies, but issued in the deeds that led to the awful death on the cross. **Sinners** indeed were these gainsayers, the representatives of all the sinners of the whole world, and nothing restricted them in their deadly opposition to the Lamb that bore all their inflictions with such patient, brave endurance. If we reckon up aright what Christ thus bore, and who it was that bore it, and why, we will surely not grow weary and lose our ὑπομονή. — And we are to consider it for this very purpose: **that ye wax not weary, fainting in your souls.** The verb ἐκλύειν means to loosen, hence to relax, become exhausted (Matth. 15, 32; Gal. 6, 9), as a runner who has to slacken his pace in the stadium. The dative ταῖς ψυχαῖς ὑμῶν is best drawn to the participle, **fainting in your souls,** which describes the inner act that accompanies the outer, the loss of courage and hope. What the trials of the Christian are will be stated in a moment, but whatever they are, a looking upon Jesus will make us strong to bear them without fainting and giving up. Nothing is sadder than to see the Christian who has made a good start in the race sink down in defeat when there is everything to inspire him and make him strong.

Ye have not yet resisted unto blood, striving against sin: and ye have forgotten the exhortation, which reasoneth with you as with sons,

> **My son, regard not lightly the chastening of the**
> **Lord,**
> **Nor faint when thou art reproved of him;**

For whom the Lord loveth he chasteneth,
And scourgeth every son whom he receiveth.

The readers of the Epistle are here reminded of the comparative lightness of their previous and present sufferings and of the character of these sufferings as chastenings of the Lord. **Ye have not yet resisted unto blood,** as others have, some of those mentioned in the previous chapter (35-37), and especially also Christ himself. The writer may also have thought of Stephen, of James, and the bloody beatings and mistreatments of others. **Unto blood** refers of course to a bloody death, but very properly includes also scourgings and blows which draw blood. This accords with the implied figure, which from a race turns now to a fight; *a cursu venit ad pugilatum,* Bengel; compare 1 Cor. 9, 24-27. The resisting and **striving** here meant is therefore not against inward sin and temptation, but **against sin** as an outward antagonist, who meets us by opposing and persecuting our faith with violent means; hence the change of the figure. "Ye have not yet resisted unto blood" furnishes a fine application to our hearers to-day, none of whom have been called upon to suffer like the martyrs of old, or like those who shed their blood for Christ in recent years at the hands of pagan uprisings in far away mission fields. If all these could bear so much, why cannot we bear something too? Is our courage and perseverance so small because we have been shielded so well by the kindness of God? Are our complaints so great because our sufferings have been so little? What would become of our endurance if bloody persecution should actually break out for us also? And let us not forget that some who gave their blood for the faith were recent converts, not trained so thoroughly in the Gospel as we are. — Our sufferings are, properly considered, only fatherly chastenings, nothing to be discouraged at, but a mark of our sonship and high position with God. **And ye have forgotten the exhortation** is read by most commentators as a question, by some as an exclamatory question, since they think this softening of what would otherwise be a sharp rebuke is more in harmony with the tenor of this entire section: "And have ye clean forgotten?" Both ἐκλανθάνεσθαι and the following ὀλιγωρεῖν occur only here in the N. T.; the former is quite strong: to forget completely. **The exhortation which reasoneth with you as with sons** is personified as though it did the reasoning. This is the more appropriate as the quotation, showing what the exhortation says, is from Prov. 3, 11-12, and the first nine chapters of this book personify the divine Wisdom (compare also Luke 9, 49). Delitzsch calls this exhortation the touching, encouraging appeal of Holy Scripture to the heart of man, entering into discourse with us as in maternal tenderness and anxiety for our welfare. By διαλέγεσθαι, to reason, is meant mutual converse or discussion. So the divine exhortation listens, as it were, to our wrong thoughts and complaints and then **reasoneth with you as with sons,** as a father explains things to his sons.

Let us prize this great condescension of God, this loving treatment of ourselves as his children, and let us not disregard his paternal words. — The Septuagint has only the word "son," but **my son** brings out the original Hebrew fully. The two dangers in our suffering are that either we may treat them too lightly, or that we may become discouraged and faint under them. **Regard not lightly** warns us against making little of the Lord's discipline, not taking it seriously as coming from him, soon casting its impressions from our minds, and going on as carelessly and indifferently as before. It is indeed remarkable how quickly some people recover from the Lord's discipline. In a few days or weeks all serious thoughts are gone again from their hearts. The word παιδεία meant only education to the pagan Greeks, but the inspired writers put into it what we understand by discipline or correction. And here the emphasis is on the latter; we are not to disregard merely the Lord's words, but likewise not his **chastening,** when he corrects and trains us with the rod of affliction. The Lord is so concerned about us that he applies also the latter, and we are so slow to listen to his words that we also need the

chastening. — **Nor faint when thou art reproved of him**
deals with the other possibility, and this is the one about
which the holy writer is here especially concerned; we are
not to give out in exhaustion, sink down in discouragement
and despair. The Hebrew has: "do not murmur," *werde
nicht unwilling,* and Delitzsch rightly says: "Resentment and
despondency have both, in times of suffering, the same
mode of expression — murmuring." The term used by the
writer of Hebrews thus interprets the original and brings
out the sense in which it is meant, an entirely legitimate
way of quoting, illuminating the word used. **When thou
art reproved of him** shows what lies in the παιδεία or
chastening; ἐλεγχόμενος points to a fault in us, which the
reproof administered is to remove. Our affliction under
trials and persecutions is to make us better children of
God; the fire of trial is to cleanse, to make our faith
brighter, our devotion to the Lord and his Word stronger,
our love for our brethren more fervent, our courage, patience and other Christian virtues finer. — The climax of
the quotation is in the comforting, encouraging reason assigned for the admonition to hold out under affliction and
persecution: **For whom the Lord loveth he chasteneth.**
The chastening of the Lord is for those whom he loves
with his great fatherly love. To realize this puts a different complexion upon all our suffering for Christ's sake.
The Lord's discipline is not a sign of his displeasure, an
evidence of his wrath and rejection of us, but a sign of
his love, an evidence of his acceptance of us and his concern for us. The moment we are properly convinced of
this, all murmuring will cease and we will gratefully submit even to what may be very painful. — **And scourgeth
every son whom he receiveth** follows the Septuagint
which reads a different punctuation of the Hebrew original
than we now have, one of which Delitzsch says that it is
to be preferred to the present Masoretic reading: "and as a
father with a son he taketh delight" (*viz.* in correcting
him, or, in him, after correction). Here we have added
the thought that such discipline is the invariable rule with

the Lord; and hence, that this is a mark of all his sons. The word **scourgeth** is quite strong and shows what is included in the chastening and reproof mentioned before; the Lord applies the rod or whip and lays stripes upon our backs. And this is one of the prerogatives of his sons, a badge of their sonship, a blessing they should highly esteem. The parent who spares the rod spoils the child. "Behold, happy is the man whom God correcteth: therefore despise not thou the chastening of the Almighty. For he maketh sore, and bindeth up: he woundeth, and his hands make whole." Job. 5, 17-18. We still thank our parents for the discipline they gave us in youth; and it is easy for us to see how some parents ill serve their children when they deal too gently with them, as did Eli of old with his wicked sons. So we, when God scourges us, must not complain and cry out: How have I deserved this? but must know that we cannot be received as sons of God or remain sons without feeling the rod at our Father's hands. And if it please him to use the enemies of our faith as rods, let us know that even this is his work and for our good. A thousand times better the scourging of his loving hand, which never lays on too much, than the scorpion whips with which the devil lashes his followers to all eternity. Our discipline will soon end when God takes his sons to their eternal home. — And so our epistle closes with a word full of the strongest comfort for all the children of God, inspiring them to keep on in faithfulness and trust under every affliction, and by persevering unto the end to win the crown of eternal life.

HOMILETICAL HINTS.

Once with waving palms and shouts of hosanna the multitudes accompanied Jesus as he made his entry into Jerusalem. But they did not know that Jesus was going to his death and what that death really meant, nor was their intention to follow him upon such a path of shame and suffering, ending in the cross. Their enthusiasm, love, and devotion was all gone when Jesus shouldered the hard burden of the cross and when at last with weary feet and faint unto death he climbed the sad hill, Calvary. To-day we are shown a different multitude, far greater than the one at Jerusalem, a very cloud of witnesses. They all accompany Jesus too, and their hearts and lips are singing his praise in far better strains than the hosannas at Jeruaselm's portals. These all know who Jesus is, indeed the cross he bore and the shame he endured is the very comfort and strength of their hearts, the one supreme excellence which draws their hearts to him. And see, every one of them is likewise marked with the cross, and some of them show where their own blood has flowed. Who are these all? They are the glorious saints of God who have fought the good fight and won the crown, looking to Jesus, the author and finisher of their faith. They are with the triumphant Savior now in his everlasting kingdom, where all suffering is ended, and light and joy reigns for evermore. And we, my friends? you children about to bow your knees before this altar? You parents and friends who have knelt there before? You little ones who shall kneel there ere long — we belong together with these witnesses of the faith, for the cross of Jesus is in our hearts also, and nothing shall turn us from our allegiance to him.

At the end of the eleventh chapter of Hebrews one of God's saints wrote the significant words: "To be continued."

Christians need not be ashamed of the company to which they belong. Truer, nobler, grander hearts never graced this earth: mighty heroes in patience, brave champions for the glory of the Lord, profound searchers into the mysteries of the Almighty, sacred singers of imperishable praise, manly confessors of the highest and holiest truth, tireless workers in the Lord's vineyard, devoted worshippers at the Savior's feet, faithful petitioners at the throne of grace, silent sufferers under the cross, comforted mourners beside the open graves, triumphant conquerors in the very hour of death. And every one of them was what he was "by faith alone." They have died, and yet they live, yea, shall live for evermore.

Here is Stephen, sinking down in a bruised heap beneath the stones hurled at him and with his dying breath praying for his murderers; James the elder quietly laying his head upon the executioner's block; James the just, the Lord's brother, crushed by being hurled from the high temple wall to the rocks beneath; Paul slain with the sword; Peter crucified head downward; Justin, the martyr, who loved truth better than life; the aged bishop Pothin, dying of his wounds in a dungeon; Ponticus, only fifteen years old, yielding up his young life amid nameless tortures; the youthful maid Blandina, placed with naked body upon a glowing iron chair and then in a net thrown to the wild beasts. Of these too it is true: the world was not worthy of them.

A foolish runner is he who enters the track with a great bag of plunder on his back. — Who are your companions? Others, who like you are running the race, spurring you on? Or worldly companions, blocking your way, turning you aside from the track, holding you back to dally with them in the pleasures that injure the soul? — Faithful confession is a strange fashion in the eyes of the world. Earnest prayer, and diligent attendance upon the Word is made mock of by many.

Looking to Jesus, the author and finisher of our faith. For without me ye can do nothing. Look with faith in his blood, with prayer to his grace, with desire to do as he did. — To cease looking upon him is to leave the fountain of life, to wander in the desert without food and drink, to surrender to the foe and yield our hands to his fetters, to perish in night and gloom where we might have lived in light and glory.

To wish not to suffer is to wish not to be a child of God. To flee from the conflict is to flee from the victory and the crown. — The joy of the Redeemer is the joy of our redemption.

There never was but one way to heaven for sinners, the one marked by the cross of Christ, with the shadow of the cross on all who go that way.

Soldiers Of The Cross:

I. *Yours is a great Captain.*
II. *Yours is a noble army.*
III. *Yours are invincible weapons.*
IV. *Yours is a gallant struggle.*
V. *Yours is a glorious victory.*

With The Cross of Jesus Going On Before.

I. *The host that follows.*
II. *The path they take.*
III. *The power they find.*
IV. *The goal they reach.*

Sure, I Must Fight, If I Would Reign!

I. Hence I pray: *Increase my courage, Lord!*
II. Hence I vow: *I'll bear the toil, endure the pain!*
III. Hence I trust: *Supported by Thy Word.*

30

Looking Unto Jesus.

I. *We trust his grace.*
II. *We heed his example.*
III. *We submit to his discipline.*

Every Christian Can Persevere Unto the End.

I. *You can accept the encouragement of the cloud of witnesses.*
II. *You can lay aside every weight and the sin that doth so easily beset us.*
III. *You can, above all, look to Jesus, the author and finisher of your faith.*
IV. *You can submit to your heavenly Father's training.*

Let Us Run With Patience the Race that is Set Before Us.

Looking

I. *To the cloud of witnesses about us.*
II. *To the Lord Jesus before us.*
III. *To the Father in heaven above us.*

C. C. Hein.

MAUNDY THURSDAY.

1 Cor. 10, 16-17.

Luther calls this text his *Herzblatt* as regards the Lord's Supper, and again he terms it a thunderbolt upon the head of errorists. Outside of the accounts of the institution of the Sacrament in the Gospels and by St. Paul this is certainly the most important *sedes doctrinae,* and therefore exceedingly precious as a text for Maundy (mournful) Thursday, the very day of the institution of the Supper. It states directly what the Supper is, and it does this in an argument which puts the special truth contained in this text, and, alas, so often rejected, beyond all question or doubt. In its doctrinal substance our text is anything but a dry or barren proposition demanding merely intellectual assent; it is one of the fundamentals of our faith, a stream of grace direct from the very fountain of salvation itself, uniting us with Christ and the brethren in a way which determines even our outward conduct (verse 21). So too this text must be preached, giving the faith of our people the nourishment and strength it needs, and their hearts a love both fervent and intelligent for the Sacrament and its fruits. Let us remember also that of all the churches in our land our Lutheran Church is the only one which has preserved in this respect what the Lord has given it, and that we must be faithful to our trust. False unionism is our greatest foe here, and against it we must stand like a rock. — If this text cannot be used on the day for which it is set, some other time should be found for a sermon on it, a time reaching as many auditors as possible. Its great subject is: *our communion with the body and blood of the crucified Savior,* whereby we are savingly united with him, and thus fraternally bound together with each other.

467

The communion of Christ's body and blood a means of salvation.

In the first 22 verses of the tenth chapter the apostle shows how dangerous it is for the people of God to become entangled in sinful license. He does this, first, by pointing to the Israel of old whom God bound to himself with the great blessings experienced in crossing the Red Sea and passing through the wilderness. The description of these blessings reminds us of Baptism and the Lord's Supper (1-4). How untrue the Israelites proved to the grace thus vouchsafed to them is brought out in detail, and a warning for us is interwoven. In the next place the apostle deals with the danger of the Corinthian Christians in becoming entangled again in idolatry. Here again he puts forward the great spiritual blessing by which God had bound them to himself as his own (16-17), and then drives home the admonitions that this must separate them from everything that would join the soul to idolatry. He begins his argument with the call to "flee from idolatry" (14), and then asks them as wise men to judge the decisive factors in the case themselves. The first of these deals with their connection with Christ, which the apostle puts in the form of a question, the answer to which is self-evident and certainly admitted by his readers: By the Lord's Supper they are placed into communion with Christ's body and blood. It is this part of the argument which forms our text. The other decisive factor is that partaking of things sacrificed to idols is communion with devils. The evident conclusion must be that these two communions exclude each other, and that any attempt to combine them is to provoke the Lord to jealousy (22). Paul might have brought forth Baptism, or faith in Christ and his Word, when he wished to emphasize the close union of the Corinthians with the Savior; he chooses the Lord's Supper, first, no doubt, because there is here a communion through eating and drinking analagous to the feasts at the idol festivals, and secondly because this communion is a constant repetition of a sacramental union, herein too analagous to the repeated idol feasts, and this the most sacred and intimate possible for us this side of eternity. He speaks of the cup first, leaving thus full room to dwell on the bread, this offering a directer analogy to the meat eaten at the idol feasts. — **The cup of blessing which we bless, is it not a communion of the blood of Christ? The bread which we break, is it not a communion of the body of Christ?** The construction of τὸν ἄρτον as an accusative by attraction to ὅν, the following relative, makes it very probable that τὸ ποτήριον is construed in the same way. As in the words of the Institution itself **the cup** is used for its contents. "They are so identified, that, without dreaming of a departure from the prose of every-day life, all the cultivated languages of men give the name 'cup' both to the thing containing and the thing contained." Krauth, *Conservative Reformation*, 778. This grammatical metonomy must be carefully distinguished from a metaphor, which is an entirely different thing, as we see for instance in Christ's prayer in Gethsemane where there was neither a literal cup nor literal contents, but only the terrible anguish figured by the word cup. — The cup **of blessing,** τῆς εὐλογίας, really: "of the blessing," is the sacramental cup over which "the blessing" is pronounced in the act of consecration. Christ's giving of thanks first made the cup a "cup of blessing," but here the reference is to our acts of consecration, as the following relative clause shows. For εὐλογεῖν here and Mark 14, 22 and Matth. 22, 20, we have in 1 Cor. 11, 24; Matth. 26, 26; Luke 22, 19, the narrower εὐχαριστεῖν, to give thanks. In substance both denote the same thing, the sacramental setting apart of the earthly elements for their intended exalted use. Thanking and blessing or praising are closely related; we frequently show our gratitude to God for his gifts by speaking of the grace and goodness of the Giver. Thus blessing includes thanksgiving. The blessing of ordinary food for the wants of the body by giving thanks (Luke 9, 16; 1 Tim. 4, 3) deals only with the natural functions of such food for the sustenance of the body in accordance with the divine purposes of providence; the sacramental blessing deals with the specific function of bread and wine for the blessed nourishment of our souls in conveying to us Christ's body and blood in accordance with the specific command and promise of Christ. — The addition: **which we bless,** brings out prominently the consecratory act as repeated at each new celebration of the Supper in accord with Christ's bidding: "This do." As Christ gave thanks and blessed the bread and wine, so now must we in celebrating the Lord's Supper; Paul's words here show that the apostles so understood the Savior. The evangelists have made no record of the words of blessing which Christ uttered in the first celebration of the Supper; they report only the words he used when he gave the consecrated elements to the disciples. The Savior's original words of blessing are therefore not to be used by us. These words were spoken, we may say, once for all, and their effect remains for all time whenever and wherever the Sacrament is celebrated in accordance with Christ's institution. *Formula of Concord,* 615, 75 *etc.* But this does not mean that now we may omit the consecration of the elements, *i. e.* the blessing or thanksgiving, for although Paul says only of the cup of blessing, *which we bless,* that it is the communion of Christ's blood; this consecratory blessing is not accidental, but essential. Philippi rightly states, *Glaubenslehre,* V. 2, 488, that the apostle makes the real presence of the Lord's body and blood depend thereon. As regards the form now to be used, everything depends on our uttering over the elements the creative institutional word of Christ already contained in his eucharistic blessing, and clearly expressed for us during his act of distribution, that word which he will acknowledge in every new celebration of the Supper and whose constant effectiveness he will maintain; wherefore also the church very correctly uses the Scripture words of the Institution itself in the consecratory act. *Accedit verbum ad elementum et fit sacramentum.* Augustine; also quoted in the Confessions, 468, 18; 330, 1. Therefore too the Formula of Concord says: "In the administration of the Holy Supper the words of institution should be publicly

spoken or sung, distinctly and clearly, and should in no。
way be omitted," the Latin adding: "and this for very many
and the most important reasons." The first is, "in order
that obedience may be rendered to the command of Christ:
This do." The second deals with the faith of the hearers,
to which the Latin adds: "besides that the elements of
bread and wine may be consecrated or blessed for this holy
use;" and then the German: "and in order that the body
and blood of Christ may therewith be administered to be
eaten and to be drunk, as Paul declares 1 Cor. 10, 16." 616,
79 *etc.* As essential to the Sacrament the Formula explicitly enumerates: *"the consecration,* or words of Institution, and the *distribution* and *reception,* or oral partaking
of the consecrated bread and wine, likewise the partaking
of the body and blood of Christ." 617, 86. — Concerning
the element thus consecrated, and thereby connected with
the creative word of Christ uttered at the first celebration, the apostle asks, fully sure of the affirmative answer
of the Corinthians: **is it not a communion of the blood
of Christ?** The reception of the consecrated element is
implied. We must note that Paul does not ask merely:
"Is it not a communion *of Christ?"* There are various ways
of entering into communion *with Christ;* the apostle here
singles out one of these ways, the most sacred and intimate
possible for us now: the communion of his blood (and
body). He is concerned here not simply with a spiritual
communion, which may take place at any time and without
an earthly medium, but with a very special communion,
that *of Christ's blood (and body),* mediated only by the
earthly sacramental element. Besides the direct statements
before us, this is shown also by his entire argument. Paul
is not warning the Corinthians simply against some form
of spiritual communion with idols, but against a participation in idol feasts, against a communion with idols through
the earthly medium of food offered to idols. Against simple
spiritual communion with devils it would have been proper
for the apostle to put some form of spiritual communion
with Christ, a communion by faith, or by contemplating

Christ's Word, or by prayer. But against the communion with devils at idol feasts through eating of flesh sacrificed to idols the apostle puts the communion with Christ's body and blood in the Lord's Supper. These two clash so directly and terribly that the argument of the apostle becomes overwhelming. Moreover, his argument is meant especially for the careless and lax Corinthians, those who would be unworthy communicants if they proceeded to attend idol feasts. As against these, however, the argument would be emptied of all force if with Zwingli and Calvin we would assume that in the Lord's Supper only bread and wine are received; for then these unworthy communicants, not receiving Christ's body and blood in eating and drinking of the consecrated elements, would not enter into communion with that body and blood and thus with Christ, and therefore not incur the terrible guilt of which Paul speaks. The mere reception of bread and wine as symbols of an absent body and blood of Christ would never arouse the jealousy of the Lord as stated by Paul (verses 21-22; 11, 29). Compare Krauth, *Conservative Reformation,* 632. Thus in a double way the apostle's argument demands that the natural sense of his words be adhered to, namely that the consecrated elements are indeed **a communion,** κοινωνία (or *participation in,* margin) of Christ's body and blood. The word is from κοινωνεῖν, to have in common, to have a share or part in. It states a connection of one thing with another by way of participation in that other. The apostle does not say that the consecrated cup *signifies* such a communion, but that it *is* such a communion; nor that the consecrated cup is a *symbol* of such a communion, but that it is *a communion itself.* We must note also that the communion of Christ's blood is predicated of the cup, *i. e.* of the earthly element as a sacramental element. Only on the basis of this elemental communion can we speak of a communion of Christ's blood for the participants in the Holy Supper. Yet we must hold fast, that the apostle is speaking of both elements, the earthly and the heavenly, only as received in the actual celebration of the Sacrament. It is the cup so used which conveys to us the blood of Christ; so that we must say, if there were no real and true connection of the cup received, with Christ's blood, there could and would be no connection between us and the blood of Christ. The how of this κοινωνία will always remain a mystery for us, since Christ has nowhere revealed it; the great fact, however, stands fast and is held fast by faith, since it is indeed revealed. The effort to remove this mystery almost always leads into error. Our church states the apostle's teaching by means of the set phrase that "in, with, and under" the bread and wine the true body and blood of Christ are communicated to us in the Supper. Of the Supper of the Lord we teach "that the true body and blood of Christ are truly present and are communicated to those that eat in the Lord's Supper" (*quod corpus et sanguis Christi vere adsint et distribuantur vescentibus in coena Domini*). *Augsb. Conf. X.* This excludes the Romish transubstantiation as well as Zwinglianism and Calvinism, all capernaitic eating and drinking, impanation, consubstantiation, and every doctrine which tries to remove the mystery of the mode. — By **the blood of Christ** is meant the blood shed for us for the remission of sins, as Christ himself states in the words of institution; his *true* blood, which truly flowed from his wounds on the cross in sacrifice for our sins. If in objection it be urged that when Christ instituted the Supper he stood visibly before the disciples, and that now his body is in heaven, we reply that the body and blood of Christ never was, and is not now, confined to only one mode of presence, a visible and local presence while on earth, and a local, supernatural presence now in the heavenly regions. His human nature was united with his divine nature, and by virtue of this union could be present in a manner far beyond what our sense and reason are able to grasp. While standing visibly before Nicodemus Christ said: "The Son of man . . . is in heaven," John 3, 13. Similarly, standing before his disciples, he said in the Sacrament: This is my body, this is my blood. The fact that at the first institution the body

of Christ was before the eyes of the disciples does not exclude that in an invisible and heavenly manner his body and
blood were communicated by means of the sacramental
bread and wine to the disciples; just as the glorious presence of Christ in heaven now does not exclude that his
body and blood as offered for our sins are now communicated to us in a supernatural manner by means of the earthly
elements in the Sacrament.   The decisive thing in both
instances is the divine Word, which is all that faith needs
and wants; when reason demands more, or denies what
the Lord says for us to believe, it arrogates to itself a
false authority and becomes the mother of unbelief.
Formula of Concord, 619, 98; 623, 119.   Krauth, 783 *etc.*

All that we have said in regard to Paul's first question
applies also to the second which parallels the first. **The
bread which we break, is it not a communion of the body
of Christ?** The word ἄρτος signifies a loaf of bread, and
the margin renders it *loaf,* which is a help in understanding
the addition: **which we break.** This breaking is for the
purpose of distribution, and for this alone. The parallel
between the cup "which we bless" and the bread "which we
break" lies in this, that the first mentions the consecration
as an essential feature, and the second mentions the distribution as also an essential feature.   Therefore, what is
done with the cup is also done with the bread, both are
blessed or consecrated, even as Christ commanded; and
what is done with the bread is also done with the wine, both
are distributed, again as Christ commanded.   Some, however, and especially they who turn the Sacrament into a
symbol, insist that this breaking of the bread, although
without counterpart in the cup, there being no pouring out
of it, is symbolic of the breaking of Christ's body in death.
Meyer even calls it "an essential symbolical proceeding."
Nebe, although Reformed, gives up this claim of his church,
and rightly. It is generally the case that they who empty
out the real essence of the Sacrament pile up unessential
symbolical features as essentials, and this even where there
are no symbols. "Bread is an inanimate thing: how can

breaking it be like the putting of a human being to death?
Breaking bread is the very symbol of quiet and peace; who
would dream of it as an appropriate symbol of the most
cruel and ignominious death? Bread is the representative
food, and used in metaphor, is the symbol of spiritual and
supernatural food. The breaking of bread is the means
of giving it as food, and taking it as food, and as a symbol,
the symbol of giving and taking a higher food. No one
would dream of the breaking of a piece of bread as the
symbol of killing a human body; and if so extraordinary
a symbolic use of it were made, it would require the most
explicit statement, on the part of the person so using it, that
such was its intent; and when he had made it, the world
would be amazed at so lame a figure." Krauth, 723. —
Is it not a communion? repeats exactly the word of
the first question, and shows that in it lies the point for
both questions. **Of the body of Christ** signifies, as Christ
says: "My body which is given for you," *i. e.* sacrificed
for our sins on the cross. For "body" and "blood" in Paul's
questions Hodge, a prominent Calvinistic dogmatician and
exegete, puts: "their sacrificial virtue," and in this way
evades the force of the apostle's words; to shield himself
the more effectually from these words he sets up the claim:
"The passage decides no point of difference," *Com.* on 1
Cor., p. 186. He is able to do this, however, only by setting
up alongside the authority of the Word "those laws of belief which God has impressed upon our nature," by which
euphonism he means reason. Such is the native clearness
and force of the apostle's words, that only by devious means
like those employed by Hodge can the truth they convey
be evaded.

The communion of Christ's body and blood a means of fraternal union.

The apostle assumes that both of his questions are
answered affirmatively by his readers. He now adds:
**seeing that we, who are many, are one bread, one body:
for we all partake of the one bread.** This rendering

assumes that "one bread" and "one body" are in apposition and both designate the union of all communicants, inasmuch as they all partake of the one sacramental bread; it thus gives one meaning to the word bread in the first clause, and another to the same word in the second. Compare the closing words in the exhortation in the Communion Liturgy. It is beyond question better to adhere to the true meaning of ἄρτος, which is that of sacramental bread throughout, as is correctly done in the marginal rendering: *seeing that there is one bread, we, who are many, are one body.* It is incorrect to make ἄρτος in the first clause the predicate of ἐσμέν, either the ἐσμέν Paul wrote, or a second one supplied in thought, for the second clause shows that the apostle means no metaphorical bread, but the actual sacramental bread. After ὅτι εἷς ἄρτος we simply supply ἐστί. The apostle is presenting an argument from the effect of the sacrament, an effect realized and felt by his readers, to the cause.which produces that effect. **Seeing that,** since, or because, **there is one bread** in the Sacrament, no matter where or when the celebration takes place, or who partici-pates, there is likewise also this effect: **we, who are many,** individuals, differing in many ways outwardly and inwardly, **are one body.** What joins us together and makes us one is the εἷς ἄρτος, the one bread. But certainly not as mere bread, or only as a symbol of Christ's body. That would not make us "one body," it would be but a weak. superficial, outward tie, without organic power. The great effect that we are actually made "one body" is due to the equally great cause, that the sacramental bread which we receive is the real communion of Christ's body. All who sacramentally receive his body are indeed "one body." Meyer infers correctly: "This union into one body by partaking of one bread could not be, if the bread were not a κοινωνία of the body of Christ, which is the efficacious cause of our being 'one body,' that which constitutes the many a unity." There is far more here than a mere comparison: as there is one bread, so we, the many, are one body. Nor is this whole statement of the apostle merely a remark by the way, a side-thought not essential to the line of his argument. On the contrary, verse 17 applies the great truth of verse 16 directly to Paul's Corinthian readers. They all, in belonging to the Corinthian congregation and assembling at the Lord's table as communicants, are made **one body,** by receiving the bread which is a participation in Christ's body (the same being true of the cup). Philippi is correct when he emphasizes the admonitory purpose which runs through Paul's words, who is aiming especially at those foolish Corinthians attending at one time the Lord's table and then the table of idols. These are the people who must know what the Lord's Supper is and what it does: it is a communion of Christ's body and blood, and by giving us that body and blood makes us "one body," utterly different from pagan worshippers united at idol feasts. Knowing and realizing this, these Corinthians should abandon their dangerous folly and thank God for ever anew, in and by the Sacrament, joining them together with his children as "one body." We to-day may well apply Paul's words to those foolish church-members who think "there is nothing wrong" in going to Christ's altar with Christ's followers one day and to a Christless altar in a Christless organization the next day. — By the "one body" Paul does not mean the communion of saints composed of all believers; for to this body belong also the children who are not communicants and do not receive the sacramental bread, and this invisible body is constituted by the tie of faith in Christ, not by participation in the Lord's Supper. By the "one body" he means the company of professing Christians who assemble outwardly at the Lord's table, who manifest their oneness by uniting in that table, and who therefore ought to be truly and inwardly one, also by receiving worthily Christ's body and blood. — This is brought out vividly by the causal clause: **for we all partake of the one bread.** In οἱ πολλοί the multiplicity is stated, in οἱ πάντες the totality: **we all** as forming one great body; we all as belonging together and bound together. The ordinary construction is μετέχειν τινός, never μετέχειν ἐκ τινος. The reading: "We all partake of the one bread" simply disregards the *ἐκ*, which the margin very properly preserves by translating: "We all partake *from* the one bread." "The one bread" is the medium for our partaking; "from" that we obtain the gift itself of which we partake, and this, as the context plainly indicates is the body of Christ, conveyed to us by the sacramental bread. Philippi emphasizes this and then concludes: "Therefore our passage contains a *dictum probans* as well for the *manducatio oralis* as for the *manducatio indignorum*, even as the one also follows from the other." *Glaubenslehre,* V. 2, 475. Compare *Formula of Concord,* 613, 64. The one bread is such not numerically, but qualitatively: "one" as regards its function in the Sacrament. The Greek article is added to refer back to the bread already mentioned before.

HOMILETICAL HINTS.

Every Word of God, and especially also this Word, demands childlike faith on our part, a trustful and satisfied adherence to what this Word discloses to us, combined with humble submission to its sanctifying influence.

There are three things which call for attention in our text: first of all, the statement regarding the heavenly gift bestowed in the Sacrament; secondly, the reference to the heavenly blessing conveyed through that gift; and thirdly, the reference to the blessed results the reception of that gift is to work in us. The first is Christ's body and blood; the second is the communion with Christ through his body and blood; the third is the union with our fellow communicants by means of Christ's body and blood.

"Blessed are they which are called unto the marriage supper of the Lamb." Rev. 19, 9.

"Blessed is he that shall eat bread in the kingdom of God." Luke 14, 15. Ps. 23, 5; 133, 1.

When we grow weary in our pilgrimage, feel how weak we are in trying to persevere unto the end, lose in some degree the comfort of our reconciliation with God; when our faith has difficulty in bearing up the soul to the heights of peace and joy in God, when our love droops and grows chilled from constant contact with the world, when our hope begins to dim and doubt whether we shall conquer in the fight and gain the victory like our Lord — then especially are we to come to the table of the Lord's communion, where his own body and blood fill us with new life and power and lift us up again to the fullest assurance of his grace and pardon, of his help and strength.

We call the Supper of our Lord *Communion.* It is that: the most holy, exalted, intimate and blessed union possible for us this side of eternity. The very name is an invitation, a· promise and assurance, an open fountain of untold blessing. All our salvation is in communion with the Lord, and the highest communion is that of his body and blood sacrificed for our sins and given us to eat and to drink for our highest assurance, joy, and peace.

Not *above* the earthly elements hovers the heavenly gift, so that one may eat of those elements and never come near that gift, but *under* bread and wine Christ's body is eaten and his blood is drunk; not *alongside* of· the elements is the heavenly gift offered, so that a double reception is necessary, the one only by the mouth, the other only by faith, but *in* the bread and wine Christ's body and blood is distributed and received; finally, not *without* bread and wine, or only by means of apparent· bread and wine is the communion of Christ's body and blood accomplished, but *with* real bread and wine, unchanged in its substance. *Smalcald* Articles 330-331. Thus our three precious prepositions ward off false conceptions on every side. (From Besser.)

In the communion of Christ's body and blood there is pardon for every distressed conscience, sealed by the very sacrifice which obtained that pardon for us. Draw near in true repentance. In the communion of Christ's body and blood there is power to hush all fear, misgivings, and doubts as to ourselves; for he who gives these gifts to us will not depart from us and leave us to ourselves. Draw near in full assurance. In the communion of Christ's body and blood there is strength for every future battle against the devil, world, and sin; for all of them have been vanquished by the sacrifice upon the cross. Draw near in joyful hope of victory.

In the Sacrament you are not to perform a great feat of faith, lifting your heart in a mighty effort to the heavenly regions to bring down to yourself the assurance of Christ's nearness and grace; in the Sacrament Christ himself stoops down to you, however weak and lowly you may be, feeds you with his own heavenly strength and grace, gives you his own body to eat and blood to drink, makes you completely his own in a communion of unspeakable grace.

Brethren the Christians called each other of old, and now

and then we use the same word of love; with a brotherly kiss
they greeted each other when they went to the Supper of the
Lord to testify to their fraternal fellowship in him in whom our
salvation is prepared. They were a communion of saints, all
partakers of one body and blood; steadfast martyrs and faithful confessors, who found in this Supper power to endure and
hold out in their severest trials; gallant hosts of fighters and
victors, who found in this gift of God strength for every battle;
pilgrims, who like Elijah of old pursued their journey in the
strength of this food unwearied to the end; weak hearts many
of them, but in whose weakness God grew strong; helpless, yet
grasping this rod and staff they were led safely through the dark
valley — what an exalted company! All of them gathering around
the one table, all of them fed by the one Lord, all of them joined
into one congregation and made one in the fellowship of love —
a true communion of saints. (From Matthes.)

"We know that St. Paul does not say here: We are all one
body of Christ, but simply: we are all one body, one company,
one congregation, just as every city is a particular body as over
against another city. From this it does not follow that all the
members of this body are holy, spiritual members, and thus have
the spiritual fellowship, but that they are one bodily company
in which there are both holy and unholy members, who are all
partakers of one bread. There is a great difference between
body and Christ's body." Luther.

But what shall we say of those who outwardly belong to
the body, but inwardly are foreign to it, who show the signs of
faith, but deny the power of faith, who bow now before Christ's
altar, and presently at some Christless altar, who take the sacred
body and blood of their Lord, but crucify him again in the company of those who spurn his body and blood? Will you be one
of these?

The Lord's Supper is a Feast of Holy Communion.

Because

I. *It unites Christ with his Christians.*
II. *It unites the Christians with each other.*

C. C. Hein.

The Essential Communion Blessings.

I. *Participation in Christ's body and blood.*
II. *Union with Christ himself.*
III. *Oneness with our fellow communicants.*

Christ's Intention in the Holy Communion.

He intends it as

I. *A seal of our pardon and salvation.*
II. *A bond of union among Christians.*

See that You Obtain the Communion Blessing.

I. *You must hunger and thirst for the reception of this blessing.*
II. *You must trust the Lord in bestowing this blessing.*
III. *You must rejoice in the possession of this blessing.*
IV. *You must exhibit the grace and power of this blessing.*

What Does the Lord's Communion Require?

I. *Empty hearts.*
II. *Receptive hearts.*
III. *Responsive hearts.*

The Lord's Communion the Crown of His Saving Gifts.

I. *He gives us his sacrificial body and blood.*
II. *He gives us his sacramental indwelling.*
III. *He gives us his sanctifying love.*

GOOD FRIDAY.

2 Cor. 5, 14-21.

"One died for all" is the caption attached to this text in the Eisenach pericope book. The great historical fact must be made to stand out distinctly on the day of Christ's death. This in its saving effects is the proper subject for Good Friday, and we certainly have it here. Two rich lines of thought are joined together in our text, the first dealing with the saving act of Christ itself, the second dealing with the saving proclamation of that act.

God reconciled the world unto himself.

Paul is explaining to the Corinthians the real motive of his work in persuading them, and men generally, to believe in Christ, so that they may appear with joy before his judgment-seat. Whether now the Corinthians think that in this work the apostle is carried away by enthusiasm and beside himself, or judge that he is of a sober mind in his zeal and earnestness, one thing is certain, they know that it is all for them (ὑμῖν), verse 13. Now follows the explanation, which unlocks all that is in Paul's heart and life as a believer in Christ and an apostle of the Gospel. **For the love of Christ constraineth us; because we thus judge, that one died for all, therefore all died; and he died for all that they which live should no longer live unto themselves, but unto him who for their sakes died and rose again.** The question whether **the love of Christ** means Christ's love for us, or our love for him, or a combination of the two (Schlatter), is clearly answered by the context which deals with what Christ did for us. Συνέχειν is to hold or keep together, to confine, *etc.*, here finely translated: **constraineth us,** yet

482

this not with any compulsion or force, but, as the nature of Christ's love suggests, filling the hearts of the apostle and his companions with the most earnest and zealous devotion to the Savior and his Gospel-work. Whoever knows in any degree the love of Christ must feel something of its constraining power; and surely, they should feel it in goodly measure who make it their life's work to proclaim that love to others. — Paul explains how this constraining power took hold of him: **because we thus judge, that one died for all, therefore all died.** This is the first and fundamental conclusion at which his judgment arrived, on which a second one rests: "and he died, *etc.*" There is only the participle: κρίναντας τοῦτο, but it is evidently causal: "because we judge;" but it is an aorist and refers to a certain time in the past: "because we *judged* this." The past time referred to is undoubtedly the moment when the love of Christ first entered the heart of Paul and he realized fully what this love meant. Then he judged this (τοῦτο): **that one died for all,** namely Christ upon the cross. The Greek heightens the effect by putting the words in this order: "one — for all — died." The emphasis is on the contrast between *one* and *for all.* The preposition ὑπέρ with the genitive may mean instead of, in the place of, or, more indefinitely, for the sake of, in behalf of, for someone's benefit. In itself it cannot settle the question here whether Christ died as our substitute, or merely in general in some way for our good. The context must show this; and here there can be no hesitation that the narrower meaning is intended, for the apostle states positively: "therefore all died." It is impossible for one to die *for* all, so that in consequence all are counted as having died in his death, without taking ὑπέρ to mean: in the stead of. And this proximate context cannot be brushed aside by pointing to the remoter context in the next verse: "who died *for* them and rose again," where ὑπέρ, because of the two actions dying and rising again, naturally means: "for their sakes." For always the question would remain how the dying of one *for* all could be equivalent to all dying, if he did not die *in their*

484 *Good Friday.*

stead. Trench makes this very plain in his *Synonyms of the New Testament,* II, 163, adducing examples from secular writers, and quoting Tischendorf at length, who refers also to N. T. passages not treating of Christ's death. The wider preposition ὑπέρ is used, where the meaning ἀντί cannot be denied, in order to include the thought that Christ's dying in our stead was also for our benefit. — One died for **all,** all men, not one excepted; God reconciled "the world" unto himself, verse 19. It is folly to limit the word "all," as the Calvinist Hodge does, to all those who accept the fruit of Christ's death; and another folly to appeal to the next statement: "therefore all died," and explain this dying of the death of an old nature in conversion, so that "all" would mean again only those who accept Christ's death in faith. Any limitation of the universality of Christ's redemptive death violates not only the present word of St. Paul but all the other statements of Scripture of like import; no more terrible error is put forth by the blindness of Bible interpreters. In ὑπὲρ πάντων there is absolutely no limitation. — **Therefore all died** draws the blessed conclusion. Christ's death is the death of all; οἱ πάντες, with the article, refers back pointedly to those mentioned by ὑπὲρ πάντων. The very ones (all) for whom Christ died, in and by his death themselves underwent death. In what sense is not stated here; merely the fact is emphasized. Christ died, and by his death paid the penalty of all; and this is the sense in which all died: all have paid the death penalty in and by his death. This is the mighty truth with which all the Gospel rings, and this is the blessed truth which every Good Friday sermon must proclaim aloud to sinners.

Paul has stated the first great truth which became his conviction (κρίναντας) when the love of Christ entered his heart. He follows it up with the second, which shows the purpose of Christ's redemptive death: **and he died for all, that they which live should no longer live unto themselves, but unto him who for their sakes died and rose again.** Again we have the complete statement:

He died for all. It is so precious and great that it bears repetition again and again. But now the emphasis is on the purpose (ἵνα) of this death. We might expect a further repetition of "all" (πάντες), a purpose relating to all alike. The apostle, however, restricts his thought to a special class, οἱ ζῶντες, **they which live.** Some commentators make this refer to the ordinary bodily or physical life. It is hard to understand how such a superficiality can satisfy them, when the same word follows at once in ζῶσιν and certainly does not mean mere physical living. To say that they who in one sense died in Christ's death still remain in this physical life and are therefore termed ζῶντες (Bachmann), is to attribute a platitude to Paul, of which no commentator should be guilty. How can anyone "live" either to himself or to Christ, unless he be physically alive? By οἱ ζῶντες, **they which live,** Paul means those who have the true life, *i. e.* who have obtained it by Christ's death; he means the true believers. Not all for whom Christ died are such. Many for whom he died, and who thus died in him, never get the life that blossomed for them in that death. Christ indeed would have all men come unto repentance and a knowledge of the truth, that they might "judge" as Paul did; but many "would not." — The apostle's argument here is not concerned with them, but with the others who like himself are οἱ ζῶντες, alive by faith in Christ's death. That death, while its first and primary intention is life and salvation for all men everywhere, has as a second intention, that all who do obtain through it life and salvation shall manifest that life and **no longer live unto themselves, but etc.** Both ζῶντες and ζῶσιν refer to the spiritual life, and the manifestation of this life here emphasized for the Corinthians is that it be an exhibition of true love to him who first loved us and died for love of us. That will mean that they **no longer live unto themselves,** as they did when the love of Christ had not yet entered their hearts and begun to constrain them; it will mean that now, knowing and rejoicing in this love they yield to its blessed constraint and live **unto him who for their sakes died**

and rose again, by devoting themselves to his service and
work, as Paul and his fellows were doing in regard to the
Corinthians and everywhere else. — The apostle mentions
not only the death of Christ: "him who for their sakes
died" in dying for all, but also his resurrection: **and rose
again,** himself now living in glory forever, and thus, although once he died, requiring and calling for their devotion and service. The context here, where Paul speaks
of devotion and service for Christ, is different from that
in verse 14; here, besides the death of Christ, it is proper
to mention his resurrection, and not only this addition of
the resurrection, but also the thought of service and devotion on our part, makes it necessary to widen ὑπὲρ αὐτῶν
into **for their sakes.** — In this grand way Paul explains
the motive of all his apostolic work to the Corinthians,
opening his whole inner life to them. He does more, he
shows what must be the inner motive and principle of
every true Christian life. His words are thus a call for
us to examine ourselves, to put away everything in our
lives whereby we still live selfishly to ourselves, as do the
children of this world who know not Christ and his love
and death; and likewise a call to look to our devotion,
whether Christ is all in all to us. Ah, there will be much
that needs mending, before we can say that Christ's purpose in dying for us is realized in us as it should be, and
as it was in Paul!

It was realized in Paul: **Wherefore we henceforth
know no man after the flesh: even though we have
known Christ after the flesh, yet now we know** *him so*
no more. A great change has taken place in Paul, one
that, however, necessarily extends in principle to every
true follower of Christ. **Wherefore if any man is in
Christ,** *he is* **a new creature: the old things are passed
away; behold, they are become new.** In Paul this result
dates from the moment the love of Christ fully constrained
him. The modifier κατὰ σάρκα must belong to the verb
οἴδαμεν, not to the object οὐδένα, because the apostle is speaking of a change which has occurred in himself; moreover,

when he wishes to connect καταˋ σάρκα with a noun or its
equivalent, he always attaches it directly to the word thus
modified. **We know no man after the flesh** means that
in thinking and judging of men and dealing with them the
apostle is no longer governed by carnal ideas, but by the
higher and holier considerations which center in Christ. He
neither approves nor disapproves, loves or hates any man,
or any man's work, from motives such as rule those who
have not experienced the love of Christ in their hearts.
And the Corinthians may draw a conclusion here in regard to the apostle's contact with themselves; in all of it
there was nothing that smacked of the flesh. Would that
the same were true of every minister of Christ, yea, of
every Christian! — The general thought thus expressed
Paul applies in a special way to Christ himself, for
his thoughts here all center upon the Savior: **even though
we have known Christ after the flesh,** in the days `be-
fore Paul's conversion when he judged of Christ with a
carnal mind in a carnal way, καταˋ σάρκα again belonging
to the verb. Then he was offended in Christ and considered him opposed to the Jewish interests, even going so
far in his opposition as to persecute Christ's followers.
To the fleshly pharisaical mind Christ was anything but
an acceptable Messiah. But Paul hastens to add: **yet now
we know** *him so* **no more;** Christ's love and the apostle's
understanding of that and of his death quickly changed
all that. What strange, foolish, pernicious thoughts men
have of Christ before their hearts are renewed by his love,
thoughts to which afterwards, like Paul here, they can
revert only with shame. Olshausen and a few others draw
καταˋ σάρκα to Χριστόν, and make the apostle say that he
was acquainted with Christ while he walked on earth; but
this introduces a strange and irrelevant thought. Whether
he actually saw Jesus in the flesh (note that he does not
use this personal name, but the one designating his office:
Christ), or not, has no bearing whatever on what he is
here writing to the Corinthians. As far as evidence goes
Paul never met the Savior during the Savior's earthly

sojourn; and here he is speaking of a different thing entirely. The Corinthians were in danger of judging of Paul "after the flesh",and thus thoroughly misunderstanding him; and worse even than that, they were in danger of judging carnally even of Christ, and thus falling into the most dangerous and deadly errors, losing the great blessings of his love and death. What Paul here says regarding himself is not only to set him right in the eyes of the Corinthians who had been listening to slanderous tongues, but at the same time to warn them against carnal ways of thinking and judging, which would prove their utter undoing. And it is for this especially that he brings. in here the reference to Christ. Away with the spurious wisdom of the flesh in what pertains to the Gospel; it is blindness, folly, falsehood, and utter loss!

The second sentence beginning with ὥστε is parallel to the first, but it presents what lies beneath the first, and therefore is in the form of a general truth, and thus also carries forward the thought begun in verse 15. **Wherefore if any man is in Christ** means living in him by faith, transplanted from the kingdom of the flesh into the kingdom of the Spirit; καινὴ κτίσις, he is **a new creature,** or, as the margin reads: there is *a new creation.* The marginal translation in the A. V.: *let him be a new creature,* has nothing to justify it in the original. By κτίσις is meant the act itself of founding, or producing, or the product of such an act; and the latter meaning applies here. The word implies an agent, who here is none other than God himself (verse 18). And the quality of newness is in contrast to the old nature before conversion (σάρξ); it is the newness wrought by regeneration and sanctification, when man becomes spiritual. — **The old things are passed away** describes the negative result of the change: the old ways of thinking and acting, the old opinions, principles, desires, aims, purposes, *etc.;* **behold, they are become new,** they have changed completely. Note the aorist παρῆλθεν, "passed away" in one past act; and the perfect γέγονεν, "have become," and thus are new still. Instead of knowing κατὰ σάρκα, the man who is renewed in knowledge after the image of God, Col. 3, 10, knows κατὰ πνεῦμα; he thus first of all knows Christ himself, and then also the things of Christ, Christ's apostles, ministers, followers, the church and all its work in the world. Blessed newness, born in us through the love of Christ and his redemptive death! No wonder Paul exclaims: ἰδού, **behold,** as if he were actually preaching to the Corinthians. Meyer says there is something triumphant in the exclamation and terse statement.

Now the thought swings back to verse 14, but with an added fulness that makes it incomparably precious: **But all things are of God, who reconciled us to himself through Christ, and gave unto us the ministry of reconciliation; to wit, that God was in Christ reconciling the world unto himself, not reckoning unto them their trespasses, and having committed unto us the word of reconciliation.** By τὰ πάντα the apostle means **all things** pertaining to the change he has just described; they **are of God,** ἐκ τοῦ θεοῦ, the true God himself is their originator. How he is this, is now set forth: **who has reconciled us to himself through Christ.** Καταλλάσσειν and ·καταλλαγή are the words for exchange, as when money is changed, or given in exchange for goods; then, of persons, it is used of the change from enmity to friendship, whether this involves that only one, or that both parties drop their difference or adjust or remove it in some other way. So God is said here to have established a reconciliation, one in which he "reconciled us to himself," removing what separated "us" from him. Nothing is said of his wrath on the one hand, or of our enmity against him, although both are naturally implied. "With καταλλαγή connects itself all that language of Scripture which describes sin as a state of enmity (ἔχθρα) with God (Rom. 8, 7; Eph. 2, 15; James 4, 4); and sinners as enemies of him and alienated from him (Rom. 5, 10; Col. 1, 21); Christ on the cross as the Peace, and maker of peace between God and man (Eph. 2, 14; Col. 1, 20)." Trench. But the observation is correct that in this act of reconciliation God is really conceived as a judge who is bound to hold against us our trespasses (verse 19), and thus his reconciling us to himself is not to be considered a mere change of mind on his part, and much less a change of mind on our part brought about by God, but we must conceive of it as a removal of the guilt which our transgressions heaped up, and for which, until that removal, the divine Judge had to hold us liable ("reckoning unto them their trespasses"). The reconciliation here meant is the change of our *relation to God* which God himself effected; and this change be wrought **through Christ** as the means or instrument, namely through his atoning death, by which God brought about a full propitiation (ἱλασμός) or satisfaction for our sins. Rom. 4, 25: "Whom God set forth to be a propitiation, through faith, by his blood." Rom. 5, 10: "We were reconciled to God through the death of his Son." The pronoun **us** in no way restricts this reconciliation, for this embraces "the world" (19); but Paul here speaks of himself and his fellow laborers, explaining how both their work and the motives with which they carry it on are "of God." — Therefore he at once adds to the fact of their reconciliation, that it was this same God who **gave unto us the ministry of reconciliation.** Διακονία is any service by which others are benefited, and **the ministry of reconciliation** is that special service, embodied in a particular office, which is connected with God's great act of reconciliation; it is the service of proclaiming this reconciliation to men, to preach and teach the Gospel of grace in Christ Jesus. — Both the reconciliation and its office is further explained: **to wit, that God was in Christ reconciling the world unto himself.** The ὡς ὅτι introducing this sentence has been ex-plained in a variety of ways by the different N. T. grammars and exegetes. Many of them make ὅτι causal, some taking ὡς ὅτι together as pleonastic, while others, together with our English versions, make it declarative. We have thus the choice of translating: "as (is the case) since;" or simply "since," or "because;" or: **to wit, that.** The causal meaning of ὅτι seems inappropriate here, since that would make

Paul adduce as proof for the fact he has stated the very fact itself: God reconciled us and gave us the ministry, *because* God reconciled the world and committed unto us the word of reconciliation (the emphasis throughout in the Greek being on "God"). We therefore prefer the declarative meaning. In verse 19 Paul states practically the same thing as in verse 18, only with added explanation and emphasis; and we may read this verse either as the apostle's own explanation to the Corinthians of what he has just said before; or, as a summary, furnished by Paul, of what "the ministry of reconciliation" is to proclaim: "to wit, that, *etc.*" The former seems most natural. These critical questions, the intricacies of which cannot be elaborated here, do not affect the substance of the great doctrine set forth; and this is the chief concern of every Gospel minister. — **God was in Christ reconciling the world unto himself.** The emphasis is on θεός and likewise on καταλλάσσων; as in verse 18: "of God." Our whole salvation is God's work, his alone. It is best not to make a separate proposition of θεὸς ἦν ἐν Χριστῷ, as Luther, Calvin, the A. V. (note its punctuation), and others do: "God was in Christ;" for evidently καταλλάσσων ἑαυτῷ has the emphasis and constitutes the point of the sentence: "God was reconciling to himself," *i. e. God* was doing this great work; and *reconciling to himself* was this mighty work. The participle with the imperfect ἦν describes the act as a process and at the same time makes the action stand out more majestically. — **In Christ** is similar to "through Christ" in the previous verse; it points to what was done by God in the death of Christ on the cross (compare verse 14): God there changed the relation of the world to himself, placing the world into a relation of peace instead of condemnation. In Christ and in Christ alone did our reconciliation take place, because he alone could offer the mighty atonement for our sins; and this he did offer, and so God made the reconciliation. — This embraced **the world,** every human being; note the "all" in verse 14. The attempt of Hodge to reduce also this word to mean only "the class of beings towards whom God was manifesting himself as propitious" (*Commentary,* 144), shows how Calvinists must violate the plain words of Scripture to make room for their limited atonement. They thus take away the one all-sufficient comfort of poor sinners, that they, every one without an exception, are embraced in "the world" which God reconciled unto himself. — The next two participles: λογιζόμενος and θέμενος are evidently parallel; but the latter is an aorist, and at the same time it states something that cannot be viewed as a part of the reconciling act itself. The two participles must therefore be taken as pointing out two important facts connected with the reconciling act of God: God was reconciling the world to himself in Christ, and so he is now **not reckoning unto them their trespasses** (μὴ λογιζόμενος, present participle, retaining its present force, and not made an imperfect by ἦν), **and having committed unto us the word of reconciliation** (καὶ θέμενος, in a past definite act, but one following the reconciling act itself). God reckoned the trespasses of the world to Christ when Christ died and paid the world's penalty on the cross, and so ever after God does not reckon these trespasses to the world, does not treat the world with wrath and condemnation, casting it from him forever, but, looking to Christ and his atoning merits, he turns all his love and grace to the world, and offers it the pardon and salvation Christ has prepared (verse 20). The αὐτοῖς, **unto them** points to the individual sinners which make up the sum total called "world," and in παραπτώματα likewise their guilt is viewed as a multitude of trespasses, not as one single mass of sin. So we may say: every single sin of every single sinner was laid on Christ, and so is not now charged against the sinner by a reconciled God; if one single sin were so charged against you or me, our hope of salvation would be shut out from the start. The universal non-imputation here spoken of as the direct result of God's reconciling act and as embracing every sinner as included already in the "world," must be clearly distinguished from the personal non-imputation of sin which takes place only for those sinners who personally accept Christ and the reconciliation God effected in him. The latter is based on the former and is always connected with faith; and it is the latter which is called "justification," or "justification by faith," in the constant language of Scripture, of our Confessions, and of our preaching and teaching generally (Rom. 3, 28; 4, 7-8; *etc.*). If we use "justification" also for the former act, we must guard carefully against confusing the two, the more as some have failed grievously in this respect.* — God changed the relation of the world to himself, he now for Christ's sake turns all his grace and favor to the sinful world. But the world of itself knows nothing about this mighty change, so God did one thing more, which the apostle puts into the statement: **having committed unto us the word of reconciliation.** The margin translates more closely: *having placed in us* this word. God put the precious word, which is to announce the reconciliation to all sinners everywhere, into the hearts of the apostles and preachers of the Gospel. Let every preacher look closely at ἐν ἡμῖν, and see that the

---

*The mistake here referred to consists of making the justification of the world, which took place at the death of Christ, the only justifying act of God, thus leaving no room for the act by which God pronounces each individual sinner free from guilt the moment he comes to faith. This error is aided by the faulty terminology: "objective justification," and "subjective justification." Usually the former is taken to mean God's justifying sentence regarding the whole world. The best name for this, if one wishes to speak of it as a justification, is: *universal justification.* By the second they who use the term generally mean the appropriation of "objective justification" through faith. It is apparent at a glance that "subjective justification" in this sense is no act of God at all, but merely a change that takes place in us. Here the full faultiness of these terms appears. When God pronounces a poor sinner who believes in Christ free from guilt, this is altogether an objective act of God, one that takes place outside of us, in heaven above. The right name for this is *personal justification.* And let us remember, this is what the Scriptures, and Confessions and all preachers and teachers in the church ordinarily and constantly term justification. See the Catechism for instance.

word of reconciliation he proclaims this day and in sermon after sermon is really in his own soul. It is not for him merely to have it in his keeping intellectually, he must possess it spiritually, as did Paul, so that the love of God and Christ which is in that word may "constrain" him with its blessed power (verse 14).

God's embassadors intreat us to be reconciled to God.

Paul's great concern is that the Corinthians may understand aright the inwardness of his office as a preacher of Christ's atonement and God's reconciliation who himself is constrained by the love of which he speaks. Of this he now writes at length in the closing verses of this chapter and in the first 13 verses of the next. We have only the opening sentences of this discussion to deal with. **We are embassadors therefore on behalf of Christ, as though God were intreating by us: we beseech** *you* **on behalf of Christ, be ye reconciled to God. Him who knew no sin he made** *to be* **sin on our behalf; that we might become the righteousness of God in him.** The apostle is drawing a deduction: **therefore,** namely since the word of reconciliation is committed to us. He begins the sentence with **on behalf of Christ**, making this emphatic. In this instance ὑπέρ cannot mean instead of, because the apostles are viewed here not as representatives of Christ, but of God, and it is he too who has given them their commission (verses 18-19). The word **embassadors** expresses the dignity of the office and work; at the same time it describes the apostles as both messengers and representatives. An embassador speaks in the name and by the authority of another, and he utters not his own thoughts, promises, offers, or demands, but those of the king or government sending him. The message of an embassador receives no authority from the messenger himself, who is only the mouthpiece of another. And yet all the authority of that other lies behind the message conveyed. If the message is rejected or the mes-

senger mistreated, the offense is all against the sovereign
who sent the embassador. Let us who are God's embassadors to-day realize this fully, but let us not make the
mistake of altering the message and word committed to
us and then thinking that God's power and authority are
still behind them. — We are embassadors, **as though God
were intreating by us;** the genitive absolute τοῦ θεοῦ
παρακαλοῦντος states an action accompanying that of the
main verb πρεσβεύομεν. These two statements go together,
the second explaining the first. Our embassadorship is as
though **God** himself is speaking, merely using the apostles
as his instruments: **by us.** But the wonder is that God,
who is infinitely great and high, should be **intreating** a
sinful, fallen, death-worthy world. What utter condescension! But this is only in harmony with what lies behind it, when God, instead of turning from the corrupt
and sin-cursed world, in Christ extends to it his grace and
pardon. Note the correlation of "Christ" and "God" in
this connection. — For Paul, to be an embassador of God,
is to exercise his office forthwith; so at once he states his
message here: **we beseech** you **on behalf of Christ, be
ye reconciled to God.** God's "intreating" is Paul's "be-
seeching;" in both words is the condescension of divine
love which seeks to win us poor sinners to accept the gifts
of that love and then to respond with an answering love.
On behalf of Christ, in his name and interest, is correct,
not "in his stead," because the embassadors are God's representatives and spokesmen. Their message is altogether in
our own interest, for our own benefit, but here, because
Christ gave his life for us, he is represented as having the
greatest interest and concern in the preaching of the Gospel
which is to bring to him the souls he so dearly purchased.
— **Be ye reconciled to God** appeals to all in general;
quisquis audiet is to take it to himself. The imperative
second aorist καταλλάγητε is passive: **be ye reconciled.** God
alone can effect the reconciliation, by taking the sin away,
which he did in Christ; man can only accept this reconciliation effected by God. And even this he is absolutely help-

less to do, until God himself comes to him with the efficacious message of reconciliation (the Word as a means of grace), full of divine love, grace, goodness, and truth, and lets it ring in his ears and heart. This message is the power by which God enkindles faith in the sinner's heart, so that he trusts the message and its author, believes, and thus appropriates the reconciliation of God for his own personal salvation, and ever after lives in the blessedness and peace of it. — Paul continues the message by showing on what the call to be reconciled rests: **Him who knew no sin he made** *to be* **sin on our behalf.** In the participial designation τὸν μὴ γνόντα ἁμαρτίαν we have γινώσκειν used with its intensive meaning, *nosse cum affectu et effectu;* Christ never knew sin, as we do, by being inclined to it, loving it, experiencing it, being inwardly touched, tainted, injured by it. Sin beat upon him from the outside, but never invaded his heart to the slightest extent. John 8, 46; I Pet. 2, 22. The subjective negative μή has been variously interpreted, as expressing God's thought concerning Christ, or Christ's own, or that of the apostle and the church. It is either the first, since it occurs in a message of God uttered by God's embassador, and also in a sentence on what God has done; or the second, matching the γινώσκειν of Christ's experience. In either case it thus becomes the third, since the church believes both God and Christ. The abstract: **sin,** ἁμαρτία, without the article, means sin in its widest range, so that sin in any and every form, whether as a condition, motive, feeling, thought, or act is denied of Christ. — Him **on our behalf** (emphasized by its position) God made sin; but, as in verse 14, ὑπέρ must mean "in our stead," because only by being made our Substitute could Christ's suffering and death under the load of our sin avail anything "on our behalf." The abstract is repeated: him God **made** *to be* **sin** (ἐποίησεν, by a definite act); it is a terse and exceedingly powerful way of saying that all sin was placed upon the sinless, spotless Lamb of God by God himself, so that in the judgment on Calvary Christ stood before God not only as *a* sinner, or even *the* *greatest* sinner, but as *the one and only* sinner in the world. And thus this "One died for all," verse 14, thereby doing what all the sinners in all the world could not have done if all had died: atoning completely for sin. — And the purpose of it all was: **that we might become the righteousness of God in him.** In the "righteousness of God" we have the opposite of the "sin" which Christ was made to be. To be righteous is to satisfy the requirements of the divine norm of right; and **righteousness** is the quality or condition which measures up to that norm. All so-called human righteousness falls far short, it is nothing but filthy rags, never a perfect spotless garment. Therefore God has prepared a righteousness himself in Christ, which is therefore properly called **the righteousness of God;** it meets every requirement of the divine judgment and is always accepted and acknowledged by him. This wonderful righteousness, of which the world never dreamed, God reveals and offers in the Gospel, Rom. 1, 17. See on this subject the text for the Third Sunday in Epiphany. Paul is even now revealing and offering it. There is but one way to obtain it, namely by faith. As God reconciled us to himself "in Christ," so also we are to become the righteousness of God **in him,** by believing in him and his atoning merits. The moment faith is enkindled in the heart by the precious message of God's righteousness in the Gospel, that moment God declares us just, *i. e.* justifies us; in that moment "the righteousness of God" is ours, as completely ours as our sin was Christ's sin on the cross; and even as God made him to be "sin" there for us, so now we are become "the righteousness of God in him." And this is what Christ died for: to reconcile the world unto God, and to justify all those who believe.

> "Jesus, Thy blood and righteousness
> My beauty are, my glorious dress:
> 'Midst flaming worlds, in these arrayed,
> With joy shall I lift up my head."

32

HOMILETICAL HINTS.

"Put off thy shoes from off thy feet, for the place whereon thou standest is holy ground," Ex. 3, 5.

Two images meet us in our text: the cross on Calvary with its priceless burden of divine love reconciling a sinful world unto God, and, kneeling in Spirit beneath that cross, the heart of one of Christ's most devoted followers, utterly constrained by that love and its wondrous manifestation. But there is more, much more: every one of the great cords that bind together the great love of him on the cross with the answering love of him who kneels beneath the cross is here pointed out to us: a world of sin wiped out by a Savior's blood, a world of sinners reconciled unto God, a divine righteousness prepared for all, a message of reconciliation sent out into all the world, a host of embassadors of God proclaiming and offering the peace wrought on the cross, hearts cleansed and pardoned by the atoning blood, faith looking with gratitude to him who wrought their pardon, a new life glowing where once the old death held dreadful sway, and thus a heavenly love holding with holy constraint those whom it has won and made wholly its own. Come, let us view the wonders of Calvary, that they may win and bless our hearts anew with heavenly light and life and peace.

"One died for all, therefore all died." One great, pure, powerful enough, paid the penalty of all, therefore in him all have paid it.

He was made sin for us; we are made righteousness in him. He took our burden of death from us, we take the gift of pardon, cleansing, and peace from him. — "As if any friend pays a debt for a friend, the debtor is freed by the merit of another, as though it were by his own. Thus the merits of Christ are bestowed upon us, in order that, when we believe in him, we may be accounted righteous by our confidence in Christ's merits, as though we would have merits of our own." *Apology,* 237, 19. — "The righteousness of faith before God consists alone in the gracious reconciliation or the forgiveness of sins, which is presented to us of pure grace, for the sake of the merit alone of Christ as Mediator, and is received alone through faith in the promise of the Gospel." *F. C.,* 575, 30.

In Christ God saw the sin of the whole world, and poured out his wrath upon it. And thus he himself established a reconciliation, by atoning for the sin that separated us from him. It was all of God. — And so also when now you and I are personally reconciled to God. God works in us the acceptance of his reconciliation. To be sure the prodigal son had to change inwardly when he returned to his father, but all the change was that he bethought himself of his father and accepted that father's pardon and reconciliation.

The whole Gospel is a message that God has reconciled us to himself. The whole work of the ministry is to proclaim to men that God has reconciled them to himself. The whole work of the church is to lead men to accept this divinely wrought reconciliation and to continue therein. But the great thing in reconciliation is always love, and here it is a love as great as he himself who wrought the reconciliation. This is the love that shines in the Gospel, that sounds forth its call through the ministry, that spreads wide the portals of the church. Let this love take hold of you and bless you with all its gifts and powers. There is no greater love than that which lifted Christ on the cross, he who will not submit to that will never find reconciliation with God, for nothing but God's great love in Christ could reconcile lost sinners to himself.

"New"—the old sin, curse, accusation, fear, darkness, death, all gone. "New"—a new cleansing, washing in the Lamb's blood, assurance from God, peace and confidence in the soul, hope and joy for all eternity, and in and over all this a new and evergrowing love kindled by the love of him who died for us and rose again.

"One Died For All."

I. *Then all are dead.*
II. *Then all may live.*
III. *Then all should love.*

The Reconciliation of the Cross.

I. *Effected by God.*
II. *Announced in the Word.*
III. *Accepted by faith.*

"In the Cross of Christ I Glory!"

I. *It crowns God's love.*
II. *It cancels my sin.*
III. *It kindles my faith.*
IV. *It compels my devotion.*

What Crowns the Cross on Calvary?

I. *God's reconciliation and righteousness.*
II. *Our devotion and love.*

The Reconciling Power of Calvary's Cross.

I. *On God's part it reconciled us unto him.*
II. *On our part it bids us to be reconciled unto him.*

THE EASTER CYCLE.

THE EASTER CYCLE.

Easter to Cantate.

The Easter cycle contains six texts, plainly divided into two section of three. The texts for Easter Sunday, Easter Monday, and Quasimodogeniti, deal directly with the great Easter miracle and its proper commemoration by the Christian church. Quasimodogeniti is made the octave of Easter Sunday, as in the old gospels and in the Eisenach gospels, and rounds out the celebration. A glance at these three texts shows how finely they are chosen to fit their respective places. In all three of them the mighty fact of Christ's resurrection stands out prominently, especially in the first. In all three of them there is exultation and festive joy. Since they are epistle texts they state not only the fact of Christ's resurrection, but at the same time the full significance of this fact as regards our salvation and the priceless blessings comprised therein and made our own. — Easter Sunday brings us the triumphant assurance: "But now is Christ risen from the dead!" Naturally, this climax of the text must be the heart of the Easter Sunday sermon. Christ is risen indeed! But at once we are shown what this resurrection means for us both objectively and subjectively: it establishes beyond all shadow of doubt the verity of the entire Gospel, the reality of Christ's atonement for our sins, the validity of our faith, the certainty of our own blessed resurrection and its accompanying hope. A richer Easter text cannot be found; the preacher will delight to use it, and his congregation to hear it. Its burden is *Christ risen; and all our salvation assured.* — Easter Monday is celebrated by only a few of our congregations in this country, but the text here set for the day is so fine that most preachers will rejoice to use it at least for Easter evening. Here again the note of triumph goes forth: "O death, where is thy sting!" And coupled with it is the fervor of gratitude: "Thanks be to God which giveth us the victory through our Lord Jesus Christ!" But as befits a text for second place, here we have the application of the great Easter truth for our daily lives. Rejoicing in our glorious victory and the hope of incorruption and immortality, we must be firm, diligent, confident all our days. So this text deals with *the full appropriation and utilization* of the great Easter blessing. — All this is rounded out by Quasimodogeniti. There is still the festival note of joy: "Blessed be the God and Father of our Lord Jesus Christ!" Then comes the story of *our living hope* centered in Christ's resurrection, dwelling in us by regeneration, guarded by God's power even in the fire of trial, and presently to be crowned with heavenly fulfilment. A rich text indeed, full of the finest festive light and joy.

The following three texts of this cycle are certainly noteworthy. Each of them contains two elements: first God's grace to us, next our acceptance and response. But there is a marked gradation, in that the first element overshadows the second, in the first text; both are about equally balanced in the second; and the second element is especially prominent in the third. Misericordias Domini brings out the central truth in all that was shown us in the Easter celebration, the very heart of the Gospel, that we are saved altogether by divine grace through faith. We may say this text deals with *grace and faith,* although the latter is mentioned only as the natural corollary of the former. — In the text for Jubilate the same thought is presented, only that now we are shown God's love in the sending of his Son and in the propitiation he wrought for our sins. This must be answered by love on our part. So the subject of the text is *love and love;* only the preacher must deal with both in the light of the Easter celebration just passed. — In the final text of this cycle, the one for Cantate, the second element receives most prominence. The sum of the text is *faithfulness,* but this founded on the risen Christ (who is once more emphatically mentioned), it is stimulated by Paul's example, and made strong and enduring by the faithful saying of him who cannot deny himself. — The two parallel lines of thought in these texts will be found highly effective: on God's part grace, love, faithfulness; and, produced by these in us: faith in God's grace, love as the answer to love, and faithfulness as the response to faithfulness.

EASTER SUNDAY.

1 Cor. 15, 12-20.

A note of triumph rings through this dramatic Easter text. We hear its first sound in the surprised question with which Paul challenges certain Corinthians: "How say some among you that there is no resurrection of the dead?" Then we hear it rising with increased power and volume as the apostle deduces one invincible conclusion after another from this false notion of the foolish Corinthians. And finally, when the last conclusion is drawn and all the Gospel and all our salvation is seen to depend on Christ's resurrection, with a mighty burst of divine assurance the triumphant note rings out: "But now hath Christ been raised from the dead, the firstfruits of them that are asleep!" This triumph must ring through the entire Easter sermon, lifting up the hearts of both the preacher and his hearers in heavenly assurance and joy. — Our text does exactly what we have a right to expect of an epistolary text for this great festival: it presents the mighty deed wrought for our salvation in all its saving power and results for us poor sinners. We see indeed, as could not be otherwise on this day, that Christ is risen, but we see at the same time what all this resurrection has wrought for us and what therefore it must mean to us. The effectiveness of our text in this respect could hardly be greater. The fact that Paul unfolds the consequences of Christ's resurrection in a negative way, by unfolding what would be the case if Christ had *not* been raised, may be used to heighten the effect of the sermon by the dramatic feature that is thus involved; only it would be a mistake to stay on the negative side and adhere to the negative form. All these negations the apostle himself turns into mighty affirmations by his closing declaration, and this, as the crowning point of the text, must govern the whole sermon. The affirmations thus resulting shatter forever these dismal negations, and thus on a dark background make the heavenly blessings of Christ's resurrection stand out the more vividly. Modern skepticism in regard to Christ's resurrection, or in regard to the resurrection in general, should certainly have no prominence in the Easter sermon; if it be necessary to treat of it especially, some other sermon should handle the subject. This day our one duty is to proclaim *Christ, risen,* and in and with that *all our salvation forever secured.* We may divide the text itself into three sections: first we have the apostle's question which furnishes the point for his discussion; next, the apostle's deductions unfolding what the denial of the resurrection implies; and finally his positive assurance to all, that Christ is raised indeed.

The question.

In the first verses of the fifteenth chapter the apostle records the central facts of the Gospel which he preached, and in connection with these he introduces a full statement of the historical proof for Christ's resurrection. He says explicitly that what he himself had thus received he conveyed to the Corinthians, and they received it on their part and were saved thereby (compare verses 1-9). He thus lays the foundation on which he builds in our text when he takes up the denial of the resurrection and shows what this must imply. Keeping this in mind we will catch the full force both of Paul's surprised question and of the powerful reply he makes to it. **Now if Christ is preached that he hath been raised from the dead, how say some among you that there is no resurrection of the dead?** With a simple δέ, **now,** the apostle makes the transition to the new side of the subject he now wishes to take up. There is no article with **Christ** in the Greek; Paul means Christ in general as he forms the basis of faith and hope for the Corinthians. He **is preached,** at this very time by the Corinthian pastors in their public assemblies and elsewhere, as the risen Christ. **That he hath been raised from the dead** summarizes this preaching, stating in a simple sentence what the Corinthians had first received through Paul's own preaching (verses 1-3) and had held fast ever since. Paul fixes this from the very start, because it is the vital point in all that he is about to say, and he intends to use it with all the power of truth there is in it. The passive ἐγήγερται, **he hath been raised,** implies God as the agent. The Scriptures say both that God raised Christ (Rom. 6, 4; 8, 11; Matth. 16, 21; 17, 23; 26, 32), and that Christ arose himself (Mark 9, 31; Luke 18, 33); in both cases the act is due to the divine power, which belongs to Christ as well as to the Father. Jesus had power to lay down his life, and to take it again, John 10, 18. Here the apostle uses the passive and makes God the agent because of the parallel he has in mind regarding our resurrection as a work of God. — **How say some among you** is an expression of surprise: how is it possible? what delusion causes this? Who the τινές are we can only surmise. Putting together what we know of the Corinthians as Greeks and their inclination to philosophic ideas and reasonings, we can say that these deniers of the resurrection were very likely a few educated members of the congregation who revived some of the notions that were prevalent among Greek men of learning. We have a parallel in the men of Athens who laughed Paul to scorn and refused to hear him longer when he mentioned the resurrection of Christ (Acts 17, 32). It is probable too that they belonged to the adherents of Apollos and were brought into the congregation after Paul had left it. — They set up the doctrine **that there is no resurrection of the dead,** that such a thing could not be, namely a rising up to life of those once dead. How they established this to their minds is not indicated, Paul deals only with the claim as such, and here it is enough for us to note that human reason in one way or another has always found objection to this doctrine and attempted to show its falseness. In Corinth, it seems, the resurrection in general was denied without reference to the

Gospel doctrine of Christ's resurrection. But Paul sees at once, what others at first failed to see: the resurrection in general cannot be denied without advancing to a denial also of Christ's resurrection. Both stand and fall together. What the denial of the latter implies is no less than a destruction of the entire Gospel in all its parts. This the apostle uses as a weapon with which to crush the error and mightily to establish and safeguard the truth.

The deductions.

Paul at once correlates the two resurrections: **But if there is no resurrection of the dead, neither hath Christ been raised.** For a moment he allows the Corinthian error to stand, but only to analyze it and bring out all that is bound up in it, and thus the more thoroughly to refute it. If there is no resurrection of the dead, then, whether the Corinthians have realized it or not, it is certain: **neither hath Christ been raised.** The resurrection deals with the body, and Christ's body was given unto death on the cross and then buried, like any human body, in the grave. He was flesh of our flesh, bone of our bone, and in this respect altogether one with us, although in person the Son of God. So it could not be argued that he was a different and higher being and therefore exempt from the rule that the dead are not raised. The apostle also disregards any such evasion of the point; it would be too far wide of the mark. — He therefore at once proceeds to build upon the solid foundation he has laid: **and if Christ hath not been raised, then is our preaching vain, your faith also is vain.** With Christ not raised, it follows of a certainty: **vain,** or *void* (margin), is both the apostolic **preaching,** and the Corinthians' **faith.** The word "vain" is repeated and put forward in both cases for emphasis; it denotes emptiness, vacuity. All Gospel preaching, every assertion and promise in it, is then hollow, with no reality back of it; and the same is then true of any "faith" or confidence resting upon such preaching; for the two belong together, the latter resting wholly on the former, and the former always intended to produce the latter. — How this is the apostle shows more fully. **Yea, and we are found false witnesses of God; because we witnessed of God that he raised up Christ: whom he raised not up, if so be that the dead are not raised.** Verse 15 stands out as a complete, independent statement and should be separated by more than a comma, as in the Greek text, from the foregoing; the English uses a period. The stress is on ψευδομάρτυρες, the force of which is augmented by the genitive τοῦ θεοῦ. The apostles would be **false witnesses,** and false in respect to **God.** Meyer makes τοῦ θεοῦ an objective genitive; not witnesses which belong to God, but which testify concerning God. This is proper because of what follows. By calling himself a witness the apostle describes his office; he has nothing of his own to convey to the Corinthians or anyone else, he conveys only what he has seen and heard and what has been entrusted to him. — The terribleness of what Paul is here writing he brings out by the explanation: **because we witnessed of God** what is not true. But "of God" is too weak for κατὰ τοῦ θεοῦ, which is really: "against God" (so also Luther), the preposition having the same force as in 4, 6; 2 Cor. 10, 5; 13, 8; Gal. 5, 17; it shows that the apostles would not only be liars, but blasphemous liars, speaking falsehood against the true God himself, saying **that he raised up Christ** (or: *the Christ,* margin): **whom he raised not up, if so be that the dead are not raised.** In order to show the enormity of the falsehood, the apostle sets it down in cold, plain words for the Corinthians to look at, and he is careful to insert the false assertion which lies at the bottom of it all, and which some in Corinth actually believed. Luther puts into Paul's mouth the following: "God forbid that I should say such a thing or let such abominable blasphemy come into my heart! Therefore, I will not permit this article of faith to be doubted, but will hold it as more certain than my own life, and will boldly continue in it, that when I lie in death and rot I shall come forth again, more beautiful and bright than this sun."

But there is another side to this denial of the resurrection by the Corinthians, which, when unfolded, displays still more the fearful consequences which it involves. In presenting this side the apostle does exactly what he did in the first instance (verse 13): he correlates Christ's resurrection with that of the dead generally. **For if the dead are not raised, neither hath Christ been raised.** This is the key to what precedes, and again the key to what follows. **And if Christ hath not been raised, your faith is vain; ye are yet in your sins. Then they also which are fallen asleep in Christ have perished. If in this life only we have hoped in Christ, we are of all men most pitiable.** Paul has already said that with Christ not risen our faith is "void," empty, with nothing real to rest on; now he adds the other thought: our faith then is also **vain,** ματαία, idle, foolish, useless; it is good for nothing, because it brings no benefit or fruit, and the word is emphatically put forward. Bengel: κενή, *sine vera re;* ματαία, *sine usu.* The two are evidently closely related, for a faith that rests on empty air can be of no use; whatever it trusts on will fail and come to nought. — This appears at once in what follows: **ye are yet in your sins,** in their guilt and condemnation; compare John 8, 21. Faith in a Savior who died but failed to rise is "vain," because he cannot free us from our sins. If there is no resurrection, there is also no redemption, no reconciliation with God, no justification, no life and salvation. If Christ is dead, then every believer is forever dead in trespasses and sins. As long as Christ, our surety, is not released, it is certain the debt is not paid, and we are held liable just as before, no matter how much we may trust in the supposed payment. Christ's resurrection is the positive proof that his sacrifice was indeed sufficient, and fully accepted as such by God. Therefore Christ was raised again for our justification, Rom. 4, 25. To reject his resurrection is to reject the efficacy of his sacrifice, and his death would be as "vain" as our faith in a dead Christ. — But there is another step: **Then they also which are fallen asleep in Christ have perished.** When Paul wrote, near Easter-time in the year 57, some of the Corinthians had already died, believing and trusting in Christ to the end. Paul uses the significant word κοιμηθέντες, **are fallen asleep in Christ;** the aorist expresses that one by one they closed their eyes for the final slumber; and to fall asleep in Christ is the beautiful Scripture expression for the Christian's death, who sinks into peaceful slumber to be awakened presently by the risen Lord to the new and glorious life in his presence. The word itself is thus a denial of the Corinthian error, a testimony to the heavenly hope of the resurrection from the dead at the last day, according to Christ's promise. **In Christ** signifies in union and communion with him by faith. What of all such, so dear to the hearts of their relatives now addressed by the apostle? One word expresses it: ἀπώλοντο, they **have perished,** they are lost forever without hope or help. Dying in their sins they have fallen into eternal damnation. In this crushing way the apostle brings home to his readers what the denial of the resurrection really means. He who persists in it writes on every believer's tomb: "Lost;" or, which is the same: "Damned." Nothing more heart-rending could be said. All the hereafter is shrouded in the blackest night; this has swallowed up those who have passed beyond, and it awaits those whose life is now swiftly passing away. And this is what those foolish Corinthians, whether they realized it or not, were putting in the place of the light and hope that shines for every believer beyond the grave; for Christ is risen indeed and become the firstfruits of them that are asleep; yea, we shall not perish, but have everlasting life (John 3, 16). — As in the first line of deductions, so now in this, the apostle makes a summary and comprehensive addition. **If in this life only we have hoped in Christ, we are of all men most pitiable.** The marginal rendering. preferred by the American Committee, is better: *If we have only hoped in Christ in this life, etc.* The correct text reads: εἰ ἐν τῇ ζωῇ ταύτῃ ἐν Χριστῷ ἠλπικότες ἐσμὲν μόνον, κτλ. The adverb μόνον stands at the end and cannot be drawn to ἐν τῇ ζωῇ ταύτῃ at the head of the sentence, as is done by the English versions; it modifies the entire sentence, making it mean: If we be no more than people who place their hope in Christ in this life. — The phrase **in this life** is not in contrast to the condition of those already dead, but is entirely general, and refers to all Christians as they live here and finally die. The perfect participle signifies a continuation of hope during the earthly life; Paul is viewing their life from the standpoint of its close. With the copula ἐσμέν the participle brings out the character and kind of the people here referred to, they are such as have kept on hoping. — To hope **in Christ** is to have our hope connected with him, deposited in him; its fulfilment depends entirely on him. If Christ is not risen then all Christians are nothing but people who spent their lives vainly hoping in Christ. — If this is all we are or can be, the apostle declares: **we are of all men most pitiable.** By this he says that all who are without faith and hope in Christ, all who are not Christians, are certainly to be pitied. They are without God and hope in this world. But it is more pitiable still to have a great hope in the heart all through life, to shape the whole life according to that hope, to crucify the flesh, to fight sin, to war against temptation, to bear the cross, to suffer reproach and many another ill, all for this hope, and then to have that hope a vacuous thing, an absolute and utter disappointment. This is Paul's commentary on a Christianity for this life without regard to what is to come after. A Christianity without a risen Christ and the sure and certain hope of the resurrection for ourselves, whatever men may say in laudation of its moral influence and good works, is worse than none.

The positive assurance.

Paul has pursued the Corinthian error pitilessly to its last desperate conclusion. He has woven a chain so ponderous and mighty that for every believer that error lies crushed and helpless forever. With a sudden dramatic turn, as effective in every way as all the reasoning he has

33

employed hitherto, he now voices the great Easter fact, which all through his previous reasoning trembled for expression in his own heart, and no doubt also in the hearts of his readers as they perused his inexorable lines. **But now hath Christ been raised from the dead, the firstfruits of them that are asleep.** Paul simply announces the great fact; he has already stated the historical evidence for it in the first section of the chapter, and that evidence strengthens the announcement now made. As a true witness testifying of God he sounds forth the clear truth of God. And that truth affords an immense relief. Like a climber in the Alps, trembling at the brink of some bottomless gulf, the rock already crumbling beneath his feet, suddenly finding himself at a turn where the path stretches safe and wide before him, so are we when from the journey to verse 19 we step over into verse 20. All the deductions the apostle has drawn rested on a mere supposition, which had entered some minds and was threatening to enter more; but it was and is utterly false. Therefore, like a house of cards all the deductions based on it fall at the breath of truth. The opposite of every one of these dreadful deductions is true, true to the utmost limit. Verse 12 must be reversed in its second half. — **But now hath Christ been raised from the dead,** and not like Jairus' daughter, or the widow's son, or Lazarus, Martha's and Mary's brother, but raised by the glory of God, lifted up into the glory which he had in the beginning with the Father, with a name that is above every name. The tomb of Joseph's garden is empty: Christ is risen indeed! — as our Savior and Redeemer, whose sacrifice avails before God, whose work is crowned with eternal success. — That would be enough, but the apostle adds: **the firstfruits of them that are asleep.** This is highly significant for all who believe in him. Paul does not bring in a line of details, as he might have done; he expects his readers to find the blessed details themselves when they reverse the conclusions he has drawn in analyzing the error. Here he sums up everything in a statement on the final result of Christ's resurrection for us all. The figure of the **firstfruits** brings up the image of a great harvest ushered in by the first sheaf which is presented as an offering to God, Lev. 23, 10. So Christ is the ἀπαρχή of **them that are asleep,** the κεκοιμημένοι (perfect participle), that have fallen into slumber and so continue asleep. The reference is not only to those who were dead when Paul wrote, but to all who sleep in Jesus. Their sleep is like that of Christ, it will end in a glorious awakening. The first sheaf ushers in all the coming harvest; it leads the great procession of sheaves. Paul thinks and speaks only of true Christians. Christ will indeed raise up all men, but he is not the firstfruits of those who rise to shame and everlasting contempt, Dan. 12, 2. The three persons whom Christ raised during his earthly ministry cannot be brought in here as part of the great resurrection, since they were merely returned to their earthly life and had to undergo death a second time. Enoch and Elijah were translated bodily to heaven and did not die at all. But the harvest has already begun, for after Christ's resurrection many bodies of the saints which slept arose, and came out of the graves, and went into the holy city, and appeared unto many, Matth. 27, 52, and, as we must conclude were then transferred to heaven. So in a twofold way the resurrection has actually begun, in Christ the firstfruits, and in a company of his saints, who now await the coming of us all.

> "Jesus, my Redeemer lives,
>   And his life I soon shall see;
> Bright the hope this promise gives,
>   Where he is I too shall be:
> Shall I fear then? Can the Head
>   Rise and leave the members dead?"

HOMILETICAL HINTS.

There is and can be no true Christianity without the risen Christ and faith in him, for Christianity is living union and communion with Christ, and this is impossible if Christ did not rise from the dead.

Not the doctrines which Christ uttered have in and by themselves conquered the world and built the church, but the living Lord himself who is ever in and with the doctrines and those who receive them by faith. Nothing is more foolish than the modern effort to hold fast those doctrines and at the same time to set aside the living Lord as unessential to the doctrines. Can you live in a house whose foundation you have removed? Ask yourself what makes the church valuable, indispensable to you, what is the highest blessing it offers you, and you will ever find, it is the Lord himself. What is the baptism of your child, if there is no living Christ to make your child his own? What is your confirmation, if you cannot enter into a covenant with the living Redeemer and be his own forever? What is every service in his house, if his name is only a name and he is not present to give you his blessings and receive your devotion? What is the Sacrament of his body and blood, if he remained in the grave and his body is dust like that of other men? There is not a single feature in our religion which in one way or another does not rest on the resurrection of Jesus from the dead. Take this away and the entire church and all Christianity sinks into ruin.

Are we to believe indeed that this earth is nothing but a great hearse, circling senselessly around the sun, and just as senselessly some day plunging into its fire to consume all these dead bones; that all that we have preached, loved, hoped, thought, and done, that was beautiful and good and true and great, shall turn absolutely into nothing? Our conscience rises in rebellion against the very idea and shouts a mighty denial, if there be a God and a Gospel at all.

You may take your choice: say, either it is possible that Christ should rise; or, it is impossible that he should rise, *i. e.* that God should break the yoke of sin and death, that God should redeem the world, rescue sinners, and lift them into eternal blessedness. What is possible or impossible in this respect God himself has told us, and the entire Bible is his Word.

Our Easter faith is no mere faith in the immortality of the soul, in a far-away beyond, but a faith in God who raised Jesus from the dead and will raise up our mortal bodies and make them like unto the body of Jesus, glorious forevermore.

For Christ only they are dead who are dead in their sins, dead in unbelief.

It was Luther who wrote in large letters on his table and the walls of his room: *Vivit, vivit,* He lives, he lives! when his enemies like a swarm of bees buzzed about him and he was ready to drop with discouragement and weariness.

The angel in Christ's tomb points to the place where the Lord lay and tells us: "He is not here!" But I point to my breast and answer him: "He is here; here is the life that he won for me from death, here is the peace he bought for me with his blood, and his living hand has placed them both in my bosom. He lives, and I have experienced the power of his life and resurrection."

See what God has done! By the resurrection of Christ he has turned this great charnel-house of death into a mighty harvest-field, and presently he will send his angel servants to bring in the golden sheaves.

For almost 1900 years the enemies of God and Christ have tried to destroy the great fact of Christ's resurrection. The world has changed tremendously in all this time, but one thing has remained, fixed, solid, immovable, the bulwark and citadel of our salvation, the great fact wrought by God himself, Christ's resurrection from the tomb. Every new effort of men to cancel that fact has only helped to overthrow the more the previous efforts of this kind. And towering beyond the reach of human hands, there it stands supreme, inaccessible to the foe, and thousands and thousands of believing hearts have been lifted aloft to stand there safe, jubilant, in the eternal light of salvation, and while foe after foe sinks down helpless in night and death, they continue their song: Halleluiah, Jesus lives!

Face your conscience, the multitude of your sins, and the damning sentence of the Law; then you will know what the apostle Paul means with his triumphant exclamation, Christ is risen from the dead. Look into the dark chamber of the tomb, see the hand of death reaching out to lay you low; then again you will know what the Gospel message of Christ's resurrection means. He who died for our sins and rose again, he alone has deliverance for us from sin and death, he alone has pardon, life, salvation.

But now is Christ Risen From the Dead!

   I. *He is risen, and we may preach it.*
  II. *He is risen, and we may believe it.*
 III. *He is risen, and we may rejoice in it.*
 IV. *He is risen, and we shall rise because of it.*

The Joyful Easter Message: The Lord is Risen, He is Risen Indeed!

I. *It establishes our faith.*
II. *It assures our forgiveness.*
III. *It guarantees our resurrection.*

C. C. Hein.

Our Confession of Faith Beside Christ's Open Grave.

I. *I believe in the communion of saints.*
II. *I believe in the forgiveness of sins.*
III. *I believe in the resurrection of the body.*
IV. *I believe in the life everlasting.*

Blau.

Faith's Easter Triumph.

I. *Over doubt.*
II. *Over sin.*
III. *Over death.*

Faith's Easter Vision.

It beholds:

I. *A living Savior in heaven.*
II. *A full pardon for every sin.*
III. *An efficient comfort in every tribulation.*
IV. *A peaceful slumber in the grave.*
V. *A glorious resurrection at the last day.*

Your Faith is not Vain.

I. *It rests on the Rock of Ages.*
II. *It rescues in every storm.*

Christ is Risen: We are of all Men Most Fortunate.

I. *Ours is a sure Gospel.*
II. *Ours is a sure faith.*
III. *Ours is a sure pardon.*
IV. *Ours is a sure hope.*

EASTER MONDAY.

1 Cor. 15, 54-58.

Easter morning brings us Paul's triumphant announcement of Christ's resurrection from the dead and a survey of the greatest blessings connected therewith. Easter Monday or — if we choose — Easter evening adds a jubilant word on the appropriation of the Easter blessings and their application to our daily lives. So the emphasis in our text rests on the thanks we owe to God for having given us the victory, and on the apostle's admonition to make full use of it in steadfastness and diligence. Our subject then should be *the full appropriation and utilization* of God's Easter blessings.

Our Easter thanks.

Paul reaches the close of his glorious chapter on the resurrection. He has taught the resurrection of Christ from the dead, and, based on this, our resurrection and the blessings connected with it; he has also described the resurrection body and the transformation which shall occur in the case of those who will still be alive at the last day. In treating of the last subject he has stated positively, "that flesh and blood cannot inherit the kingdom of God," verse 50, *i. e.* the kingdom in its eternal completion; be strengthens this by adding: "neither doth corruption inherit incorruption." Flesh and blood is our body in is present condition and form; and we must observe the distinction between the body as such, and the condition or form in which it may be. Jerome has well said: *Alia carnis, alia corporis definitio est; omnis caro est corpus, non omne corpus est caro.* Our bodies as they are now cannot enter heaven and the eternal world, they must be changed. That which is corruptible in them

519

must be removed and replaced by incorruption. *Corrupti-bile corpus, quale post lapsum factum est.* Calov. Sin has introduced corruption, and this must be swept out completely. On these fundamental truths the closing words of the apostle rest. They apply to all believers, whether they pass through death before reaching the kingdom, or undergo the sudden transformation at the last day. — **But when this corruptible shall have put on incorruption, and this mortal shall have put on immortality, then shall come to pass the saying that is written, Death is swallowed up in victory. O death, where is thy victory? O death, where is thy sting? The sting of death is sin; and the power of sin is the law: but thanks be to God, which giveth us the victory through our Lord Jesus Christ.** — There is something grand and solemn in the way Paul repeats the words of the 53rd verse in the first verse of our text. He strikes the chords of a triumphal song and he makes them ring out full and strong. Some of the old authorities omit the clause: "this corruptible shall have put on incorruption," but the best evidence shows that the words are genuine; they certainly heighten the effect of the entire statement. By lengthening the conditional part of the sentence, the apostle keys up the more our expectation as to what the conclusion will bring. — **When** this corruptible shall have put on incorruption refers to the last great day when all the dead shall arise from their graves. Their bodies shall come forth then, but without any trace of the corruption of sin that once affected them. — **This corruptible,** like the following **this mortal,** designates the body in its corrupt and mortal condition; the demonstrative **this** sounds as if, in writing the words the apostle were pointing to his own body. "Corruptible," destructible, perishable, subject to decay, is the wider term, including what is expressed by "mortal," which designates a particular mode, a destruction or passing away by means of death. The duplication is like that of Hebrew poetry, beautiful in its parallelism and rhythm, and markedly enriching the thought. What a sad condition our bodies are

in, "corruptible" and "mortal," even though the effects of
salvation have already set in and shed many a blessing upon
us. — Corruption itself cannot inherit incorruption (50),
but that does not mean that this body of ours, corruptible
now, can not eventually put on **incorruption,** a new condition and form, one that overcomes and expels forever the
old condition and form; a condition in which every trace
of sin and its harmful effects is gone, and there is in its
place the glory, beauty, and power of an eternal, indestructible life, that which Peter calls "an inheritance incorruptible and undefiled, and that fadeth not away, reserved in
heaven for you," 1 Pet. 1, 4. **Immortality** is the other
name for it, a condition free from the power of death, and
any deterioration or change which death works, fadeless
with the unchanging powers of the eternal life. — The apostle uses the figure of a garment: **shall have put on,**
ἐνδύσηται, the aorist subjunctive after ὅταν, followed by the
regular future γενήσεται. Not that corruption and mortality
shall merely be covered up and hidden from view by having
a mantle of incorruptibility and immortality cast over it,
for these two exclude each other so completely that whoever puts on the new garment first lays off the old, just as
when we are clothed in the garment of Christ's righteousness we lay off the garment of sin and guilt and the filthy
rags of our own righteousness. What a glorious moment
that shall be, when the Lord "shall fashion anew the body of
our humiliation, that it may be conformed to the body of his
glory, according to the working whereby he is able even to
subject all things unto himself," Phil. 3, 21. "Therefore,"
writes Besser, "the grave grieves no Christian, even though
it takes a long while until God's grain comes up. To those
who have fallen asleep the thousand years of their rest in
the grave will appear just like the twinkling of the eye
which transforms those who remain. And with perfect insight into God's ways both will unite in saying Amen to
God's way of turning what is mortal into immortality."—
Then shall come to pass the saying that is written introduces a quotation from Is. 25, 8; what the prophet ut-

tered in a **saying** will then be turned into actual reality (τότε γενήσεται) ; what **is written,** and thus as the Word of God is infallible, will be shown to be so by the outcome. **Death is swallowed up in victory** reproduces the Hebrew: "He (Jehovah) swallows up death forever," rather than the free Septuagint rendering: "Death, having prevailed, swallowed up men." Only the active form is changed by the apostle into the passive to suit the present connection. The Hebrew *lazenach,* which Delitzsch and Koenig render "forever," is probably from *nezach,* to shine or be victorious, and Paul translates it as the Septuagint does in some places: εἰς νῖκος (later form for νίκη), **in victory;** margin: *victoriously.* Paul thus quotes Isaiah closely. **Death** is the destructive power that produces in us corruption and mortality; and this fearful power will itself be **swallowed up,** consumed, and thus made to disappear completely and forever. "And death shall be no more," Rev. 21, 4. Luther: "The Scriptures announce how one death (Christ's) devoured the other (ours)." — In his *Introduction to the Holy Scriptures,* 7th ed., II, 340 and 346, Horn notes the difference between the quotation from Isaiah, which the apostle introduces because of its actual fulfilment at the last day, and the next quotation from Hos. 13, 14, which the apostle merely appropriates as expressive of his own thought. This mode of using the words or thoughts of another, because of their special force or beauty, is frequent among all good writers, and an adornment of style. It is not intended as an exact quotation, but as a free adaptation of the language or thought of another, sometimes in an entirely new and different setting. The N. T. writers thus frequently employ O. T. statements, because their minds are full of the thoughts and words of the old prophets. — Paul sees death forever conquered, and therefore sings his song of triumph over the vanquished foe, using the dramatic questions of Jehovah recorded by the prophet, but adapting them in a new form to his own special purpose: **O death, where is thy victory? O death, where is thy sting?** It ought to be plain that the apostle here intends only an allusion to what the prophet wrote, and no more; he does not intend a quotation in the usual manner, which is indicated also by the absence of any formula for introducing a quotation. Where the prophet had "death" in the first question, and *sheol* in the second, the apostle, according to the best Greek texts, used **death** in both. The same freedom is exercised in the questions themselves; in the second "sting" is taken from the Septuagint; the A. V., following the *textus receptus* has it in the first question. The Hebrew *sheol* is the place where death's power is displayed. All men are therefore said to pass into *sheol,* since all must give up this life and undergo death. The difference that divides men in death is generally disregarded in the O. T. use of the term *sheol,* or rather the full light of revelation does not yet illumine the threshold of eternity when the prophets speak of passing into *sheol.* The Septuagint used the term *hades* for *sheol* in our passage, and frequently elsewhere. *Hades,* however, goes beyond the indefinite Hebrew *sheol;* in the N. T. it is used to signify "hell," the place of torment for the damned. The light of revelation in the N. T. shows distinctly the great difference between men in death: the blessed and righteous pass at once into Paradise, into the hands of the Father and of Christ, into heaven, whereas the unbelieving and wicked are cast into *hades,* that is hell. The godly never enter *hades;* and it is a perversion of Scripture to imagine *hades* as having two compartments, one called Paradise, a preliminary abiding place for the blessed after death, and another called "hell," a preliminary abiding place for the damned. The fact that even some otherwise good commentators put forth this error only goes to show how delusive such false notions may be. For a good discussion of the entire subject compare Zietlow, *Der Tod,* 63 *etc.* and 87 *etc.* In our passage the A. V. has for the second question "grave," and in the margin "hell," probably on account of the *hades* in the Septuagint; the best texts, however, show that Paul used, in his free adaptation, "death" for both questions, and this for *sheol* in our passage is altogether acceptable. — When death is swallowed up forever, or swallowed up in victory, death's **victory,** which for a while seemed so real and great, will be gone. It filled the earth with graves and dead men's bones, laying low even the people of God, but in reality death was only an instrument in the hand of another, and having done its temporary work, is thrown aside, and for us all God steps in with a new work, a glorious resurrection from the dead, which reverses all death's apparent victory. — As with the victory, so with the **sting** of death. A κέντρον is a goad or any sharp pointed instrument, such as was used to drive oxen, or for purposes of torture; then also it is used for the sting of a scorpion or bee, the quills of a porcupine, *etc.* We may say therefore: death drove us all with his sharp goad, pierced us through with its instrument of torture, and laid us into the grave; or, death inflicted its poisonous sting upon us, and thus slew us. But this instrument of its power is gone forever when Christ calls our bodies from the grave. The apostrophe to death is highly dramatic and powerful, bringing out all the exultation and triumph in Paul's heart. — The apostle explains the figurative language he has used: **The sting of death is sin;** "as through one man sin entered into the world, and death through sin; and so death passed unto all men, for that all sinned," Rom. 5, 12. If there were no sin, or if we were perfectly exempt from sin, no death could touch us. Death operates always and everywhere through sin. Men have tried to play with "the sting of death" and yet escape its stroke; they have always tried in vain. — And **the power of sin is the law,** for sin itself is the transgression of the law, ἁμαρτία is to miss the mark set by the law as the expression of the divine will. So sin is always connected with God's law, which never mildly submits or consents to be broken, but always resents transgression and reacts with divine wrath upon the sinner who transgresses it. This too has been tried, with sad reiteration, to sin, and then to escape the power of sin which is the law; but every sin is broken law, and broken law strikes the sinner down. This then is how death keeps on in its destructive work: sin and the law are behind it.   Even now when Christians come to die they are not spared all the bitterness of death which results from sin and the law as the power of sin, for in death we still need a last repentance. Old Matthias Claudius said on his deathbed: "I have studied all my life to be ready for this hour, yet I did not think it would be as serious and severe as this." And Vinet writes: "On the countenance of death, however blessed it may appear, there still rests a reflection of the wrath of the Highest." Men may despise life, but that does not say that they have really made ready to die; and they may despise death, but that does not say they have really conquered death. — Only brief is the apostle's explanatory statement; his triumphant joy has one more glorious note to add, a deep, strong note of gratitude to God: **but thanks be to God, which giveth us the victory through our Lord Jesus Christ.** All this glorious **victory,** the resurrection to life with all that it implies of triumph over sin, death, and the condemnation of the law, it is God who is the Author and the Giver of it; and therefore the apostle's gratitude is all laid at the feet of God's throne. The present participle τῷ διδόντι, **which giveth,** shows that the giving takes place now already; we have the victory now as a present possession. "Beloved, now are we children of God, and it is not yet made manifest what we shall be. We know that if he shall be manifested, we shall be like him; for we shall see him even as he is." 1 John 3, 2. Some think the present participle merely marks the certainty of the future victory, that we *shall* have it as surely as if we *now* had it; but there is no need to disregard thus our actual present possession of the final victory. — God gives it to us now **through our Lord Jesus Christ,** as the Savior who atoned for our sins, conquered death, satisfied the law, brought immortality and life to light, and now transfers all the spoils of his victory to every believer. Let us remember, through him alone can we escape our direst foe; in the dark hour of death his rod and his staff alone can comfort us. Paul's thanks have echoed through the whole world, and wherever there were other possessors of the divine gift of everlasting victory through Christ they have made the apostle's fervent words their own.

Our Easter duty.

The great 15th chapter of First Corinthians concludes with a mighty call to duty. As when the women on the way from the open tomb met Jesus the risen Savior, and when Mary Magdalene saw him beside the tomb, all found themselves employed as messengers to convey the joy to others, so our Easter victory, every possession of it, gives us a great and blessed work to do. **Wherefore, my beloved brethren, be ye steadfast, unmoveable, always abounding in the work of the Lord, forasmuch as ye know that your labor is not vain in the Lord.** It is by far best to make this **wherefore,** ὥστε, reach back through the entire chapter and not to connect it only with τῷ διδόντι. — Verse 50 has the address "brethren" for the apostle's readers; here it is intensified by an affectionate addition: **my beloved brethren.** They are one with him in possessing the great victory through our Lord Jesus Christ, and this oneness unites them in a holy love, higher than mere affection (φιλεῖν) such as is otherwise found abundantly among men; therefore the ἀγαπητοί from ἀγαπᾶν. — **Be ye steadfast, unmoveable,** γίνεσθε, "become," and so "be." The word for **steadfast,** ἑδραῖοι, means sitting, and thus fixed, firm, unmoving, settled. It evidently refers to the inner faith, conviction, and character of the Corinthians. With a victory so great, their first duty is to be firmly and fully settled in it, so that they realize its greatness and glory, its preciousness and power, and abide in it with souls happy and thankful. So many are inwardly unstable, like water or sand, never settling down solidly in the Gospel and its glorious faith. Their hearts are fixed elsewhere, and as vain as those other things are so vain is their attachment to them. Easter hearts must be steadfast hearts, and every new Easter must make them more steadfast still. — **Unmoveable** is companion to "steadfast," ἀμετακίνητοι, from κινεῖν, to set in motion or shift, hence: not moved, shifted from your position. This refers to outward solicitation or attack. There are always foes to assail our Easter faith, sometimes striking it directly, then coming with subtle error to compromise our confession, and again trying to draw us into sinful conduct contrary to our Lord's will. Thus they would make slaves of us who are victors in Christ. Against them all stand "unmoveable" in the power and might of your Easter faith. — So rooted and grounded, so fortified and valiant in defense, let us add one thing more: **always abounding in the work of the Lord.** Here every word is eloquent with meaning. **Abounding,** περισσεύοντες, means: being more than enough, being rich to superfluity. What a word for the thousands who work, pray, testify, give, suffer as little as possible! But with our wealth of heavenly spoils and our eternal victory in Christ, we can and must "abound." — **In the work,** in real work, effort, labor; we are not called to idleness and mere enjoyment, and the time of our rest will come anon at eventide. The noblest, grandest, most profitable, most enduring work in the world is the work **of the Lord.** His church is full of it, he has instituted it, he gives the strength for it, it is altogether his, and every one of us has his full share of it to do. If there were no victory in him for us, then would we have nothing to do. Now we have; find your share of it, do it, superabound in it, revel in it, glory in it. — And this not for a day, but **always,** in youth and in age, in pleasant as well as in somber days, when many work with us and when we plod on alone, whether we have done ever so much already and others have done hardly anything at all — "always," πάντοτε. — And this is to cheer us on: **forasmuch as ye know that your labor is not in vain in the Lord.** By κόπος is meant our toil and weary effort, our sweat and our strain in the work; earnest workers are bound to experience that. But we ourselves know from the Lord himself that our labor is not **vain,** or *void,* **in the Lord.** "'In the Lord" and "void" do not and cannot harmonize. Our effort cannot be illusive, empty, hollow, as long as it is in him. Other effort is. When men make money, honor, or anything earthly their god, they may work hard, they may succeed in their way, but the whole undertaking has no foundation and basis worth while, and every exertion that brings such laborers nearer their goal is as vain as if they had not made it and not gone forward. There is something to every labor done in the Lord, a blessing for the laborer and a blessing for those labored for, both from the Lord. — So while we look forward in triumphant Easter hope and thankfulness, let us grow ever firmer in our faith, ever more diligent in our love.

HOMILETICAL HINTS.

Easter proclaims an immortality not only for half of our being, the soul alone, but a resurrection of the flesh, an immortal existence of spirit, soul, and body in eternal blessedness.

Not only the end of our earthly course, already its beginning bears the mark of death, and is subject to its influence and consuming power. Every breath we take decreases the sum-total allotted to us of God. Every step bears us nearer to the grave. Every day that we greet in the brightness of sunshine after the darkness of night shortens the term granted us for our stay here on earth. Every day sinking to its close calls to us: Soon, soon will the day of your life reach its close! Every year approaching its final hour preaches with new earnestness: Remember, to know thine end and the measure of thy days, what it is; that thou mayest know how frail thou art. Ps. 37, 4. Every slight indisposition of the body is a messenger reminding us of death. Every part of our life bears the stamp of mortality. Matthes.

"Death is swallowed up in victory." It has actually become part of the victory. Death is surely here yet, but it has been placed into God's plan of redemption for us. It belongs together with the things that work together for our good. It has changed its function entirely. From a master of the world it has become the servant of him who has now assumed the mastery unto himself. Willingly it follows the triumphal chariot of our great Easter Conqueror. From a jailor it has become a gate-keeper, from a curse it has changed into a blessing, from a destroyer of all our happiness, an usher into a happiness that never ends. Now death is not the end, but only a transition into a perfect, endless state. Riemer.

It may be, as we often hear, that death comes as a relief to those whose sufferings have been severe. But the despair which is so ready to exchange the apparently greater evil for one that seems less, certainly cannot be called deliverance. Nor is this true firmness, but only the breaking down of all hope. There is no deliverance in death except death be the servant of him who said to the poor malefactor: To-day shalt thou be with me in Paradise. Riemer.

To be free from death — is the longing of the whole world. Impossible, except we are freed from sin. To be free from sin — is the earnest desire of the soul. Impossible, except we are freed from the law. To be free from the law — is the sighing and groaning of those who have all their lives long felt the bondage of: Thou must, and: Thou must not! But this too is impossible, except we attain the glorious liberty of the children of God through Jesus our Redeemer.

If the true life does not begin for you here on earth; it will never begin. — Only what has begun to live here will endure and outlast death.

Since Easter the entire complexion of our life and our work in this world has changed. If our life were reduced to the short span between our first earthly bed and our last, then we would have to narrow down all our plans and undertakings accordingly. Temporary aims and inferior motives would dominate all our activity. Even if we would add as our highest effort the work of social uplift and betterment, still we would not get beyond the life and activity of a well regulated ant heap. The thing for which a man works is what lends value to his work. If he must strive only for a good income, for an easy, comfortable existence, for a good name among men, for a few honors and pleasures, for a little good to his fellow men, then he does not rise above the little circle of this fleeting, transient life. All his work would after all, no matter how well done, be vain or void. But the Easter faith lifts our whole existence onto a higher plane. Now eternity is our outlook; eternal blessings and results for us and others are our goal. Our labor is not in vain in the Lord.

Neither Rome nor Geneva, neither Babel nor Sodom shall induce us to exchange our sure and certain hope in Christ's salvation for the poor efforts of man's ability, the dark mystery of an absolute election with a limited atonement, the hollowness of doubt and a life only for what these earthly days can bring.

34

Steadfast and unmovable we will remain amid the shifting winds
of human opinion and the motley aims of human wisdom and
shrewdness, trusting in the rock of the divine Word with Christ,
the risen Savior as our inspiration, guide, and eternal goal.

God Hath Given us the Victory.

I. *Rejoice in it.*
II. *Thank him for it.*
III. *Make full use of it.*

Thanks be to God Which Giveth Us the Victory Through our Lord Jesus Christ!

I. *A thanks as abounding as is the gift.*
II. *A thanks as enduring as is the victory.*

Death is Victory.

I. *Dying — is the name of the battle.*
II. *Sin — is the name of the foe.*
III. *Christ — is the name of the victory.*

A. Stoecker.

Our Walk in the Easter Triumph.

I. *Death's fear leaves us.*
II. *Incorruptibility and immortality beckon us.*
III. *Firmness and confidence possess us.*

Easter Makes us Steadfast and Immovable.

I. *By giving us an eternal hope.*
II. *By filling us with exhaustless strength.*

Death is Swallowed up in Victory.

I. *See it in Christ's empty tomb.*
II. *Believe it at every Christian's grave.*
III. *Demonstrate it in your own devoted life.*

QUASIMODOGENITI.

1 Pet. 1, 3-9.

Quasimodogeniti is treated as the octave of Easter in the old pericope systems, and completes the festive celebration of the great Easter event. Our text thus belongs together with the two that precede it and rounds out what they have presented. And this it does in an admirable way. Observe its festive tone of exultation: "Blessed be the God and Father of our Lord Jesus Christ." Note also the distinct mention of the great Easter fact: "the resurrection of Jesus Christ from the dead." The real subject of the text is *the living hope* which the resurrection has brought us. This is presented as our own by virtue of the new birth, and is thus identified with our very life as Christians. The text thus presents the Easter blessing in its most intimate and perfect appropriation, an appropriation which is to continue through all our lives, for we are told how God guards us by his power, preserves us in every trial, and brings us at last to the end of our faith, which is the full realization of our hope, even the salvation of our souls. There are really only two sentences in our text, and they may serve as the most natural division of the apostle's thought.

The resurrection and our hope.

We have already stated the particulars concerning Peter's First Epistle, in connection with the text for Oculi, which the reader may compare. The apostle is writing to people troubled and discouraged because they had to suffer somewhat for their faith, not indeed martyrdom or bloody persecution, but more or less hatred and ill-will from their heathen surroundings. Peter's aim is to overcome this troubled condition of mind on the part of his readers and to inspire them with new courage, patience and fortitude. So in the very first sentences, after the formal greeting, he holds up before them, with a triumphant, joyful note in his words, their great and glorious hope in the resurrection of Jesus Christ from the dead, a hope to overcome every trial of faith, infallibly certain of fulfilment, and unspeakably great in what it shall bring. **Blessed** *be* **the God and Father of our Lord Jesus Christ, who according to his great mercy begat us again unto a living hope by the resurrection of Jesus Christ from the dead, unto an inheritance incorruptible, and undefiled, and that fadeth not away, reserved in heaven for you, who by the power of God are guarded through faith unto a salvation ready to be revealed in the last time.** — Peter begins the body of his letter with the very same words as Paul his letter to the Ephesians (1, 3) and his second letter to the Corinthians (1, 3): **Blessed** *be* **the God and Father of our Lord Jesus Christ.** Εὐλογητός (supply εἴη) has a passive meaning: God "be praised;" it is used only of God in the N. T. **The God and Father of our Lord Jesus Christ** is a full and solemn designation for the God of our salvation, found frequently with Paul, and used also by James. When God is called "the Father of our Lord Jesus Christ," our Savior is declared to be the true and essential Son of God. If we connect the genitive also with "God," as some think necessary: "God of our Lord Jesus Christ," our Savior is referred to also as man; as such he himself cried on the cross: "My God, my God!" and said to Mary Magdalene after his resurrection: "I ascend unto . . . my God." But Meyer is right, the expression is quite rare in the Epistles (only Eph. 1, 17); moreover, Peter is not elucidating only the relation of God to Christ, but is naming God for us. As such he calls him first of all: ὁ θεός **God,** the true God; and then adds that he is the **Father of our Lord Jesus Christ,** to designate him as the God of salvation. Peter includes himself in the possessive **our,** which embraces all believers. It is worth noting that the apostles

praise God again and again when they dwell on his great
deeds for our salvation. He deserves our praise with far
greater earnestness and fervor than we usually render. —
The blessing for which Peter praises God is put in the
form of a participial clause: **who according to his great
mercy begat us again, etc.** Κατὰ τὸ ἔλεος states that mercy
moved God, and that in begetting us he also adhered to
mercy as the principle and norm of his action. The **mercy**
of God is his pity for our sad condition; its being **great**
is especially mentioned, just as in a similar connection in
Eph. 2, 4: "being rich in mercy . . . . quickened us,
etc." Dead and doomed forever in our trespasses and sins,
God, moved and guided by his great pity for us, **begat us
again,** ἀναγεννήσας ἡμᾶς, brought us into a new life. Although
the verb used is peculiar to Peter, it expresses the same
thing called the new birth by John (3, 3), quickening by
Paul, Eph. 2, 5-6; Col. 2, 13; and a new creation, Eph.
2, 10; Gal. 6, 15. We are begotten again when the life
from God is implanted into our souls: it is the same as
faith in Christ, filling the heart with new powers, new
thoughts, motives, volitions, *etc.*, so that indeed a new
creature results. — Peter writes: begat us again **unto a
living hope;** this menas that the new life has put into our
hearts "a living hope," the opposite of an empty, false,
deceptive hope. This hope is not "lively" (A. V.), or
"living," because it is bright, active, and strong in us, but
because God guarantees and produces its fulfilment. All
men have some sort of hope, but while so many deceive
themselves with the dead hopes of their own making, we
who are born of God have a living hope which rests on
his promises and power. When the hopes of others go to
pieces in the last flood, ours will sail triumphantly into the
harbor of eternal fulfilment. — The addition: **by the resurrection of Jesus Christ from the dead** modifies not
"living," but "begat us again." The resurrection of Christ
was the crowning point of his redemptive work; it showed
that he was indeed the Son of God and Savior of the world,
and that his dying sacrifice was sufficient to cancel the sins

of the world and to satisfy the righteousness of God.
Christ's resurrection is thus the heart of the Gospel; as
such God manifested it to the apostles and had it proclaimed
by them to others. Many believed, and were thus truly
"born again by the resurrection of Jesus Christ from the
dead." By being instrumental in producing the new birth
Christ's resurrection also wrought the living hope connected
with that birth; for his resurrection guarantees the resurrection and final salvation of all who believe in him. There
is a fine correspondence between: ὁ ἀναγεννήσας . . .
ζῶσαν . . . δι' ἀναστάσεως. — Another modifier follows:
**unto an inheritance incorruptible and undefiled, and
that fadeth not away, reserved in heaven for you.** Like
the two preceding phrases this one also depends on the main
verb "begat us again," but it forms a parallel and virtual
opposition to the first, "unto a living hope," and brings out
in an impressive way what the treasure of our hope really
is. It is **an inheritance** which comes to us as the children
of God begotten of him again, and thus heirs of God (Rom.
8, 17), each receiving his allotted portion. It seems unnatural, with κληρονομία in such close connection with
ἀναγέννησις, to drop, as Meyer insists, the entire conception
and imagery of "inheritance" and make the word mean only
"a possession" in general. Our inheritance is the heavenly
kingdom in all its glory; and the idea of inheritance applies
also in this respect that the kingdom is ours now already,
while as yet we have not entered upon its possession and
enjoyment. We have it, but it is ours in a living hope. —
This inheritance is **incorruptible,** neither moth, rust, thieves,
or any other destructive force can in any way injure it like
the inheritances of earth, which even if a man obtains them
are all subject to corrupting forces and are thus transient,
unenduring, and passing away (verse 7). Again it is
undefiled, no sin can taint it in any way. It is the inheritance of the saints in light, so pure and lofty that we
can give our affections to it without reserve, something we
cannot do with the inheritances of earth. In addition it
fadeth not away, it is imperishable. There is nothing about

it that withers, decreases, or declines, no disappointing change. Stoeckhardt finely adds, that our first delight in entering the world of glory will never lessen or change, in all eternity our enjoyment will be equally intense and strong. And Besser says: Ever enduring freshness and beauty of youth in ever youthful delight will fill the hearts of the heavenly heirs. We will never tire of the heavenly manna. Huss, the martyr at Constance, combined the three attributes: Our inheritance will never lose anything through age or sickness on our part, or any damage to itself; it will never be marred by impurity; and it will never lessen in its delight for having been enjoyed long. — But Peter mentions still another quality: **reserved in heaven for you, who by the power of God are guarded through faith unto a salvation ready to be revealed in the last time.** Two thoughts are here combined: the inheritance is reserved and kept for us, and we are guarded and kept for it. The passive τετηρημένην (κληρονομίαν) points to God as the one who watches, takes care of, and thus guards and keeps the inheritance for us. Many an earthly heir has lost his inheritance through unsafe guardians; but not so we. And here the apostle changes the first person to the second: εἰς ὑμᾶς, **for you,** applying what he says in the directest way to his hearers, to comfort and cheer them. — This is enhanced by the significant addition: **who by the power of God are guarded etc.** The faithful guardian of the inheritance faithfully guards also the heirs. This he does ἐν δυνάμει, in or by his power; Luther translates: *aus Gottes Macht.* The verb φρουρεῖν is a military term, with which also δύναμις harmonizes, and suggests foes. We are amid many perils, but the Keeper of Israel sleeps not nor slumbers. It is a grave misapprehension, both of Scripture teaching and of the actual facts in the Christian life, to imagine that God's omnipotent power comes upon our faith and makes it strong and steadfast; that God's almighty power penetrates our hearts with its might and so lifts up our faith when foes beat it down, and preserves it to the end. Stoeckhardt in this way connects: **by the power of God** with the

added phrase **through faith;** and he supplements this idea
by interpreting Eph. 1, 19 so as make faith a product of
God's omnipotence in the first place: "who believe according to that working of the strength of his might *etc.*"
(omnipotence), omitting the very important comma after
"believe." Faith, however, is never filled with strength by
the divine omnipotence, but by the divine grace, *i. e.* by the
gracious activity of the Holy Spirit, who operates through
the Word of God and the holy Sacraments as the means of
grace; just as this efficacious grace, and not the simple
omnipotence of God, first creates faith in us. Omnipotent
power deals not with the strengthening of our faith, but
with the checking of our foes. These, if left free to do
as they wish, would overwhelm us and the work grace has
accomplished in us. Against these God in his almighty
power guards us, and the military term is exactly in place.
God's power marked the circle beyond which Satan dared
not go in trying Job. The royal power of Christ keeps his
church so that the gates of hell cannot prevail against it.
"The angel of the Lord encampeth round about them that
fear him and delivereth them." P. 34, 7. "We pray . . .
that God would guard and keep us, so that the devil, the
world, and our flesh may not deceive us, nor entice us
into misbelief, despair, and other great shame and vice:
and though we be assailed by them, that still we may finally
prevail, and obtain the victory." Luther. Some commentators make "the power of God" here signify the Holy
Ghost, or his gracious power. This is doctrinally safe, but
exegetically incorrect, for the text points to neither by the
word δύναμις θεοῦ. — **Through faith unto salvation** is connected in the Greek and ought to be read together; Hofmann connects "by the power of God through faith," as if
the power were exercised through·the faith as a means, but
φρουρουμένους stands between ἐν δυνάμει and διὰ πίστεως,
separating the two and indicating thus where the latter
belongs: διὰ πίστεως εἰς σωτηρίαν. Faith is not the means
whereby God does the guarding; his power chooses whatever means it may need. Faith is the subjective means

whereby we attain final **salvation,** our inheritance in
heaven. The thing that guards both us and our faith is
God's omnipotent power, and the purpose of this guarding
is that through faith we may attain salvation. — Our final
inheritance is still hidden from view, safe in God's keeping,
but it is **ready to be revealed in the last time.** Everything
is completed for its unveiling, nothing further needs to be
done in preparing and obtaining the salvation itself. **The
last time** is already here, no new period for additional
work, such as Chiliasts for instance imagine, will follow.
In a little while the great curtain will be drawn aside; then
we will behold our inheritance and enter upon its eternal
enjoyment. — In this highly effective way Peter comforts
and cheers his discouraged readers, and bids us all keep in
mind the resurrection of Jesus Christ from the dead and
the certain fulfilment of our living hope.

The resurrection and our joy.

The apostle now makes direct mention of the trials
his readers had to undergo, and shows how in the midst
of them their living hope in the great salvation to come
fills them with the highest joy. **Wherein ye greatly rejoice, though now for a little while, if need be, ye have
been put to grief in manifold temptations, that the proof
of your faith,** *being* **more precious than gold that
perisheth though it is proved by fire, might be found
unto praise and glory and honor at the revelation of
Jesus Christ: whom not having seen ye love; on whom,
though now ye see him not, yet believing, ye rejoice
greatly with joy unspeakable and full of glory: receiving
the end of your faith,** *even* **the salvation of** *your* **souls.** —
The connection with the foregoing is quite close, in fact
the entire section to verse 12 is one grand period, rich
both in the variety and grandness of its expression, as
also in the greatness and power of its thought. **Wherein
ye greatly rejoice** refers to the apostle's entire foregoing
statement, or, as some suggest, to "the last time" (verse 5)
through which we are now passing and at the end of which

our salvation shall be revealed. The former seems preferable, although in substance there is little difference, as
the thing that causes our joy is the great hope that is ours
through the new birth by the resurrection of Christ. The
apostle uses a verb which signifies an abounding or exceeding joy, ἀγαλλιᾶσθε, **ye greatly rejoice,** as if he wished to
set this joy in triumphant opposition to the grief he now
mentions. So Christ on the eve of his departure from his
disciples and in the face of the great grief they were to
experience, said to them: "These things have I spoken
unto you, that my joy may be in you, and that your joy
may be fulfilled." John 15, 11. — We who prize our great
Easter hope aright will continue in exceeding joy, even if
the apostle's word applies also to us: **though now for a
little while, if need be, ye have been put to grief in
manifold temptations.** Our trials are now **for a little
while** only; they cannot and do not continue indefinitely.
The ὀλίγον of Peter reminds us of the μικρόν of Christ,
John 16, 16. Moreover, these trials come only **if need be,**
if in the counsel of God they are necessary for us. They
do not befall us by chance, nor are they at the pleasure of
our foes; God's hand is over us, and he permits our trials
only for our good. Peter is by no means minimizing the
afflictions of his readers, but he certainly does not justify
us in thinking of our hurts as greater, longer, and worse
than they really are. — **Ye have been put to grief** expresses the distressing effect which the trials had on Peter's
readers; they were not stoical and callous, but felt distressed and hurt by their bitter experiences in following
the risen Christ. Peter knew by his own experience how
they felt. But he uses the aorist participle λυπηθέντες,
"grieved," while he writes ἄρτι, "now," εἰ δέον, "if need be,"
and the present tense ἀγαλλιᾶσθε, "ye greatly rejoice;" the
latter, we must note, expresses continued joy, going on and
on without cessation, while the aorist participle refers to
single inflictions of grief, which, though they occur now
and as there is present need, yet are quickly left behind,
while the great joy still goes on. — The readers of Peter

thus find themselves grieved **in manifold temptations,** or *trials* (margin), for every ill which they suffered at the hands of their enemies tested their faith, and this in a variety of ways. The foes of our faith are always inventive and know how to diversify their attacks, hurting us often in new and unexpected ways.

After placing the exceeding joy over against the brief, though necessary, grief, the apostle points to the purpose of such trials on the part of his readers. In an effective figure he unfolds the image which the word "trials" perhaps suggested to him, which however Christians generally have found so true and appropriate that they have constantly used it since. The purpose of your being put to grief by manifold temptations for a little while is: **that the proof of your faith,** *being* **more precious than gold that perisheth though it is proved by fire, might be found unto praise and glory and honor at the revelation of Jesus Christ.** James writes similarly: "Count it all joy, my brethren, when ye fall into manifold temptations, knowing that the proof of your faith worketh patience" (1, 3). By δοκίμιον, which is either the same as the other form δοκιμεῖον, or a neuter adjective used as a noun, here is meant the fact of your being tested or assayed like precious metal (Cremer), the successful **proof** which demonstrates the genuineness **of your faith;** the . *proving,* as the margin of the American Committee renders it in the James passage. — This proof Peter describes as **more precious than gold that perisheth though it is proved by fire,** πολυτιμότερον (τοῦ δοκιμίου) χρυσίου κτλ, the bracketed word being supplied in thought. Our faith is compared with gold, and our trials of faith with the testing out of gold by fire. But the gold **perisheth though it is proved by fire;** it is a poor earthly thing and like all earthly things, even though its value is shown for a while, it must pass away. Our faith, and the testing which it undergoes is far superior. Gold at most can buy only a few earthly things. but faith embraces Christ and his righteousness, and thus in and through him eternal salva-

tion. Now if gold, perishable though it is, because of its
temporal value be put through a process of purification by
fire, how much more should not faith, with its external
value for us, undergo a purifying operation? We must
remember that while we live here on earth our faith is
by no means free from impurities; frequently there is
mixed with it a false confidence, a trust in ourselves and
our own righteousness, or perhaps a lack of that clear
knowledge which sees salvation in Christ alone. So God
sends us fiery trials as there is need, in order to destroy in
our faith every impurity and admixture, and to leave it
fixed wholly and alone upon Christ and his merits. "In
the fiery oven the straw burns, but the gold is purified."
Augustine. And Luther writes: "The fire does not lessen
the gold, but makes it pure and bright, removing any admixture. So God lays the cross upon all Christians, in
order to purify and cleanse them well, that their faith may
remain pure, even as the Word is pure, and that we may
cling to the Word alone and trust in nothing else. For
we all need such a purifying and cross greatly because of
our old, gross Adam." — God's purpose is that the proof
of our faith, in its successful result, **might be found unto
praise and glory and honor at the revelation of Jesus
Christ.** The passive εὑρεθῇ points to God; he will examine
us and our faith at the last day, and blessed are we if he
finds that the testing has shown our faith to be genuine. .
Such a test is in itself for us "unto praise and glory and
honor," and will then be shown to be such by the final
judgment of God "at the revelation of Jesus Christ," when
at the last day he shall appear in his glory. But this our
praise, glory, and honor is the product of God's gracious
work in producing and perfecting our faith in us, and
therefore redounds unto his praise, glory, and honor. The
heaping up of these terms is for greater emphasis; and
even so they but faintly express what God wishes to bestow upon us. We shall have **praise** of God when he shall
acknowledge our faith before all the world, and this will
be **glory and honor,** a priceless distinction, at the same

time, far above anything the world is able to bestow.
"Blessed is the man that endureth temptation: for when
he hath been approved, he shall receive the crown of life,
which the Lord promised to them that love him." James
1, 12. Thus, Stoeckhardt writes, our suffering, which at
first seems a contradiction of glory, is the very way God
has ordained for us to attain to glory, the *via regni.*

The thought of the praise, glory, and honor which
shall be ours at the revelation of Jesus Christ makes
Peter's heart expand with joy in anticipation, and all
this joy he centers in the risen Christ, now in glory, then
to be revealed and seen by us: **whom not having seen ye
love; on whom, though now ye see him not, yet believing, ye rejoice greatly with joy unspeakable and full
of glory: receiving the end of your faith,** *even* **the salvation of your souls.** Usually we love one whom we
have seen and by actual intercourse have come to prize
highly, and our love then continues even after he is removed from our sight (ἰδόντες, aorist). But Peter's readers
had never actually seen Jesus and thus formed his acquaintance; yet they loved him with the full devotion of
spiritual love (ἀγαπᾶτε). With the apostle this was different, for he had seen Jesus with his own eyes, also after
his resurrection. This contrast between himself and his
readers he here implies as noteworthy. — And it is the
same with their faith: **on whom, though now ye see him
not, yet believing.** They believe on him, rest all their
heart's confidence on him as·their Savior, although they
do not see him with their eyes (ὁρῶντες, present). The
negative οὐ with ἰδόντες simply refers to the fact of their not
having seen Jesus, while the following μή with ὁρῶντες
refers to the thought of Peter's readers; they love Jesus,
although they never saw him, and they believe on him,
although they realize that they do not see him. Peter may
here have thought of the foolish demand of Thomas: "Except I shall see in his hands the print of the nails, and
put my finger into the print of the nails. and put my hand
into his side, I will not believe;" and of the word of Jesus:

"Blessed are they that have not seen, and yet have believed." John 20, 25 and 29. — Instead of using a finite verb, πιστεύετε, the apostle turns this into a participle, πιστεύοντες, and adds ἀγαλλιᾶτε as the finite verb, making the construction slightly irregular. **Ye rejoice greatly with joy unspeakable and full of glory,** while in the present tense, anticipates the moment when we "receive the end of our faith, even the salvation of our souls." So the joy of which verse 6 spoke as now in our hearts because of our regèneration and living hope, shall continue and finally be a joy unspeakable and full of glory (verse 8) when that hope is fully realized. It is **unspeakable** because no language of which we are now masters can possible give adequate utterance to it; not until we see with our eyes him whom we have so long loved and believed in will our tongues be loosed to sing the heavenly hymns of praise. So also our present joy may anticipate somewhat the glorious joy to come, but not until we ourselves leave this state of humiliation and trial and receive the end of our faith, "the crown of life," James 1, 12, will our joy itself be completely **full of glory,** or *glorified,* as the margin translates more closely. Our present trials cannot endure long, soon our faith will be turned into sight, our suffering into glory. The apostles who have already seen Jesus in his humiliation and in his glorification will see him again; who will describe the unspeakable joy of that event? And we who have seen him only as he is revealed to us in his Word shall behold him as he is. with these our glorified eyes; we shall know him as we ourselves are known. And this joy shall never cease nor sink below the exaltation and ecstacy of its first outburst. — The immediate cause of this final joy is explicitly stated: **receiving the end of your faith,** *even* **the salvation of** *your* **souls.** We shall carry away salvation as our possession, to own and enjoy it as our gift from the hand of God. **Salvation** in the sense of eternal deliverance is **the end of our faith,** the goal toward which faith from its very start is directed. We indeed have salvation now in that we are delivered from sin and guilt the moment we believe; but this is salvation only in its first stage, to be followed by the final stage when Christ shall receive us into eternal glory. "When the chief Shepherd shall be manifested, ye shall receive the crown of glory that fadeth not away." 1 Pet. 5, 4. It is called the salvation **of souls** not in distinction from the body, nor as pertaining especially to the soul, the body merely sharing the soul's deliverance (Bengel). "Soul," ψυχή, here designates the person, the real being itself which is saved, not merely a certain part of it. Stoeckhardt finely adds that perdition then means the loss of the soul, the greatest calamity that can befall man's entire person or being. Peter has been called the apostle of hope, as Paul has been called the apostle of faith, and John of love; his claim to the name is fully established by these words from his pen, which mark out a shining, radiant path from the trials through which we now pass to the eternal glory around the throne of our risen Savior.

HOMILETICAL HINTS.

In reading Peter's words on hope we must not slip across the word "lively" or "living" too quickly. This is the very feature which distinguishes our hope from all the other hopes which men carry in their bosoms and which are born dead when first they enter the heart. Even when they blossom into fulfilment they soon shed their petals and no abiding fruit follows. To cling to such hopes as a real satisfaction for the soul is worse than to dream of winning the grand prize when one has not even entered the lists. Our hope is "living" because Christ lives, lives in eternal glory, and by faith in our hearts, and with divine grace and power will unite us with himself.

Heaven is a holy land, and no sin-stained creature can possibly enter it. Man, whoever he may be, must be born anew, if he is to reach that Canaan. Our natural birth gives us the hope of a longer or shorter life on earth, but this is bound to end in death and perdition because of sin. Only a new birth implants into our hearts the life that endures in glory forever. From this germ alone there will grow a new man and in his soul a living hope, which is more than the poor makeshifts of the sad and downcast, trying to lighten their burdens for a little while.

An inheritance is given over into the full possession of the heir when he reaches his majority. — Incorruptible, undefiled, and that fadeth not away are all negative terms; they bring out what our hope really is by contrasting it with other hopes. The real glory, beauty, sweetness, grandness of our heavenly inheritance no earthly words can adequately express. Even salvation is a negative term, for it means rescue and deliverance from sin; what our estate shall be when salvation is forever complete we cannot fully know until we enter upon that estate.

As the day is already in the dawn, so is our final salvation in the faith and hope that now brightens our hearts when the Gospel of Christ's resurrection sheds its grace upon us. — The future is ours, the eternal future. — It is easy to contend and endure when the palm and the crown beckon us in our trials.

They speak falsely who say that Christianity bids us starve and suffer here, and comforts us only with uncertain hopes of a grand future. Their falseness is also folly when they proclaim as the true gospel the doctrine that the future will take care of itself, and that our chief duty is to make this life fair and lovely. No, we are not deluding ourselves. It requires an alert mind, enlightened eyes, sound sense and judgment, and the grace of God itself, for us to see through the shams of the world and to fix our hearts and hopes upon the treasures that never fail.

He who has no eternity has no time: no time that is worth while, no true object to which to devote himself, no peace, joy, and hope to cheer him as the years slip by. No sure and glorious eternity means travel through a desert, where only empty cisterns are found and nothing but delusive mirages mock the soul. — The Christian life is not made of dust, rests not on the sand of human opinion, is not written in fading, earthly words, is not invented by human wisdom; but its life is of God, it rests on the living Savior Christ, it is written in the imperishable words of divine truth, it is designed by God who will crown it with eternal blessedness.

He who knows no assured eternity divides his times of suffering into weeks of suffering, and these into days of suffering, and these into hours that seem endless. He who rejoices in the eternal hope is lifted across all suffering and now already anticipates the happiness that is in store for him. — As the sculptor strikes the rough block of marble with his chisel and mallet, slowly but surely the beautiful statue emerges. So God uses our trials to form in us the image of himself in ever fairer and more perfect lines.

In the shadows of the deep valley the traveller at eventide sees the far-off mountain-tops lit up with the golden radiance of the sun. So we plod on wearily in the shadow, but the glory of our eternal sun shines on yonder heights, and presently we shall be lifted up to rejoice in its fadeless light for evermore.

Our Living Hope.

I. *It is absolutely certain.*
II. *It lights up all our earthly life.*

The Power of Christ's Resurrection.

I. *It produces a new life in us here.*
II. *It lifts us into an eternal life hereafter.*

Schapper.

"Blessed be the God and Father of our Lord Jesus Christ!"

This is
I. *Our song of joy at Eastertide when we look up to the risen Christ.*
II. *Our hymn of comfort while we plod on through earthly trials.*
III. *Our shout of exultation when at last we enter upon our eternal inheritance.*

We are Heirs of an Inheritance Incorruptible, Undefiled and That Fadeth not Away.

I. *God has made us such by a new birth.*
II. *God trains us as such during our earthly life.*
III. *God receives us as such at the last great day.*

The Riches of our Easter Faith.

I. *A living hope.*
II. *An abiding comfort.*
III. *An endless joy.*

The Heavenly Heirs and Their Priceless Inheritance.

I. *God has prepared it and keeps it for them.*
II. *God has made them heirs and keeps them for the inheritance.*

35

MISERICORDIAS DOMINI.

Eph. 2, 4-10.

From the festive celebration of the glorious Easter event, which extended from Easter Sunday to Quasimodogeniti, we now turn to the three Sundays which are to carry the afterglow of the festival into our hearts, Misericordias Domini, Jubilate, and Cantate. The first of these sets before us the infinite grace of God which has wrought our salvation in Christ Jesus: "for by grace have ye been saved through faith." But this is done in a rich Easter setting; Paul writes of the God of grace that he "quickened us together with Christ, and raised us up with him, and made us to sit in the heavenly places, in Christ Jesus." This is the heart of the text and gives it a special appropriateness for the present Sunday. Grace to be grace, however, shuts out entirely all human merit. This lies already in the description of God's work of grace as our spiritual resurrection from the death of trespasses and sins; it lies likewise in the reference to faith by which alone the salvation of God's grace is made our own. But it is so important that the apostle brings it out fully by itself in several additional emphatic statements, bestowing all the praise and honor for our present salvation on God alone. So we may say our subject for this Sunday is *grace and faith*. We are quickened together with Christ through faith by the work of God's grace (4-7), and for the glory of God's grace (8-10).

Quickened together with Christ by the work of God's grace.

In the first grand period of his letter to the Ephesians Paul praises God for the wealth of spiritual

546

blessings bestowed upon them in Christ Jesus (1, 3-14);
this he follows up with a petition that they may be filled
with wisdom and knowledge to understand the greatness of these blessings and of God's gracious workings
in them (15-23). In the second chapter the apostle then
reminds the Ephesians of the central work of God's
grace in them, of their spiritual resurrection and present
salvation, the whole of which must be attributed to this
grace of God alone. The first three verses of this
chapter, while they constitute part of the opening sentence of our text, are not included in the text, because
their contents is sufficiently referred to in what follows;
to omit them is the easier since the apostle, after the
long qualifying statements in the first verses, takes up
the thread of his thought in verse 4. **But God, being
rich in mercy, for his great love wherewith he loved us,
even when we were dead through our trespasses, quickened us together with Christ (by grace have ye been
saved), and raised us up with him, and made us to sit
with him in the heavenly** *places,* **in Christ Jesus.** — The
first verse of our chapter begins with the object of the
sentence: καὶ ὑμᾶς, to which at once an elaborate modifying
statement is attached. Having reached its end the apostle
starts anew by stating the subject of his sentence, **God,**
adding δέ, **but,** to bring it out the more, and to contrast it
with the object ὑμᾶς whose sad condition he has just described. This contrast appears also in the addition:
being rich in mercy. God pitied the condition of the
Christians (note the change from "ye" to "we") when they
lay dead in their trespasses. Instead of casting them away
in anger or disgust, as they richly deserved, their sad lot
stirred the merciful heart of God. The greatness and
abundance of that mercy is described by the figurative
adjective **rich;** there was a boundless wealth of mercy in
God's heart, and all its richness was for us in our dire
and deadly poverty. — The apostle dwells on this point:
for his great love wherewith he loved us. He uses διά
with the accusative, "on account of," "for the sake of his

great love," *i. e.* to satisfy it. It is this love that moved
God to do what he did for us poor sinners. No wonder
the apostle calls it **great,** which corresponds to the previous
"rich." Nobody can measure out its greatness and vast-
ness. The repetition: **love wherewith he loved us** emphasizes this love in its greatness by telling of its activity.
The aorist ἠγάπησεν is used because the apostle has in mind
a signal act in which that love manifested itself. Meyer
makes this the reconciling death of Christ, of which, however, there is no hint in the text. The act that Paul had
in mind from the first verse on, when he spoke of the
Ephesians having been dead in trespasses and sins, was
that of quickening such dead. In ἥν (ἀγάπην) ἠγάπησεν we
have a cognate accusative (Winer 32, 2). **Love** is the
wider term, including as special forms or varieties, according to the persons loved, mercy and grace. Mercy is the
love for those in distress; grace for those who are unworthy of love and loving help. Grace is the love that
thus goes out to damnable sinners; mercy the love that
goes out to miserable sufferers. — **Even when we were
dead through our trespasses** brings in once more the object of the sentence, which the apostle had mentioned to
begin with (verse 1), only that now he uses the wider first
person instead of the second ("we all," verse 3). The καί
emphasizes ὄντας, and thus lays stress on the fact as it
existed when the love of God wrought the great change.
We were **dead,** the apostle writes, still lying in spiritual
death wrought **through our transgressions,** when God
quickened us. There is a mighty contrast between this
death and the quickening which ended it. A man still dead
is utterly unable to do anything for himself, least of all
in obtaining life. The apostle's statement here, like others
of the same kind, excludes all synergism in the divine
work of regeneration and conversion. A dead man can
do absolutely nothing in preparing himself for the reception
of life. If he is made alive this must be wholly the work
of another. Death and quickening also exclude the idea
of a gradual transition from the one state to the other.

There are no stages between the two: a man is either dead, or he is alive; with the first spark of spiritual life in his soul death ends. But it is a grave mistake to urge the imagery of death in the unregenerate to such a degree as to shut out the efficacious power and operation of the Word of God as a means of grace. When God quickens the dead sinner this is not in every respect like the raising for instance of Lazarus from the tomb. God does not simply by an instantaneous word of his absolute omnipotence call us into spiritual life, but by the preaching and teaching of the Gospel so works upon the dead heart that finally the spark of life, or true faith, is kindled in it. How this is done we see in the examples of Christ's and the apostle's teaching and preaching when it succeeded in implanting faith. — Paul speaks of this divine work when he says that God **quickened us together with Christ.** The verb fits the object, ὄντας ἡμᾶς νεκρούς, exactly: a new life was introduced by God into the dead by the means of grace. The inner connection with sin, death, and damnation was broken, and a new union and connection with God established. This is quickening, making alive, regeneration. The σύν in συνεζωοποίησεν with the following dative τῷ Χριστῷ (not: *in* Christ, margin) connects our quickening with that of Christ, who for our sins lay dead in the tomb, and was quickened and brought to life again by the glory of the Father who accepted his all-sufficient sacrifice. There is more here than a mere similarity; our quickening is not merely like Christ's in some important feature. On the other hand we must not identify the two, as some commentators do, making Christ's quickening itself that of all his believers. The σύν is not that strong. There are two separate acts of God, one in regard to Christ, and the other in regard to us, but both inwardly and truly connected. Our quickening is the outcome and result of Christ's quickening; the life put into us by God through the means of grace is the very life which Christ by his resurrection brought to light. Besser says that God's saving act has two arms as it were, an Easter arm by which it raised up Christ from the dead, and a Penecostal arm by which it now raises up the spiritually dead with Christ. Tit. 3, 3-5. The parallel passages, Col. 2, 12-13 and Rom. 6, 3-11, connect our quickening with baptism, and show that it consists in the generation of faith. In this respect they go beyond what the apostle states here, but the act he describes is the same in all these passages. Calov makes the fine statement: *Vivificati sumus in ipso ut redemptore et ad spem certam ut in capite nostro.*

At this point the apostle inserts a brief parenthetical statement, in order to emphasize the point he wishes his readers to note especially: **by grace have ye been saved.** The entire act of God in saving us is the outcome of his grace. This word heads the sentence and carries the emphasis. It is added to the "love" and "mercy" mentioned before in order that the character of the divine agency in our salvation may be fully brought out. Our salvation is altogether a gratuitous gift of God. We are not in the least worthy of being saved, we are worthy only of being abandoned, rejected, condemned. And this is the marvel that rings through all the Gospel, that in spite of our total unworthiness God saved us. In declaring it the apostle slips back to the second person, ἐστέ; he is not merely making a statement in a general way, but impressing a fundamental truth upon his Ephesian readers. It is for each of us to realize for his own person: God's grace has saved me! Bengel: *Gratiam esse docet proram et puppim.* Paul calls the Ephesians σεσωμένοι, people whom God has rescued from the terrible death in which they lay, and who are therefore such rescued people still. It is counted a great thing to rescue someone from the danger of bodily death, but God's grace delivered us from a worse death when we were already slain by its fearful power. Men count themselves fortunate when they are snatched from an impending death, but what shall we say of our blessedness in having been brought forth out of spiritual death itself and set into a new and heavenly life?

After the parenthesis the apostle adds two more

verbs to describe fully the greatness of God's saving
act: **and raised us up with him, and made us to sit with
him in the heavenly** *places,* **in Christ Jesus.** The Scriptures say both of Christ, that he was "quickened" (1 Pet.
3, 18), and that he was "raised up" from the dead. The
latter usually includes both, and yet we can distinguish two
sides to the great act, one the restoration of life to Christ's
dead body, and the other the bringing forth of the living
and glorified Christ from the tomb that had received his
dead body. In the same way the apostle here speaks of
our being quickened and **raised up.** God gives us the
spiritual life in connection with the risen Christ, and makes
us go forth to live in the newness of this life. This fuller
statement of his gracious work enhances its greatness and
blessedness in our eyes. — But after forty days Christ
ascended to heaven and was seated at the right hand of
God. And this too, in our connection with Christ, has
its counterpart in us: **God made us to sit with him in the
heavenly** *places.* Harless is right when he insists on the
aorists here used; they must not be overlooked or changed.
Paul is speaking, not of something that shall occur, but of
something that did occur. Moreover, τὰ ἐπουράνια are not
simply *bona,* but *loca.* Bengel, however, observes that the
apostle does not say: *in dextra; Christo sua manet ex-
cellentia.* God has made us sit indeed in **heavenly places,**
but Christ alone sits at God's right hand. The heavenly
places in which God has made us sit are located in the
kingdom of heaven which he has established here on earth.
Compare Phil. 3, 20; Col. 3, 3b. This is the counterpart to
the glorious kingdom above and at the same time its threshold. All the great blessings of heaven are conveyed to
us now in the church on earth, and we are set as the children of God in the midst of them. Instead of lamenting
because of our hard condition in this sinful world, we
ought to sing praises unto God for having elevated, honored, and blessed us in such a heavenly way already in this
life. The high and prideful places of earth are dung-heaps
compared with the heavenly places in Christ's kingdom.

where we sit in the presence of God and our Savior, in
company and communion with the children of God, his
saints and heirs, at the table of his Word and Sacrament,
under the shadow of his goodness and love. — And all this,
raising us up and making us sit in heavenly places, the
apostle says once more, God has done **in Christ Jesus,** in
connection and in union with him, in whom alone all our
salvation is found. — Some commentators, like Meyer,
refer this quickening *etc.* to our bodily resurrection and
glorification, interpreting the aorists to mean that all this
has virtually been done for us already, namely in the
resurrection and glorification of Christ, in which the consummation of our salvation is assured.   But this is forced,
both from the standpoint of grammar and language, and
from that of sober truth and reality.   God's act of saving
us plainly refers to what he has already done for us, and
what in consequence we now actually enjoy; and the final
reference to good works, in verse 10, settles the question,
that the apostle speaks of things past and present, and
not merely of those future made virtually ours now
already in Christ.

Still the heavenly future is not forgotten.   In all
that God has done and does for us now he has in view
this purpose: **that in the ages to come he might shew
the exceeding riches of his grace in kindness toward us
in Christ Jesus.**   Besser points out that **toward us** settles
the meaning of the entire clause.   The apostle speaks of
the same persons throughout; to those whom God has
made alive and elevated in Christ Jesus he intends forever to show the exceeding richness of his grace in kindness in Christ Jesus.   While what he does for us beyond
doubt has its bearing also on those who come after us, this
is not the apostle's thought here.   **The ages to come** are
the ages of eternity, when God's saving work shall have
reached its glorious goal in us.   Then he purposes to **show**
before all the angels and saints in heaven **the exceeding
riches of his grace in kindness** toward us.   To the love,
mercy, and grace already mentioned **kindness** is now

added as a special manifestation of grace. By χρηστότης is meant benignity and sweetness, such as invites to familiar intercourse and sweet converse, and bestows all manner of good (Trench, *Synonyms of the New Testament*, II, 58 *etc.*). Christ's ministry was full of this kindness; some of its fairest displays we see in his reception of the sinful woman, his blessing of little children, and his words of comfort and healing. In heaven, with everything sinful forever and completely removed from us, all the kindness of God as our loving Father shall be poured out upon us. Who can describe all the sweetness and loveliness of it! But even as here all our salvation rests in Christ alone, there also the goodness or kindness of God shall still be connected with him. Our heavenly delights will all be **in Christ Jesus.**

Quickened together with Christ for the glory of God's grace.

The brief parenthetical exclamation: "by grace have ye been saved," betrays the thought that underlies the apostle's entire exposition in this section. We see it also in his using so many different terms for the divine motive power in saving us: love, mercy, grace, kindness. This underlying thought comes out fully now and is set forth in all its main features in a terse, energetic way: **for by grace have ye been saved through faith; and that not of yourselves: *it is* the gift of God: not of works, that no man should glory. For we are his workmanship, created in Christ Jesus for good works, which God afore prepared that we should walk in them.** — All that the apostle has said concerning God's great act of saving us as well as concerning his purpose for the ages to come rests completely on the grace of God: **for** — it is just as I have said — **by grace have ye been saved through faith.** Again **grace** heads the sentence, but this time it has the article, τῇ χάριτι: this very grace of which the apostle has been speaking. The personal note is likewise retained: **ye,** ye Ephesians, **have been saved,** rescued

from spiritual and eternal death, and are now in this
blessed condition. — An important new thought, however,
is added: ye have been saved **by faith,** by living trust in
Christ and his redemptive work. In Col. 2, 12 the apostle
says directly: "Ye were also raised with him through
faith in the working of God," A. V.: "of the operation of
God." God accomplished his purpose of delivering us
from death when by his Word and Spirit he kindled faith
in the hearts of the Ephesians. Notice that διὰ πίστεως is
connected with the passive σεσωμένοι which implies God as
the agent. Faith is not something that we do on our part
towards our salvation, but something that God produces in
our hearts to accomplish in us his great purpose. We
indeed do the believing, but it is God who brings us to
believe, and in this way saves us. Faith is the ὄργανον
ληπτικόν, *die Nehmehand,* as the dogmaticians say, by which
God appropriates to us individually the gifts of his grace.
In the business of salvation faith is considered only as
to its receptive quality, not as to its operative quality. But
on this very account faith is essential, and he that believeth
not is damned, because he does not receive the salvation
offered and brought to him. Thus "grace" and "faith" are
always correlatives. "As often, therefore, as mention is
made of mercy" — and it is the same with grace — "we
must keep in mind, that faith is there required, which receives the promise of mercy. And, again, as often as we
speak of faith, we wish an object to be understood, *viz.*
the promised mercy." In the German we read: "As often
as the Scriptures speak of faith, they mean the faith that
builds on pure grace." Apology, 93, 55; Mueller, 97, 56.
— So important is this matter that the apostle adds several
explanatory specifications. The first is: **and that not of
yourselves.** The τοῦτο refers to the verb, the act and fact
of our being saved; and οὐκ ἐξ ὑμῶν denies categorically that
this is due in any manner to the Ephesians themselves. The
source and origin of their salvation is wholly in God. As
little as a dead man can do anything toward making himself alive, so little can the spiritually dead do the least

toward obtaining spiritual life. — Instead of salvation being in any way due to ourselves, the apostle says: *it is* **the gift of God,** or, more closely: "God's **is the gift,** his and his alone, and in the form of a gift, gratuitous, freely bestowed by his abounding grace and mercy, this gift which the Ephesians had in possession. We poor sinners are not even in a condition to go to God and beg such a gift from him; he himself devised the whole plan of it and made it ours by his grace through the hand of faith. — **Not of works** explains more definitely what lies in the previous specification "not of yourselves." As grace would be excluded, if our being saved were due to ourselves, so faith would be excluded, if our being saved were due to works. A salvation "of ourselves" would, of course, exclude also faith, just as a salvation "of works" would exclude grace, but the apostle has the former parallel, in which the latter lies embedded. Among all our "works" before our quickening and resurrection there was not one that God could find pleasure in, or that could move him to save us; they were all wide of the mark, and deserved nothing but condemnation. — And so in the work of salvation it was and is now 'the divine intention: **that no man should glory;** 1 Cor. 4, 7. When we consider what it cost God to save us by his grace through faith, namely the sacrifice of his Son on the cross, we will see why he must want all human glorying and boasting shut out. And indeed, nothing now so militates against his grace and what it does for our salvation as the glorying of self-righteousness, including that of Pelagianism and synergism. To know what grace is, and to have saving faith in that grace is to glory in the Lord, 1 Cor. 1, 32; 2 Cor. 10, 17.

> "All glory be to God on High.
> Who hath our race befriended."

How completely all boasting on our part is shut out the apostle shows by stating in the form of further proof just what God did, and had to do, in order to save us. For **we are his workmanship created in Christ Jesus etc.**

The entire context shows that the apostle is not speaking of God's work in first calling man into being, but of his work in calling our new life into being by quickening and raising us up from the dead. He now turns to the first person again: **we,** making his words applicable to every Christian. No matter who we are, whether an apostle like Paul, or a young babe in arms regenerated of water and the Spirit: we all are **his workmanship.** "His" is placed forward for emphasis: *"His* workmanship are we." As this is true of our entire being as men, so it is true of our being as children of God: "Know ye that the Lord he is God: it is he that hath made us, and not we ourselves; we are his people, and the sheep of his pasture," Ps. 100, 3. By **workmanship** something that God has made is meant, and this making is at once described as creative: **created in Christ Jesus etc.** In κτίζειν we have the equivalent of the Hebrew *barah,* to call into existence from nothing. Paul has in mind a close parallel between the first creative act, when God called man into being, and this second act, likewise creative, when God called our spiritual life into being. Of course, there are great differences, but as regards the essential point both acts are alike. God is the one who alone could do these wondrous works, no one else had the ability or power required; and both are works by which he produced something from nothing. Where there was no being, and no part of any being, God called into existence Adám and Eve; and again where there was no life, nor any part of life, nothing but spiritual death. God brought into existence the spiritual life that is in us. The former he did by his omnipotence, by which also he blessed the first pair that they should multiply on earth; the latter he did by his grace, and this grace works alike in each individual through the divinely appointed means. This difference is brought out by the addition: **in Christ Jesus,** which means more than that now we are in Christ Jesus as a result of God's work in saving us; it says directly that the whole work itself, from beginning to end, took place in connection with Christ Jesus. "Wherefore if any man is

in Christ, he is a new creature," 2 Cor. 5, 17. Gal. 6, 15;
Eph. 4, 24. Paul here emphatically reiterates what he said
before that we were quickened together with Christ, raised
up with him, made to sit in the heavenly places in Christ
Jesus, and blessed with all God's kindness in the ages to
come in Christ Jesus. Just as our redemption is in Christ
Jesus, so our new creation and personal possession of this
redemption is in him. He is the specific life element outside of which the spiritual creative process cannot possibly
occur; the very life that is now in us is the life that Christ
brought to light and gave to us as a heavenly gift. — But
the chief emphasis is on the addition: **for good works,
which God afore prepared that we should walk in them.**
So completely is the idea of our salvation being due to
works of ours shut out that all good works on our part
are the result of God's saving work in us. Harless correctly says that on the basis of this apostolic declaration
Lutheran theology has ever taught: *Bona opera non
praecedunt justificandum, sed sequntur justificatum.* **Good
works** are such as God esteems good; thoughts, words, and
deeds in which the righteousness and holiness of the new
life manifests itself. Such works are an utterly impossible
thing before our quickening; only the new creature in
Christ Jesus is able to bring them forth. And this is God's
purpose that every one of us who lives in Christ should
produce the fruits of such a life. "Herein is my Father
glorified, that ye bear much fruit; and so shall ye be my
disciples." John 15, 8. Not in order to be saved, but because we are already saved, are we to do good works. As
the sun was created to shine, the rose to give forth its
delightful odor, the bird to fly, so we were created anew
to do good works, and thus to glorify him who created us
what we are in Christ Jesus. What a lesson for those also
who are slothful in good works and always wait to be
driven! — The addition: **which God afore prepared that
we should walk in them,** states that long in advance of
our doing a single good work God himself prepared and
made ready the good works in which afterwards he wanted

us to walk. All the ways in which we can now manifest
our holiness and righteousness are God's design and preparation; we need not puzzle and search what may please
God, he has long ago mapped out our course. The apostle
does not say here that God prepared *us* that we should
walk in good works (so Luther), but that he prepared the
good works themselves; οἷς is in attraction after ἔργοις
ἀγαθοῖς instead of ἃ, not instead of ἐφ' οἷς. Nor is προητοίμασεν
in the sense of foreordained, which would require προορίζειν;
God prepared our good works. This he did in Christ
Jesus: "our walk in him is our walk in them." Stoeckhardt
writes: "Christ, in whom we live and move and have our
being, makes us partakers of his gifts and virtues; is
formed in our life and walk; his holiness, purity, humility,
gentleness, goodness, tenderness, kindness, *etc.* shine forth
in our walk as Christians. And thus all self-praise is excluded. A true Christian does not boast even of the true
good works which flow from his regeneration, his faith.
To God alone belongs the honor for what we are and do
as Christians." — **That we should walk in them** means:
as in our native and proper element, keeping within the
safe lines which they indicate, and never wandering beyond.
Ambularemus, non salvaremur aut viveremus. Bengel.
Thus Paul carries the praise of God's grace through con-
sistently to the end, and it is the grace that comes to us in
Christ Jesus, our risen and glorified Savior, alone.

HOMILETICAL HINTS.

"Self-righteous souls on works rely,
And boast their moral dignity;
But if I lisp a song of praise,
Grace is the note my soul shall raise.

'Twas grace that quickened me when dead,
And grace my soul to Jesus led;
Grace brings me pardon for my sin —
'Tis grace subdues my lusts within. . . .

Through endless years of grace I'll sing,
Adore and bless my heavenly King;
I'll cast my crown before his throne,
Saved by his sovereign grace alone."

Can there be anything more precious for the sinner than the word "grace"? It unlocked heaven and gave us Christ; it removed the mountain of our sin, and placed in its stead the eternal favor of God; it took away death, and put life in its stead; it canceled our condemnation, and gave us divine pardon; it took us from darkness and translated us into the kingdom of life and light; it removed our misery and filled us with hope, light, and joy. And all this did grace do because of itself alone, and not because of anything in us, because there was absolutely nothing in us, save sin and guilt and utter condemnation.

"What all our faith must rest upon,
Is grace, free grace through his dear Son."

This is the wonder of grace, that we who were dead have been made alive; that we in whom there is nothing good are declared to be righteous and acceptable to God; that we who know and feel our guilt are pardoned and freed; that we who were in the grasp of hell are made heirs of heaven; that we who trembled on the brink of perdition are led into Paradise.

Not until a man truly believes in Christ does he judge correctly concerning his previous condition. It may be that then he lived merrily on, but within his soul everything was dead. There was no connection with God, no appreciation of his Word and kingdom. A man in this condition need not feel at all unhappy. For when God and his Word are strangers to us, we do not really know sin, either that there is such a thing, or what it really is. The sad thing about one dead in sin is that he does not realize the sin, but imagines himself a capable and respectable person. We must not think that those dead in sin are always openly wicked. The greatest danger is that people considered entirely honorable and estimable fail utterly to understand their true spiritual condition. They imagine that they are entirely right in refusing to concern themselves about God and in pursuing their course according to their own notions. Men who have fallen into open sin often come readily to the conviction that things cannot go on thus. In the condition of spiritual death there are many differences and degrees. But one thing is alike in them all, in spite of any differences there is nothing but death as long as the life from God is absent. Riemer.

As long as we are dead in sins we prize most highly what we are able to make of ourselves. But when we are saved by grace we prize most highly what God makes of us.

We certainly have a right to ask, what the new life is like. God makes a man the opposite of what sin has made him: where sin slew him, God gives him life; where sin made him a child of the devil, God makes him his own child; where sin turned all his thoughts and purposes toward the world, God turns them toward himself.

No man can tell just what life, the real essence of life, is. We cannot lay bare the thing that causes the plant to grow, flower, and fruit; we cannot see, measure, or weigh what animates the beast of the field. So with our own natural life; we cannot touch and handle it like a material thing. And in this respect spiritual life resembles all other life: it is a mysterious and wonderful thing, far above our powers of penetration to fathom and analyze. But if we cannot tell just what the life itself consists of, we do know the moment anything has life and is alive. The plant grows and thrives, and we see its new leaves and development; the animal displays its wonderful powers, and we follow its movements and actions; man puts his bodily and mental powers into operation, and we see a thousand things that he does — he is alive, because he eats and drinks, talks and laughs, works and plays, builds and buys, *etc.* When all this ceases, and the body crumbles to dust, we know that he is dead. So also is the spiritual life manifested by the activities natural to it. The man who turns to God and Christ, worships and adores his Savior, eats and drinks of heavenly food, serves God in true love and fights sin, grows in grace and holiness, is certainly spiritually alive; we see that he has been quickened, raised up with Christ, and made to sit in the heavenly places. He who cares nothing for Christ, does not receive his Word and gifts, fails to worship, confess, serve and obey him, drifts on in sin and the love of the world, that man is spiritually dead. And as the odor of death emanates from a decaying body, so the intolerable odor of ungodliness and sin emanates from the spiritually dead, and they who have the true life detect it and turn from it.

So completely is God the author of our spiritual life that even the works in which this life expresses itself are all his work and preparation. He designed the straight and narrow way and gives us power to walk thereon. He kindled the love in our hearts, and set before us all the opportunities and means whereby to exercise it. Every deed by which we rightly honor him and truly serve our fellow men goes back to God who devised it and makes it possible for us to perform it.

See What the Grace of God Has Done for me!

I. *It has given me a wonderful salvation.*
  1. A rescue.
  2. A new life.
  3. A spiritual resurrection.
  4. A re-creation.
  5. A heavenly exaltation.

II. *In a wonderful way.*
  1. By grace.
  2. In the form of a gift.
  3. Through faith.

By Grace:

I. *My confession of faith.*
II. *My biography.*

The Central Pillars of our Evangelical Faith.

I. *By grace alone.*
II. *Through faith alone.*

Our Spiritual Quickening Through the Grace of God.

I. *The death, from which we were quickened.*
II. *The power of Christ's resurrection, by which we were quickened.*
III. *The new life, unto which we were quickened.*

What Does it Mean to be Saved by Grace?

I. *It means deliverance from sin, death, and perdition.*
II. *It means quickening, resurrection, sitting in the heavenly places*
III. *It means humility, gratitude, good works.*

Our Salvation the Gift of God.

I. *By grace.*
II. *In Christ.*
III. *Through faith.*

36

JUBILATE.

1 John 4, 7-14.

The great salvation which was completed and set before all the world by the resurrection of Christ from the dead rests on the infinite grace of God, and on his unspeakable love. After the celebration of the great Easter event, which extends to the Sunday after Easter, we therefore have two texts, one dealing with the divine grace, the other with the divine love. Each of them includes the corresponding corollary, for grace is intended to be received by faith, and love calls forth love in return. This is the setting in which we find our present text. Unlike the preceding one there is no direct reference here to Christ's resurrection, yet we have the comprehensive statements that the Son of God was sent to be a propitiation for our sins, and to be the Savior of the world. It is proper for us to take both in their fullest meaning as including what was done when God raised up him who died for our sins and by his resurrection made him manifest as indeed the Savior of the world. It was thus that God displayed all the fulness of his saving love, that love which calls forth an answering love in the hearts of all who accept it. And this love of ours, begotten of the love of God, must go out to our brethren, yet in doing so unites us most intimately to God, the author of love. The entire text thus deals with the manifestation and blessed results of *love,* first of the love of God toward us, and then of our love in return.

God's love to us.

John is speaking of the divine character of love in the words which immediately precede our text, and he

562

ends with the great statement: "God is love," of which
Besser rightly says: "Love is not so much a quality
which God *has,* as rather the all-embracing total of what
he *is.*" And Bengel adds that this little sentence, God is
love, brought to John, in the brief moment of writing it,
more sweetness than all the world is able to give."
Gerhard calls love "a practical definition of God." The
entire doctrine of Scripture concerning God is summed
up in the brief sentence: ὁ θεὸς ἀγάπη ἐστίν. But John at
once adds what is essential for us who are in this sinful world: God who is love has manifested himself as
love toward us, and this in the most wonderful and
blessed way. **Herein was the love of God manifested
in us, that God hath sent his only begotten Son into
the world, that we might live through him. Herein is
love, not that we loved God, but that he loved us, and
and sent his Son *to be* the propitiation for our sins.**
— John is setting down a great historical fact: ἐφανερώθη
ἡ ἀγάπη, **the love of God was manifested.** He adds the
article; God is love, and *this* love of his was manifested.
So in the manifestation we see and experience God himself as that which he really is. His love came forth and
showed itself so that men could actually see and feel it. It
might have remained in the inner life of God, exercising
itself between the persons of the Godhead, or in the glorious confines of the heavenly world, going out to the blessed
angels of God as objects worthy of its attention. But behold, — a thing which transcends all our poor earthly
reason — God manifested his love to a fallen world; John
3, 16. **In us** is more correctly given by the margin: *in our
case;* the German would be *an uns.* Ἐν ἡμῖν is not the
same as εἰς ἡμᾶς, toward us, or unto us; nor is "in us"
here the same as "in our hearts," in a subjective, personal
experience of God's love. John's thought is rather that
we ourselves are the blessed objects of God's love; its
entire manifestation is one by which God concerns himself
with us who were in such dire need; it is a manifestation in regard to us. — For it consists of this **that God**

hath sent his only begotten Son into the world, that we might live through him. This sending embraces not only the incarnation, but the entire work of the Son in the world. In his entire *missio,* as it occurred here on earth, the love of God stood displayed; and that not only for us to see and know, but for us to receive and experience in its saving results. God sent us not only messengers to tell us in mighty words of his love; these too he sent, great prophets of old, the last of whom was the Baptist. At last, however, he sent **his only begotten Son,** begotten as **his Son** from all eternity, of one essence with the Father, eternal and infinitely glorious. It is unfortunate that a commentator like Zahn should reduce the appellation μονογενής (John 1, 18) to the wonderful generation of Christ in the womb of the virgin Mary. The term refers to something far greater, for it is not applied to the Son of man, or to the assumption of his human nature, but to the Son of God. To be sure, John did not write: "the only begotten God;" but in showing how improper this would be Zahn disregards entirely that the apostle did write: "his (God's) only begotten Son." While no man can possibly tell what the eternal generation of the Son really signifies, we do know that it makes the Son truly equal with the Father, of one essence with him, yet distinct in person. And so we perceive his divine glory and exaltation above all the creatures of God however great. The only begotten Son could and did bring us more than any and all previous messengers of God. While they came with the message of God's love and evidences and proofs of it, the Son brought us this love itself in all its fulness and saving power. — For the only begotten Son was sent **that we might live through him,** that through his person and work we who were dead in sins might be delivered from our terrible bonds and made partakers of the true life, in eternal union and communion with God. The verb ζάω has ἀποθνήσκω, to die, as its opposite. He who lives through the Son of God has the life that really deserves the name, and death has no more power over him. Even temporal death can only lead him, like a humble servant, to a fuller enjoyment of that wonderful life which has become his through Christ. When the apostle writes: "that **we** might live through him," he indeed speaks only of the true Christians, and of the divine intention and purpose as it concerns this limited number, since the gift of life has actually been made theirs. The Scriptures often do this; compare verse 10. Yet this in no way means to exclude the others from the saving purpose of God in sending his Son, who is the Savior of the whole world, verse 14, although many refuse to accept him and the life he has obtained for them.

By means of a parallel statement the apostle emphasizes what he has just said and makes his thought still clearer: **Herein is love, not that we loved God, but that he loved us, and sent his Son** *to be* **the propitiation for our sins.** The stress is on God as the foundatain and author of love, and on the manner in which his love secured life for us sinners. John is not speaking of love in general, as if he were taking all love together and stating what its essential features are. He is speaking of the love that is really and truly love, fully deserving the name; of this he says: **Herein is love** (ἡ ἀγάπη) **not that we loved God, but that he loved us.** He puts these two in the strongest opposition. It is a mistake to imagine that the love which deserves the name emanates from us, and rises up from our hearts to God; the exact reverse is true, this love is altogether of divine origin: ἡ ἀγάπη τοῦ θεοῦ ἐστιν; it is a flame from above, flashing down into our hearts and igniting them with love. There was no such thing as our loving God while we were in our sins; all ideas of that kind are an empty delusion. If love depended on us in this respect, there never would have been any such thing. The sinner hates God and turns in enmity against him, as long as sin controls him. Even what he calls "love" in his dealings with friends, associates, and his fellow men does not deserve the name of true love (ἡ ἀγάπη). And with love in this sense foreign to us there is shut out any possibility of our calling forth the love of God upon us by our first loving him. Before ever we knew what true love was, God's love went forth to us, enfolded us in its heavenly radiance, and by its heavenly power started to kindle the light of love in us.

The two statements: "the love of God was manifested," and: "God loved us," belong together; likewise: "God sent his only begotten Son into the world," and: God "sent his Son to be the propitiation for our sins." All four, moreover, must be taken together as a whole. The love of God is not something hazy, vague, indefinite, a mere inactive feeling in the .bosom of God; his love at once expresses itself in the fullest and most adequate manner: he **sent his Son,** and since we were sinners, under the curse and doom of sin, he sent him *to be* **the propitiation for our sins.** How little this excludes other men we see in 1 John 2, 2: "and not for ours only, but also for the whole world." To understand this "propitiation" we must take in its full meaning the designation **his Son,** · which is none other than the second person of the Godhead, born man of the virgin Mary. The word translated **propitiation,** ἱλασμός, is from ἱλάσκομαι, to appease or conciliate to one's self. In biblical usage it is never God who is propitiated, but our sins, or we sinners (Heb. 2, 17; Luke 18, 13); so here Christ is called the propitiation **for our sins,** περί with the genitive, concerning, or in the matter of our sins. Westcott explains that Christ by his atoning death altered the character of that which from without occasioned a necessary alienation of God from us, and opposed an inevitable obstacle to God's fellowship with us. Christ covered our sin, and thus removed it out of the way. In ἱλασμός, which occurs in the N. T. only here and in 1 John 2, 2, we have more than in ἱλάστης, the propitiator. Christ does not propitiate alone, but, as Trench points out, he at once propitiates and is himself the propitiation: "The two functions of priest and sacrifice, which were divided, and of necessity divided, in the typical sacrifices of the law, met and were united in him, the sin-

offering by and through whom the just anger of God
against our sins was appeased, and God was rendered
propitious to us once more." *Synonyms*, II, 140. By
Christ as our propitiation God reconciled us unto himself
(compare καταλλάσσειν in the text for Good Friday, 2 Cor.
5, 18-19); the effect of the ἱλασμός is the καταλλαγή. This
then is love in its true and real sense, that God stooped
to us in our sins, and covered with the atoning blood of
his only begotten Son these sins of ours, which otherwise
he could not but hate and punish, thus placing us into
an entirely new relation to himself. There was no change
in God, for he is love from all eternity; but there was a
mighty change in regard to us and our sins, in that now
there is provided a complete propitiation and expiation for
them. By this propitiation the way is opened for us into
everlasting life. Every one who believes in Christ has this
life; freed from his sin and guilt by God's justifying grace
on the basis of Christ's propitiatory merits, he is made
God's own beloved child and shall bask in the sunlight
of his love for evermore.

Our love in return.

John has been setting forth the great fact of God's
love and its saving manifestation in an objective way; using
the historical aorist he has told his readers what God has
done for them in his only begotten Son. Yet the apostle has
also taken care of the subjective element by employing the
pronoun "we," which implied that as true believers his
readers had accepted the love of God and the propitiation
and life which is wrought for them. Now, on the basis of
what God has done and what "we" have received at his
hands, the apostle places the effective conclusion: **Beloved,
if God so loved us, we also ought to love one another.**
Writing of love John's own heart glows with love; bidding
others to love, he himself displays love. So he addresses
his readers again as in verse 7: **beloved.** Let every
preacher of the Gospel make an application for his own
benefit at this point. — He uses the conditional form: **if**

God so loved us, but he has already shown that the condition is fulfilled, to which he points with the word **so.** The conclusion is therefore established, and no one who has experienced the love of God can possibly deny it: **we also ought to love one another.** Our possession and enjoyment of God's love necessarily involve this obligation. You cannot sit in the sunshine of God's love and remain cold toward those who there sit beside you. "It is in itself unthinkable," writes Dryander, "and a miserable self-delusion to imagine we can comfort ourselves in grief and guilt with the love of God and receive at the Lord's table the gift of divine love and forgiveness, while at the same time our hearts remain hard and loveless." When the apostle writes **one another,** he means our fellow believers, although, of course, he does not wish to exclude other men from the activity of our love. But those who alike receive God's love form one body, and this body, so intimately connected with God and his love, is naturally the first and foremost field for the exercise of our love; nor will there be a wider reach of true love, if the narrower one is impossible for us. The verb is again ἀγαπᾶν, love in the true and exalted sense of the word, higher, because of its spiritual quality, than φιλεῖν, the love of affection and personal attachment which may be altogether without this quality.

John now sets forth what it really means for us to have and exercise such love: **No man hath beheld God at any time: if we love one another, God abideth in us, and his love is perfected in us: hereby know we that we abide in him, and he in us, because he hath given us of his Spirit.** The perfect tense τεθέαται, **hath seen,** and the adverb **at any time,** are intended to cover all the past experience of John's readers. At no time did any of them rest his eyes upon God; manifestly, because this is impossible, since God is invisible. An actual seeing with the natural eye is meant, not a spiritual seeing with the eye of faith; for so we all have seen God, and see him still in his Word and Sacrament. But John does not mention this invisibility of God to show why our love must go out now, not to God directly, but by way of the brethren. If this had been his thought he would most likely have used the present, and not the perfect tense. Moreover, it is both God's will, and entirely possible for us, to love God directly although he is invisible; by spiritual communion with him, by converse with his Word, by service rendered to honor and please him in worship and works of many kinds we certainly can exercise our love to God directly. — The apostle's idea is that though we have never seen God, yet **if we love one another, God abideth in us.** This means more than that such love is an evidence of God's presence in our hearts, from which to draw the conclusion that he has been working in us. Certainly, where the God of love has entered, there he will have wrought love. The apostle, however, has the future in mind: **God abideth in us,** day by day, never leaving us; and in this regard he says that only when we exercise the love God has implanted into our hearts, does he remain in us. The condition of his presence is ever that from the blessedness of his love to us we impart love to the brethren. We indeed cannot see God, yet if we love one another, the invisible God of love is most really present in us. To show such love is to exercise what constantly flows to us from the presence of God in us. To cease such love is to be empty of God and far from him. So the world has not God, and knows him not; its distinctive mark is self-love, selfishness, and even what it pleases to call "love" and "charity," and by which it often makes an impressive outward display, never reaches up to the love which is born of God and the saving work of his Son. Where gold alone will answer all the brass in the world must be thrown aside. — But not only will God abide in us, if we love one another, John adds: **and his love is perfected in us.** Commentators are puzzled by the genitive ἡ ἀγάπη αὐτοῦ, whether this is subjective or objective. Some at once take the easiest explanation and make it the latter: our love to God is made perfect, if we love one another, ignoring the intervening clause. On the other hand, it is certain that God's love to us, as this love is in him, cannot be made perfect, for it is so already; this idea is therefore at once excluded. But John has just spoken of God abiding in us, and, of course, he abides in us together with his love to us. The thought is thus entirely natural, and in fact the first to suggest itself, that with him permanently abiding in our hearts his love to us also reaches its consummation, **is perfected in us.** The fact is that our love to God never is really perfected in us in this life, even if we love the brethren well; there is always some corner of our heart still darkened by selfish thought. It is therefore decidedly best to make the genitive subjective: God's love reaches its real goal in us when now God permanently abides in us; then his love will have full play to mold us according to his will. And love's desire is ever to be thus perfected in the closest union and communion with the object that is loved. — **Hereby we know,** John adds, **that we abide in him, and he in us, because he hath given us of his Spirit.** The apostle has just shown that everything depends on God abiding in us; for if he is in us, the blessed work of his love will be accomplished in us. So we must accept his love and respond to its impulse in loving one another. But how shall we know **that we abide in him, and he in us,** that we are truly one with God? The answer to this implied question does not lie in our love to one another, or even to God directly. This is evidence indeed, but sometimes, when our love grows weak and faint, this evidence would be correspondingly weak. Note the full expression for the mystical union: **we in him, and he in us.** Of this we are altogether sure, **because he hath given us of his Spirit.** With the Son God has also given us his Spirit (1 John 3, 24), or, as the apostle here says "of his Spirit," of his divine fulness, power, and grace. This divine gift is evidence not from us, but from God that he and we are in communion. For the Spirit of God is his heavenly medium for reaching our hearts; and this Spirit is the direct opposite of the world and its spirit. Wherever the Spirit has been given his presence is felt and known; for he draws us away from the world and its selfish and godless ways, he lifts

us ever upward to God, to the things of God, and to the
love of God's people. Every stirring of the Spirit within
us is evidence that we can depend on it that God is united
with us, even in times when we have grown weak and discouraged. When this Spirit no longer moves in us, rebuking, admonishing, comforting, strengthening, guiding,
enlightening us, then indeed our hearts are empty and
dead, and then neither true love nor the desire for it will
be in them.

But the fundamental thing in all these realities
is the one which John mentioned in the beginning of
our text, and to which he now once more returns, as
the foundation of everything: the sending of the Son
as our Savior. **And we have beheld and bear witness
that the Father hath sent the Son** *to be* **the Savior of
the world.** The apostle is speaking of himself and his
fellow apostles, as the verbs plainly show. They have seen
with their own eyes, not the Son alone, but the entire mission of the Son. They saw the Only Begotten from the
Father (John 1, 14) as he carried out his great redemptive
work and completed it on the cross and by his resurrection
from the dead. And what they thus **have beheld** and
looked upon with their eyes (compare 1 John 1, 1) during
those precious days when they lived and walked with
Christ, they now **bear witness** to and testify to all men
everywhere as the chosen messengers of God. Their witness
has reached us also, and we hear it gain in John's words:
that the Father hath sent the Son the Savior of the world.
In the name **Savior,** σωτήρ, we have that precious title
which centers all our rescue and salvation in the Son of
God; he, and he alone, wrought our deliverance, and without him there is no hope for sinners. And he is truly the
Savior **of the world,** of all men of all nations and ages,
not one excepted. It is folly for Ebrard to discount this
comforting statement by writing: "The question, whether
Christ came with the design to save all the individuals of
this unredeemed world, or only a portion of them, does
not in the most distant way enter into the text." This

question so completely and fully enters into the text that
its most positive affirmative answer is the very text itself,
and its denial a subversion of the text. Luther gives us
the apostle's true meaning when he declares concerning
himself, that as surely as he belongs to the world, so surely
also did Christ redeem him. — The whole text lies summed
up in the admonition with which Dryander closes his excellent sermon: "Let us bring to God these hearts of ours,
bleeding from a thousand wounds which sin and the world
have struck in them, that he may heal them with his love.
Consecrated and sanctified by him who is love, let us consume ourselves in order to show by a life of love that we
know him." So shall his love not be in vain for us.

HOMILETICAL HINTS.

A king asked the poet Simonides: "What is God?" The poet
requested a day's time to find an answer, and then another and
another, until finally he declared: "The longer I think of it, the
less I know." Not one who was wiser than all others, but a simple
fisherman from Galilee, John, the apostle, has given the answer
which none of the wisest of the world could ever discover of
himself: "God is love." — You do not feel the power of the spring
sunshine when you merely see it trembling in the foliage outside:
you must step out into its glowing beams. Likewise you will never
know the greatness of the word, that God is love, as long as you
try to penetrate it with your reason and analyze it with your
speculation — and who is able even to do that? — You must go out
into the warm radiance of this love and expand under its heavenly
warmth, then you will know in your own soul that God has loved
you. Dryander.

From him also the following: "It is not that John of himself
has made the momentous discovery of what God is, but God himself
revealed it to the apostle in the school of the Savior, in communion
with Jesus Christ. Herein was the love of God manifested in us,
that God hath sent his only begotten Son into the world."

Yes, we believe, God is love. That is an easy thing as long
as we are in health, have plenty of money, and live in the sunshine
of good fortune. Then, like a lark rising aloft over verdant fields
our Jubilate will warble and sing: God is love. But ask the men

in prison cells, whether they believe that God is love. They will reply, that there is no God at all, and if there is that he is cruel and a God of hate. They will say that they are no worse than thousands of others, and yet are deprived of liberty and joy. How can the God of love permit a world-order like that? Ask the laborer who toils and sweats at his daily tasks and grumbles at his wrongs, that he must lead a life of hardship while others enjoy ease and plenty; ask him whether he believes that God is love, and he will give you the same kind of an answer. Shall we inquire also of the grief-stricken beside the freshly turned grave, or of the sufferers on their beds of pain, whether God is love? He who is uniformly fortunate, with abundance of earthly treasures and enjoyments, he lightly speaks of the love of God — but is that all the word means? Riemer.

As long as we talk of God's love and think only of the candy of our wishes, we have never yet known that love.

The victory of God's love is on Calvary; the triumph of his love, in Christ's open tomb; the glory of his love in all those who now live through Christ. — To know God's love is to prize the sacrifice that love made; to share its power; to serve in its kingdom.

The greatest thing in the world is not anything of the world at all; it is the heavenly love of God in Christ Jesus his Son. — To make Christ less than the Son of God is to reduce God's love, to cheapen the propitiation for our sins, to lose the riches of that love.

John makes a surprising turn. We rather expect him to say: "If God so loved us, we also ought to love him." Instead he says: "We also ought to love one another." But he implies that thus we will both love God and show that love as we should.

It seemed strange and incomprehensible to the heathen observers of the first Christians, that they should love each other even before they had known each other. Their derisive word was precious testimony nevertheless: "Their Lawgiver has persuaded them that they are all brethren!"

Our love to men is service to God. — The Gospel of self-interest is the agnosticism of God's love in Christ Jesus. — Love, says Augustine, then do what thou wilt.

Whatever your position in life, whether rich or poor, high or humble, old or young, man or woman — whoever you may be, you cannot be such, that this commandment of love does not apply also to you. Live for your business, your property, your calling, your family, your art, your philanthrophy — yea, take the highest goal known to human enterprise: it will never satisfy. But open your heart to the love of God, proclaim that love, and let it unite you with your brethren, and you will live a life that is full of joy — *jubilate*, now, and evermore!

The Gospel of love is as young to-day as when John penned it, yea, as when God in eternity conceived it. If the world stands ten thousand years more, yea, when it has been transformed by the great change of the last day, this preaching of love will not have grown old and outworn.

It is the hight of lovelessness to let men's souls go on to perdition, while we provide a thousand charities for their bodies. — The love of the brethren is not to put them into opposition to others, but to increase their magnetic powers, so that they may win others for a similar love.

No one is superfluous on earth as long as he is able to love, and let none complain that he has no real calling in life while he is still able to attend to the work of this his calling of love. Dryander tells of Twesten calling on his friend and colleague Nitzsch at the university of Berlin, while the latter lay on his death-bed. Pointing to his poor old, faded body the patient sufferer said: "I can no longer see, nor hear, nor work; I can — only love." But this was enough.

Jubilate! Rejoice in the Love of God!

   I. *Appreciate its sacrifice.*
  II. *Live in its communion.*
 III. *Respond to its prompting.*

The Greatest Gifts of God's Love.

    I. *His Son.*
   II. *Propitiation.*
  III. *Life.*
  IV. *Love.*
   V. *Indwelling.*

True Love is Divine.

  I. *It emanates from God.*
 II. *It is exercised in God.*

Latrille.

The Fullness of God's Love.

  I. *Its highest manifestation.*
 II. *Its most blessed fruit.*

Matthes

The Life That is Born of Love:

I. *Must ever rejoice in that love.*
II. *Must ever thrive and grow in that love.*
III. *Must ever do the works of that love.*

God's Love in Christ Jesus the Fountain of our Life.

I. *Our life is the gift of that love.*
II. *Our life is to be the evidence of that love.*

CANTATE.

Cantate completes the Easter cycle, hence this beautiful text on *faithfulness* or *perseverance*. Once more the great Easter thought is to be presented effectively to our hearers, in the admonition: "Remember Jesus Christ, risen from the dead," and in the added promise: "If we die with him, we shall also live with him." In the two previous texts the chief stress was on God's grace and love, here it is evidently on our conduct. We are to persevere in faithfulness unto the end; and in order that we may, are to keep in remembrance the risen Savior, let the example of his faithful apostle encourage us, and cling to the sweet assurance of the promise, which the corresponding threat throws into greater relief. Accordingly as we combine or keep apart what is said of Christ and of the apostle himself, we have two or three sections in the text.

Remember Jesus Christ, risen from the dead.

Paul's intention in writing the words of our text to Timothy is quite plain. The apostle is urging his "son Timothy" to bear himself as a faithful soldier of Jesus Christ, and tells him in picturesque and striking language what the chief requirements are in this regard, verses 4-7. But Timothy, like every soldier of Christ, needs more than this. In order that the admonition may find a ready, joyous, hopeful response, there must also be ample encouragment, and this is what the apostle now supplies from the rich fund at his disposal. Lest we ever grow discouraged, let us remember Jesus Christ, whom also Paul himself followed so faithfully to the end; and let us keep before our eyes the great promise

576

with its stern alternative. — **Remember Jesus Christ, risen from the dead, of the seed of David, according to my gospel.** In as few words as possible, but these compact with meaning, Paul sets Christ before Timothy for his encouragement. Luther has finely translated the present imperative μνημόνευε: *Halt im Gedaechtnis,* keep in memory. Timothy is not to think of Christ only once, or occasionally, but is to bear him in mind constantly. Paul writes the full name **Jesus Christ,** our Savior, the Messiah. Both his person and his saving office are thus referred to, and these in connection with each other. — The terse addition: **risen from the dead** is not a confessional formula, as some have thought, but a summary statement of Paul's preaching and teaching which hinged entirely on the resurrection of Christ. This, of course, implies his vicarious suffering and death. The perfect passive participle ἐγηγερμένον, from ἐγείρειν, "having been raised up," and thus now **risen,** marks the permanent condition of Jesus Christ; he lives now and triumphs in his victory over sin and death. As such a glorious Savior he is to be constantly present to the mind of Timothy for his encouragement. His victory is our victory; by it we are assured of success in our fight. The foes which Christ overcame cannot hurt us now; Christ lives to aid and help us every day; and his example marks the path which we are to follow, and can follow, by his help. — Without a connecting word Paul adds: **of the seed of David,** which has been variously interpreted. Some are satisfied to take it merely as a reference to Christ's human nature, as Rom. 1, 3-4; others bring in the typical relation of David to Christ; and still others, more correctly, read the words as a designation of Christ's royal Messiahship. The real purpose of this reference to Christ's descent from David cannot be found as long as we disconnect it from the resurrection of Christ. The two belong together: it was he who was of the seed of David that was raised up from the dead. The passage which illuminates this is Acts 2, 29-30. Peter there describes

37

Jesus as the one in whom God's sworn promise to David
was fulfilled: "that of the fruit of his loins, according to
the flesh, he would raise up Christ to sit on his throne."
David "seeing this before, spake of the resurrection of
Christ" (A. V.). So Paul here views Christ as the promised
seed of David, risen from the dead, and occupying the
throne of David forever as our Messiah-King. God's great
promise to David has actually been fulfilled, namely in
Christ's resurrection and elevation to the eternal throne. —
And this, Paul says, **according to my gospel** (Rom. 2, 16;
16, 25). It is the actual contents of the glad message
which it was his life's work to proclaim. The promise to
David and the preaching of Paul are one and the same
thing, only the latter recounts the fulfilment of the former.
Timothy is to keep in memory the great apostle's teaching,
then there will be no lack of valor and courage on his part.

Paul's own example.

What Paul urged Timothy to do he himself did with
diligence and thoroughness; it is what must be demanded of every preacher, lest he preach to others and
himself be a castaway. So the apostle writes: **wherein
I suffer hardships unto bonds, as a malefactor; but the
word of God is not bound. Therefore I endure all things
for the elect's sake, that they also may obtain the salvation which is in Christ Jesus with eternal glory.** Ἐν ᾧ,
wherein, refers to εὐαγγέλιον, but to this gospel as Paul
actively and energetically proclaimed it. Timothy was
in the same position, also having the office of the
ministry. Paul's example therefore applied very directly
to him. Living and working in the Gospel, the apostle
writes: **I suffer hardship unto bonds;** he means that
all manner of evil comes upon him and inflicts pain and
distress, and this in his case has now reached the climax
of imprisonment. Paul was in bonds, a prisoner in Rome
on trial for his life, at the very time when he wrote
these words; they must have affected Timothy greatly when
he first read them. The best chronology makes this the

2 Tim. 2, 8-13.

second and final imprisonment of the apostle, which ended
with his martyr death not long after. See the introduction
to Stellhorn's *Pastoralbriefe Pauli*, I, 7 etc. — On what plea
Paul was now imprisoned we are unable to say, but he must
have been charged with some grave offense, since he says
that he was made to suffer **as a malefactor,** a criminal in
the eyes of the law. The word implies that Paul felt deeply
both the wrong and the shame of his persecution. Yet
Christ had forewarned all his disciples of this very thing,
Matth. 10, 24-25, and when Paul was now in the midst of
it, he took it as part of his soldier-lot (verse 3), bore it
willingly, bravely, even joyfully, and inspired others to do
the same, whatever they might be called on to bear. Seeing
him going thus valiantly to an unjust and cruel death, shall
we, who are called to trials far less severe, prove unfaithful
and fail to persevere to the end? — We catch an interesting
glimpse of Paul's way of thinking in the side-statement he
now throws in: **but the word of God is not bound.** His
own person does not matter much (compare Phil. 1, 12 etc.,
also 18, text for Septuagesima), just so the Gospel is not
checked. In thinking of himself his mind cannot but revert
to the Gospel. Speaking of his bonds, he at once notes that
the precious Gospel is not bound. No chain has ever been
invented for it; it goes on freely in its conquering course.
When the voice of one of its preachers is hushed, another
will be raised up by the Lord; yea, the bonds and suffering
of God's messenger will themselves proclaim his Son's name
in the very midst of his foes. Old Chrysostom wrote: "They
bind the hands, but not the tongue." And Bengel explains
οὐ δέδεται by the two words: *Expedite currit.* This is because it is the Word **of God,** who himself lends wings to
his Gospel. — **Therefore,** διὰ τοῦτο, is drawn by some to
what precedes, in order not to bring together in one sentence
two phrases with διά and the accusative: "On this account
I endure all things on account of the elect." Yet this,
although by no means smooth, is not so unusual in Paul's
writing; moreover, to read: "but the word of God is not
bound διὰ τοῦτο, on this account," *i. e.* on account of my

imprisonment, makes Paul deny what could hardly have been in his mind, namely the thought that the Gospel was altogether bound up with the fortunes of his own person. **Therefore** goes with what follows: because the Word of God is not bound;" it is this which gives Paul comfort, strength, and joy, so that he can say: **I endure all things for the elect's sake.** In πάντα, **all things,** he summarizes his past, present, and any future sufferings. Gladly he endures (ὑπομένω) them all, stands up under them and bears them patiently and perseveringly (ὑπομονή — patience). — **For the elect's sake** again shows that Paul's great concern is not his own person, his bodily safety, comfort, good fortune, or his personal honor among men. These things influence too many of us, even in the ministry; and so also our people, who are ever inclined to put selfish earthly advantages above the interests of the church and even their own spiritual good. But the apostle rejoiced to serve others, even if it were, as now, by his patient example of suffering. **The elect** are those whom God chose as his own "from the beginning unto salvation in sanctification of the Spirit and belief of the truth," 2 Thess. 2, 13; those whom he foreknew and foreordained to be conformed to the image of his Son, Rom. 8, 29. The question whether Paul meant only the elect of his own time, or also those of later times, which some commentators raise, introduces a distinction which the apostle in no way suggests. He is concerned about God's people generally, and would like to serve them all. He does not use the term ἐκλεκτοί in the Calvinistic sense, as the fixed number chosen absolutely and unconditionally to eternal life, but in the biblical sense of saints and believers chosen as such in Christ Jesus, who must make their calling and election sure, 2 Pet. 1, 10. These, while they stand, must take heed lest they fall, and therefore need all the help and encouragement God provides for them. — So the apostle is earnestly desirous, **that they also may obtain the salvation which is in Christ Jesus with eternal glory.** He willingly gives himself to suffer, and if need be to die, in order that his example of faithfulness and perseverance may be one

of the means in God's hands for keeping his children faithful and true to the end. Stellhorn has the following fine
explanation: "Paul's patience in his greatest undeserved
suffering was an actual proof of the divine power of the
Gospel which he believed and preached; it was this for
every one who heard of it and did not wilfully harden
himself against such proof, and it thus served to make them
willing toward the Gospel and to confirm and keep them
therein." When the apostle says: **to obtain the salvation,**
he means the final salvation which is bestowed at the last
day; so Peter writes, 1 Pet. 1, 9: "receiving the end of your
faith, even the salvation of your souls." The modifier **with
eternal glory** makes this perfectly plain.   There is no
article with σωτηρία: "to obtain salvation," there being only
this one, and no other.   It is **salvation in Christ Jesus**
because found and obtained only in him. "Therefore the
entire Holy Trinity, Father, Son, and Holy Ghost, direct
all men to Christ, as the Book of Life, in which they should
seek the eternal election of the Father." *Formula of Concord,* 661, 66. "But they should hear Christ, who is the
Book of Life and of God's eternal election of all God's children to eternal life; who testifies to all men without distinction that it is God's will that all men who labor and are
heavy laden with sin should come to him, in order that he
may give them rest and save them, Matth. 11, 28." 661, 70.

The Lord's final faithfulness.

The thought of final salvation with glory leads the
apostle to state explicitly what will take place at the
last day when Christ in his eternal faithfulness will
fulfil both his promise to those who have been faithful
and his threat to the faithless. **Faithful is the saying:
For if we died with him, we shall also live with him:
if we endure, we shall also reign with him: if we shall
deny him, he also will deny us: if we are faithless, he
abideth faithful; for he cannot deny himself.** — The
apostle uses the expression: **Faithful is the saying**
repeatedly, 1 Tim. 1, 15; 3, 1; 4, 9; Tit. 3, 8, and inva-

riably to bring out the reliability and trustworthiness of some general truth. A number of commentators think that in our text this assurance must refer to what Paul has just said, since it is followed by a sentence with γάρ, which seems to state a reason why the saying is faithful. The margin has this view when it translates: *Faithful is the saying; for etc.* But this leaves us altogether in doubt as to what the "saying" is that is thus pronounced "faithful." In what precedes Paul tells us why he endures all things so steadfastly, he utters no general truth. But in what follows he does utter such a truth, and that with poetical rhythm in an elevated tone. — This then is the faithful saying upon which Timothy, and every one of us, can depend with absolute certainly: **If we died with him, we shall also live with him; etc.** It is evidently intentional that there is first an aorist: συναπεθάνομεν, "died;" next a present tense: ὑπομένομεν, "endure;" and finally a future: ἀρνησόμεθα, "shall deny." Commentators are pretty well agreed that the dying with Christ here spoken of refers to the bodily death of martyrdom; and they choose as parallels passages like Rom. 8, 17 and Phil. 3, 10, while they reject Rom. 6, 8: "But if we died with Christ, we believe we shall also live with him," since this speaks of our dying with Christ in conversion, and thus becoming partakers of his atoning death for us. But in spite of this consensus and the ground on which it is built, namely that the context does not suggest the latter kind of death, but rather the former, this interpretation is unsatisfactory. Paul is stating a blessed, encouraging general truth, one of the great promises of the Gospel, applicable to every true Christian: "If **we** died with him, **we** shall also live with him; *etc.*" To narrow this down, so that his words apply only to a few who die a martyr's death, is certainly improper. The aorist, as in Rom. 6, 8, most naturally points to a definite past act; especially is this the case here where we have three conditional sentences all built alike, and a progress of tenses in the three conditions, first an aorist, then a present, and finally a future. Neither Paul nor Timothy had as yet reached martyrdom. It is hardly satisfactory to say, as is generally done, that the aorist is used merely to indicate time prior to the following future tense; this is especially unsatisfactory when we look at the two following sentences. Finally, why should Paul mention death first, and then enduring, when evidently, if a martyr's death is meant, the enduring of persecution and suffering would precede the death? — The faithful saying or promise of the Gospel which we are all to remember for our encouragement is twofold: **If we died with him, we shall also live with him: if we endure, we shall also reign with him.** When Paul writes: "if we died," he takes it for granted that we did so die, and that therefore we indeed shall live. He means the death to sin in repentance, that which is fundamental for our entire personal salvation. The σύν in the verb refers to Christ: "We have become united with him by the likeness of his death," Rom. 6, 5. Christ "died unto sin once," Rom. 5, 10, completely atoning for it; in this death we have joined him, becoming partakers of it, when we turned in repentance from sin and in faith to Christ. Only they who thus die with Christ **shall also live with him** to all eternity. The promise of life with Christ is entirely general and properly applies to all believers, and by no means only, or in a special sense, to martyrs. Think of all the glorious future before you, and thus keep your heart valiant and strong during the brief time of your earthly sojourn and trial. — On this fundamental promise rests the other, which is by no means only a weak repetition, as the other interpretation makes it, or an anti-climax to the first promise, but a mighty and glorious addition: **if we endure, we shall also reign with him.** Paul was enduring when he wrote the words, even as he had died with Christ; Timothy likewise. And this word applies to every one of us who now endures, that is holds out with patience under persecution and trial. Some indeed are called upon to resist even unto blood, Heb. 12, 4, to endure a great fight of afflictions, Heb. 10, 32, and like Paul count not their lives dear in the defense of the Gospel, Acts 20, 24. Here then is where Paul touches upon martyrdom. To all who endure the promise is sure: **we shall also reign with him** in the glorious kingdom to come. Note well that it is more to reign than it is to live. The promise is thus magnified to those who endure and possibly undergo death for the Gospel. The Scriptures repeatedly promise this reigning to those who endure: Rev. 3, 21; 20, 4 and 6; 2, 10; Luke 19, 17 and 19; 22, 29-30. What it signifies we shall not fully know until we enter that glorious world. Buechner says that it includes the possession of higher powers in an extensive field of operation, the exercise of a mighty influence in Christ's kingdom, and the triumph with Christ over all the foes whose last effort was defeat. Daechsel, like other millennarians, brings in the chiliastic notion of a reign on earth when the millennial kingdom shall be established, a notion utterly foreign to the apostle.

But there is a reverse to this promise, a mighty warning against faithlessness: **if we shall deny him, he also will deny us.** The verb means to disown, refuse, say no. Any and every permanent denial of Christ is meant, by act as well as by word. In the early church the heathen authorities often demanded a denial of Christ by attempting to force Christians to offer pagan sacrifices. But the apostle puts no restrictions into the word, save that the denial pertains to former confessors and believers. If they lose their faith, turn again to human wisdom, subversive error, worldly living, then the saying is sure: **he also will deny us.** Here both the condition and the conclusion are in the future tense, because the apostle would speak of such denial on any Christian's part only as a remote possibility. Alas, it has often become a sad present reality! Where Christ will disown those who proved unfaithful to him in spite of all his grace and gifts, he has himself said: "But whosoever shall deny me before men, him will I also deny before my Father which is in heaven," Matth. 10, 33. Nothing more terrible can be imagined than the words: "I never knew you; depart from me, ye that work iniquity."

Matth. 7, 23. — The apostle adds: **if we are faithless, he abideth faithful; for he cannot deny himself.** Here faithless and faithful are opposites, and the latter is explained by the clause with γάρ. Christ cannot be false to himself and his Word, whether that Word be a promise or the reverse. If he were to deny himself, disown his own Word, or prove untrue to his character as righteous, holy, and truthful, he would no longer be God. Cremer points out that πιστός, used of God or Christ, refers to his promises. Accordingly, some understand Paul to say here, that even if we prove untrustworthy and deny Christ, his promise stands nevertheless, remains uncanceled, so that we may return in repentance and be accepted. While this is certainly true, the entire context (note the three conclusions with the future tenses) points to the final judgment as the time when we shall find Christ absolutely faithful and in no way denying himself. In that solemn hour he will fulfil both his promises and his threats; and it is for us now to shape our conduct accordingly in faithful endurance to the end.

HOMILETICAL HINTS.

To remember Jesus Christ, risen from the dead, of the seed of David, is more than to carry the story of his resurrection about in the memory or mind; it means to carry Jesus Christ himself in our hearts, in true and living faith. This is more than to think or speak of him once in a while, perhaps to recall him in time of special distress; it means to let him dominate our lives, to have him ever present with us, to be in constant communion with him, to live and depend on him day by day, to serve and honor him with our whole being. Thus Paul remembered him, and thus he bade Timothy do.

The name and fame of great men lives for a time in the world, then finally sinks into forgetfulness. The same thing may happen with Jesus' name, if we impress it only upon our memories when we hear of him in preaching and teaching. Soon other impressions blot out his image on the tablets of the mind; concerns and interests that seem far more important crowd him out of our thoughts. If we recall him and his great work it will be only like something which once we knew — a dead monument that remains where it is, not a living, saving power that ever goes with us.

The Christians in Timothy's time were prone to lay great stress on genealogies, legendary interpretations of ancient Jewish histories, for purposes of instruction after the manner of the old Jewish-Alexandrine philosophy. Perhaps Paul had these in mind (1 Tim. 1, 4; Tit. 3, 9), when he emphasized the genealogy of Jesus as "of the seed of David."

Human fashions and opinions are always changing, but Paul's Gospel is the same to-day as when he wrote of it in his Roman prison.

It is remarkable that the very men who insist that the laws of nature are immutable, imagine that the spiritual laws of divine truth and righteousness may be changed at will to accommodate themselves to their special requirements at any time. But the faithful sayings of God cannot change: he who will not die with Christ cannot live with him; he who refuses to endure shall not reign.

Look at faithful Paul, devoted unto Christ till his last breath; then look at Judas, the faithless traitor, who sold his Master for the price of a slave. Think of faithful Timothy, who heeded his spiritual father's admonitions in all things; then consider Demas, who turned again to the love of the world. Consider Barnabas and his generous offering in the first church; then mark well the hypocritical Ananias and Sapphira, who tried to steal the honor that did not belong to them. Which will you choose — the faithfulness of the former, or the faithlessness of the latter?

See in the pierced hands and feet of Jesus the signs of his faithfulness. What is the cross that we adore but the symbol of his faithful obedience to his heavenly Father? And now, as he sits on his throne of glory, with the name that is above every name, it is his faithfulness that is thus distinguished. He could not deny himself; he cannot, at the last great day.

Paul's great concern were his fellow Christians, the chosen children of God. For them he labored, suffered, and finally gave up his life in martyrdom. In this he followed Christ, who thought only of us and our salvation when he lived, suffered, and died here on earth. It is the Lord's will ever to bind us together with others, and our faithfulness to Christ is to show itself in the way in which we serve those for whom he has made us responsible. Cain did not think himself his brother's keeper; but from Christ and the apostles down, every child of God holds himself responsible for others. — What will you have at the last day? Shall your own children, relatives, former friends and associates rise up to curse you, because you considered only yourself and allowed them to go on to destruction? Do you not know that one of the tortures of the damned will be the accusation of those whom they helped on to a like damnation? Or will you have the gratitude of this or that child of God, perhaps of many, who shall come to you in that glorious life above to thank you for faithful admonitions, warnings, instructions, and a good. example, by which they were aided in reaching the heavenly goal? Do you not know that among the sweetest joys of heaven there shall be expressions of gratitude from one saint to another?

We shall all meet him who abideth faithful at the last great day. And before the Faithful One nothing shall avail us but faithfulness.

A faithful heart needs never to practice deception. Let men examine its conduct, let God himself come and see. But he who is faithless is constantly intent on hiding his falsehood. He needs all sorts of excuses, pleas, explanations, justifications, all as false as the faithlessness they are to hide. And already in this life these fig-leaves are often torn away, and he is left stark naked before the eyes of men, false, lying, hypocritical, traitorous, apostate wretch that he is. But if he should deceive men to the very end, he cannot deceive the Faithful One, who will deny him at last.

Remember Jesus Christ, and he will not forget or deny you.

Would You be Faithful?

Then
  I. *Remember the risen Savior.*
 II. *Remember his faithful apostle.*
III. *Remember your responsibility to others.*
 IV. *Remember the Lord's final faithfulness.*

Remember Jesus Christ, Risen From the Dead.

  I. *On whom all our faith rests.*
 II. *In whom all our lives center.*

Heffter.

What Must Every Servant of Jesus Christ Keep in Mind?

  I *That Jesus Christ is risen from the dead.*
 II. *That we must pass through much tribulation into the kingdom of God.*
III. *That the Lord cannot deny himself.*

Heffter.

Remember Jesus Christ, According to Paul's Gospel.

   I. *In confession.*
  II. *In trials.*
 III. *In death.*

Paul's Legacy: "Remember Jesus Christ, of the Seed of David, According to my Gospel."

   I. *A priceless treasure of saving grace.*
  II. *A sweet fountain of divine comfort.*
 III. *A glorious crown of everlasting hope.*

Be Faithful to the Faithful One!

   1. *In confessing his Gospel.*
  II. *In performing his work.*
 III. *In bearing his cross.*
 IV. *In trusting his promise.*

THE PENTECOST CYCLE.

THE PENTECOST CYCLE.

Rogate to Trinity Sunday.

This cycle needs an introduction less than any other. It is the briefest of all, and three of its five texts are assigned to festival days, each of which bears its own distinct character. It is necessary, however, to note that the texts here presented adhere to the Epistle idea, which, as already shown in previous cycles, differs decidedly from the gospel idea. The three festival texts in this cycle do not present the festival facts as such, and are not intended to describe them as such or to dwell on their details. The preacher who expects this will be disappointed and ought to take up one or the other of the gospel texts. The epistle texts take the great festival facts set forth in the gospel texts for granted and build on them as their foundation. The result in each case must be a sermon which indeed refers to the festival fact, but elaborates at length the special Gospel truth founded on that fact and the special blessing of God thus made our own. All the riches of God's grace are thus thrown open to the preacher, and his task will be to fill his mind and heart with them so that he may convey them fully and adequately to his hearers.

The very first text contains a thought that is significant for the entire cycle. Rogate, of course, deals with the subject of prayer, but in this text we are to deal not with individual, but with congregational prayer. An examination of the other texts will show that all of them deal with the idea of the church as the great communion of saints, in which each individual believer is only one of the units. This broadens the entire cycle, and brings to the consciousness of our hearers the fundamental truth that God means us to be members of one great body, viewed as such by

591

him, endowed with blessings as such, and finally to be gathered from all the ends of the earth in his eternal kingdom of glory. So Rogate deals with general and with intercessory prayer.

The text for the Ascension festival is built on the exaltation of Christ. But instead of setting forth this great deed of God, it shows what the consequences of it are for us who are now partakers of Christ's death and resurrection, while we still live here on earth. All God's people must set their minds on heavenly things, and must be content to wait for the manifestation of glory which shall be theirs when Christ returns at last.

Exaudi is altogether in line with this exalted theme of the festival immediately preceding. We are shown in detail what wondrous things God has done regarding our Savior, when he crowned his work by lifting him up to be the head over all to the church. Very decidedly the thought of the church as one great spiritual body is here brought out, and the connection of the church with Christ, the eternal Lord of all, as its Head.

Then follows the chief festival in the cycle, Pentecost. It says nothing at all about the gospel event which occurred in Jerusalem, the outpouring of the Holy Spirit upon the first disciples, its subject is the great work of that Spirit, namely the building of the church as the communion of saints throughout all the ages. The Holy Spirit erects a holy temple in the Lord, a habitation of God in the Spirit. What the gospel text can bring in only incidentally, is here the main subject, and one of supreme importance for all Christian hearers. — The text for Pentecost Monday is here omitted; it is Eph. 4, 11-16, and deals with the inner work of the Spirit in building the church.

The grandest text in the entire cycle is the one for Trinity Sunday, rounding out the entire festival half of the church year. In one grand sweep it reaches from eternity to eternity. Its three sections connect themselves with the three persons of the Godhead, thus bringing out the doctrine of the Holy Trinity in a glorious manner. The entire plan of salvation, from its first inception in eternity to its final consummation in eternity, is presented in all its main features. The emphasis all through the text is on the work of God in our salvation, thus building our faith on the foundation which cannot fall. The entire text is a mighty hymn of praise, beginning with this note in its fullest power, and returning to it as in a refrain at the end of each of the three sections. The wealth of this text is so great and vast that the best preacher can hope to present only a part of it to his hearers. — A second Trinity text is offered in 2 Cor. 13, 11-13; it contains the N. T. benediction, and thus summarizes what the first text presents *in extenso.* — The Pentecost cycle as a whole, and the text for Trinity Sunday in particular, connect the entire first or festival half of the church year in a fine manner with the second or non-festival half. The Triune God has established the church; its development, life, character, and consummation follows in natural order.

ROGATE.

1 Tim. 2, 1-6.

The subject of prayer is so important that one Sunday in the church year is especially devoted to its consideration. Both the gospels and epistles selected for Rogate deal with some phase of prayer; and our present text presents the duty and blessedness of *public or congregational prayer for all men in general*. Nothing is said concerning the Holy Spirit in this connection, although this is the first text in the Pentecost cycle. The preacher will himself supply any reference in this direction which he may deem necessary. But the text has a wealth of its own in another direction. It shows the connection of Christians with the state and its authorities, and with the human race in general, bringing out in a glorious way the universality of divine grace and redemption, and basing on this our duty of public and general prayer. This text then goes together with the general prayer provided for our congregations in the morning liturgy and offered up every Sunday morning after the sermon in the pulpit, or — which is far preferable — just before the close of the service at the altar. A sermon in this line will certainly be highly beneficial. We have here, first, the exhortation to such prayer, and, secondly, the reason for making it.

Paul's exhortation to general prayer.

Timothy was the pastor of the congregation at Ephesus, and Paul is writing him concerning his office and work, instructing him how to manage both in a God-pleasing and efficient manner. After warning him against false doctrine and heretical teachers in the first chapter of the Epistle, the apostle takes up the conduct

of the public services and tells Timothy what must be
done to meet the requirements of the Gospel. It is thus
that Paul comes to speak of general prayer at public
worship. **I exhort therefore, first of all, that supplications, prayers, intercessions, thanksgivings, be made for
all men; for kings and all that are in high place; that
we may lead a tranquil and quiet life in all godliness
and gravity.** — The connection with what precedes
(οὖν) is quite general. Timothy is to war the good war-
fare, holding truth and a good conscience, unlike some who
have taken a different course (verses 18-20 of chapter 1).
Of course, he is to do this in his office of pastor at Ephesus
and general assistant and representative of Paul in directing
the work at other places. **Therefore** he must observe the
following things, which the apostle finds it necessary to
mention in particular, beginning with what concerns public
worship. — **I exhort first of all** brings up the first matter,
which is followed by others, verse 8: "I desire therefore;"
verse 12: "I permit not;" compare 3, 14. In παρακαλῶ
there lies the thought of helpfulness toward Timothy as
Paul's assistant. He is given, in the form of exhortation,
directions such as he needs for his work, and reasons for
them, which are to serve both in guiding him personally and
in guiding the people with whom he has to deal. This first
matter concerns congregational prayer and its proper scope.
This is to be general, both in employing **supplications,
prayers, intercessions, thanksgivings,** and in embracing
all men. Congregational prayer, naturally, presupposes individual prayer on the part of Timothy and the members of
his congregation. This the apostle takes for granted, and
here emphasizes that besides such prayer the entire congregation is to unite in coming to the throne of grace, as indeed
was customary from the very beginning on, Acts 1, 14; 2,
42. By using four different terms for such prayer, and
these in the plural, the apostle brings out the comprehensiveness of such prayer and indicates the fulness with which
Christian congregations are to address God. The first three
terms: "supplications, prayers, intercessions" form a closely

related group, not really so many different kinds of prayer, but prayer contemplated from different sides and in different respects. Trench. **Supplications,** δεήσεις from δέομαι, are requests or petitions, which imply need and want on our part. We stretch out our empty hands unto God in order that he may fill them with his gifts. The word is general and often used also of requests to men. The second term, **prayers,** προσευχαί, signifies devotions or acts of worship, and is restricted to sacred use, like the German *Gebete* as distinguished from *Bitten*. It involves honor to God on our part. The third word **intercessions,** ἐντεύξεις, implies childlike confidence on our part; it is from ἐντυγχάνειν, to fall in with a person, to draw close to him so as to enter into familiar speech and communion with him. Trench, who brings this out at length, adds that the English rendering "intercessions" did not originally denote prayers for others, as we now understand the word. This must be noted in preaching, since all three terms, in fact also the fourth are meant in an intercessory sense: "for all men" *etc*. Stellhorn, in his *Pastoralbriefe Pauli*, correlates the three by saying that, while they all relate to requests on our part, the first implies that we be humbly mindful of our great need of the gifts and blessings of God, who alone is able to bestow what is good and wholesome; and the second, that we come to God with due reverence, recognizing him as the Lord of lords, the great God of heaven and earth, before whom we must bow in the dust; and the third, that we draw nigh to him in childlike trust and freedom, telling him all that we wish, knowing that as our Father he will indeed give us what is needful and salutary. It is certainly necessary for every congregation and every pastor who leads his congregation in general prayer to bear these implications in mind. Thoughtless prayer, idle drifting of the mind while the pastor reads the prayer, is the very opposite of what Paul here sets forth as so necessary for us all. — Besides humble, worshipful, trustful requests to God we are to utter also **thanksgiving,** εὐχαριστίαι, grateful acknowledgments for past mercies. These are never to be absent from our

praying (Phil. 4, 6; Col. 4, 2), for however sad our condition may be at any time, we always enjoy great and undeserved blessings. In heaven our wants shall indeed cease,
but our thanksgiving will still continue, will indeed be
larger, deeper, fuller than here; for only there will the redeemed know fully how much they owe to their Lord; and
this, while all other forms of prayer in the very nature of
things will have ceased in the entire fruition of the things
prayed for. Trench. — This general and complete form of
prayer is to be made **for all men,** ὑπέρ, in their behalf, for
their benefit. It is well to pause at this point, that we may
take in the full force of the apostle's Gospel requirement.
As God loves all men, so we are to be concerned about all.
Some we can reach with our personal influence and word,
but how many are wholly beyond us? And even those
whom we can reach God must help us to influence aright.
All of them, therefore, we must include in our prayers.
Some near and dear to us may be far away at the time; our
prayers will bring a blessing to them. Those that are hostile to us and refuse to hear us we are still able to reach by
our prayers. "A true Christian," writes Stellhorn. "always
prays for his neighbor; for this is the greatest love he can
show him, although he who really prays for his neighbor
will also be ready at all times to assist him as he is able and
there may be need. Here no man is to be excluded, not
even our enemy, Matth. 5, 44. The more wicked a man
shows himself, also toward us, the more he needs our intercession. How often do we forget that, and how necessary is therefore the apostle's admonition, both for the
preacher and his congregation! How often would things
be better in a family, a congregation, a larger church body,
if men would pray more diligently, not only for themselves, but also for each other, and for others! How often
do we deem other things more necessary at the time, if not
in theory, at least in practice; and yet the very first admonition of the apostle who labored more than all the rest,
and who certainly was not an inactive pietist, is: Pray —
for all men! Pray for them when they are in bodily or

spiritual need and danger; give thanks for them when they have received help! Pray that in their station and calling they may live and work to the honor of God and the blessing of their fellow men, and may finally be saved; thank God for the good he has done and still does through them. This is the best and most necessary thing we are able to do."

The apostle's politics are world-wide, yet they harmonize well with patriotism and citizenship in whatever country one may reside. Our prayers are to be intercessions also **for kings and all that are in high place,** that is for the persons at the supreme head of the government, as were the Roman emperors in Paul's time and royal personages governing one or the other land in particular, and in addition all others in governmental authority. It need hardly be said that the apostle is not endorsing monarchy as the only form of government by mentioning **kings;** ὑπὲρ βασιλέων, without the article, means kings as such. In a republic this includes the president. **All that are in high place** takes in every other governmental official. The church has a special interest in them all, whether they are Christians or not. We are to pray for them as men, as we do for others, and then also as men to whom is committed the welfare of many others, including important interests of the church. — This is shown by the addition: **that we may lead a tranquil and quiet life in all godliness and gravity.** There is no practical difference ἤρεμος, still, gentle, **tranquil,** and ἡσύχιος, still, **quiet,** at ease and peace. The two convey the one idea: absence of anything that may disturb, harass, or trouble the church, like hostility, oppression, and persecution, or in general wicked laws, wicked administration of law, wicked wars, or other evil measures. Our prayers then must be: "Cause Thy glory to dwell in our land, mercy and truth, righteousness and peace everywhere to prevail. . . . Graciously defend us from all calamities by fire and water, from war and pestilence, from scarcity and famine." By βίον διάγειν the apostle means our life in its earthly environment. — He adds **in all godliness and gravity** because these are the

Christian characteristics of our life, **godliness,** purity and
reverence toward God in all our thoughts and actions,
and **gravity,** dignified and worthy conduct toward our fellow men. There is a close connection between "a tranquil
and quiet life" and such "godliness and gravity." If the
former is absent the latter, at least for the weaker members of the church, is very hard to maintain. Hostility of
the government toward the church, and grave political dis-
turbances are bound to react detrimentally upon the congregation and individual Christians affected. Some are always incited to questionable conduct under such circumstances, and not a few may make shipwreck of their faith.
Our interests as Christians are bound up to a considerable
extent with the interests of our country and those of its
citizens generally. In praying for the government we are
thus led by a double motive, love for the good of our land
and all its inhabitants, including those in responsible positions, and love for the good of the church and all its members. Both are safeguarded and fostered alike when our
government acts righteously, justly, wisely, tolerantly with
all its people.

Paul's reasons for requiring general prayer.

**This is good and acceptable in the sight of God our
Savior; who willeth that all men should be saved, and
come to the knowledge of the truth.** Whatsoever is
morally **good** is καλόν, beautiful in the eyes of God, and
at the same time **acceptable,** in this case a prayer which
God delights to receive and answer. Both designations
receive their special force from the addition: **in the sight
of God our Savior,** the stress being on the word "Savior."
He is the God whose great purpose and work is to rescue
us from the curse and power of sin. Therefore it is entirely in harmony with God's thought and will when we pray
for all men, including those who are in authority, that they
may put nothing in the way of the Gospel, yea, accept it
for their own persons. Our entire text is dominated by
the term **all men,** which here occurs for the second time,

and is followed in the fifth verse by the equivalent "all." It is a terrible thing for Calvin, in his Commentary, to say of this passage that all who use it in opposing his doctrine of predestination "are subject to puerile hallucination," that Paul means only that no people or class of men is excluded from salvation (*"apostolus simpliciter intelligit, nullum mundi vel populum, vel ordinem a salute excludi*), that he is speaking here only of the different races of men, not of individuals as such, and this merely because he wishes the class of kings and rulers also included. By such wretched pleas Calvinists evade the clear statements of Scripture. We have here what the dogmaticians call the antecedent will of God, which is again and again expressed in Scripture in the plainest possible way, Ez. 33, 11; John 3, 16; 2 Pet. 3, 9. That God really wants all men to be saved is evinced by his providing and offering the efficacious means of salvation to all: who willeth that all men should be saved **and come to the knowledge of the truth.** This **truth** is the Gospel, the power of God unto salvation to every one that believeth, Rom. 1, 16; and **the knowledge,** ἐπίγνωσις, of the truth is the saving apprehension of the Gospel in its contents, which is the same as faith. Nor is it that the Gospel is merely held out to us, and we then of ourselves bring forth the saving knowledge or faith which apprehends it. If this were the situation, no man on earth would be saved, for none of us can by his own reason or strength believe in Christ or come to him. The truth itself works knowledge and faith in us. And it is God's will that this should occur in every man's heart; on his part he has omitted nothing to attain this result. If it is not attained it is because a man wilfully and persistently opposes the saving influence of the Gospel, as did Jerusalem, Matth. 23, 37.

The apostle establishes the universality of God's saving will by pointing to the unity or oneness of God, and likewise to the oneness of the Mediator: **For there is one God, one mediator also between God and men,** *himself* **man, Christ Jesus, who gave himself a ransom**

for all; the testimony *to be borne* **in its own times.** The oneness of God is without question among Christians; equally without question then must be the oneness of his will regarding men. Whatever he originally wills regarding mankind, he must will equally for all, for he is one, and they all are one in trespasses and sins. It is impossible, Paul argues, that in the one God there should be contradictory wills; polytheism may have such wills, having a variety of gods, monotheism cannot. — But the case is still stronger: there is **one mediator also between God and men.** Here again the oneness is emphatic. As there is only one will regarding our salvation, so there is only one way to salvation, namely through the mediation of Christ and faith in him. God's will was not an idle wish regarding all men, as Calvinists sometimes argue to escape the doctrine of universal grace, it was a true will expressing itself fully and completely in action by sending **a mediator between God and men;** not between God and *some* men, but θεοῦ καὶ ἀνθρώπων, God and *men* as such, the whole human race, including every one who is man. Except in Hebrews, in connection with διαθήκη, this is the only passage in which μεσίτης, **mediator,** is used of Christ; it designates him according to his office and work in uniting again God and men who had been separated by sin. — It is emphatically added of this Mediator: himself **man, Christ Jesus, who gave himself a ransom for all.** In regard to Christ there is not only his oneness as a Mediator, but in addition his humanity. Inasmuch as he is "himself man," a human being, he evidently counts for all who like him are human. Hofmann. *The Lutheran Commentary* finely summarizes: "One God, the God of all, through one Mediator, the Mediator of all, is the twofold pledge of one salvation for all . . . The one God wills the salvation of all, and the one Mediator undertakes the redemption of all." As man this Mediator could and did act for men. — His full personal and official name is added: **Christ Jesus,** making the statement the more impressive. This Mediator who is man is the Messiah, the Anointed One, Matth. 3,

16-17, Jesus, the Savior, in whom the saving grace of God our Savior (verse 3) has appeared fully for all men. — In one comprehensive statement the mediatorial work of Christ is now described: **who gave himself a ransom for all.** This act of his was possible to him only as a man; he **gave himself** in the supreme sense of the word when he died on the cross. That was a voluntary act of his; for no man could take his life from him, he laid it down of himself, even as he took it again, John 10, 18. His voluntary sacrifice reveals all the greatness and nobility of his love, and settles once and for all the charge of injustice against God, in that he should have unjustly punished the innocent instead of the guilty. Christ gave himself willingly, assuming all our guilt and penalty, and God accepted this all-sufficient gift or sacrifice in our behalf. **A ransom,** ἀντίλυτρον, is more than a λύτρον, a price; it is decidedly a price paid for another or for others, ἀντί, in their stead. This establishes the doctrine of substitution (Rom. 3, 25; Eph. 5, 2) or exchange. By giving himself into death Christ made himself our substitute, and in our stead suffered the penalty of our sin and guilt. — And this he did **for all,** ὑπὲρ πάντων, in behalf of, for the benefit of all, which with ἀντίλυτρον plainly signifies also: in the place of all. Here once more that word full of the mightiest comfort for poor sinners is uttered with emphasis: **all** — not one excepted. Meyer combines the following passages: The entire human race lay bound in the power of darkness, Col. 1, 13, and could not free itself, Matth. 16, 26; then Christ came and paid the necessary ἀντίλυτρον, even himself, his own life, Matth. 20, 20; and so obtained for us all the priceless σωτηρία. — The addition τὸ μαρτύριον καιροῖς ἰδίοις, **the testimony** *to be borne* **in its own times,** is an apposition to the entire preceding sentence (Bengel: an accusative absolute), not merely to the relative clause. This **testimony** is not one implied in the act of Christ's giving himself into death, thus on his part declaring God's universal grace to men (a thought true enough in itself, but not stated here), but the testimony of the Gospel as proclaimed by the preachers of the Gospel, for Paul adds: "whereunto I was appointed a preacher and an apostle . . . , a teacher of the Gentiles in faith and truth." It is a testimony because it reports an objective fact, and because they who testify have had actual spiritual experience of it. **In its own times** denotes the times of the New Testament, after the ransom was paid for all; they extend till Christ's return on the last day. Before this, in the times of the Old Testament, there were and could be only prophecies and promises of what God would do in his grace through the Messiah for Israel and all· men. When the blessed work was done and all completed, the times had arrived for its full proclamation to all the world.

HOMILETICAL HINTS.

Was there ever a Christian who did not pray? Was there ever a great man in the church of God whose greatness did not appear in the power and frequency of his praying?

Rogate, pray ye! But not only each for himself; *rogate* is plural, we must all pray together, as one great body of God's children, and in prayers worthy of such a body which is set to be the light of the world, in prayers for all men.

Riemer reports in his sermon on this text that one of his members honestly told him at one time that the most tiresome part of the service was the general prayer at its close. It is only too true that devotion generally lags at this point, the congregation listening patiently and permitting the pastor to do the praying, as if that were part of his work. What so many of us lack is the proper conception of congregational activity at the services. We are not to be merely an audience, but a congregation. We are not only to receive, but also to contribute. We are not so many individuals only, but so many parts of a whole, with blessings and duties as such. All the great interests of the kingdom of God, all the best interests of men generally in our city, state, country, and the whole world are our concern.

Many prayers are born of necessity, but necessity drives us, and we never get very far in this way. There is a better training-master, he to whom the apostles went with the request: "Lord, teach us to pray!"

Blood and language are strong human ties; a stronger one is intercession.

The early Christian church would have had reason enough to criticize the government of their time; they left that to others and prayed for kings and all others in authority. That was more effective. Worldly men fly to revolution in order to get relief, and generally fall into greater evils than the ones they try to abolish by such means; Christian men resort to prayer.

The Fatherhood of God and the brotherhood of man is an empty thing without the mediatorship of Christ. All creatures must call God their Creator, and all alike are the work of his hands. In Christ the Redeemer we are lifted above this creature-level, to that of immortal souls with an eternal spiritual destiny.

Prayer is all-embracing. There is no need either of body or soul which it does not embrace, according to the promise: "Whatsoever ye shall ask the Father in my name, he will give it you." Do we long for enduring intercourse with our heavenly Father? he bids us: "Pray without ceasing." Everywhere the misery and wretchedness of life meets our eyes, here some great calamity, there some great sorrow, and as great as our sympathy may be, our hands are so often tied and unable to render help. One great resource is left to us: "Thine is the power!" But who will count the blessings we all receive day by day, many of them unconsciously and while we sleep: "Bless the Lord, O my soul; and all that is within me, bless his holy name. Bless the Lord, O my soul, and forget not all his benefits!"

The Lord's Prayer is written in the plural. It is a prayer for the congregation and the entire church. In many churches the bells ring when the congregation reaches this prayer in its service, in order that all who are prevented from being present may also fold their hands and join their brethren in this general prayer.

Too many churches lay the emphasis on social, civic, economic, earthly betterment and imagine they have advanced greatly since the days of Paul; God lays the emphasis for us and all men on Christ, his mediatorship, his ransom, the testimony of the Gospel, eternal salvation.

Many forget to pray altogether; others think it enough to pray only for themselves, or for some others, or in a limited way.

Our Mighty Obligation to Pray for all Men.

I.   *Because the same God extends the same saving love to all.*

II   *Because the same Savior paid the same ransom for us all.*

III. *Because as the Church of this same God and Savior we stand in relation to all.*
   1) As part of all.
   2) Influenced by others (hence: "Kings", *etc.*).
   3) Influencing others, by the silent but immensurable power of prayer, by the eloquent testimony of the Gospel.

The Grandness of Christian Prayer.

As seen in its
   I. *Basis.*
      a) One God.
      b) One Redeemer.
      c) One salvation.

   II. *Scope.*
      a) One and all.
      b) Low and high.

   III. *Character.*
      a) Supplications.
      b) Devotions.
      c) Communings.
      d) Thanksgivings.

What Makes True Congregational Prayer so Acceptable to God?

It agrees
   I. *With the world-wide grace of God.*
   II. *With the world-wide sacrifice of Christ.*
   III. *With the world-wide scope of the Gospel.*

The Value of Christian Intercession.

It is shown
   I. *In the love it exhibits.*
   II. *In the people it includes.*
   III. *In the blessings it secures.*

The Highest Duty we Owe the State and the Government.

   I. *Godly living.*
   II. *Intercession.*
   III. *Gospel testimony.*

The Kind of Priests our Times Need.

Men
   I. *Rooted and grounded in Christ.*
  II. *Full of the testimony of the Gospel.*
 III. *Bearing others on their hearts.*

ASCENSION.

Col. 3, 1-4.

Heavenly-mindedness must characterize those whose hearts are joined to Christ seated at the right hand of God. This is the sum of our text and presents the proper epistle thought for the festival in a direct and effective manner. The fact of Christ's ascension forms the basis; on this rests the application, first in the form of an admonition (1-2), and secondly in the form of a great promise or assurance (3-4).

If then ye were raised together with Christ, seek the things that are above, where Christ is, seated on the right hand of God. Set your mind on the things that are above, not on the things that are upon the earth. Paul here begins the second half of his Epistle which deals with the ethical features of the Christian life. The conditional form of the first sentence with **if** is not meant to render the matter problematical, as if perhaps the Colossians were not raised together with Christ. The apostle takes for granted that they were, and bases his first admonitions on this fact as real. Yet the conditional form serves to make each of his readers silently ask himself, whether in his own case this condition is indeed fulfilled as the apostle assumes. The connecting οὖν, **then**, refers back to verse 20 of the previous chapter, where the apostle speaks of dying with Christ; they who have died with him were also raised with him, since these two always go together. Meyer is right in his observation when he says that this refers not only to our dying unto sin and rising unto a new life, but to our becoming partakers of Christ's death and likewise of his resurrection, Rom. 6, 4 etc. By our Baptism and faith in Christ we are joined together with Christ (σύν) that in his resurrection we have also been raised and planted into a new life. We are thus no longer in the old dead life, but in a new living life, growing out of Christ's atoning death and justifying resurrection applied to each of us personally. — The result must be what the apostle demands: **seek the things that are above, where Christ is, seated on the right hand of God.** "The things that are above" are the treasures and riches of our salvation in their fullest possession and enjoyment. While they include, of course, heaven itself and the blessedness of the glorified state; they by no means consist of these alone. They that seek shall find, heaven at last, but also day by day the things that here precede heaven and are certainly from above, peace, purity, righteousness, and joy in the Holy Ghost in ever richer measure. **Where Christ is, seated on the right hand of God** is added to show the exalted character of these treasures and at the same time to connect them with our Redeemer. Their home and origin is not on this sinful earth, where lasting treasures cannot be found, but "above," in the presence of our glorified Lord. — **The right hand of God,** Ps. 110, 1, "is no fixed place in heaven, as the Sacramentarians assert without any ground in Holy Scriptures, but is nothing else than the almightly power of God, which fills heaven and earth, in which Christ is placed according to his humanity, really, *i. e.* in deed and truth, without confusion and equalizing of the two natures in their essence and essential properties." *Formula of Concord,* 629, 26 *etc.* Christ's being **seated** on the right hand of God is his exercise of the divine majesty and power according to his human nature, in infinite exaltation and glory. The things that we are to seek are therefore found where this majesty and power of Christ is exercised; they are connected with him in his royal exaltation; he is their heavenly source and dispenser. It would be a serious mistake indeed, if on this day of Christ's ascension we would think of his exaltation at God's right hand only after the manner of Enoch's or Elijah's glorification, or that of the saints who arose after Christ's resurrection and were taken bodily to heaven. Our

divine blessings flow from the power and majesty of God
as exercised by our exalted loving Savior. He indeed presented himself in glorious form to the heavenly spirits,
when he ascended on high, and this vision of him is granted
to them still. So also our bodies are to be glorified at last
and become like his. But at the same time Christ entered
into the heavenly mode of existence exalted over all creature
limitations, far above all the heavens, governing all things,
and filling all things; and this according to his human nature. Philippi, *Glaubenslehre* IV, 1, 185. This is the sense
in which Christ is above, seated on the right hand of God;
and thus our heavenly treasures are in his exalted hands,
to be dispensed to us who seek them. — **Set your minds
on the things that are above** emphasizes the inward impulse and disposition from which the act of seeking should
proceed. Lightfoot writes: "'You must not only *seek*
heaven, you must *think* heaven." Here also we have the
contrast: **not on the things that are upon the earth,** as
emanating from earth and belonging to it. This does not
mean that we are to disregard, in monkish asceticism, all
earthly things, such as work, occupation, food, family and
business relations, and the thousand and one things that
pertain to our earthly existence. In so far as God has appointed these things to us we are to attend to them, and he
himself bids us do this with all care and faithfulness. But
we are not to "set our minds on them," to center our hearts
and lives on their possession and enjoyment. They are
ever to be secondary, and to be brought into subservience
to the things that are above. All earthly things shall fade
at last and pass away, even the fairest, purest, and best;
what then will they do who have set their hearts and minds
on them, and not on the things that are above? Ewald
argues that while Paul uses these general expressions: "the
things that are above," and "the things that are upon the
earth," he still has in mind the teaching of the false
prophets who were disturbing the Colossian Christians.
These men made much of meat and drink, holy days, Sab-

bath, *etc.*, outward ordinances: Handle not, nor taste, nor touch, severity of the body, *etc.* (Col. 2, 16-23), and by this show of wisdom and false humility they put a shadow in place of the substance Christ. They minded earthly things and not heavenly, and earthly things of the worst sort, like thousands to-day who expect to win heaven by their own efforts. Certainly the admonition is in place: Neither seek nor set your heart upon follies of this kind, but keep them fixed upon Christ alone, the truth, righteousness, liberty, and service which he gives us from his heavenly throne above. Only so will we be safe and ourselves be received into his glorious presence at last.

Paul adds the reason for his admonition: **For ye died, and your life is hid with Christ in God.** The aorist ἀπεθάνετε marks a definite past event, one included already in the previous statement: "ye were raised together with Christ." If the Colossians were raised, they must have died. Both events are connected with Christ; to die with him is to enter personally into the saving communion of his death for us. This had occurred for the Colossians when they came to faith in Christ; then they died to sin, to the world, to their entire former mode of life, and to all that formed the heart and center of that life. With that death a fact, how could they any longer set their minds, in the old way, on the things that are on earth? A dead man no longer responds to the solicitations of the things that once moved him; he will not stretch out his hand to grasp the gold you may offer him, or to take the pleasure that beckons him; so the Christian, dead with Christ, has a dead eye, ear, and heart for all the vain and transient things of the world. In place of his old life there is a new one, infinitely superior in every way. — **And your life is hid with Christ in God.** This is the spiritual life which is ours now by faith. To make it future eternal life forsakes the entire connection of this life with Christ's resurrection. Paul is speaking after the manner of John: "Beloved, now are we the children of God, and it is not yet made manifest what we shall be." 1 John 3, 2. — This wonderful, heavenly life

differs entirely from the old worldly life which clung to
the visible treasures and pleasures of earth and found its
substance and full satisfaction in them. It is **hid with
Christ in God;** hid in the sense that its real form and
heavenly character is veiled and covered up from the eyes
of the world, and to a great extent from the eyes of
Christians themselves. It is like a pearl, hidden as long as
it lies in the shell. Chrysostom. This life, Luther says,
you have not yet in yourselves by feeling, but in Christ by
faith. Even when Jesus walked among men, they failed to
recognize him as he really was. Isaiah wrote truly: "He
is despised and rejected of men . . . he hath no form
nor comeliness." And it is so still, since he has gone to the
Father; the world disregards him altogether. But our life
is **hid** (κέκρυπται, has been and still is) **with Christ in God.**
It is completely bound up "with Christ," in fact he himself
is our life, John 14, 6; 2 Cor. 4, 10-11; 1 John 5, 11-12. And
as Christ is "in God" John 14, 10-11, so also is our life. All
its springs are in him, all its joys, treasures, and activities
center in him. The world ever looks down, and not up, and
so it cannot see the real form of this life and understand
what this life is. What did the men of Paul's time make
of him? One said, he was beside himself, others called
him a babbler when he proclaimed the resurrection of Jesus.
His preaching a Christ crucified was a stumblingblock and an
offense. So it is with the world generally as regards our
life. It does not understand him who is risen on high and
lives and reigns to all eternity (comp. Rom. 6, 10), nor those
whose life he is. — Ewald lays stress on the word "hid"
and puts this in contrast to the ideas of the false Colossian
teachers who made the Christian life a thing of legal reg-
ulations, ordinances, and observances. "The kingdom of
God is not eating and drinking, but righteousness and peace
and joy in the Holy Ghost." Rom. 14, 17. "The kingdom
of God cometh not with observation . . . the kingdom of God is within you." Luke 17, 20-21. This interpretation lends a special significance and appropriateness
to Paul's choice of the word κέκρυπται, and, as already

stated above, points the way to a fine line of application. — Without a connecting particle the apostle proceeds: **When Christ,** *who is* **our life, shall be manifested, then shall ye also with him be manifested in glory.** This is the great Christian hope, the crown of our life in Christ. Paul's words are a repetition of Christ's promise to all his believers, John 5, 28-29; 14, 3; *etc.* Our life is "hid with Christ," because he is **our life** (margin: *your life*), dwelling in our hearts by faith. He is hidden now; the apostles beheld his visible ascension to heaven, gazing after him until a cloud received him out of their sight. Since then his visible presence has been removed from our eyes. But he **shall be manifested,** when he shall return in glory, and all the angels with him, and shall sit on the throne of his glory, all the nations of the earth gathered before him for final judgment. So also the angels declared at his ascension: "Ye men of Galilee, why stand ye looking into heaven? this Jesus, which was received up from you into heaven, shall so come in like manner as ye beheld him going into heaven." Acts 1, 11. — As our life is hid now since he is our life, so our life shall be manifested when he at last is manifested. Now and to all eternity our life is bound up with him. Paul writes: **then shall ye also with him be manifested in glory,** appear in your own persons as what you really are, sons of God, coheirs of Christ, kings and princes of God. Body and soul shall shine **in glory,** made like unto Christ. The day of humiliation shall give place forever to the day of exaltation. Christ's word shall be fulfilled to the uttermost: "Where I am, there shall also my servant be." John 12, 26.

HOMILETICAL HINTS.

The Word of God furnishes us, as far as is necessary, an inventory of the things that are above. God has revealed so much, and again concealed so much, in order that our love for the truth in seeking the things that are above, and our obedience to the

Word of God and what it offers us, might have occasion to prove itself. Rieger.

He who dies before he dies will not die when he dies. Matthes.

Only a Savior who has died is able to rise and ascend with rejoicing and triumph; only one who has died with him is able to look up after him, like the men of Galilee, with joy and hope.

Do you find here on earth many things that are beautiful, grand, delightful, attractive, satisfying? Well, God made the world, and sin marred it. Remember that he likewise made heaven, and sin did not mar that. If you find many things so fine in this world, what will heaven be? But the worst that sin has done is that it made all earthly things transitory. Being marred, they must all be made over, not one of them can abide. Therefore none of them can satisfy, even if we set our hearts on them; they will fade and die at last, just as we fade and die in our earthly life. But the heavenly things, unmarred by sin, endure forever. Set your hearts on them, in them you may have joy for evermore.

Many men think and talk of heaven, and where Christianity prevails even worldly men talk of a hope of heaven. But heaven is for none of us except we see Christ in it, our crucified Christ at the right hand of the divine glory. In him and in him alone lies our hope of heaven. He alone can take from us what bars us out of heaven, and he alone by his exalted power and glory can lift us up from death and the grave and set us into heaven. All hopes that are not built on him, are delusive mirages which at last leave the soul to parch and perish in the arid desert of death.

You know the question of the disciples before the Lord's ascension: "Lord, wilt thou at this time restore again the kingdom to Israel?" They kept dreaming to the last of a heaven on earth, and many still hold the dream and want it realized. Here is the answer: "Your life is hid with Christ in God." Here we must be content to live by faith, not by sight. Here we must wear the garment of humility, not the robes of glory. Here we must bear the cross, and cannot already wear the crown. Here we must fight, war against temptation, strive against the flesh, suffer hardship as a soldier, — there at last we shall reign.

It will be a terrible day when the Christ whom so many denied is manifested at last in the fulness of his glory, and when at the same time all that was in their hearts and lives is manifested as what it really was. Then they will shrink in terror from their own hideous, inexcusable, damnable unbelief, their contradiction of the Lord's Word, their wilful adherence to sin, their evil lusts and passions. Bare and naked shall they stand in the sight of the great King and of all angels and men. — But what a glorious hour for every believer! Then shall they see manifested the Savior and

Lord in whom they trusted so confidently, and his glory and power will rejoice the believers' hearts. And we ourselves shall be manifested — all our faith and trust will shine out, and the Lord will acknowledge it; all our seeking of the things that are above, all the love and Christian grace that Christ has wrought in us. And our sins? We shall be manifested as cleansed and purified by the Savior's blood. O glorious day! Would that it were already here!

Three Rays From the Portal Which Received Our Ascending Lord.

I. *One falls upon Christ's throne above.*

  a) His glorification the proper close of his earthly career as our Savior.
  b) His exaltation, in the exercise of all the divine power and majesty, the continuation of his saving work.

II. *One falls upon Christian hearts below.*

  a) Christ is our hidden life.
  b) Striving for the things that are above our one life-task.

III. *One falls upon the union of Christ and the Christians.*

  a) Christ will draw us up to himself.
  b) He shall be manifested, he who is our life.
  c) We shall be manifested with him in glory.

Our Hearts are in Heaven.

I. *Our Lord is there.*
II. *Our soul's treasures come from there.*
III. *We ourselves shall go there.*

"And in Jesus Christ, His Only Son, our Lord . . . Ascended Into Heaven."

I. *My Lord and King.*
II. *My fount of grace.*
III. *My everlasting hope.*

Sursum Corda!

I. *Because we are dead to the world.*
II. *Because our life is hid with Christ.*
III. *Because we shall appear with Christ in glory at last.*

"Heavenward Doth Our Journey Tend."

I. *"Here we roam a pilgrim-band."*
II. *"Yonder is our native land."*

Do You Believe in Christ's Ascension?

Attest it
I. *By remaining dead to sin.*
II. *By living with Christ in God.*
III. *By seeking the things that are above.*
IV. *By rejoicing in the hope of glory.*

EXAUDI.

Eph. 1, 15-23.

There are two salient points in this grand text, one in the word *knowledge:* "a spirit of wisdom and revelation in the knowledge of him, having the eyes of your heart enlightened, that ye may know," *etc.;* the other in the climax of what the apostle prays that his readers may know, namely *Christ* in his heavenly exaltation, verses 20-23. The Eisenach pericope book points to the latter with its superscription: "Gave him to be head over all things to the church." This makes the subject for the sermon: *Christ in his exalted relation to the church.* Our text thus connects itself closely with the festival of the Ascension, less closely with that of Pentecost. There is no mention of the Holy Spirit; even the knowledge that Paul desires for his readers is viewed as the gift of "the God of our Lord Jesus Christ, the Father of glory." Yet we must bear in mind that the exaltation of Christ as the Head of the church is the foundation of the entire Pentecostal grace of the Spirit, for it is this our exalted Head who sent down the Spirit from on high and now by this Spirit rules his body, the church. The text for Pentecost joins itself in a fitting manner to our present text in that it describes the church of God as "a holy temple in the Lord," "a habitation of God in the Spirit." — The exalted tone of the opening verses of the Epistle, 3-14, continues throughout our text. The entire nine verses constitute one grand sentence, like a mighty strain on some magnificent organ with all the stops drawn. It is difficult to find points of division; the current and sweep of the apostle's words is so strong that we are carried straight on to the glorious end. It must suffice for us to make an incision

616

at the point where Paul begins to speak of Christ especially, either at the end of verse 18, or after the words "who believe" in verse 19.

The hope God has given us in Christ.

Paul, first of all, blesses God for his heavenly grace and gifts to the Ephesians (verses 3-14), then he speaks of his intercessions for them, that they may increase in the knowledge of Christ, and he mentions in detail some of the important parts of this knowledge. **For this cause I also, having heard of the faith in the Lord Jesus which is among you, and** (margin: *the love*) **which** *ye show* **toward all the saints, cease not to give thanks for you, making mention** *of you* **in my prayers.** — All that Paul had said of the grace of God and its rich gifts, in verses 3-12, he could apply to his Ephesian readers directly, in verses 13-14. They had believed, they were sealed with the Holy Spirit of promise. **For this cause** refers to this situation; the apostle means to say: Because we Christians have been so greatly blessed, and ye Ephesians have become partakers of these wonderful blessings, **I also,** making my action correspond to that of God, include you in my thanksgivings and prayers. — Paul had been away from Ephesus a long while, and now wrote from his prison in Rome where he lay awaiting trial. But he knew how things were with the Ephesians: **having heard of the faith in the Lord Jesus which is among you.** It is a mistake to conclude from these words that Paul was not personally acquainted with the people to whom he thus wrote, or, at least, that the majority of them were strangers to him. It was just as possible and natural for him to get news from his friends, as to secure information concerning strangers. Paul most likely was anxious to hear from the congregation he had gathered and served for three years, and may have made special efforts to get news during his long wait in Rome. He had been successful, and the news was good news; it told of **the faith in the Lord Jesus which is among you,** the living trust in the hearts of the

Ephesians resting on the Savior, rooted and grounded in
him: πίστις ἐν κτλ. There is no actual difference between
καθ' ὑμᾶς and the simple ὑμῶν, except that the latter, as
Stoeckhardt points out, may embrace the entire faith of
the Ephesians back to its beginning, while the former
would refer only to the faith as it was at the time Paul
heard of it. The substitution for the simple genitive is peculiar to later Greek, and occurs already in the N. T. — The
American Committee is certainly right in contending that
the text and the margin should change places. It is in
vain to try to extract an acceptable meaning from the
reading: "faith which ye show toward all the saints;" while
everything is clear the moment we read: **love which** *ye
show* **toward all the saints;** compare 1 Thess. 1, 3; 2
Thess. 1, 3; Col. 1, 4. Love is the product of faith, an
evidence of its life and genuineness. Chrysostom calls the
two "a wonderful pair of twins;" and Bengel says that love
to all the saints is the characteristic mark of Christianity,
John 13, 35; 15, 12. Some lay all the emphasis on love
alone and care nothing about contending for the faith once
for all delivered unto the saints (Jude 3), and for the
good confession of faith which is the first duty of every
believer. They would raise fruit without planting the
tree that bears it; they would pluck flowers without growing the peculiar plant which alone bears them. But all
their "mighty works" of which they boast so pridefully,
even if done by Jesus' name, will not be acknowledged by
the Lord, Matth. 7, 22-23. Would that every one of our
congregations were famed for its faith and love! — The
good report which Paul heard from Ephesus had the effect
that his thoughts kept turning to this former place of his
labors. I **cease not,** he writes, **to give thanks for you,
making mention** *of you* **in my prayers.** The apostle was
grateful to God for all the good that blossomed out of the
Gospel in Ephesus, and doubly so because he himself had
first planted the good seed there. In his dreary imprisonment the triumphs of the Gospel in the fields of his labors
made him happy and lightened his bonds. Paul usually has

a genitive with μνείαν ποιεῖσθαι, and here, if ὑμῶν is not genuine, — the best texts omitting it — we must supply its equivalent as necessary to express the apostle's meaning. Paul bore all his congregations on his heart, and in his prayers diligently remembered them. Here was one of the hidden springs of his success, which it is well for every pastor and officer in the church to bear in mind.

Besides thanksgiving Paul has intercession for the Ephesians. Having such great spiritual blessings it is most necessary that they know and realize fully what these blessings are, their greatness and preciousness. Too often we take God's finest. gifts as a mere matter of course, and the result is that we finally lose them. So in his prayers Paul adds intercession to thanksgiving. This he indicates by at once stating the contents of his intercessory prayers: **that the God of our Lord Jesus Christ, the Father of glory, may give unto you a spirit of wisdom and revelation in the knowledge of him; having the eyes of your heart enlightened, that ye may know what is the hope of his calling, what the riches of the glory of his inheritance in the saints, and what the exceeding greatness of his power to us-ward who believe.** — Passages like Mark 6, 25; 9, 30; 10, 37 show plainly that ἵνα here has lost its final force, and simply introduces the contents of the apostle's prayer. The hellenistic optative δῴη (for δοίη; comp. also Blass 23, 4) indicates an earnest wish on the apostle's part, by which he places the matter in God's hands. Some prefer the Ionic subjunctive δώῃ, which would also be very unusual.* Our R. V. translates as if a subjunctive were used: **that God may give.** — God is called **the God of our Lord Jesus Christ,** after the manner of Jesus' own words, John 20, 17: "my God and your God;" Matth. 27, 46; compare Eph. 1, 3. It is certainly true that God is "the God of our Lord Jesus Christ" only according to Christ's human nature; but for the Ephesians Paul means to bring out that the God to

---

*Compare *Friedrich Blass' Grammatik d. neutest. Griechisch.* 4th ed. by Albert Debrunner, § 369, 1 and § 95, 2.

whom he and they go in prayer is the God who sent Jesus
Christ into our flesh to work out our salvation, the God
who attested his work with word and deed, the God to
whom Christ returned when the work of redemption was
done. As the God of our Lord Jesus Christ God is our
God, the God of infinite mercy and grace in Christ Jesus,
our Father in Christ Jesus. — This God of our salvation is
at the same time **the Father of glory,** our Father to whom
all the divine and heavenly glory belongs. The δόξα is
that which distinguishes God as God, his infinite greatness,
excellence, perfection, and majesty. It is the sum of all
the divine attributes and excellencies. — Both parts of this
double designation pertain to the blessings which Paul requests for the Ephesians. Since God is the God of our
Lord Jesus Christ, we may freely ask of him the full
knowledge of Jesus and the blessings that are ours in him,
as Paul does here for the Ephesians; and since he is the
Father of glory, we, his children, may freely ask him to
help us see and realize this glory of his as it manifiested
itself in the resurrection and exaltation of Christ (verse
20, *etc.*). — The gift which the apostle desires for the
Ephesians is **a spirit of wisdom and revelation in the
knowledge of him.** The question whether πνεῦμα here
signifies the Holy Spirit who fills our hearts with wisdom
and revelation, or a new spirit in our hearts having wisdom
and revelation, is decided by the two English versions in
favor of the latter view; therefore: **spirit,** without the
capital letter. The reason for this is the explanation which
the apostle adds: by "a spirit of wisdom and revelation" he
means in particular: "having the eyes of your heart enlightened, *etc.*" This connection is disregarded by a number of good commentators, who then understand the apostle
to mean the Holy Spirit; though sealed by him already
(verse 13), they may yet receive him in fuller measure.
But it is best to adhere to the connection indicated. **A
spirit of wisdom** is one that applies its blessed knowledge
in the right manner; and a spirit **of revelation** is one that
has more and more of the truth revealed to us by God.

Both this wisdom and this revelation are to be given to us **in the knowledge of him.** The apostle uses ἐπίγνωσις, because he means the knowledge which really apprehends God, true heart-knowledge, not merely that of the intellectual faculties; αὐτοῦ is best referred to God, as in the following verses. "This is life eternal, that they should know thee the only true God, and him whom thou didst send, even Jesus Christ." John 17, 3. Thus to know God is to apprehend his counsel of salvation and to receive his saving gifts, in all of which he makes himself known to us as he really is. "Christian knowledge does not consist of certain finished intellectual apprehensions, certain doctrinal statements and formulas impressed upon the memory, but in a living and constantly growing experience of the saving truth, in an ever fresh apprehension of what the grace of God has given us in Christ Jesus." Besser. Paul's prayer for the Ephesians must therefore become our own prayer for ourselves and others.

The apostle explains his meaning more in detail by the addition: **having the eyes of your heart enlightened, that, etc.** It is simplest to make the accusative πεφωτισμένους τοὺς ὀφθαλμούς depend on the preceding δώη as an apposition to πνεῦμα κτλ.; still some prefer to make it an accusative of specification. The **heart** here designates the center and the organ of our personal life, and as such includes not only the emotions and sensibilities, but also the intellect and the will. **The eyes of the heart** are the spiritual powers of sight. Paul's prayer is that God may give the Ephesians an inward sight that is **enlightened** by his saving truth. — And he specifies what great truth he has in mind: **that ye may know** (εἰς κτλ.: toward this that ye may know) **what is the hope of his calling, etc.,** *i. e.* the hope put into your hearts by God's efficacious calling which made you his children The apostle has mentioned faith and love before, now he adds that other part of our spiritual life and activity, hope. The Ephesians are to know fully what this hope is, its substance and quality, its certainty and preciousness, its heavenly superiority over all mere human and self-made hope. — **What the riches of the glory of his inheritance in the saints** describes the object of our hope. "What a full, grandiose heaping up of terms, actually symbolizing the importance of the subject." Meyer. The object of our hope is **his inheritance,** God's, which he made our own by his calling, when he brought us to faith in Christ. The Ephesians are to know and realize **what the riches of the glory** of this inheritance really is. Being the inheritance which "the Father of glory" bestows upon his children, it has not only glory, but riches of glory. Our heavenly state shall shine with wondrous splendors; in us the divine glory shall be reflected. 1 Cor. 2, 9. But the addition **in the saints** shows that the apostle conceives of "the riches" as now already the property of the saints or believers. Although they have not as yet entered upon their heavenly inheritance, they are infinitely rich in being able to call it their own as children and heirs of God. And they are the only ones with whom such wealth is found, all others are wretchedly poor, the riches of their inheritances going no farther than earth. How necessary for the Ephesians and all of us to realize this! — From the hope in our hearts Paul looks up to the object of that hope, the heavenly inheritance, and then he looks up still farther to the divine power which guarantees this inheritance to us. The Ephesians are to realize this as the pinnacle of all: **and what the exceeding greatness of his power to usward who believe,** εἰς ἡμᾶς, extending toward us his children and heirs, τοὺς πιστεύοντας. It is over us now and always, and we must know its **exceeding greatness,** far beyond any other power, thus rendering the fulfillment of our hope and the execution of God's gracious plans in giving us this hope certain beyond any doubt. If the realization of our hope depended on our own power, nothing but fear could fill our hearts, for we are so weak and frail that we would most likely lose our inheritance. But God's power is over us, and all is safe.

The power which makes our hope certain.

Our only reason for making a division at this point
is that the apostle speaks of Christ in all that now follows; in reality there is no break at all. Paul has said
what he desires the Ephesians to know, their hope, their
inheritance, and God's power behind both; he now proceeds with a phrase that governs and shapes all that
follows to the end of the text: **according to that working
of the strength of his might which he wrought in Christ,
when he raised him from the dead, and made him to sit
at his right hand in the heavenly** *places,* **far above all
rule, and authority, and power, and dominion, and every
name that is named, not only in this world, but also in
that which is to come.** — On what does κατὰ τὴν ἐνέργειαν
κτλ. depends? In his third indirect question the apostle
speaks of "the exceeding greatness of his (God's) power to
us-ward," and now he continues by showing what this
great power has accomplished in the case of Christ. This
connection in the thought itself is so close and evident, that
it cannot be set aside in order to reach farther back to
find what κατὰ κτλ. modifies, as some do who connect with
τὸ εἰδέναι, or even with ζωή. The exceeding greatness of
God's power to us-ward, which the apostle is so concerned
about us knowing, is **according to that working of the
strength of his might which he wrought in Christ, when
he raised him from the dead, etc.;** so, if we know aright
what God's power, displayed in Christ's resurrection and
exaltation, is, we shall understand what his power now is
to us-ward. — Hofmann, followed by Wohlenberg, connects κατὰ τὴν ἐνέργειαν κτλ. with the participle πιστεύοντας,
making the apostle say that the faith of the Ephesians is
due to God's power. This is also the exegesis of the Mis-
sourian controversialists, who use it without question.
Meyer shows its incorrectness by pointing to the undeniable
fact that τοὺς πιστεύοντας is merely an incidental modifier of
ἡμᾶς and could be omitted entirely without really changing
the sense. The apostle writes: "us who believe," because

he wishes to include himself and believers generally, not merely the Ephesians and himself. Harless finds the connection with πιστεύοντας "meaningless" as far as the line of thought is concerned, and "unsuitable" as to expression, since Paul, who is very careful in the use of the prepositions never writes πιστεύειν κατά. Ewald adds that it is out of the question to make the lengthy elaboration extending on through verses 20-23 modify the incidental participle πιστεύοντας. The fact is, the apostle is not showing at all how faith is produced in us, least of all that it is produced by God's great might; he is telling us how he prays that we may know aright the great power of God behind our inheritance and hope, and then he describes this power to us by showing what it has already done in the resurrection and exaltation of Christ. Stoeckhardt and the Missourians use their incorrect exegesis mainly to secure a proof passage for their peculiar doctrine that faith is caused by the omnipotence of God. "He (Paul) would have us realize that we owe our faith to the power and might of God, which is stronger than everything else, to the almightiness of God, which . . . masters everything resisting it." The bringing forth and preserving of faith Stoeckhardt calls "the greatest triumph of the divine almightiness." Wilful resistance, which our Confessions predicate only of those in whom the Holy Spirit can not have his work, he attributes alike to all men, saying that they all resist God with "the intensest exercise of their power;" and this resistance then is met and crushed by the exercise of God's omnipotence. This entire conception is an importation into the apostle's words and into Scripture generally. Conversion and faith are never ascribed to God's omnipotence, but always to the efficacy of his mercy and grace. The former brooks no resistance, as the Scriptures constantly declare; the latter does, Matth. 23, 37. If God converts by omnipotence the question stares us in the face: Why does he exercise his omnipotence only upon a few? and there remains nothing but the Calvinistic answer: Because this is his mysterious, absolute, sovereign will! An exegesis that produces such results stands self-condemned. — In order to emphasize the power of God Paul combines three terms: the **working of the strength of his might;** ἰσχύς is **might,** as God possesses it, *vis, virtus;* κράτος is **strength,** as God exercises it; and ἐνέργεια, **working,** is the activity itself, when the strength of the might is put forth in some definite operation or task. — As with the great Head of the church, so with the members, in regard to their inheritance and hope: his power to us-ward, we must know and realize, is according to that working of the strength of his might **which he wrought in Christ, when he raised him from the dead, and made him to sit at his right hand in the heavenly** *places,* **etc.** Paul teaches by concrete example; he recites the actual deeds of God by which he crowned the saving work of Christ: the resurrection from the dead, and the enthronization in supreme glory and majesty. The application we are to make to our own case is assuring indeed: according as God completed the saving work of Christ in so triumphant a manner, so he will complete the work in us that we may attain the hope and enter upon the inheritance that is ours in Christ. — The ἐν τῷ Χριστῷ is just as it stands: **in Christ,** and not: "upon Christ," which Stoeckhardt is anxious to ward off by translating "through Christ," certainly out of place here. God wrought mightily and gloriously indeed "in Christ," namely in his human nature, when he raised him from the dead and exalted him. The participle καθίσας is far better attested than ἐκάθισεν; both ἐγείρας and καθίσας here denote action simultaneous with the main verb ἐνήργησεν, or ἐνήργηκεν, and the latter participle is transitive: **made him to sit,** as in 2, 6; 1 Cor. 6, 4; 10, 7; 2 Thess. 2, 4, although most frequently used intransitively. — God's **right hand** is wherever God is; it is his infinite glory, power, and majesty. Christ's sitting at God's right hand is his complete exercise of that glory, power, and majesty. In the **heavenly** places, ἐν τοῖς ἐπουρανίοις signifies the heavenly world into which Christ ascended visibly, and whence he

40

shall come again in like manner as he ascended thither. "So then the Lord Jesus . . . was received up into heaven, and sat at the right hand of God." Mark 16, 19. Compare also the remarks on the previous text. Our living connection with the risen and glorified Christ makes all that God did in him so comforting for us who look forward to a glorification with Christ. God's power cannot fail us who believe; only unbelief will lose all that is thus prepared for us in Christ. — In further description of Christ's exaltation Paul adds: **far above all rule, and authority, and power, and dominion.** He has in mind the angelic spirits of heaven; the abstract terms, however, can hardly be said to signify different ranks of angels, nor can we determine a gradation among the terms, either in an ascending or descending scale. Meyer, for instance, attempts this, but his efforts are not convincing. It is sufficient to know that God has endowed his angels in various ways and assigned them glorious fields for the exercise of their power. Not only above, but **far above,** ὑπεράνω, them all is Christ in his exaltation, including even **every name that is named, not only in this world, but also in that which is to come,** *i. e.* every being or power, or influence that exists at all, whether good or bad, and is named or designated in some way. "Let any name be uttered, whatever it is, Christ is above it; is more exalted than that which the name so uttered affirms." Meyer. "We know that the emperor precedes all, though we cannot enumerate all the ministers of his court: so we know that Christ is placed above all, although we cannot name all." Bengel. Compare Phil 2, 9. **Not only in this world, but also in that which is to come** takes in the entire world-age, and beyond that the eternity to come. Αἰών is *age* (margin), *seculum*, then the world as it exists in time, and, more ethically, the course and current of this world's affairs. Since this course and current is full of sin **this world**, αἰών οὗτος, came to be used with an evil connotation, and αἰών μέλλων, "the world to come," was placed over against it. This **world to come** shall be ushered in by Christ at his second coming, but in reality it exists now already, and we may now taste the powers thereof (Heb. 6, 5), but since we still wait for its full blessedness it is called "the world to come." Far above all that we shall ever know or name even in the heavenly world is Christ our exalted Lord. — **And he put all things in subjection under his feet, and gave him to be head over all things to the church, which is his body, the fulness of him that filleth all in all.** Christ was not only exalted above all things, but God **put all things in subjection under his feet,** made him the absolute ruler and master of all. Again this refers to the human nature of Christ and its participation in the *idiomata* or attributes of the divine by virtue of the personal union. Him whom they once nailed to the cross God made the absolute Lord of all. It would be wrong to restrict πάντα, **all things,** to the enemies of Christ; even Ps. 8, 6, from which the apostle takes this sentence as expressing his own thought (compare 1 Cor. 15, 27) does not suggest this restriction. The Psalm speaks only of man as the ruler of earth, the apostle elevates the word on man's dominion in using it of Christ and includes far more than the creatures of earth, namely all things created by God, whether in earth, or heaven, or hell, Phil. 2, 10-11. Man's earthly dominion is only a reflection of Christ's universal dominion. Every one of his foes, even Satan himself, thus lies beneath our Redeemer's feet. — This, of course, includes also all believers in so far as they are also creatures of God, but Christ stands in a special relation to them: God **gave him to be head over all things to the church, which is his body.** The church, ἐκκλησία, is here the entire body of believers, the communion of saints; compare Gal. 1, 13; 1 Cor. 12, 28; 15, 9; Acts 20, 28 *etc.* Sometimes the word is applied to a single congregation. To this church God **gave** Christ by a special act of his power and grace when he raised him from the dead, glorified and exalted him. He gave him, however, not merely to be the ruler and lord of the church, as he is ruler and lord of all things, but as **head over all things** to the church, **which is his body.** This headship is different

from the one pertaining to all created things. In the sense
of a head to his own body Christ belongs only to the church
by the special gift of God. His **body,** σῶμα αὐτοῦ, is a
spiritual organism, in which the life of the Head pulsates.
Certainly as such a Head Christ also rules the church; his
Word is its law, and his Spirit moves and controls every
member; but this is a different rule from that of the universe generally, it grows out of the gracious, saving
spiritual connection of the church with Christ — yet this is
the same Christ whose exaltation over all creatures is
supreme. It needs little reflection to see what all this means
for our inheritance and hope:

> "Can the Head
> Rise and leave the members dead?"

All this points also to the greatness of the power of God
to us-ward; here we see its blessed working revealed in a
way that fills us with the strongest possible comfort and
joy. — The apostle's addition: **the fulness of him that
filleth all in all** divides the commentators. In what sense
is the church the πλήρωμα, the **fulness** of Christ? The answer would be simple if the word could be taken in the
passive sense: "that which is filled by Christ who filleth all
in all;" and not a few commentators interpret in this way.
But the fact is that in all the other fifteen places in the
N. T. the word is used in an active sense, and this is true
of the language generally. We are compelled to understand πλήρωμα as: "that which fills something else," in this
instance Christ himself. The apostle explains more fully,
and without a figure, what his thought is in calling the
church "the body" of Christ the Head over all. As Ewald
puts it: "Without the church he, the Head over all, would
still fall short of what he really was to be. The church is
the complement of his being, necessarily belonging to him,
the exalted Mediator of salvation." Wohlenberg has the
same interpretation. Stoeckhardt uses Eph. 3, 19; 4, 13,
to show that fulness here must mean the full measure of
Christ's gifts, powers, and virtues; but this is only a

weakening of the passive sense of "fulness," Christ's gifts *etc.* filling the church, instead of Christ himself. — There is a paradox in calling the church the fulness **of him that filleth all in all.** The supremacy of Christ over all things is not one merely of influence, but of presence: Christ is in and through all, filling the universe. Our dogmaticians emphasize that this refers to the risen and exalted Christ, therefore to his human nature; this nature participates in the divine attribute of omnipresence. It is certainly wrong to restrict the word "all" in any way, the entire connection showing all things are indeed meant. **All in all** is all in every respect, all completely. What a wonderful thing that the church should be the body, and indeed the fulness, of him who holds so exalted a position and himself fills all in all! But such is the power of God to usward, and such the measureless depth of his saving grace.

HOMILETICAL HINTS.

The knowledge of the glory of the living God is not the piling up of dead intellectual ballast, but the securing of an interest-bearing capital. Matthes.

There would not have been much faith and love in Ephesus if there had not been considerable knowledge; to increase both the apostle prays for more knowledge. True knowledge in the kingdom of God is power.

Much stress is laid in our times on active faith, and we frequently hear about practical Christianity. Some people become so practical finally that they consider faith itself unpractical, and regard works of love as the only thing really worth while. They fail to see that you must have the tree to obtain the fruit. Riemer. — Where there is living Christian faith, there you will find serious inquiry regarding God and his work in the world.

A faith that holds to nothing definite will not hold out when put to the test at last. — It is remarkable with what little knowledge some Christians get along. They hear a few harrangues by some evangelist, take a dose of Gospel billingsgate, submit to a few morality lectures, shake the preacher's hand, and then are ready to go out and convert others. As with them, so with many of us, we are not concerned about the wealth of saving knowledge that should be ours.

The strongest thing on earth is death; but God raised up Christ, our Redeemer, from the dead. The highest personages on earth are princes, kings, emperors; but God placed Christ, our Redeemer, above all rule, authority, power, and dominion in the world to come. The greatest foe is Satan and his hellish kingdom; but God put all things under Christ's feet. This is not only supreme power, but supreme saving power — the power which is enlisted in our cause to lift us at last to eternal glory. "Worthy is the Lamb that was slain to receive power, and riches, and wisdom, and strength, and honor, and glory, and blessing. . . . . Blessing, and honor, and glory, and power be unto him that sitteth upon the throne, and unto the Lamb for ever and ever." Rev. 5, 12-13. — All things God has put under Christ's feet: whatever will not obey and follow him like sheep must be tamed and conquered and crushed by him like wolves and ravenous beasts.

In making the Lord of all our Head God gave him to us; in making us his body God gave us to him. — The head with its brain fibers controls every member of the body, and with every pulse-beat the blood of the body rises to the head to bring back a life of human intelligence to the members of the body. So Christ is the Head of the church, and so we as his body draw life from him. — The church without Christ would be a decapitated corpse, its heart forever still in death. Christ indeed would be a living and independent Head without the church, but isolated, bodiless, without the body whose Savior he is (Eph. 5, 23). Besser. So highly does Christ esteem the church, writes Calov, and so tenderly does he love it, that in a certain sense he considers himself incomplete and maimed, if he is not joined to us and we to him as his fulness, as is the head with its body. — The Bridegroom cannot be such without the bride; the Firstborn among many brethren (Rom. 8, 29) could not have this title, if there were no such brethren born after; the chief head of the corner (Eph. 2, 20-22) would not be this if no stones were built upon it for a habitation of God in the Spirit.

Christ ascended on high. Christ sends his Spirit from on high.

Christ at the Right Hand of God.

I. *Lord over all.*
II. *Head to the church.*
III. *Fountain of faith, love and hope.*

Christ in His Exaltation the Head of the Church.

Behold:

    I. *What this gives to the church.*
    II. *What this makes of the church.*
    III. *What this guarantees for the church.*

Our Living Relation to the Exalted Redeemer.

    I. *We are his body.*
    II. *He is our hope and inheritance.*

The Power of God to Us-Ward.

    I. *Displayed in Christ's exaltation.*
    II. *Operative for our salvation.*

The Spirit of Wisdom and Revelation in the Knowledge of God.

    I. *It brings forth faith, love, and hope.*
    II. *And faith, love, and hope live upon it.*

The Knowledge we Need for our Faith.

    I. *A knowledge of God's mighty saving deeds.*
    II. *A knowledge of God's mighty saving purposes.*

Adapted from Riemer.

PENTECOST.

Eph. 2, 19-22.

Pentecost, the festival of the outpouring of the Spirit, is the birthday of the Christian church, and our epistle text has for its subject the great work of the Holy Spirit, the Christian church, the *habitation of God in the Spirit.* In this respect our text agrees well with the old epistle for the day, which describes the first general beginning of the church on the day of Pentecost, when three thousand souls turned in faith to Christ. Our brief text speaks of the members, the foundation, and the growth of the Christian church.

The members.

Beginning with the 11th verse the apostle addresses in particular the Gentile Christians at Ephesus, showing how they were made equal with the Jewish Christians in their position as members of the Christian church. In the 19th verse, with which our text begins, the apostle sums up briefly what he has said on this subject, and adds a word on the growth of the church in general. **So then ye are no more strangers and sojourners, but ye are fellow-citizens with the saints, and of the household of God.** Ἄρα οὖν is a favorite way with Paul of introducing a conclusion or summary drawn from his preceding discussion; see, for instance, Rom. 5, 18; 7, 3 and 25; 8, 12; 9, 16 and 18; *etc.* The Gentiles were at one time separate from Christ and without God in the world, but the blood of Christ changed that, verse 12-13. Jews and Gentiles were both redeemed by the cross. And in Ephesus those who believed, Jews and Gentiles alike, were united in one, both having access in one Spirit unto the

632

Father. At Jerusalem, on the day of Pentecost, this glorious work began, when the Gospel was preached in so many different languages. It continued at Ephesus, and throughout the world, since that day. Millions of Gentiles have followed those to whom Paul addressed this section of his Ephesian letter. To us all to-day the words apply directly: **So then ye are no more strangers and sojourners.** By **strangers,** ξένοι, the apostle understands foreigners, people who are not citizens; the addition **sojourners,** πάροικοι, indicates that they have moved in from elsewhere and dwell alongside of the citizens, but without sharing their rights and privileges. So the Gentiles were foreigners as far as the O. T. theocracy was concerned; they did not belong to it. Even when they lived in the Jewish country or near the Jews elsewhere, they had none of their high prerogatives. As long as they adhered to their idolatry the πολιτεία τοῦ Ἰσραήλ with all its spiritual blessings was closed to they. Some commentators think that Paul has reference to what the Gentiles might have become in O. T. days, if they had accepted Judaism, namely guests and associates of the Jews, a sort of second-class citizens in the old theocracy, not full citizens as now in the Christian church; but this entire idea is foreign to the apostle and in no way suggested by the words "strangers and sojourners." Paul is evidently placing over against each other what the Gentile Christians at Ephesus once actually were in the days of their heathenism, and what they now were through faith in Christ. — **But ye are fellow-citizens with the saints, and of the household of God.** The contrast is strong: ἀλλά; and there is special emphasis in the repetition of ἐστέ: **ye are** — remember it and rejoice in it! **Fellow-citizens with the saints** means citizens of God's kingdom just like the saints: "saints together with the saints," Ewald. It would be a strange restriction to make **saints** here mean only Jewish Christians, or, as has been suggested, the patriarchs of old. The saints are those who are sanctified by the blood of Christ and brought to a new and holy life; true Christians in general. The Gentile

Christians addressed by Paul belong to this class. "Fellow-citizens with the saints" is the opposite both of "strangers" and "sojourners." Behold, God hath enlarged Japhet and made him to dwell in the tents of Shem, Gen. 9, 27. Someone has finely said: "The Bible is Shem's tent, but by means of the Greek language Japhet entered into it." — But the apostle goes beyond the figure of a polity or city, adding a term expressive of still closer association: **and of the household of God**. The οἰκεῖοι are the members of a house or family. So David says: "I will dwell in the house of the Lord for ever," Ps. 23, 6; and the sons of Korah: "How amiable are thy tabernacles, O Lord of hosts!" Ps. 84, 1. Of Christ we read Heb. 3, 6: "Whose house are we." In the kingdom to come we shall sit at the same table, like members of one great family, with Abraham, Isaac, and Jacob. To be of the household of God is to have him as our Father, to be his children and heirs, to enjoy the riches of his grace and the care and tenderness of his love. There is nothing higher for any human being. It is much to be a happy properous citizen of a great empire under a wise, mighty, beneficent ruler; it is certainly far more to be a prince and child of that ruler himself, dwelling in his own royal palace.

The foundation.

A new figure follows the two already employed: **being built upon the foundation of the apostles and phophets, Christ Jesus himself being the chief cornerstone.** The emphasis is on the final genitive absolute: "Christ Jesus *etc.*," which dominates the entire imagery and brings out our connection with Christ in a way that forms an advance over the strong figure of the household immediately preceding. We are not only members of God's household, but actually built together into one solid and enduring structure with the chief corner-stone Christ. The Ephesian Gentile Christians were built upon the apostolic foundation and the corner-stone Christ when they were brought to faith and baptism. Then God himself made them living stones and fitted them into the temple (ἐποικοδομηθέντες, passive participle) that actually grows like a living thing, verse 21. Besser says it is an idle question whether by **the foundation of the apostles and prophets** Paul meant the persons of these men, or the Gospel they preached. Since the building is composed of personal stones, Christ and the believers, no doubt the persons of the apostles and prophets are also meant. Yet we are not built upon these persons merely, as believers who preceded us in embracing Christ; in this manner we of a later day rest on all the believers who went before us. We are built on "the foundation (τὸ θεμέλιον, the groundwork) of the apostles and prophets" because of their office and work. The **apostles** were Christ's chosen embassadors and messengers, commissioned to preach the Gospel to all the world. To this day the apostles are "the foundation" of the church, its solid and enduring ground-work, because they still preach to us, and we to-day believe their word and doctrine. The **prophets** are mentioned after the apostles, and there is no separate article with προφητῶν; the one article with both apostles and prophets shows that they together form one category or class, yet this need not indicate that the two words refer to the same persons. It does not appear in any way why the apostles, although of course they had the gift of prophesying, should here be spoken of as prophets. The other passages in which prophets are mentioned (Eph. 3, 5; 4, 11; 1 Cor. 12, 28) indicate that here N. T. prophets are meant, the associates and fellow workers of the apostles, endowed with a special gift. This explanation is preferable to the one which refers the word to the prophets of the O. T. days, especially those who wrote the books of the O. T.; the reason is that Paul is speaking of the Christian church as it was being built after the completion of Christ's work. In the O. T. times the Gentiles were "strangers and sojourners," although the O. T. prophets had done their work already in those days: now the believing Gentiles are fellow citizens of the saints. The objection that the N. T. prophets can-

not be placed beside the apostles, because the church of
future times does not rest on them, is without force, since
some of the apostles left no written records, while some
of the assistants of the apostles did, namely Mark and
Luke. Even those apostles and prophets who recorded
nothing nevertheless did their work in building the church
by their authoritative teaching, the substance of which
the others put into permanent written form through divine
inspiration. So we to-day rest on the foundation of the
preaching and teaching of all the apostles and prophets
of Christ. Nor does this set aside the O. T. prophets or
the O. T. itself; Christ himself, as well as his apostles
and prophets, bring us the fulfillment of what the O. T.
promises. The N. T. prophets indeed themselves rest on
the testimony of the apostles, yet the Lord gave them
special gifts and offices, and Paul magnifies their work as
it deserves (1 Cor. 14, 1). — The essential and distinctive
thing about this structure is now added: **Christ Jesus
himself being the chief corner-stone.** The αὐτοῦ belongs
to Χριστοῦ Ἰησοῦ. The apostle has already described Jesus
to his readers; in chapter 1, 20-23 we see him risen from
the dead and exalted gloriously, and in our chapter, verse
13, his atoning blood is emphasized. He who constitutes
the chief corner-stone is **Christ Jesus,** the Messiah and
Savior of the world, who has executed his redemptive
work and now with royal power carries God's plan of
salvation to completion. This Savior and his work is the
sum and substance of all apostolic preaching, the burden
of all true prophetic utterance. He is the sun that shines
with heavenly grace and splendor in all the inspired
writings. As regards the building he is **the chief corner-
stone,** ἀκρογωνιαῖος (λίθος). Ewald is right when he insists on a more careful interpretation of the figure here
presented. In 1 Cor. 3. 11 Christ is called the foundation;
here the foundation and the corner-stone are viewed sepa-
rately and must not be thrown together when the figure is
explained. By "the chief corner-stone" the apostle does
not mean merely a stone at the corner connecting the two

walls of Jewish and Gentile Christians, a mere connecting link; nor a stone which holds together the entire building, a thing which a corner-stone cannot properly be said to do; nor a stone which carries the entire structure of the building, which would make a foundation of the stone; finally also not the chief stone which completes the foundation. All these interpretations deviate from the real function of a corner-stone, which is to determine the lines, the direction, the character and kind of the building. Thus the corner-stone belongs to the foundation and determines the chief angle, thereby governing the rest. It is the one stone which is most significant in the entire structure. In the church of God this chief stone is Christ Jesus himself; he and his work determine, shape, govern everything else about the building. Isaiah prophesied of Christ: "Behold I lay in Zion for a foundation a stone, a tried stone, a precious corner-stone, a sure foundation," 28, 16. Both Peter and Paul repeat this prophecy, 1 Pet. 2, 6 and Rom. 9, 33. Gerlach adds the remark that in our passage Christ is ranged alongside of the apostles, because their word like that of Christ forms the foundation of the church, John 14, 12; 17, 20, yet he is superior to them as he is the chief corner-stone and governs the entire building including the foundation. In this respect the figure of the head of the church resembles that of its chief corner-stone.

The growth.

The Christian church as a building is not yet finished, new stones are constantly being added. So the apostle writes of Christ, the chief corner-stone: **in whom each several building, fitly framed together, groweth into a holy temple in the Lord; in whom ye also are builded together for a habitation of God in the Spirit.** There is no figure in the phrase **in whom,** namely in Christ, not "upon whom." "In Christ" here means in living communion with him, through faith. The subject of the sentence is πᾶσα οἰκοδομή, not as the *Recepta* reads πᾶσα ἡ οἰκοδομή; the article is missing. Hence we cannot translate: "the whole building," although this would suit the context well, πᾶς without the article never having this meaning. **Each several building,** or *every building* (margin) would be correct linguistically, only the apostle is speaking of one great structure, not of several. "Every building" would also be too indefinite; we should expect him to designate more closely that he intended certain buildings called congregations — if such had been his meaning. The correct rendering is nearly like that of the A. V.: **all building,** *i. e.* all that has been or is being erected on the foundation. The great building is still growing, but every part of it is growing in Christ. in union and communion with him. Whatever is apart from him, no matter how grandly it rises, and how much labor is spent upon it, is not a part of the church, the communion of saints; it is a foreign, worldly, hostile structure, even if men call it the church. — The apostle adds the participial modifier: **fitly framed together.** This conveys what the Apostles' Creed expresses by "the communion of saints." All true believers are intimately joined together in one spiritual structure; one stone fits up to, matches, and is joined to the other with complete exactness, and so the entire structure as it progresses constitutes one harmonious and beautiful whole. Christ dominates every stone in it. We have a faint idea of what this means when we contemplate some grand cathedral composed of thousands of stones, yet all wrought together to produce one magnificent result. Jews and Gentiles hated each other, but in the Christian church they were made one and dwelt in loving communion with each other; so also other differences among men are overcome by the complete inner spiritual harmony that rules in the *Una Sancta.* Stoeckhardt writes: Christians have a new way about them, they have the mind of Christ, they live not to themselves, but serve each other in love. They admonish, comfort, edify each other. Each looks not only to his own things, but also to the things of others. One bears the others burdens, and bears with the other's weaknesses and faults. The strong help to support the weak. All the apostolic admonitions to love, unity, and the exercise of brotherly virtues rest on this inner relation of oneness among the members of Christ's church. That such admonitions are still necessary shows that the temple of the Christian church is not yet entirely finished even in those who have come to faith. The sad and painful divisions that still show themselves indicate that there is still work to do, yet the inner spiritual oneness and harmony already existing in faith, and working itself out more and more in love, must not be overlooked and disregarded. — Of this spiritual structure the apostle writes: it **groweth** into a holy temple (or *sanctuary*, margin) **in the Lord.** The verb αὔξει is the present tense, not future, as Ewald strangely reads it; it is a regular classic alternate to αὐξάνειν. We may say of a building that it grows, becomes larger, as its walls and towers rise higher and higher under the builder's hands. The Christian church is thus still in process of growth; every new believer is another stone upon its glorious walls. And to aid in this work of building by missionary and pastoral labors is the grandest occupation on earth. Sometimes the church seems to be at a standstill, progress appears lacking, heathenism and unbelief hold their own and even seem to make inroads on the church, Christian workers hang their heads and lament. But God's work never stops; the church grows, sometimes secretly; the gates of hell cannot prevail against it. If some fall away, remember: "They went out from us, but they were not of us; for if they had been of us, they would have continued with us; but they went out that they might be made manifest how that they all are not of us." I John 2, 19 — The church grows **into a holy temple in the Lord;** that is what it will ultimately be when the growth is finished, but that is also what the church is now already as the growth proceeds. **Holy in the Lord** (Christ) belongs together; some make the prepositional phrase depend on the verb, but this is already modified by the relative "in whom" at the head

of the sentence; the latter can hardly be drawn to the
participle, "fitly framed together," distant from it. Christ
dwells in the church, and thus makes it a true temple and
therefore holy. The holiness all emanates from him. All
who constitute the temple are in him, and he forgives their
sins. and puts his Spirit into their hearts to sanctify them in body, soul and spirit. "Know ye not
that ye are a temple of God, and that the Spirit of
God dwelleth in you?" 1 Cor. 3, 16. — A special application is made of all this to the Gentile Christians at Ephesus:
**in whom ye also are builded together for a habitation
of God in the Spirit.** The relative **in whom** is parallel to
the one in the previous verse; its antecedent is the same.
In fact the entire verse is an applicatory parallel to verse
21. The Gentile Christians were already built together
with the other Christians, yet the apostle uses the present
tense: **are builded together,** because the work in them was
still in progress. Even while they read this Epistle of
Paul, as Besser writes, they were being edified and builded
together more and more. The σύν in the verb has the same
meaning as in the previous compounds: together with other
believers. *Extra ecclesiam nulla salus;* you cannot be saved
apart from Christ, the chief corner-stone, nor apart from
those who are builded upon him. Let nothing ever separate you from your fellow believers! — **For** (really: *into*)
a habitation of God in the Spirit is like the preceding:
"into a holy temple in the Lord." "Habitation of God"
defines exactly what is meant by "a holy temple in the
Lord." The glory of the church is that God dwells within
her, even in every one of her members. John 14, 21. **In
the Spirit** cannot mean merely "in the spirit" or spiritually
(Ewald); the reference to the Trinity in Paul's statements here is too plain to be ignored; compare the same
thing in verse 18. Nor is ἐν instrumental, "through the
Spirit," as Meyer would make it in connecting the phrase
with the verb; it has its ordinary first meaning: "in," as in
the three instances immediately preceding. The church is
God's habitation "in the Spirit," in union and communion

with the Holy Spirit, according to Jesus' own promise to
the disciples: "And I will pray the Father, and he shall
give you another Comforter, that he may be with you for
ever, even the Spirit of truth." John 14, 16-17. This
promise has been fullfiled, the Spirit has been given us,
and in him we and all Christians live and move and have
our spiritual being. As a holy temple in the Lord, and a
habitation of God in the Spirit, the glory of the church is
not in anything outward, but in this inward and hidden
union with the Triune God. The full revelation of this
glory shall come when the last sinner is made a member of
the church and the Lord returns in majesty and power.

HOMILETICAL HINTS.

There are many Christian churches, so-called. Which one is
meant here? Certainly not some outward section of what is commonly called Christendom, not even our own Lutheran Church.
Nor, if we are generous enough to include all the churches that in
any way call themselves Christian, can they be meant here as a
visible outward body. On this day of the outpouring of God's Holy
Spirit our eyes are fixed on the holy temple in the Lord which he
has erected and made the habitation of God in the Spirit, namely
the church which we confess in the apostolic symbol: "I believe in
the holy Christian church, the communion of saints."

It is no air-castle, this wonderful structure erected by the
great master-builder, the Spirit of God.

When Spener came to die he desired to be buried in a white
shroud and a light-colored coffin, saying: I have all my lifelong
mourned over the sad condition of the church. My white shroud
is to attest that I die in the hope of better things for the church of
the future. — So we often speak of the lowly condition of the
church and allow our hearts to become sad; this day the inner glory
of the church is to fill our hearts with joy.

The enemies of the church thought they had forever buried
out of sight the great corner-stone Jesus Christ. But lo, when the
rubbish was cleared away on Easter day, when the tomb was opened
and death's seal shattered, there stood the chief stone of the corner
laid solidly and gloriously in place by God himself, and the great
structure of the Christian church began to rise.

41

Once the disciples pointed out to Christ the grand pillars and foundation stones of the Jewish temple, the pride of all the nation. But the Lord told them how presently destruction would overtake this temple, and not one stone would remain upon another. The dome of Christ's spiritual building alone will endure to all eternity.

The foundation of the apostles and prophets still stands to-day, the living Word which they recorded and handed down to all future generations. One generation after another has attacked the impregnable rock of Holy Scripture; they have turned to dust, it still stands unshaken and sublime. *Verbum Dei manet in aeternum.*

What are men in their natural sinful state but loose, useless boulders lying around to no purpose but to block the way, rocks of offense, stones of stumbling. If they are to serve their proper purpose, if at last they are not to be cleared away with the useless building rubbish, they must be taken in hand by the great master builder, dressed and trimmed with his heavenly tools and lifted into place in the great spiritual house of God.

Do not make the mistake of trying to build yourself, thus interfering with the Holy Spirit's work.

Edification is far more than a slight moving of the heart, a sweet stirring of the emotions, a little moral instruction. To be edified is to be filled with Christ, to be built up in the saving truth of apostolic teaching, to be inwardly renewed in faith and love by the Holy Spirit.

Pentecost does not produce outward uniformity, but inward union; in multiplicity oneness, in variety harmony. The church is a glorious cathedral, not a long, flat; dreary factory-building.

Do not ask only: Have I the Spirit? but also: Has the Spirit me?

We are to be framed together and builded together; we are to be fellow citizens with many others, members of the grandest household on earth. This union with others is essential in our being built upon the foundation of the apostles and prophets, Christ Jesus being the chief corner-stone. You cannot be joined to Christ and controlled by his Spirit without being joined to many brethren, growing together with them, laboring and suffering with them, and finally lifted to glory with them.

Praise God for the Holy Spirit and His Blessed Work!

I. *He has built the church.*

    1) Christ the corner stone, in his divine-human person, in his mediatorial work.

    2) The foundation of the apostles and prophets, the Gospel in its fulness, in the inspired Scriptures, in its constant proclamation.

    3) The building fitly framed together, the increasing communion of believers.

II. *He has made us through faith members of the church.*

    1) We are no longer strangers and sojourners.

    2) We are God's people, fellow citizens in his kingdom, adopted, re-born children of his house, living stones in his temple, a habitation in which he dwells.

    8) Who can describe fully the blessedness of our position?

III. *He is bestowing upon us the richest blessings of the church.*

    1) The Triune God dwells in us.

    2) The complete Gospel is ours.

    3) The fellowship of the saints is ours.

    4) The hope of eternal glory is ours.

The Cathedral of the Christian Church.

I. *Its mighty corner-stone.*

II. *Its solid foundation.*

III. *Its magnificent walls and towers.*

IV. *Its crowning glory* (the indwelling of God).

                            —Adapted from Matthes.

Our Joy in the Holy Christian Church.

We rejoice when we contemplate:

I. *Its impregnable foundation.*

II. *Its world-wide extent.*

III. *Its final consummation.*

The Mighty Building of the Christian Church.

I. *Solid.*

II. *Vast.*

III. *Fitly framed.*   Harms.

What is the Church?

I. *The communion of saints.*

..II. *The ground and pillar of the truth.*

III. *The temple of God.*

                                Stoecker.

Our Spiritual Home, the Church.

I. *It received us through a spiritual birth.*
II. *It furnishes us spiritual sustenance.*
III. *It offers us spiritual communion.*

———

TRINITY SUNDAY.

Eph. 1, 3-14.

For Trinity Sunday this is an admirable text. The day demands that we preach on the Trinity; and, answering to this, our text actually falls into three sections describing one after another in an exalted manner the work which each person of the Godhead wrought for our salvation, rendering due praise to God for it all. The proper way to preach the mystery of the Trinity is to connect it throughout with the plan of salvation, since God has revealed to us the deep things of his being for the very purpose of making us understand properly the work he has done for us. — But our text stands at the end of the entire festival half of the church year; it is the keystone of the great arch we have built with all the previous texts. At the same time it constitutes the portal for the second half of the church year, the long line of after-Trinity Sundays. Our text fills its place admirably also in this respect. In fervent and glowing language it sums up all the blessed work of God which we have considered in detail in the festival cycles through which we have passed, and renders due praise to God. The elaborate Trinity cycle deals with the Christian life which has its fountain in what God has done for us; before we take up the details of this life in the long line of after-Trinity texts, we are offered here an impressive summary of what God has wrought for us. With that like a sun shining on our pathway we are in the best possible position to go on and view piece by piece what the Christian life must contain when it appropriates the riches of God's grace in Christ Jesus through the Holy Spirit. — Our general theme then is: *The Triune God, the God of our salvation.* We see what the Father has done, in verses 3-6; what the Son has done, in verses 7-12; and what the Holy Spirit has done, in the concluding verses.

The Father's part in our salvation.

Paul begins the body of his Epistle to the Ephesians with a grand note of praise, magnifying God for his mercy and grace to us all in Christ Jesus. In doing this he goes back beyond time, recounting what God did for us already in eternity. **Blessed** *be* **the God and Father of our Lord Jesus Christ, who hath blessed us with every spiritual blessing in the heavenly** *places* **in Christ: even as he chose us in him before the foundation of the world, that we should be holy and without blemish before him in love: having foreordained us unto adoption as sons through Jesus Christ unto himself, according to the good pleasure of his will, to the praise of the glory of his grace, which he freely bestowed on us in the Beloved.** The opening words of this section: **Blessed** *be* **the God and Father of our Lord Jesus Christ**, are identical with 1 Pet. 1, 3, and have been considered in the text for Quasimodogeniti, to which the reader may refer. Note the recurrence: εὐλογητὸς . . . ὁ εὐλογήσας . . . ἐν εὐλογίᾳ : *Blessed be . . . who hath blessed . . . with blessing.* The verb εὐλογεῖν (to speak well of some one, to praise) is used both for the utterance of blessing, and for the actual bestowal of blessing. The former is the sense when we bless God, the latter usually when God blesses us, and this invariably in the N. T. Our entire text describes the gifts with which God **hath blessed us.** When Paul writes **us,** he means himself and his readers whom he addresses as οἱ ἅγιοι καὶ πιστοὶ ἐν Χριστῷ Ἰησοῦ, "the saints and the faithful in Christ Jesus." All who are such to-day rightly apply his words to themselves. — God has blessed us **with every spiritual blessing in the heavenly** *places* **in Christ.** To bless with blessing is emphatic; and **every** blessing is comprehensive, not a single spiritual gift that we need is absent. This wealth of blessing is **spiritual,** not merely because it is for our spirits and differs from bodily blessing, but because it emanates from the Spirit of God. The two English versions translate ἐν τοῖς ἐπουρανίοις: **in the heavenly** *places,* while Luther and some others have: *in himmlischen Guetern.* Cremer takes the expression to mean the entire sum of heavenly treasures; *i. e.* of those that belong to the heavenly order of things. The same phrase occurs in 1, 20; 2, 6; 3, 10; 6, 12, and throughout refers to *loca,* not *bona,* as Stoeckhardt correctly says. Soden adds that naturally the divine act of blessing occurs in heaven, the glorious dwelling-place of God and all blessed spirits, yet here the "blessing" itself is described as in heaven, bearing a heavenly character, and coming down to us from heaven. — **In Christ** belongs to εὐλογήσας: in him, in union and communion with him. This involves also, we may say, "through Christ," and "for Christ's sake," but includes more than either or both of these phrases. The Lutheran Commentary is right: "Union and fellowship with Christ are implied." And such union and fellowship always involves divinely wrought faith. Ewald accordingly says, that when God blessed us in Christ, "he beheld the recipients of this blessing as enclosed in Christ." Luther brings this out richly when he interprets our passage: "This is the heavenly blessing which the holy Christian church, or Christendom, has through Christ: that one is free from the law, sin, and death, that one becomes righteous and alive, that one has a gracious God; namely, a joyful confident heart, a joyful conscience, knowledge of Christ, a true and certain understanding of the Scriptures, the gifts of the Holy Spirit, good courage toward God, and the like." When the apostle writes of God that "he hath blessed us in Christ," this means an actual bestowal of blessing, an act that occurred for the Ephesians when they were brought to faith in Christ by means of the Gospel.

By ἐξελέξατο (middle voice), **he chose us,** the apostle declares that God picked us out and appropriated us unto himself by a special divine act. The preposition in the verb points to a mass or number out of which the choice was made; here the entire fallen race is meant, the world.

In view of the Hebrew equivalent *bachar,* and the O. and N. T. use of ἐκλέγεσθαι, ἐκλεκτοί, and ἐκλογή, it is a mistake to obliterate the distinctive meaning of a choice out of many, and to make the word mean simply that God appointed us to something. But the same thing applies to ἡμᾶς, **us,** which here refers to Paul and the Ephesian ἅγιοι καὶ πιστοὶ ἐν Χριστῷ Ἰησοῦ, and of course applies to all others who are believers in Christ. The divine election did not take place in an arbitrary manner; God did not reach blindly into the mass of fallen humanity and choose whom he happened upon. He chose the persons here described. Since his choosing took place in eternity, before the world began or ever a human being was created, God must have forseen ἡμᾶς. This is so evident and necessary that even the strictest Calvinist does not venture to deny it. With the omniscience of God thus admitted in regard to the world generally and the persons whom God chose for himself, it is altogether arbitrary to restrict this omniscience to the mere fact that such persons would come to exist in time; God beheld both their existence and the success of his work in leading them to permanent faith in Christ, the Redeemer. As such ἅγιοι καὶ πιστοὶ ἐν Χριστῷ Ἰησοῦ he chose them for his own, *i. e.* unto eternal salvation. It was an act of supreme grace. — This is brought out especially by the addition: **in him,** in Christ. Just as we are now "the saints and the faithful *in Christ Jesus,"* and as God blessed us with all blessing *in Christ,* so he chose us already in eternity *in Christ.* Compare also verses 6 and 7. Throughout faith is implied, and to eliminate it is to alter the apostle's meaning and make him say that, without seeing anyone by faith in Christ, God, merely on the basis of Christ's universal redemption, selected a fixed number of the fallen race for his own, either in an altogether arbitrary manner, or according to some mysterious and unknown rule. This is to attribute false human speculation and deduction to the apostle as his own inspired thought. The old exegetes construed ἐν αὐτῷ with ἡμᾶς: "us in Christ," *i. e.* by faith, forseen of God. Stoeckhardt complains that even Abbott, Hofmann, and Ewald of modern times do the same, or interpret as if this were the construction. He might have named others. Wohlenberg says pointedly: "in Christ = included in Christ, and this including is conditioned by faith." Winer writes, p. 348: "The formula ἐν Χριστῷ constantly refers to the εἶναι, generally in a concise manner;" and he explains this in a note: "In so far as the Christian is in the most living (the most intimate, hence the ἐν) communion with .Christ (by faith)." He explicitly declares that ἐν Χριστῷ (κυρίῳ) never means *per Christum,* "through Christ," as Stoeckhardt nevertheless translates; this would be διά, as Paul also has it in verse 5 where he means "through." But though we have the best grammatical authority for construing: ἡμᾶς ἐν αὐτῷ, still since the previous clause connects ἐν Χριστῷ with the participle εὐλογήσας, so here it seems best to construe ἐν αὐτῷ with the verb ἐξελέξατο: God chose us in Christ, the action itself took place in Christ. But this by no means eliminates faith, since Christ and this merit is here considered not merely as the *causa meritoria* objectively and in general as *aquisita* for all men, but as the *causa meritoria* of our election, subjectively, *appropriata,* made ours by faith. The verb and its object belong together, both are connected with Christ. "If the sphere of an action is Christ, the objects of that act must also be within that sphere, or else they would be beyond the sphere of the action itself." Schmitt, *Columbus Theol. Mag.,* Vol. 25, 346. And this is the reason why the modern exegetes so generally include faith. — Our Lutheran dogmaticians summed this up in the technical phrase: God elected *intuitu fidei,* in view of faith: in view of the all-sufficient merits of Christ appropriated by divinely wrought faith. They never considered faith in this connection as in any way the work or merit of man, but as solely the gift of God, produced in our hearts altogether by the efficacious work of God's Holy Spirit operating through the means of grace. This excludes synergism completely. The phrase "in Christ" may be taken to include the entire plan of salvation from its very beginning up to and including the *discretio personarum*, the election of the persons found by faith in Christ and finally brought to glory; this is *the wider form* of the doctrine of predestination, presented finely in the Formula of Concord, 652, 13-24, the so-called *first tropus.* When, however, the divine act of choosing us "in Christ" is considered only in connection with the persons chosen, and all else left out, we have the narrower form of doctrine, the so-called *second tropus,* employed by the Lutheran theologians after the time of the Formula of Concord. Both forms are doctrinally one, only the former takes in more than the latter. Each has its special use: the wider excludes synergism, for in detailing the plan of salvation great stress is laid on the divine activity as the sole power which works our salvation; the narrower excludes Calvinism, for in pointing to the truth that God chose only those who believe in Christ, the arbitrary and absolute predestination of a mysterious few is overthrown. One of the gravest errors of to-day is to mingle the two forms, especially to predicate of the narrower what pertains only to the wider. — The divine act of election occurred **before the foundation of the world** (2 Thess. 2, 13), before the work of creation began, in eternity. — The purpose of God's election is indicated already by the middle voice of ἐξελέξατο: he chose us for himself, for his children and heirs. But this is stated directly: **that we should be holy and without blemish before him.** As in Col. 1, 22 this refers to our justification, not to our sanctification. The apostle writes εἶναι: "to be holy *etc.*," not γίνεσθαι: "to become holy *etc.*" **Before him** also plainly refers to the judgment of God, who pronounces those alone holy and blameless whom he finds in Christ by faith. No righteousness of ours avails before God, but ever does he accept the righteousness of Christ held by faith. Compare also Eph. 5, 27, which settles the claim of Stoeckhardt that **holy and without blemish** always signifies the acquired holiness of Christian life, and not the imputed holiness of faith in Christ. When God chose us for his own he wanted us truly as such, as indeed "his sons through Christ Jesus," verse 5, having "our redemption through his blood, the forgiveness of our trespasses," verse 7. **Holy** signifies without sin; **without blemish,** so that no charge can be brought against us.

In love must be construed with the following participle, as we have it in the marginal translation: *having in love foreordained us.* It refers, not to our love, but to God's as the inner cause of his gracious act, and is placed first in order to make it emphatic. **Having foreordained us unto adoption as sons through Jesus Christ unto himself** declares that in his elective act God, already in eternity, determined that we should be his sons forever. . The υἱοθεσία, like the foregoing "holy and without blemish," refers to the final judgment and what then follows, to which our state of grace in time leads up and in which it culminates. We find the same thing in Rom. 8, 29: "foreordained to be conformed to the image of his Son, that he might be the firstborn among many brethren." The aorist participle προορίσας here does not denote an act prior to the action of the aorist verb ἐξελέξατο, but an action involved in the verb and simultaneous with it: in choosing us God foreordained us to eternal sonship in heaven. This is an adoption and sonship **through Jesus Christ,** made possible and realized only through the Mediator Jesus Christ and his redemptive work. Apart from him and outside of him no sonship is possible for sinners, and of course no election and predestination unto eternal salvation. Formula of Concord, 661, 66 and 70. **Unto himself** rounds out the term "adoption as sons;" it is an adoption which connects us with God, by it we are made his children, God's very own. — The entire act of God as here set forth by the apostle is **according to the good pleasure of his will,** which indicates not only the free resolution of the divine will, in being prompted by nothing outside of God himself, least of all by any merit or worthiness of ours, but indicates as well his mercy and grace (εὐδοκία). Our election is not a matter merely of the will of God, considered in an absolute sense, but of his good and gracious

will. According to Cremer εὐδοκία means the free will of
God whose content is something good, Matth. 11, 26; Luke
2, 14; 10, 21; Phil. 2, 14. To identify "the good pleasure"
of God with his "will," as some have done, is to eliminate
an essential element from the apostle's thought in favor of
Calvinistic ideas. Nor is the will of God here meant as a
mysterious and secret will, as such writers have imagined,
for Paul says explicitly in verse 9 that God "made known
unto us the mystery of his will;" this he did in the Gospel,
in the entire plan of salvation.—These thoughts are brought
out still further by the addition: **to the praise of the glory
of his grace, which he freely bestowed upon us in the
Beloved.** God's grace is the favor which he bestowed upon
us unworthy sinners, and this is full of glory in that it
manifests in a wonderful manner the highest excellence of
God. We see this glory shining forth especially in his
electing grace; and wherever and whenever this and all its
results is made known, there is, and must be, honor and
praise of God, just as Paul also breaks out in words of
blessing when he speaks of it all to his Ephesian readers.
Note the similar expressions in verses 12 and 14: "unto
the praise of his glory," dividing our text into three formal
sections. The relative clause points out, that sonship
"through Jesus Christ" has actually become ours. Freely,
graciously, without our merit it was made our own in him
who in a supreme sense is termed **the Beloved,** because God
was well-pleased in him. The A. V. had the reading ἐν ᾗ
instead of ἧς, and translated: "'wherein he hath made us
accepted in the beloved." But the best texts all have the
genitive, which is an attracted accusative, the apostle having
in mind χάριν χαριτοῦν; but others insist that the attracted
form must be the dative, the grace being the means *"wherewith* God endued us" (margin). Winer, § 24. The verb
ἐχαρίτωσεν might mean that God made us gracious, but the
entire context shows that the apostle meant: God bestowed
grace upon us.

The Son's part in our salvation.

The closing words of the previous section form an easy transition to what now follows. Thus far the dominating thought was in the elective act of God back in eternity, now the apostle dwells on the divine blessing as made ours at the present time: **in whom we have our redemption through his blood, the forgiveness of our trespasses, according to the riches of his grace, which he made to abound toward us in all wisdom and prudence, having made known unto us the mystery of his will, according to his good pleasure which he purposed in him unto a dispensation of the fulness of the times, to sum up all things in Christ, the things in the heavens, and the things upon the earth.**

The line of thought in brief is this: we have our redemption . . . according to the riches of his grace . . . according to his good pleasure. Paul's sentence is not rambling, but carefully and symmetrically, even if elaborately, built. In verse 3 "who hath blessed us *etc.*" begins the description of the blessing bestowed on us in eternity; here, in verse 7, "in whom we have our redemption *etc.*" begins the description of the divine blessing as actually realized in time. And this description divides into three sections, each beginning in the same way: "in whom *etc.*," here in verse 7, and similarly in verses 11 and 13. In each case, Wohlenberg rightly remarks, **in whom** is more than outward mediation; Christ did more than to obtain and transmit these blessings to us, he made them ours by taking us into communion with himself. And this again includes faith, as in verses 3 and 4. The same is true of the verb: **we have.** While objectively all men have been redeemed, and there is forgiveness in Christ's blood for all, yet only of true believers can it be said that they *have* the redemption and forgiveness in Christ. Our great treasure is: **our redemption through his blood,** our liberation wrought by the payment of a ransom or price, and this price Christ's own blood. The mention of **blood,** instead of death, points to the sacrificial act of Christ, when as the Lamb he was slain for our sins. Besser says, when the heavenly treasures are mentioned Christ and his blood are bound to be brought in. — By the apposition: **the forgiveness of our trespasses,** the apostle brings out the essential effect of Christ's redemption for all believers. Our **trespasses,** every act by which we fell instead of standing upright, incurring guilt and the wrath and punishment of God, are forgiven, no longer charged against us. For the sinner the sweetest word in the Bible is ἄφεσις, **forgiveness,** the removal of his sins so that they shall not come back forever, as far as the east is from the west, Ps. 103, 12. The apostle is speaking to believers concerning themselves, not concerning men generally; hence it is a perversion of his words for Stoeckhardt to say that in and with the redemptive act of Christ the sins of all men were actually pardoned. God forgives the sins only of those who repent and believe; the sins of all others are "retained," John 20, 23; on such the wrath of God abides, and they are condemned already, John 3, 36 and 18. Forgiveness or justification is that act of God by which, the moment faith is kindled in a poor sinner's heart, he is pronounced free from guilt and declared just, for the sake of the merits of Christ. Besser says this is the life-sap in the tree of grace. As a hen gathers her chickens under her wings, holding them safe, so we who are "in the Beloved" by faith are safe from every sin, no penalty can touch us. Ps. 32, 1.

All this is **according to the riches of his grace, which he made to abound toward us in all wisdom and prudence, having made known unto us the mystery of his will.** Our having redemption and forgiveness is due altogether to God's **grace,** his unmerited kindness and favor toward us sinners. The **riches** of his grace is its greatness and magnificence, which comes to view, not only in the pardon pronounced upon us, but especially also in the work of the Gospel upon our hearts. God did more than to give us a taste of his grace, he made it **abound toward us in all wisdom and prudence;** ἧς is an attracted ἥν, not ᾗ *wherewith he abounded* (margin), and the verb ἐπερίσσευσεν is transitive. His Gospel filled us with its divine **wisdom,** the living apprehension of Christ and his blessed work for us, and with **prudence,** the ability to apply this wisdom in our lives (Col. 1, 19). "Wisdom apprehends God's acts, knows and understands his counsel of grace; prudence refers to what we must do, deals with our duties and the best way to perform them; wisdom sees what God has done, prudence orders our own doing," Braune. The addition **all** is comprehensive: wisdom and prudence of every kind. Some commentators refer wisdom and prudence to God, which indeed may be done. — God made his grace abound thus toward us, when he **made known unto us the mystery of his will,** when by the Gospel he enlightened our hearts and brought us to faith. **The mystery of his will** is not some special secret resolution or determination of God, but the contents of his saving will, Eph. 6, 19; Col. 1, 26. This was hidden and unknown to men, until God revealed it by sending out his messengers to proclaim it abroad, Col. 1, 25. Paul thus praises God by describing in a glorious manner his work of grace upon the believers, justifying them for Christ's sake by bringing them to faith in the Gospel.

But there is still more to be said. The apostle is bent on bringing out the full blessedness and glory of God's work, as we have noted already in his use of the comprehensive terms: "every spiritual blessing," "the glory of his grace," "the riches of his grace," "which he made to abound." So he continues: **according to his good pleasure which he purposed in him unto a dispensation of the fulness of the times, to sum up all things in Christ, the things in the heavens, and the things upon the earth.** On top of the first κατά, verse 8, there is now placed another, verse 10, embracing the other and going beyond it. God's **good pleasure** (εὐδοκία) **which he purposed in him** (Christ) is indeed the same good pleasure as in verse 5, his free and gracious purpose of salvation; but here its contents are described in a special manner. God προέθετο, set for himself, purposed his good pleasure **unto a dispensation of the fulness of the times** (margin: *seasons*). Time is here conceived as a series of epochs or periods, and these reach a fulness as God's plans are carried to completion in them. **The fulness of the times** is thus the N. T. era, beyond which there shall be no more earthly era. God's plans are now culminating. Compare Gal. 4, 4. **A dispensation** of the fulness of the times is an administration, a management with regard to this period; the word οἰκονομία reminds us of the proper management of a household. In five parables God is described as a householder, and the imagery connected with the term is utilized in various ways. Throughout the N. T. — The thing now that God purposed and set for himself, the sum and substance of his good pleasure, for this dispensation of the fulness of the times, is nothing less than: **to sum up all things in Christ, the things in the heavens, and the things upon the earth.** There is no use in trying to limit **all things** here, especially when Paul adds: **the things in** (really *upon*, margin) **the heavens, and the things upon the earth.** Heaven and earth are meant, and all that is therein, not merely angels and believers. In Phil. 2, 10, where simply the exaltation and eternal power of Christ are set forth, we have the addition: "and things under the earth." But in our passage the powers of evil are treated as eliminated by God when his dispensation and administration of the Gospel times shall be completed. The thing that God purposed and is now bringing to its consummation is: **to sum up all things in Christ,** ἐν τῷ Χριστῷ, *the* Christ, in whom he has elected and justified us. The verb ἀνακεφαλαιώσασθαι is not derived from κεφαλή, head, and accordingly does not mean to make Christ the head of all things, as in verse 23; it is from κεφάλαιον, hence: "to gather in one," A. V., to summarize, as for instance when all the commandments are summed up in one statement, Rom. 13, 9. So God purposed to sum up all things in Christ for himself (middle voice). Christ is to be the center of all things in heaven and earth. All that disrupts and disturbs now shall be eliminated completely and forever, and for all the things in heaven and earth there shall be one grand harmony in Christ Jesus. This glorious work Paul sees in full progress now, and its consummation is absolutely certain. No wonder that he blesses God and uses the richest language he is capable of in doing so! — There is no room here to take up the many different interpretations and constructions proposed by the various commentators for verses 9-11; we have confined ourselves to a brief presentation of the best positive results, so also in the next section. We may yet add that the apostle's words afford no hint whatever of the so-called restitution of all things in Christ, which some have tried to find here and elsewhere in Scripture.

The apostle has shown what he *have* (ἔχομεν, verse 7) in Christ, and this in connection with God's great world-plan; he now adds what we *are* and *are to be* in Christ, in whom all things are to be summed up: **in him,** *I say,* **in whom also we were made a heritage, having been foreordained according to the purpose of him who worketh all things after the counsel of his will; to the end that we should be unto the praise of his glory, we who had before hoped in Christ.**

The reader must notice this constant repetition of **in him,** and its peculiar force. All our blessings are found in Christ and are ours in Christ alone. Here the phrase is markedly emphatic, followed as it is by the relative **in whom.** Just as commentators diverge in regard to ἀνακεφαλαιώσασθαι, so in regard to κληρωθῆναι. The A. V. translates ἐκληρώθημεν: "we have obtained an inheritance," *i. e.* were made heirs: while the R. V. has: "we were made a heritage." The latter seems preferable, as it brings out the full passive sense. Some attempt to hold to the etymological meaning: "we were chosen by lot," as in verse 4: ἐξελέξατο, but Harless is right, the verb reminds one too strongly of κλῆρος, κληρονομία, κληρονόμος, κληρονομεῖν, and the apostle's phrase in verse 14: ἀρραβὼν τῆς κληρονομίας, all dealing with the thought of inheritance. This then is the new thought added by the

•42

apostle: **we were made a heritage.** Just as Israel of old was God's heritage in former ages, Deut. 4, 20, so now are we who believe in Christ. In all the great universe which is to be summarized in Christ, we hold this special position: "'Ye are an elect race, a royal priesthood, a holy nation, a people for God's own possession, that ye may show forth the excellencies of him who called you out of darkness into his marvelous light," 1 Pet. 2, 9. The subject lies in the verb (we), and there is not the slightest indication that Paul means any others than the ἡμεῖς he has been speaking of all along, himself and the Ephesians, and by implication all other believers (verse 1). It is preposterous to assert that in ἐκληρώθημεν the apostle is speaking only of himself and other Jewish Christians as distinguished from Gentile Christians, and that the limitation thus suddenly introduced is indicated by the participial clause at the end of verse 12: τοὺς προηλπικότας κτλ. Yet there are venerable commentators who follow this exegetical tradition and seem to be satisfied with it. Meyer is right, if such a distinction between Jewish and Gentile Christians were intended we would have to have a strongly contrasted ἡμεῖς and ὑμεῖς, and this is absent; in verse 13 ὑμεῖς is Paul's direct address to all his readers, now omitting reference to his own person. — God made us his inheritance when he brought us to faith, but this is in accord with his eternal plan and purpose: **having been foreordained according to the purpose of him who worketh all things after the counsel of his will.** Stoeckhardt is bound to make πρόθεσις mean nothing but the bare determination of God by which he settles irrevocably that something shall be done, *i. e.* whatever the context may be made to indicate. But the word is used here and elsewhere concerning our salvation, and means the *saving* purpose of God which he has fully revealed in his Word. It was in accordance with this purpose of salvation that God foreordained us to be his heritage; and since he is one **who worketh all things after the counsel of his will,** he has carried out his purpose, he has made us his heritage, and he will crown this work at last just as he has purposed.

The counsel of his will is the plan on which God's will
has settled; it is not the power of omnipotence, but the plan
and provision, the means and influence which his grace employs in the work of our salvation. — **To the end that we
should be unto the praise of his glory, we who had before
hoped in Christ,** εἰς τὸ εἶναι κτλ., is a statement declaring
God's intention and purpose in foreordaining us and making us his heritage. We are to be **to the praise of his glory,**
εἰς ἔπαινον δόξης αὐτοῦ: our whole condition as God's heritage
is to glorify God, or, in other words, to proclaim, magnify,
and extol the attributes of God which constitute his glory,
his mercy and grace in Christ Jesus especially. Paul himself with pen and tongue gives us an example of what God
intends concerning all of us. This divine purpose will be
fully realized when we enter the perfection, where no discordant note of sin shall disturb the harmony of our praise.—
It ought to be plain that **we** (ἡμᾶς) here refers to all Christians in general; for it continues the "we" that runs all
through the preceding verses without a break or alteration,
and the predicate here connected with "we" beyond question
applies to all Christians as such: all of them God has made
his heritage and foreordained to the end that they should
be unto the praise of his glory. But a participial modifier is
attached to ἡμᾶς, it is placed at the end of the clause:
τοὺς προηλπικότας ἐν τῷ Χριστῷ: **we who had before hoped in
Christ.** Harless, Stoeckhardt, and others think that this
modifier limits ἡμᾶς, and thus also the "we" in ἐκληρώθημεν to
the Jewish Christians in Ephesus, since they had hoped in
Christ before (πρό) he appeared. This idea is an importation into the text, a misconception in regard to πρό, and as
restricting the scope of the preceding "we" on the very face
of it incorrect. Note too that the apostle is here winding up
the second grand section of his thought, the one on the Son
and our salvation (verses 7-12); how could he possibly at
the last moment alter the "we" that runs through the entire
section, in fact takes up and carries forward this "we" from
the first section (3-6)? Even outwardly the close of each
section is plainly indicated by the repetition of the striking

phrase: to the praise of God's glory (see verses 6, 12, and 14), which the preacher will do well to note and utilize in a sermon for Trinity Sunday. The third grand section begins with ὑμᾶς, "ye," since now, omitting reference to himself, the apostle addresses the Ephesians as such, in a personal and direct manner. — The modifier τοὺς προηλπικότας in no way limits ἡμᾶς, but describes ἡμᾶς. The sense is that God wanted "us" to be to the praise of his glory, namely Paul and the Ephesian Christians, and thus naturally all Christians everywhere, "us" namely **who have before hoped in Christ** (note the margin: *have,* for the perfect participle, which in our English would be rendered by the pluperfect in a finite tense). The πρό thus refers to our present state as contrasted with the glorious state to come; we now hope in Christ and continue in this hope, afterwards our hope shall be realized in glorious sight, when we shall see Christ as he is. Ewald takes the entire phrase together: εἰς ἔπαινον δόξης αὐτοῦ τοὺς προηλπικότας ἐν τῷ Χριστῷ, making the whole of it express God's intention concerning us (Christians), so that our hoping now, in advance of the glory to come, redounds to the glory of God. This combines the whole statement in a compact manner and is quite acceptable. In substance there is scarcely any difference from the explanation we have given.

The Holy Spirit's part in our salvation.

The last part of Paul's great hymn of praise for the heavenly blessings of God is addressed to the Ephesians as such, bringing this home to them personally, and in fact all that precedes likewise, because it all hangs most closely together: **in whom ye also, having heard the word of the truth, the gospel of your salvation, — in whom, having also believed, ye were sealed with the Holy Spirit of promise, which is an earnest of our inheritance, unto the redemption of** *God's* **own possession, unto the praise of his glory.** — Again we have **in whom,** for in no part of the work of salvation can we leave Christ; here the connection is: "in whom

. . . ye were sealed." **Ye also** refers to all the
Ephesians. Besser is certainly right when he says that
neither here, nor before, these words, could the first
readers of the Epistle have perceived that the apostle intended a distinction as between Jewish and Gentile Christians. Some insert a predicate here: "ye also were made a
heritage;" or: "ye also hoped;" or simply: "ye also are (*i. e.*
in him)." None is necessary as ὑμεῖς is the evident subject
of ἐσφραγίσθητε. — **Having heard the word of the truth,
the gospel of your salvation** points to a blessed fact in
regard to the Ephesians; Paul himself had been the bearer
of that Gospel to them. **The word of the truth** is the word
which consists altogether of truth, or the quality of which
is truth. It is the **gospel** or glad news concerning their
salvation, telling of all that God had done for them and
meant to work in them in order to save them. — The R. V.
makes the second **in whom** parallel with the first, as we
see by the preceding dash and the following comma; the
A. V. similarly. Yet some prefer: "in whom having also
believed," *i. e.* believed in Christ, or in the Gospel. Paul
mentions the believing especially, in fact refers to it a second
time in verse 15. The great blessing he now intends to set
forth is conditioned on the hearing and believing of the
Gospel. — And this is the blessing: **ye were sealed.** With
the kindling of faith in their hearts by the Holy Spirit
through the Gospel, that Spirit himself was given them as
the seal to mark and stamp them as belonging now to God
(his heritage) and as intended for him forever. A seal is
affixed to indicate ownership, or to make a thing safe
and inviolable, or to attest a thing and certify to it; in
σφραγίζεσθαι, with εἰς following there is also the idea that the
object sealed is to be kept for the purpose for which it has
been set apart. Here, as Hofmann says, all these specific
meanings flow together, and since the sealing is an inner
act in the heart of him who is sealed, it is intended for him
especially, to know and realize that he belongs wholly to
God, and must not fall away again to the world. "The
Spirit himself beareth witness with our spirit, that we are

children of God," Rom. 8, 16; 1 John 5, 10. — We are sealed
with the Holy Spirit of promise, a divine, a living seal,
and thus a proper mark for the divine life implanted in us;
promised by God himself through the prophets and the Son
and therefore called: "the promise of the Father," Acts 1,
14; Luke 24, 49; compare Acts 2, 33; Gal. 4, 14. — This
Spirit the apostle calls **an earnest of our inheritance,** using
the masculine relative ὅς because of the gender of the noun
following; ἀρραβών is pledge-money, caution-money guaran-
teeing complete future payment. So the Spirit is God's
pledge to us that he will in due time give into our possession
all that he has promised. As God has fulfilled the vital
promise that he would give us his Spirit, so he will fulfil
the rest of his great promises. — Ye were sealed, writes the
apostle, **unto the redemption of God's own possession,
unto the praise of his glory.** A future redemption is
meant, the final deliverance from all evil through the λύτρον
of Christ. Instead of saying: "Ye were sealed . . . unto
your redemption," the apostle generalizes, for all through
this text he has the entire church of God in mind: "unto
the redemption of the possession." This is not a possession
that we have, but one that God has: "the purchased possession," A. V., the one acquired by God, purchased with his
own blood, Acts 20, 28; *God's* **possession,** as the R. V.
rightly interprets in its translation. The αὐτοῦ in the next
phrase belongs to both: "his possession . . . his glory."
God's entire heritage is meant (compare verse 11), all his
people who believe in him; 1 Pet. 2, 9, where the same term
occurs. With the Ephesian believers they shall stand at last
in the perfect glory and blessedness of heaven; for this they
were endowed with the Spirit of promise. And this too, as the
culmination of all God's great saving acts, shall be **unto the
praise of his glory.** To make this marked repetition of the
ultimate purpose of God in all his saving work merely
incidental, as Ewald would have us do, is simply an
exegetical mistake. As Paul, all through this text, emphasizes the causality of God in our salvation, beginning back
in eternity, and extending on to all eternity, so he brings

out at the end of each description of the divine acts **the
praise of his glory.** And for Trinity Sunday we can have
no grander or more blessed refrain than this, referring first
to the Father, then to the Son, and finally to the Holy Spirit,
the great Three in One:

Soli Deo Gloria.

HOMILETICAL HINTS.

When an airship passes over our heads, we drop our most
important work and gaze after it. Is it more wonderful than this
message from the world beyond the stars themselves: God has
chosen us in Christ Jesus before the world began to be his own
forever? Day and night we ought to ponder it and drink in the
blessedness of it; for the airship is gone in a moment, but this
truth of our salvation shines in the heavens like a sun that never
sets.

"In Christ!" Chosen in him; having redemption and forgiveness in him; all things eventually to be summed up in him;
sealed in him to eternal glory. Thus from eternity to eternity, on
through all the course of time, there shines one broad pathway of
light: Christ. And all whom God saw and sees in him he takes
for his own; all else he casts away forever

We love to complain, Paul begins with thanksgiving and blessing, even though he writes in a prison. — Christ arose to heaven
with his hands outspread in blessing, and the blessing has flowed
down upon us ever since.

Beholding us in Christ, placed there by his own blessed work,
God chose us to be his heritage forever. Here is the heavenly
fountain and source of our salvation: in God, in God alone! — In
Christ by faith excludes every vestige of human merit. — In the
Beloved we are beloved. All that makes us so is from God, in
Christ.

Noblesse oblige! Let God's children be an honor to their
Father. Let the worms of the dust that he has raised so high
glorify him with the gifts he has given them.

The blood of Christ is the only price that will free the sinner's
soul. — The forgiveness of sins, pronounced upon us by God in
heaven for Christ's sake, is the only pardon that endures to eternity.

God's plans embrace the universe. Christ is the crown of all,
and everything in heaven and earth is assigned its place with

reference to him. Our position is that of his special heritage, his blood-bought brethren. All his foes shall be crushed beneath his feet.

Fanatics have dreamed of a miraculous sealing of the Spirit, attested by visions, direct revelations, a self-invented sanctity and unction. God's sealing takes place when we hear and believe his Word, when the Spirit works our justification and sanctification. This is the true seal. Every baptized child bears it, and every Christian who by faith retains his baptismal grace. — Does your sin distress you? Does the cross of Christ comfort you? Does the absolution in Christ's name rejoice you? Does the call to obedience find a response in you? Does the hope of salvation in Jesus delight you? Then the seal is plainly impressed upon your soul. Hold fast the earnest of your inheritance, and your name shall be called when the eternal inheritance is divided to all the sons of God.

Glory be to the Father, and to the Son, and to the Holy Ghost, as it was in the Beginning, is Now, and ever Shall be, World Without End. Amen.

I. *The Father hath chosen us.*
   1) The Father is the source of our salvation.
       With the Son and the Spirit he formed the plan of salvation.
       In Christ he chose every believer for his own.
       By his Spirit's grace we are now adopted sons.
   2) Praise ye the glory of his grace!

II. *The Son has redeemed us.*
   1) The Son is the source of our salvation
       He redeemed us with his blood.
       He sent us the Gospel of God's gracious will.
       He forgave our sins.
       He has assigned us a glorious position in his great kingdom.
   2) Live to the praise of his glory!

III. *The Holy Spirit hath sealed us.*
   1) The Holy Spirit is the source of our salvation.
       He brought us to faith in the Gospel.
       He marks us as God's possession.
       He makes us certain of eternal deliverance
   2) Go on in sure and certain hope to the praise of his glory!

The Good Pleasure of God's Will.

Manifested

    I. *By the Father, who chose us for sonship.*
    II. *By the Son, who redeemed us for sonship.*
    III. *By the Spirit, who confirms us in sonship.*

Paul Ebert.

The Gospel of the Triune God.

A proclamation of

    I. *The Father, who hath blessed us.*
    II. *The Son, in whom we have redemption.*
    III. *The Spirit, who is the earnest of our inheritance.*

Arthur Kuhlmann.

"In Christ."

    I. *Chosen.*
    II. *Pardoned.*
    III. *Sealed.*

The Divine Guaranties of our Eternal Salvation.

    I. *Election.*
    II. *Redemption and forgiveness.*
    III. *Sealing.*

Our Joyful Trinity Faith.

    I. *I believe in the love of God.*
    II. *I believe in the grace of Jesus Christ.*
    III. *I believe in the communion of the Holy Ghost.*

CPSIA information can be obtained
at www.ICGtesting.com
Printed in the USA
BVHW031114180819
555871BV00004BA/81/P